THE OXFORD HANDBOOK OF

MONSTERS IN CLASSICAL MYTH

THE OXFORD HANDBOOK OF

MONSTERS IN CLASSICAL MYTH

Edited by

DEBBIE FELTON

OXFORD
UNIVERSITY PRESS

Great Clarendon Street, Oxford, OX2 6DP,
United Kingdom

Oxford University Press is a department of the University of Oxford.
It furthers the University's objective of excellence in research, scholarship,
and education by publishing worldwide. Oxford is a registered trade mark of
Oxford University Press in the UK and in certain other countries

Published in the United States of America by Oxford University Press
198 Madison Avenue, New York, NY 10016, United States of America

British Library Cataloguing in Publication Data
Data available

Library of Congress Control Number: 2023942612

ISBN 978–0–19–289650–6

DOI: 10.1093/oxfordhb/9780192896506.001.0001

Printed and bound by
CPI Group (UK) Ltd, Croydon, CR0 4YY

CONTENTS

PART II: MONSTERS IN ANCIENT FOLKLORE AND ETHNOGRAPHY

PART III: INTERPRETING THE MONSTERS

PART IV: THE RECEPTION OF
CLASSICAL MONSTERS

FIGURES

Abbreviations

ANS	American Numismatic Society
AO	Antiquités orientales collection number (Louvre Museum)
ATU	H-J. Uther, *The Types of International Folktales*, 3 vols. (Helsinki, 2004)
Austin-Bastianini	C. Austin and G. Bastianini, *Posidippi Pallaei quae supersunt omnia* (Milan, 2002)
BAM	F. Köcher et al., *Die babylonisch-assyrische Medizin in Texten und Untersuchungen* (Berlin, 1963–)
BAPD	Beazley Archive Pottery Database (https://www.cvaonline.org/carc/pottery)
BNJ	I. Worthington (ed.), *Brill's New Jacoby* (Leiden, 2006–)
BNP	H. Schneider et al. (eds.), *Brill's New Pauly*, 22 vols. (Leiden 2002–2011)
CAF	T. Kock, *Comicorum Atticorum Fragmenta*, 3 vols. (Leipzig: Teubner, 1880–8)
Cornell	T. J. Cornell (ed.), *The Fragments of the Roman Historians*, 3 vols. (Oxford, 2014)
DCPP	E. Lipinski (ed.), *Dictionnaire de la civilisation phénicienne et punique* (Paris, 1922)
DELG	P. Chantraine, *Dictionnaire étymologique de la langue grecque* (Paris, 1968–80)
DK	H. Diels and W. Kranz (eds.), *Fragmente der Vorsokratiker* (6th edn., 1952)
FGrH	F. Jacoby, *Die Fragmente der griechischen Historiker* (Leipzig, 1923–)
Fowler	R. L. Fowler, *Early Greek Mythography*, vol. 1 (Oxford, 2000)
fr./frr.	fragment/fragments
K.	Kouyunjik (Nineveh) collection number (British Museum)
LIMC	L. Kahil et al. (eds.), *Lexicon Iconographicum Mythologiae Classicae* (Zurich, 1981–99)
LP	E. Lobel and D. L. Page, *Poetarum Lesbiorum Fragmenta* (Oxford, 1955)

LSJ	H. G. Liddell, R. Scott, H. S. Jones, and R. McKenzie (eds.), *A Greek–English Lexicon: Ninth Edition with a Revised Supplement* (Oxford, 1996)
MAN	Museo Arqueológico Nacional collection number (Madrid)
MNB	Monuments de Ninive et de Babylone collection number (Louvre Museum)
MW	R. Merkelback and M. L. West, *Fragmenta Hesiodea* (Oxford, 1967)
OCD	*Oxford Classical Dictionary*
OEAANE	E. Meyers (ed.), *The Oxford Encyclopedia of Archaeology in the Ancient Near East* (Oxford, 1997)
OED	*Oxford English Dictionary* (online edition) (Oxford, 2000–)
Page, *PMG*	D. L. Page, *Poetae Melici Graeci* (Oxford, 1962)
Peter	H. Peter (ed.), *Historicorum Romanorum Reliquiae*, 2 vols. (Leipzig, 1870–1914)
PBerol.	*Berlin Papyri*; see https://berlpap.smb.museum/sammlung/?lang=en
PBingen	*Papyri in Honorem Johannis Bingen Octogenarii*; see https://berlpap.smb.museum/p-bingen/?lang=en
PCairo	G. Daressy, *Catalogue général des antiquités égyptiennes du Musée du Caire.* Nos. 24001–24990. Fouilles de la Vallée des Rois (1898–1899) Fasc. 1. (Cairo, 1902)
PEG	A. Bernabé (ed.), 1987. *Poetae epici Graeci. Testimonia et fragmenta.* Pars I (Bibliotheca Scriptorum Graecorum Romanorum Teubneriana). Leipzig.
PG	J. P. Migne (ed.), *Patrologiae cursus completus: Series Graeca* (Paris, 1857–1904)
PHermitage	
PL	J. P. Migne (ed.), *Patrologiae cursus completus: Series Latina* (Paris, 1884–1904)
POxy.	*Oxyrhynchus Papyri* (Oxford, 1898–)
RE	A. von Pauly, G. Wissowa, and W. Kroll (eds.), *Real-Encyclopädie der classischen Altertumswissenschaft* (Stuttgart, 1884–1937)
Roscher, *Lex.*	W. H. Roscher (ed.), *Ausführliches Lexicon der griechischen und römischen Mythologie* (Leipzig, 1884–1937)
schol.	scholion / scholia
Suda	Greek Lexicon formerly known as *Suidas*
Suppl. Hell.	H. Lloyd-Jones and P. Parsons (eds.), *Supplementum Hellenisticum*, Texte und Kommentare no. 11 (Berlin, 1983)
Thilo–Hagen	G. Thilo and H. Hagen, *Servii Grammatici qui feruntur in Vergilii carmina commentarii* (Leipzig, 1881–1902)

ABBREVIATIONS OF CLASSICAL AUTHORS AND TITLES AS USED IN THIS VOLUME

Ael.	Aelian
NA	*De natura animalium*
VH	*Varia historia*
Aesch.	Aeschylus
Ag.	*Agamemnon*
Cho.	*Choephoroe*
Eum.	*Eumenides*
PV	*Prometheus vinctus*
Ant. Lib., *Met.*	Antoninus Liberalis, *Metamorphoses*
Apollod.	Apollodorus
Bibl.	*Bibliotheca*
Epit.	*Epitome*
Apul., *Met.*	Apuleius, *Metamorphoses*
Ap. Rhod., *Argon.*	Apollonius Rhodius, *Argonautica*
Ar.	Aristophanes
Av.	*Aves*
Eq.	*Equites*
Ran.	*Ranae*
Vesp.	*Vespae*
Arist.	Aristotle
Gen. an.	*De generatione animalium*
Part. an.	*De partibus animalium*
[Phgn.]	*Physiognomonica*
Pol.	*Politica*
Ath.	Athenaeus
Bacchyl.	Bacchylides
BD	*Book of the Dead*

Cic.	Cicero
Fam.	*Epistulae ad familiares*
Tusc.	*Tusculanae disputationes*
Claud.	Claudian
CM	*Carmina minora*
DRP	*De raptu Proserpinae*
Dio Chrys., *Or.*	Dio Chrysostomus, *Orationes*
Diod. Sic.	Diodorus Siculus
Eur.	Euripides
Bacch.	*Bacchae*
El.	*Electra*
Hec.	*Hecuba*
Hel.	*Helena*
HF	*Hercules furens*
Hipp.	*Hippolytus*
IT	*Iphigenia Taurica*
Med.	*Medea*
Phoen.	*Phoenissae*
Eust.	Eustathius
Il.	*Ad Iliadem*
Od.	*Ad Odysseam*
Hdt.	Herodotus
Hes.	Hesiod
Cat.	*Catalogus mulierum*
Op.	*Opera et dies*
Theog.	*Theogony*
Hippolytus, *Haer.*	*Refutatio omnium haeresium*
Hom.	Homer
Il.	*Iliad*
Od.	*Odyssey*
Hor.	Horace
Ars	*Ars poetica*
Carm.	*Carmina*
Epod.	*Epodi*
HT	*Hieronyman Theogony*
Hyg.	Hyginus

Fab.	*Fabulae*
Poet. astr.	*Poetica astronomica*
Hymn. Hom. Ap.	*Hymnus Homericus ad Apollinem*
Isid., *Etym.*	Isidore, *Etymologiae*
Luc.	Lucan
Lucian	
Ind.	*Adversus indoctum*
Philops.	*Philopseudes*
Salt.	*De saltatione*
Ver. hist.	*Verae historiae*
Lucr.	Lucretius
DRN	*De rerum natura*
Lycoph.	Lycophron
Alex.	*Alexandra*
Macrob. *Sat.*	Macrobius, *Saturnalia*
Marcus Aurelius	
Med.	*Meditations*
Mart.	Martial
Nic. *Thēr.*	Nicander, *Thēriaca*
Nonnus	
Dion.	*Dionysiaca*
Ov.	Ovid
Am.	*Amores*
Ars. am.	*Ars amatoria*
Fast.	*Fasti*
Her.	*Heroides*
Met.	*Metamorphoses*
Tr.	*Tristia*
Paus.	Pausanias
Petron. *Sat.*	Petronius, *Satyrica*
Philostr.	Philostratus
Her.	*Heroicus*
Imag.	*Imagines*
VA	*Vita Apollonii*
VS	*Vitae sophistarum*

Phlegon, *Mir.*	Phlegon, *Mirabilia*
Pind.	Pindar
Isthm.	*Isthmian odes*
Nem.	*Nemean odes*
Ol.	*Olympian odes*
Pyth.	*Pythian odes*
Pl.	Plato
Cra.	*Cratylus*
Euthphr.	*Euthyphro*
Euthyd.	*Euthydemus*
Leg.	*Leges*
Phd.	*Phaedo*
Phdr.	*Phaedrus*
Resp.	*Respublica*
Plin.	Pliny the Elder
NH	*Naturalis historia*
Pliny the Younger	
Ep.	*Epistulae*
Plut.	Plutarch
Mor.	*Moralia*
De Is. et Os.	*De Iside et Osiride*
Vit.	*Vitae parallelae*
Cim.	*Cimon*
Nic.	*Nicias*
Thes.	*Theseus*
Polyb.	Polybius
Prop.	Propertius
Quintilian	
Inst.	*Institutio oratoria*
RT	*Rhapsodic Theogony*
Sall.	Sallust
Hist.	*Historiae*
Schol. ad Eurip. Phoen.	*Scholia on Euripides' Phoenissae*
Sen.	Seneca (the Younger)
Ep.	*Epistulae morales*
Herc. fur.	*Hercules furens*

Oed.	*Oedipus*
Phaed.	*Phaedra*
Serv.	Servius
in Verg. Aen.	*Commentarii in Vergilii Aeneidem*
Sid. Apoll., *Carm.*	Sidonius Apollinaris, *Carmina*
Sil., *Pun.*	Silius Italicus, *Punica*
Solin.	Solinus
Soph.	Sophocles
OT	*Oedipus tyrannus*
Trach.	*Trachiniae*
Stat., *Theb.*	Statius, *Thebaid*
Steph. Byz.	Stephanus Byzantinus
Suetonius	
Aug.	*Divus Augustus*
Tertullian	
De anim.	*De testimonio animae*
Theoc.	Theocritus
Id.	*Idylls*
Thuc.	Thucydides
Timotheus of Gaza	
De an.	*De animalibus*
Tzetz.	Tzetzes
ad Lyc.	*Scholia ad Lycophronem*
Chil.	*Chiliades*
Val. Flacc., *Argon.*	Valerius Flaccus, *Argonautica*
Varro, *Rust.*	Varro, *De re rustica*
Veg. *Mil.*	Vegetius, *De re militari*
Verg.	Vergil
Aen.	*Aeneid*
Ecl.	*Eclogues*
G.	*Georgics*
Xen.	Xenophon
Cyn.	*Cynegeticus*
Cyr.	*Cyropaedia*
Hell.	*Hellenica*

Contributors

Mercedes Aguirre is Honorary Professor of Greek Philology in the Universidad Complutense in Madrid. She is also Honorary Research Fellow at the University of Bristol, and a Life Member of Clare Hall in the University of Cambridge. Her main areas of published research are Greek literature, Greek mythology and iconography, and the modern reception of Greek mythology. She is the author of *Reflejos del mito griego: Diosas y heroínas en la pintura prerrafaelita* (Madrid, 2006), and co-editor of *Fantasmas, aparecidos y muertos sin descanso* (Madrid, 2014). With Richard Buxton she has co-authored *Cyclops: The Myth and Its Cultural History* (Oxford, 2020). She has also published several novels and short stories, some of them inspired by Greek mythology although situated in our contemporary world, for instance *Mythical Tales of the Everyday World* (2nd bilingual Spanish–English edn., Madrid, 2022), and *El cuadro inacabado* (Madrid, 2013) and its English version, *The Unfinished Painting* (Kibworth, 2020). Webpage: www.mercedesaguirrecastro.com.

Eirini Apanomeritaki is a Visiting Fellow at the University of Essex in the Department of Psychosocial and Psychoanalytic Studies. She serves on the executive committee of the Centre for Myth Studies in Essex. Her research focuses on psychoanalytic theory, mythology, and comparative literature.

Camilla Asplund Ingemark is Senior Lecturer in Ethnology at the Department of Cultural Anthropology and Ethnology, Uppsala University/Campus Gotland, Sweden. Her fields of interest include oral narrative, ancient folklore, folklore and literature, the history of emotions (especially in the ancient world), Old Norse Studies, and environmental humanities. She has worked with ancient Roman folk narrative, nineteenth-century Finland-Swedish folk tales and legends, and contemporary vernacular conceptions of climate change. Her most recent book is *Representations of Fear: Verbalizing Emotion in Ancient Roman Folk Narrative* (Helsinki, 2020), co-authored with Dominic Ingemark.

Emma Aston is Professor of Classics at the University of Reading, United Kingdom. She is the author of a book on hybridism in Greek religious iconography, *Mixanthrôpoi: Animal-human Hybrid Deities in Greek Religion* (Liège, 2011), as well as articles on Greek religion and myth. She also works on the history and culture of ancient Thessaly, and is currently completing a monograph on that region, to be published by Liverpool University Press.

Peter Adrian Behravesh is a writer, editor, and musician. His essay, 'The Vault of Heaven: Science Fiction's Perso-Arabic Origins', received the 2018 Walter James Miller Memorial Award for Student Scholarship in the International Fantastic. For his work as the audio producer of the fantasy fiction podcast *PodCastle*, Peter has received the British Fantasy Award and has been nominated for the Hugo Award and the Ignyte Award. His interactive novel, *Heavens' Revolution: A Lion Among the Cypress*, is forthcoming from Choice of Games. When he isn't crafting, crooning, or otherwise consuming stories, you'll find Peter hurtling down a mountain, sipping English Breakfast tea, or sharpening his Farsi (though usually not all at once).

Leanna Boychenko is Associate Professor of Classical Studies at Loyola University Chicago. Her research focuses on Archaic Greek and Hellenistic poetry, Ptolemaic Egypt, and cultural and literary connections between Greece and Egypt. Her current project examines Callimachus' *Hymns* and their role as a political tool for Ptolemaic legitimation.

Persephone Braham is Professor of Spanish and Latin American Studies at the University of Delaware. Her research is on monsters and monstrosity in Latin America, and she also writes and teaches about Latin American film, urban space and power, gender and sexuality, and the Caribbean. Her book *From Amazons to Zombies* was described as 'An accessible and super generative study of how monstrosity—including the cannibal—was a trope used by European colonizers because they were idiots' (Joseph Pierce).

William Brockliss is Bradshaw Knight Professor of the Environmental Humanities, Director of the Center for Culture, History and Environment, and Associate Professor of Classics at the University of Wisconsin-Madison. He is the author of *Homeric Poetry and the Natural Environment* (CHS, 2019), is currently writing *Horror in Ancient Epic*, and teaches a course on ancient Greek and Roman monsters.

Richard Buxton is Emeritus Professor of Greek Language and Literature and Senior Research Fellow in the University of Bristol. He is also a Life Member of Clare Hall in the University of Cambridge. His main research interests are ancient Greek literature, especially tragedy, and Greek mythology. Among his many books are *Imaginary Greece: The Contexts of Mythology* (Cambridge, 1994), *The Complete World of Greek Mythology* (London, 2004), *Forms of Astonishment: Greek Myths of Metamorphosis* (Oxford, 2009), *The Greek Myths that Shape the Way We Think* (London, 2022), and, co-authored with Mercedes Aguirre, *Cyclops: The Myth and Its Cultural History* (Oxford, 2020). His works have been translated into more than a dozen languages. From 2006 to 2012 he was President of the Foundation for the *LIMC*. He is committed to bringing an informed awareness of ancient Greece, and particularly its mythology, to the widest possible public. Webpage: https://richardgabuxton.co.uk.

Susan Deacy is a Classicist who specializes in ancient Greek religion, mythology, history, gender and sexuality, and in the experiential applications of classical mythology.

She is Professor of Classics at the University of Roehampton, where she has worked since 2004, and the co-founder of the Network ACCLAIM: Autism Connecting with Classically Inspired Mythology. She won a National Teaching Fellowship in 2015 for her work towards diversifying Classics, is Principal Fellow of the Higher Education Academy, and was elected as a Fellow of the Society of Antiquaries of London in 2021. Her latest book is *What Would Hercules Do? Lessons for Autistic Children Using Classical Myth* (Warsaw, 2023), and her current projects include lessons for autistic children based on monsters, notably Medusa.

Ryan Denson received his PhD from the University of Exeter in 2023, completing his thesis on ancient beliefs about sea monsters and sea people. His research interests concern the supernatural in antiquity, folklore, and the ancient imagination. He has published 'Divine Nature and the Natural Divine: The Marine Folklore of Pliny the Elder' for a special issue of the journal *Green Letters* on the interdisciplinary theme of folklore and ecocriticism (2021). Other recent publications include 'Procopius and the Lord of the Demons: The Synthesis of the Demonic Justinian' (2022) in the *Journal of Late Antiquity,* and a chapter on 'Order Among Disorder: Poseidon's Underwater Kingdom and Utopic Marine Environments', for the edited volume *The Ancient Sea: Utopia and Catastrophe in Classical Narratives and Their Reception* (Oxford, 2022).

Julia Doroszewska is Research Fellow at the Faculty of History, University of Warsaw. Her research interests include imperial Greek and Latin prose, predominantly the ancient novel and late antique hagiography, as well as ancient folklore. In her studies of ancient mentality, she combines literary studies with anthropological approaches (particularly the concept of liminality). She has published on Plutarch and Apuleius as well as on Phlegon of Tralles, to whom she dedicated a monograph titled *The Monstrous World: Corporeal Discourses in Phlegon of Tralles' Mirabilia*. She is currently conducting two research projects: *Epiphanies of the Saints in Late Antique Literature* and *Thinking of Thinking: Conceptual Metaphors of Cognition in the Plutarchan Corpus*, both of which are funded by the National Science Centre in Poland.

Debbie Felton is Professor of Classics at the University of Massachusetts Amherst. Her research focuses on folklore of the monstrous and supernatural. Her books include *Haunted Greece and Rome: Ghost Stories from Classical Antiquity* (1999), *Monsters and Monarchs: Serial Killers in Classical Myth and History* (2021), and the edited volumes *Landscapes of Dread in Classical Antiquity: Negative Emotion in Natural and Constructed Spaces* (2018) and *A Cultural History of Fairy Tales in Antiquity* (2021). Professor Felton has also been the editor of the journal *Preternature* since 2015. She enjoys bringing research on classical antiquity into the public sphere, and has appeared in various media (newspapers, radio, TV, blogs, podcasts, webinars) in the US and Europe, including *Coast to Coast AM, The Monster Professor, Weird Tales, CBS Mornings, Classical Wisdom,* and *New Books Network.*

Luba Freedman is a Jack Cotton Professor Emerita in the Art History Department at the Hebrew University of Jerusalem and a researcher into Italian Art of the fifteenth and sixteenth centuries in Florence, Rome, Venice, Parma, and Correggio. Professor Freedman understood early on that she wanted to specialize in the History of Italian Renaissance Art, emphasizing its Classical heritage. Her MA and doctorate were completed at the Hebrew University under the supervision of the department's founder and Israel Prize winner, Professor Moshe Barasch. Professor Freedman has written five books and over fifty articles on masterpieces of the visual arts, including three studies on works of Italian poets: Petrarch, Boccaccio, and Tasso. She has also collaborated on editing a book of articles that deal with mythology. In all her publications, she stresses her constant interest in Classical and Christian subjects and in Aesthetics.

John B. Friedman, Professor Emeritus of English and Medieval Studies at the University of Illinois at Urbana Champaign, has been a Visiting Scholar at the Center for Medieval and Renaissance Studies at the Ohio State University since 2014. His many publications include *The Monstrous Races in Medieval Art and Thought* ([1981] 2000), *Book of the Wonders of the World* (with Kathrin Giogoli and Kristin Figg, 2018), and dozens of journal articles and book chapters on a broad range of medieval topics, including Chaucer, clothing, animals, and, of course, monstrous peoples.

Dr Liz Gloyn is Reader in Latin Language and Literature at Royal Holloway, University of London, UK, where she is currently Co-Director of the Centre for the Reception of Greece and Rome. She has previously worked at the University of Birmingham and Rutgers, the State University of New Jersey. Her research interests beyond classical reception studies explore the intersection between Latin literature, the Roman family, and ancient philosophy. She is the author of *The Ethics of the Family in Seneca* (Cambridge, 2017) and *Tracking Classical Monsters in Popular Culture* (Bloomsbury, 2020).

Dr Greta Hawes is Research Associate at the Center for Hellenic Studies. Her research focuses on Greek myth, and especially on ancient forms of interpretation and the ways the Greeks used stories to make sense of the landscapes around them. She is author of *Rationalizing Myth in Antiquity* (Oxford, 2014) and *Pausanias in the World of Greek Myth* (Oxford, 2021), and editor of *Myths on the Map* (Oxford, 2017). She co-directs MANTO, a dynamic dataset of Greek myth, and directs Canopos, an open access repository for translations of mythographic texts.

Marianne Govers Hopman is Associate Professor of Classics at Northwestern University. Her research focuses on Archaic and Classical Greek poetry, with special interests in literary theory, feminist studies, animal studies, post-humanism, and the environmental humanities. She has published articles on Homer, Athenian tragedy, and the Greek hymns. She is the author of *Scylla: Myth, Metaphor, Paradox* (Cambridge, 2012), and the co-editor (with Renaud Gagné) of *Choral Mediations in Greek Tragedy* (Cambridge, 2013). Her current research project explores the fifth-century BCE tragedy *Prometheus Bound* as an attempt to come to grips with the question of how humans and their inventions fit into the world.

Dominic Ingemark is Senior Lecturer in Classical Archaeology and Ancient History in the Department of Archaeology and Ancient History at Uppsala University, Sweden. His research interests include ancient folklore (particularly ancient Roman folk narrative), Roman social history, Roman foodways, Roman horticulture and agriculture, Roman glass, and Roman–native relations (focusing on Roman Iron Age Scotland and Scandinavia). His most recent book is *Representations of Fear: Verbalizing Emotion in Ancient Roman Folk Narrative* (Helsinki, 2020), co-authored with Camilla Asplund Ingemark.

Derrek Joyce received his MA in ancient Greek and Roman studies from Brandeis University in 2018 and has since been operating as an independent scholar. His research interests include classical mythology and folklore, the evolution of Graeco-Roman gods from ancient religious practices to those of the modern day, and interpretations of the monstrous in current media. Beyond literature, he enjoys expanding his understanding of horticulture and exploring the possibilities 3D printing technologies bring to the preservation of material culture and to gaming hobbyists.

Kenneth F. Kitchell, Jr. is a Professor Emeritus of Classics from Louisiana State University and the University of Massachusetts Amherst. His fields of interest include Greek and Latin pedagogy, and animals and animal lore in classical antiquity and the Middle Ages. Among his recent books are *Albertus Magnus and the Natural World*, with Irven Resnick (Reaktion 2022); *Albertus Magnus De Animalibus: A Medieval Summa Zoologica*, also with Irven Resnick (Ohio [2018] 2020); and *Animals in the Ancient World A–Z* (Routledge 2014), chosen as a *CHOICE Magazine* Outstanding Academic Title for 2014. He resides in Tennessee where he continues his research and is under contract to publish *The Animal World of the Ancient Greeks* with Katia Margariti (Routledge) and the first ever translation of Thomas of Cantimpré's *De natura rerum* with Irven Resnick (Catholic University Press).

Janek Kucharski is Associate Professor in the Department of Philology at the University of Silesia in Katowice. His main research interests are Athenian oratory and tragedy as well as Greek folklore, although he sometimes ventures into other areas such as Homer and the reception of antiquity in Byzantium. He is the author of annotated Polish translations of Hyperides (2016), Antiphon and Dinarchus (2021), and Demosthenes (forthcoming), and co-editor of *The Makings of Identities in Athenian Rhetoric* (London, 2020).

Jennifer Larson is Professor of Classics at Kent State University. Her research interests include ancient Mediterranean religions and magic, Greek poetry, ancient gender and sexuality, and classical mythology. She is the author of five books including *Understanding Greek Religion: A Cognitive Approach* (Routledge, 2016) and *Greek Nymphs: Myth, Cult, Lore* (Oxford, 2001). As a research affiliate of Oxford University's School of Anthropology and Museum Ethnography, Jennifer works with Seshat: Global Databank to test hypotheses about the role of religion in world history, and is a Seshat Board member.

Genevieve Liveley is Professor of Classics and Turing Fellow at the University of Bristol. Her particular research interests are in the story frames, schemata, and scripts that programme cultural myths and sociotechnical narratives. She is the author of *Narratology* (Oxford, 2019) and a number of books and papers on Augustan literature—including *Ovid's Love Songs* (Duckworth, 2005) and *A Reader's Guide to Ovid's Metamorphoses* (Continuum, 2011).

Carolina López-Ruiz is Professor of the History of Religions, Comparative Mythology, and the Ancient Mediterranean World at the University of Chicago Divinity School. She is the author of *When the Gods Were Born: Greek Cosmogonies and the Near East* (Harvard, 2010), and has edited the anthology *Gods, Heroes, and Monsters: A Sourcebook of Greek, Roman, and Near Eastern Myths in Translation* (2nd edn., Oxford, 2018). She has also co-edited or authored several volumes on colonial relations in the western Mediterranean and Phoenician studies. In her most recent book, *Phoenicians and the Making of the Mediterranean* (Harvard, 2021), she offers a fresh appraisal of cultural contact and the Phoenicians' agency during the so-called orientalizing period.

Dunstan Lowe is Senior Lecturer in Latin Literature at the University of Kent. He has published articles on a range of Latin authors, and the book *Monsters and Monstrosity in Augustan Poetry* (Ann Arbor, 2015). His other main research interest is classical antiquity in digital games, a subject he helped to establish by co-editing (with Kim Shahabudin) *Classics for All: Reworking Antiquity in Mass Culture* (Cambridge Scholars, 2009). He has also published on topics in ancient science and folklore, including monumental weathervanes and magnetic levitation.

Justine McConnell is Reader in Comparative Literature and Classical Reception at King's College London. She is author of *Black Odysseys: The Homeric Odyssey in the African Diaspora since 1939* (2013), *Derek Walcott and the Creation of a Classical Caribbean* (2023), and (with Fiona Macintosh) *Performing Epic or Telling Tales* (2020). She has also co-edited four volumes on the reception of Graeco-Roman antiquity.

Katarzyna Marciniak is Professor and Director of the Centre for Studies on the Classical Tradition (OBTA) at the Faculty of "Artes Liberales", University of Warsaw. In 2011 she established the international programme *Our Mythical Childhood*, bringing together scholars from various continents in the aim of studying the reception of classical antiquity in children's and young adult culture. She is a laureate of the Loeb Classical Library Foundation Grant, the Alexander von Humboldt Foundation Alumni Award for Innovative Networking Initiatives, and the European Research Council Consolidator and Proof of Concept Grants. She has published on classical reception, children's and young adult culture, and Cicero. She edited *Chasing Mythical Beasts: The Reception of Ancient Monsters in Children's and Young Adults' Culture* (2020).

Fiona Mitchell's research focuses on Greek literature, iconography, and myth. Her work explores the use of monstrosity and bodily abnormality, creation narratives, and ancient conceptions of time. She published *Monsters in Greek Literature: Aberrant Bodies* *in Ancient Cosmogony, Ethnography, and Biology* in 2021. Her current work examines the use of personification in the representation of time and its origins.

Andrea Murace, who graduated in Classics from the University of Siena, Italy, is currently a PhD student in Classics at Roma Tre University and at Nice-Côte d'Azur University. His main research areas include Greek literature (particularly of the Late Antique and Byzantine periods) and archaeology. He is interested in the human-animal relationship in the ancient world, at the level of ethics, hunting, paradoxography, and zoological knowledge.

Daniel Ogden is Professor of Ancient History in the University of Exeter, having previously taught at Hobart and William Smith Colleges, Oxford University, and University College of Swansea. He has published three books on the ancient dragon: *Drakōn: Dragon Myth and Serpent Cult in the Greek and Roman Worlds* (2013); *Dragons, Serpents and Slayers in the Classical and Early Christian Worlds: A Sourcebook* (2013); and *The Dragon in the West* (2021). His other books include *Greek and Roman Necromancy* (2001); *Aristomenes of Messene* (2003); *In Search of the Sorcerer's Apprentice: The Traditional Tales of Lucian's Lover of Lies* (2008); *Perseus* (2008); *Magic, Witchcraft and Ghosts in the Greek and Roman Worlds: A Sourcebook* (2nd edn., 2009); *The Legend of Seleucus* (2017); *The Werewolf in the Ancient World* (2021); and *The Strix-Witch* (2021). He is the editor of *A Companion to Greek Religion* (2007) and *The Oxford Handbook of Heracles* (2021).

Simon Oswald is Assistant Professor in the Department of Classics at the University of Massachusetts Amherst. His research ranges widely across the fields of archaeology and linguistics, and particularly one of the most important intersections between the two, epigraphy.

Madadh Richey is Assistant Professor of Hebrew Bible at Brandeis University. She studies discourses of myth, magic, and religion within and around the Hebrew Bible and the ancient Middle East. Her current book project, *Visions of Gods and Monsters*, explores religious and social functions of divine-combat images in visual art of the Levant and Mesopotamia during the Iron Age (*c*.1175–550 BCE). Professor Richey is an epigrapher of Northwest Semitic inscriptions and publishes newly discovered and recently rediscovered texts in Hebrew, Ugaritic, Phoenician and Punic, and Aramaic.

Brett M. Rogers is Professor of Greek, Latin, and Ancient Mediterranean Studies at the University of Puget Sound—a sublime place replete with monsters: in addition to local interest in the sasquatch, the regional ice hockey team is the Kraken and the place is overshadowed by Mount Tahoma (in the words of Marianne Moore) 'An Octopus | of ice'.

Christina A. Salowey is a Professor of Classics at Hollins University. Her professional interest in ancient Greek mythology and religion combined with a personal interest in the environment and nature has led to her research into the interplay between the geology of the Mediterranean landscape and mythical stories to explain the natural forces that sustain and threaten human existence. She has published elsewhere on Heracles and his confrontations with forces of the landscape, especially rivers, contributed studies on women commemorated in grave monuments, and enjoys the interdisciplinary investigations that the study of the ancient Greek world demands.

Antonella Sciancalepore is a specialist of medieval literature and culture, currently working as a research fellow at the Institut de Civilisations, Arts et Lettres of the Université Catholique de Louvain (Belgium). She has a PhD in Interpretation, Philology of Texts, and History of Culture from the University of Macerata and the University of Edinburgh. She has published two books and several articles on human-animal relations, non-human identity, and female sovereignty in medieval French and Occitan literature. Her upcoming book *At the Edge of Human* discusses how human-animal hybrids in medieval literature and encyclopaediae (1200–1450) work as thought experiments about the limits of the human. Her main research topics include animals, monsters, and environment representation in medieval European culture.

Hannah Silverblank is a Mellon Postdoctoral Fellow in Critical Classical Reception at Brown University (2022–4). Her research focuses on how meaning is constituted and exchanged across time, languages, species, and embodied differences. Her in-progress book project, *Listening to the Monster in Greek Poetry*, tunes into the monster's cosmic positioning in more-than-human worlds by attending to the aesthetics of non-human sonic expression in ancient Greek poetry. Several of Silverblank's recent and forthcoming publications have focused on the role of disability and/or queerness in translation theory, lexicography, reception theory, and the occult arts and sciences. Silverblank received her DPhil. in Classical Languages and Literature at the University of Oxford in 2017, and she taught in various Humanities departments at Haverford College from 2017 to 2022.

R. Scott Smith is Professor of Classics and Chair of the Department of Classics, Humanities, and Italian Studies at the University of New Hampshire, where he has taught since 2000. His major field of study is ancient myth and mythography, with special focus on the intersection of mythography, space, and geography. He is currently co-director of a digital database of Greek myth, MANTO: https://manto.unh.edu. In addition, he is interested in how mythography operates in scholia and commentaries and is undertaking a student-supported project to translate mythographical narratives in the Homeric scholia, Servius, and other scholiastic texts. He also produces the podcast *The Greek Myth Files*: https://manto-myth.org/gmf.

Dr Benjamin Eldon Stevens works in two main areas: classical receptions, with focuses on underworlds and afterlives, science fiction/fantasy/horror, and film; and Latin literature, which he has studied for cultural histories of the senses and ideas about language including silence. He is the author of *Silence in Catullus* (Wisconsin, 2013) and co-editor of *Classical Traditions in Science Fiction* (Oxford, 2015), *Classical Traditions in Modern Fantasy* (Oxford, 2017), *Frankenstein and Its Classics* and *Once and Future Antiquities* (both Bloomsbury, 2018); he is also a published translator of French and Spanish. A graduate of the University of Chicago (PhD 2005) and Reed College (BA 1998), he has taught at Bard College, Hollins University, Bryn Mawr College, Trinity University, and Howard University.

Stephen M. Trzaskoma is the Dean of the College of Arts and Letters at California State University Los Angeles. He has published widely on the surviving novels from ancient Greece and on Greek and Roman myth and mythography. He is the co-editor, with R. Scott Smith, of the *Oxford Handbook of Greek and Roman Mythography* (2022), *Writing Myth: Mythography in the Ancient World* (2013), and *Apollodorus' 'Library' and Hyginus' 'Fabulae': Two Handbooks of Greek Mythology* (2007).

Dr Arngrímur Vídalín is Assistant Professor of Old Norse Literature at the University of Iceland, Reykjavík, School of Education. He has been a visiting scholar at Harvard University (2016), the University of Silesia in Katowice (2016), and the University of Copenhagen (2014 and 2018). His current projects include a book about Grettis saga and a critical edition of the fourteenth-century manuscript AM 194 8vo., now also known under the title 'Narfeyrarbók', as discussed in his chapter in this volume.

Marchella Ward (Chella) is the Tinsley Outreach Fellow at Worcester College, Oxford where she splits her time equally between research in classical reception and work to dismantle the inequities and biases that structure access to Higher Education. Her research focuses on the role of the classical in the ways that bodies are made meaningful, and she is particularly interested in how the ancient world is weaponized in contemporary ableisms and in the racialization practices of European empires. Her first monograph, on the role of the classical in ableist tropes about blindness, is forthcoming with Cambridge University Press. Chella also writes frequently for non-specialists and for children—her first children's book, *A Journey Through Greek Myths* (2020) has been translated into four languages. From September 2022 she will be Lecturer in Classical Studies at the Open University.

Jesse Weiner is Associate Professor of Classics at Hamilton College in Clinton, New York. He has published numerous articles on Greek and Latin literature, drama, and classical reception studies with strong interests in monumentality, memory, aesthetics, and gender studies. He is co-editor of *Frankenstein and Its Classics: The Modern Prometheus from Antiquity to Science Fiction* (Bloomsbury Academic, 2018) and *Searching for the cinaedus in Ancient Rome* (Brill, 2023). In public humanities, he has worked with Ancient Greeks/Modern Lives and his work has appeared in *History Today* and *The Atlantic*.

Lorenz Winkler-Horaček is a professor of classical archaeology at the Freie Universität Berlin, where he is also the curator of the Berlin Cast Collection (Abguss-Sammlung Antiker Plastik). He received his doctorate from the University of Heidelberg in 1991 and worked for fourteen years at the University of Rostock. He habilitated in 2004 and transferred to the Freie Universität Berlin in 2007. His field of research is heavily image-based and covers both the Greek and Roman periods. Its primary focus is on monsters and mixed creatures in early Greek art as well as cultural contacts between Greece and the Near East. Another area of his work is in the field of visual communication in the Roman Empire, especially visual strategies for establishing power. Additionally, he focuses on the history of plaster casts. He has curated numerous exhibitions on archaeological themes at the Berlin Cast Collection and organized events with contemporary artists.

Vanda Zajko is Associate Professor in Classics in the Department of Classics and Ancient History at the University of Bristol. Dr Zajko has wide-ranging research interests in the reception of classical myth and literature, especially in psychoanalytic theory, feminist thought, and literary empathy. Her many publications include *Laughing with Medusa: Classical Myth and Feminist Though* (co-edited with Miriam Leonard, Oxford, 2006) and *Classical Myth and Psychoanalysis: Ancient and Modern Stories of the Self* (co-edited with Ellen O'Gorman, Oxford, 2013).

Notes on Usage

When dealing with materials from various cultures from across the ancient Near Eastern and Mediterranean worlds, questions of orthography and other usages inevitably come up. To ensure a certain level of consistency within the volume, we were asked to standardize our spellings to Latinate versions of Greek and other foreign language names. So, even in chapters dealing solely with Greek literature, art, and architecture, readers will find Latinate spellings rather than transcriptions of the Greek: 'Uranus' rather than 'Ouranos', for example, and 'Cyclopes' rather than 'Kyklopes'.

We were faced with many other orthographic issues, some necessitated by house style, others optional. For example, we had to choose among variant spellings even of Latinate versions, and so (for example) have 'Orthrus' rather than 'Orthus' for the canine brother of Cerberus, and 'Ammut' rather than 'Ammit' for the Egyptian goddess. Similarly, we had to make choices regarding specific versus generic uses of the names for various monsters and monster groups, and have used capitalized 'Sirens', 'Harpies', 'Sphinx', and the like when referring to the Odyssean Sirens, the Apollonian Harpies, and the Theban or Gizan Sphinx, but lower-case 'sirens', 'harpies', 'sphinx', and so on when referring to generic versions of these monsters, such as the sphinxes used decoratively in ancient Anatolia or in Renaissance art. In contrast, the Tritons and Nereids are capitalized throughout as deriving from paternal names (Triton, Nereus). The Giants (Gigantes) who were the children of Gaea are capitalized; 'giant' elsewhere is not. The Cretan Labyrinth is capitalized but other labyrinths are not. Heracles' Twelve Labours as a group are capitalized, but individual labours are not. In short, we cannot list the hundreds of orthographic rules that ended up being applied across all forty chapters, but wanted to make readers aware that there is a method behind what might otherwise seem like arbitrary choices.

Lastly, we acknowledge that 'the ancient Near East', while still the more common appellation applied in classical studies for the region stretching from Mesopotamia through Anatolia and the Levant and environs, reflects the perspective of the nineteenth-century British Empire, especially with respect to the pre-Islamic period (whereas the usage of 'Middle East' developed in the twentieth century with reference to the modern geopolitical region). A more accurate designation going forward might perhaps be 'Western Asia'.

INTRODUCTION
Monster Theory and Classical Myth

DEBBIE FELTON

WHY MONSTERS?

MYTHICAL monsters are marvellous. They are also often menacing and malevolent. Physically and geographically, whether they have impossibly composite bodies or dwell on environmental boundaries or transgress perceived societal norms, they demonstrate a unique marginality. But monsters are often also misunderstood. They do not exist in myth only to provide foils for heroes, or simply to represent inexplicable aspects of the natural world, though such functions certainly remain crucial for many of the creatures discussed in this volume. Rather, monsters and their characteristics also provide a broad perspective on a wide variety of ongoing cultural concerns. Aside from informing us about how ancient Mediterranean peoples perceived their environment and interacted with it, the monsters of classical myth—here including the ancient Near East, Egypt, and the Graeco-Roman world—constantly provide us with paradigms for new approaches to ancient material. In this volume, readers will find famously familiar monsters not just in their original contexts of two and three thousand years ago, but also in relation to their relevance for the modern world.

MONSTER THEORY AND CLASSICAL STUDIES

Nearly every chapter in this volume draws on what we call 'monster theory', a phrase coined by medieval scholar Jeffrey Jerome Cohen in his edited volume *Monster Theory: Reading Culture* to describe the study of monsters and their meanings within and beyond their cultural contexts. Monsters, Cohen and his contributors argued, symbolically express a society's anxieties; if we think about why a culture engenders this or that monster, we may better understand that culture (1996: 3). Although monster theory originated in medieval studies, Cohen stressed that monsters from the distant past remain highly relevant to conceptions of the monstrous in the immediate present. And, in fact, classicists had started thinking about monsters at around the same time: Catherine Atherton's 1998 *Monsters and Monstrosity in Greek and Roman Culture* gathered five papers in one volume that was acknowledged as 'a very important book for all who are interested in better understanding an unfortunately often-neglected topic', with the observation that 'despite the enormous bibliography on each specific monster, not much has been said until now about what a monster is, what it represents and why it is "good to think with" ' (Giordani 2003).[1]

Atherton's collection, having been assembled around the same time as Cohen's work, understandably did not incorporate his ideas, and lacks specific acknowledgement of many characteristics that have since come to be widely associated with monsters, such as hybridism, morphological distortion, and boundary transgressions (both physical and behavioural). Similarly, Atherton's contributors do not address female monstrosity, philosophical or psychological interpretations, and other such considerations in any detail. Her collection's vital contribution, however, was to acknowledge that—as many later scholars of monster theory have observed—monsters tend to be culturally determined.[2] Each culture has its own anxieties and fears, its own definitions of what is 'normal' and acceptable. And even within cultures people have different viewpoints about what constitutes 'the monstrous'. So, as Liz Gloyn points out, rather than being able to settle on a shared definition of 'monster', creating a consensus about the concept, whether for classical or modern monsters, 'would be far from straightforward' (2020: 3).

For peoples of the ancient Near East and Mediterranean, at least, monsters embodied a variety of general unconscious fears: the potential of chaos to overcome order; the potential victory of nature against encroaching human civilization, and of irrationality over reason; and even of the little-understood nature of the female in contrast with the male. These ancient stories repeatedly presented monsters being conquered by gods and men, as the perceived forces of order, civilization, reason, and patriarchy inevitably prevailed in ancient thought (Felton 2012: 103). Monsters also provided a means to express fear of the Other—any individual or group seen as different in a fundamental way from the culture telling the story. Whereas the Other can often be someone (or a group) of a different skin colour, social class, religion, sexual orientation, and the like, this was rarely the case in antiquity, where the Other was most often a different, faraway people. For example, from ancient Greece to medieval Europe, people received reports of the Cynocephali (a 'dog-headed' people) living in India, largely without questioning

---

[1] The phrase 'good to think with', now often applied to monsters, originates with Claude Lévi-Strauss' 1962 *Totemism* (in a completely different context).

[2] See e.g. Porada (1987: 1), Bremmer (1997: 2), Atherton (1998: x), Cohen (1996: 4), Gilmore (2003: 9), Asma (2009: 1–15); cf. Felton (2012: 103–31).

the existence of such hybrid humans but instead accepting that such oddities were likely to exist on the fringes of the known world.

This conception remained distinct from the theriomorphic deities of the Egyptians, such as the jackal-headed Anubis—just one of many possible examples of the ongoing connection between monstrosity and the divine. Some ancient cultures had no specific terminology for things we might consider monstrous, but instead encompassed them under the general concept of 'spirits'—not humans, not gods, but something in between; as Madadh Richey points out in Chapter 2, 'no language first written in the ancient Middle East includes a word whose semantics map mostly—and, for many languages, even partially—on to those of English "monster"', and Leanna Boychenko discusses a similar semantic issue for the concept of monstrosity in Egyptian culture in Chapter 3. But for Greece and Rome, a partial clue to the ancient conception of 'monster' around the Mediterranean comes through the language they used to signify such beings, as many other chapters in this volume indicate. The Greek term *teras* referred both to portents from the gods and, in a more concrete sense, a physical monstrosity, something deformed; hence our modern term 'teratology', which refers not only to mythologies about marvellous, unusual, and inhuman physical creatures, but also to the scientific study of congenital abnormalities. The English word 'monster' itself comes from the Latin *monstrum*, etymologically linked with the verbs *monere* ('to warn') and *monstrare* ('to show'). A *monstrum*, to the Romans, originally denoted any manifestation of divine will that breached 'the natural order, provoking awe or at least shock', but eventually came to be the closest thing to a regular Latin term for any physically anomalous being (see Lowe 2015: 8–9).

So, for the purposes of this volume, readers will find that 'monster' refers to a variety of creatures, most of them exhibiting physical anomalies such as an excess or deficit of limbs, unusually large size, and/or jarring hybridity, and all of them, in some way or another, transgressing literal or metaphorical boundaries. Often their main purposes in the stories are to act as disruptive agents, though such disruption may come only when they find their status as guardians threatened. At a minimum, these creatures prove unsettling in their unexpectedness; at a maximum, they pose dire threats to humans and human attempts to settle into and impose order on the natural world.

And, as representatives of the natural world (preferably one devoid of humans), monstrous creatures in ancient myths almost invariably dwelled in places outside settled, urban areas, such as mountains, caves, cliffs, and other natural, often liminal locations bordering on or largely untouched by human settlement. The farther from major urban centres people went, it was believed, the more likely they were to encounter the monstrous, and the edges of known civilization were particularly rife with strange, threatening creatures (see van Duzer 2012). The Sphinx, for example, lived on Mount Phikion outside the city of Thebes; the Cyclops Polyphemus and his kin lived in caves; the snaky-haired Medusa and her Gorgon sisters traditionally were said to live on a rocky island in the Mediterranean. Similarly, bodies of water including lakes, marshes, and the often-hostile sea held many monsters (Boardman 1987; Denson 2022). As Jan Bremmer observed, such locations are not surprising since wilderness is where 'unordered' things such as monsters belong (1997: 3). The chapters in this volume often highlight this geographical liminality.

ORGANIZATION OF THE VOLUME

To show a progression of sorts in how we have perceived mythical monsters from antiquity across the millennia, this volume presents these monsters within four different if inevitably overlapping parts. The first and longest introduces readers to the most well-known monsters of the ancient world, including those that played significant roles in creation myths and hero quests—Typhoeus, the Gorgons, the Hydra, the Theban Sphinx, Scylla and Charybdis, the Minotaur, and many others. The second part covers monsters that appear mainly in ancient folklore and ethnography rather than in relation to heroes: ghosts, child-snatching bogeys, and unusual peoples such as the Cynocephali. The third part provides various interpretations of classical monsters, examining their representations in art and architecture from antiquity to the Renaissance and explaining the most widely used theoretical approaches, including psychoanalysis, cognitive theory, and disability studies. The fourth and final part examines the tradition and reception of classical monsters in later literature and art, often drawing upon the theories explained in Part III to explain the adaptation and significance of classical monsters in other cultures, such as Persian, Scandinavian, Afro-Caribbean, and Latin American, and in specific literary genres, including young adult literature, science fiction, fantasy, and fan fiction. We have also aimed for a broad audience, and to that end have tried to keep theoretical and other field-specific jargon to a minimum.

A MATTER OF PERSPECTIVE

The importance of the various perspectives offered in this volume may be summed up with an Aesopian fable, 'The Satyr and the Traveller'. Here, the creature 'normally' considered as monstrous is the satyr, whose hybrid human-animal mixture varied across Greek and Roman culture from having a horse's ears and tail (the former) to having a goat's ears, tail, legs, and even horns (the latter), but whose 'monstrous' behaviour was limited to human-like drunkenness and unsuccessful attempts to seduce nymphs or the occasional human female. Similarly, centaurs (half-horse, half-human) were known for being violent drunks, a notable exception being Chiron, who, unlike his brethren, was highly educated by the god Apollo in various skills (including medicine, music, astronomy, and archery). Over time, satyrs, unlike centaurs, were portrayed less as ribald and more as a type of nature spirit that guarded the woodland. This fable provides a helpful example of the shifting and relative cultural conceptions of what was considered anomalous and therefore monstrous:

When rough winter set in with thick frost, and every field stiffened under the hard ice, a traveller found himself stuck in a dense fog. The path was no longer visible, preventing him from continuing. The story goes that a satyr, one of the guardians of the forest, took pity on the man and offered to shelter him in his cave. The satyr, as a native of the wild countryside, was straightaway both amazed and greatly afraid upon observing the immense power of the man. For first, to restore some vitality to his freezing limbs, the man thawed his hands by blowing hot air onto them. After the cold had dissipated, he began to enjoy the generous hospitality of his host; the satyr, eager to show off country life, had set out the best of what the forest had to give, and offered a bowl filled with hot Lyaean wine, so that its warmth would spread through the man's limbs and relieve the chill. But then the man cringed at touching the hot bowl with his lips and blew again—with a cool breath! At this, his host, utterly terrified, was dumbstruck at the double portent [*monstro*], and, driving the man out into the woods, ordered him to go far, far away. 'I do not want anyone ever to come into my cave again', said the satyr, 'who breathes two different ways from the same mouth!' (G 368)[3]

Adrados (1999–2003: 3.50) points out that this anecdote provides a metaphorical attack against lies and duplicity, as it ironically highlights *man's* unreliable, deceptive dual nature, rather than overtly referencing the 'monstrous' dual nature of the hybrid satyr, who instead appears as a perfectly normal representative of nature. The satyr, rather than the human, exhibits the emotions in this story: he pities (*miseratus*) the lost traveller, but then feels awe (*miratur*) and extreme fear (*pavet, perterritus*) and is stunned (*obstipuit*) at what he perceives as the highly unnatural and therefore monstrous ability demonstrated by his guest. That is, the satyr demonstrates the emotions typically associated with *human* reactions to monsters (Felton 2021).

Such cultural relativity was not an entirely new perspective. The fifth-century Greek historian Herodotus provides an anecdote about Darius, king of the Persians, that illustrates how monstrous one culture's customs can seem to another:

During his reign, Darius summoned the Greeks of his court and asked them for what price they would be willing to eat their fathers' bodies when they died, and they replied that they would not do it for any amount. Darius next summoned those Indians called 'Callatiae', who eat their parents; in the presence of the Greeks, who understood through a translator what was being said, he asked what it would take for them to burn their dead fathers. Horrified, the Callatiae cried out that Darius should not speak such ill-omened words—so firmly entrenched are one's customs. (3.38.3–4)

This sort of perspective-taking appears much more frequently in modern adaptations of classical monsters, as this volume's later chapters illustrate. Such stories help remind

---

[3] I use the numbering system of Laura Gibbs (2008) (G). The Latin text is Avianus, fable 29 (*c.*400 CE); for the folk-tale type, see ATU 1342, Uther (2004: 144). All translations from Latin and Greek are my own unless otherwise indicated.

us that 'monstrosity' need not equal 'evil', and more recent studies on the monstrous tend towards inclusive treatments of the alterity represented by physically anomalous bodies and non-normative behaviour (see e.g. Emmrich 2020: 7–29). By studying the concepts of monsters and monstrosity across cultures and time, we learn about the shifting concerns of those cultures and observe how monsters represent various aspects of the unknown, the inexplicable, and the feared. But we also learn how to face what causes us discomfort and dread, to make peace with it, and, with any luck, to change our attitudes towards the monstrous by empathizing with it.

ACKNOWLEDGEMENTS

I am inexpressibly grateful to all the contributors in this volume for their expert knowledge on the subject matter, their amazing patience with the editing process, and their perseverance through very difficult pandemic times. This project began in 2020, and all the authors involved were affected by COVID-19 in one way or another, whether from the relatively manageable loss of library access to the irreparable loss of family and friends. I am especially grateful to those who joined us late in the process to replace contributors who were for various reasons unable to continue their chapters. Thanks also to my agent, Jill Marsal, of Marsal Lyon Literary Agency; to our editors at Oxford University Press, most specifically Charlotte Loveridge and Henry Clarke, for shepherding this project through to publication; and to Jim and Alex, for putting up with me during yet another long, intricate project.

WORKS CITED

Adrados, F. R. 1999–2003. *History of the Greco-Latin Fable*, 3 vols., trans. L. A. Ray. Leiden.

Asma, S. T. 2009. *On Monsters: An Unnatural History of Our Worst Fears*. Oxford.

Atherton, C., ed. 1998. *Monsters and Monstrosity in Greek and Roman Culture*. Bari.

Boardman, J. 1987. ' "Very Like a Whale"—Classical Sea Monsters', in *Monsters and Demons in the Ancient and Medieval Worlds: Papers Presented in Honor of Edith Porada*, ed. A. E. Farkas et al., 73–84. Mainz am Rhine.

Bremmer, J. 1997. 'Monsters en fabeldieren in de Griekse cultuur.' *Vereniging van Vrienden Allard Pierson Museum: Mededelingenblad* 68: 2–5. Amsterdam.

Cohen, J. J. 1996. 'Monster Culture (Seven Theses)', in *Monster Theory: Reading Culture*, ed. J. J. Cohen, 3–25. Minneapolis.

Denson, R. 2022. 'Sea Monsters and Sea People: The Marine Realm in the Greco-Roman Imagination.' PhD thesis, University of Exeter.

Emmrich, T. 2020. *Ästhetische Monsterpolitiken: Das Monströse als Figuration des eingeschlossenen Ausgeschlossenen*. Heidelberg.

Felton, D. 2012. 'Rejecting and Embracing the Monstrous in Ancient Greece and Rome', in *The Ashgate Research Companion to Monsters and the Monstrous*, ed. A. S. Mittman and P. J. Dendle, 103–31. Farnham.

Felton, D. 2021. 'Monsters and the Monstrous: Ancient Expressions of Cultural Anxieties', in *A Cultural History of Fairy Tales in Antiquity*, ed. D. Felton, 109–30. London.

Gibbs, L. 2008. *Aesop's Fables*. Oxford.

Gilmore, D. 2003. *Monsters: Evil Beings, Mythical Beasts, and All Manner of Imaginary Terrors.* Philadelphia.

Giordani, M. 2003. 'Review: C. Atherton, *Monsters and Monstrosity in Greek and Roman Culture.* Nottingham Classical Literature Studies vol. 6: 1997; Bari: Levante (2000 printing).' https://bmcr.brynmawr.edu/2003/2003.04.15/. Accessed 18 January 2023.

Gloyn, L. 2020. *Tracking Classical Monsters in Popular Culture.* London.

Lowe, D. 2015. *Monsters and Monstrosity in Augustan Poetry.* Ann Arbor.

Porada, E. 1987. 'Introduction', in *Monsters and Demons in the Ancient and Medieval Worlds: Papers Presented in Honor of Edith Porada*, ed. A. E. Farkas et al., 1–11. Mainz.

Uther, H.-J. 2004. *The Types of the International Folktale: A Classification and Bibliography: Based on the System of Antii Aarne and Stith Thompson.* Helsinki.

van Duzer, C. 2012. '*Hic Sunt Dracones*: The Geography and Cartography of Monsters', in *The Ashgate Research Companion to Monsters and the Monstrous*, ed. A. S. Mittman and P. J. Dendle, 387–435. Farnham.

PART I

MONSTERS IN THE ANCIENT MEDITERRANEAN AND NEAR EAST

CHAPTER 1

··

MONSTERS IN CREATION NARRATIVES OF ANCIENT GREECE AND ROME

FIONA MITCHELL

··

INTRODUCTION

CREATION narratives tell the story of how the world came to exist in its current form. In this process, we usually see the cosmos develop from a muddled or empty primordial state into a more ordered and differentiated one. Monstrous bodies play a significant role in this development. In Greek and Roman narratives, monstrous bodies tend to appear after the very first group of deities, who often embody the spaces in which the rest of creation takes place (e.g. the earth and the sky), and before anthropomorphic deities become the rulers. In some instances, monsters are part of the process in which different types of bodies proliferate before the unviable ones fade out. In most ancient narratives, however, monsters are creatures which must be overcome by anthropomorphic deities and their heroic offspring. In this victory over creatures with different bodies, the gods demonstrate both their pre-eminence and that of the ordered cosmos to which their bodies belong. In either case, monsters and their anthropomorphic counterparts demonstrate the process of creation through the change in types of bodies that exist at different times. In this way, they mark out the chronological boundary of the human world by highlighting a time when forms that are now impossible were present in the world.

MONSTROUS FAMILIES IN HESIOD'S
THEOGONY

Hesiod's *Theogony* ('Origin of the Gods') is our earliest Greek account of creation, and probably the most influential cosmogony in Greek and Latin literature. Hesiod seems to have composed the poem in the eighth century BCE. As its title suggests, the *Theogony* narrates the origins of the gods and the cosmos from the very first deities, down to the births of heroes. While it focuses on the Greek pantheon and the emergence of the Olympian deities as the rulers of the cosmos, the poem reflects significant influences from Near Eastern texts (López-Ruiz 2010). In particular, the story of the conflicts between generations of the gods shows correspondences to the Hittite *Song of Kumarbi*, and the conflict between Zeus and his final opponent, Typhoeus, bears similarities to the conflict between Marduk and Tiāmat in the Babylonian *Enūma eliš*.

The *Theogony* explains the development of the cosmos through a genealogy of the gods. Although the first four gods—Chaos, Gaea, Tartarus, and Eros—simply come into being and Gaea (Earth) produces Uranus (Sky) parthenogenically, sexual reproduction is usually the process by which areas of the cosmos are created. The poem's narrative drives strongly towards a final version of the cosmos in which Zeus rules over a clearly ordered and divided cosmos (Clay 2003: 152–3). Monsters play an important role in demonstrating the progression of the cosmos into its final form: as the cosmos moves away from its earlier stages, characterized by a lack of order, the creatures that physically manifest this disorder are removed from the cosmos by being killed or imprisoned.

In the *Theogony*, individual branches of the family tree gather similar beings together into groups (West 1966: 34, 244). The monsters exist in three specific branches. Many of them are the children of Phorcys and Ceto, a pair of divine figures associated with the sea. A smaller number are the offspring of Gaea and Uranus. Typhoeus is the child of Gaea and Tartarus. Thus, while the monsters are still related to the gods, they are separated from the Olympians because they belong to a different part of the family. This genealogical distance corresponds to physical and social distance: the Olympians in Greek literature and art were usually depicted with beautiful and idealized anthropomorphic bodies, in contrast with the hybrid monsters. The *Theogony* also presents the Olympians as having clear speech and eating divine food, whereas the monsters often have distorted or animal voices and eat raw flesh. So, while the monsters are related to the Olympians, they are also kept at a distance that marks how they fail to live up to the idealized natures of the ruling gods.

The offspring of Phorcys and Ceto are the most physically diverse group of monsters, and several are hybrids (Fig. 1.1). Echidna is 'half a quick-eyed beautiful-cheeked nymph, but half a monstrous snake' (Hes. *Theog.* 298–9).[1] The Chimaera has multiple

---

[1] Translations of Hesiod are from Most (2006). Below, all translations of the Orphic theogonies are my own; translations from Ovid's *Metamorphoses* are from Miller (1916); translations of

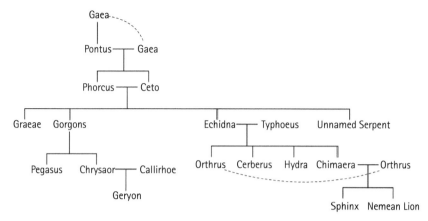

FIGURE 1.1 Genealogical table of the monsters descended from Phorcys and Ceto, according to Hesiod. Dotted lines indicate the repeated appearance of individuals; double lines highlight the instances of uncertain parentage.

Credit: Fiona Mitchell.

animal heads: one of a lion, one of a goat, and one of a snake (321–2). Others seem to be abnormal versions of a single creature, such as the Nemean Lion (327–32), Orthrus (a dog, 309), and the unnamed 'terrible snake' that guards the golden apples (333–5). Lions, dogs, and snakes recur in other family members: the Sphinx has a lion component, Cerberus is canine, and the Hydra is serpentine. Some of the family have multiple heads: Cerberus has fifty (312) and the giant Geryon has three (287). This group thus combines hybridity with excessive features.

It is not only these creatures' bodies that do not fit into one category, but also their behaviours. This is most evident in the case of Echidna, described as 'not at all similar to mortal human beings or to the immortal gods' (Hes. *Theog.* 295–6). She inhabits a divine home as she lives in 'glorious mansions' (303), but she is also described as 'eating raw flesh' (300). This diet is also a characteristic of Cerberus (311). Thus, the creatures in this group are not only unlike animals or humans, but also unlike the gods, despite their genealogical connection. Unsurprisingly for a group of creatures with unclear physical boundaries, their genealogy is also blurry: sometimes the mother of a particular creature is not named, and the text refers vaguely to 'she' (295, 319, 326). Thus, for this family branch, the exact lineage—which Hesiod provides for most other beings—appears to be less important than having these monsters connected to one another and separated from the Olympians.

These monsters seem to exist primarily to be killed by heroes: the Hydra and Nemean Lion are slain by Heracles (Hes. *Theog.* 332), Medusa by Perseus (280), and the Chimaera by Bellerophon (325). By killing such monsters, the heroes remove creatures which do

Empedocles are from Kirk et al. (1983); and translations of Lucretius follow Rouse (1924) with minor adaptation.

not fit into the version of the world we live in (clearly, we do not live alongside them). The heroes therefore participate in the transformation of universe into its final structure under the rule of Zeus.

The children of Uranus and Gaea make up a smaller, but no less significant, group of monsters. In addition to the Titans, Gaea and Uranus produce two trios of physically strange children (Hes. *Theog.* 139–53): the Hecatoncheires ('Hundred-Handers') and the Cyclopes ('Circle-Eyes'). Rather than being hybrids, they are characterized by their excess or lack of certain body parts. These Hesiodic Cyclopes are key allies of Zeus: they provide him with the thunderbolt (141, 503–6), a tool that allows him to defeat both the Titans (687–710) and Typhoeus (853–68; see the chapters by Brockliss, and Aguirre and Buxton in this volume). The Hecatoncheires also ally with the Olympians in the battle against the Titans (654–88). These groups do not therefore need to be killed off by the Olympians or their heroic offspring because they contribute to their rule.

The *Theogony* presents the Hecatoncheires and the Cyclopes as substantially different from the hybrid children of Phorcys and Ceto. In addition to being allies of the Olympians, they appear more physically and socially like the gods. Although they have the 'wrong' number of body parts, they are essentially anthropomorphic. In addition to being skilled craftsmen, the Cyclopes can speak fluently like the Olympians (Hes. *Theog.* 654–63), they consume divine food (640), and one marries a daughter of Poseidon (817–19). Although some children of Phorcys and Ceto appear to possess some civilized features (Echidna's 'glorious mansions', 303), none of them speak or demonstrate any technical skill. The treatments of these groups differ significantly. Instead of being killed, the Hecatoncheires are confined to the underworld as 'the trusted guards of aegis-holding Zeus' (735). The Cyclopes are not referenced again in the *Theogony*. Despite their broadly anthropomorphic forms, the Cyclopes and Hecatoncheires still have no place in the worlds of mortals or the Olympians.

The single most important monster in the *Theogony* is Typhoeus, the final opponent Zeus must overcome before securing his divine kingship. Typhoeus embodies a complex hybridity. His body consists of both anthropomorphic and serpentine elements: he has hands, feet, and shoulders (Hes. *Theog.* 823–4), but also a hundred snake heads which have eyes burning with fire (825–7). However, his hybridity is most apparent in his voices. He sounds like multiple animals:

> At times [he made] the sound of a loud-bellowing, majestic bull, unstoppable in its strength, at other times that of a lion, with a ruthless spirit, at other times like young dogs, a wonder to hear, and at other times he hissed, and the high mountains echoed from below. (831–5)

He incorporates all the animals that we see in the bodies of the children of Phorcys and Ceto. His combination of so many dangerous animals establishes him as an appropriate opponent to Zeus in contrast to the less powerful creatures defeated by the heroes.

In addition to the animal elements, he is (almost) like the gods. He speaks 'as though for the gods to understand' (Hes. *Theog.* 831). His similarity to them suggests his capacity to pose a threat to them, but this godlike quality combined with the animal sounds highlights his difference. His inability to communicate meaningfully marks him as outside the Olympian social grouping, in contrast to the Hecatoncheires (654–63). Since sound forms such an important part of his characterization, Typhoeus' battle with Zeus takes place largely through sound. Zeus uses one united noise: the thunder from his thunderbolt, which causes the different parts of the cosmos to resonate: 'the earth echoed terrifyingly, and the broad sky above, and the sea, and the streams of Ocean, and Tartaros in the earth' (839–41). Typhoeus' voices can only make the mountains echo (835), a distinction that marks Zeus' greater power. Zeus' thunder, moving through each of those separate sections of the universe, marks out the ordering process that the world has undergone as a result of his kingship (Goslin 2010: 365–6). It also demonstrates his ability to affect both entities that produced Typhoeus (Gaea and Tartarus), and thus his ability to defeat the monster. It is striking that the weapon he uses to complete this sonic battle is produced by monsters, the Cyclopes (141). We see in both his defeat of Typhoeus and his choice of weapon, Zeus' control over even the most unruly elements of the universe (Brockliss 2017–2018: 135–6).

Since the text presents the final cosmos as an ordered one ruled by Zeus, the monsters in the *Theogony* stand in opposition to the anthropomorphic primary deities. The defeat of these monsters by heroes marks the point at which the cosmos transitions into our world, since we can see that they do not inhabit it. The violence of this process reinforces the idea that these abnormal bodies are fundamentally opposed to the nature of the cosmos under Zeus' rule. As in the generational conflicts that lead to their supremacy—between Uranus and Cronus, then Cronus and Zeus—the Olympians establish the final cosmic order through violence. The monsters in the *Theogony*, therefore, exist to be defeated or removed so that our world can exist as it does now and to show the Olympians and the heroes establishing the final, and correct, order.

Benign Monstrosity in the Orphic Theogonies

The Orphic theogonies are a group of creation narratives attributed to the mythical poet Orpheus. These texts, surviving only as fragments in quotations from later authors, diverge from Hesiod's more traditional cosmogony by having different primordial deities and placing particular emphasis on the god Dionysus, describing his death and resurrection. The earliest text, the Derveni Papyrus, dates to the fourth century BCE; it is a commentary on an earlier text, which could date back to the fifth century (West 1983: 77, 81–2). There are varying opinions in the scholarship regarding whether the Orphic theogonies are linked to religious practices because there are some ritual items (such as gold tablets) which are associated with attempts to ensure a positive afterlife and which bear the names of Dionysus (Bernabé 2008: 291–2; Edmonds 2013: 63–8).

However, the fragmentary nature of the literary and material evidence means that this connection is uncertain.

Two of these texts are of particular interest here for their inclusion of hybrid deities: the *Hieronyman Theogony* and the *Rhapsodic Theogony*. The *Rhapsodic Theogony* survived to a later date and we have a larger number of fragments, but both texts present a very similar narrative and so can be examined together (see Rappe 2000: 148–9; Bernabé 2008: 293; Mitchell 2021: 49–52). In contrast to Hesiod's *Theogony*, the Orphic theogonies preserve parts of a less-well-represented mythological tradition. Although they share broadly the same sequence of primary deities (Uranus, Cronus, Zeus), the Orphic theogonies present a creation narrative with some significant differences. The earliest deities are a pair of hybrid creator deities, in this case Chronos (Time) and Phanes (who is born from an egg produced by Chronos) rather than Uranus and Gaea. The foregrounding of time and the birth of a creator from an egg suggest possible connections to Egyptian texts (especially the Coffin Texts) and Indian texts (e.g. the *Matsya Purana* and the *Laws of Manu*; see Mitchell 2018). Additionally, in the final stages of the Orphic narratives, Zeus transforms into a snake to father Dionysus. The progression of the cosmos is not, therefore, towards a complete separation of human and animal bodies, but one that seems to maintain more of the fluidity and strangeness of the primordial period.

The first creator deity is Chronos, a god of time (Greek *chronos*). Deified versions of time appear only rarely in Greek sources (e.g. Ap. Rhod. *Argon*. 4.672–82). In the Orphic theogonies Chronos seems to represent eternal or imperceivable time; for example, he has the epithet *agēraos* ('unageing'). His body is also unusual; in the *Hieronyman Theogony* he combines multiple hybrid elements:

> He is a serpent with the heads of a bull and a lion attached to him, and between them he has the face of a god, and wings on his shoulders. (*HT* fr. 76.I)

Two nearly identical fragments reiterate this description (*HT* frr. 76.II and IV). The combination of lion, bull, human, and snake has led to suggestions that Chronos is connected to the Zodiac, although it is unclear whether this association is the cause or the result of his hybridity (Brisson 1985: 44; West 1983: 192–3; Mitchell 2021: 54–6). We can also see a strong similarity to the animals that make up Typhoeus' body and voices in the *Theogony*, although Chronos has a substantially different role.

Chronos creates the elements needed for the cosmos to exist. For example, he produces Aither, Chaos, and Erebus in the *Hieronyman Theogony* (fr. 78), and Aither and Chaos in the *Rhapsodic Theogony* (fr. 111). These figures represent the vague spaces within which the rest of creation takes place: Aither, associated with brightness, is usually part of the sky; Chaos is a gap or chasm; Erebus is a dark subterranean space. In the Orphic theogonies, Chronos, as a personification of time, also provides a chronological context for creation often missing from other Greek accounts. In both texts he creates the egg from which Phanes, the next creator deity, emerges (*HT* frr. 79.I, 79.II; *RT* fr. 114). In the *Hieronyman Theogony*, the upper half of the egg's shell becomes Uranus and the lower half Gaea (e.g. fr. 80.IV). Thus, in the Orphic theogonies, hybrid creatures, even those composed of dangerous animals, are not inherently threatening. Instead, their bodies point to a heavily creative period in which the divisions between divine, human, and animal have not yet been established.

This benign hybridity continues in Phanes, who also has a monstrous body made up of the same elements as that of Chronos, but in a different form. Only one description of him survives from the *Hieronyman Theogony*:

> [a] double-bodied god had gold wings upon his shoulders, he had growing upon his sides the heads of bulls, upon his head a monstrous serpent resembling the forms of every kind of wild animal. (fr. 80.I)

The references to shoulders, sides, and a head indicate an anthropomorphic form, with animal elements attached. The snake 'resembling the forms of every kind of wild animal' points to a limitless hybridity.

Fragments from the *Rhapsodic Theogony* also provide details about Phanes' appearance. One contains a description similar to that in the *Hieronyman Theogony*, in which the deity has 'the heads of a ram, a bull, a lion' (fr. 129.I). Other *Rhapsodic Theogony* fragments seem to refer obliquely to these multiple heads, by referencing multiple sets of eyes, faces, and horns (frr. 131, 132, 133). Phanes' hybridity, like that of Typhoeus, also manifests in his voice: 'he sends forth the bellows of a bull or those of a flashing-eyed lion' (fr. 130). Additionally, the *Hieronyman Theogony* consistently refers to Phanes as male (e.g. 'the son of Aither', frr. 124, 125), but one place the *Rhapsodic Theogony* states that Phanes (under an alternative name, Erekepaios) 'is both female and father' (fr. 134) and another refers to Phanes as 'androgynous' (fr. 121). This combination of male and female highlights his capacity for creation, appropriate for a god who produces the physical universe.

Phanes' birth marks the point at which the physical world comes into being. In both the *Rhapsodic* and *Hieronyman Theogony*, Phanes emerges from the egg produced by Chronos, but the mechanism by which this creates the world differs. In the *Hieronyman Theogony* Phanes' birth is associated with the origin of Uranus and Gaea. In the *Rhapsodic Theogony*, Phanes' birth marks the moment the physical world is revealed not through physical creation but through illumination (e.g. frr. 117, 121). This origin seemingly connects with Phanes' name, likely associated with the Greek verb *phainō* ('bring to light' or 'appear'). Phanes is also connected to light in other parts of the *Rhapsodic Theogony*: fr. 123 describes him as too bright to be seen by anyone other than Night, and fr. 127 describes him as invisibly illuminating the cosmos. Elsewhere, fragments reference him riding on a chariot eternally (frr. 172.II, 172.III, 173), suggesting some sort of role as a sun deity.

The sun's emergence indicates the differentiation of night and day. Thus, Phanes' birth marks a new and more tangible form of time than that which existed under Chronos. This change is mirrored in the more concrete nature of the things he creates: the home of the gods, the sun, moon, stars, earth, sea, and the first mortals (*RT*, frr. 152, 153.II, 153.III,

159). Whereas Chronos creates intangible deities, Phanes makes the physical world. His birth therefore marks a fundamental shift in the nature of the cosmos.

Phanes is not the final creator. This role is given to Zeus, who recreates everything produced by Phanes in order to become the primary deity. Zeus does this by consuming Phanes: 'he had taken the form of all things into his hollow belly' (*RT* fr. 241). Specifically, he takes in the sea, earth, underworld, rivers, gods, and 'whatever had come to pass and whatever was yet to come' (fr. 241; cf. 240.I). Zeus' creative capacity is also connected to animal forms: he is not consistently anthropomorphic in the *Rhapsodic Theogony*, but becomes a snake to father Persephone by Demeter and again to father Dionysus by Persephone. In the *Rhapsodic Theogony*, Dionysus is fundamental to the origin of humans; when the Titans consume him, Zeus retaliates by killing them with his thunderbolt. The resultant ash becomes the matter from which humans are created, and Dionysus is resurrected (*RT* frr. 302, 318, 320, 326). Thus, even humans are hybrids: our bodies contain a combination of Titan and Olympian elements produced in an abnormal event. Hybridity is therefore an important element in the creation of both Olympians and mortals in the Orphic theogonies.

Clearly, some elements of these Orphic creation narratives differ from what appears in Hesiod's *Theogony*. Although Zeus consumes Phanes to take control of the cosmos, the Orphic theogonies do not generally present monstrous creatures as violent. Instead, the two most important creative figures are complex and benign hybrids. Indeed, the level of violence displayed in the changing generations of gods also varies considerably from that in the *Theogony*. Phanes was the first ruler (*RT* fr. 167) and his immediate successor, Night (*RT* fr. 169.II), receives the role through peaceful action: Phanes 'placed the glorious staff into the hands of the goddess Night, in order that she would possess royal honour' (*RT* fr. 168). The transitions of power between Uranus and Cronus, and between Cronus and Zeus, still occur violently, but intergenerational violence is not ubiquitous.

Although Chronos and Phanes share physical similarities with Typhoeus, they have fundamentally different roles in their respective narratives. Typhoeus poses an explicit threat to the divine order of the Olympians. In contrast, Chronos and Phanes create the world that the Olympians later rule. There are two key reasons for these differences. First, these characters appear at different points in the creation process. Chronos and Phanes exist at the beginning of creation and enable it. Bodies that do not adhere to expected categories are not surprising or threatening because these categories do not yet fully exist. Typhoeus, in contrast, appears at the end of the creation process. Ordered categories (such as 'god', 'mortal', 'animal') are already in place, and Typhoeus' existence undermines the categories that now define the cosmos and are a fundamental part of Zeus' rule. Second, the narrative endpoints are different. In the *Rhapsdic Theogony*, at least, the narrative does not end when Zeus gains power; instead, we get the story of Dionysus. The end of this text, then, focuses on a god associated with blurring categories such as male/female or human/animal. Thus, the hybrid bodies of the early deities do not seem antithetical to the final form of the cosmos. The characteristics of the Orphic theogonies allow monsters to exist without needing to be destroyed. Instead, they are active and important participants in the creation of the cosmos.

Ovid's Violent and Monstrous Creation Story

Ovid is unusual for a Roman poet in composing an explanation of the world's creation. Writing a few years earlier, Vergil includes a very brief creation narrative in *Eclogue* 6, and Ovid's own *Ars amatoria* provides an appropriately eroticized cosmogony (2.467–88), but the creation story in Ovid's *Metamorphoses* (7 CE) more closely resembles some Greek accounts. Like Hesiod, he uses a divine genealogy as part of his cosmogony. In this narrative, Ovid includes the Giants and the Cyclopes, albeit with forms somewhat different to those in Hesiod. Given that the shapes and transformations of bodies are fundamental to the *Metamorphoses*, the physical nature of the creatures that existed at the beginning of the world are significant. Although the creatures presented in the cosmogonic section (Giants and Cyclopes) do not undergo metamorphoses, their presence at the beginning of the text points to the role of bodily strangeness that will run throughout the text (Bernabé 2018: 212). They are also significant in terms of placing Ovid's work within a generic framework: Ovid's references to the Gigantomachy link his poem to the genre of epic (Lowe 2015: 190–214; Myers 1994: 14).

The Giants appear early in the *Metamorphoses* within the narrative of the Myth of Ages. During the description of the Race of Iron (*Met.* 1.151–62), Jupiter refers to their attack on Olympus and subsequent defeat. We get an indication of their immense strength and potential threat: they 'essayed the very throne of heaven, piling huge mountains, one on another, clear up to the stars' (1.152–3). But Ovid does not reference any physical features here, just the use of their blood by Terra (Earth) to produce humans, whose own tendency towards violence parallels that of the Giants (1.157–62). Slightly later, when describing his rage at the cannibalistic and impious behaviour of Lycaon, Jupiter refers to the Giants' hybrid and excessive body parts:

> I was not more troubled than now for the sovereignty of the world when each one of the serpent-footed giants was in act to lay his hundred hands upon the captive sky. (1.182–4)

With this reference to excessive hands and serpentine features, Ovid recalls the physical qualities of both Typhoeus and the Hecatoncheires in Hesiod. In his *Fasti*, a poem about the origin of various Roman festivals, Ovid gives the Giants one thousand arms in addition to their serpentine legs (*Fast.* 5.37). The number of their limbs may be fluid, but their excessiveness lies at the core of their representation in Ovid's work. His Cyclopes, however, are closer to their Hesiodic counterparts as Jupiter receives a thunderbolt 'which Cyclopean hands had forged' (*Met.* 1.259).

In addition to having specific connections with epic literature, the Giants' attack on Olympus has political associations. Ovid compares this event to the murder of Julius Caesar by his fellow Romans (*Met.* 1.200–1), characterizing it as a hubristic and futile attack on the established order. This comparison has distinctly ambivalent connotations for Augustus, both as the emperor at the time the text was written and as the adopted son of Caesar. At this point in the text, Jupiter demonstrates a capacity for great violence: he defeats the Giants and destroys the world with a flood in order to start again. Ovid thus presents Jupiter as an extremely powerful and threatening figure (Segal 2001: 79–80, 84). Indeed, we see Jupiter's threat extends to the home of the gods: in defeating the Giants, he 'shattered Olympus' when he used his thunderbolt (Ov. *Met.* 1.154). This section might be read, therefore, as characterizing Augustus as a potential threat to both his enemies and those around him.

In the *Metamorphoses*, Jupiter floods the earth after witnessing the abhorrent behaviour of Lycaon, king of Arcadia. Jupiter transforms Lycaon into a wolf when, after rejecting Jupiter as a god and attempting to kill him, the king tries to serve Jupiter a meal made from human flesh (1.221–31; see Liveley in this volume). Lycaon's transformation, which Ovid describes only briefly, would initially seem to reflect a change from one coherent being (human) to another (wolf). However, the narrative focuses on the ways in which Lycaon does *not* completely transform:

> He turns into a wolf, and yet retains some traces of his former shape. There is the same grey hair, the same fierce face, the same gleaming eyes, the same picture of beastly savagery. (1.237–9)

Since the human Lycaon already manifested the qualities of a wolf, a complete transformation is not required. His metamorphosis physically reflects his inhuman and uncivilized nature. This episode is significant not only in its narrative of the punishment for hubris, but also because it demonstrates that the blurring of bodies and transformations resulting from divine anger are themes present from the beginning of the poem (Feldherr 2011: 41–8).

Lycaon's actions cause not only his own transformation, but also that of the entire world. When Jupiter floods the earth, the world's geography becomes inverted: dolphins swim among oak trees (*Met.* 1.302–3) and the sea reaches the tops of mountains (1.309–11). The cosmos thus partially reverts to its unformed beginnings. Only after this process does our generation of humans come into being. The beginning of our world, then, is established by an act associated with hybridity and violence.

ACCIDENTAL MONSTERS IN EMPEDOCLES

Monsters do not appear only in mythological creation narratives; we also see them in philosophical discourse. The Greek Presocratic philosopher Empedocles (fifth century

BCE), whose work survives only in fragments, explains our world's origin as a result of a cycle during which Love (*philotēs*) and Strife (*neikos*) have precedence at alternating times (e.g. frr. 14 and 16).[2] Love draws all parts of the universe together until it becomes a unified mass; Strife separates the universe until is entirely divided. The origin of living beings occurs during the transition of control from Strife to Love. At this time, body parts come together in a variety of combinations. Empedocles describes the early stages of the process:

> Here sprang up many faces without necks, arms wandered without shoulders, un-attached, and eyes strayed alone, in need of foreheads. (fr. 50)

Once these individual pieces cohere, larger body parts begin to come together. Some combinations are unsuccessful:

> many creatures born with faces and breasts on both sides, man-faced ox-progeny, while others again sprang forth as ox-headed offspring of man, creatures compounded partly of male, partly of the nature of female, and fitted with shadowy parts. (fr. 52)

Thus, rather than being a process that follows human-like procreation, or one that is guided by a demiurge or creator, the development of living beings is a result of trial and error.

This version of creation differs significantly from what we see in the genealogical narratives of Hesiod, the Orphic theogonies, and Ovid. However, there are some significant overlaps. First, Love is a significant figure both in Empedocles and Hesiod. In the *Theogony*, Love (Eros) is one of the first four deities and drives the sexual desire that causes the gods to procreate and thus to populate the cosmos. Although a different version of Love (*philotēs*) appears in Empedocles, Love is still presented as a driving force developing the cosmos, which is based in desire. Second, disordered bodies again highlight the progression of the cosmos in this text as in the others discussed above. Although, because of the cyclical nature of Empedocles' cosmology, the universe does not have a final form in which our bodies must exist as they are eternally, the time preceding ours is still characterized by bodies (such as human-animal hybrids) that no longer fit into our world. Therefore, these monsters are not simply mythological figures, but beings that provide a way of thinking about how we came into existence and how we divide our own era from those that came before us.

---

[2] Fragment numbers from Wright (1981).

Strange Bodies in Lucretius'
De rerum natura

In its philosophical approach to creation, Lucretius' first-century BCE didactic epic *De rerum natura* ('On the Nature of Things') is closer to Empedocles than to the mythological accounts. Lucretius' philosophical beliefs mean that his work rejects traditional religious ideas, such as the active involvement of the gods in the mortal world, and promotes Epicurean philosophical ideas and atomism (the theory that all parts of the universe are composed of tiny particles). Although the narrative sequence in which aspects of the cosmos come into being is familiar from the mythological accounts—spaces, followed by celestial phenomena, then living beings—the recognizable world comes into being through atoms 'attempting every combination and motion' (*DRN* 5.428).

Much like Empedocles' example of ox-faced men, Lucretius provides specific examples of early failed attempts at bodies (Furley 1970; Sedley 1998):

> the androgyne, between man and woman yet neither, different from both; some without feet, others again bereft of hands; some found dumb also without a mouth, some blind without eyes, some bound fast with all their limbs adhering to their bodies (*DRN* 5.839–42)

These descriptions of unsuccessful early versions of humans demonstrate, by their abnormality, the 'correct' forms of bodies. We are expected to have a particular shape (i.e. one that includes hands and feet), and to be able to move in particular ways. We must be able to communicate and absorb sensory information. By failing in these respects, these earlier beings cannot participate in society: they 'could do nothing and go nowhere, could neither avoid mischief nor take what they might need' (5.843–4). In this case, we have a clear instance of bodily difference used to define the expected nature of humans by providing examples of creatures which do not meet these expectations.

Lucretius' list of failed bodies is not just concerned with the way that we fit into society, but with our ability to continue it through procreation. The first of the apparently failed beings, the androgyne, points to the importance of this theme. Lucretius demonstrates his concern with this idea by highlighting the inability of 'abnormally' formed creatures to reproduce. He explains that to do so, living beings need specific things: nourishment, the ability to emit seminal fluid, and sexual reproduction (*DRN* 5.849–54). If these needs are not met, living beings cannot exist eternally and are not able to continue to survive into our time.

Lucretius later reinforces his rejection of 'abnormal' bodies when he explicitly states that hybrids of the sort that are made up of two different creatures are not possible: 'Centaurs never existed, nor at any time can there be creatures of double nature and twofold body combined together of incompatible limbs' (*DRN* 5.878–9; see Hawes in this volume). He then explains that different creatures develop at different rates and have different dietary requirements, and therefore cannot exist in hybrid bodies (5.883–900). Time seems particularly important in framing abnormal bodies: the earlier, failed beings could explicitly not exist in a way that would allow them 'by procreation to forge out the chain of generations' (5.850). They lack capacity to produce a future for themselves. Lucretius explicitly presents his objection to hybrids in terms of time; these creatures are chronologically distinct from us; they help delineate 'our' world from the one that preceded us.

Despite the differences in their texts, Lucretius does cover one of the same major episodes as Ovid: the Gigantomachy. Lucretius does not describe the Giants physically and they are not, themselves, key figures but fit into the broader philosophical context. In contrast to Ovid, whose Gigantomachy marked an impious political action, Lucretius uses the Giants' attack on the gods as a positive model of Epicurus' rejection of traditional religion (Hardie 1986: 209–13; Kronenberg 2005: 407): 'neither fables of the gods could quell him, nor thunderbolts, nor heaven with menacing roar' (*DRN* 1.68–9). The 'thunderbolts' (*fulmina*) in particular recall Jupiter's traditional weapon. Here, then, an episode often portrayed as an instance of hubris points to the action that must be taken against an established institution to enact a positive change. It is likely for this reason that Lucretius downplays the monstrosity of the Giants and employs a more idealized version of their description. Lucretius has rejected abnormal bodies elsewhere; comparing such monstrous creatures as the Giants to Epicurus would be undesirable. Nevertheless, he retains these monsters in this discussion of the nature of the world and how it came to be.

CONCLUSION

Monsters frequently appear in Greek and Roman creation narratives, even those which do not frame their ideas within an explicitly mythological setting. Within these narratives, monsters must eventually disappear because we can see that they do not exist in the world around us. In some accounts gods or heroes remove them, often violently. In others, they were failed experiments that could not survive. In this way, they participate in the explanation of how the world came to be as it is. They help to demarcate the progression the cosmos has undergone in the transition between an empty space or unformed mass to our current world. Monsters exist in and physically manifest a time in which the boundaries that define our would had not yet been established.

In marking out our world and our time from the ones that preceded us, these monsters perform a fundamental role. They are creatures against which we define ourselves. This is perhaps most readily apparent in the accounts of Empedocles and Lucretius, in which strange bodies appear as failed attempts to create humans. However, we can also see this in the other texts discussed above. The monstrous creatures in Hesiod and Ovid—the children of Phorcys and Ceto, Typhoeus, the Giants—are presented as opponents to anthropomorphic heroes and gods and are inevitably defeated by them. In this way we can see how anthropomorphic bodies are centralized in cosmogonies because creation narratives are fundamentally stories about how we and our world came into being.

SUGGESTED READING

Gregory (2007) provides a broad overview of ancient Greek cosmological traditions. On relationship between Greek and Near Eastern creation narratives see López-Ruiz (2010) and West (1997). For further discussion of monsters in Hesiod and the Orphic theogonies more generally, see Mitchell (2021). Clay (2003) addresses the conflict between monsters and heroes and the hybridity of both groups in Hesiod's *Theogony*. On the use of monsters in Augustan literature, see Lowe (2015), and Myers (2004) on cosmology in Ovid specifically.

WORKS CITED

Bernabé, A. 2008. 'Teogonías órficas', in *Orfeo y la tradición órfica: un reencuentro*, ed. A. Bernabé, F. Casadesús, and E. Albrile, 291–324. Tres Cantos.

Bernabé, A. 2018. 'La Cosmogonía de las *Metamorfosis* de Ovidio y las *Rapsodias* órficas.' *Emerita* 86/2: 207–32.

Brisson, L. 1985. 'La Figure de Chronos dans la théogonie orphique et ses antécedents iraniens', in *Mythes et représentations du temps*, ed. D. Tiffeneau, 37–55. Paris.

Brockliss, W. 2017–2018. 'Olympian Sound in the *Theogony* and the *Catalogue of Women*: Sweet Music and Disorderly Noise.' *Classical Journal* 113/2: 129–49.

Clay, J. S. 2003. *Hesiod's Cosmos*. Cambridge.

Edmonds, R. G. 2013. *Redefining Ancient Orphism*. Cambridge.

Feldherr, A. 2011. *Playing Gods: Ovid's Metamorphoses and the Politics of Fiction*. Princeton.

Furley, D. 1970. 'Variations on Themes from Empedocles in Lucretius' Proem.' *Bulletin of the Institute of Classical Studies* 17: 55–64.

Goslin, O. 2010. 'Hesiod's Typhonomachy and the Ordering of Sound.' *Transactions of the American Philological Association* 140: 351–73.

Gregory, A. 2007. *Ancient Greek Cosmogony*. London.

Hardie, P. H. 1986. *Virgil's* Aeneid: *Cosmos and Imperium*. Oxford.

Kirk, G. S., J. E. Raven, and M. Schofield, eds. 1983. *The Presocratic Philosophers*. Cambridge.

Kronenberg, L. 2005. 'Mezentius the Epicurean.' *Transactions of the American Philological Association* 135/2: 403–31.

López-Ruiz, C. 2010. *When the Gods Were Born: Greek Cosmogonies and the Near East*. Cambridge, MA.

Lowe, D. 2015. *Monsters and Monstrosity in Augustan Poetry*. Ann Arbor.

Miller, F. J., trans. 1916. *Ovid*: Metamorphoses *Books 1–8*. Cambridge, MA.

Mitchell, F. 2018. 'The Universe from an Egg: Creation Narratives in the Ancient Indian and Greek Texts', in *The Indian Ocean in Antiquity: Political, Cultural and Economic Impacts*, ed. M. A. Cobb, 171–90. London.

Mitchell, F. 2021. *Monsters in Greek Literature: Aberrant Bodies in Ancient Greek Cosmogony, Ethnography, and Biology*. Abingdon.

Most, G., ed. and trans. 2006. *Hesiod*. Cambridge, MA.

Myers, K. S. 1994. *Ovid's Causes: Cosmogony and Aetiology in the Metamorphoses*. Ann Arbor.

Rappe, S. 2000. *Reading Neoplatonism: Non-discursive Thinking in the Texts of Plotinus, Proclus, and Damascius*. Cambridge.

Rouse, W. H. D., trans. 1924. *Lucretius:* On the Nature of Things. Cambridge, MA.

Sedley, D. N. 1998. *Lucretius and the Transformation of Greek Wisdom*. Cambridge.

Segal, C. 2001. 'Jupiter in Ovid's *Metamorphoses*.' *Arion* 9/1: 78–99.

West, M. L., ed. 1966. *Hesiod:* Theogony. Oxford.

West, M. L. 1983. *The Orphic Poems*. Oxford.

West, M. L. 1997. *The East Face of Helicon: West Asiatic Elements in Greek Poetry and Myth.* Oxford.

Wright, M. R. 1981. *Empedocles: The Extant Fragments*. New Haven.

CHAPTER 2

··

MONSTERS IN ANCIENT NEAR EASTERN MYTH AND RELIGION

··

MADADH RICHEY

INTRODUCTION

THE monsters imagined by inhabitants of the ancient Near (or Middle) East—an area extending roughly from the Nile and Bosporus in the west to the Zagros Mountains in the east—certainly served as both inspiration and foil for inhabitants of the Aegean world and points further west. One finds dragons, griffins, merpeople, and even a single Cyclops populating this region's visual art and texts, spanning from before the rise of writing (*c.*3000 BCE) through increasingly intense interactions with Hellenistic culture in the wake of Alexander's conquests. Histories of individual ancient Middle Eastern monsters and how they influenced monsters of the broader Mediterranean world mostly have yet to be written; some exemplary studies include Angelini (2018), Höpflinger (2010), and Winkler-Horaček (2011, 2015). I will focus less on the mechanics and direct lines of such influence than on the world of ancient Middle Eastern monstrosity in and of itself—especially ancient Mesopotamia and the Levant—in the hope of providing a catalyst for future studies.

This chapter does not—and indeed cannot—present merely another list of ancient Middle Eastern monsters, with which monsters of the central and western Mediterranean might be compared. For readers seeking such registers, the most useful of the many available resources include, for Mesopotamia, Wiggermann (1994) and Green (1994); for Egypt, Lucarelli (2010); and for the Levant, the large (if often idiosyncratic) *Dictionary of Deities and Demons in the Bible* (van der Toorn et al. 1999). Two things are sometimes lost in these inclusive bestiaries: on the one hand, the recurring tropes attendant to the monstrous, and on the other, the lurking ambiguities about how the monstrous is both constituted and deployed in these ancient contexts. It bears remembering that no language first written in the ancient Middle East includes a word whose semantics map mostly—and, for many languages, even partially—onto those of English 'monster', the rubric under which we, as scholars, have learned to analyse animate entities manifesting aspects of anatomical hybridity (cf. Boychenko in this volume). This is likely part of the reason why, while substantial progress has been made outlining the above-mentioned recurring tropes relevant to such entities, ancient Middle Eastern monsters remain an unruly class. It is not always clear who should be in the monster club and who should be out. Two entities whose anatomies or activities might lead one to expect parallel functions often behave very differently from one another. And the list of apparent problems goes on. In the interest of drawing attention to these less heralded realities, I focus less on pithy generalities—'ancient Middle Eastern monsters are or do x, y, or z'—and more on how ancient sources subvert standards and laws. In attending to such ambiguities, I will demonstrate that ancient Middle Eastern monsters provide more than background for later Mediterranean complexity. The monster is manifold as far back as one can travel.

Fuzzy Oppositions: Monster Assistants, Pets, and Alter Egos

In reading about ancient Middle Eastern monsters, one commonly encounters the assertion that the monstrous is somehow equivalent to the evil or even the chaotic and is therefore opposed to the good and its analogues, such as gods and kings. While such discursive constructions of monstrosity do occur, they only obtain universally if the monstrous is pre-emptively defined as that which is evil or chaotic, a definition doomed to miss important things about ancient Middle Eastern constructions of both real and imaginary entities. Again, because no ancient Middle Eastern language has a lexeme (word or words) whose semantic range overlaps precisely with that of the English word 'monster', neither such a definition, privileging evil or chaos, nor any other can be grounded in ancient Middle Eastern lexical usage. We can therefore adopt in our investigation a pragmatic definition of 'monster' that both reflects contemporary colloquial and/or deeply theorized usage of that term and reveals important information about ancient Middle Eastern entities, concepts, and texts. The delineation of the monstrous as that which is threateningly but also attractively hybrid is both colloquially and theoretically informed (e.g. Carroll 1990: 27–35; Halberstam 1995; Cohen 2006), and a pursuit of monstrosity as hybridity continues to produce meaningful insights. In the ancient Middle East, the monster as hybrid does *not* always occupy an unambiguously evil pole and is, especially, not always or even often opposed to the (perfect) divine, largely because ancient Middle Eastern monsters tend to appear as associates or even doubles of the gods.

Two complexes of literary material from Mesopotamia helpfully manifest this associative tendency. First, the late second-millennium BCE Babylonian Akkadian epic of Gilgamesh, written out by the scholar Sîn-lēqi-unninni, is a tremendous and well-known literary achievement.[1] But *Gilgamesh* is also the outgrowth of diverse earlier literary traditions, especially in the Sumerian language (Edzard 1990, 1991, 1993; Fleming and Milstein 2010), as well as being the near contemporary of other texts about the hero, including in Hittite (Beckman 2019). Both the standard Babylonian edition and many other *Gilgamesh* texts include vignettes in which the hero and his companion Enkidu journey to the Cedar Forest of Lebanon and there battle a terrifying monster known as Ḫuwawa in Sumerian and Ḫumbaba in Akkadian. Ḫumbaba is a paradigmatic monster; he is not only hybrid but also gigantic. He fights by both traditional combat and a magical control of the winds. When Gilgamesh and Enkidu at last defeat him, Gilgamesh bags his head as a trophy (Richey 2021a: 348–55). Importantly, though, this encounter between giant and heroes does not act merely as a conservative fable illustrating how monster conquest begets lasting fame. Within the logic of the narrative, Ḫumbaba is something of a sympathetic character; he guards the Cedar Forest because he has been deputized by Shamash (the sun god) and the other deities to do so. Gilgamesh and Enkidu's unprovoked, glory-seeking attack is, in at least one version, directly condemned by the gods under Enlil's leadership (Edzard 1990: 190; Fleming and Milstein 2010: 189). In fact, at this point in the standard epic (and after a parallel slaying of the goddess Ishtar's beloved 'Bull of Heaven'), the heroes' fortunes take a significant downturn. Enkidu soon dreams of his own death and thereafter perishes; Gilgamesh, mourning pitiably, stumbles off to the steppe and the edge of the world. This beloved Mesopotamian text therefore serves neither as an exhortation to fight monsters nor as an authorization that the hybrid must be destroyed. It claims, rather, that the most fearsome creatures may have been specifically designed by the gods for difficult protective tasks in distant, rugged terrain, and they are there best left alone. Not only the literary epic but also the abundant apotropaic visual art of Ḫumbaba (Graff 2012)—which likely influenced later Mediterranean *gorgoneia* (see both Lowe and Oswald in this volume)—regularly remind the ancient viewer about these principles.

Second, there exist at least two versions of the second- and first-millennium Akkadian epic of Anzû, in which the eponymous lion-griffin monster steals the magical Tablet of Destinies from the king of the gods, Enlil, while the latter is preoccupied in his bath (Vogelzang 1988; trans. Foster 2005: 555–78). What has put Anzû in such a proximate position to the high god is difficult to reconstruct from the fragmentary manuscripts that cover the text's beginning, but from what survives it looks as though Enlil and the other gods observe the monster's birth, as well as his bodyguard suitability. Enlil himself then, in the process of assigning functions to all divine beings, accords Anzû a position as his own personal protector. Only from this position does Anzû have the opportunity

---

[1] George (2003); other recent academic translations incorporating additional fragments include Foster (2019), George (2020), and Helle (2021).

to observe Enlil in his greatest vulnerability and then conceive and fulfil a desire to seize the Tablet of Destinies, an emblem or source of the high god's power. In this epic, therefore, the monster is trusted but immediately breaks that trust. When Ninurta, the only god brave enough to resist Anzû, goes out against him, he emerges victorious only by tricking the Tablet-possessing monster into incanting his own demise (Studevent-Hickman 2010). That Anzû is, for a while at least, able to wield the Tablet of Destinies as effectively as any god troubles any simplistic excision of him into a wholly separate category of monster. The epic of Anzû warns against letting the monster get too close, lest he take ultimate power for himself. But that such a warning was felt to be necessary and powerful reveals that alliance with the monstrous was a thinkable, if dangerous, relation.

The classic context in which most contemporary audiences encounter pre-Hellenistic Mesopotamian monster visual art—namely the palace relief sculptures of the later Neo-Assyrian kings—is also far more beholden to the associative than to the oppositional tradition of monster–deity interaction (Kolbe 1981; Ataç 2010: 145–201). Almost the only surviving piece of Neo-Assyrian monumental relief sculpture depicting an actual combat with a monster is the relief from one of the entrances to the temple of the god Ninurta at the ancient city of Nimrud. In this relief—appropriated by Austen Henry Layard in the 1850s and now in the British Museum (BM 124751–2; Kolbe 1981: 71–7, pl. 8.1)—Ninurta, holding double-edged trident lightning bolts, pursues Anzû. The latter cranes his head over his shoulder, as if warning his foe with a mighty roar. A mirrored but otherwise identical relief was discovered by Layard's expedition across the entrance passageway from this one and left in situ (Gadd 1938: pl. 15). But other than these, extensive archaeological activity in the Middle East has revealed just one Assyrian relief sculpture suggesting a god–monster confrontation: a fragmentary relief from Tell Šēḫ Ḥamad (Assyrian Dūr-Katlimmu), a provincial administrative centre on the Ḫabur River. On this fragment, only the top of a god's head and the upper portion of what is likely an antagonistic *mušḫuššu* dragon are visible, but they do appear to face off, and the god's raised axe is clearly aimed at the snake's head (Kühne 1984).

Some Assyrian written sources hint at a wider tradition of similar representations (Engel 1987). A building inscription of King Sennacherib (r. 705–681 BCE) claims that he constructed an *akītu*-house sanctuary for the New Year festival outside Aššur whose bronze gate depicted scenes from the epic poem *Enūma eliš*, in which the high god—Aššur in Assyrian manuscripts, Marduk in Babylonian—opposes the rising of Tiāmat, the personified watery abyss, and her brood (Lambert 2013). Among these was an image of 'the gods going before [Aššur …] and arranged behind Aššur, Tiāmat with the creatures of her womb, whom Aššur, king of the gods, goes to fight' (K.1356:9–12, in Grayson and Novotny 2014: 222–5 [no. *Sennacherib* 160]). The language here clearly implies an illustration of the direct combat, with the good gods led by the imperial deity Aššur arrayed on one side and the evil monsters led by Tiāmat on the other. No such representation, unfortunately, survives, and this ekphrastic (image-descriptive) text is relatively unusual in its assertion of depicted divine confrontation involving monsters.

What does survive in ninth- to seventh-century BCE Assyrian monumental relief sculpture are abundant individual and small-group representations of those creatures. The oldest come from the central building at Nimrud—perhaps a temple, perhaps to be attributed to the reign of Aššurnaṣirpal II (Meuszynski 1976)—and consist of two images of the *girtablullû* 'scorpion-man' (AO 19850; N-A 12/74, in Meuszynski 1976: 39, pl. 9a), here standing alone but named among monsters and children of Tiāmat in various contexts, including *Enūma eliš* (Kolbe 1981: 79–83). Although Aššurnaṣirpal's Northwest Palace, also at Nimrud, contains no such images, later kings would begin to incorporate static images of other monsters into their visual artistic programmes. Sargon II's palace at Dūr-Šarrukīn (present-day Khorsabad; see Albenda 1986) included two relief sculptures of a *laḥmu* 'hairy hero' (AO 19861–2; Kolbe 1981: 89–96, pl. 10.2–3), a giant anthropomorph clutching a lion and popularly but erroneously identified with Gilgamesh (Wiggermann 1981–1982). A seascape from the same palace shows a *kulullû* 'merman' and *aladlammû* 'winged bull' benevolently accompanying ships (AO 19889; Maul 2000: 29–34). These occasional representations are multiplied dramatically in the art of Sennacherib's Southwest Palace and Aššurbanipal's North Palace, both at Nineveh (Barnett et al. 1998; Barnett 1976). In the former, one finds the oldest Assyrian monumental representations of the lion-headed *ugallu*, already in great number (Green 1986: 197–204). The latter adds to its own multiple images of this creature the only known Assyrian images of the *urdimmu* 'dog-man' and *urmaḥlullû* 'lion-centaur' and one of only two known monumental images of the *mušḫuššu* 'dragon' (Ellis 2006; Kolbe 1981: 121–32). In all cases, though the monsters may appear threatening, they are engaged in no directly antagonistic activity. The question thus arises: what is their role in this palatial art?

The answer is complex, but the semantics of these monstrous relief sculptures proceed largely from the implicit contrast between their antagonistic aspect in literary texts like *Enūma eliš* and their passive, even supportive, functions in the visual art. In the Neo-Assyrian palatial relief programmes described above, monsters like the *ugallu* and the *mušḫuššu* are carved beside entryways and along hallways. Lacking composition-internal enemies, their threatening postures imply that the object of such postures are understood to be found in the real world. The relief monsters guard against potential and actual invaders of the Assyrian king's central space. This deployment of such fearsome creatures would imply to the viewer knowledgeable of literary traditions that the monsters had really been tamed and appropriated by the king, whose power was thereby magnified. The palatial relief programmes strongly imply that monsters with which Ninurta, Aššur, Marduk, and other great gods fought valiantly have now—paradoxically but therefore impressively—been brought into the service of the king himself.

The idea that the king or god could be glorified by exploiting fearsome monsters is of course not limited to this palatial relief art. The same impulse sits behind the frequent first-millennium Assyrian and Babylonian depictions, especially on cylinder seals, of gods standing on or even running astride large hybrid creatures (Ornan 2005: 80–6; Richey 2019: 201–39). These figurations conceptually extend a tradition of showing gods riding fearsome terrestrial beasts, like various storm-gods on their bulls or Ishtar on her lion. Literary texts from Mesopotamia and beyond, too, assert that gods are proved particularly potent due to their ability to command and even domesticate monstrous antagonists. In Ugaritic myth from ancient Syria, for example, one finds various monstrous enemies of the storm god Baʿlu and his sister ʿAnatu described as 'beloved' ones of the high god ʾIlu, whose authority over the whole cosmos—even its chaotic elements—is thereby stressed (Smith 2001: 33–5; Pitard 2007; Richey 2018). Moreover, Hebrew Bible poetic texts declare Yahweh to hold sway over such monsters as Behemoth and Leviathan (Smith 2001: 36–40; Ballentine 2015: 87–8; Ayali-Darshan 2020: 197–203), in one case even going so far as to characterize the former, a huge and muscular swamp-dwelling beast, as 'the first of God's works' and the latter, a scaly sea monster, as the deity's plaything (Job 40:19, 29).

MONSTERS AT THE MARGINS: BEYOND IMAGINARY GEOGRAPHY

It has become almost a cliché that the monstrous and the marginal are associated with one another in many traditions. Such associations were observed long before Jeffrey Jerome Cohen's 'Monster Culture' canonized them into an often simplistically received 'thesis': 'the monster dwells at the gates of difference' (1996: 7). But what is marginal naturally depends on the location of one's centre. For the ancient Middle East, especially in the late second and early first millennia BCE, it is usually most productive to analyse Mesopotamia as central, since polities located in this area largely dominated the surrounding areas politically, economically, and culturally. For an ancient affiliate of Assyria or Babylonia, literary monsters were often imagined to inhabit geographical extremes, as with Gilgamesh and Enkidu encountering Ḫumbaba in the distant Cedar Forest of Lebanon. In the Sumerian epic Lugale (van Dijk 1983; trans. Jacobsen 1987: 233–72), Ninurta battles the mountain monster Asag in the rocky wilderness. Several Neo-Assyrian kings boast of having hunted and killed fantastic animals in such exotic places as the shores of the Mediterranean (e.g. Tiglath-Pileser I; see Engel 1987: 69–74). The expected pattern is obvious enough to be perennially observed by modern scholars as a constitutive feature of Mesopotamian imaginary geography (e.g. Sonik 2012: 107; Feldt 2015a; Konstantopoulos 2021). But this positioning is not simply a reflex of some common human psychological tendency. It also reflects the cultural contexts in which the denizens of Mesopotamia encountered—and from which they adapted—visual artistic motif and compositional strategies for representing monsters in the first place.

The Neo-Assyrian royal proclivity for depicting monsters in palatial relief sculpture was not an *ex nihilo* invention of these kings. Rather, it mixed and melded two distinct traditions of monstrous visual art.[2] The first of these was the Kassite (c.1600–1150

---

[2] In addition to what follows, the influence of monstrous art from Urartu, Assyria's northern neighbour, merits future detailed exploration; see, for now, the brief survey in Jakubiak (2011).

BCE) and other Babylonian fashion of decorating so-called boundary stelae, popularly known as *kudurrus*, with relief sculptures of hybrid creatures (Slanski 2003). *Kudurrus* stood as monuments commemorating the granting or ownership of land, and they were covered both with inscriptions guaranteeing that ownership and with images of gods and monsters, who presumably acted as notional enforcers (Paulus 2014; Seidl 1989). Even if *kudurrus* did not appear on literal property boundaries (Slanski 2000; 2003: 55–62), their textual descriptions associated these boundaries with monstrous figures. And for Assyrians encountering *kudurru* art especially on their southern peripheries, the art of this geopolitical frontier became paradigmatically monstrous, likely reinforcing local beliefs about the cosmic position of hybrid beings.

The second influencing tradition was the similar but originally independent late second- and early first-millennium BCE Syro-Anatolian (often 'Neo-Hittite' or 'Luwian') habit of depicting hybrid creatures in both relief and round sculpture, then positioning them primarily as guardians of city-gates and palaces. Such deployments of monsters—which range from winged sphinxes to bird-, bull-, and lion-men—are attested at nearly every Iron Age site from which substantial relief carvings survive, including Carchemish, Ḥalaf (Gōzān), and Zincirli (Šamʾal), in modern southeastern Turkey and northern Syria (Orthmann 1971: 306–50). One of the two surviving Assyrian relief sculptures of divine combat—the Tell Šēḫ Ḥamad *mušḫuššu* stele—is clearly based on Syro-Anatolian illustrations of gods confronting monstrous snakes that, unlike the Assyrian piece, reflect a common tradition in their immediate context. These prototypes are found across a range of sites, from Malatya in the northern Amanus to ʿAšāra (Terqa) on the Euphrates (Orthmann 1971: 437–9). A newly discovered analogue from the area of Erzin, on the plain of Issos, indicates an even wider distribution of this motif than previously thought (Ensert et al. 2008). The Syro-Anatolian practice of positioning such sculptures in city and palace gates certainly influenced later Assyrian palatial arrangements, and even the individual supernatural motifs of Assyrian art are often visibly based on Syro-Anatolian precursors (Winter 1982).

For the Assyrians, both Babylonia and Syro-Anatolia were indeed on the margins of the empire, and their conquest of these regions over the course of the ninth and eighth centuries BCE represented first an ambition and then a reality, achieved by the most militarily successful kings. The incorporation of monsters into Assyrian palace art therefore does not merely assert the geo- and topographical separation of monsters but rather the ability of the ideal Assyrian king to cross seemingly uncrossable lands and to harness the wild powers that he finds there. There is substantial continuity between the earlier Assyrian claim to have retrieved fearsome beasts from the frontier and the more implicit appropriation of purely imaginary visual artistic monsters. These monsters reassured Assyrian literati as to their cultural power and superiority over prestigious yet subjugated Babylon (Ataç 2010: 180), but, notably, this same ideology was simultaneously directed to northwestern Syro-Anatolian neighbours. This latter visual artistic relationship also cannot be boiled down to mere passive 'influence'.

Over the course of the first millennium BCE, though, the spread of monsters relative to Mesopotamia was not only centripetal—as evidenced by, among other things, two artefact corpora that, in the Levant and Anatolia, were strongly influenced by Mesopotamian techniques and traditions, namely amulets and seals (both cylinder and stamp seals). In the case of the former, for example, amulets depicting the Mesopotamian baby-killing demon Lamaštu appear sporadically at Levantine sites in this period (Götting 2011). Lamaštu was characterized by anatomical hybridity—leonine head, exaggeratedly feminine anthropomorphic body, avian legs—and apotropaic incantations describe her as monstrous both in terms of her animalistic features and in aspects of her improperly gendered presentation (Richey 2021b). Some Lamaštu amulets in the west are almost certainly Assyrian imports, brought by Mesopotamian officials or traders who intended the pieces for their personal protective use or who planned to sell well-made exotic goods to locals. This is true of several amulets from Zincirli, as well as an isolated find from near Beth Guvrin in the foothills of southern Israel. Other Levantine Lamaštu amulets, though, were likely manufactured on the margins of the Assyrian Empire. At least one interesting artefact suggests, too, that the artisan responsible did not speak Akkadian (as might be expected), but a local Aramaic dialect. This artefact is the recently republished Lamaštu amulet from Zincirli, which depicts the demon in strikingly Syro-Anatolian style and, below the protective figures incised perfunctorily on the reverse, names the amulet's likely owner, Bar Qurḥu, with an alphabetic Aramaic inscription (DeGrado and Richey 2017). This artefact provides excellent evidence that not only practitioners in Mesopotamia but also ordinary folk in the Syro-Anatolian region were actively representing and concerned with the dangerous invasions of monstrous demons into their very homes.

This one amulet is far from the only indication that those in the west were beginning to learn about and fear Mesopotamian demons and to combat them with apotropaic artefacts and their own spoken magic (DeGrado and Richey 2021). Statuettes and amulets of the first-millennium Mesopotamian demon Pazuzu (Fig. 2.1), who often functions in art as Lamaštu's nemesis, are widespread not only in Assyria and Babylonia but also throughout Syria (Tell Šēḫ Ḥamad, Carchemish, Sultantepe, Zincirli) and even the southern Levant (Megiddo, Beth Shean, Beth Shemesh; Heeßel 2002). Like Lamaštu, Pazuzu originated in Mesopotamia, and he is monstrous, having a canine head (sometimes horned and/or bearded), four wings, a humanoid upper body, avian legs, a scorpion tail, and a prominent penis. Most inscribed artefacts of Pazuzu feature cuneiform script, but precisely one statuette is inscribed in alphabetic Aramaic with a four-line protective charm (DeGrado and Richey 2019). Now in the Ashmolean Museum, this statuette of uncertain provenance was reportedly purchased at San al-Hagar (ancient Tanis) in the late nineteenth century. Its language nevertheless suggests that its owner was an Aramaic-speaker from the western provinces rather than a speaker of Akkadian. Like the Aramaic-inscribed Lamaštu amulet from Zincirli, then, this statuette suggests that originally Mesopotamian monsters crossed putative cultural borders just as easily as did the Babylonian and Syro-Anatolian monumental monsters that came from these peripheral regions.

In sum, just as the Assyrians received monumental monsters from their frontiers and accordingly conceptualized monsters as geographically marginal, they soon gave

FIGURE 2.1 Bronze statuette of Pazuzu, first millennium BCE (MNB 467).

Source: Wikimedia / PHGCOM. CC BY-SA 3.0.

back armies of miniature demons. The entire complex of this tradition soon spread even further west. From both Anatolian and Levantine bases, by land and by sea, the monstrous iconography of the ancient Middle East spread westward to the Aegean and beyond in the so-called orientalizing revolution. In southwestern Anatolia, for example, both monumental and glyptic Lycian traditions of hybrid theriomorphic art, drawing on older Hittite and other Anatolian compositions, are well-attested through at least the fourth century BCE (Colas-Rannou 2020). Phoenician ivories and metalwork often

FIGURE 2.2 Monumental relief from Pozo Moro, Spain (MAN Inv. 1999-76-A).

Source: Wikimedia / Luis García. CC BY-SA 3.0.

depict hybrid creatures, seemingly in an extravagant attempt to heighten the aesthetic quality of luxury goods; this tradition of hybrid art combined with local practices to produce such monsters as those on the c. fifth-century BCE tower monument at Pozo Moro, Spain (Almagro-Gorbea 1983). Here, in addition to a multi-headed hydra-like creature, the relief depicts snake-headed but otherwise grotesque anthropomorphic bicephalics who appear to be consuming something (children?) from bowls as well as a pig, who lies belly-up on the main table (Fig. 2.2; Azize 2014). The snake creatures of Pozo Moro are 'ancient Middle Eastern' monsters only via their affiliation with Phoenician settlement in the area, but the story of the spread of monster iconography from east to west must recognize that this material, too, speaks to a ferment of hybridity, both anatomical and cultural.

CONCLUSION

The twenty-first century has yielded several attempts to define in conceptual and even psychological terms what the hybrid anatomies of ancient Middle Eastern monsters might have meant for a human onlooker (e.g. Wengrow 2014; Maiden 2020: 133–76). Such projects, however, are only the latest in a long line of monster hermeneutics that begin in ancient Mesopotamia itself. To conclude, it is worth reflecting briefly on two of the dominant modes of such theorizing in the ancient Middle East.

First, monsters of the ancient Middle East were understood as embodiments of various threats to the human, especially illness and death, such as the fashioning of Lamaštu as an explanatory icon for illnesses of childbirth and infancy. In this respect, Lamaštu is emblematic of broader Mesopotamian thought, which often assigns disease to the realm of the demonic. Entire compendia of incantations and rituals were written for protection against illness-causing 'evil demons'—UDUG.ḤUL in Sumerian, *utukkū lemnūtu* in Akkadian—and such texts do occasionally describe the anatomical oddities and hybridities of these demons (Geller 2016). Especially before the first millennium BCE demons other than Lamaštu were rarely depicted in visual art, but Pazuzu has his own developed iconography, and some other disease demons, such as a recently discovered 'epilepsy demon', sometimes receive visible form (*BAM* 202; Arbøll 2019). Although they usually appear to act of their own accord, such monstrous figures could also be imagined as deployed by human magical practitioners (e.g. the paradigmatic sorceress of the *Maqlû* incantation series; Abusch 2016: 293–6). Interestingly, one defended against these evil influences not only by speaking protective incantations, but also by appropriating them and reversing their influence onto the evil practitioner themselves (Abusch 2016: 302). A similar logic is at play in the household deployment of buried ceramic monster figurines to guard against evil (Rittig 1977; Nakamura 2004); the best guard against a monster is an even more fearsome monster, whose loyalty to its human originator is apparently assured by the creative process itself (Feldt 2015b).

Second and finally, the Mesopotamian monster is often treated, like those of other contexts, as an omen, or sign, of both good and ill to come. Teratological omen series abound in the cuneiform record; the most extensive of these is the omen collection *Šumma izbu*, 'If an anomalous foetus ...' (Leichty 1970; De Zorzi 2014), which renders geopolitical and other predictions from the anatomies of malformed births. But this compendium is merely one refraction of an extremely diverse and detailed strain of reflection on the meanings of 'monstrous births', both human and animal (Maul 2003: 62–4; De Zorzi 2017). There are some indications that this 'science' was also pursued on the Mediterranean coast, e.g. in the local language of the Late Bronze Age city-state of Ugarit (*c.*1550–1200 BCE; Pardee 2007), perhaps even providing a link between the Mesopotamian manifestation of teratology and its many later European parallels. In this case, the ancient Middle East would again stand at the roots of much later monstrous traditions.

Suggested Reading

Recent introductory overviews to monsters and demons in Mesopotamia include Konstantopoulos (2019) and Verderame (2012). For a sense of the complexity of individual monsters, Heeßel's (2011) brief exposition of Pazuzu is especially recommended. Readers interested in emerging literary and queer theoretical approaches to Mesopotamian monsters might begin with Richey (2021b), on Lamaštu's threatening femininity. Ballentine (2015) and Grafius (2020) are good starting points for exploring biblical monsters; the former focuses on monsters' ancient Middle Eastern mythological contexts and the latter on the promise of the contemporary horror genre for understanding biblical monster narratives. The use of monsters in non-Mesopotamian magic, with a focus on Aramaic in Iron Age Syria, is accessibly summarized in DeGrado and Richey (2021).

Works Cited

Abusch, T. 2016. *The Magical Ceremony* Maqlû: *A Critical Edition*. Leiden.

Albenda, P. 1986. *The Palace of Sargon, King of Assyria: Monumental Wall Reliefs at Dur-Sharrukin*. Paris.

Almagro-Gorbea, M. 1983. 'Pozo Moro: El monumento orientalizante, su contexto socio-cultural y sus paralelos en la arquitectura funeraria ibérica.' *Madrider Mitteilungen* 24: 177–294.

Angelini, A. 2018. *Dal Leviatano al drago: Mostri marini e zoologia antica tra Grecia e Levante*. Bologna.

Arbøll, T. P. 2019. 'A Newly Discovered Drawing of a Neo-Assyrian Demon in *BAM* 202 Connected to Psychological and Neurological Disorders.' *Journal des médicines cunéiformes* 33: 1–31.

Ataç, M.-A. 2010. *The Mythology of Kingship in Neo-Assyrian Art*. Cambridge.

Ayali-Darshan, N. 2020. *The Storm-God and the Sea: The Origin, Versions, and Diffusion of a Myth throughout the Ancient Near East*. Tübingen.

Azize, J. 2014. ' "Child Sacrifice" without Children or Sacrifice: The Pozo Moro Relief.' *Ancient Near Eastern Studies* 51: 263–77.

Ballentine, D. S. 2015. *The Conflict Myth and the Biblical Tradition*. Oxford.

Barnett, R. D. 1976. *Sculptures from the North Palace of Ashurbanipal at Nineveh (668–627 B.C.)*. London.

Barnett, R. D., E. Bleibtreu, and G. Turner. 1998. *Sculptures from the Southwest Palace of Sennacherib at Nineveh*. London.

Beckman, G. M. 2019. *The Hittite Gilgamesh*. Atlanta.

Carroll, N. 1990. *The Philosophy of Horror, or Paradoxes of the Heart*. New York.

Cohen, J. J. 1996. 'Monster Culture (Seven Theses)', in *Monster Theory: Reading Culture*, ed. J. J. Cohen, 3–25. Minneapolis.

Cohen, J. J. 2006. *Hybridity, Identity, and Monstrosity in Medieval Britain*. New York.

Colas-Rannou, F. 2020. *Créatures hybrides de Lycie: Images et identité en Anatolie antique (VIe–IVe siècle avant J.-C.)*. Rennes.

DeGrado, J., and M. Richey. 2017. 'An Aramaic-Inscribed Lamaštu Amulet from Zincirli.' *Bulletin of the American Schools of Oriental Research* 377: 107–33.

DeGrado, J., and M. Richey. 2019. 'The Aramaic Inscription of the Ashmolean Museum Pazuzu Statuette and Ancient Middle Eastern Magic.' *Semitica et Classica* 12: 17–64.

DeGrado, J., and M. Richey. 2021. 'Discovering Early Syrian Magic: New Aramaic Sources for a Long-Lost Art.' *Near Eastern Archaeology* 84: 282–92.

De Zorzi, N. 2014. *La serie teratomantica* Šumma izbu: *Testo, tradizione, orizzonti culturali*, 2 vols. Padua.

De Zorzi, N. 2017. 'Teratomancy at Tigunānum: Structure, Hermeneutics, and Weltanschauung of a Northern Mesopotamian Omen Corpus.' *Journal of Cuneiform Studies* 69: 125–50.

Edzard, D. O. 1990. 'Gilgameš und Huwawa A. I. Teil.' *Zeitschrift für Assyriologie und vorderasiatische Archäologie* 80: 165–203.

Edzard, D. O. 1991. 'Gilgameš und Huwawa A. II. Teil.' *Zeitschrift für Assyriologie und vorderasiatische Archäologie* 81: 165–233.

Edzard, D. O. 1993. *'Gilgameš und Huwawa': Zwei Versionen der sumerischen Zedernwaldepisode nebst einer Edition von Version 'B'.* Munich.

Ellis, R. S. 2006. 'Well, Dog My Cats! A Note on the *Uridimmu*', in *If a Man Builds a Joyful House: Assyriological Studies in Honor of Erle Verdun Leichty*, ed. A. K. Guinan et al., 111–26. Leiden.

Engel, B. J. 1987. *Darstellungen von Dämonen und Tieren in assyrischen Palästen und Tempeln nach den schriftlichen Quellen.* Mönchengladbach.

Ensert, H. K., et al. 2008. 'The Stele of Erzin.' *Adalya* 11: 35–46.

Feldt, L. 2015a. 'Religion, Nature, and Ambiguous Space in Ancient Mesopotamia: The Mountain Wilderness in Old Babylonian Religious Narratives.' *Numen* 63: 347–82.

Feldt, L. 2015b. 'Monstrous Figurines from Mesopotamia. Textuality, Spatiality and Materiality in Rituals and Incantations for the Protection of Houses in First-Millennium Aššur', in *The Materiality of Magic*, ed. D. Boschung and J. N. Bremmer, 59–95. Paderborn.

Fleming, D. E., and S. J. Milstein. 2010. *The Buried Foundation of the Gilgamesh Epic: The Akkadian Huwawa Narrative.* Leiden.

Foster, B. R. 2005. *Before the Muses: An Anthology of Akkadian Literature*, 3rd edn. Bethesda.

Foster, B. R. 2019. *The Epic of Gilgamesh*, 2nd edn. New York.

Gadd, C. J. 1938. 'A Visiting Artist at Nineveh in 1850.' *Iraq* 5: 118–22.

Geller, M. J. 2016. *Healing Magic and Evil Demons: Canonical Udug-hul Incantations.* Berlin.

George, A. R. 2003. *The Babylonian Gilgamesh Epic: Introduction, Critical Edition and Cuneiform Texts.* Oxford.

George, A. R. 2020. *The Epic of Gilgamesh: The Babylonian Epic Poem and Other Texts in Akkadian and Sumerian*, 2nd edn. London.

Götting, E. 2011. 'Exportschlager Dämon? Zur Verbreitung altorientalischer Lamaštu-Amulette', in *Exportschlager: Kultureller Austausch, wirtschaftliche Beziehungen und transnationale Entwicklungen in der antiken Welt*, ed. J. Göbel and T. Zech, 437–56. Munich.

Graff, S. B. 2012. '*Humbaba/Huwawa*.' PhD dissertation, New York University.

Grafius, B. 2020. *Reading the Bible with Horror.* Lanham, MD.

Grayson, A. K., and J. Novotny. 2014. *The Royal Inscriptions of Sennacherib, King of Assyria (704-681 BC), Part 2.* Winona Lake, IN.

Green, A. 1986. 'The Lion-Demon in the Art of Mesopotamia and Neighbouring Regions.' *Baghdader Mitteilungen* 17: 141–254.

Green, A. 1994. 'Mischwesen. B. Archäologie. Mesopotamien.' *Reallexikon der Assyriologie* 8/3-4: 246–64.

Halberstam, J. 1995. *Skin Shows: Gothic Horror and the Technology of Monsters.* Durham, NC.

Heeßel, N. P. 2002. *Pazuzu: Archäologische und philologische Studien zu einem altorientalischen Dämon.* Leiden.

Heeßel, N. P. 2011. 'Evil against Evil: The Demon Pazuzu.' *Studi e materiali di storia delle religioni* 77: 357–68.

Helle, S. 2021. *Gilgamesh: A New Translation of the Ancient Epic.* New Haven.

Höpflinger, A.-K. 2010. *Schlangenkampf: Ein Vergleich von ausgewählten Bild- und Textquellen aus dem griechisch-römischen und dem altorientalischen Kulturraum.* Zurich.

Jacobsen, T. 1987. *The Harps That Once . . . Sumerian Poetry in Translation.* New Haven.

Jakubiak, K. 2011. 'Some Remarks on Fantastic Creatures in Urartian Art and Their Religious Aspects.' *Acta Archaeologica Pultuskiensia* 3: 71–8.

Kolbe, D. 1981. *Die Reliefprogramme religiös-mythologischen Charakters in neuassyrischen Palästen: Die Figurentypen, ihre Benennung und Bedeutung.* Frankfurt.

Konstantopoulos, G. 2019. 'Deities, Demons, and Monsters in Mesopotamia', in *Ancient Mesopotamia Speaks: Highlights of the Yale Babylonian Collection,* ed. A. W. Lassen, E. Frahm, and K. Wagensonner, 45–55. New Haven.

Konstantopoulos, G. 2021. 'Migrating Demons, Liminal Deities, and Assyria's Western Campaigns.' *Advances in Ancient Biblical and Near Eastern Research* 1: 131–48.

Kühne, H. 1984. 'Tall Šēḫ Ḥamad/Dūr-katlimmu 1984.' *Archiv für Orientforschung* 31: 170–8.

Lambert, W. G. 2013. *Babylonian Creation Myths.* Winona Lake, IN.

Leichty, E. 1970. *The Omen Series* Šumma izbu. Locust Valley, NY.

Lucarelli, R. 2010. 'Demons (Benevolent and Malevolent)', in the online *UCLA Encyclopedia of Egyptology,* ed. W. Wendrich et al. https://www.uee.ucla.edu.

Maiden, B. E. 2020. *Cognitive Science and Ancient Israelite Religion: New Perspectives on Texts, Artifacts, and Culture.* Cambridge.

Maul, S. M. 2000. 'Die Sieg über die Mächte des Bösen: Götterkampf, Triumphrituale und Torarchitektur in Assyrien', in *Gegenwelten zu den Kulturen Griechenlands und Roms in der Antike,* ed. T. Hölscher, 19–46. Leipzig.

Maul, S. M. 2003. 'Omina und Orakel. A. Mesopotamien.' *Reallexikon der Assyriologie* 10: 45–88.

Meuszynski, J. 1976. 'Neo-Assyrian Reliefs from the Central Area of Nimrud Citadel.' *Iraq* 38: 37–43.

Nakamura, C. 2004. 'Dedicating Magic: Neo-Assyrian Apotropaic Figurines and the Protection of Assur.' *World Archaeology* 36: 11–25.

Ornan, T. 2005. *The Triumph of the Symbol: Pictorial Representation of Deities in Mesopotamia and the Biblical Image Ban.* Göttingen.

Orthmann, W. 1971. *Untersuchungen zur späthethitischen Kunst.* Bonn.

Pardee, D. 2007. 'La Tératologie au sein de la "science" ougaritienne', in *Monstres et monstruosités dans le monde ancien,* ed. J. Pérez Rey, 261–74. Paris.

Paulus, S. 2014. *Die babylonischen Kudurru-Inschriften von der kassitischen bis zur frühneubabylonischen Zeit.* Münster.

Pitard, W. T. 2007, 'Just How Many Monsters Did Anat Fight (*KTU* 1.3 III 38–47)?', in *Ugarit at Seventy-Five,* ed. K. L. Younger, 75–88. Winona Lake, IN.

Richey, M. 2018. 'Ugaritic Monsters I: The ʾatūku "Bound One" and Its Sumerian Parallels.' *Ugarit-Forschungen* 49: 333–65.

Richey, M. 2019. 'Visions of Gods and Monsters: Levantine and Mesopotamian Iconographies of Divine Combat and Their Textual Impressions.' PhD dissertation, University of Chicago.

Richey, M. 2021a. 'Goliath among the Giants: Monster Decapitation and Capital Display in 1 Samuel 17 and Beyond.' *Journal for the Study of the Old Testament* 45: 336–56.

Richey, M. 2021b, 'The Mesopotamian Demon Lamaštu and the Monstrosity of Gender Transgression', in *Religion, Culture, and the Monstrous: Of Gods and Monsters,* ed. J. P. Laycock and N. L. Mikles, 145–56. Lanham, MD.

Rittig, D. 1977. *Assyrisch babylonische Kleinplastik magischer Bedeutung vom 13.–6. Jh. v. Chr.* Munich.

Seidl, U. 1989. *Die Babylonischen Kudurru-Reliefs. Symbole mesopotamischer Gottheiten.* Freiburg/Göttingen.

Slanski, K. E. 2000. 'Classification, Historiography and Monumental Authority: The Babylonian Entitlement *narûs* (*kudurrus*).' *Journal of Cuneiform Studies* 52: 95–114.

Slanski, K. E. 2003. *The Babylonian Entitlement* narûs (kudurrus*): A Study in Their Form and Function.* Boston.

Smith, M. S. 2001. *The Origins of Biblical Monotheism: Israel's Polytheistic Background and the Ugaritic Texts.* Oxford.

Sonik, K. 2012. 'Mesopotamian Conceptions of the Supernatural: A Taxonomy of *Zwischenwesen*.' *Archiv für Religionsgeschichte* 14: 103–16.

Studevent-Hickman, B. 2010. 'Language, Speech, and the Death of Anzu', in *Gazing on the Deep: Ancient Near Eastern and Other Studies in Honor of Tzvi Abusch*, ed. J. Stackert, B. N. Porter, and D. P. Wright, 273–92. Bethesda, MD.

van der Toorn, K., B. Becking, and P. W. van der Horst, eds. 1999. *Dictionary of Deities and Demons in the Bible*, 2nd edn. Leiden.

van Dijk, J. 1983. *LUGAL UD ME-LÁM-bi NIR-ĜÁL: Le Récit épique et didactique des Travaux de Ninurta, du Déluge et de la Nouvelle Création*, 2 vols. Leiden.

Verderame, L. 2012. ' "Their Divinity is Different, Their Nature is Distinct!" Nature, Origin, and Features of Demons in Akkadian Literature.' *Archiv für Religionsgeschichte* 14: 117–27.

Vogelzang, M. E. 1988. Bin šar dadmē: *Edition and Analysis of the Akkadian Anzu Poem.* Groningen.

Wengrow, D. 2014. *The Origins of Monsters: Image and Cognition in the First Age of Mechanical Reproduction.* Princeton.

Wiggermann, F. A. M. 1981–1982. 'Exit *Talim*! Studies in Babylonian Demonology, I.' *Jaarbericht ex Oriente Lux* 27: 90–105.

Wiggermann, F. A. M. 1994. 'Mischwesen. A. Philologisch. Mesopotamien.' *Reallexikon der Assyriologie* 8/3–4: 222–46.

Winkler-Horaček, L., ed. 2011. *Wege der Sphinx: Monster zwischen Orient und Okzident.* Rahden.

Winkler-Horaček, L. 2015. *Monster in der frühgriechischen Kunst.* Berlin.

Winter, I. J. 1982. 'Art as Evidence for Interaction: Relations between the Assyrian Empire and North Syria', in *Mesopotamien und seine Nachbarn: Politische und kulturelle Wechselbeziehungen im alten Vorderasien vom 4. bis 1. Jahrtausend v. Chr.*, ed. H.-J. Nissen and J. Renger, 355–82. Berlin.

CHAPTER 3

SPAWNED FROM THE NILE

Egyptian Monsters in Graeco-Roman Culture

LEANNA BOYCHENKO

INTRODUCTION

IN *Parliament of the Gods*, a comic dialogue in Greek by the second-century CE author Lucian, the gods have decided to expel foreigners and resident aliens from their roster. Momus, blame personified, leads the charge and singles out Anubis for ridicule: 'And you, you dog-faced Egyptian bandaged with linen, who are you, buddy, or how do you think you're worthy of being a god, howling as you do?' (10.1–3).[1]

Momus mocks Anubis' animal head and his linen wrappings, the latter probably referring to mummification. Zeus, however, responds by saying that Egyptian gods may seem strange to the uninitiated, but that it is really a matter of symbolism (*ainigmata*). Indeed, Momus calls the Egyptian gods 'ridiculous' (*geloitera*), but harsher criticism goes out to the satyrs of Dionysus' crew, whom he calls monstrous (*terastios*, 5.3) and strangely formed (*allokotos*, 4.15). Here, Egyptian gods may be embarrassing, but they are not monsters despite having hybrid forms, which are quite typical of Graeco-Roman monsters like the Chimaera, sphinxes, and satyrs, whom Momus specifically blames.

Lucian's criticism was by no means new. Over five hundred years earlier, a fragment from the comedy *Poleis* by the Middle Comedy poet Anaxandrides strikes a similar chord. The context and the identity of the speaker are unfortunately lost, as the fragment is preserved in the work of a much later author, Athenaeus of Naucratis (late second century CE), in a discussion of eels (7.299f. = fr. 39 Kock 1–8). The speaker declares that he cannot be an ally to the Egyptian he is addressing, partially due to cultural differences in the roles of animals and gods: 'You worship the cow while I sacrifice it to the gods. You consider the eel the greatest deity while we consider it the greatest of delicacies....

---

[1] All translations are my own unless otherwise noted.

You honour the dog, but I beat it.' We have Anubis again, here called a dog, as well as Atum, the Egyptian creator god symbolized by snakes and eels. As far as the Greeks were concerned, the Egyptian gods are not monstrous—simply unfit for worship and better for other things.

There certainly are cases where Greek and Roman monsters resemble Egyptian gods. The bull-headed Minotaur, for instance, has the same composition as the sacred Egyptian Mnevis bull, usually depicted fully as a bull but sometimes as bull-headed with a human body. The Greek sphinx, usually portrayed as having the head of a woman, body of a lion, and wings of an eagle, mirrors some depictions of Astarte, a West Semitic goddess adopted by Egypt from Syria and Canaan. Full-face depictions of gorgons with their tongues sticking out are reminiscent of the Egyptian god Bes. Perhaps these Egyptian gods inspired the appearances of Greek and Roman monsters, but the case of Astarte shows possible other influences as well. Egyptian influence on Greek and Roman culture is easily found, but Egyptian monsters themselves are somewhat more elusive and can be difficult to distinguish even in an Egyptian context. Below, we will first examine different types of divine entities in Egyptian sources and then turn to examples of their influence on constructions of monsters in Greece and Rome.

EGYPTIAN GODS, DEMONS, AND MONSTERS

Egyptian gods can be anthropomorphic (humanoid), zoomorphic (animal-formed), and therianthropic (part animal, part human). While some gods often hold one form, others take various shapes. Cosmic gods like Shu, god of the air, and Nut, goddess of the sky, tend to be anthropomorphic, as do geographic gods like Hapi, god of the Nile flood. In contrast, Horus, king of the gods, can appear as a human, a hawk, or a hawk-headed human. Still, not all Greeks and Romans found the Egyptian gods laughable, regardless of their forms. The fifth-century BCE Greek historian Herodotus claims that, 'nearly all the names of the gods came from Egypt to Greece' (2.50) although he refrains from discussing most aspects of Egyptian religion. The closest Herodotus comes to mentioning Egyptian monsters is in his description of Egyptian fauna (2.68–75): he includes dangerous animals like crocodiles and hippopotamuses and misunderstood animals like 'harmless' horned snakes (truly deadly vipers), the phoenix (identified by some Egyptologists as the avian deity Bennu, a heron associated with the sun god Re), and unexplained flying snakes (which are depicted in Egyptian art, though Herodotus claims to have seen their skeletons). But these are still clearly animals, not monsters, however strange they might have seemed to a Greek audience. That said, deadly animals certainly existed in Egypt and could be viewed as a threat and take the expected role of a monster in a story. For instance, 'The Tale of the Doomed Prince', from Egypt's Eighteenth Dynasty (1550–1295 BCE), tells of a prince fated to die at the hands of a crocodile, snake, or dog.

While some narrative Egyptian myths exist, many of our Egyptian sources on the gods are primary religious texts like the *Book of the Dead*—(Faulkner et al. 2015)—a funerary text that arose in the New Kingdom (*c.*1550 BCE). Such texts name deities and sometimes describe their appearances, but rarely explain or analyse their roles. Instead of telling stories, much Egyptian mythology communicates through symbolism or allusion. This makes it difficult to pin down exactly how the Egyptians understood and categorized divinities and how they envisioned the monstrous. Certain deities were frightening, dangerous, and sometimes called the 'enemy', but Egyptian has no clear word for 'monster'. In fact, a single word in Egyptian encompassed all divine creatures: *nTr*, translated as 'god'. Scholars often use the word 'monster', however, especially to describe Ammut, Seth, and Apophis.

Despite the universal term for 'god', divine power was regional and unequal. There are at least three versions of the gods' origin story, associated with the cities of Hermopolis, Heliopolis, and Memphis, and each city features a different god as its creator. Still, the boundaries between different divinities could be weak due to syncretism, a practice in which two or more gods coexisted and fused but still retained their own characteristics and identity. For example, the gods Re and Horus could manifest as the syncretic Re-Horakhty, 'Re who is Horus of the Two Horizons', the 'chief of the gods' linked to the pharaoh.

In general, great gods—usually members of the primordial families—were differentiated from lesser gods, among whom were underworld deities now classified by Egyptologists as 'demons' and other underworld beings known as 'cavern' and 'gate' deities. Even so, one of the great gods, Osiris, appears in the underworld's Hall of Justice among lesser 'judgement' deities and another great god, Seth, has many monstrous and demonic characteristics. At the same time, he is himself a slayer of monsters.

Demons, cavern, gate, and judgement deities are associated with the Duat, the Egyptian underworld, and appear in funerary texts, some carved or painted on tomb walls. The names of demons sometimes are written in red ink—a colour usually reserved for marking the titles, beginnings, and section headings of texts—and are marked at the end of the word with the semantic marker for 'enemy' or 'death' (the hieroglyph known as 'man with an axe in his head'; these markers are called 'determinatives'). Demons' names often correspond to their frightening activities—for example, the Butcher, the Horrifier, and the Cutter. While demons often act as guardians and protectors of both humans and other gods, they also cause illness and disease. Demons lack the overarching power of the great gods, but function as helpers and intermediaries, either being sent out by greater gods or invoked by magic spells.

Since the Egyptians believed that demons, despite their occasional benevolence, could also cause harm, they frequently depicted demons as knife-holding hybrid figures sometimes composed of different animals (e.g. Ikenty, a cat-headed bird), sometimes with multiple heads. Other demonic characteristics include walking backwards and having opposite-facing features, such as eyes in the back of one's head (Szpakowska 2009: 800), an idea perhaps reflected in Herodotus' description of Egyptians doing everything completely backwards (2.35). Not until the New Kingdom (sixteenth to eleventh centuries BCE) did demons become recipients of cult worship, and they became increasingly popular under Greek and Roman rule (Lucarelli 2010: 9).

While demons travel between the worlds of the living and the dead, cavern divinities are relegated to the Duat and live in underworld caves, dealing out punishment and killing enemies of the god Re, often by beheading them. They also protect the deceased who successfully pass judgement and become members of the blessed dead (known as 'the justified', or 'true of voice'). Cavern deities take a variety of shapes, including the forms of humans, mummies, serpents, catfish-headed gods, and even the great gods ('Spell of the Twelve Caves', *PCairo* CG 24742; Spell 168, *BD*, Faulkner et al. 2015: 140–1). It was customary to leave offerings to these gods either to help the deceased or in hope of assistance for oneself in the afterlife.

Gate deities guard the many gates of the underworld. To pass into the afterlife, the deceased must know these deities' secret names. One especially significant gate deity is the giant snake Apophis, discussed below; other gate deities have more illustrative names like Swallower of the Damned; Existing on Maggots; and Mistress of Anger, Dancing on Blood (Wilkinson 2020: 81–2). Many of these deities are therianthropic and hold knives.

Judgement deities reside in the Duat's Hall of Justice at the Great Tribunal, where the heart of the deceased is weighed against the feather of truth. If the heart is heavier than the feather, indicating a life of crime and falsehood, the monster Ammut swallows it up (Fig. 3.1). Specific deities punish specific crimes; for example, the Bone Breaker eponymously punishes liars, and the Eater of Entrails similarly punishes perjurers (Wilkinson 2020: 83; Spell 125, *BD*, Faulkner et al. 2015: 129–30).

Egyptian underworld deities are in many ways analogous to Greek chthonic deities, i.e. gods and monsters of the underworld. The three-headed dog Cerberus, guardian

FIGURE 3.1 Ammut and the Weighing of the Heart in the Egyptian *Book of the Dead* from the Papyrus of Ani, *c.*1250 BCE.

Source: British Museum. Public domain.

of the entrance to Hades, may be frightening, but like a gate deity his job is to guard more than to harm; his multiple heads allow him to watch many directions at once. The Erinyes (Furies) could be invoked for vengeance and were thought responsible for disease and destruction, but they also received cult worship and act as protectors in their other roles, such as the Eumenides (Kindly Ones). Neither underworld group—Greek or Egyptian—is inherently evil, but still potentially dangerous.

Now that we have an overview of the Egyptian source material, we will turn to examples of how the Greeks and Romans incorporated Egyptian monsters into many of their significant cultural institutions, from literature and art to politics and religion. We begin with a giant snake in the Middle Kingdom's 'Tale of the Shipwrecked Sailor' (c.1940 BCE) and its connections to the *Odyssey* (eighth century BCE), before examining Apollonius Rhodius' reframing of a battle in the *Book of the Dead* as a contest between the sorceress Medea and the giant Talos in his *Argonautica* (third century BCE). Next, we explore the heart-swallowing demon Ammut and her connections to the Greek and Egyptian sphinx, before ending with Cleopatra VII, the dangerous ruler of an Egypt viewed as monstrous after the break-up of Rome's Second Triumvirate.

The 'Tale of the Shipwrecked Sailor' and the *Odyssey*

Egypt is present from the very beginning of Greek literature, briefly mentioned in the *Iliad*, in which Egyptian Thebes is proverbially linked to wealth (9.381–2). Our earliest detailed description of Egypt in Greek literature, however, appears in the *Odyssey*, where the Greek king Menelaus tells Odysseus' son Telemachus about being stranded in Egypt on his way home from Troy. He describes Egypt as a land of riches, education, and knowledge: along with expensive gifts of silver and gold, his wife Helen returns with a drug that erases sorrow and pain. Menelaus' Egypt is also a magical and mysterious land where his adventures include being aided by a goddess and wrestling the sea god Proteus (*Od.* 4.351–585).

In contrast, when Odysseus finally returns home to Ithaca, he describes Egypt as a more realistic place. Disguised as a Cretan, he tells a series of lies, and these 'Cretan Lies' portray Egypt as a land of trade wholly populated by men, who are ruled by a pious king who saves the hero's life (*Od.* 14.278–84). Even in our earliest sources, then, Egypt was multifaceted and could appear both exotic and familiar. The *Odyssey* does more than provide an early Greek appraisal of Egypt, however; it also reflects the influence of an Egyptian story, the 'Tale of the Shipwrecked Sailor', which provides a model for the hostile and helpful forces on Odysseus' journey.

The 'Shipwrecked Sailor', our oldest preserved Egyptian story, dates to Egypt's Twelfth Dynasty (c.2000–1900 BCE). We have only one copy, preserved on a papyrus (*PHermitage* 1115), but references to the story in later texts provide proof of its popularity. Although rather short at 189 lines, the 'Shipwrecked Sailor' shares many formal characteristics with the *Odyssey*. Also written in verse, it similarly begins *in medias res*, contains repetitive formulaic language, and includes a tale within a tale told by a first-person narrator. The two works also have similar plots. In each, a man survives a shipwreck while all his companions drown, and he washes up on a magical island where he receives guidance on how to return home. Most importantly, each protagonist is characterized as a 'clever' man who saves himself with his ability to know what to say. Storytelling constitutes a major theme throughout the narratives, along with the powers of speaking, listening, and remembering.

The monster of the 'Shipwrecked Sailor' turns out not to be very monstrous after all, at least in his behaviour. His first appearance, however, is startling indeed. The sailor washes up on an island full of golden age imagery: lush foliage teeming with beautiful fruit and an abundance of fish and fowl for food. Suddenly, the narrator thinks he hears thunder or perhaps the sea. Trees crack. The earth shakes. A giant golden snake, 30 cubits long with a 2-cubit-long beard and eyebrows of lapis lazuli appears. This serpent approaches the narrator, demanding to know what he wants, and threatens his life. The narrator faints. Upon recovering, he tells the story of his shipwreck to the snake, who provides the sailor with instructions on how to return home. The snake then tells his own tragic story. After four months a boat arrives, and the snake sends the sailor back home with many riches.

Egypt is a snaky place. The so-called Snakebite Papyrus (589–525 BCE, Brooklyn Museum 47.218.48a–f) details remedies and treatments for snakebites and lists thirty-four different kinds of snakes. No wonder, then, that snakes held many and mixed meanings for the Egyptians. On the one hand, cobras were closely associated with different goddesses and appear as the uraeus (the cobra rearing from the front of a crown), symbolizing kingship. Several goddesses (and some gods) are depicted with a snake head on a human body; only in Roman times did these Egyptian deities have the body of the snake and the head of a woman, like Graeco-Roman monsters. Snakes can also be monstrous, like Apophis, the giant snake embodying chaos, who attacks the solar boat of the sun god Re every night. Another divine snake, Mehen, protects Re on the journey. So prevalent are snakes that they even slithered their way into the Egyptian writing system: the horned viper represents the sound 'f' in hieroglyphs and the cobra represents 'second d', equivalent to the sound 'dj'.

The snake in the 'Shipwrecked Sailor' is the avatar of a god, as demonstrated by his body of gold and lapis lazuli, such ornate decoration being a regular feature of statues of the gods. The story's imagery also connects him to Re. The snake's tragic story relates how there were once seventy-five snakes, all relatives, dwelling on the island. One day, a star fell from the sky and killed all but him, since he was away at the time. In a religious text known as the 'Litany of Re', Re has seventy-five forms, linking this snake to the god. The snake calls himself 'the Lord of Punt', a land whose exact location is still debated, but which probably lay southeast of Egypt, since the Egyptians called Punt the 'Land of the God', the land of Re where the sun rises. Still, as R. B. Parkinson (1997: 99 n. 17) explains, 'the identity of the serpent is presented as an obscure metaphor' and there is no consensus on which deity he represents.

The snake adds to the island's preternatural interpretation when he calls it 'this is-land of *ka*' (Blackman 1972: 114), which may be a metaphor for the underworld. The *ka* was the life force of a person, the part of the soul that survived after bodily death. The island's fruit trees are cultivated, which further connects the snake and his island to the underworld: in Egyptian necropolises, gardens were planted in front of tombs to pro-vide sustenance and shelter for the souls of the deceased. The *Book of the Dead* and other funerary texts depict underworld gardens, which served the same purpose. If the snake's island represents the underworld, then the sailor, like Odysseus, undergoes a *katabasis* and spiritual rebirth before returning home.

Towards the end of the story, the sailor learns that he will never see the island again, as the snake tells him it will 'become waters' (Blackman 1972: 154). Scholars commonly understand this cryptic phrase to mean that the island will sink underneath the ocean, another indication of its otherworldly, liminal status (Baines 1990: 62). This resembles the fate of Scheria, the Phaeacians' island-home in the *Odyssey*: Poseidon threatens to surround their city with a mountain (13.149–52), cutting them off from the rest of the world as retribution for aiding Odysseus—thus making it, like the snake's island of *ka*, a place to which one cannot return.

Unlike Menelaus, who had to wrestle Proteus when the sea god shape-shifted into snake form (4.457), Odysseus himself never encounters any snakes in the *Odyssey*. Still, many of the *Odyssey*'s adventures share themes and elements of the Egyptian shipwrecked sailor's encounter with the snake. For example, the sailor first perceives the snake as a threat—it even carries off the sailor in his mouth at one point—but the snake turns out to be benevolent. Similarly, Odysseus encounters the ghost of Teiresias in the frightening environment of Hades, but the seer gives Odysseus important prophecies and advice for his return home. Likewise, the goddess Circe first meets Odysseus' crew with hostility, turning the men into swine when they arrive on her island, but upon realizing that Odysseus has the aid of Hermes she becomes helpful and instructs Odysseus how to return home. Perhaps it is no coincidence that Circe is the daughter of Helios, the sun, just as the snake of the 'Shipwrecked Sailor' is linked to the sun god Re.

Many other details suggest the influence of the 'Shipwrecked Sailor' on the *Odyssey*, including similar descriptions of the ships' crews and a shipwrecked man huddling under bushes before exploring his new location. Indeed, this is one of several Egyptian stories and poems that has left its mark on early Greek literature, although a formal study of the subject still needs undertaking.

Battling Monsters in the *Book of the Dead* and the *Argonautica*

Seth, the Egyptian god of chaos and confusion, exemplifies the paradoxically harmful yet benevolent nature of many Egyptian deities. On the one hand, he is violently mon-strous: he kills his brother Osiris, thus bringing death into the world, and in a fight with his nephew Horus over Osiris' throne, he rapes Horus and rips out his eye. On the other hand, Seth represents kingship and serves as a protector of the god Re. Seth usually appears therianthropic in form, but the animal whose forked tail, long, rounded head, and tall, rectangular ears he bears remains unidentified and is simply referred to as the 'Seth animal', possibly a hybrid creature.

As part of his association with chaos, Seth's domain included the desert and foreign countries, and he was linked to foreign gods like the Semitic Baal. Epithets such as 'wrongdoer', 'his name is bad', and 'evil one' reinforce his negative associations and, as with demons, his epithets are sometimes accompanied by the determinative for 'enemy'. The Seth animal itself can serve as a determinative, marking chaotic words like 'tumult', 'illness', and 'storm'. The Greeks identified Seth with Typhoeus (Hdt. 2.144.2), a chaos monster and enemy of the gods (see Brockliss in this volume).

Reflecting Seth's more positive side, Egyptians sometimes named their children 'Seth-is-kind' and 'Seth-is-great'. Indeed, Eugene Cruz-Uribe (2009) argues that Seth's primary association should be with power and might rather than chaos. Certainly, the balance between chaos and order formed an essential part of life for the Egyptians. Seth therefore provides a necessary chaotic force to ensure cosmic balance and order.

In the *Book of the Dead*, Seth appears as protector of order and slayer of monsters in the 'Chapter for Knowing the Souls of the Westerners' (Spell 108, *BD*, Faulkner et al. 2015: 127). The *Book of the Dead*'s individual chapters, known as spells, describe the underworld and instruct the deceased on their journeys into the afterlife. Stretching into Roman times, the texts range in quality and so were probably widely available. Misreadings and duplicate spells in some copies point to a symbolic importance beyond the ability of their owners to read them. We have many examples from the Hellenistic period (332–330 BCE), called the Ptolemaic period for Egypt specifically, since during that time it was ruled by the Ptolemies, successors to Alexander the Great.

Despite his name, which suggests that he was from the island of Rhodes, the Hellenistic poet Apollonius Rhodius most likely belonged a new generation of Greeks born in Egypt. While the content of the *Argonautica*—Jason's quest for the Golden Fleece aided by the sorceress Medea—is steeped in Greek tradition, the epic has close ties to the political and cultural climate of Ptolemaic Egypt, where the Ptolemies were building Egyptian temples, worshipping Egyptian gods, and styling themselves as pharaohs while still preserving Greek traditions. Anatole Mori (2008) shows that figures in the poem reflect members of the Ptolemaic family, although the characterizations are more complicated than one-to-one correspondence. Jackie Murray (2014) persuasively dates the epic to 238 BCE, the year Ptolemy III introduced a new calendar and received extended cultic honours. With this in mind, we can read the *Argonautica* as an honorific poem for Ptolemy III.

Apollonius' poem also contains many allusions to Egyptian mythology, religion, and tradition. Susan Stephens (2003) examines the voyage of the Argo in the *Argonautica* as a reflection of the voyage of the Egyptian solar bark. In Egyptian theology, Re, the sun god, leaves the sky at night to travel through the underworld in his solar bark and must defeat the snake Apophis before returning to the sky and being reborn. Sometimes Re himself, in various forms like Re-Horakhty or even a cat, battles Apophis; at other times Seth helps Re fight, as in *Book of the Dead*, Spell 108. In the *Argonautica*, Apollonius uses this cosmic fight as a model, transforming it into a battle against the bronze man Talos.

Spell 108 describes Apophis' attack on the solar bark. As the sun sets, the bark descends westward into the underworld and approaches a tall mountain guarded by Apophis, a serpent 30 cubits long—the same length of the snake in the 'Shipwrecked Sailor'. Apophis turns his eyes against the crew to hypnotize them, but Seth uses his magic power (and an iron spear) to save the ship. Seth orders Apophis to retreat and cover his face. He calls himself the 'great magician' who has the power to conquer the snake.

In the *Argonautica*, Apollonius describes a parallel fight. There, the remaining crew of the Argo has finally escaped from their near-death adventures in Libya and arrives at Crete, only to find Talos, a giant man of bronze, guarding the shores. He attempts to prevent the sailors' landing by throwing rocks at them from a high cliff. The Argonauts, at this point extremely exhausted from their arduous journey, need Medea's magical knowledge and courage to defeat Talos. She enchants the bronze guardian with her eyes, driving him mad so that he grazes his ankle—the only vulnerable place on his body. The ichor keeping him alive gushes out, and he collapses (Ap. Rhod. *Argon.* 4.1638–88).

The parallelism is striking. In both episodes, a boat approaches a high cliff and encounters a hostile force. The monstrous entity is then defeated by someone on the boat who is an outsider in some way: Medea as a woman, a witch, and a foreigner, and Seth as a god of chaos and king of foreign lands. Moreover, Spell 108 takes place in the underworld, while in the *Argonautica*, the Argonauts also sail west towards the sunset, and the following episode of the epic plunges them into darkness, symbolizing death (Stephens 2003: 232–3). There are also some verbal parallels between the two passages, suggesting that Apollonius was familiar with the *Book of the Dead*.

Apollonius' battle echoes the action of Spell 108 but complicates the relationship between monster and monster-slayer. In Spell 108, Apophis, the foe, uses his eyes to overcome the crew, while Seth uses a spear to stop him. In the *Argonautica*, Medea, on the protagonists' side, uses her eyes as a weapon, giving her qualities of both Apophis and Seth. Apollonius also masterfully mixes Greek and Egyptian tradition: Talos' rock-throwing recalls the *Odyssey*'s Cyclopes and Laestrygonians, especially since he, like them, is a giant. Instead of a snake, Talos is a bronze man, the last of an earlier age of men, described as 'ash-tree born' (*Argon.* 4.1641), which recalls Hesiod's *Works and Days* (143–55; eighth century BCE), grounding Talos in Greek mythic tradition.

The *Argonautica* does not lack snakes, however. In one episode, Jason sows the earth with a serpent's teeth, which grow into armed men (3.498–9); in various others, Heracles kills a giant snake guarding the apples of the Hesperides (4.1393–1410), the seer Mopsus dies of a snakebite (4.1502–36), and even the Argo itself becomes a snake in a simile (4.1540–7). In an earlier passage that Stephens (2003) calls a doublet of the Talos episode, Medea conquers another giant snake, the guardian of the Golden Fleece, enchanting the snake's eyes by sprinkling a magical potion in them (*Argon.* 4.123–66). When we first hear of this serpent, we learn that he was born from Earth on the spot where Typhon's blood had dripped after the monster was wounded by Zeus' thunder-bolt (2.1206–15). Since the Greeks equated Typhoeus (Typhon) with Seth, Apollonius' allusion to Egyptian tradition in the *Argonautica* becomes even more complex: Medea defeats a monster associated with Seth, who plays the role of both monster and monster-slayer, just as she later has qualities of both monster and monster-slayer in the battle against Talos.

HYBRID ANIMAL ENTITIES: AMMUT, THE SPHINX, AND OTHERS

The Egyptian monster Ammut is part lion, part hippopotamus, and part crocodile—the three deadly man-eaters of Egypt. Images of Ammut generally give her the face of a crocodile with a lion's mane, the front legs and torso of a lion, and the hind legs of a hippopotamus. This hybridity symbolizes that she is inescapable by land or water. Ammut sometimes appears on tomb walls but is primarily associated with two scenes in the *Book of the Dead*: the weighing of the heart and the presentation of the deceased to Osiris. Ammut's name means 'Swallower of the Dead': her role was to devour the hearts of the impure, preventing them from entering the afterlife.

While Ammut's hybridity should mark her as especially dangerous, the goddess Taweret, composed of the same three animals, is a beneficial deity, frequently depicted on apotropaic amulets that were especially popular among pregnant women. Taweret appears with the head of a hippopotamus, the hands and feet of a lion, and the tail of a crocodile—a different combination of Ammut's deadly trio. Taweret's popularity grew in Graeco-Roman Egypt, but her early influence on the broader Mediterranean world can be seen on Minoan seals from Crete, which evince her influence on the Minoan genius, a hybrid deity often depicted bringing offerings and libations to the gods (Weingarten 1991; see also Kitchell in this volume). The god Bes played a similar apotropaic role. Leonine, tailed, and sometimes winged, Bes usually appears as a dwarf, frequently ithyphallic, often dancing. While most figures in Egyptian art are portrayed in profile, Bes typically meets the viewer face-on, with a protruding tongue (for images, see Bagh et al. 2021). Thus, Bes can variously resemble a Greek satyr or a *gorgoneion*. Both Taweret and Bes are sometimes classified as demons, but their frightening aspects also help make them effective guardians. Bes, like Taweret, became very popular in Graeco-Roman Egypt and in this context occasionally wears a *bulla*, a protective amulet worn by Roman children.

Ammut, with the epithet 'Great of Death', is a little scarier, usually depicted crouching expectantly near the scales of justice like an eager dog begging for scraps (Fig. 3.1). Over time, however, she becomes more leonine and similar to the Greek sphinx in posture—still crouching, but with her head held high. Ammut loses most of her crocodile and hippopotamus aspects, and although she never gains wings or a human head, scholars believe her image was influenced by the Greek sphinx, a monster also closely associated with death (van Dijk 2001). The relationship between the Greek and Egyptian sphinxes is an interesting case, since it seems that the Egyptian sphinx influenced the Greek version, which in turn came back to influence the Egyptians in Ammut's metamorphosis (cf. López-Ruiz in this volume). The Egyptian sphinx (*Ssp-anx* 'living image'), associated with the god Re as well as with the pharaoh, is a beneficial guardian thought to symbolize the combination of human intellect and the brute strength of beasts, an idealized quality of rulers.

Another sphinx-like divinity is the West Semitic goddess Astarte, borrowed from Canaan and Syria. While Astarte can be purely anthropomorphic, sometimes she appears as a winged hybrid creature very similar to the Greek sphinx. Astarte was both a goddess of love and fertility as well as a goddess of war, but in Egypt this latter association became most prominent, especially in her role of protector of the king's chariot in battle. She also accompanied the god Seth as his wife: her fierce battle rage complemented his chaos. Astarte's dangerous side ties her more closely to the Greek sphinx, a killer of men.

CLEOPATRA AS *MONSTRUM*

Cleopatra VII (r. 51–30 BCE), last of the Ptolemies, came into power when Egypt was already a client state of Rome. She tried to reclaim Egypt's independence and, although she ultimately failed, she left an indelible imprint on history—and, to some, a monstrous reputation. Many of our ancient sources concerning Cleopatra notably consist of Roman propaganda after her defeat by Octavian—the future emperor Augustus—at the Battle of Actium (31 BCE).

Plutarch's *Life of Antony,* written more than a hundred years after Cleopatra's death, provides our most complete overview of the queen, but we also get glimpses of her in works by her Roman contemporaries, including the poets Horace, Vergil, and Propertius, who depict her as a flirtatious seductress, a controlling whore, and a monstrous queen leading a brigade of monstrous gods. In his *Elegies*, Propertius calls her the 'Prostitute-queen of incestuous Canopus' (3.11.39) and Horace laments Antony as 'A Roman man, alas, enslaved to a woman' (*Epod.* 9.11–12). While Cleopatra's lack of sexual restraint is the prevailing theme, a close second is that of men's fear. Lucan (39–65 CE), in his *Pharsalia*, an epic poem about the Roman civil war, succinctly sums up the anxiety that not just a woman, but a *foreign* woman, will control Rome—and Roman men:

> She terrified the Capitol (if it's possible!) with her *sistrum*
> and pursued Roman standards with unwarlike Canopus,
> seeking to lead Pharian triumphs with Caesar captured.
> And there was doubt in the waters off Actium
> whether a woman—and not even a Roman one—would rule the world.

(10.63–7)

Vergil's description of Aeneas' shield strongly influenced Lucan's depiction: the shield is decorated with scenes illustrating key moments of Roman history, from Romulus and Remus' infancy to Octavian's triumph after the Battle of Actium. Here Vergil places Octavian on one side to represent order, the people and the senate, and the gods of Rome. On the opposite side, Antony and Cleopatra represent the Other, with Cleopatra called his 'unspeakable' (*nefas*) Egyptian wife (*Aen.* 8.688). Cleopatra uses her *sistrum*—a type of rattle used in religious rites—as a sort of war trumpet and we see her death foreshadowed by twin serpents. The Egyptian gods stand off against the Roman gods: Anubis is barking again, although here the gods are not laughable, but full-blown 'monsters, gods of every race' (*omnigenumque deum monstra*, 8.698).

Similar descriptions appear in Horace's 'Cleopatra Ode' (*Carm.* 1.37), which begins *nunc est bibendum*, 'now it's drinking time', to celebrate Octavian's victory. Here, both Cleopatra's entourage and the queen herself are monstrous. Cleopatra's depiction in this poem is complex; scholars still debate the precise meaning of the phrase describing her, *fatale monstrum*, which means 'deadly monster', 'fateful portent', or perhaps both (1.37.21). On the one hand, Cleopatra is unbridled, frenzied, and drunk on fortune (or even just drunk), but on the other she is also a brave woman who would rather die than be led on display through the streets of Rome.

Across the ancient Mediterranean and to this day, powerful women across the world are vilified and depicted as monsters (Zimmerman 2021). In Cleopatra's case, the image of her as a decadent slut who commands monsters—or is a monster herself—has become the primary way she is remembered. Instead of viewing her through the lens of Roman propaganda, however, I suggest that, by way of conclusion, we look to a papyrus giving a tax exemption to a Roman citizen in Egypt (*PBingen* 45) The papyrus is written in Greek, the language of the Ptolemaic administration. Peter van Minnen (2000) has argued that only the ruler of Egypt could grant this exemption and that ruler would be none other than Cleopatra. Underneath the exemption is a one-word Greek imperative, most likely written by the queen herself: *ginesthoi* ('Let it be done!'). And so, we can let Cleopatra have the last word, since the Romans were right about at least one thing that she knew how to do: command.

CONCLUSION

The emperor Decius is the last Roman ruler whose name we have carved in Egyptian hieroglyphs, honouring him as pharaoh (249–251 CE). The very latest extant hieroglyphs comprise an inscription known as the Graffito of Esmet-Akhom and are preserved with an inscription dating them to 394 CE, under the rule of the Roman emperor Diocletian. We can see this as an end of sorts to a long relationship between Egypt and Greece and later with Rome. Different moments in this relationship build a larger picture of classical monsters and their sources. We have looked at the early influence of the 'Shipwrecked Sailor' on the *Odyssey*, the impact of Egyptian religion and the *Book of the Dead* on our only remaining epic of the Hellenistic period, the metamorphosis of a monster from a scene in the *Book of the Dead*, and finally, an Egyptian queen whose near success made her a monstrous threat to Rome. These are just a few examples demonstrating how Egyptian culture influenced classical monsters. Indeed, Egypt's broader influence on Greece and Rome has still not been sufficiently studied; there is much left to examine regarding the relationship of Egypt's literature, society, and art to its Mediterranean context, particularly when it comes to monsters.

SUGGESTED READING

Hart (2005) and Wilkinson (2020) provide good introductions to the Egyptian pantheon. Graves-Brown (2019) explores Egyptian demons. Fischer (1987) provides a rare examination of the Egyptian idea of the monstrous. Loprieno (1996) has an edited volume covering many different aspects of Egyptian literature. Parkinson (1997) has translations of Middle Egyptian poems, and Borghouts (1978) is a treasure trove of Egyptian spells in translation. Mori (2008) writes about the Ptolemies in the *Argonautica*, while Stephens (2003) examines Egyptian influence on Hellenistic poetry. For Cleopatra, Jones (2006) collects primary sources in translation, and Roller's (2010) biography examines her life and times through the lens of our ancient sources. For the phrase *fatale monstrum*, see Simone (2019), which reviews the scholarship on the topic and provides a fresh look at Horace's ode.

WORKS CITED

Bagh, T., et al. 2021. *Bes: Demon God, Protector of Egypt*. Copenhagen.

Baines, J. 1990. 'Interpreting the Story of the Shipwrecked Sailor.' *Journal of Egyptian Archaeology* 76: 55–72.

Blackman, A. M. 1972. *Middle-Egyptian Stories*. Brussels.

Borghouts, J. P. 1978. *Ancient Egyptian Magical Texts*. Leiden.

Cruz-Uribe, E. 2009. 'Stḥ ꜣ pḥty "Seth, God of Power and Might".' *Journal of American Research Center in Egypt* 45: 201–26.

Faulkner, R. O., O. Goelet, and E. von Dassow. 2015. *The Egyptian Book of the Dead*. San Francisco.

Fischer, H. G. 1987. 'The Ancient Egyptian Attitude toward the Monstrous', in *Monsters and Demons in the Ancient and Medieval Worlds: Papers Presented in Honor of Edith Porada*, ed. A. E. Farkas, P. O. Harper, and E. B. Harrison, 13–26. Mainz.

Graves-Brown, C. 2019. *Daemons and Spirits in Ancient Egypt*. Swansea.

Hart, G. 2005. *The Routledge Dictionary of Egyptian Gods and Goddesses*, 2nd edn. New York.

Jones, P. J. 2006. *Cleopatra: A Sourcebook*. Norman, OK.

Kock, T. 1884. *Comicorum Atticorum fragmenta*, vol. 2. Leipzig.

Loprieno, A., ed. 1996. *Ancient Egyptian Literature*. Leiden.

Lucarelli, R. 2010. 'Demons (Benevolent and Malevolent)', in the online *UCLA Encyclopedia of Egyptology*, ed. W. Wendrich et al. https://www.uee.ucla.edu.

Mori. A. 2008. *The Politics of Apollonius Rhodius' Argonautica*. Cambridge.

Murray, J. 2014. 'Anchored in Time: The Date in Apollonius' *Argonautica*', in *Hellenistic Poetry in Context*, ed. A. Harder, R. F. Regtuit, and G. C. Wakker, 247–84. Leuven.

Parkinson, R. B. 1997. *The Tale of Sinuhe and Other Ancient Egyptian Poems, 1940–1640 BC*. Oxford.

Roller, D. W. 2010. *Cleopatra: A Biography*. Oxford.

Simone, A. 2019. 'Horace's Protean Cleopatra (*Carm.* 1.37).' *Classical Philology* 114/3: 506–16.

Stephens, S. 2003. *Seeing Double: Intercultural Poetics in Ptolemaic Alexandria*. Berkeley and Los Angeles.

Szpakowska, K. 2009. 'Demons in Ancient Egypt.' *Religion Compass* 3/5: 799–805.

van Dijk, J. 2001. 'Hell', in the online *The Oxford Encyclopedia of Ancient Egypt*, ed. D. B. Redford. Oxford. https://www.oxfordreference.com/display/10.1093/acref/9780195102345.001.0001/acref-9780195102345.

van Minnen, P. 2000. 'An Official Act of Cleopatra (with a Subscription in Her Own Hand).' *Ancient Society* 30: 29–34.

Weingarten, J. 1991. 'The Transformation of Egyptian Taweret into the Minoan Genius.' *Studies in Mediterranean Archaeology* 88: 3–20.

Wilkinson, R. 2020. *The Complete Gods and Goddesses of Ancient Egypt*, 2nd edn. New York.

Zimmerman, J. 2021. *Women and Other Monsters: Building a New Mythology*. Boston.

CHAPTER 4

TYPHOEUS, AGENT OF DISORDER

WILLIAM BROCKLISS

INTRODUCTION

MONSTERS are figures of disorder whose corporeal peculiarities, unruly behaviours, and extreme otherness threaten the physical structures of the universe and the conceptual distinctions that undergird human attempts to make sense of the world (Cohen 1996). Typhoeus (also Typhaon, Typhon, Typhos) represents perhaps the most extreme instantiation of disorder of all monsters of the Greek and Roman tradition. The poets and artists of ancient Greece and Rome associate him with several related themes: disordered or otherwise unusual family relations, a disorderly body, disorderly sounds, and the capacity to engender disorder in the cosmos and on earth. Writers also draw on Typhoeus to illustrate disorder in human communities and the human soul, and to explore conceptual pairings important to their poems and treatises, such as reason and madness, music and noise.

ORIGINS AND EARLY GREEK REPRESENTATIONS

The monster's disorderly qualities are echoed in figures from other mythologies, whom scholars have identified as antecedents of, or parallels to, Typhoeus in the ancient Greek and Roman tradition. Martin West places the monster in an Eastern Mediterranean context, adducing Near Eastern tales of battles between the king of the gods and an unruly challenger (1997: 300–4). Some of these antagonists exhibit serpentine attributes, as with the Sumerian Azag, who 'hisses like a serpent' (301). The violent conflict between the two divinities may cause widespread destruction on earth. In a separate study, West likens Greek descriptions of Zeus' battle with Typhoeus to stories of battles between storm-gods and their snaky adversaries in other Indo-European traditions; for example, in the Vedic tradition of ancient India, the god Indra defeats Vṛtra, 'a huge serpent', while in Norse mythology Thor subdues 'the Miðgarð Serpent' (2007: 256, 259).

Our earliest Greek representations of Typhoeus are found in texts that date from the Archaic period (eighth to sixth centuries BCE). In his studies of Near Eastern and Indo-European parallels, West focuses on Hesiod's *Theogony* (eighth century BCE), which details the generations of the gods and explains how the current order of the universe came about. Zeus' defeat of Typhoeus, who represents the final challenge to his rule, constitutes the last major episode of the poem. As with the non-Greek stories discussed by West, the Hesiodic monster has serpentine characteristics, and his conflict with Zeus disturbs the cosmos. Hesiod's treatment of Typhoeus also incorporates motifs that become characteristic of later Greek tales about the monster, such as irregular reproduction or a disorderly physique.

The *Theogony* refers to figures named Typhaon and Typhoeus, who seem to be one and the same character (West 1966: 252). Such varied nomenclature became the norm in later sources, which make no distinction between figures called Typhoeus, Typhaon, Typhon, or Typhos. We find Typhaon in a section of the *Theogony* known as the 'Catalogue of Monsters' (270–336). The monsters of the *Theogony* reveal their disorderly qualities in part through their unruly fertility (Clay 2003: 12–30, 150–61), and Typhaon is no exception; the 'Catalogue' relates how he 'mingled in love' with Echidna and thereby fathered Orthrus (the two-headed hound of the three-headed Geryon), Cerberus (the fifty-headed dog of Hades), the snaky Hydra, and possibly other monstrous children. Such prolific reproduction exceeds the poem's norms, though its mechanism (sex) is unremarkable. So long as we can identify this Typhaon with Typhoeus, we next hear of the monster in a tale of his birth and his conflict with Zeus. Typhoeus himself is the product of sexual reproduction: his parents Earth and Tartarus unite 'in love, through golden Aphrodite' (*Theog.* 822). An unusually precocious infant, Typhoeus emerges into the world with the capabilities of a mature being and, immediately after his birth, challenges Zeus' supremacy (836; cf. West 1966: 389).

Hesiod's monster is remarkable for his disorderly physique. The *Theogony* details Typhoeus' physical characteristics, as do Greek vase paintings from the sixth century BCE and later. The characteristics the poem attributes to Typhoeus differ, however, from those in visual art (see *LIMC*, s.v. 'Typhon'). We hear that 'from his shoulders there were a hundred heads of dread, glaring snakes, licking with dark tongues, and the eyes in his wondrous heads darted forth fire under the brows' (*Theog.* 824–7).[1] Visual representations likewise associate Typhoeus' body with snakes, but unlike Hesiod's description, some of these representations show a figure with a snaky lower half and a human-like head (e.g. Fig. 4.1), perhaps because a painter could not reasonably fit

---

[1] All translations are mine.

FIGURE 4.1 Zeus fights Typhoeus; hydria (water-jar) from Euboea, *c.*540–530 BCE. Staatliche Antikensammlung, Munich.

Source: Wikimedia / Bib Saint-Pol. Public domain.

one hundred heads on a vase. This and other artistic renderings also depart from the *Theogony* insofar as they give Typhoeus wings, possibly to indicate his divinity.

In a further detail clearly more suited to literature than to the visual arts, the *Theogony* explores the soundscape created by Typhoeus, which contrasts with other sounds described in the poem. The monster voices a disorderly mixture of horrendous noises. His confused vocalizations suit a newborn creature with adult capabilities, since they mix the mature and the immature (the sounds of puppies and a bull; see Brockliss 2017/ 18: 141). They also confuse different categories of being, as Typhoeus mingles animalian cries with sounds uttered 'as if for the gods to understand' (*Theog.* 829–35; Goslin 2010). But even if his utterances are sometimes comprehensible to the gods, his cacophonous performances contrast starkly with music that the poem associates with Zeus—namely, the orderly song of the Muses, who celebrate Zeus' supremacy on Olympus and inspire the orderly music of the *Theogony* itself (Goslin 2010).

In the *Theogony*, Typhoeus' disorderly nature reveals itself most of all in his tumultuous battle with Zeus. Following Zeus' defeat of the Titans, Typhoeus emerges as the last and greatest challenger to Zeus' rule, who 'would have ruled both mortals and immortals' if Zeus had not taken notice (837). Though Typhoeus is a male divinity, his association with Earth may suggest a last attempt by that goddess to promote matriarchal forces in the cosmos, in preference to Zeus' patriarchy (Clay 2003). The poem thus indicates an alternative, possibly matriarchal path that the universe could have taken had Zeus lost the battle.

The account of the battle, however, undermines the distinctions between Typhoean disorder and the order guaranteed by Zeus. Zeus defeats Typhoeus with thunder and lightning, thus fighting 'fire with fire' both literally and figuratively (Ogden 2013: 218). He suppresses his monstrous, noisy, fiery-eyed adversary with noisy, fiery weapons that were themselves produced by the physically monstrous Cyclopes (*Theog.* 139–46; Brockliss 2017/18). Zeus also ends Typhoeus' challenge to cosmic order at the cost, albeit temporarily, of disrupting the peace in all the major realms of the cosmos: he sets fire to the earth, sea, and heaven, and the noise of the battle causes consternation even in the lower world (*Theog.* 847–52).

Typhoeus' disorderly nature is also evident in his enduring threat to human communities after the battle. Having defeated the monster, Zeus confines him in Tartarus, the divine prison-house. Typhoeus, however, continues to play havoc with human seafaring and agriculture: while other gods are the source of useful winds, Typhoeus is the origin of destructive winds that imperil sailors with storms at sea and ravage fields with dust clouds (*Theog.* 869–80). Indeed, Typhoeus' name may have influenced the formation of the English 'typhoon' (cf. *OED*, s.v.).

We find another early depiction of Typhoeus in Homer's *Iliad*, an epic poem set during the Trojan War and dating to around the same time as the *Theogony*. As with *Theogony* 869–80, the Iliadic passage may depict the defeated Typhoeus. But if so, the context is different: while the Hesiodic Typhoeus engenders disorder on earth, the Homeric poem incorporates the monster into a simile that suggests the disorderliness of a human community:

> They then go as if the whole earth were consumed by fire;
> And the earth beneath was groaning, as under Zeus the Thunderer
> In his anger, whenever he lashes the earth around Typhoeus
> In Arimi, where they say is the bed of Typhoeus;
> Thus the earth groaned greatly under their feet
> As they came; they crossed the plain very quickly. (2.780–5)

This simile compares the noise generated by the Greek soldiers gathering at Troy with the din unleashed by Zeus' thunderbolt, but, as often in the *Iliad*, other details in the imagery introduce resonances beyond the explicit point of comparison. At 2.780–5, such details recall events and images from earlier in Book 2. When Agamemnon proposes that the Greeks abandon the siege of Troy, the soldiers run for the ships, but Odysseus restores order by striking them. With the mutiny suppressed, the generals muster the troops for battle, and a sequence of seven similes describes the soldiers' movements and their leader, Agamemnon. A lengthy catalogue of the Greek forces then interrupts the story, and the Typhoeus simile occurs shortly after the narrative resumes. The reference to 'Zeus the Thunderer' assailing Typhoeus (2.781) recalls a comparison of Agamemnon with 'Zeus the Thunderer' (2.478), while the description of Zeus lashing 'the earth around Typhoeus' (2.782) echoes the physical punishments that Odysseus deals out to the troops, thereby associating the soldiers with a monster whose disorderly tendencies would have been familiar to audiences from mythic tradition. The soldiers' insubordination finds a parallel in Typhoeus' challenge to Zeus' rule.

There are, however, discrepancies between the *Iliad*'s descriptions of the soldiers and its depiction of Typhoeus, which serve to emphasize the chaos associated with the monster and his divine rival. Even if the Greek soldiers lack discipline, once chastised they do not resume their mutiny. Indeed, they show no such insubordination in the remainder of the epic, and never again is a leader such as Odysseus obliged to employ force against them. In the Typhoeus simile, however, Zeus lashes his foe multiple times. His continued punishment of the monster suggests that Typhoeus retains the potential to sow confusion. If so, Zeus' anger is understandable: unlike his Hesiodic equivalent, whom Zeus defeats decisively, the Iliadic Typhoeus invites punishment repeatedly. Zeus' control over his dangerous antagonist seems therefore less secure than Agamemnon's over his troops. And once again, Zeus' own actions are a source of disorder. As in his battle with the Hesiodic monster, the earth groans and catches fire.

Our last major treatment of the monster from the Archaic age occurs in the *Homeric Hymns*, a set of poems from the seventh and sixth centuries BCE describing the actions and attributes of the Greek gods. Though composed later than the *Iliad*, the hymns employ similar language to that of the Homeric epics. The *Homeric Hymn to Apollo* tells a story involving Typhaon and his similarly monstrous foster-mother, a giant snake (*drakainan*, 300), who was the original inhabitant of Delphi. Though unnamed in the hymn, she is elsewhere known as Delphyne (Ogden 2013: 42–4). The hymn departs from most other sources in the events that it depicts and shows innovations in its treatments of Typhaon's origins, early history, and position relative to Zeus' supremacy. Nonetheless, some of the themes treated in the episode intersect with those found in other texts: the *Homeric Hymn to Apollo* associates Typhaon with unusual modes of reproduction, a disorderly body, and the ability to wreak havoc.

Typhaon emerges from a string of unusual births produced antagonistically, in a contest between the king and queen of the gods (*Hymn. Hom. Ap.* 305–52). Hera, incensed that Zeus was able to engender Athena without her involvement, gives birth on her own to Hephaestus. But she finds her disabled offspring unsatisfactory and decides to create a second child by slapping the earth. Her parthenogenesis of Hephaestus is thus followed by an act of generation that, in the context of the Homeric hymns and epics, is irregular in two respects: it represents the union of two female divinities, Hera and Earth; and it is achieved through physical contact between the two but not through sexual intercourse. The Earth becomes pregnant from the encounter and later gives birth to the monster Typhaon.

The unusual origins of Hephaestus and Typhaon are matched by their unusual physical characteristics. While the Olympian gods are otherwise non-disabled and physically powerful, Hephaestus is weak and has shrivelled feet (*Hymn. Hom. Ap.* 316–17). His half-brother, Typhaon, is 'like neither gods nor mortals' (351). The hymnist does not elaborate, but the suggestion of a creature outside the normal categories of human or divine physiques is in keeping with other Greek portrayals of monsters. The extraordinary appearance of the two gods is also consistent with disturbing treatments of maternity, disability, and monstrosity in other ancient Greek texts. In his *Generation of Animals*, for instance, Aristotle asserts that 'monstrous' births arise when the influence of material provided by the mother is not tempered by the father's seed (4.767a–769b). Some infants who would nowadays be regarded as disabled fall into Aristotle's category of the 'monstrous' (see Garland 1995). For ancient readers following Aristotle's reasoning, the unusual appearances of the disabled Hephaestus and the monstrous Typhaon would be no surprise: neither child has a father.

Despite his unusual origins and physical traits, however, Typhaon's prenatal development and infancy follow the sort of trajectory we might expect for a young human. Earth requires a full year to gestate Typhaon (*Hymn. Hom. Ap.* 343), a period similar to that of a human mother. Moreover, unlike the Hesiodic Typhoeus, Typhaon does not spring into action shortly after leaving the womb. The hymn's monster requires nurture, like any regular infant, and is not yet ready to challenge the gods. Accordingly, when Apollo eventually intervenes, he does battle not with the young Typhaon but with the Delphic snake, who becomes the monster's foster-mother.

Both Typhaon and his foster-mother favour disorder. The snake is both monstrous and a scourge to the humankind: 'a wild monster, big, well-fed, who used to effect many evils for humans on the earth, evils not only for them but also for their long-shanked sheep, since she was a blood-red bane' (*Hymn. Hom. Ap.* 302–4). These lines suggest that she dined on the sheep and perhaps also on the humans mentioned here (cf. 355–6, 364–6). In the end, Apollo slays the snake, ridding the future site of his oracle of a potential hazard to worshippers and their sacrificial flocks. At the same time, by defeating Typhaon's monstrous foster-mother, Apollo suppresses an unruly female being, thus supporting his father Zeus' regime (Clay 2006: 17–94). As with the Hesiodic tale of Typhoeus, then, the *Homeric Hymn to Apollo* depicts the victory of patriarchal forces associated with Zeus. The cursory reference to Apollo's attack on the snake in lines 357–8, however, indicates the ease of his victory: in contrast with Zeus' prolonged contest with Typhoeus in the *Theogony*, Apollo simply shoots the Delphic serpent with one of his arrows.

In the *Homeric Hymn to Apollo*, Typhaon is left alive, and, though he remains peaceful while under the care of the snake, the hymnist suggests his future capacity to wreak havoc. He introduces the monster as 'dread, difficult, a pain for mortals' (306), a description repeated in line 352. Unlike the Hesiodic Typhoeus, the last major challenger to Zeus, Typhaon seems to emerge at a time when Zeus has already established control over the cosmos (Clay 2006). Nonetheless, if he is anything like the child Hera wishes to engender, he may challenge Zeus' kingship of the gods: Hera hopes that her child will 'be pre-eminent among the immortal gods' (*Hymn. Hom. Ap.* 327) and 'no way inferior to [Zeus] in might' (338). The dangerous Typhaon is therefore a suitable fosterling for the marauding snake: he is the gift of 'an evil thing to an evil thing' (354). As the offspring of only females, Typhaon shares the snake's capacity to upset the patriarchal order guaranteed by Zeus.

TYPHOEUS IN CLASSICAL GREECE

Greek writers' fascination with Typhoeus continued into the Classical age of the fifth and fourth centuries BCE. The monster's next significant appearance occurs in the *First Pythian Ode* by the Greek poet Pindar, who composed the poem for Hieron of Syracuse, in celebration of his victory in a chariot race in 470 BCE. As in the *Theogony*, the din produced by the monster, here named Typhos, contrasts with the harmonies of the Muses (*Pyth.* 1.14, 23–6; Passmore 2018). And while the *Theogony* associates the Muses' performances with Zeus' regime, here their song strikes fear into Zeus' enemies, including 'hundred-headed Typhos' (*Pyth.* 1.13–16). Moreover, as at *Theogony* 869–80, Zeus has already conquered the monster. In Pindar's ode, the defeated Typhos is the source of the smoke and flames of Mount Etna in Sicily, under which he is imprisoned (1.17–28), but his volcanic performances pose no more threat to Zeus than the destructive winds of the *Theogony*, which are a problem only for mortals.

As in the *Iliad*, however, differences between the portrayals of humans and gods indicate that divine power dynamics may be more complicated than their mortal equivalents. The ode creates parallels between Hieron's kingship and that of Zeus, and readers might compare Zeus' victory over Typhos with Hieron's over his mortal enemies (Meister 2019). But whereas Hieron's power among men appears untrammelled, the ode offers a more qualified portrait of Zeus' supremacy. Typhos no longer challenges Zeus, and while the music of the lyre lulls his fellow Olympians to sleep, Zeus seems immune to its soporific effects. Nonetheless, the Muses exercise power over symbols of Zeus' might: the lyre owned jointly by Apollo and the Muses lulls Zeus' eagle to sleep and quenches his fiery thunderbolt. Music, associated with watery imagery, counteracts fire, both that of Typhos and that of Zeus (*puros*, *Pyth.* 1.6, 21: Barker 2003).

The description of Zeus' slumbering eagle, moreover, recalls other stories where Zeus himself falls asleep and thereby risks relinquishing control over the cosmos. Barker (2003) compares Pindar's ode with *Iliad* 14, where Hera incapacitates Zeus with the help of the god Sleep, the most significant challenge to Zeus' pre-eminence in the Homeric epics. Similarly, a story related by Epimenides (*FGrH* 457 F8), tells how Typhoeus takes advantage of Zeus' slumber to mount an assault on Olympus. As in Epimenides' tale, the presence of Typho(eu)s in Pindar's poem accompanies suggestions of limitations to Zeus' supremacy, though the ode places greater emphasis on the power of music than on that of the monster.

Typhon reappears as a smoky, fiery creature in Plato's *Phaedrus*, where Socrates offers a mundane explanation for a strange story (229d–230a): people say that the Athenian princess Oreithyia was raped by Boreas, the North Wind, but in fact she was blown off a cliff while playing. Socrates expresses a lack of interest in similar attempts to explain away stories of monsters such as the Chimaera or the Gorgons, because not yet having understood himself, he finds it unreasonable to enquire into other affairs. Nonetheless, he draws on that incarnation of monstrous disorder, Typhon, to pose a question about his own nature: 'I'm considering whether I might be a beast more complicated [*poluplokōteron*] and fierier/smokier [*epitethymmenon*] than Typhon, or a tamer and simpler [*haplousteron*] animal, whose nature has a share in something divine and without puffery [*atyphou*]' (230a). Socrates, then, rejects the practice of providing rationalizing explanations for tales of monsters (see Hawes in this volume), only to offer a monstrous allegory of his own. While the *Iliad* uses Typhoeus as an image for disorder in a human community, here the figure of Typhon illustrates disorder in an individual human soul.

While not referring explicitly to the disorderly physique and behaviours traditionally associated with Typhon, Socrates' language nonetheless hints at them. His term *polyplokōteron* ('more complicated') evokes the monster's snaky windings (*plokai*). His words also offer an explanation for Typhon's name, which tallies with the monster's traditional associations: with the term *epitethymmenon*, Socrates creates an etymological link—possibly a correct one (pro: Beekes 2010; contra: Chantraine 1968–1980)—between Typhon and a verb associated with smoke and flame, likewise from the root *typh-* (*epityphomai*). He reinforces this link through use of the adjective *atyphou* to describe the opposite set of characteristics. The term combines the negative prefix *a-* with the root *typh-* and normally means 'not puffed up' (LSJ, s.v. *atyphos*)—i.e. not conceited, not arrogant. But given the uses of *typh-* elsewhere in this passage of the *Phaedrus*, here it also indicates someone who is 'not *epitethymmenos*'—that is, not filled with fire and smoke—or 'not Typhonesque'. All these meanings are consonant with the Hesiodic Typhoeus, who is not only associated with fire but who also has the arrogance (the 'puffery') to challenge Zeus' governorship of the cosmos (Griswold 1986: 40).

Socrates' words at *Phaedrus* 230a imply that, if he turns out to have a Typhonesque nature, this would be an unwelcome discovery. His subsequent comments are not, however, consistent with a straightforward dismissal of Typhonesque qualities. Typhon's arrogant, 'puffed-up' plan to conquer the cosmos suggests a being of limitless appetites (Griswold 1986: 40–1), and we might expect that, when Socrates proceeds to discuss desire and the soul, he will endorse non-Typhonesque reason and restraint. And initially he does just that. Phaedrus recites a speech praising the non-lover's self-restraint over the lover's desire; Socrates responds by criticizing the lover as a creature devoted to pleasure, but then corrects himself with a defence of love in which he recommends the divinely inspired madness of the lover over self-restraint (*sōphrosynē*), which has a human origin (244d). The contrast between Typhonesque qualities and a non-Typhonesque nature with 'a share in something divine' anticipates this endorsement of divine influences. Nonetheless, the lover's madness seems more in line with the fiery, ambitious Typhon than with his 'tamer' opposite.

TYPHOEUS IN THE ROMAN EMPIRE

Greek texts produced under the Roman Empire develop motifs from earlier representations of Typhoeus, but with a focus on the dichotomies of reason and unreason, harmony and disharmony. In his treatise on Isis and Osiris, the biographer, philosopher, and religious scholar Plutarch (c.46–c.120 CE) uses the name Typhon in place of that of the Egyptian god Seth (*De Is. et Os.* 367d, 371b; see Boychenko in this volume). Such a treatment of a foreign deity is consistent not only with the custom of syncretism that was prevalent under the Roman Empire—the habit of identifying gods from other religious traditions with one's own—but also with a long-established practice of using elements from Greek culture to interpret foreign religions (Griffiths 1970). And though Plutarch ultimately rejects Egyptian religion in favour of Greek philosophical insights (Richter 2001; Domaradzki 2021), he devotes much of the treatise to the development of parallels between figures and motifs from Egyptian sources and elements of Greek mythology.

The creation of such parallels influences Plutarch's representation of Typhon, causing him to develop in new ways the sorts of cosmic themes apparent in other representations of Typhoeus. Of our other Greek sources, only *Iliad* 2.780–5 so much as hints that the monster might repeatedly destabilize the cosmos. In Plutarch's treatise, however, Typhon's disorderly nature poses a constant threat to his fellow gods: he represents fundamental negative forces, forever conflicting with the positive forces of Osiris, his sister/consort Isis, and their allies. Plutarch thus incorporates Typhon into a dualistic conception of cosmic forces (Griffiths 1970; Petrucci 2016).

While Isis is associated with wisdom and Osiris with life-giving waters, Typhon fosters confusion, fire, and destruction. When he introduces Typhon, Plutarch deploys an etymological pun similar to that used by Plato's Socrates. He associates the monster's name not with *epityphomai*, however, but with another verb from the same root, *typhoō*, used in a metaphorical sense to denote mental confusion: Typhon is 'demented' (*tetyphōmenos*) 'because of ignorance and deception' (*De Is. et Os.* 351f). Typhon is also responsible for 'the emotional, Titan-like, irrational, and impulsive element in the soul' (371b), though the soul in question appears to be that of the cosmos and not, as in the *Phaedrus*, that of an individual human (Brenk 1999: 232–3; Petrucci 2016: 338–40). Elsewhere in the treatise, Typhon's fiery qualities manifest in the heat and droughts that he causes. But he is also responsible for *all* the destructive forces of the natural world, including the harmful winds produced by the Hesiodic monster (369a). Plutarch's Typhon also differs from his enemies in his associations with rupture and separation: Typhon emerges prematurely and violently from his mother's side, he attempts to tear up the sacred account guarded by initiates into the cult of Isis, and he dismembers Osiris. Isis and her allies, by contrast, represent forces of combination and reintegration, who undo the damage wrought by Typhon: Isis reassembles the sacred account and, most notably, the body of her brother Osiris.

In revenge for Osiris' suffering, Typhon's enemies mutilate him. A statue in the Egyptian town of Kopto depicts Horus, son of Isis and Osiris, holding Typhon's genitals, presumably having first removed them from the offending god. Horus thereby deprives Typhon of 'energy and strength' (*De Is. et Os.* 373c). These details are reminiscent of an episode from Hesiod's *Theogony* where Cronus castrates Uranus and thereby overpowers him (159–206), but Horus' actions also represent a fitting riposte to Typhon's aggression against his father Osiris: when Typhon divides up Osiris' body, only the phallus is lost irrecoverably, eaten by fish after Typhon throws it into the Nile.

Plutarch, however, follows this description of Horus with a tale in which mutilation is answered by recombination, thus reinforcing the associations of Isis and her associates with reintegration. Hermes—the Egyptian Thoth and, according to some, Isis' father—'removed Typhon's sinews and used them for strings' (*De Is. et Os.* 373c). While the lyre of the Muses and Apollo strikes fear into Pindar's Typhos, here the lyre is the product of Hermes' manipulation of Typhon's body. According to Plutarch, the moral here is that 'reason makes harmony from disharmonious elements, setting them in order, and does not obliterate the power of destruction but lames it' (373d). The story thus suggests that musical harmony results not from the qualities of individual notes but from the manner of their arrangement, which must be in accordance with reason. Typhon's sinews, each of which produces a note on Hermes' lyre, are combined disharmoniously in his body. Such notions accord with other portrayals of Typhon, where he both possesses disorderly body parts and produces disorderly sounds. By contrast, Isis and Hermes are associated with music. As Hermes' actions indicate, such gods can arrange notes, which by themselves have no share in harmonics, in a rational fashion, and thereby engender harmony.

At the same time, Plutarch's interpretation of the stories of Hermes, Horus, and Typhon reminds us that Typhon's unruly forces are never completely banished from the cosmos. Despite such obvious setbacks as the removal of his sinews, Typhon's destructive power is lamed but not obliterated, and Plutarch revises the Hesiodic account of Typhon's parentage so as to emphasize Typhon's eternal challenge to more constructive gods: he proposes that we substitute the names Isis, Osiris, and Typhon (in that order) for Earth, Eros, and Tartarus, the first beings to appear in the Hesiodic cosmos. Tartarus, Typhon's father in the *Theogony*, is thereby identified with Typhon himself, and his enmity with Isis and Osiris is projected back into the first divine generation. Zeus' last opponent in the *Theogony* becomes a destructive force present at the birth of the cosmos.

Typhon also figures significantly in a text roughly contemporary with Plutarch's treatise, an early imperial compendium of mythology known as the *Library* (first or second century CE) attributed to Apollodorus. The *Library* is of interest not only for the motifs that it preserves, some of which must derive from sources that we no longer possess, but also for the ways in which it combines those motifs into compelling stories, as in its unique version of the tale of Typhon (*Bibl.* 1.6.3). As with Plutarch's treatise, the *Library's* account of Typhon includes the themes of dismemberment and the theft of sinews, but this time Zeus and not the monster is the victim. And while the *Library's* version focuses on Typhon's challenge to Zeus, it intersects only partially with details familiar from Hesiod and Pindar. As in the *Theogony*, the *Library's* Typhon is the product of Earth and Tartarus, but his disorderly physique echoes portraits of the monster from multiple sources. His one hundred snake's heads (this time sprouting from his hands) recall the Hesiodic and Pindaric versions, but his human-like torso, wings, and snaky lower half resemble representations in visual art, such as in Fig. 4.1.

The *Library*'s Typhon mounts a more serious challenge to Zeus than in the *Theogony*. The monster's assault causes such alarm among the immortal deities that they flee to Egypt and hide themselves in the form of animals (cf. Ov. *Met.* 5.321–31; Ant. Lib. *Met.* 28.2–3; Fontenrose 1980: 75; Ogden 2013: 217). Like his Hesiodic equivalent, the *Library*'s Zeus lashes Typhon with thunder and lightning. But he also engages his opponent at close quarters with a sickle, rendering himself vulnerable to Typhon's monstrous form. Typhon succeeds in incapacitating Zeus with his snaky coils and lays hold of the sickle, with which he strips away the god's sinews, the source of his strength. Typhon thus inflicts on Zeus the very punishment that he receives at the hands of Hermes in Plutarch's treatise, though in the absence of a precise date for the *Library*, we cannot know whether one text influenced the other.

The *Library*'s account of how Zeus rallies and defeats Typhon further departs from the other versions discussed here. The *Theogony* depicts the victory of the anthropomorphic Zeus, supplied with weapons by the physically monstrous Cyclopes, over an opponent who is disorderly in both appearance and behaviour. The *Library*'s version involves further physically monstrous characters on each side, though once again Typhon is allied with female divinities and Zeus with male. Typhon deposits Zeus and his sinews in a cave under the protection of Delphyne, a half-serpent, half-girl, in an attempt to prevent Zeus from regaining his strength. But Zeus is freed with the help of Hermes and the monstrous god Aegipan ('Goat-Pan'—perhaps a form of the god Pan, or perhaps a separate divinity), who steal and refit the sinews.[2] Zeus then attacks Typhon once more with thunderbolts and, as in Pindar's ode, traps him beneath Mount Etna. The volcano's fires in this case, however, result from the lightning Zeus employs to subdue Typhon rather than from the monster's continuing rage.

TYPHOEUS IN LATE ANTIQUITY

Nonnus' epic poem, the *Dionysiaca*, is the last ancient Greek text to describe Typhoeus. The poem focuses mostly on Dionysus' military campaigns in India but incorporates many other tales besides, including the story of a character called variously Typhoeus, Typhon, and Typhaon. At the time of the work's composition in the fifth century CE, writers continued to engage with themes from Greek mythology, but such elements existed alongside and in dialogue with Christian motifs. In keeping with such a cultural milieu, we can identify intersections between Nonnus' depiction of Dionysus and Christian representations of Christ (Shorrock 2011).

We would, however, be hard-pressed to identify Christian influences in Nonnus' depiction of the monster whom, for convenience, I shall call 'Typhoeus'. Other authors

---

[2] Despite the absence of explicit references to musical themes, the verb used for fitting the sinews, *harmozō*, can also refer to the tuning of musical instruments: cf. LSJ, s.v. I.5.

of late antiquity drew on Greek tales about defeats of snaky adversaries, including Typhoeus, in their creation of stories such as that of St George and the dragon (Ogden 2013: 383–426), but Nonnus' account of Typhoeus alludes neither to St George nor to other Christian figures. We cannot, for instance, read Zeus' conflict with Typhoeus as an allegory for God's battle with Satan: Nonnus' Typhoeus is no fallen angel, and his lustful Zeus bears little resemblance to the Christian God. Rather, Nonnus' depiction of Typhoeus represents a final development of themes from the sorts of non-Christian sources described above. In particular, the poem offers an innovative treatment of the monster's relationship with harmony and cosmic order.

Nonnus' monster has a more complicated relationship with music than in other sources. Here, he is 'a lover of song' (*Dion.* 1.415), and his enemies exploit his 'excessive susceptibility' to music to gain the upper hand (Hardie 2005: 118). When Zeus sets aside his thunderbolts, Typhoeus steals not only those weapons but also Zeus' sinews. To win back both items, Zeus hatches a plan with the mortal Cadmus, to whom he promises the hand of Harmonia, in recognition of the fact that by helping to overcome Typhoeus he will become the 'defender of cosmic harmony' (*Dion.* 1.397). Cadmus tries to lure Typhoeus away from Zeus' weapons with a beautiful tune on his pipes. Typhoeus later compares Cadmus' pipes unfavourably with Zeus' thunderbolt, which he adopts as his own *organon* (1.432), meaning both 'tool' and 'musical instrument' (LSJ, s.v.; Shorrock 2001: 122; Hardie 2005: 117). Nonetheless, Typhoeus leaves the cave where he is guarding Zeus' weapons in pursuit of Cadmus' music. Cadmus harnesses the monster's love of music again when he deceives Typhoeus into releasing the sinews, on the pretext that he is going to use them to fashion a lyre to celebrate the monster's victory, much as the Hesiodic Muses celebrate Zeus' supremacy. When Cadmus plays another tune on his pipes, the monster 'hear[s] the harmony' (*Dion.* 1.520) and is 'bewitched' (1.521, 534).

Once again, however, Typhoeus' vocalizations and actions distance him from musical sound. Like the Hesiodic monster, Nonnus' Typhoeus is remarkable for the chaotic mixture of noises that he produces (*Dion.* 1.156–7; 2.250–6, 367–70). Yet the *Dionysiaca* offers a clearer picture than does the *Theogony* of the relationship between Typhoeus' disorderly body and his vocalizations. Nonnus' monster possesses the heads of lions, bulls, puppies, and snakes, and he emits sounds appropriate to those animals (*Dion.* 2.380–3, 610–14). By contrast, though the term *rhoizeskh'* (*Theog.* 835) may indicate the hissing of Typhoeus' snake-heads (West 1966: 388), Hesiod does not describe the monster as having body parts matching the other sounds that he produces. Moreover, while Zeus' battle with the Hesiodic Typhoeus fills the cosmos with noise, Nonnus' monster poses a threat to music associated with the fabric of the cosmos. According to the goddess Victory as she tries to rouse Zeus to fight back, Typhoeus' assault on the Olympians has dissolved not only the ties that bind the four elements (*Dion.* 2.215–16) but also the 'unbreakable bonds of [cosmic] harmony' (2.222).

Such a being might seem opposed to the harmonious sound of poetry. Perhaps, when Nonnus shows Zeus defeating his noisy adversary, he distances his epic from a Typhoean soundscape (Shorrock 2001: 121–5; Maciver 2016: 533–8). But as Philip Hardie (2005: 121–2) points out, Typhoeus' vocalizations have something in common with the poetics of the *Dionysiaca*. While Typhoeus makes the sounds of several different beasts, an earlier passage connects Nonnus' poetic project with the shape-shifter Proteus, who imitates the forms of multiple animals: from the outset, Nonnus' poem espouses a poetics of multiplicity and variety (1.12–33; cf. Shorrock 2001: 20–3). The poem, then, may not imply a simple disjunction between Typhoean noise and poetic harmony but instead aligns itself with a multifarious and unruly aesthetics. Nonnus thus adopts a poetic mode suitable for his prolific, forty-eight-book poem.

CONCLUSION

Most of the time, our sources characterize the monstrous Typhoeus as the great opponent of structure and sense, whether in the form of the divine order that undergirds the cosmos or of the sort of harmonies and arguments instantiated by our poems and philosophical treatises. Typhoeus, the 'perfect anti-Zeus' (Blaise 1992: 362) or, in his own fantasy, the 'master of the universe, a new Zeus' (Braden 1974: 869), threatens to install a regime of chaos in place of Zeus' orderly dispensation. Some of our authors associate Typhoean chaos with unruly matriarchal forces, such as Earth, Hera, or the Delphic snake, who are the opponents of Zeus and his male deputies, such as Apollo, Hermes, and Aegipan. In Homer, Hesiod, and Pindar, Typhoeus also offers a fascinating glimpse of a raucous soundscape alien to and disruptive of the sort of musical harmony closely associated with poetry in the ancient world. And in the context of cultures that valued reason or of the philosophical writings produced by those cultures, such as the works of Plato and Plutarch, Typhoeus stands as one of antiquity's most compelling explorations of reason's opposite, irrationality.

For Zeus to rule the cosmos, for philosophical arguments to be constructed, or for poetry to be sung, it might seem that Typhoeus and his powers must be decisively banished. Our sources do not, however, engage in a simple dismissal of Typhoeus and of the forces that he represents. While Typhoeus' disorderly plans for the cosmos do not materialize, he nonetheless endures in the worlds of these authors, even after he engages with inimical forces. In some works, such as those of Hesiod and Pindar, he continues to plague mortals with wind or fire. Other authors, such as Homer and Plutarch, indicate that he retains the potential to challenge his divine antagonists. Philosophers, moreover, may identify a role for the passions alongside reason and for elements of the soul as consistent with Typhoean forces as with their contraries. While Plutarch sets Typhoean ignorance against Isiac wisdom, Plato's Socrates finds room for a species of madness, a concept introduced by the figure of Typhon.

Typhoean noise also intrudes into the soundscape of poetry. While Typhoeus' cacophonous performances fail to silence poetic song, the Hesiodic Zeus creates a monstrous din in response to Typhoeus, thereby adopting the wild language of his adversary. For the duration of their battle, chaotic noise reigns. Finally, Nonnus' *Dionysiaca* reimagines this lord of illogic and noise as a musical being. And in this way, one of the last artistic experiments of pagan antiquity hints that a Typhoean soundscape of irreducible multiplicity might make a contribution to poetics.

Suggested Reading

For Indo-European parallels for the figure of Typhoeus, see also Watkins (1995: 448–63). Ogden (2013) studies Typhoeus in the context of serpentine figures from Greek mythology, Fontenrose (1980) in the context of myths of Delphi. Discussions of the ancient works mentioned above and of the place of Typhoeus within them include Ballabriga 1990 and Blaise 1992 (Hesiod); Barker 2003 (Pindar); Griswold 1986 (Plato); Griffiths 1970 (Plutarch); Braden 1974, Shorrock 2001, and Hardie 2005 (Nonnus).

Works Cited

Allen, T. W., ed. 1912–1920. *Homeri opera*, 5 vols. Oxford.

Ballabriga, A. 1990. 'Le Dernier adversaire de Zeus: Le Mythe de Typhon dans l'épopée grecque archaïque.' *Revue de l'histoire des religions* 207/1: 3–30.

Barker, A. D. 2003. 'Lullaby for an Eagle', in *Sleep*, ed. T. Wiedemann and K. Dowden, 107–24. Bari.

Beekes, R. S. P. 2010. *Etymological Dictionary of Greek*. Leiden.

Bernabé, A., ed. 2017. *Himnos homéricos*. Madrid.

Bernardakis, G. N., P. D. Bernardakis, and H. G. Ingenkamp, eds. 2009. *Plutarchi Chaeronensis Moralia*, vol. 2. Athens.

Blaise, F. 1992. 'L'Épisode de Typhée dans la *Théogonie* d'Hésiode (v. 820–885): La Stabilisation du monde.' *Revue des études grecques* 105: 349–70.

Braden, G. 1974. 'Nonnos' Typhoon: *Dionysiaca* Books I and II.' *Texas Studies in Literature and Language* 15/5: 851–79.

Brenk, F. E. 1999. ' "Isis Is a Greek Word": Plutarch's Allegorization of Egypt', in *Plutarco, Platón y Aristóteles*, ed. A. Pérez Jiménez, J. García López, and R. M. Aguilar, 227–38. Madrid.

Brockliss, W. 2017/18. 'Olympian Sound in the Hesiodic *Theogony* and *Catalogue of Women*: Sweet Music and Disorderly Noise.' *Classical Journal* 113/2: 129–49.

Burnet, J., ed. 1901. *Platonis opera*, vol. 2. Oxford.

Chantraine, P. 1968–1980. *Dictionnaire étymologique de la langue grecque*. Paris.

Clay, J. S. 2003. *Hesiod's Cosmos*. Cambridge.

Clay, J. S. 2006. *The Politics of Olympus: Form and Meaning in the Major Homeric Hymns*, 2nd edn. London.

Cohen, J. J. 1996. 'Monster Culture (Seven Theses)', in *Monster Theory: Reading Culture*, ed. J. J. Cohen, 3–25. Minneapolis.

Domaradzki, M. 2021. 'The Lotus and the Boat: Plutarch and Iamblichus on Egyptian Symbols.' *Transactions of the American Philological Association* 151/2: 363–94.

Fontenrose, J. E. 1980. *Python: A Study of Delphic Myth and Its Origins*. Berkeley and Los Angeles.

Frazer, J. G., ed. 1921. *Apollodorus: The Library*, 2 vols. Cambridge, MA.

Garland, R. 1995. *The Eye of the Beholder: Deformity and Disability in the Greco-Roman World*. Ithaca, NY.

Goslin, O. 2010. 'Hesiod's Typhonomachy and the Ordering of Sound'. *Transactions of the American Philological Association* 140/2: 351–73.

Griffiths, J. G. 1970. *Plutarch's De Iside et Osiride*. Cardiff.

Griswold, C. L., Jr. 1986. *Self-Knowledge in Plato's Phaedrus*. New Haven.

Hardie, P. R. 2005. 'Nonnus' Typhon: The Musical Giant', in *Roman and Greek Imperial Epic*, ed. M. Paschalis, 117–130. Herakleion.

Maciver, C. A. 2016. 'Nonnus and Imperial Greek Poetry', in *Brill's Companion to Nonnus of Panopolis*, ed. D. Accorinti, 529–48. Leiden.

Maehler, H., ed. 1987. *Pindarus, Pars I: Epinicia*, 8th edn. Berlin.

Meister, F. J. 2019. 'Hieron and Zeus in Pindar'. *Classical Philology* 114/3: 366–82.

Ogden, D. 2013. *Drakōn: Dragon Myth and Serpent Cult in the Greek and Roman Worlds*. Oxford.

Passmore, O. 2018. 'Typhoeus and "Ty-phonics" in Pindar, *Pythian* 1.26 and Hesiod, *Theogony* 834'. *Mnemosyne* 71/5: 733–49.

Petrucci, F. M. 2016. 'Plutarch's Theory of Cosmological Powers in *De Iside et Osiride*.' *Apeiron* 49/3: 329–67.

Richter, D. S. 2001. 'Plutarch on Isis and Osiris: Text, Cult, and Cultural Appropriation'. *Transactions of the American Philological Association* 131: 191–216.

Shorrock, R. 2001. *The Challenge of Epic: Allusive Engagement in the Dionysiaca of Nonnus*. Leiden.

Shorrock, R. 2011. *The Myth of Paganism: Nonnus, Dionysus and the World of Late Antiquity*. London.

Vian, F., ed. 1976. *Nonnos de Panopolis: Les Dionysiaques, Chants I–II*. Paris.

Watkins, C. 1995. *How to Kill a Dragon: Aspects of Indo-European Poetics*. Oxford.

West, M. L, ed. 1966. *Hesiod: Theogony*. Oxford.

West, M. L. 1997. *The East Face of Helicon: West Asiatic Elements in Greek Poetry and Myth*. Oxford.

West, M. L. 2007. *Indo-European Poetry and Myth*. Oxford.

CHAPTER 5

....

THE GIANTS

Children of Gaea

....

CHRISTINA A. SALOWEY

INTRODUCTION

....

ACCORDING to the Greek poet Hesiod (*c.*700 BCE), whose epic *Theogony* ('Origin of the Gods') presented a widely influential version of the ancient Greek creation story, the earth goddess Gaea gave birth to the Giants after a full circle of the year from the time when she engineered the emasculation of her consort, the sky god Uranus. After soaking up the blood dripping from the wound, she conceived and gestated the monstrous beings. Cronus, a son of Uranus, had accomplished his father's mutilation after his mother, Gaea, had provided him with a sickle to avenge the cruel imprisonment of her children, of which there were three groups: Cronus and his siblings (the Titans), the Hecatoncheires or 'Hundred-Handers' (Kottos, Briareos, and Gyes), and the Cyclopes. Of all her children by Uranus, only Cronus stepped up to perform the deed that led to the creation of the arrogant race known as the Giants (*Theog.* 177–86). Their origin from Gaea is reflected in their various Greek and Latin names, all meaning 'born from earth': *gēgenēs* (e.g. Aesch. *PV* 353; Eur. *Bacch.* 996), *gigas*, *gigantes* (Eur. *Phoen.* 128; Soph. *Trach.* 1058), *terrigena* (e.g. Ov. *Met.* 5.325; Luc. 3.316).

Even after punishing Uranus, Gaea remained enraged about his treatment of her children. Although Hesiod does not relate the episode, later poets tell how Gaea deployed the Giants against the sky, where Zeus and the Olympians now resided, an attack that became known as the Gigantomachy, a clash of the gods and Giants for control of the cosmos. The narrative of the Gigantomachy was a prominent theme in Greek, Roman, and Etruscan art and literature for over nine hundred years. Sometimes hyperbolically related, sometimes discredited and disbelieved, the Gigantomachy persisted as both a rollicking good tale and a metaphor for the destruction of overpowering antagonists who threatened a political or religious world order. Other scholars and encyclopaedic works have compiled the immense quantity of representations of the theme (Vian 1951,

1952; *LIMC*, s.v. 'Gigantes'; Gantz 1993: 443–54), so here I will present only the most in-fluential representations in literature and art, concentrating on innovative expositions of the story. I will first emphasize the changing appearance and the individual narratives of prominent Giants and then outline the different regions where the battles were said to have been fought and these Giants laid to rest, since the geomorphological characteristics of these areas have been ascribed to these earth-born creatures.

Birth and Characterization

Hesiod outlines the birth of the Giants (*Theog.* 183–7), but does not mention their most famous exploit, the Gigantomachy. The Giants are engendered from Uranus' blood and are characterized as large and fully armed, 'shining in armour, holding long spears in their hands' (185–6).[1] The trappings of the warrior remain the standard visual representation of the Giants in art until the Hellenistic period, although even then indications remain that the tradition of the armed Giant survives (e.g. Ap. Rhod. *Argon.* 3.1225–7).

Later sources adopt a snake-legged appearance and emphasize the Giants' hybridity, referring to them as 'many-bodied' and 'two-bodied' in reference to their anguine appendages (Diod. Sic. 1.26; *Bell. Pun.* fr. 4 Powell). Ovid, a Roman poet of the first century CE, has Zeus describe them as beings with one hundred arms (*Met.* 1.183–4), conflating the Giants' battle against the Olympians with the Titans' battle against the Hundred-Handers, a confusion that possibly arose from passages in the plays of the fifth-century BCE tragedian Euripides (*Hec.* 466–74; *IT* 221–4; see Gantz 1993; Vian 1952: 169–74). Ovid's Zeus also describes them as snake-footed (*anguipedum*, *Met.* 1.184)—a striking *hapax legomenon*, as Ovid uses *serpentipedes* elsewhere (Anderson 1996: 170; Ov. *Tr.* 4.7.17). Nonnus, a Greek epic poet of the fifth century CE, similarly characterizes the Giants as multi-handed, and makes their tresses serpentine (*Dion.* 1.18; 25.87–8, 205–9; 48.46–50). In the mythography of Apollodorus (*c.* second century CE), the Giants are 'unrivalled in the size of their bodies, unconquerable in their strength, these creatures, awe-inspiring in their appearance, manifested with long hair falling from their heads and chins and with the scaly feet of snakes' (*Bibl.* 1.6.1). Other authors commented that their 'feet ended in the coils of snakes', indicating their low status (Macrob. *Sat.* 1.20.9; Serv. *In Verg. Aen.* 3.578). The second-century CE Greek traveller Pausanias opined that Giants with snakes for feet was an absurd story, since a monstrously large body dug up in the Orontes river was human in all parts of its body (8.29.3–4). Claudian (late fourth century CE), in his unfinished Latinate epic on the Gigantomachy, stresses that their warrior function and serpent form were established at their birth: 'There was a sound; thickly they burst out and not yet born, they already prepare their arms for war and

---

[1] All translations are the author's unless otherwise noted.

they challenge the upper gods, twisting their hissing path with twinned course' (*CM* 52.6–8). Sidonius Apollinaris, a fifth-century CE Roman writer from Gaul, imagines the Giants as venomous, with scaly legs ending in serpent-heads, taking the image to ridiculous extremes: 'thus, the insolent youthful band, endowed triply with snake attributes, treading the earth with hungry foot, were running, a thing to be marvelled at, as they step on their heads' (*Carm.* 9.82–4).

Homer provides a lineage for the Giants when the disguised Athena reveals that Eurymedon, who ruled over the 'insolent' (*hyperthumoisi*) Giants, was the great-great-grandfather of Arete, Phaeacian queen and wife of Alcinous (*Od.* 7.58–9). At the end of the banquet held in honour of Odysseus, Alcinous characterizes the Giants as a 'wild tribe' (*agria phula*, 7.206), Similarly, the early Greek poets highlight the Giants' excessive nature, calling them 'overbearing/arrogant' (*hyperphialous*, Bacchyl. 15.62) and boastful (*megalauchon*, Pind. *Pyth.* 8.20).

EXTENDED GIGANTOMACHY NARRATIVES

To provide context for the individual narratives of frequently named Giants, I now turn to the major comprehensive versions of the Gigantomachy in art and literature. While the surviving early literature preserves the suitably violent parturition for this transgressive race, the sources barely allude to the details of the Giants' attempts to destroy and reshape the cosmic realm. Abundant artistic representations from the sixth and fifth centuries BCE, however, fill this narrative gap, and the consistencies of these compositions suggest that the artists may have been guided by an epic poem (Vian 1952: 169). A fragment of Xenophanes, a Presocratic philosopher and poet, impugns the morality of epic poems on the battles of the Giants, centaurs, and Titans, thus providing evidence that such works had been authored (DK 21B1).

A highly influential, early sculpted relief of the Gigantomachy served as the north frieze on the Siphnian Treasury at the Sanctuary of Apollo at Delphi, dated to 520 BCE (Daux and Hansen 1987). The frieze preserves a synopsis of the main battleground confrontations, the names of several Giants, and an example of the archaic–classical iconography for the cosmic struggle. The Olympian combatants, mainly striding to the right, battle against the Giants, primarily moving and facing to the left, in the attire of hoplites. Many gods and goddesses in this crowded sculpted relief are recognizable from their standard attributes: e.g. a fully armed Athena with her aegis and Hermes dressed in a *pilos*, his characteristic pointed hat. Some identifications are trickier, due to the damaged nature of the frieze. In Fig. 5.1, the striding male figure with a skin knotted around his neck has been shown to be Dionysus rather than Heracles, identified by a crown of ivy, a fawn skin around the waist and a panther skin shield (Lenzen 1946; Vian 1951: 106; Brinkmann 1994). Themis drives the chariot pulled by lions, one of whom bites a fleeing Giant on the hip. Apollo and Artemis precede them to the right, fighting side by side with arrows and quivers on their backs. Other parts of the frieze figures can

FIGURE 5.1 Gigantomachy, north frieze from the Siphnian Treasury in the Sanctuary of Apollo at Delphi.
Left to right: Two Giants, Dionysus, Themis in a chariot drawn by lions and Giant in front, Giant attacked by lion, Apollo and Artemis, fleeing Giant, one supine vanquished Giant, and three Giants carrying shields.

Source: Wikimedia / Fingalo. CC BY-SA 2.0.

be obscure at first glance, but barely visible inscriptions aid in interpreting the scene. (Brinkman 1985; *LIMC*, s.v. 'Gigantes' 3, for possible identifications).

Further right, not visible in Fig. 5.1, is a large gap in the frieze, which has been plausibly restored with Zeus' chariot group, on parallel with comparable scenes in contemporary vase painting (Moore 1977). This scene would have placed the most prominent combatants in the battle, i.e. Zeus and Heracles, in the centre of the relief. Heracles, a half-mortal participant, was an essential component for victory and is a pronounced figure in most artistic versions of the Gigantomachy (Salowey 2021). Following the surviving horses of Zeus' chariot, in the foreground, a goddess, who turns back to finish off a Giant stretched out under the horses, has been variously identified as Hera or Aphrodite, but no accompanying inscription survives. The comic element of the goddess of love moving in the opposite direction to all the other divinities in a scene of warfare makes that identification a more tempting choice. Several conquered Giants are identified by accompanying labels: Ephialtes, Porphyrion, Biatas, Astarias, and Alcyoneus, with a strikingly frontal, grimacing face (Brinkman 1985: 94 [N7], 103 [N22],

97–8 [N11–12]). The fragmentary far-right end is very mutilated but may show Poseidon's battle against Polybotes. Since sculpted frieze reliefs were a relatively new form of art in this period, this extended visual narrative would have been remarkable to Delphic pilgrims processing up the sacred way almost as co-combatants against the Giants with the very recognizable Olympian gods (Neer 2003: 141–5). The Olympians fight as Iliadic heroes, in hand-to-hand combat from the backs of chariots, against Giants who appear in phalanx formation, unique in Archaic art (Stewart 1997: 89).

While no epic literary versions survive or are alluded to in the Classical period, the theme of the Gigantomachy was parodied in comedy and referenced in tragedy and philosophy, indicating that the story was familiar to the fifth-century audience. The plot of Aristophanes' *Birds* is loosely based on the Gigantomachy, and in it the protagonist Pisthetairos claims to have the resources of six hundred Porphyrions—Porphyrion being the king of the Giants—and is clothed in leopard skins for an attack on Zeus (1246–52, a possible reference to Dionysus' attire). Hegemon of Thasos, a late fifth-century comic poet, composed a parody on the Gigantomachy that was performed on the day the unwelcome news of the Athenian defeat at Syracuse arrived (413 BCE), and kept the Athenians laughing as they hid their tears from spectators from other cities in the audience (Ath. 9, 406e = *CAF* I.700). In Euripides' *Cyclops*, a Silenos, praying to Dionysus, wonders if he really helped Dionysus in a battle against Enceladus or if he dreamed it (5–9), a humorous critique on the reality of the battle.

In Athens, the battle narrative was woven into a peplos, or long dress, presented to the goddess Athena at the Panathenaia festival, re-established in 566 BCE (Ridgway 1992: 122–4). This celebration of Athena's role in the victory of the gods over the Giants kept the narrative at the forefront of the Athenian imagination (Callicrates, *FGrH* 124 F5; Aristoteles fr. 637, ed. Rose 1967; Shear 2021: 39–50). The peplos, paraded through the streets of Athens on a cart, was a prominent visual moment of pride for the Athenians: their tutelary goddess was an influential martial force against this attack on the cosmic order. Subsequently, the theme is abundantly represented on Attic black-figure vases, votive offerings on the Acropolis (*LIMC*, s.v. 'Gigantes' 104–23; Shapiro 1992: 38), and major sculptural groups of the Archaic and Classical periods—most notably the pediment of the precursor to the Athenian Parthenon (*LIMC*, s.v. 'Gigantes' 7), the west pediment of the temple of Apollo at Delphi (*LIMC*, s.v. 'Gigantes' 3; Ridgway 1993: 292–6), and the metopes on the west side of the Classical Parthenon (*LIMC*, s.v. 'Gigantes' 18). Playwrights referenced not only specific Giants and the battle (Eur. *HF* 177–9, *Ion* 1528–9; Ar. *Av.* 823–31), but also the representation on the peplos (Ar. *Eq.* 566; Eur. *Hec.* 466–74; *IT* 222–4; Stamatopoulou 2012). Socrates, in dialogue with Euthyphro, enquires whether he believes in the war between the gods and Giants, as the poets tell it and as it is represented by renowned artists, 'especially the peplos, full of such embroideries that is led up to the Acropolis during the Great Panathenaia' (Pl. *Euthphr.* 6b–c; cf. *Resp.* 2.378b–c).

In the fourth century BCE, the rationalization of the myth as a tale of violent, telluric forces begins to appear and the battle is moved from Pallene to the volcanic regions of Southern Italy (Timaios, *FGrH* 566 F86). The Giants' fate to be entombed underneath the ground becomes an explanation for the fiery and earth-shaking nature of volcanic mountains, like Mount Etna. Apollodorus' later description of the battle seems to rely on the figurative monuments of the sixth and fifth centuries BCE but adds details derived from innovations of that period (*LIMC*, 'Gigantes' 192). Hellenistic poets rarely refer to the battle, although captivating vignettes of the struggle do appear, like Apollonius' mentions of one Giant's cuirass (*Argon.* 3.1225–7; see below) and Helios rescuing an exhausted Hephaestus (3.232–4).

The Great Altar of Zeus at Pergamon, dated between 185 and 165 BCE, preserves the premier representation of the Gigantomachy, offering vivid portrayals of several prominent duels as well as magnifying the participation of many previously unsung minor divinities (*LIMC*, s.v. 'Gigantes' 24; Ridgway 2000: 19–66; Coarelli 2017). In the 113 metres of the frieze decorating the building's exterior, the artists represented the Giants primarily as anguiform but also as animal-headed creatures and fully human armed warriors. The frieze was approached from the rear where the most illustrious divine defenders—Zeus, Athena, and Heracles—are represented (Fig. 5.2). Zeus takes on three Giants, both human and serpent-legged, pinning one to his right with a thunderbolt, while his eagle takes on an older Giant from above. Heracles is evidenced in the fragmentary scene by some remnants of his lion skin, combined with the fact that the fallen Giant just to the right of Zeus pulls an arrow from his chest (Simon 1975: 18). To the right of this scene, the vignette of Athena taking on Alcyoneus and Gaea is distinguished by its vigorous movement and its legible narrative. Athena grabs the winged Alcyoneus to her left by the hair, as he reaches out to disengage her arm—to no avail, by the look on his face. Athena strides boldly to the left, as Nike flies in to crown her victorious. Below Athena, Gaea emerges from the ground, her face mirroring the look of anguish on that of her son, unable to help him or fight back. The poignant inclusion of Gaea heightens the emotional impact of the scene. The brilliant and energetic conquests of the gods against the fearsome and wild Giants on this frieze would have encouraged visitors to Pergamon to equate the victories of their own rulers (the Attalids) over their enemies to the actions of Olympians maintaining the cosmic order in the face of such a violent attack (Coarelli 2017: 200).

FIGURE 5.2 Gigantomachy from the Great Altar of Zeus at Pergamon.
Left to right: Giant with thunderbolt, Zeus, Giant with eagle of Zeus over his head, Giant with remnant of Heracles' lion skin dangling over him, space, winged Alcyoneus, Athena, Gaea emerging from ground, Nike flying in from the right.
Source: © Staatliche Museen zu Berlin, Antikensammlung. Photo: Johannes Laurentius, Inv. no. AvP III.2 GF 15-17.

After the Augustan age, the Gigantomachy experiences a revival, despite—or maybe because of—the disdain of the topic expressed by many elegiac poets, including Horace, Ovid, and Martial (e.g. Hor. *Carm.* 2.12.6–9; Ov. *Am.* 2.1.11–18; Mart. 9.50.5–6). Ovid, however, seems to have written an epic Gigantomachy in his youth (Owen 1924), and Martial promises Julius Cerialis, a Roman writer and friend, that 'it is permitted for you to recite without interruption your Giants' during a dinner party (11.52.17). Other epic treatments survive only in fragments. Dionysius, a geographer from the time of Hadrian, wrote a *Gigantias*, and Philostratus reports that the philosopher Scopelianus wrote a much-imitated *Gigantia* (*VS* 1.21.5). Claudian referred to the theme extensively in his writings as a way to aggrandize imperial victories, but fragments of two Gigantomachies written by him, one in Greek and one in Latin, also survive (Platanauer 1922; Ludwich 1897: 167–75; see also Cameron 1970).

NAMED PARTICIPANTS
IN THE GIGANTOMACHY

There is considerable variation in narrative tales and in surviving inscriptions on works of art regarding the names of the Giants and the gods who dispatched them. Nine Giants—Porphyrion, Alcyoneus, Ephialtes, Clytius, Eurytus, Hippolytus, Mimas, Enceladus, and Polybotes—are mentioned in more than one source and we even have some information about their escapades.

In most sources, Porphyrion is finished off with Heracles' arrow (Pind. *Pyth.* 8.12–18; Hor. *Carm.* 3.4.50–6). Apollodorus supplies the surprising detail that Zeus inspired in the Giant lust for Hera (*Bibl.* 1.6.2). As Porphyrion tore her robes and would have forced her, Hera cried for help and Zeus struck him dead with a thunderbolt. Porphyrion's name, meaning 'purple', provides an etymological reinforcement to his kingship of the Giants, as the dye used for purple was expensive enough that it was reserved for royalty. In his unfinished Latin epic poem, Claudian alludes to a possible duel between Apollo and Porphyrion, an idea that may have originated in Pindar (*Pyth.* 8.12–19 and schol. Pind. *Pyth.* 8.15; *LIMC*, s.v. 'Porphyrion' 444). Claudian has Terra (Gaea) encourage her son, claiming that 'Delphic laurel will bind you ... and you will control the Kirrhan temples' (*CM* 52.35). Later in the poem, Porphryion is propelled through the sea by his serpentine legs and tries to uproot Delos, the island sanctuary of Apollo, to hurl it at the heavens (*CM* 52.114–15).

Alcyoneus, Porphyrion's brother, after being pierced by Heracles' arrows, revived upon falling on the ground, for the battle was fought in the land of his birth, Pallene, and he was considered immortal while there (see below). Athena advised Heracles to drag him outside the border, where the Giant then died (Apollod. *Bibl.* 1.6.1), a technique the hero had also used against the Giant Antaeus in Libya on a separate occasion (Gantz 1993: 417). Pindar knows Alcyoneus as a herdsman (*Isthm.* 6.32), and treats his death at the hands of Heracles as an isolated act accomplished with the help of Telamon, a hero from Aegina (*Nem.* 4.25–30), a variant supported in multiple vase paintings in which Heracles ambushes a sleeping Giant (*LIMC*, s.v. 'Alkyoneus' 1–30). Alcyoneus was not listed as a combatant in the Gigantomachy until the Roman period. The tradition of Heracles fighting this huge monster at Phlegras in Thrace (Pind. *Isthm.* 6.32–6) later drew the episode into the Gigantomachy narrative (Gantz 1993: 445; Vian 1952: 217–21).

Ephialtes, who was shot in one eye by Apollo and the other by Heracles (Apollod. *Bibl.* 1.6.2), is named in Hyginus' list of Gaea's sons (*Fab. praef.*) and labelled as a fallen Giant on the Siphnian Treasury (Brinkmann 1985: 94 [N7], figs. 45–6). The Ephialtes in the Gigantomachy has nothing to do with the Ephialtes, son of Poseidon and Iphimedeia (*LIMC*, s.v. 'Aloadai' 570), who tried, along with his brother, Otos, to pile Mounts Ossa and Pelion onto Mount Olympus to attack the gods (e.g. Hom. *Od.* 11.305–20; *Il.* 5.385–91; Apollod. *Bibl.* 1.7.4).

Clytius, Eurytus, and Hippolytus, though named as participants in the Gigantomachy, receive only passing mention in the extant sources. Clytius was killed by the chthonic goddess Hecate, who had joined the Olympians in their battle, brandishing her torches (Apollod. *Bibl.* 1.6.2), a scene represented vividly on the Great Altar of Zeus at Pergamon (*LIMC*, s.v. 'Gigantes' 24). Eurytus was killed by Dionysus' thyrsus and Hippolytus by Hermes' sword (Apollod. *Bibl.* 1.6.2; Hyg. *Fab. praef.*).

The death of Mimas has the most variations in both art and literature. He is depicted and labelled in several figural scenes (*LIMC*, s.v. 'Gigantes' 2, 24, 105, 318), and the chorus in Euripides' *Ion*, while surveying the sculptural works in the sanctuary of Apollo, view a Gigantomachy scene in which Mimas is incinerated by a thunderbolt of Zeus (214–15). Mimas' breastplate ends up in the possession of Heracles' descendant Aletes, a gift from Ares who won it in the battle (Ap. Rhod. *Argon.* 3.1225–7). Claudian, also reporting the god of war as Mimas' conqueror, says that Ares shattered the Giant's skull with a spear and provides the imaginative detail that Mimas' human form died, but the serpents of his lower half lived on, ferocious in their hissing (*CM* 52.85–91). In a description of the Gigantomachy on Athena's shield in a marriage hymn by Sidonius Apollinaris, Mimas flings the island of Lemnos at Athena's aegis to avenge the death of his brother, Pallas (*Carm.* 15.24–6). Apollodorus reports that Hephaestus kills Mimas with an anvil (*Bibl.* 1.2.6).

Greek sources often portray Enceladus as Athena's opponent (e.g. Eur. *HF* 907–9; Hor. *Carm.* 3.4.55–8; Paus. 8.47.1; *LIMC*, s.v. 'Gigantes' 342–54). Roman sources, however, predominantly present Enceladus as the king of the Giants; as such, he usually confronts Zeus, who entombs him under Mount Etna (e.g. Verg. *Aen.* 3.578–82; Stat. *Theb.* 4.8; Sid. Apoll. *Carm.* 6.27–8). The name derives from the ancient Greek *kelados*, meaning loud noise, din, or clamour. Roman poets capitalized on this etymological association to establish Enceladus as the booming voice of Mount Etna after the Giant's imprisonment there (Stat. *Theb.* 3.593; 12.274–5; Claud. *DRP* 2.156–62; 3.122–3). Writing under the Roman Empire, the Greek poet Nonnus, as an advocate for Dionysus, has the wine god roast the Giants, including their leader, Enceladus, with his torches (*Dion.* 25.90; 48.67–70).

Poseidon chased down Polybotes and broke off and threw a piece of the island of Cos, called Nisyrus, to trap him underground (Apollod. *Bibl.* 1.6.2; Strabo 10.5.16). Pausanias reports that the Coans believe the attack occurred at Cape Chelonas, across from the island of Nisyrus. In some versions, Zeus first knocked Polybotes down and Poseidon next buried him. This struggle may be what appears on the final fragment of the north frieze of the Siphnian Treasury, comprised of a chariot driven by the sea god's wife, Amphitrite, a composition on parallel with vase paintings of the same period (*LIMC*, s.v. 'Gigantes' 105).

LOCATION OF THE GIGANTOMACHY

Apollodorus offers that 'some say that the Giants were born in Phlegrae, others in Pallene' (*Bibl.* 1.6.1), and those two toponyms are used for the battle throughout the ancient sources (Vian 1952: 189–91, 217–18; Mayor 2000: 194–202; Salowey 2021: 239–41). Most early Greek authors locate the encounter at Phlegras (e.g. Hes. *Cat.* fr. 43a65 MW; Pind. *Nem.* 1.67–9). Some authors conflate the two locations (e.g. Hdt. 7.123), and Polyaenus explains that Pallenians fleeing Troy were abandoned at Phlegras and lent their name to the place (7.47). The names became interchangeable, and both are attached to the westernmost 'finger' of the Chalcidice peninsula just east of Thessaloniki.

In many regions, palaeontological discoveries of the bones of large prehistoric animals may have encouraged the Gigantomachy's geographical placement. Large bones were observed and connected with the Giants at Pallene (Solin. 9.6; Philostr. *Her.* 8.18; Chuvin 2017: 267), Crete (Diod. Sic. 5.71), Rhodes, Arcadia, and Campania (Mayor 2000: 317 n. 9). All areas today contain fossil beds (Mayor 2000: 195–6, 305 n. 26). *Phlegras*, a Greek word used to identify any place associated with volcanic agency, became a most suitable name for the battlefield since later descriptions conceptualized the vanquished Giants as suppressed underground by mountain-wielding Olympians to act as strong earthquakes and fiery eruptions.

This connection of the Giants with volcanic landscapes drew other locales into the cosmic struggle, most notably the famously volatile region of Campania. The plains near the northwestern flank of Mount Vesuvius were also known as the Campi Phlegraei, or Phlegraean Fields, and imprisonment of the Giants is often located here (e.g. Timaeus, *FGrH* 566 F89; *LIMC*, s.v. 'Gigantes' 192). The Giant Mimas was deposited under Prochyta (modern-day Procida) and Typhoeus under Imarmine (modern-day Ischia). Silius Italicus, when describing Hannibal's visit to Baiae, has the guide give credit to Hercules for entombing the Giants there and producing a volcanic wasteland: 'they say that Giants prostrate under a Herculean mass shake the earth all round and burn widely the fields with a panting breath' (*Pun.* 12.143–5).

CONCLUSION

The representation of the Giants always anchors them firmly in the realm of Gaea and the earth. They are terrestrial beings striving for an unnatural place in the firmament, who, in the end, are forcefully reimprisoned in the regions that produced them. They make themselves known in the rumblings of volcanoes and in the shaking of the land, as they attempt to cross that boundary again into the upper air. Their overreach makes them monstrous, and their excessive strength and violence make them a symbol of chaotic forces let loose on a civilized world. The story of their spectacular defeat, a comeuppance for their hubris, makes their victors shine all the more brightly.

SUGGESTED READING

The Roman mythographer Apollodorus provides the most complete ancient literary narrative of the Gigantomachy, although more colourful details of the Giants' appearance, behaviour, and mode of capture are sprinkled throughout a millennium of ancient literature, some of which is noted in this chapter. Vian and Moore's entry 'Gigantes' in the *LIMC* is an expanded and updated version of Vian (1951), providing a chronological listing of the works of art carrying representations of the Giants, usually in their most prominent role, as antagonists in the Gigantomachy. Every listing in the *LIMC* provides the provenance, current location, date, brief description, and bibliography for each work of art. Additionally there is a summary of trends in iconography for the depiction of the Giants in concluding sections. The *LIMC* entry and Vian (1952) together provide a broad overview of the literature, art, and interpretations of the Giants and Gigantomachy. For the non-francophone, Gantz (1993) offers a great English synopsis of the literary history of the Giants' myth and some of the controversies, but with little mention of artistic depictions. In a recently published colloquium on the Giants in the western and eastern Mediterranean, Massa-Pairault and Pouzadoux (2017) add to Vian's work by incorporating some recent artistic discoveries as well as expanding on the treatment of the theme in Etruscan art.

WORKS CITED

Anderson, W. S., ed. 1996. *Ovid's* Metamorphoses, *Books 1–5*. Norman, OK.

Brinkmann, V. 1985. 'Die aufgemalten Namenbeischriften an Nord- und Ostfries des Siphnierschatzhauses.' *Bulletin de correspondance hellénique* 109/1: 77–130.

Brinkmann, V. 1994. *Die Friese des Siphnierschatzhauses: Beobachtungen zum formalen Aufbau und zum Sinngehalt*. Munich.

Cameron, A. 1970. *Claudian: Poetry and Propaganda at the Court of Honorius*. Oxford.

Chuvin, P. 2017. 'Typhée, ultime avatar des Géants? Pérégrinations d'un mythe à travers l'Anatolie', in *Géants et gigantomachies entre Orient et Occident*, ed. F.-H. Massa-Pairault and C. Pouzadoux, 263–75. Naples.

Coarelli, F. 2017. 'Il "Grande Altare" di Pergamo: Cronologia e contesto', in *Géants et gigantomachies entre Orient et Occident*, ed. F.-H. Massa-Pairault and C. Pouzadoux, 193–201. Naples.

Daux, G., and E. Hansen. 1987. *Fouilles de Delphes*, vol. 2: *Le Trésor de Siphnos*. Paris.

Gantz, T. 1993. *Early Greek Myth: A Guide to Literary and Artistic Sources*, 2 vols. Baltimore.

Lenzen, V. F. 1946. *The Figure of Dionysos on the Siphnian Frieze*. Berkeley and Los Angeles.

Ludwich, A. 1897. *Eudociae Augustae, Procli Lycii, Claudiani Carminum Graecorum Reliquiae*. Leipzig.

Massa-Pairault, F.-H., and C. Pouzadoux, eds. 2017. *Géants et gigantomachies entre Orient et Occident*. Naples.

Mayor, A. 2000. *The First Fossil Hunters: Paleontology in Greek and Roman Times*. Princeton.

Moore, M. B. 1977. 'The Gigantomachy of the Siphnian Treasury: Reconstruction of the Three Lacunae.' *Bulletin de Correspondance Hellénique* 4: 305–35.

Neer, R. T. 2003. 'Framing the Gift: The Siphnian Treasury at Delphi and the Politics of Public Art', in *The Cultures within Ancient Greek Culture*, ed. C. Dougherty and L. Kurke, 129–49. Cambridge.

Owen, S. G. 1924. 'Ovid's *Gigantomachia*', in *P. Ovidi Nasonis Tristium Liber Secundus*, ed. S. G. Owen, 63–81. Oxford.

Platnauer, M. 1922. *Claudian with English Translation*. London.

Ridgway, B. 1992. 'Images of Athena on the Akropolis', in *Goddess and Polis: The Panathenaic Festival in Ancient Athens*, ed. J. Neils, 118–42. Princeton.

Ridgway, B. 1993. *The Archaic Style in Greek Sculpture*. Chicago.

Ridgway, B. 2000. *Hellenistic Sculpture II: The Styles of ca. 200–100 B.C.* Madison.

Rose, V. 1967. *Aristotelis qui ferebantur librorum fragmenta*. Leipzig.

Salowey, C. 2021. 'The Gigantomachy', in *The Oxford Handbook of Heracles*, ed. D. Ogden, 235–50. Oxford.

Shapiro, A. 1992. 'Panathenaic Amphoras: Their Meaning, Makers, and Markets', in *Goddess and Polis: The Panathenaic Festival in Ancient Athens*, ed. J. Neils, 29–52. Princeton.

Shear, J. 2021. *Serving Athena: The Festival of the Panathenaia and the Construction of Athenian Identities*. Cambridge.

Simon, E. 1975. *Pergamon und Hesiod*. Mainz.

Stamatopoulou, Z. 2012. 'Weaving Titans for Athena: Euripides and the Panathenaic *peplos* (*Hec.* 466–74 and *IT* 218–24).' *Classical Quarterly* 62: 72–80.

Stewart, A. 1997. *Art, Desire, and the Body in Ancient Greece*. Cambridge.

Vian, F. 1951. *Répetoire des Gigantomachies figurées dans l'art grec et romain*. Paris.

Vian, F. 1952. *La Guerre des Géants: Le Mythe avant l'époque hellénistique*. Paris.

CHAPTER 6

···

DRAGONS

···

DANIEL OGDEN

INTRODUCTION: DEFINITIONS OF THE
CLASSICAL *DRAKŌN*

···

THE Greek term *drakōn* (plural: *drakontes*) was borrowed into Latin as *draco* (plural: *dracones*), where it jostled with the native equivalent *serpens* (plural: *serpentes*) before ultimately giving us the modern English 'dragon'. The best way to understand the terms *drakōn* and *draco* in their classical contexts is as defining 'a large (land-based) snake and something more'. By 'something more' I mean a supernatural or sacred quality or affinity, or additional or exceptional physical or behavioural attributes (cf. Riaño Rufilanchas 1999; Ogden 2013a: 2–4; 2021: 9). At the realistic end of the spectrum the term attached to the very real snakes maintained in shrines, most famously the in- cubation shrines of the healing god Asclepius (Ogden 2013a: 310–17; cf. Riethmüller 2005; Renberg 2017: esp. 1.115–270, 634–49, 689–713), where they served as the benign serpent-god's avatars, and where their licks or nips may even have helped in the healing of the patients (Angeletti et al. 1992; Ogden 2013a: 367–370). It is difficult to pin down the species deployed in this way: the literary descriptions and iconographic representations, such as they are, are vague, and more than one species may have been in use. However, the best guess is the large but gentle Four-lined Snake (*Elaphe quatuorlineata*), which responds phlegmatically to human handling, and is today the star of the *Serpari* festival in honour of St Dominic at Cucullo (Abruzzo). A remarkable archaeological discovery has recently confirmed the presence of this species already in Classical Greece (Ogden 2013a: 372–9; Gambari 2017: 77–83). No 'monsters' here!

Forms and Narratives

But there are 'monsters' indeed at the fantastical end of the spectrum, namely the great *drakontes* of Panhellenic myth that find themselves pitted against gods and heroes. Let us pass some of the principal pure-form *drakontes* of myth in review, roughly in the chronological order of their first attestation either in literature or in iconography (which is not, of course, necessarily the order in which their myths came into existence).

Typhon

The title of 'earliest *drakōn*' should rest with Typhon (aka Typhoeus and Typhaon), attested from *c.*700 BCE (Hes. *Theog.* 820–80). He is 'earliest' because his cosmic battle against Zeus for the throne of heaven, which culminates in the god burying him in the earth (e.g. under Etna), is an example of the so-called combat myth in which the thunderbolt god fights a serpentine foe (see Ogden 2013a: 40–8; 2021: 375–82 for discussion; 2013b: 39–44 for the principal sources in translation). This combat myth is widespread amongst the earlier civilizations of the Near East and boasts a deep Indo-European heritage (amongst more recent discussions, see Rodríguez Pérez 2008: 23–68; Noegel 2015; Bachvarova 2016: 250–65). And he is a *drakōn* despite the fact that the term is only occasionally applied to him (see, however, Hes. *Theog.* 825; Strabo 16.2.7) and despite the fact that he is canonically represented as a complex hybrid. In art and literature alike he is represented as some form of 'anguiped', humanoid above the waist and serpentine below it (see Fig. 4.1 in this volume; *LIMC*, s.v. 'Typhon'), though he can be represented with multiple additional heads of all sorts. But his fundamental identity as a *drakōn* has now been revealed by the publication of a Corinthian alabastron vase of *c.*575–550 BCE (Arvanitaki 2012). On this we see a striding, bearded figure wielding a thunderbolt, which he holds up in his right hand ready to hurl or dash against a large, pure-form serpent, which he grasps by the throat with his left. Only Zeus wields the thunderbolt, and Typhon is his only opponent with a serpentine aspect; the serpent, accordingly, must be Typhon, revealed at last in his purest and most basic form (see further Brockliss in this volume).

The Hydra

The Hydra, attested from *c.*700 BCE (initially in art: *LIMC*, s.v. 'Herakles' 2019–20), is a marauding dragon. Ancient authors rarely designate this multi-header explicitly as a *drakōn*, because they tend to refer to her simply by her proper name (or title), but she is indeed designated as a *drakōn* in, for example, tragedy (Soph. *Trach.* 834; Eur. *Phoen.* 1134–8). 'Hydra' signifies 'Water Snake', appropriately so given that she is born in and makes her home in the Lernaean marsh in southern Greece. Perhaps she guards its spring, Amymone, just as others in this list are water guardians, but, if so, the claim does not survive explicitly in the extant sources. The most canonical version of her defeat at the hands of Heracles during the hero's second labour is well known. As Heracles lops off one of her heads with his sickle, two more grow in its place. Heracles gets the better of her by having his assistant, his nephew Iolaus, sear the stumps as he lops (Ogden 2013a: 26–33, 2013b: 50–6; see further Aguirre and Buxton and Fig. 11.1 in this volume).

Ladon

Ladon, the *Drakōn* of the Hesperides maidens, associated with the Far West and attested from c.700 BCE (Hes. *Theog.* 333–6), is a gold-guarding dragon. He is most commonly represented as single-headed, though in art he is sometimes given two or three heads, and in literature sometimes a hundred. In his canonical story he guards the golden apples of the Hesperides maidens by hanging in the tree with the fruit, where he is tended by the girls, who offer him drinks. According to some sources, Heracles, on his eleventh labour, clubs Ladon to death to take the apples. According to other sources, which are tricky to reconstruct, one of the Hesperides maidens falls in love with Heracles and helps him to steal the apples from the immortal and unsleeping serpent by distracting the creature with a drink or even contriving to send him to sleep with a magic potion (Ogden 2013a: 33–40; 2013b: 57–62). However, Hesiod gives us a tantalizing glimpse of an earlier story, with a brief vignette of Ladon brooding over the apples in a cave lair inside the earth, in the manner we have come to associate with Fafnir, the famous treasure-guarding dragon of Norse myth.

Drakōn of Ares

The *Drakōn* of Ares, attested from the earlier sixth century BCE (Stesichorus F96 Finglass), is a water-guarding dragon. Ares sets him to guard the virgin spring of Dirce or Thebe, at the site of the future city of Thebes in central Greece; by some accounts the spring is located within the dragon's own cave lair. The Phoenician Cadmus comes into conflict with the creature when he needs to take water to make a sacrifice to initiate the foundation of his new city. He is usually said to kill the *drakōn* with a rock. He then sows half of its teeth in the ground to produce the originators of his city's population; these men, the *Spartoi* ('Sown Men'), are said to spring up from the ground ready-armed. Later, Ares punishes Cadmus with a period of servitude for killing the sacred *drakōn*. Moreover, the end of Cadmus' life is unfathomable. He migrates to Illyria with his wife Harmonia, where he becomes king of the Encheleis, the (snake-affiliated?) 'Eel-people'. There he and Harmonia are transformed into *drakontes* in turn, before being translated to Elysium. Perhaps the metamorphosis is intended as a further gesture of compensation and restitution demanded of Cadmus by Ares—though, oddly, Harmonia is the god's own daughter (see Ogden 2013a: 48–54; 2013b: 109–18).

Python

The marauding Dragon of Delphi is first attested, in the *Homeric Hymn to Apollo*, as female, in the form of Delphyne (300–9, 349–73; *c.*590 BCE). But thereafter, with rare exceptions, the creature is represented in the male form of Python. The battle against Apollo, in which Python meets his doom, is initiated when the oracle tells him that the god, not yet born, is destined to kill him. Accordingly, he harries the pregnant Leto, but she is able, nonetheless, to give birth to her son, who proceeds, still a babe in arms, alongside his twin sister Artemis, to shoot Python with his bow and arrows (Hyg. *Fab.* 140). The rotting (*pythein*) of the serpent's huge carcass—as opposed to the serpent's personal name itself—is then said to have given Delphi its alternative name of Pytho (see Ogden 2013a: 40–8; 2013b: 39–44).

Drakōn of Colchis

The *Drakōn* of Colchis, attested first in art on a cup by the painter Douris (*c.*480–470 BCE; *LIMC*, s.v. 'Iason' 32), is another gold-guarding dragon and, like Ladon, hangs in his tree to guard his golden treasure, in this case the Golden Fleece. The maiden-witch Medea serves as his keeper, feeding him with her herbs and potions. Medea is usually said to have drugged the serpent (as opposed to killing him) so that Jason, with whom she has fallen in love, can take the Fleece (Ogden 2013a: 58–63; 2013b: 125–33). As with Ladon and Python, the first attestation is also the most anomalous: the cup shows the dragon, magnificently realized, regurgitating Jason in an episode unknown in the surviving literature: evidently the early stages of this more martial assault on the serpent had not gone well for the hero (Fig. 6.1). Perhaps the dragon is unable to digest Jason because he is protected by Medea's invincibility lotion (cf. Ap. Rhod. *Argon.* 3.1246–8). Medea herself, incidentally, is of further interest as a veritable Mistress of Dragons (Ogden 2013a:198–209): her Colchis pet aside, she conjures up phantom *drakontes* for Pelias with her drugs; her Chariot of the Sun is drawn by (initially wingless) flying *drakontes*; and upon teaching the Marsi of Italy, later to be known as a race of snake-blasting sorcerers, how to control their serpents, she comes to be recognized as their goddess Angitia (a folk etymology based on *anguis*, 'snake'). The *Drakōn* of Colchis is also indirectly associated with the sowing of dragon's teeth. According to Apollonius of Rhodes, before approaching it, Jason has had to deal with the Spartoi produced from the other half of the teeth of the *Drakōn* of Ares, which Athena had given to Aeetes, king of Colchis and Medea's father (*Argon.* 3.1176–90, 1278–407; 4.123–66). It seems likely that in an earlier version of Jason's story these episodes were inverted, and that the dragon's teeth sown derived not the remote *Drakōn* of Ares but from the (just-slain) *Drakōn* of

FIGURE 6.1 Dragon on red-figure cup tondo (interior) painted by Douris, *c*.480–470 BCE. Vatican Museums, inv. 16545.

Source: Wikimedia / Shii, public domain.

Colchis itself—in precisely the way, in fact, that Ray Harryhausen sensibly reconstructed Jason's story in his classic stop-motion-animation film *Jason and the Argonauts* (1963, dir. Don Chaffey).

Drakōn of Nemea

The *Drakōn* of Nemea, attested from the earlier fifth century BCE (Bacchyl. 9.10–14), is another water-guarding dragon. He is set by Zeus to guard the spring of Langia in the god's sacred grove at Nemea in southern Greece. When the slave-nurse Hypsipyle puts her baby charge Opheltes down in the grass to fetch water for the Seven against Thebes (the seven champions making their way through Nemea en route to Thebes, to fight for its throne), the dragon kills him with a flick of his tail; it is not clear whether this is deliberate. The Seven then avenge the child by slaying the serpent before founding the Nemean Games to commemorate the lost boy (see Ogden 2013a: 54–8; 2013b: 119–24).

Hera's *Drakōn* Pair

Attested from *c*.480 BCE, the *drakōn* pair sent by an envious Hera against Heracles (*LIMC*, s.v. 'Herakles' 1650) resemble Python in that they are killed by a baby—indeed, again by a twin baby. Heracles throttles them with his bare hands. Whereas Apollo's twin sister Artemis is able to help him against Python, Heracles' twin brother Iphicles can give him no support—but then he is merely the son of the mortal Amphitryon, whereas Heracles is the son of Zeus, the seed of the two fathers having mingled in Alcmene's womb (Ogden 2013a: 63–5; 2013b: 45–9).

Overlapping Motifs

Most of these great *drakontes* of Panhellenic myth, and indeed almost all antagonist *drakontes* in Greek myth, share some default motifs in their traditions: they all tend to be fiery (of mouth or eye), to emit a pestilential breath (both qualities are imaginative extrapolations of the effect of viper venom, which causes an intense burning sensation), and to inhabit caves (the imaginative extrapolation of the snake's hole, duly inflated to match the *drakōn*'s gargantuan size). But, beyond these default motifs, it will be immediately apparent that these major dragons of Panhellenic myth overlap in some of their other leading motifs, as illustrated in the accompanying Venn diagram (Fig. 6.2).

The diagram is in some senses arbitrary (should we really differentiate baby Heracles from adult Heracles?), simplistic (how are we to accommodate significant variants, as in the Delphic case?) and over-schematic, to be sure, but it retains some value in highlighting an *equilibrium effect of the system of Panhellenic myth*, which *tends to tolerate the repetition of non-default, leading motifs in two of its major* drakōn-*fight traditions, but no more*. Our query about whether the Hydra should also be considered a spring guardian helps make a useful point: spring guardianship may be considered a motif in the Hydra tradition, but, given that it is unexpressed, it can hardly be considered a *leading* motif. And there was no bar on such leading motifs recurring in more local and minor traditions: the *Drakōn* of Thespiae is still permitted to maraud (Paus. 9.26.7–8); Heracles (yet again) may still overcome the serpent of the river Sangaris (Hyg. *Poet. astr.* 2.14). This limitation upon the repetition of leading motifs has the effect of bestowing a sense of variety upon the major Panhellenic dragon-fight narratives, one that contrasts markedly with the stories of the hagiographical dragon-fight tradition (of which more anon), and indeed with the prolific dragon-fight stories of Germanic mythology (for which, see Lionarons 1998; Rauer 2000; Evans 2005; Acker 2012, 2013; Ogden 2021: 309–73).

Drakontes are seldom favoured with personal names (Ogden 2013a: 151–5). 'Hydra' may appear to be an exception to this rule, but we recall again that the word *hydra* signifies 'water snake', so that the designation (and Greek did not differentiate between upper and lower case) may be more of a title than a name as such. When *drakontes* are

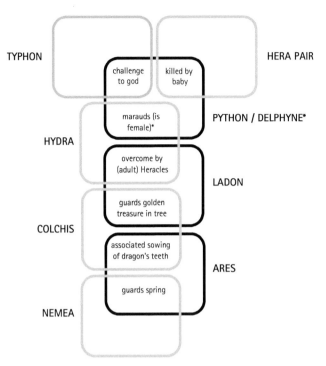

TYPHON

challenge
to god

killed by
baby

HERA PAIR

marauds (is
female)*

PYTHON / DELPHYNE*

HYDRA

overcome by
(adult) Heracles

LADON

guards golden
treasure in tree

COLCHIS

associated sowing
of dragon's teeth

ARES

guards spring

NEMEA

FIGURE 6.2 Venn diagram of overlapping leading motifs in the principal Panhellenic dragon-fight myths.

indeed given personal names, they tend to be shaped by the structure of the word itself, i.e. SYLLABLE + -ōn. We have already encountered Ladon and the metathetical pair of Python and Typhon. The case of 'Typhon' in particular demonstrates the peculiar pull of this name structure: by the fifth century BCE this form of the dragon's name had come to predominate in common use, superseding the earlier variants Typhoeus and Typhaon. Another example of dragon-naming can be gleaned from second century CE, when the prophet Alexander of Abonouteichos achieved great popularity in the regions around the Black Sea. As we learn from Lucian's excoriating biography, *Alexander* or *the False Prophet*, he found himself a large and compliant snake, to which he attached an artificial humanoid head, and promoted it as the manifestation of 'the New Asclepius' (the old Asclepius too having been a *drakōn* at heart, like the healing avatars of his sanctuaries). When he had to choose a name for his new creation, Alexander was guided by established practice: Glycon, 'Sweetie' (see Robert 1980: 393–421; Petsalis-Diomidis 2010: 14–66; Ogden 2013a: 325–30).

The source traditions for the great Panhellenic dragon-fights confront us with a striking paradox. In most cases (that of Typhon being a notable exception) the most expansive and elaborate accounts of the battles—and those that show a concerted interest in the psychology of the creature itself—are preserved for us in the Latin sources, not the Greek ones (e.g. Ov. *Met.* 3.28–98, on the *Drakōn* of Ares; Val. Flacc. *Argon.*

8.54–121, on the *Drakōn* of Colchis). The Romans clearly loved their *dracones*. And yet there seem to have been no dragons indigenous to early Roman myth (that ever-elusive thing) and, more remarkably still, the Romans seem to have felt little need to invent new dragons for themselves. The one clear exception to the last rule, and it is a fairly spectacular one, is the tale of the battle of Regulus and his army against the enormous *serpens* of the Bagrada River in Libya during the course of the First Punic War, first attested in a fragment of the mid-first-century BCE historian Q. Aelius Tubero (F8 Peter = F11 Cornell), but retold in glorious detail by the first-century CE epic poet Silius Italicus (*Pun.* 6.140–282). The dragon is eventually overwhelmed by the army's newfangled catapults (Ogden 2013a: 66–7; 2013b: 141–5). How do we account for the apparent Roman upsurge in dragon-fight representation (Ogden 2021: 42–58)? Is it a reflex of the ubiquity of images of friendly dragons in Roman culture? One thinks here of Asclepius, living in the heart of the city on the Tiber Island, whose 292–291 BCE journey there from Epidaurus in the form of a great serpent is beautifully narrated by Ovid (*Met.* 15.665–94; cf. Ogden 2013a: 310–17). And of genius loci serpent-pairs that continue to decorate so many shrines, both domestic and at street corners, in Pompeii and Herculaneum, and which must once have decorated the capital itself in similar proportions (Flower 2017: esp. 63–75; cf. Tinh 1992). Or does the upsurge lie in the tendency of Latin poets to attempt to surpass the scene types they found both in their Greek models and in the writings of their Roman rivals? Or did it lie in the authors' experiences of the beast fights of the arena? Or is the apparent Romanness of the upsurge merely illusory? Do our Roman authors rather merely recreate dutifully an upsurge in the celebration of the dragon fight in the Hellenistic Greek literature that is now largely lost to us? That which does survive offers us accounts of some interest of the Colchis Dragon (Ap. Rhod. *Argon.* 4.123–66) and Hera's serpent pair (Theoc. *Id.* 24, esp. 10–33, 56–9, 82–100).

HYBRID FORMS

'And something more': the claim that the ancient *drakōn* was, by default, a pure serpent in form requires a small but intriguing qualification. In art, from some point already in the seventh century BCE, the *drakōn* often sports a human beard; from the fourth century BCE the beard can often be joined by a balancing crest. These features are seldom noticed in the literary sources (some rare examples at, e.g. Posidippus 15 Austin-Bastianini; Nic. *Ther.* 443–4), which offer little help in divining their significance. The beard cannot normally be construed as a differentiator of a male serpent from a female one (despite Ael. *NA* 11.26): the female Hydra, for instance, often boasts a full set of beards on each of her multi-heads. The only available conclusion is that the beard serves rather as an (optional) differentiator of supernaturalness: in other words, that it serves, precisely, as a differentiator of a *drakōn* from a common-or-garden snake. The conceit was probably borrowed from Egyptian art, in which the beard could serve as a non-gender-specific

marker of divinity, for snakes as well as other creatures; so it is that statues of the female pharaoh Hatchepsut are bearded, pharaohs being divine. We may also point to the
c.2200 BCE 'Tale of the Shipwrecked Sailor', which features a gold and lapis lazuli serpent
30 cubits in length with a beard of 2 cubits in length (Lichtheim 1973–1980: 1.211–15; see
Ogden 2013a: 155–61; 2021: 28, 56, 60–1).

We can say a little more on gender. A female of the species could be designated by the
fundamentally male term *drakōn*, as in the case, once again, of the Hydra. But Greek
did also develop a paired term characterized for femaleness, *drakaina*, 'dragoness'
(Ogden 2021: 59–83). This was not used much, but, when it was, it seems usually to have
evoked not a pure serpent in form, but rather a female anguiped, i.e. a creature similar
to the evolved Typhon, with a female-humanoid upper half and a serpentine lower one.
Examples falling into this category include various 'Echidnas' or 'Vipers' (Hes. *Theog.*
295–308; Hdt. 4.8–10; *Acts of Philip* 8.4 [G], 8.16 [V]); Delphyne (Apollod. *Bibl.* 1.6.3);
Harmonia (Eur. *Bacch.* 1357–9); Hecate (Lucian, *Philops.* 22); some of the (ever-Protean)
lamiae (e.g. Dio Chrys. *Or.* 5.12–15); and Campe (Nonnus, *Dion.* 18. 236–67).

The powerful concept and imagery of the *drakōn* tended to colonize the other great
monsters of Greek myth. The notorious hair of the Gorgons consists not merely of
snakes, but actually of *drakontes* (their *drakōn* nature in this context being determined
presumably more by their supernaturalness than by their size). And the Gorgons' particular terrible power, that of being able to turn humans and animals to stone, they
surely derive from their serpentine attachments: the power represents an imaginative extrapolation of the widespread (though apparently mistaken) folk-belief that
snakes hypnotize and freeze their prey before devouring it (e.g. Luc. 9.619–99; Ogden
2013a: 92–8; 2013b: 82–96; cf. Lowe in this volume). Let us note here that the ancient
folk-etymology, deriving the noun *drakōn* from the verb *derkomai* (of which the
aorist—equivalent to the English preterite, i.e. simple past tense—participle form is
drakōn), 'look', continues to fascinate many (including Riaño Rufilanchas 1999: 172;
scepticism at Ogden 2013a: 173). The Chimaera's *drakōn* tail makes up a relatively
small physical proportion of her body, but we cannot doubt that it is the *drakōn* that
is the key to her distinctive modus operandi, that of burning up the landscape around
her with her terrible breath (e.g. Hom. *Il.* 6.152–95; Ogden 2013a: 98–104; 2013b: 75–81;
cf. Smith in this volume). And similarly even Cerberus, whose Chimaera-like *drakōn*-
tail and Gorgon-like *drakōn*-pelt, more familiarly represented in art than in literature (*LIMC*, s.v. 'Herakles' 2553–628, though note Hecataeus *FGrH* / *BNJ* 1 F27), would
seem to derive his toxicity from his serpentine element, when, dragged forth from
the underworld by Heracles (him again!) and terrified by the unaccustomed daylight,
he slavers or vomits over a harmless plant native to the region, transforming it into
the deadly aconite (Herodorus of Heracleia F31 Fowler; Ov. *Met.* 7.406–19; Ogden
2013a: 104–15; 2013b: 63–74; cf. Joyce in this volume). On one occasion too Cerberus
is said to have turned an unnamed man to stone—evidently borrowing from the
Gorgons' repertoire, as the snake hair he shared with them licensed him to do (Ov.
Met. 10.64–7).

THE CLASSICAL DRAGON'S EVOLUTION IN MEDIEVAL CHRISTIANITY: FORM AND NARRATIVE

So how did the ancient dragon, in essence just a massive serpent with a fiery breath, evolve into the sort of dragon that any small child can recognize today, the creature with a more animalian head, a fatter central body, legs, and wings? It did so under two pressures (Ogden 2021: 84–136). The modern dragon's overall body-shape resembles less that of the ancient *drakōn* than it does that of its ancient marine cousin, the sea monster or *kētos* (*cetus*): this massive, serpentine, coiling, but fishtailed creature did indeed sport an animalian head, a fatter central body and a prominent pair of fore-flippers that often, in later art, morphed into legs, this perhaps under the influence of the charming form of the hippocamp, a horse before and sea monster behind (Boardman 1987; cf. Ingemark and Asplund Ingemark in this volume).

For all the common qualities of the *drakōn* and the *kētos*, the pagans had kept the two creatures largely distinct at the conceptual level. But this began to change with Hellenistic Jewish and then Christian thinking. From the first the Septuagint, the version of the Hebrew Bible translated into Greek for the Ptolemies in Alexandria during the third and second centuries BCE, used both terms interchangeably and seemingly randomly in its representation of the Bible's monsters Leviathan and Rahab (see e.g. Job 26:5–14, where both terms are deployed). Jerome would subsequently follow suit in compiling his Latin Vulgate (405 CE). And when we come to an early patristic work, *The Shepherd of Hermas*, of *c*.130–50 CE, we find Hermas having a vision in which he is attacked by a fire-breathing, land-lubber creature that is manifestly a *drakōn* in form but is termed rather a *kētos* (vision 4). The second pressure to which the pagan *drakōn* was subject in Christian thought was its merging with the winged but otherwise humanoid demon, the fallen angel. The notion of such winged demons is present in Christian thought already by the time of Tertullian's 197 CE *Apology* (22). In the late fourth-century BCE *Acts of Philip*, the saint encounters a great *drakōn* that presides over a brood of fifty lesser ones. These are transformed into flying demons when the saint duly compels them, using exorcistic techniques, to build a church for him, each of them taking to the air to fetch a column for the edifice (11.2–8 [A]; cf. Amsler 1999; Ogden 2013a: 387–91; 2013b: 207–19).

By the turn of the fifth century CE no lesser patristic luminaries than Augustine and Jerome again were taking it for granted that dragons (*dracones*) were flying creatures (Jerome, *Commentary on Isaiah* 13.21–22, PL xxiv. 163, *c*.395–400 CE; August., *Commentaries on the Psalms* 148.9 on v.7, *c*.392–417 CE). After the collapse of the Roman Empire in the West we rather lose track of the dragon's iconography, but it re-emerges in the tradition of illustrated manuscripts. By the ninth century CE these deliver to us, amongst other variants, a fully formed modern dragon. Amongst the various forms scampering over the pediments decorating the Eusebian canons with which the *Gospels of Hincmar* are prefaced, for example, is a brown creature with an animalian head, from which he breathes forth fire, a fattish central body, from which descend a pair of legs in the position in which a *kētos* would have sported its fore-flippers, a serpentine tail, and a pair of wings (Reims, Bibliothèque Municipale, MS 7, fo. 19). In short, he is a perfect 'wyvern' (this convenient word derives ultimately from the Latin *vipera*, 'viper', via Old French *wivre*). It would take the wyvern some centuries more to acquire, on a consistent basis, the second pair of legs that we in modern times prefer our dragons to possess. It is at around the turn of the fifteenth century that the four-legged type becomes properly established, this again in the context of iconography (e.g. Hans von Judenburg, chestnut-wood sculpture St George, *c.*1400 CE: Metropolitan Museum of Art, 64.280).

As to medieval Christian narrative, the dragon colonized hagiography at an early stage: it is attested already from the later second century CE, first in the *Acts of Thomas* (30–3; cf. Bremmer 2001). The dragon fight, in which the saint aligned himself with God in his battles against the great biblical serpents, Leviathan-Rahab, the Serpent of Eden, and the Revelation Dragon (confined to the abyss by the archangel Michael), continued to thrive in saints' biographies for a millennium and a half, and in an intensely conservative way: the fights described at the end of the tradition would have been fully meaningful to the authors of those still at its commencement, and not the least conservative aspect of the tradition consists in the striking fact that the saintly dragon tends to retain its pure vermiform shape even as its cousins in other genres and other media evolve into the wyvern in the way we have just described. Included among the more prominent dragon-fighting saints are the further apostles Andrew and Philip, and after them Sts Clement of Metz, Samson of Dol, Silvester, and many others (Ogden 2013a: 383–426; 2013b: 187–256; and esp. 2021: 139–308).

The ideal schema of the hagiographical dragon fight, of which hundreds if not thousands of examples survive, proceeds along the following lines (cf. Ogden 2021: 165–259). A dragon resides in a cave, a well, a tomb, a grove, or an island. From its lair it makes marauding attacks upon sheep, cattle, and human communities. It breathes forth its caustic venom as fire, smoke, or a pestilential miasma, the last of which sickens and kills the locals; it can also poison the spring upon which they depend. A saint, duly petitioned, fasts, prays, dons spiritual armour (most typically a shield of faith), and approaches the lair. He subjects the dragon with further prayers or the sign of the cross; it bows its head and fawns like a pet. The saint leashes its neck with a slight garment (most typically a stole). As he parades the creature before them, the locals are converted or confirmed in their own faith. Sometimes the dragon is identified with a demon and cannot therefore be killed, only subjected to exorcistic banishment. It is sent off to the wilderness or hurled into the abyss, with the latter conceptualized as the underworld, opened up for the purpose; or it is plunged into the depths of the sea. At other times the dragon is indeed a mortal creature to be killed. The saint can merely command it to die; as it does so, it vomits forth venom or bursts open. Or the saint can deploy a simple weapon that mirrors one of the dragon's own, his own breath or spittle (which scalds the dragon) or indeed fire. The dragon's carcass still constitutes a biohazard: as it rots it releases venom-laden gas into the atmosphere. Sometimes it is removed with ox-carts, having been hacked into sections. Conversion aside, the deed produces more tangible monuments: a hermitage for the saint to retire into, or a church or a monastery, sometimes located within the cave from which the dragon has been ejected. The hands-off approach to dragon-dismissal or even dragon-slaying renders the activity an equal-opportunities one and a certain number of female saints do partake of it alongside their male counterparts: e.g. Eudocia of Heliopolis, Margaret of Pisidian Antioch, and Victoria.

CONCLUSION: ST GEORGE AND THE DRAGON

To speak today of dragon and saint in the same breath is to evoke, for most readers, the image of St George. But, for all its fame, his dragon fight is of a rather unusual variety by saintly standards. The earliest extant narrative account of his fight is preserved in a Georgian manuscript of the eleventh century CE, though in iconography he had been spearing dragons since the seventh century CE (Patriarchal Library, Jerusalem, cod. 2). George kills the dragon of Lasia with his sword and thereby delivers from it the princess Sabra (as she will eventually be known), the daughter of the city's king Selbius, the virgin having been offered to it as a placatory sacrifice (see Delehaye 1909: 45–76; Walter 2003: 109–44; Ogden 2021: 295–302).

Incidentally, the sacrifice of virgin girls to dragons is rarer than one might imagine. In classical texts attractive boys are sacrificed to the Dragon of Thespiae and the dragon-like Lamia-Sybaris (Paus. 9.26.7–8; Ant. Lib. *Met.* 8), but girls are given only to sea monsters (e.g. Hesione to the *Kētos* of Troy and Andromeda to the *Kētos* of Ethiopia-Joppa: see Ingemark and Asplund Ingemark in this volume). On the hagiographical side, the rare examples of dragons receiving girl sacrifices include the Dragon of (Syrian) Antioch, killed when the father of its latest victim throws the relic thumb of John the Baptist into its mouth (Theodore Daphnopates, *Oratio in translationem manus S. Praecursoris Antiochia Constantinopolin* 12–13, *PG* cxi, pp. 617–18, tenth century CE; cf. Ogden 2021: 238–43).

The unusualness of George's battle consists in his military status and his consequent deployment of martial methods, at once old-fashioned (harking back to the pagan) and newfangled (saluting the rise of chivalry). In this respect he belongs to an exclusive club of two, the other distinguished military dragon-slaying saint being Theodore Tyron, with whom he is often mirrored in his earlier iconography (this from the seventh century CE again; see Delehaye 1909: 12–43; Walter 1999; 2003: 44–66). George's most typical iconography, in which he is shown spearing a supine or backwards-turning dragon from the back of his rearing horse, goes back—via the imagery of the early Christian anonymous 'holy rider' figure—all the way to Bellerophon, who was to be found spearing the backwards-turning Chimaera below, from the back of his rearing Pegasus, already from *c.*660 BCE (*LIMC*, s.v. 'Pegasos' 152; Ogden 2013a: 102; 2021: 302–5). This brings us back, more or less, to the point at which we began.

SUGGESTED READING

The principal sources of interest for the subject, those of classical myth and Christian hagiography alike, are collected in translation in Ogden (2013b); those for the cult of the *drakōn*-god Asclepius are collected in the impressive Edelstein and Edelstein (1945). The views put forward here have been developed in two substantial monographs on the *drakōn*, Ogden (2013a and 2021), and these may be consulted for further detail on all matters. German surveys are to be found in Merkelbach (1959) and Röhrich (1981), the latter with a folkloric perspective; Sancassano (1997) offers a survey in Italian, Riaño Rufilanchas (1999) in Spanish. An excellent introduction to the great *drakontes* of Panhellenic myth more particularly is provided by Fontenrose (1959); the ever-reliable Gantz (1993) offers careful exposition of the developing stages of the sundry traditions; note also Watkins (1995) (a most useful quarry of material, marshalled in the service of an untenable argument). For their iconography the best starting point is the various dedicated articles in the admirable *LIMC*; on *drakōn* iconography more generally see the varied books of Mitropoulou (1977) (regrettably samizdat), Grabow (1998) and Rodríguez Pérez (2008). Boardman (1987) supplies the standard treatment of the classical *kētos*. An outstanding introduction to dragons in the hagiography of the Latin West is to be found in Rauer (2000) (this despite the fact that this fascinating book is addressed primarily to *Beowulf*); cf. also Privat (2000). Walter (2003) offers the best introduction to the Byzantine military saints, George and Theodore Tyron. The question of the dragon's evolution is addressed in a rather different way by Khalifa-Gueta (2018).

WORKS CITED

Acker, P. 2012. 'Death by Dragons.' *Viking and Medieval Scandinavia* 8: 1–21.

Acker, P. 2013. 'Dragons in the Eddas and in Early Nordic Art', in *Revisiting the Poetic Edda: Essays on Old Norse Heroic Legend*, ed. P. Acker and C. Larrington, 53–75. London.

Amsler, F. 1999. *Acta Philippi*, 2 vols. Turnhout.

Angeletti, L., et al. 1992. 'Healing Rituals and Sacred Serpents.' *The Lancet* 340: 223–5.

Arvanitaki, A. 2012. 'Ο Δίας εναντίον ενός δράκοντα: μια διαφορετική απεικόνιση του μύθου της αναμέτρησης του Δία με τον Τυφώνα στην Κόρινθο', in *Κεραμέως παίδες. Αντίδωρο στον Καθηγητή Μιχάλη Τιβέριο από τους μαθητές του*, ed. E. Kephalidou and D. Tsiaphaki, 171–8. Thessaloniki.

Bachvarova, M. R. 2016. *From Hittite to Homer: The Anatolian Background of Ancient Greek Epic*. Oxford.

Boardman, J. 1987. 'Very Like a Whale—Classical Sea Monsters', in *Monsters and Demons in the Ancient and Medieval Worlds,* ed. A. E. Farkas, 73–84. Mainz.

Bremmer, J. N., ed. 2001. *The Apocryphal Acts of Thomas*. Leuven.

Delehaye, H. 1909. *Les Légendes grecques des saints militaires*. Paris.

Edelstein, E. J., and L. Edelstein. 1945. *Asclepius: A Collection and Interpretation of the Testimonies*, 2 vols. Baltimore.

Evans, J. D. 2005. ' "As Rare as They Are Dire": Old Norse Dragons, *Beowulf*, and the *Deutsche Mythologie*', in *The Shadow-Walkers: Jacob Grimm's Mythology of the Monstrous*, ed. T. Shippey, 207–69. Tempe, AZ.

Flower, H. I. 2017. *The Dancing Lares and the Serpent in the Garden: Religion at the Roman Street Corner*. Princeton.

Fontenrose, J. 1959. *Python: A Study of the Delphic Myth and Its Origins*. Berkeley and Los Angeles.

Gambari, S. 2017. *La grotta dei serpenti tra medicina e folclore*. Rome.

Gantz, T. 1993. *Early Greek Myth: A Guide to Literary and Artistic Sources*, 2 vols. Baltimore.

Grabow, E. 1998. *Schlangenbilder in der griechischen schwartzfiguren Vasenkunst*. Münster.

Khalifa-Gueta, S. 2018. 'The Evolution of the Western Dragon.' *Athens Journal of Mediterranean Studies* 4: 265–90.

Lichtheim, M. 1973–1980. *Ancient Egyptian Literature*, 3 vols. Berkeley and Los Angeles.

Lionarons, J. T. 1998. *The Medieval Dragon: The Nature of the Beast in Germanic Literature*. Enfield Lock.

Merkelbach, R. 1959. 'Drache.' *Reallexikon für Antike und Christentum* 4: 226–50.

Mitropoulou, E. 1977. *Deities and Heroes in the Form of Snakes*, 2nd edn. Athens.

Noegel, S. B. 2015. 'Jonah and Leviathan: Inner-Biblical Allusions and the Problem with Dragons.' *Hen* 37: 236–60.

Ogden, D. 2013a. *Drakōn: Dragon Myth and Serpent Cult in the Greek and Roman Worlds*. Oxford.

Ogden, D. 2013b. *Dragons, Serpents and Slayers in the Classical and Early Christian Worlds: A Sourcebook*. New York.

Ogden, D. 2021. *The Dragon in the West*. Oxford.

Petsalis-Diomidis, A. 2010. *Truly Beyond Wonders: Aelius Aristides and the Cult of Asklepios*. Oxford.

Privat, J.-M., ed. 2000. *Dans la gueule du dragon: Histoire—ethnologie—littérature*. Sarreguemines.

Rauer, C. 2000. *Beowulf and the Dragon*. Cambridge.

Renberg, G. H. 2017. *Where Dreams May Come: Incubation Sanctuaries in the Greco-Roman World*, 2 vols. Leiden.

Riaño Rufilanchas, D. 1999. 'Δράκων', in *Τῆς φιλίης τάδε δῶρα: Miscelánea léxica en memoria de Conchita Serrano*, 171–86. Madrid.

Riethmüller, J. W. 2005. *Asklepios: Heiligtümer und Kulte*, 2 vols. Heidelberg.

Robert, L. 1980. *A travers l'Asie Mineure: Poètes et prosateurs, monnaies grecques, voyageurs et géographie*. Paris.

Rodríguez Pérez, D. 2008. *Serpientes, dioses y héroes: el combate contra el monstruo en el arte y la literatura griega antigua*. León.

Röhrich, L. 1981. 'Drache, Drachenkampf, Drachentöter', in *Enzyklopädie des Märchens, Handwörterbuch zur historischen und vergleichenden Erzählforschung*, ed. K. Ranke et al., 3. 787–820. Berlin.

Sancassano, M. 1997. *Il serpente e le sue immagini: Il motivo del serpente nel poesia greca dall'Iliade all'Orestea*. Como.

Tinh, T. T. 1992. 'Lar, Lares', in *LIMC* 6/1: 205–12.

Walter, C. 1999. 'Theodore, Archetype of the Warrior Saint.' *Revue des études byzantines* 57: 163–210.

Walter, C. 2003. *The Warrior Saints in Byzantine Art and Tradition*. Aldershot.

Watkins, C. 1995. *How to Kill a Dragon: Aspects of Indo-European Poetics*. Oxford.

CHAPTER 7

....

THE 'MONSTER-HARBOURING SEA'

Sea Monsters and Sea Serpents in Ancient Myth

....

DOMINIC INGEMARK AND
CAMILLA ASPLUND INGEMARK

INTRODUCTION

....

ATTITUDES toward the sea in antiquity were highly ambivalent. Many passages about the sea in ancient Greek and Roman literature were of a profoundly negative nature, but we can also point to a fair number of positive ones. Plato expresses this ambivalence in the following way:

> For the sea—albeit its proximity to the land is sweet for the purposes of everyday life—is truly 'an exceedingly briny and bitter neighbour'; for by filling her markets with gain from retail trading, and engendering untrustworthiness and faithlessness in people's souls, it makes the city faithless and unfriendly both to itself and, in like manner, to others as well.[1] (*Leg.* 4.704–5)

The notion of the corrupting sea was a recurring theme, as were the dangers of sailing the seas, which were linked to the dread of drowning and being deprived of burial rites. Also, there was a deep-seated fear of the monstrous creatures that dwelt beneath the waves.

Aristotle discusses the common argument that the communications enabled by sea travel were of a profoundly corrupting nature and seen as unfavourable to good governance, but contends that if these shortcomings were avoided, proximity to the sea could be advantageous

---

[1] All translations from Greek and Latin are by Camilla Asplund Ingemark.

(*Pol.* 7.1327a). The sea was of fundamental importance—indeed a prerequisite—for most Greek cities, many of which were situated along coastal areas. Plato even likened the Greeks living in cities around the Mediterranean to 'frogs around a pond' (*Phd.* 109b).

In contrast, the city of Rome was not geographically situated directly by the sea, and although Rome came to evolve into a seafaring nation, the Roman sources reflect a society more focused on land and landowning (Janni 2015: 24–7). In Cicero's *Republic* the sentiments of Plato are in many respects reiterated. In this work we find the view that the ultimate cause of the downfall of Carthage and Corinth was their relationship to the corrupting sea: their very location, bordering on the sea; sailing the seas in their quest for profit; importing not only foreign merchandise but also foreign ways and vices; abandoning agriculture and the pursuit of arms (2.3.6–2.4.9).

While sailing in many respects was more practical than travelling on land (Casson 1974: 149–50; Meijer and van Nijf 1991: 133–4), it was potentially perilous; sudden storms—even in the summer—wrecked and sank ships. Most sailing took place during the summer, due to the difficult and dangerous weather conditions during the winter. The early Greek author Hesiod gave stern advice to his brother not to set sail when the fierce winds of the late autumn and winter had begun (*Op.* 618–93). Roman sources speak of this as the 'closed sea' (*mare clausum*): a period between late autumn and early spring when the ships stayed in the ports (Veg. *Mil.* 4.39).

Indeed, sudden storms could hit at any time of the year, and Lucretius warns of trusting the false and alluring smile of the calm sea, arguing that the true nature of the sea is both treacherous and violent (*DRN* 2.551–67). Drowning at sea was deemed a particularly pitiful kind of death, as this meant being denied burial rites and deprived of a proper grave (Huskinson 2011: 118), instead ending up as fodder for the fish that dwelled in its depth, and not finding rest in the afterlife (Prop. 3.7; Verg. *Aen.* 6.317–71). This recurrent literary topos appears throughout antiquity, for instance in Homer where Odysseus, fearing for his life on a raft in full storm, wishes that he had died in battle at Troy and been given a burial by his comrades (*Od.* 5.299–312). Horace in turn laments the unburied bones of those who drowned at sea, describing the sea's lust for destruction as insatiable (*Carm.* 1.28.15–36).

The violent and destructive nature of the sea was perceived as perilous not only for those who travelled it, but even for land itself, and Pliny the Elder in his *Natural History* portrays the opposing elements of sea and land as being in a perpetual struggle, the sea 'snatching and devouring' land (Beagon 1992: 159–61). Given the sea's violent nature, it comes as no surprise that the watery depths were thought to host a variety of fear-inspiring creatures. Horace, for example, expresses the dread the sea evoked in people—dread not only of sudden storms with high seas, but also of terror in the shape of 'swimming monsters' (*monstra natantia, Carm.* 1.3.18). Some of these monstrous creatures were factual, such as whales, sharks, and giant octopuses, whereas others were figments of the imagination, such as the giant sea monsters in Graeco-Roman myth.

FOES FROM THE DEEP:
OCTOPUSES AND KILLER WHALES

Out on the open seas there were encounters with animals perceived as being particularly ferocious and a lethal threat to sailors: killer whales and sharks, and sightings of other fearsome creatures such as whales and giant octopuses (e.g. Paus. 2.34.2; Plin. *NH* 9.3.8). In the ancient sources we also find stories of monstrous sea creatures leaving the deep seas and entering several famous harbours, thereby transgressing the barriers between sea and land, nature and civilization, their natural habitat and the rightfully human domain (Asplund Ingemark 2008; Asplund Ingemark and Ingemark 2020: ch. 10).

In Aelian's *On the Nature of Animals* we find a story of a gargantuan octopus which had come 'to despise and disdain the food from the sea' (13.6) and, to satisfy its appetite for salted fish, had entered a warehouse filled with amphorae owned by Spanish merchants. In its distorted state of mind, the octopus has come to scorn its natural diet of seafood, an exclusive and expensive cuisine in human contexts. As a result of laziness and corruption this octopus prefers imported foodstuffs, even though small salted fish were typically regarded as an inferior and tawdry type of foodstuff (Cic. *Fam.* 9.16.7). At night the octopus enters the warehouse through a filthy sewer, crushing the sturdy amphorae with its strong tentacles to access their contents. To stop the thefts, not knowing who was responsible, the merchants leave a slave to guard their goods. Alone, he could not tackle this fearsome and fierce creature, but on the following night the merchants manage to kill the marauder after a bloody fight. This story was said to have taken place in Dicaearchia (Roman Puteoli) in the Bay of Naples (Ael. *NA* 13.6). A similar story, found in Pliny the Elder and set in Carteia (Spain), tells of an octopus leaving the sea and coming onto land to steal salted fish (*NH* 9.48.92).

Another story of a monstrous sea creature infringing on and threatening the human world is found in Pliny's *Natural History*. In this case, a killer whale, too lazy to pursue its natural prey and motivated by its unnatural cravings, leaves the deep seas to instead feed on imported raw hides from a sunken ship in Ostia, the harbour city of ancient Rome. The killer whale is confronted and killed, in this case by Roman soldiers led by a highly unexpected hero: the emperor Claudius himself (9.5.14–15).

The view that the sea was a source of moral corruption is in these cases embodied in creatures that stem from the sea itself. That must have been viewed as an interesting twist to the stories. The moral message is man's dominance over nature, regardless of the brute force of these creatures.

EMERGING FROM THE DEEP SEAS:
MYTHICAL SEA MONSTERS

Turning from monstrous sea creatures in the legends to the sea monsters in ancient myth, we find horrifying beasts sent out by the gods to punish those who had incited their ire. These myths must have been profoundly popular, for not only are they found in the texts of numerous ancient authors, but many constellations were also named after the key characters in one of them, the Andromeda myth: the Ethiopian princess Andromeda; Cetos, the sea monster that threatened to devour her; and Perseus, the hero who saved her (Coleman 1983: 226).

The Andromeda story revolves around a recurring theme in Greek myth: mortals who have the audacity to compete with the immortal and inherently superior gods. In antiquity, such audacity was known as *hubris*—behaviour that did not acknowledge one's limits as a mortal. Those who exhibited hubris typically faced truly terrifying punishments. This would have been the case with Andromeda, had not a hero intervened. The story, usually set in Ethiopia but sometimes in Jaffa, begins with Queen Cassiopeia's boastful claim that either her own or her daughter Andromeda's beauty exceeded that of the sea-nymphs, the Nereids. This provoked the anger not only of the Nereids but also, more importantly, of Poseidon, the Lord of the Sea. Poseidon first punishes Cassiopeia's boast by sending a massive flood and a giant sea monster that plagued the region (Apollod. *Bibl.* 2.4.3; Manilius, *Astronomica* 5.538–55). The second, even more severe, punishment comes when an oracle reveals that the only way to free the land of Poseidon's wrath is for the king and queen to allow their beloved daughter Andromeda to be devoured by the sea monster Cetos.

Luckily for the royal family the story takes another turn, when the hero Perseus, returning from his successful quest to behead the Gorgon Medusa, finds Andromeda chained to a rock as he flies by on his winged sandals. Wearing the cap of Hades on his head, a sword in his right hand, and the head of Medusa in his left, he slays the dreadful monster that has emerged from the depths of the sea (Achilles Tatius, *Leucippe and Clitophon* 3.7). When he wants to marry the fair maiden new problems arise, however, as her betrothed plots to kill Perseus. But by showing the horrendous head of Medusa, Perseus turns his competitor into stone (Apollod. *Bibl.* 2.4.3; Hyg. *Fab.* 64). As William Hansen points out, folk-tales of this tale type, in which a hero rescues a princess by slaying a monster, are known as 'The Dragon Slayer' (ATU 300) and appear worldwide (2002: 119–23).

Another ancient Greek myth that belongs to this tale type is that of the Trojan sea monster, a story with many similarities to that of Andromeda. Indeed, Hansen has convincingly argued that these two stories were based on the same widespread folk-tale (2002: 119–23). Aside from the many analogous plot points, the characters themselves were related to each other: the hero who slew the Trojan sea monster was none other than Perseus and Andromeda's great-grandchild Heracles (Diod. Sic. 4.9).

This story revolves around the dire consequences of defrauding others, leading ultimately to the dethroning and death of the perpetrator, King Laomedon of Troy. Following a revolt against Zeus, Apollo and Poseidon were forced to pay a penance in the form of serving the mortal king for a full year. They themselves were disguised as mortals, and their true nature as immortal gods remained unknown to Laomedon. According to Homer, Poseidon built Troy's city walls, while Apollo attended to the king's cattle at Mount Ida (*Il.* 21.434–60).

Rather than receiving their promised payment from the king, however, the gods were swindled, leaving them enraged and lusting for revenge. Apollo punished the king by sending a pestilence to Troy (Diod. Sic. 4.42; Apollod. *Bibl.* 2.5.9), while Poseidon plagued the country with massive flooding:

> and he turned back all his waters to the shores of avaricious Troy, and flooded the land until it resembled a sea, and he carried off the farmer's crops and submerged their fields beneath his waves. (Ov. *Met.*11.207–10)

Moreover, the infuriated Poseidon sent a sea monster to Troy, a monster that could be appeased only by being fed humans. King Laomedon's own daughter, the fair maiden Hesione, was chosen by lot and chained to a sea cliff to be sacrificed to the monster (Diod. Sic. 4.42). Again, a parent's hubris was to be punished in the worst imaginable way: having to give up a beloved daughter. On his travels after his ninth labour, Heracles happens to see the chained Hesione. The hero promises to save Laomedon's daughter, asking in exchange the king's twelve immortal horses. While Heracles saves Hesione by slaying the sea monster, the king reneges on his promise, revealing once again his false nature (Apollod. *Bibl.* 2.5.9).

Also set at Troy is the story of Laocoön which, like many myths, has several variants. The best-known version goes as follows. In an attempt to finally conquer Troy after nearly ten years of battle, the Greeks resort to trickery. At Odysseus' suggestion, they build a large, hollow wooden horse and conceal several dozen soldiers in it. They leave the horse on the shore by Troy, while the Greek fleet moves out of sight to make it seem as though they had sailed back to Greece. Some Trojans look at the horse with amazement and awe and want to bring it into the city, but Laocoön utters these words of warning: 'Whatever it is, I fear the Greeks, even when they bring gifts' (Verg. *Aen.* 2.49). Then he violently hurls a spear in the side of the horse, eliciting a hollow moan from inside, which, unfortunately for the Trojans, was ignored.

The next event in this story illustrates the immense powers of the gods, especially Poseidon's and Athena's, and the vanity of trying to oppose their will. While soon thereafter performing the ritual sacrifice of a bull, Laocoön is attacked by sea serpents (Fig. 7.1):

> But lo! from Tenedos, over the peaceful depths (I tremble as I tell it) twin serpents with immeasurable coils were pressing upon the sea and moving towards the shore together. Their breasts were raised over the tides and their blood-red crests

FIGURE 7.1 Laocoön and his sons attacked by sea serpents. First-century BCE copy of a Hellenistic original, *c*.200 BCE.

Source: Wikimedia / Marie-Lan Nguyen. Public domain.

rose above the waves. The remaining part traversed the sea behind and their backs swelled out in immense coils; there was a noise as the sea frothed. And now they were reaching the shore and with their glowing eyes tinged with blood and fire, they were licking their hissing mouths with quivering tongues. We scattered feeble at the sight. They made for Laocoön in a straight line; and first both serpents encircled the small bodies of his two sons and with their bites fed upon the wretched limbs. (Verg. *Aen.* 2.203–15)

This stands in stark contrast to the stories of Andromeda and Hesione. Firstly, Laocoön, as a respected priest of Apollo and/or Poseidon, is depicted as a man of high moral standing and hence not culpable for the sorry fate of himself and his sons, unless hurling a spear in the side of the Trojan horse is interpreted as sacrilege (Verg. *Aen.* 2.229–31; Hyg. *Fab.*135). Secondly, opposing the will of the divine proves to be deadly: Laocoön and his sons perish.

In another version, the people of Troy had brought this calamity on themselves. Angry with their former priest of Poseidon since his devotions could not prevent the arrival of the Greeks, they had stoned him to death. The Trojans then failed to observe the god's cult for ten years. When they believed the Greeks had left, and in gratitude finally wished to perform a sacrifice to Poseidon, Laocoön was chosen by lot to do this. The long-standing neglect might have made Poseidon demand recompense through the sacrifice of Laocoön and his sons (Ogden 2013: 143). Indeed, more generally both Vergil and Petronius describe Laocoön himself in the manner of a sacrificial victim (Ver. *Aen.* 2.223–4; Petron. *Sat.* 89).

In yet another version, Laocoön had committed sacrilege, defiling Poseidon's temple by having intercourse with his wife in front of the god's image, and this transgression had to be expiated by his death and that of his sons (Serv. *In Verg. Aen.* 2.201). Alternatively, Laocoön had married and begotten children against Apollo's will, and Apollo sent the serpents in revenge (Hyg. *Fab.*135). There is a stronger moral thrust in these latter variants, where Laocoön himself is far from blameless.

SEA MONSTERS MADE MANIFEST: NATURE AS A SOURCE OF INSPIRATION

While the sea monsters in ancient art and literature firmly belong to the supernatural sphere, these stories were probably in part inspired by the natural world. The 'monster-harbouring sea' was home to many creatures that invoked fear as well as awe, and various scholars touch upon the question of which different species inspired the ancient imagination. The theories presented by these scholars are in our view by no means mutually exclusive; on the contrary, they are complementary, for to understand this rich and varied material a single explanation does not suffice. There are convincing arguments to suggest multiple sources of inspiration ultimately deriving from the animal kingdom.

Firstly, one main inspiration was animals that could be encountered in the contemporary world, both in the Mediterranean and in the Atlantic and Indian Oceans beyond. Some scholars have proposed marine animals such as whales, orcas, and sharks as the inspiration for sea monsters generally (Waugh 1961: 361–3; Coleman 1983: 229–30; Papadopoulos and Ruscillo 2002: 206–7); indeed, the same Greek word, *kētos*, denotes all three animals as well as the sea monsters of myth, such as the one that attacked Hesione (*Suda*, s.v. *kētos*; Felton 2012: 114). The Greek word also provides the base for the English word *cetology*, the study of whales.

When it comes to sea serpents specifically, one can point to several sources of inspiration. Emily Vermeule (1979: 183) suggested giant oarfish, which in their body and skin certainly resemble the mythical sea serpents. Land-living snakes may also have been another model, for their body shape as well as for their jaws and teeth (Stothers 2004: 220). Moray eels were another likely source, given the resemblance between how these mythical sea serpents are depicted in the literary accounts and the real-life physical appearance of moray eels. The Mediterranean moray (*Muraena helena*), for example, is serpentine, with strong jaws and sharp teeth. Sea monsters in myth are sometimes described as having triple jaws (Hom. *Od.* 12.89–92; Philostr. *Imag.* 12), and moray eels have double jaws—pharyngeal jaws that constitute a 'second set' of teeth, contained within the animal's throat, or pharynx, distinct from the primary or oral jaws. Moreover, they live in crevices, not unlike sea monsters abiding in caves (Mehta and Wainwright 2008). Overall, it seems plausible that sea monsters were, to some extent, inspired by this actual species. Such eels were also thought to be able to come out of the sea and onto land (Ael. *NA* 1.50; *BNP*, s.v. 'Moray').

Secondly, besides living animals of the open seas, the bones of beached whales may have constituted a source of inspiration for the massive sea monsters of ancient myths, given the fact that whalebones are occasionally found in archaeological contexts (Papadopoulos and Ruscillo 2002: 187). Equally, ancient sources describe finds of massive bones believed to have originated from sea monsters. For instance, Pausanias mentions the colossal bones publicly displayed outside Corinth (2.10.2). Suetonius says that the emperor Augustus had a collection of huge bones consisting of 'land and sea monsters, commonly called giants' bones, and the weapons of heroes' (*Aug.* 72). And Pliny references how Marcus Aemilius Scaurus, aedile in 58 BCE, brought back a skeleton of gargantuan size from Jaffa to Rome, claiming it had once belonged to the sea monster that had threatened Andromeda (*NH* 9.4.11). Clearly, massive bone finds were associated with myths of sea monsters and the heroes who slew them.

Thirdly, fossil remains of long extinct animals, such as giant giraffes, mammoths, and mastodons, exposed by erosion, may have inspired some ancient conceptions of sea monsters. Adrienne Mayor has compellingly argued that literary and historical accounts concerning colossal bones, often ascribed to mythical giants and monsters, were in fact fossils (2001: 64–5, 138–9). One strong piece of iconographic evidence Mayor discusses is a late Corinthian column-krater (*c.*560–540 BCE) possibly portraying Heracles' heroic rescue of Hesione from a fierce sea monster. There can be little doubt that the head of this monster depicts a fossil skull jutting out from a rock (Mayor 2000; 2001: 157–62; also Monge-Nájera 2020).

Other truly terrifying natural phenomena associated with sea monsters were tsunamis, rare though they might have been (Papadopoulos et al. 2014: 81). Some classical scholars have argued that these myths were inspired by actual tsunamis, an argument also put forward by certain seismological experts (Smid 1970; Forsyth 1975; Papadopoulos 2005: 181). Several myths tell of massive floods that in some cases brought with them a sea monster as a result of Poseidon's wrath (Apollod. *Bibl.* 2.4.3;

2.5.9; Manilius, *Astronomica* 5.538–55). Euripides' *Hippolytus* and Seneca the Younger's *Phaedra* describe towering tidal waves sweeping in from offshore in the form of the Bull of the Sea, a monstrous creature that ended Hippolytus' life (Eur. *Hipp.* 1198–225; Sen. *Phaed.* 1000–49), sent by the same vengeful sea god:

> Then suddenly the sea roared prodigiously from its depths and rose to the stars. No wind blew upon the sea, no part of the peaceful sky rumbled, and a storm all of her own put the sea's calm in motion.... The huge sea rises into an enormous wall.... the whole sea bellows, all the cliffs on every side resound in response, and, swelling with a monster, the flood rushes toward the land. (Sen. *Phaed.* 1007–10, 1015–26)

That the devastating effects of tsunamis were described as the result of divine fury is hardly surprising, nor is their association with sea monsters.

CONCLUSION

In many ways the negative Graeco-Roman views of the sea—as a very real, often lethal, threat with terrifying creatures dwelling in its depths—are mirrored in the myths of monstrous sea creatures. Most of these stories carry a clear moral message of right and wrong. To the Greeks and Romans alike, tilling the soil was associated with virtue, whereas sailing the seas was often connected with corruption and vice. A small number of Roman legends about monstrous sea-living creatures, such as colossal octopuses and killer whales who had left their natural habitat and abandoned their habits, came to embody these notions of the sea carrying with it corruption.

Clearly the sea evoked many emotions, and in myth, the presence of Poseidon and the ills he brought with him in the form of massive floods, tidal waves, and sea monsters heightened the drama. The myth of Andromeda teaches a lesson via Cassiopeia's boastful attitude. The myth of Hesione, in turn, highlights the deceit of her father, King Laomedon, in failing to fulfil his promises, first to Poseidon and Apollo, and subsequently to Heracles. The story of Laocoön, at least in the Roman versions preserved, usually portrays a man of impeccable moral standing.

Sometimes, however, these clear moral messages were not accepted at face value, and the ancient texts include other points of view on whether these punishments were justified or not. Was it right to let Andromeda suffer for her mother's folly, or to punish Hesione for her father's misbehaviour? Ovid, for example, describes the god Ammon, who had bidden 'innocent Andromeda' to suffer her mother's penalty, as 'unjust' (*Met.* 4.670–1). Valerius Flaccus, also sympathetic to a sacrificial maiden, provides Hesione's own perspective (*Argon.* 2.470–92). In this respect, the stories were not only conduits for a simple moral, but perhaps also tools in more sustained discussions of right and wrong, where the conclusions were far from self-evident.

SUGGESTED READING

For Greek and Roman perceptions of the sea, see Beaulieu (2016), Lindenlauf (2004), and Janni (2015), who emphasize the ambivalent attitudes—the sea as harmful and hostile, yet also benevolent and a bringer of wealth—held in Graeco-Roman thought. Two in-depth discussions on ancient myth, including those treated in this chapter, are found in Hansen (2002) and Ogden (2013). Hansen approaches these stories from a folklore as well as a Classics perspective, providing greater insights into the influence of oral tradition. Ogden's work focuses on dragons, both land-living and sea-dwelling, and provides the reader with detailed discussions of the various myths.

WORKS CITED

Asplund Ingemark, C. 2008. 'The Octopus in the Sewers: An Ancient Legend Analogue.' *Journal of Folklore Research* 45/2: 145–70.

Asplund Ingemark, C., and D. Ingemark. 2020. *Representations of Fear: Verbalising Emotion in Ancient Roman Folk Narrative*. Helsinki.

Beagon, M. 1992. *Roman Nature: The Thought of Pliny the Elder*. Oxford.

Beaulieu, M.-C. 2016. *The Sea in the Greek Imagination*. Philadelphia.

Casson, L. 1974. *Travel in the Ancient World*. London.

Coleman, K. M. 1983. 'Manilius' Monster.' *Hermes* 111/2: 226–32.

Felton, D. 2012. 'Rejecting and Embracing the Monstrous in Ancient Greece and Rome', in *The Ashgate Research Companion to Monsters and the Monstrous*, ed. A. S. Mittman and P. J. Dendle, 103–31. Farnham.

Forsyth, P. Y. 1975. 'Seneca, Thera, and the Death of Hippolytus.' *Classical World* 69/2: 113–16.

Hansen, W. 2002. *Ariadne's Thread: A Guide to International Tales Found in Classical Literature*. Ithaca, NY.

Huskinson, J. 2011. 'Bad Deaths, Better Memories', in *Memory and Mourning: Studies on Roman Death*, ed. V. Hope and J. Huskinson, 113–25. Oxford.

Janni, P. 2015, 'The Sea of the Greeks and the Romans', in *Brill's Companion to Ancient Geography*, ed. S. Bianchetti, M. Cataudella, and H.-J. Gehrke, 21–42. Leiden.

Lindenlauf, A. 2004. 'The Sea as a Place of No Return in Ancient Greece.' *World Archaeology* 35/3: 416–33.

Mayor, A. 2000. 'The "Monster of Troy" Vase: The Earliest Record of a Vertebrate Fossil Discovery?' *Oxford Journal of Archaeology* 19/1: 57–63.

Mayor, A. 2001. *The First Fossil Hunters: Paleontology in Greek and Roman Times*. Princeton.

Mehta, R. S., and P. C. Wainwright. 2008. 'Functional Morphology of the Pharyngeal Apparatus in Moray Eels.' *Journal of Morphology* 269: 604–19.

Meijer, F., and O. van Nijf. 1991. *Trade, Transport and Society in the Ancient World*. London.

Monge-Nájera, J. 2020. 'Evaluation of the Hypothesis of the Monster of Troy Vase as the Earliest Artistic Record of a Vertebrate Fossil.' *Uniciencia* 34/1: 147–51.

Ogden, D. 2013. *Drakōn: Dragon Myth and Serpent Cult in the Greek and Roman Worlds*. Oxford.

Papadopoulos, G. A. 2005. 'Two Large Tsunamis in the Prehistory of the Aegean Sea: The Minoan Tsunami (~17th Century BC) and the Troy Tsunami (~13th Century BC)', in *Proceedings of the 22nd International IUGG Tsunami Symposium, Chania, Crete, 27–29 June, 2005*, ed. G. A. Papadopoulos and K. Satake, 181–5. Chania.

Papadopoulos, G. A., et al. 2014. 'Historical and Pre-Historical Tsunamis in the Mediterranean and Its Connected Seas: Geological Signatures, Generation Mechanisms and Coastal Impacts.' *Marine Geology* 354: 81–109.

Papadopoulos, J. K., and D. Ruscillo. 2002. 'A *Ketos* in Early Athens: An Archaeology of Whales and Sea Monsters in the Greek World.' *American Journal of Archaeology* 106/2: 187–227.

Smid, T. C. 1970. ' "Tsunamis" in Greek Literature.' *Greece & Rome* 17/1: 100–4.

Stothers, R. B. 2004. 'Ancient Scientific Basis of the "Great Serpent" from Historical Evidence.' *Isis* 95/2: 220–38.

Vermeule, E. T. 1979. *Aspects of Death in Early Greek Art and Poetry*. Berkeley and Los Angeles.

Waugh, A. 1961. 'The Folklore of the Whale.' *Folklore* 72: 361–71.

CHAPTER 8

ART HORROR

Medusa and Her Sister Gorgons

DUNSTAN LOWE

INTRODUCTION

MEDUSA is arguably the best known of all mythological monsters from the ancient Mediterranean world; she was undeniably the most visible. The only mortal among three Gorgon sisters, she was beheaded by the Greek hero Perseus, who then gave her head to the goddess Athena for safe keeping. Her decapitated head seems to have provided the basis for the design known to art historians as the *gorgoneion* (pl. *gorgoneia*), which appears on thousands of art objects throughout Greek and Roman history, though its style changes profoundly over time, as does the narrative connected with it. The Greeks used the term *gorgoneion* itself ('Gorgon-object') only for a single famous example, the horrific round face glaring confrontationally at the viewer from upon the shield of Athena's gold-and-ivory statue in the Parthenon.

The *gorgoneion* otherwise usually lacks any context, but several recurrent features link it with Medusa as described in narrative sources: it is female (with rare exceptions) and has Medusa's characteristic snaky hair, or at least snake-like curls. Whole scenes from the story of Perseus also appear in ancient art, though less frequently. The earliest definite image of Medusa (700–660 BCE) is one such scene on a terracotta storage jar found at Thebes in central Greece. It shows Perseus looking away as he puts his sword to Medusa's neck: she is depicted with a woman's long hair (which he grasps with the other hand) and long skirt, though she has a centaur's body, which is surprising because it occurs nowhere else in extant ancient art or literature (Fig. 8.1).

Homer, the earliest author to mention Gorgons, refers only to images of a head. Image and text are in constant dialogue throughout the tradition of Medusa and her two sister Gorgons, which belongs within the larger story of the hero Perseus. This tradition thematizes image-making from the start, while during the Greek Classical period and beyond, storytellers added the motifs of Medusa's victims becoming statues, and of her

FIGURE 8.1 Perseus kills a centaur-bodied Medusa: detail from incised pithos, *c.*660 BCE. Louvre Museum, CA 795.

spilt blood producing its own creations. Nearly three thousand years later, the Gorgons look quite different from the way they did in ancient art and text, especially because they were reimagined in twentieth-century visual media. Contemporary narratives about Medusa show equally significant changes.

Both the story of the Gorgons and the *gorgoneion* image date back to the early Archaic period (seventh century BCE), though it is debatable which inspired the other, or whether they gradually converged (Ogden 2008: 37). We can state two definite observations: that textual narratives and visual depictions emphasize very different aspects of the Gorgons, and that in both media Medusa changed profoundly over several centuries. Various literary and artistic representations turned her from a bestial threat into a young woman, usually beautiful and often a victim. This spectrum of treatments within classical antiquity has provided room for a rich diversity of interpretations among modern critics, especially those concerned with gender and sexuality. Reinterpretations in modern art and popular culture also vary greatly, as Medusa continues to provoke the imagination and change with the times.

In its most developed form, the classical legend of Medusa and her sister Gorgons forms the lengthiest episode in the life of Perseus, a son of Zeus by the mortal princess Danaë of Argos. He was fated to kill his grandfather Acrisius who, in an attempt to avoid the prophecy, abandoned mother and baby at sea in a chest. They washed up on the island of Seriphos, whose king, Polydectes, eventually came to hate the grown-up Perseus for obstructing his courtship of Danaë. Polydectes therefore sent him on a seemingly impossible mission: to fetch 'the Gorgon's head', which Perseus achieved with the help of his patron goddess, Athena. The Gorgons are fast and frightening monsters with snakes for hair: Stheno and Euryale ('Mighty' and 'Wide-Leaping') are immortal and Medusa ('Queen') is not, though she can turn men to shapeless stones just by looking at them. The gods give Perseus several tools: a reflective shield for avoiding Medusa's direct gaze, a hooked sword for lopping off her head, a bag to put it in, a cap that renders him invisible, and winged sandals for escaping Stheno and Euryale afterwards. Perseus finds Medusa sleeping and beheads her. Two 'children' spawn from her neck: the winged horse Pegasus, and a being named Chrysaor ('Golden Sword') who later sires another monster, the triple-bodied Geryon. Perseus weaponizes Medusa's severed head to turn his enemies to stone, just as his great-grandson Heracles would equip himself with the Nemean Lion's hide and Hydra's poison. Separately, perhaps later, Athena herself wears the Gorgon's frightful face into battle on her aegis. This protective item used by Zeus and Athena was imagined as a shield, breastplate, or shawl: it was thought to get its name from 'goat' (*aix*) and was imagined as a goatskin patterned with scales. These may represent rattling metal plates: Homer says that the aegis 'roars like a hundred thousand serpents' and 'has a hundred gold tassels' (*Il.* 4.17), though in Classical Greek art, it is often fringed with snakes instead. The serpent-like roaring, scaly pattern, and fringe of snakes all suggest affinity with a snake-haired *gorgoneion*. Euripides is the only ancient source to suggest that the aegis is actually the Gorgon's skin (*Ion* 987–97).

In later incidents, Medusa's blood itself proves potent in multiple ways. Leaking onto the seaweed where Perseus first rests her head, it creates red coral that sea-nymphs can wear as jewellery (Ov. *Met.* 4.747–50). Dripping from his bag during flight, her blood spawns poisonous snakes across the Libyan desert (Ap. Rhod. *Argon.* 4.1516–17; Luc. 9.629–35). Bottled drops of it have magical powers to kill or cure (Eur. *Ion* 989–1017; Apollod. *Bibl.* 2.4.2–33.10.3). But all these revivals of Medusa's dangerous nature take place through the actions of Perseus or other men, and from her point of view they are unintended. This is very different from what happens with the toxic blood of a male monster, the centaur Nessus. When Nessus tries to abduct Heracles' bride Deianira, Heracles shoots him with a poisoned arrow—one that he had dipped in the toxic blood of another monster, the Hydra (see Deacy in this volume). Nessus intentionally uses his own tainted blood for revenge, by convincing Deianira that it is a love charm; when she finally uses it on Heracles, he too is fatally poisoned. Nessus' blood has one effect, which he chooses; Medusa's head and blood have many effects, but none are her choice. In short, for whatever reason, Perseus' story puts Medusa in a passive role throughout.

The Gorgon Myth in Narrative Sources

The Medusa story told above actually took shape over many centuries, with a lengthy, complex development of both narrative and images (Hirschberger 2000), during which the ancient Gorgon figure changed radically. To put it most simply, an originally fierce, bestial monster gradually became passive, feminine, and sympathetic. However, the change occurred gradually, producing inconsistency but also nuance as artists and authors added or changed various components.

The first mentions of Gorgons, including Medusa, in Greek literature date from the Archaic period (c.800–480 BCE). Homer, the earliest textual source, stands apart from the rest: the *Iliad* and *Odyssey* say nothing about Medusa or indeed any Gorgon narrative. Perseus is mentioned only once (*Il.* 14.319–20) and for a separate reason. Homer makes only a handful of references to a nameless 'Gorgon', whose terrifying face decorates Agamemnon's shield (11.36–7) and Athena's aegis (5.741–2). Also, Hector's terrifying glare is compared to that of 'the Gorgon' (8.348–9); finally, Odysseus hurriedly ends his visit to Hades in case Queen Persephone sends 'the head of the Gorgon, that terrible monster' for him (*Od.* 11.633–5). These references all imply that the *gorgoneion* design was well known by at least the seventh century BCE, and probably earlier.

In contrast, another poem from the early seventh century BCE, Hesiod's *Theogony* ('Birth of the Gods'), outlines a much more detailed story. The poem is mainly a catalogue of family trees—of gods and monsters alike—but Hesiod names three Gorgon sisters, Stheno, Euryale, and Medusa (*Theog.* 276), then says that Medusa had sex with Poseidon in a flowery meadow—a typical setting for erotic encounters in Archaic poetry, as with Hera seducing Zeus in *Iliad* 14. Hesiod makes no further comment except to add that Medusa 'suffered greatly' and that Perseus cut off her head, producing Pegasus and Chrysaor. This leaves the nature of Poseidon's intercourse with Medusa ambiguous, whereas six centuries later the Roman poet Ovid portrays it as rape. In Ovid's version, which relocates the event to a temple of Athena, even Medusa's ability to petrify was inflicted on her against her will. Poseidon's act violates them both: Athena's only means of punishment is to make the beautiful Medusa so ugly that people turn to stone when they see her. Since Greek gods are unfailingly fertile, we can infer from all versions that Poseidon conceived Pegasus and Chrysaor. Surprisingly, Hesiod's earliest version does not explain why Perseus beheaded Medusa, or mention anything unusual about the three sisters except that two of them were immortal. The reference to Medusa's sufferings does, however, anticipate much more sympathetic treatments in later centuries.

In the *Shield of Heracles*, a sixth-century BCE poem mainly devoted to outlining the eponymous shield, one scene describes Perseus escaping with the Gorgon's head while the other Gorgons pursue him (216–37). They are said to have protruding tongues, gnashing teeth, glaring eyes, and snakes as girdles, all fashioned from precious metals, enamel, ivory, and glass-paste. The anonymous author signals this scene as unreal in several striking ways: The golden figure of Perseus is wearing his cap of invisibility, and the severed head is inside the bag across his back, but both are visible. More surprisingly, the Gorgons' feet make the metal clang as they move (231–3), and Perseus' winged sandals really make him fly: 'his feet did not touch the shield and yet were not far from it—a great wonder to describe, since he was not supported anywhere' (216–18).[1] Also, notably, the face of Fear (*Phobos*) occupying the shield's centre has bared teeth and glaring eyes, sounding very much like the *gorgoneion* decorating various shields in art and myth, including the one carried by Agamemnon in the *Iliad*, mentioned above. In view of later accounts, we naturally see Homer's 'Gorgon' image and the Gorgon characters described in the *Theogony* and *Shield of Heracles* as separate facets of the same story. Yet they may be independent, and not fully combined until the early Classical period.

Some of the best-known elements of Medusa's story appear only after Homer and Hesiod in a complex visual–textual evolution. One example is Perseus' *harpē*, a straight sword with a curved blade branching off from one side: this only begins to replace a simple straight sword in art from the late sixth century BCE. Another example is the names of Medusa's sisters: Hesiod's *Theogony* provides both, and they seem to be accepted gradually. In the early fifth century, Pindar names Euryale (*Pyth.* 12.6–27), but two earlier Archaic sources do not name either: the pursuit scene on the cedarwood 'Chest of Cypselus', most likely carved in the same period, labelled only Perseus (Paus. 5.18.5), and the slightly later *Shield of Heracles* says only that Perseus carries the head of one 'Gorgon' while other Gorgons chase him (223–37). One Medusa narrative from the fifth century BCE looms large for us because it includes several details in Perseus' story that would later become standard, namely, the version of the historian Pherecydes of Athens (fr. 11 Fowler). For example, though he remains silent about the names of Medusa's sisters, Pherecydes includes the hooked sword seen earlier in art. He is our earliest source for Perseus using a mirror—held up by Athena and Hermes—with which to safely view Medusa, as well as for Athena being extensively involved, especially when she mounts Medusa's actual head, not just an image of it, on her aegis like a trophy. From this point onwards, Athena becomes part of the patriarchal male suppression of female power that is the myth's most obvious allegory for modern audiences. Athena is a powerful goddess who directs and supports Perseus' actions and even profits from them, but this is consistent with her roles in other myths, which include supporting two other male heroes, Jason and Odysseus, and defending patriarchal institutions.

Our fullest Medusa narrative from antiquity comes relatively late, from around the end of the first century BCE, but deserves special attention because it has been so influential. Ovid, in his epic poem *Metamorphoses* (4.614–20, 77–803) tells Perseus' story by starting with his rescue of Andromeda, then giving the Medusa exploit as a flashback as Perseus narrates the story at the festivities afterwards. Next, Ovid provides an extended narrative of a murderous brawl started by Perseus' rival, and the hero's deliberate manner of ending it by wielding Medusa's head to turn all his enemies to stone. Ovid's narrative of the Gorgon myth diverges from Vergil's earlier *Aeneid*, a far more

---

[1] All translations are my own unless otherwise indicated.

conventional epic. Like Homer in the *Iliad*, Vergil refers to Medusa's head on three occasions and only in passing (2.615–16, 6.288–9, 8.435–8). Vergil's references closely imitate Homer's: one in the underworld and the other two on military equipment, all frightening to the onlooker. By contrast, Ovid apparently invented several story elements, which seem to be motivated by his career-long preoccupation with themes of beauty and artistry. For example, Perseus uses his own shiny shield (instead of one held by a divine helper) to see Medusa, as if ogling her while she sleeps. Also, apart from Perseus' first target, Atlas (who becomes the mountain of that name), the petrified victims become perfectly lifelike statues rather than shapeless rocks, and Medusa's blood turns seaweed into decorative coral, to the delight of the sea-nymphs. These new details all embed acts of viewing into the story; the coral in particular emphasizes Medusa's femininity, offering a very different aesthetic from that found in Archaic poetry.

Later descriptions of Medusa in Roman literature stay restricted to epic poetry, perhaps because her integral role in the Perseus myth kept her in the heroic past. Lucan's *Pharsalia* is a historical epic, but also contains supernatural interludes that match its mood of grim horror, and he foreshadows an outlandish series of deaths by snake poison with a retelling of Medusa's story. Lucan focuses on her beheading but adds original details. For example, Lucan's Medusa has destroyed birds, animals, and entire tribes of Ethiopians with her petrifying glare (9.649–52); and she is feared by her own sisters (9.646–7), implying that she is the only Gorgon with such a power. In a particularly original touch, Lucan metaphorically equates Medusa's snakes with human hair: they are styled in women's fashion, she combs them (though they drip venom in the process), and after the beheading, Athena wafts them down across Medusa's face to shield Perseus. This all makes Medusa sound more feminine—and dangerous—than ever: it may be a riff on Ovid's portrayal, as his influence on Lucan is occasionally detectable. Another development occurs in the fifth century CE with the poet Nonnus' vast mythological epic, the *Dionysiaca*. This unorthodox compendium of mythical characters brings Perseus, wielding Medusa's head, into battle against Dionysus. Dionysus protects himself with a special amulet (*Dion.* 47.590–606), though his beloved Ariadne is turned to stone—the first known reference to a woman falling victim to Medusa, more than a thousand years after Homer and Hesiod first mention the Gorgon.

GORGONS AND MEDUSA IN VISUAL SOURCES

In Archaic art, the Gorgons (like most monsters) look fierce and ugly with exaggerated and stylized features, as with the *gorgoneion*, whose eye-catching glare proved so popular in most artistic media. Its shape was convenient for circular spaces, especially the inside of a Greek kylix or wine-cup, where it confronts the drinker eye to eye as a playful visual joke. In a related design theme, these cups were often also decorated with one large pair of eyes on their exterior surface, so that when the drinkers held the cups to their lips the eyes stared out at the viewer. Consequently, these shallow drinking vessels have been nicknamed 'eye-cups'.[2]

When Archaic artists depict whole-figure Gorgons, the face is still a mask-like *gorgoneion*, suggesting that the rest of the body came later. The most famous example is the Medusa on the pediment of the temple of Artemis in Corcyra on the island of Corfu (see Fig. 23.1 in this volume). Marconi has shown that this huge-headed figure developed stylistically from isolated heads and female faces on earlier temples (2007: 11–12). The massive sculpture, standing almost 3 metres high, has tusks and bared teeth, snake-hair styled into tight curls, and outspread wings; its legs are angled to symbolize swift flight. It must have made the unusually massive temple—the first we know of to be built entirely in stone—even more imposing, especially when brightly painted as it originally would have been. This Gorgon wears a short-skirted woman's tunic, its girdle made of two living snakes entwined, as described in the *Shield of Heracles*. On either side, identifying her as Medusa and foretelling her demise, are a miniature Pegasus (whose rear legs are visible on the viewer's left), and Chrysaor. Yet flanking them in turn are two large mountain leopards which configure this Medusa as a *potnia theron* ('Mistress of the Animals'), a very ancient visual motif dating back to the proto-Greek Minoan civilization. It seems as if, rather than capturing one moment in the story as described in the *Shield of Heracles*, the sculptor built a narrative scene around the *gorgoneion* in an experimental way, by working with elements of a fixed artistic repertoire.

The *gorgoneion* remained popular throughout antiquity in ceramics, painting, mosaics, and sculpture, and while scenes from the Perseus myth continued to appear, they were used less frequently and diverged into a separate tradition. Medusa's narrative has a natural affinity with the visual arts, since it concerns a monster being turned into a viewable object, and textual portrayals of Medusa frequently seem to allude to visual ones. As we have seen, new stories about the creation of images and artefacts aggregated around the core event of her death. Visual media could play with the concept of image-making too: from the Classical period onwards, images of the myth sometimes include reflections of Medusa on Perseus's shield (Taylor 2008). Indeed, the very act of portraying Medusa's face might be seen as fundamentally playful, since it implies that the viewer risks fatally turning from an active subject, viewing the art, into a passive stone object.

The *gorgoneion* resembles earlier designs in the art of the Near East, and some theorists have made arguments that the Greek Medusa myth first came about, and perhaps kept evolving, through misreadings of unfamiliar artistic conventions (see Richey in this volume). It would be naïve to suggest that the *gorgoneion* in art was mistaken for a disembodied head, which then somehow inspired the story of a decapitated Gorgon, or that the stylized, C-shaped locks of hair shown in some Archaic *gorgoneia* were mistaken for rearing snakes, since it is impossible to say whether the image or the story emerged first. At a later stage, one could make a more plausible argument about Pherecydes' claim

---

[2] See https://www.clevelandart.org/art/1926.514#.

that Athena put the actual head of Medusa on her aegis: perhaps this was a way to merge the decapitation story with an existing visual tradition of a *gorgoneion* on Athena's shield. These speculations are tempting, though impossible to prove, and in any case the Gorgon tradition was well established as a supernatural myth (involving the 'magic' of petrifaction) very early in the history of Greek culture.

The *gorgoneia*'s transition from glaring masks into more feminine, beautiful, and passive faces was first divided into three stages by Roscher (1879), and these are still broadly accepted. The earliest style, with its large eyes, heavy features, and broad (usually tusked) grin, gives way to a second, more human-like style that often even has a neck-stump clearly identifying it as Medusa's severed head. The third style is more beautiful and pathetic, monstrous only in its snaky hair (and occasionally a small pair of wings on its head). Roscher presents these as phases in a gradual process of development, though Topper (2007) convincingly argues that the 'beautiful Medusa' began as an inversion of the ugly first type, led by vase-painters portraying parodic versions of the Perseus story, and that the two coexisted for some time. It seems that, as tastes changed, the beautiful counterpoint eventually became more popular than the Archaic original. Overall, the *gorgoneion* follows broader trends in ancient Greek art, including a general trend towards naturalism, though also towards ideals of beauty. From a modern perspective, the potential for horror seems surprisingly restrained, and even the arresting glare of the Archaic *gorgoneion* loses favour in Classical Greek art, never to regain popularity in classical antiquity.

POWER AND DISEMPOWERMENT

Scholarly interpretations of Medusa, especially in psychoanalysis and anthropology, have focused on the social implications of her femininity. Because they theorize a myth or proto-myth underlying our ancient sources and are not based on specific images or texts, they therefore put more weight on the later humanized portrayals than on the earlier bestial ones. Perseus' act of taking Medusa's head is generally allegorized as patriarchal authority repressing female power, sexual or otherwise. In a brief and half-finished article, Freud (1941) interprets Medusa's head as a combination of vagina and phallic snakes, and her petrifying ability as a combination of fear and sexual arousal. This psychosexual approach strongly influenced twentieth-century scholarship on Medusa, especially the structuralist model of Jean-Pierre Vernant (1989), who connects her with a certain Baubo, Demeter's elderly servant who comically exposed her genitals to relieve Demeter's mourning. Vernant believes that the Baubo in written sources is also represented by small female figurines found at Priene, on which the belly is a woman's face and the external genitalia provide the chin. An equally important response to the same Freudian model is Hélène Cixous's (1976) feminist inversion, which celebrates Medusa as a powerful symbol of a historically repressed female identity, including sexuality. Cixous's metaphor of a 'laughing' Medusa who mocks the patriarchy lent its name to a collection of feminist approaches to classical literature (Zajko and Leonard 2006). Scholarly explanations have generally followed trending social attitudes and will undoubtedly continue to do so. For example, in recent decades Medusa's femininity has become highly politicized, because of her power (which can literally kill anyone in sight) and, increasingly, because of her role as a victim of unprovoked male violence. There is much evidence to support this in the features that set the Gorgons apart from other ancient Greek monsters.

According to their portrayals in antiquity, Medusa and her sister Gorgons are much less powerful than they look. Despite their ferocious teeth and famous speed, they do not physically injure anyone, and are only a danger when subjected to the onlooker's gaze; in the Archaic and Classical sources, Medusa does not turn anyone specific to stone while she is alive. No ancient Greek or Roman text says that Medusa is even awake when Perseus cuts off her head, and some make clear that his opportunity came when she was asleep. The short summary in the mythographer Apollodorus' *Library* even specifies that Perseus found all three Gorgons asleep (2.4.2), a bestial yet intimate image reminiscent of the monstrous Erinyes in Aeschylus' tragedy *Eumenides*, who are described as sleeping on the temple steps. Apollo's priestess calls them Gorgon-like, but far uglier (49–53). Medusa therefore always had the potential to be a sympathetic victim, though no authors take this approach before the late Classical and Hellenistic periods, when her looks become softer and more girlish, even beautiful. Ovid's origin story for Medusa also elicits sympathy for her: the girl's great beauty makes her a victim not once but twice, first when Neptune rapes her in Minerva's temple, and then when a furious Minerva disfigures her, changing her most admired feature—her hair—to 'foul snakes' (*turpes hydros*, *Met.* 4.801). Medusa is unique among classical monsters in that the Perseus narrative is almost an antidote to the aggressive glare of the *gorgoneion* so commonly seen in art. If that glare belongs to Medusa, who was asleep in the story until she was killed, then whenever we see it she must already be dead and in the hands of another. In the context of this disempowering narrative frame, the *gorgoneion* naturally became progressively more human over time, as it harmonized with the theme that Medusa has no actual agency. It remains debatable whether the humanization brings out the myth's true meaning or merely transforms it to suit Classical, Hellenistic, and later Roman tastes.

Overall, the stories about Medusa make her death far more consequential than anything she does while alive, as evidenced in part by the way that her surviving sisters simply fade away after the Archaic period. We hear only about their wails of grief which, according to Pindar, inspired Athena to imitate them by inventing the double pipes or *auloi*, a widely used musical instrument with a wailing, bagpipe-like sound (*Pyth.* 12.6–27). Such an imitation of course comprises another appropriation of the Gorgons by Medusa's conquerors. In some ways, danger returns after Medusa's death in the form of spontaneous fertility: Chrysaor is 'born' from her body and will eventually father Geryon, a monstrous enemy for Perseus' own descendant Heracles; the blood from her snake-haired head starts another lineage by spawning snakes in Libya's desert. Both generative acts echo the monstrous fertility of Gaea (Mother Earth in Greek myth), but they are exceptional. The rest of the time, the powers embodied in Medusa's head and blood are co-opted for divine and mortal advantage, particularly by her killers Perseus and Athena. To sum up, textual sources grant very little agency to the living Gorgon figures and connect them closely with the supreme act of disempowerment that is Medusa's execution. There could scarcely be a more striking contrast with the assertive, even confrontational gaze of the *gorgoneion* design, at least in its earliest forms.

THE GORGONS AFTER ANTIQUITY

Although the *gorgoneion* remained part of the visual and architectural repertoire across Europe, notably on the flag of Sicily (using a design found on Sicilian coins from the fourth century BCE), only after the Middle Ages did classically influenced artists bring Medusa and her sister Gorgons back into the popular imagination. During the twentieth century, they entered fantasy entertainment within the bestiary of mythological beings; they are now well established among the monsters in visual media. A turning point came in the Renaissance with Cellini's celebrated bronze sculpture *Perseus with the Head of Medusa*, completed in 1554. The statue imitated the usual portrayal of Perseus in Roman frescoes, like the one in the Villa San Marco at Stabiae: a heroically naked Perseus in a winged helmet holds Medusa's head aloft with his left hand, clutching his sword in the right. Cellini invented his own statue base to form part of the scene, which shows Medusa's naked corpse, trodden underfoot and gushing blood.

Horrific violence is again the focus in Caravaggio's 1597 painting of Medusa, whose head, recently severed, now grimaces horribly, spraying blood; by contrast, Bernini's marble bust from the 1640s shows Medusa alive and indeed beautiful, but with a tormented expression. These portrayals all focus on Medusa's suffering, a theme that distances them from their models in classical art—even Cellini's triumphalist Perseus.

The twentieth century brought a new strand of the tradition in which gorgons or medusas become numberless wild species, though this phenomenon seems unconnected to the ancient rationalizing explanations of the myth featuring an entire race of gorgons—for example, the first-century BCE historian Diodorus Siculus positions Medusa as a queen of the Gorgons, a race of female warriors at war with the Amazons (3.52.4–55.3) This twentieth-century shift appears to begin with Charles G. Finney's novella *The Circus of Dr Lao* (1935), in which Dr Lao identifies his captive 'medusa', a snake-haired woman whose gaze turns people to stone, as a variety local to northern Mexico. This suits the text's overall conversion of mythological beings into zoo animals, with real-world habitats and often unsettling biological realities (this medusa's snakes tussle over a lizard). The Hammer horror movie *The Gorgon* (1964, dir. Terence Fisher), loosely adapting the myth, was nevertheless influential for many years: the title character, named after the Fury 'Megaera', is an ancient spirit periodically inhabiting a noblewoman. The movie retains the three essential mythological details: the titular Gorgon has snaky hair, turns men to stone, and is ultimately beheaded. As a species, 'medusas' later reappear in the tabletop role-playing game *Dungeons & Dragons*, from its original 1974 release onwards. Its strong influence over early computer role-playing games is largely why Medusa and various gorgons have frequently appeared in digital games with fantasy settings.

Portrayals of Medusa in modern visual media have varied with popular taste, as a few prominent Hollywood examples demonstrate. Medusa was sculpted and animated by Ray Harryhausen for the climactic scene of the *Clash of the Titans* movie (1981, dir. Desmond Davis), which proved very influential. This version was untraditional in several ways: she occupies a subterranean chamber on the 'Isle of the Dead' instead of living on the traditional remote western island of Sarpedon or in Libya, as ancient sources say. She has a blue-green body that is naked and covered in rough scales, rather than the human-like body clad in Greek (or foreign) dress imagined in ancient art; her face is snake-fanged and devilish, and she hisses gutturally: she is clearly female, but bestial and aggressive (Harryhausen and Dalton 2009). Two other features that Harryhausen introduced, a bow and arrows and a huge rattlesnake-tail, have become the default for many contemporary visual representations of gorgons. Screenwriter Beverley Cross may have borrowed the snake-tail and cavernous lair from a more obscure figure, Echidna the snake-woman, sister to the Gorgons in Hesiod's *Theogony* (295–305).

In the twenty-first century, two cinematic Medusas have been beautiful and charming until they attack with their petrifying powers. One is 'Aunty Em', a dangerous recluse disguised with sunglasses and turban in *Percy Jackson & The Olympians: The Lightning Thief* (2010, dir. Chris Columbus), based on Rick Riordan's 2005 novel about a modern-day teenage Perseus. Uma Thurman portrays this character as both sad and glamorous; her dangerous gaze is suppressed by her sunglasses. The same year produced Louis Leterrier's darker remake of *Clash of the Titans*, in which Medusa is once again a hissing monster lurking in ruins, though with a beautiful face; in moments of rage, however, her visage becomes snake-like and delivers a petrifying glare, as when 'Aunty Em' removes her sunglasses. Harryhausen's 1981 Medusa had eyes that glowed when she petrified people, but the gaze of this 2010 Gorgon has developed into a controllable weapon that she can use at will. This is related to another change in twenty-first-century visual media, that Medusa and her sister Gorgons are often scheming villains—an ambiguous form of empowerment. In DC Comics, Medusa is a supervillain nemesis of *Wonder Woman* and her rival in beauty; in Marvel Comics, Medusa recurs as a villain who mainly appears in *Incredible Hercules*, while the Gorgons have numerous descendants, including the warrior Delphyne Gorgon, who is allied with Wonder Woman's Amazons. In general, gorgon figures in popular culture are essentially snake-witches, with serpentine characteristics in varying degrees. Whether petrifaction is a superpower or not, they can often control it.

Medusa is now a canonical monster-type in modern fantasy media, from video games such as Konami's *Castlevania* franchise and *Assassin's Creed: Odyssey* (2018), to contemporary fiction. Within a broader trend of reimagining ancient myths from alternative points of view, contemporary authors have given voices and central roles to mythical women, such as Penelope (Atwood 2005) and Lavinia (Le Guin 2008). Medusa has received similar retellings with feminist approaches across a range of themes: intimacy with Perseus (Burton 2021); sisterhood and pregnancy (Hewlett 2021); Cixous-style feminist allegory (Zimmerman 2021); and tragedy with some dark humour (Haynes 2022). As in classical antiquity, Medusa remains one of the most popular monsters across a wide range of creative media.

CONCLUSIONS

Contrary to how ancient authors and artists imagined her, Medusa is now often identified with female power, especially as cause for anger against patriarchal oppression and masculine violence. Among recent fictional portrayals, many intentionally subvert Medusa's legendary victimhood, instead depicting her as beautiful and independent—though often styling her as villainous. Medusa remains one of the most popular monsters from the ancient world, as part of a vivid and familiar narrative full of supernatural fantasy; she also remains topical, evoking fundamental concerns in gender politics. One defining feature of the ancient Medusa tradition is that most—probably all—of the authors and artists who portrayed her were men. Although this is no longer true (at least since Harriet Goodhue Hosmer's sculpted bust of around 1854), some male artists have intriguingly identified themselves with Medusa. Cellini put a self-portrait on the back of Perseus' helmet and his signature across the hero's swordbelt. Giambattista Marino, in his 1620 poem 'La Galeria', identified himself with a statue of Medusa (ll. 13–16), and Caravaggio even gave the decapitated monster his own face. Another playful twist on the artist's relationship with Medusa appears in Canova's statue of Perseus holding Medusa's head (two versions, 1800–1801 and 1804–1806): Perseus is looking directly at Medusa's face, as a visual pun on the fact that he is made of stone. More recently, Luciano Garbati's 2008 sculpture *Medusa with the Head of Perseus* reversed the roles of the two characters, and a decade later the piece became emblematic of protests against sexism and gender discrimination. There was a subsequent backlash among some protesters, who saw misogyny in the portrayal of Medusa as a beautiful lifelike nude. In an added nuance, Garbati used his own face for the victim Perseus, continuing the tradition of self-portraits described above. Medusa's gaze is evidently transformative even for those trying to see through her eyes.

SUGGESTED READING

Ogden (2008) gives the best summary of the Medusa myth within a thorough and accessible study of Perseus. Wilk (2000) focuses on Medusa, though his conclusion that the *gorgon-eion* represents a drowned person's face is unconvincing. Jameson (1990) interprets the myth of Perseus and Medusa as an initiation ritual, citing a wealth of early sources. Feldman (1965), for whom Medusa is a vestige of a deposed matriarchy, effectively documents the apotropaic function of the *gorgoneion*. Mack (2002) interprets Medusa's power as that of the objectifying gaze, which Perseus then transforms into the power of representation. Garber and Vickers (2003) provide an anthology of different disciplinary approaches to Medusa.

WORKS CITED

Atwood, M. 2005. *The Penelopiad.* Edinburgh.

Burton, J. 2021. *Medusa: The Girl Behind the Myth.* London.

Cixous, H. 1976. 'The Laugh of the Medusa', trans. K. Cohen and P. Cohen. *Signs* 1: 875–93.

Feldman, T. P. 1965. 'Gorgo and the Origin of Fear.' *Arion* 4: 484–94.

Finney, C. 1935. *The Circus of Dr Lao.* New York.

Freud, S. 1941. 'Medusa's Head', trans. J. Strachey. *International Journal of Psycho-Analysis* 22: 69.

Garber, M., and N. J. Vickers, eds. 2003. *The Medusa Reader.* New York.

Haynes, N. 2022. *Stone Blind: Medusa's Story.* London.

Hewlett, R. 2021. *Medusa.* Bristol.

Hirschberger, M. 2000. 'Das Bild der Gorgo Medusa in der griechischen Literatur und Ikonographie.' *Lexis* 18: 55–71.

Jameson, M. H. 1990, 'Perseus, the Hero of Mykenai', in *Celebrations of Death and Divinities in the Bronze Age Argolid*, ed. A. W. Persson, 213–23. Stockholm.

Le Guin, U. K. 2008. *Lavinia.* Orlando, FL.

Mack, R. 2002. 'Facing Down Medusa: An Aetiology of the Gaze.' *Art History* 25: 571–604.

Marconi, C. 2007. *Temple Decoration and Cultural Identity in the Archaic Greek World: The Metopes of Selinus.* Cambridge.

Ogden, D. 2008. *Perseus.* Abingdon.

Roscher, W. H. 1879. *Die Gorgonen und Verwandtes.* Leipzig.

Taylor, R. 2008. *The Moral Mirror in Roman Art.* Cambridge.

Topper, K. 2007. 'Perseus, the Maiden Medusa, and the Imagery of Abduction.' *Hesperia* 76: 73–105.

Wilk, S. R. 2000. *Medusa: Solving the Mystery of the Gorgon.* New York.

Vernant, J.-P. 1989. 'Au miroir de Méduse', in *L'individu, la mort, l'amour: Soi-même et l'autre en Grèce ancienne*, ed. J.-P. Vernant, 117–29. Paris.

Zajko, V., and M. Leonard, eds. 2006. *Laughing with Medusa: Classical Myth and Feminist Thought.* Oxford.

Zimmerman, J. 2021. *Women and Other Monsters: Building a New Mythology.* Boston.

CHAPTER 9

···

THE CHIMAERA

···

R. SCOTT SMITH

INTRODUCTION

THE Chimaera, a fire-breathing monstrous mix of lion, goat, and serpent, takes its name from that middle part: the Greek *chimaira* means 'she-goat'. Perhaps surprisingly, the specific hybridity involving just animals makes the Chimaera rather uncommon among major Greek monsters. Monstrous creatures in the Greek imagination generally fall into three types, with the largest category being human-animal hybrids, such as centaurs. Another type involves multiplying limbs or heads, as with the Hydra. The third category includes exaggerated or prodigious forms of a single creature, such as the Calydonian Boar. The Chimaera's triple animal hybridity—a unique feature—makes for a striking visual representation but also becomes a vivid model for thinking about hybridity more broadly. This is true not only of antiquity (see Pl. *Resp.* 588c; Sen. *Ep.* 113.9) but also of the adoption of the term 'chimera' in the early twentieth century for biological organisms featuring genetic material from different sets of parents (Winkler 1907; *OED*, s.v. 'Chimera', 3d). Meanwhile, the Chimaera's biological impossibility, which prompted rationalizing and allegorizing explanations even in antiquity, has easily led the term 'chimera' to mean 'an imaginary entity', its most common use in the modern period (*OED*, 3b).

In classical myth, monsters like the Chimaera often function as foils for Greek gods and especially heroes to overcome—challenges to display their prowess, strength, and cunning. In one radical exception, it is Heracles who vanquishes the Chimaera, as depicted on a vase by an artist known for such variants (see Dunbabin 1953: 1180–2). But traditionally the conquering hero is Bellerophon, assisted by another hybrid creature, the flying horse Pegasus. Although Bellerophon hails from the Greek Argolid, his victory over the Chimaera is invariably set across the sea in southern Anatolia. The myth's location, combined with other seemingly Near Eastern elements in the broader version told by Homer, has led to claims that the Chimaera, Pegasus, and even Bellerophon originated in Near Eastern cultures, or at least were inspired by them. Even so, we must be careful not to elide the *origins* of the Chimaera with the *setting* and *context* of the narratives in which it appears, all of which are strictly embedded in the Greek context.

WHAT IS THE CHIMAERA?

Although readers may have familiarity with the 'canonical' image of the Chimaera with its three heads, perhaps best represented in the famous bronze statue from Arezzo (Fig. 9.1), the Greeks never quite settled on the exact nature of the monster. The reason for this is largely because Homer's description in *Iliad* 6 is minimal and vague. Also, ancient writers had to account for the fact that the creature took its name from the goat, hardly the most terrifying of animals. This not only caused some consternation among ancient interpreters but also has given rise to some rather contemptuous opinions from modern critics, who have called the Chimaera 'piteous rather than terrific' (Roes 1934: 21) and 'the oddest and least satisfying of the mythical monsters' (West 1966 on Hes. *Theog.* 255). Such an unsatisfying combination did not prevent the myth from being one of the earliest depicted in Greek art.

Our first written reference to the Chimaera's form appears in the *Iliad*, when the Lycian Glaucus recounts his lineage to Greek Diomedes (6.145–211). The story displays

FIGURE 9.1 The bronze Chimaera of Arezzo, *c.*400 BCE.

a 'fascinating cluster of oriental details and motifs' (West 1997: 365). As Glaucus tells it, his grandfather Bellerophon hails from Ephyre, ruled by King Proetus of Argos. The king's wife, here named Anteia, lusts after the young man. When he rejects her, she goes to Proetus and falsely accuses Bellerophon of attempting to violate her. Believing his wife, Proetus sends the youth to her father, a king in Lycia unnamed in Homer but called Iobates elsewhere, with a tablet containing 'grievous signs' (sēmata lugra, 6.168). After receiving Bellerophon hospitably, the king had the tablet interpreted, and, apparently acting on its unrevealed contents, sends him against the Chimaera, which he defeats. Realizing that Bellerophon was loved by the gods, the king gave him land and his other daughter to wife; Bellerophon fathered three children by her, one of whom bore 'Lycian' Sarpedon, and another the Glaucus now telling the story to Diomedes.

Here is Homer's description of the Chimaera:[1]

> First the king ordered him to kill the invincible [amaimaketēn]
> Chimaera, which was of divine stock, not of mortals,
> in front a lion, in back a serpent, in the middle a goat [chimaira],
> dreadfully breathing out [apopneiousa] the might of blazing fire.
> This Bellerophon killed, trusting in the portents of the gods.
>
> (Il. 6.179–83)

While the account seems straightforward, several issues need to be addressed. First, it is unclear what amaimaketos, translated above as 'invincible', actually means; Homer uses it again later of the Chimaera (Il. 16.329), while Hesiod applies the term to the fire vomited by the monster (Theog. 319). Modern critics, following ancient commentators on Homer (schol. [T] Erbse and Eustathius on Il. 6.179, 16.329 = 2.281, 3.283 van der Valk), have tried to etymologize it in various ways. One suggestion is mēkos to emphasize its 'size'; this assumes that Hesiod somehow misunderstood the term. Another is maimaō, 'rush', with an intensive alpha added at the beginning, providing the meaning 'furious'. Still another suggestion is machomai, 'fight', with an alpha privative added that negates the meaning, so 'unconquerable' or 'irresistible'.

Perhaps more crucially, what is the participle apopneiousa, 'breathing out', modifying? The closest noun is chimaira, so if the participle modifies this, the fire-breathing part of the creature would be the goat in the middle. The mythographer Apollodorus interprets it this way (Bibl. 2.31), and we have a c.575 BCE Greek vase illustrating just that (LIMC, s.v. 'Chimaira' 21). But if line 181 is parenthetical, describing the Chimaera as a whole, then it could be that the lion's head at the front is the fire-breathing part—as we find on a vase from c.650 BCE housed in the Boston Museum of Fine Arts (Schmitt 1966: 342, MFA 95.10, no. 400) and in Euripides, who calls the creature a 'fire-breathing lioness' (El. 474).

[1] All translations are mine.

One difficulty here is that Homer specifies parts, not heads. Hesiod clarifies: '[the Chimaera] had three heads, one of a menacing lion, one of a goat, and one of a snake, a mighty serpent' (*Theog.* 321–2). But Homer's description is completely open to interpretation: is there a goat's head, or is it merely a goat body? Are there back legs, or does it trail off into a serpent? And if there are back legs, are they of the goat or of the lion? In fact, Homer's account is so ambiguous that it led to a *zētēma* (a question of interpretation) in Homeric scholarship. An ancient commentator on the passage exemplifies some of the issues (schol. [T] *Il.* 6.181b Erbse):

> If the greater and front part is the lion's, it should have been called 'Lion'. So, the whole is a goat, from which it got its name, but it has the head of a lion and a tail of a snake. Therefore, it is depicted breathing fire from the lion's mouth. Hesiod is misled when he says it was 'three-headed'.

While this explanation—based on the central principle of 'interpreting Homer through Homer' (i.e. without recourse to later traditions)—solves an apparent problem with the name, most visual representations of the Chimaera from the earliest period, which generally depict a goat's head emerging from the body of a lion or (more rarely) a lioness, follow Hesiod's description. Homer's vagueness could, and did, lead to different visualizations of the monster. In terms of the serpent part, for instance, while most artistic representations simply replace the lion's tail with a snake, a stone from the island of Melos and two Athenian vases show the back part of the lion turning into the body of a large, coiled serpent—which perhaps better fits 'the creature verbally described by Homer' (Schmitt 1966: 343; Jacquemin 1986: #98, 99). Certainly there was room to play with the Chimaera's form, as evidenced by the playful depictions on an Etruscan vase (550–525 BCE) housed in the Basel Antikenmuseum (inv. Zü 399 [1 inv.]): opposite a fearsome depiction of a Chimaera formed on a male lion's body is a female version that has just given birth, suckling what looks like a lion cub but may very well be a baby Chimaera, with a budding serpent's tail but no goat head yet (Krauskopf 1986: 263, no. 38, 'lion-baby').

Genealogical Connections

The genealogical information for the Chimaera depends entirely on Hesiod's catalogue of monstrous beings descended from Ceto ('Sea Monster') and Phorcys (a primeval sea god) at *Theogony* 270–336. This passage has its own textual difficulties, including a line with awkward Greek describing the Chimaera as 'fearsome and great and swift-footed and mighty' and merely repeating *Iliad* 6.181–2. Furthermore, as is common in Hesiod's catalogue of monsters, we cannot be entirely sure who the Chimaera's parents are because the antecedent for the pronoun 'she' is unclear in the phrase 'and she bore the Chimaera'. Consequently, modern scholars have proposed various mothers: Ceto (with

Phorcys), the *fons et origo* of the whole catalogue of monsters; the Hydra, the closest feminine monster to the relative pronoun; and Echidna (with Typhon), which would make the Chimaera the sibling of several other multi-headed creatures, including Orthrus, Cerberus, and the Hydra, as well as of the hybrid Sphinx and the Nemean Lion. Later mythographical sources interpreted Hesiod to mean Echidna (e.g. Apollod. *Bibl.* 2.31; cf. 3.52 and Hyg. *Fab.* 151). Of course, it may be unwise to look for certainty in Hesiod's catalogue of monsters. As Jenny Strauss Clay explains, the genealogical confusion adds to the impression 'that the cosmic process of individuation does not fully operate within this tribe', where the 'entire brood is characterized by promiscuous combinations of features and qualities' (1993: 115). In other words, just as these monstrous beings are a confused tangle of different limbs and creatures, so too are their genealogical associations tangled and confused.

Hesiod adds one detail not found explicitly in Homer: the Chimaera is killed by both Bellerophon *and* the flying horse Pegasus (*Theog.* 325; cf. *Cat.* 43a.81–7 MW). Possibly Homer's 'trusting in the portents of the gods' refers obliquely to Pegasus, but in subsequent literature and art the winged horse is front and centre. Pindar sets Bellerophon's bridling of Pegasus, made possible by Athena, specifically in Corinth at the spring of Peirene (*Ol.* 13.60–92); how Pegasus can be integrated into the story of Iobates—does Bellerophon just show up with the horse?—is perhaps a question we should not ask. Although in most depictions Bellerophon overcomes the Chimaera from above, with a spear, some artistic variations show him carrying a sword or striking at the Chimaera with a spear from below—the latter case probably being in the interest of artistic composition (Stibbe 1991). Most vividly, a fragment of Euripides' *Sthenoboea* captures the dramatic moment (fr. 665a): 'I strike into the Chimaera's throat and a tongue of fire | lashes me and scorches the beating wing of this creature [Pegasus].' Without context, we cannot tell whether this presupposes the version, known only from late scholiastic sources, in which Bellerophon attaches lead to his spear and thrusts it into the lion's mouth, whereupon the lead melts and somehow kills the beast (Tzetz. *ad Lyc.* 17; Eust. *Il.* 16.324–41, 3.283.5 van der Valk).

Pegasus, the offspring of Poseidon and Medusa (herself the offspring of Phorcys and Ceto), also has a claim to monstrosity via its physical hybridity, though its support of a hero casts it in a positive light, as does its role as bearer of Zeus' thunder and lightning (Hes. *Theog.* 286; Eur. fr. 312).

THE ORIGIN OF THE CHIMAERA AND THE LYCIAN CONTEXT

The Lycian context announced in *Iliad* 6 is further reinforced in Book 16, where we learn that Amisodarus, presumably a king, reared the Chimaera 'to be a bane for many' (16.328–9; cf. Apollod. *Bibl.* 2.31). That Amisodarus is Lycian is supported by the fact that his two sons, Atymnius and Maris, are soldiers in Sarpedon's Lycian contingent;

etymological analysis of these three names suggest origins in southern Anatolia (Brügger 2018: 150–2, 154; Janko 1995: 357–8). Later, Amisodarus' Lycian connection was used to create a logical eponym for Sidake, a town in Lycia named after his daughter (Steph. Byz. s.v. *Sidakē*). Later writers also place the Chimaera in Lycia, although they disagree as to the exact location.

Lycia served as a crossroads for Greek speakers, native Anatolian cultures, and travellers from further east, so, naturally, much scholarly effort has gone into trying to establish where the image of the hybrid Chimaera originated and to account for the Near Eastern elements in the fuller Bellerophon myth. Many studies have compared the Chimaera to various hybrid creatures from the Hittite world, Cilicia, Mesopotamia, and Luristan (Soldi 2012; Roes 1934, 1953; Tritsch 1957). And yet, while scholars have industriously searched for the missing link between the Chimaera and these earlier hybrids, the Chimaera's form depicted in early Greek literature and art is nowhere to be found in Anatolia or further east (Jacquemin 1986: 256; Iozzo 2012: 113). Perhaps we can at best say that the Chimaera is 'a composite monster which in two at least of three elements agree with Late Hittite iconography' (West 1997: 365). Another study asserts that the Chimaera's origin may derive from the lion-goat companion of the Cilician god Sandas (Mastrocinque 2007), though Bellerophon's connection to Cilicia seems secondary and late, and the presence of the serpent is not easily accounted for. Though doubtlessly inspired by such antecedents, the Chimaera appears to be a particularly Greek creation.

Others have looked to etymology to explain the goat and the fire-breathing nature of the beast, noting that 'Chimaera' may be based somehow on the Semitic root *chmr*, 'fire', 'burning asphalt'—perhaps inspired by the continuous flames erupting from Mount Olympus in Lycia (Malten 1925: 136–7). If so, the monster's name would be a clever bilingual pun and would account for the ingenious but feeble addition of a goat—the 'fire-breather'—to a pre-existing monstrous form. But the idea that the Chimaera was wholly a personification of a natural phenomenon, a concept fashionable in the early twentieth century, seems unlikely. Furthermore, as we have seen, it remains unclear whether the monster's goat portion was originally the fire-breathing part, which further complicates such a theory.

Despite the number of Near Eastern elements uncovered by scholars in the broader Bellerophon myth (West 1997: 364–7; Bachvarova 2016: 421–6, 440–3), we can still only speculate as to how or even when these elements were combined and resulted in the stories told by Homer, Hesiod, and later authors, though various proposals have been put forward. For example, the core myth could possibly belong to the Mycenaean or early Iron Age, reflecting a period of exchange between Mycenaean Greeks and Lycians (Ziskowski 2014: 85). Alternatively, a Greek poet in the court of Lycia may have composed an early Lycian epic, later used by Homer (Frei 1978). Or perhaps the story was invented by 'one or more bilingual poets who had access to both Greek and Syro-Anatolian traditions [who] introduced the obvious Near-Eastern elements of the story' (Bachvarova 2016: 426). In any case, the myth and its characters were embraced by city states in the Argolid and adopted in Corinthian art quite early (Ziskowski 2014; Schmitt 1966). By the mid-sixth century BCE, coinage in Corinth was bearing the likeness of

Pegasus and starting in the fifth century in Sicyon (a city near Corinth) the Chimaera itself was featured on many coins. Bellerophon's cultic associations in Lycia are, by contrast, late and seemingly owed to Hellenization, and the Chimaera figures rarely in art or coinage of the region (Keen 1998: 211–12).

Conclusion: Interpretations

Of course, the Chimaera's monstrous hybridity was deemed impossible according to the laws of nature by later authors who sought to rationalize these stories and often went to absurd lengths to explain how earlier poets and storytellers came up with obviously fabulous creatures and events (see Hawes in this volume; Hawes 2014). Socrates' famous rant against rationalizers includes the Chimaera along with the Hippocentaurs, Gorgons, and other 'inconceivable and portentous natures' (Pl. *Phdr.* 229c–e). As an ancient commentator of unknown date on the *Iliad* bluntly puts it, 'perhaps a he-goat [*chimaros*] raised in a goat-herd went feral; it certainly did not have varied parts, as Hesiod fabricates' (schol. [T] *Il.* 16.328–9; see also Eust. *Il.* 16.324–41, 3.858 van der Valk).

The fullest rationalizing account appears in the late fourth century BCE, in Palaephatus' *On Unbelievable Tales* (28). Palaephatus objects to the very idea of a flying horse (it would be too heavy and does not exist now), the ability of the hybrid parts of the Chimaera to digest the same food, and the notion of a fire-breathing animal. Furthermore, which head would the creature obey? Following his typical approach, Palaephatus reveals the 'real' story and explains how it became mythologized. The Chimaera (he says) was no monster, but simply a well-forested mountain located in King Amisodarus' jurisdiction. The mountain featured a chasm that vomited fire; along the approaches on either side were a lion and serpent that terrorized the woodsmen. Bellerophon, a Corinthian exile, arrived on his ship named *Pegasus* and set fire to the forest, killing the beasts. This perfectly ordinary event was then mythologized through a misunderstanding of the statement by locals: 'Bellerophon came with *Pegasus* and destroyed Amisodarus' Chimaera.' Other rationalizing accounts can be found in Plutarch, *On the Virtues of Women* (247f–248c).

The Chimaera was subjected not only to rationalizing interpretations, but also to allegorizing ones. An ancient commentator on the *Iliad* suggests that Homer was not being literal, but rather was likening aspects of the soul to different animal forms: the lion represented the soul's keenness of sight; the serpent's pliancy, the agility of the soul; and the fiery breath, the aggressive 'spiritedness' (*thumos*; schol. [D] 6.182). Eustathius offers a long list of such allegorical interpretations, for instance that this hybrid creature symbolizes the ills of the soul: gluttony, desire, shamelessness, temper, etc. (Eust. *Il.* 6.179, 2.281 van der Valk).

The sixth-century CE mythographer Fulgentius, in his Christianizing *Mitologiae* offers an improbable etymology in the service of moralizing (3.1): the name 'Chimaera' derives from *cymeron*, 'wave of desire', perhaps related to the common use of 'Chimaera' as a name for a courtesan. The three heads, then, represent the three stages of love: the lion, the onrush of desire; the randy goat, the consummation of love; and the serpent, the poisoned pill of remorse after the fact. Bellerophon, Pegasus, and Antia (Anteia) are likewise etymologized to serve the Christian rejection of lust. Such an interpretation, with Bellerophon 'the wise counsellor' using Pegasus 'the fountain of wisdom' to defeat lust as embodied by the Chimaera, was easily picked up in the medieval period (Valeriano, *Hieroglyphica* 147–8; Bernardus, *On Vergil's Aeneid* 6.287–8; Lydgate, *Reson and Sensuallyte* 3370–82; Fraunce, *Countesse of Pembrokes Yvychurch* 28v–29r).

SUGGESTED READING

Iozzo (2012) and Gantz (1993: 22–3, 312–16) are good starting points for a general discussion of both literary and artistic representations. For a comprehensive catalogue of images, see the two articles in *LIMC*: Jacquemin (1986) (Greece) and Krauskopf (1986) (Etruria). Individual studies on art of note are Schmitt (1966) (Archaic period) and Ziskowski (2014) (Corinthian in Archaic period). On possible Near Eastern antecedents for the Chimaera's form a good starting point is Soldi (2012). On Near Eastern elements in the wider Bellerophon myth, see West (1997: generally, but 364–7 for the Homeric Bellerophon myth) and Bachvarova (2016: 421–43).

WORKS CITED

Bachvarova, M. R. 2016. *From Hittite to Homer: The Anatolian Background of Ancient Greek Epic*. Cambridge.

Brügger, C. 2018. *Homer's Iliad: The Basel Commentary*, trans. B. W. Millis and S. Strack, ed. D. Olson. Boston.

Clay, J. S. 1993. 'The Generation of Monsters in Hesiod.' *Classical Philology* 88: 105–16.

Dunbabin, T. J. 1953. 'Bellerophon, Herakles and Chimaera', in *Studies Presented to David Moore Robinson*, vol. 2, ed. G. E. Mylonas and D. Raymond, 1164–84. Saint Louis.

Frei, P. 1978. 'Die Lykier bei Homer', in *Proceedings of the 10th International Congress of Classical Archaeology, Ankara-Izmir*, ed. E. Akurgal, 819–27. Ankara.

Gantz, T. 1993. *Early Greek Myth: A Guide to Literary and Artistic Sources*, 2 vols. Baltimore.

Hawes, G. 2014. *Rationalizing Myth in Antiquity*. Oxford.

Iozzo, M. 2012, 'The Chimaera, Pegasus and Bellerophon in Greek Art and Literature', in *Myth, Allegory, Emblem: The Many Lives of the Chimaera of Arezzo*, ed. G. C. Cianferoni, M. Iozzo, and E. Setari, 113–37. Rome.

Jacquemin, A. 1986, 'Chimaira', in *LIMC* 3. 249–59. Zurich.

Janko, R. 1995. *The Iliad: A Commentary*, vol. 4. Cambridge.

Keen, A. G. 1998. *Dynastic Lycia: A Political History of the Lycians and Their Relations with Foreign Powers, c.545–362 B.C.* Leiden.

Krauskopf, I. 1986. 'Chimaira in Etruria', in *LIMC* 3. 259–69. Zurich.

Malten, L. 1925. 'Bellerophontes', *Jahrbuch des deutschen Archäologischen Instituts* 40: 121–60.

Mastrocinque, A. 2007. 'The Cilician God Sandas and the Greek Chimaera: Features of Near Eastern and Greek Mythology Concerning the Plague.' *Journal of Ancient Near Eastern Religions* 7: 197–217.

Roes, A. 1934. 'The Representation of the Chimaera.' *Journal of Hellenic Studies* 54: 21–5.

Roes, A. 1953. 'The Origin of the Chimaera', in *Studies Presented to David Moore Robinson*, vol. 2, ed. G. E. Mylonas and D. Raymond, 1155–63. Saint Louis.

Schmitt, M. L. 1966. 'Bellerophon and the Chimaera in Archaic Greek Art.' *American Journal of Archaeology* 70: 341–7.

Soldi, S. 2012. ' "Chimaeric Animals" in the Ancient Near East', in *Myth, Allegory, Emblem: The Many Lives of the Chimaera of Arezzo*, ed. G. C. Cianferoni, M. Iozzo, and E. Setari, 91–109. Rome.

Stibbe, C. M. 1991. 'Bellerophon and the Chimaira on a Lakonian Cup by the Boreads Painter', in *Greek Vases in the J. Paul Getty Museum*, 5. 5–12. Malibu.

Tritsch, F. J. 1957. 'The Lycian Chimaera', in *Proceedings of the Twenty-Second Congress of Orientalists*, vol. 2, 67–78. Leiden.

van der Valk, M. 1971–1987. *Eustathii Archiepiscopi Thessalonicensis Commentarii ad Homeri Iliadem Pertinentes*, 4 vols. Leiden.

West, M. L. 1966. *Theogony*. Oxford.

West, M. L. 1997. *The East Face of Helicon: West Asiatic Elements in Greek Poetry and Mythology*. Oxford.

Winkler, H. 1907. 'Über Pfropfbastarde und pflanliche Chimären.' *Berichte der Deutschen Botanischen Gesellschaft* 25: 568–76.

Ziskowski, A. 2014. 'The Bellerophon Myth in Early Corinthian History and Art.' *Hesperia* 83: 81–102.

CHAPTER 10

....

CERBERUS, HOUND OF HADES

....

DERREK JOYCE

INTRODUCTION

....

MODERN audiences may be familiar with Cerberus (Greek: *Kerberos*) from one of his roles in popular culture. In young adult literature, he served as inspiration for J. K. Rowling's Fluffy, the three-headed, foul-breathed dog guarding the trapdoor leading to a set of underground chambers at Hogwarts in *Harry Potter and the Sorcerer's Stone* (1997). The creature also appeared as himself in Rick Riordan's *The Lightning Thief* (2005), residing underground beneath the city of Los Angeles and acting as guardian of the land of the dead. He has gained a substantial online presence due to his appearance in Supergiant Games' popular role-playing video game *Hades* (2020), where his sole purpose is to be petted by Zagreus, the main protagonist and son of the god Hades, during his attempts to escape his father's domain. He also had a brief cameo appearance in Walt Disney Animation Studios' 2021 animated film *Encanto*, where he is first shown confronting Heracles[1] and then again being defeated by the character Luisa Madrigal.

True to these depictions, in classical mythology this monstrous, multi-headed dog was charged with guarding the entrance to Hades, the Land of the Dead, where his primary function was to prevent the souls of the dead from leaving, as the poet Hesiod (*c.*700 BCE) writes:

> A terrible hound keeps guard without pity and has a wicked system: he wags both his tail and ears alike to those entering, but he does not allow them to go back again, instead, keeping close watch, he eats whomever he catches going outside the gates of Hades and dread Persephone. (*Theog.* 769–73)[2]

---

[1] For the purposes of standardization, the spelling 'Heracles' is used throughout, except in instances where the source material being quoted or cited uses 'Hercules'.

[2] Translations provided by the author unless otherwise noted.

He must also keep the living out, although he apparently failed regularly at this duty, given the number of mortals who managed to infiltrate Hades on his watch (Felton 2014: 77). While Cerberus is not the protagonist of any myths, he features prominently in the story of Heracles and appears briefly in those of other heroes, notably Orpheus, Theseus, Aeneas, and Psyche.

ETYMOLOGICAL CONSIDERATIONS

Before delving into the main stories that feature Cerberus, it is worth noting that often the naming conventions for humanoids and monsters in classical mythology are very on the nose and will either denote the character's role, highlight a prominent trait, foreshadow their fate, or simply state what they are. For example, the names Zeus and Jove—the chief gods in the Greek and Roman pantheons respectively, gods of lightning and fertility—derive from the Proto-Indo-European (PIE) root *dewos-, meaning 'god' or 'shining'. Arachne comes from either the Greek word *arakhnē* or *arakhnēs*, meaning 'spider's web' and 'spider' respectively, alluding to the girl's metamorphosis into a spider (Ov. *Met.* 10.21–2). For a non-mythical example, 'hippopotamus' is a clear compound of the Greek *hippos* and *potamos* ('horse' and 'river').

Cerberus is an example of a character that does not have this luxury. All attempts to provide etymologies for his name have been, as Ogden (2013b: 105) succinctly puts it, 'intriguing, but not yet successful'. Conversations regarding the origins of Cerberus' name trace back to Servius' *Commentary on the Aeneid of Vergil* (late fourth to early fifth century CE). The grammarian equates Cerberus to the earth itself and reports that his name is said to come from the Greek *kreoboros*, meaning 'fed on flesh' (Serv. *In Verg. Aen.* 6.395). At some point following its entrance into the written record, however, the name 'Flesh Eater' fell to the wayside and was dismissed as a folk etymology. This happened as well to the suggestion put forth in the Byzantine *Etymologicum Graecae Linguae Gudianum*, which states that Cerberus comes from *karbaros*, meaning 'heavy-headed', due to the beast having three heads (Sturtz 1818: 316).

Not until the mid- to late-nineteenth century was there a renewed interest in an etymology for the name 'Cerberus'. Unlike their predecessors, however, scholars of this period shifted their focus away from the Greek language and began to incorporate comparative linguistics into their approach, hoping to find the answer in PIE or one of its child languages. The first and by far most popular of these suggested that 'Cerberus' derived from the Sanskrit *śabála*, meaning spotted (cf. Mayrhofer 1956–1976: 1.175 and 3.297–8). This etymology was swiftly rejected by other scholars, such as Frisk (1960–1972: 828–9; also Chantraine 1968: 519; Lincoln 1991: 96; Beekes 2016: 678), but remains prevalent in conversations about Cerberus' name today because of its likeness to modern naming conventions for pets, and many people—typically, internet browsers who are unaware of previous conversations on the matter—have grown fond of the idea that Hades, the gloomy and intimidating Lord of the Dead, had a dog named 'Spot'.

Lincoln, following his dispute of *śabála*, offers an alternative: Cerberus and Garmr, the hound that guards Hel, an afterlife realm in Norse mythology, share the common PIE root *gher-, whose meaning is related to the English 'growl' (1991: 96–106). Beekes and Ogden both doubt the validity of this claim, with Beekes (2016: 678) denouncing it as 'unfounded speculations', and Ogden (2013b: 105) offering that the names of the two dogs must come from two different PIE roots—*ker- and *gher-.

The final two propositions come from an informal conversation on the social media platform Twitter (now X) involving the blog *Sententiae Antiquae*, Prof. D'Angour of the University of Oxford, the Proto-Indo-European Lexicon, and user Bhrigu the Bard. Through their conversation and collective backgrounds, they were able to theorize that Cerberus could have also stemmed from the Proto-Turkic *kara-boru* ('black-wolfhound') or the Phoenician root *klb-ʿrz ('hound of the earth'; *Sententiae Antiquae* 2018). Ultimately, though, further study on these two options would need to be done prior to calling them anything more than musings.

Monstrous Aspects

Homer mentions the 'hound of Hades' only in passing (*Il.* 8.368; *Od.* 11.623–5), leaving Hesiod as our earliest source for the creature's name and origin. Cerberus, who 'eats raw flesh' (Hes. *Theog.* 311; cf. Ogden 2013b: 109–10), is one of the several monstrous children born from the union of Typhoeus, the anguiped giant defeated by Zeus (see Brockliss in this volume), and Echidna, a composite creature whose upper body was that of a nymph and lower half was that of a serpent. Besides Cerberus, this pairing resulted in the births of some of the most well-known monsters of classical mythology. According to Hesiod, Cerberus is the brother of the Chimaera, the Lernaean Hydra, and Orthrus, who, like Cerberus, was a multi-headed watchdog with a serpent for a tail; he served the giant Geryon (*Theog.* 304–25). In contrast to Cerberus, however, Orthrus is consistently described in literature after Hesiod as having two heads. The second-century CE mythographer Hyginus, meanwhile, makes no mention of Cerberus' relation to Orthrus, instead including Scylla, the Sphinx, the dragon of Colchis, and the dragon of the Hesperides among his siblings (Hyg. *Fab. praef.* 151).

Given his monstrous parents and siblings, it is no surprise that Cerberus is, in most of his iterations, a composite of canine and serpentine parts. Hesiod describes Cerberus as a fifty-headed dog who stands guard before the palace of Hades (*Theog.* 769–70). The Greek poet Pindar (*c.*518–438 BCE) gave the creature at least one hundred heads (F249a/b SM); in the first-century BCE, the Roman poet Horace (*Carm.* 2.13.34) and the satirical *Apocolocyntosis* (13.3) continue this minor tradition. Most writers, however, gave Cerberus only three heads, along with multiple snakes sprouting from his body to represent his chthonic nature. This depiction grew to the point of popularity that by the late Roman Republic, the epithet *triceps* ('three-headed') primarily became associated with Cerberus (e.g. Cic. *Tusc.* 1.10), though also used for Hecate (*Met.* 7.194). Apollodorus

(*Bibl.* 2.122), Ovid (*Her.* 93–4), Vergil (*Aen.* 6.417–22; *G.* 4.483), and Seneca (*Herc. fur.* 783–97) all describe Cerberus as having three heads, a draconian tail, and snakes along his body.

From Greek vase paintings of the sixth to the fourth centuries BCE, we learn that the additional serpents can appear as a leonine mane, as a trail along his spine running parallel to his rib bones, or a combination of the two. But many of these depictions limit the dog to two heads, most likely due to a combination of space issues and the difficulties of creating depth while painting in profile, as was common at the time (Fig. 10.1; *LIMC*, s.v. 'Hades' 141; 'Herakles' 2558, 2583, et al.; Ogden 2013b: 106). Occasionally, Cerberus has a serpent tail and snakes emerging only from his heads and/or paws (e.g. *LIMC*, s.v. 'Herakles' 2554, 2581, 2616). Authors such as the third-century BCE poet Euphorion denote the dog's composite form exclusively with a serpent tail (fr. 121), which can appear in art literally or as a tail stylized after a serpent (*LIMC*, s.v. 'Hades' 127, 135; 'Herakles' 2570, 2582, et al.; 'Hermes' 526). Of course, some writers entirely neglect to mention Cerberus' connections to *drakontes*, making his only physical descriptor his additional heads (Hyg. *Fab.* 32, 151; Stat. *Theb.* 2.27, 52; Ov. *Met.* 6.19).

FIGURE 10.1 Heracles and Cerberus, depicted with a serpent tail and only two heads. Attic red-figure amphora by the Andocides Painter, *c.*530–520 BCE.

Source: Durand Collection, 1836, F 204. Public domain.

https://commons.wikimedia.org/wiki/File:Herakles_Kerberos_Louvre_F204.jpg

Through the second-century CE travel writer Pausanias we learn that the early Greek historian Hecataeus of Miletus (*c.*550–476 BCE) favoured a different form for Cerberus altogether: Cerberus was not a composite creature, but rather a serpent that was referred to as the 'hound of Hades' for its deadly bite, and it was this monster that Heracles brought back to his cousin Eurystheus for the last of his Twelve Labours. This description of Cerberus is part of a larger, almost euhemeristic explanation for two things: first, why a cave in Laconia in southern Greece is associated with Heracles' final task, even though the cave contains no path leading underground; and second, why the idea that the gods have a physical space underground where they collect souls is difficult to believe (3.25.5–7). But this description also engages with the tradition of another classical monster archetype: by styling Cerberus as a serpent, Hecataeus adapts the story into a typical dragon-slaying myth—wherein a visiting hero subdues a dragon that is a known blight to the local flora and fauna—and merges it with the established canon of Heracles. Given the extensive evidence contemporary with Hecataeus establishing that the canine-composite form was the one most people envisioned for the creature, it seems unlikely that Hecataeus' cave-dwelling serpent was more than part of a minor or regional variant of the myth.

Of course, other ancient authors focused on Cerberus' canine aspects and made attempts to rationalize the creature into a different, less-than-fantastical form. The Greek historian Philochorus (*c.*340–261 BCE) rationalizes the story of Heracles saving Theseus from Hades for attempting to abduct Persephone by setting it in the mortal sphere, with Hades and Persephone as mortal rulers. Cerberus here is just a very large dog, one big enough to have devoured Theseus' companion Pirithous (*FGrH* 328 F18b; Ogden 2013a: 73). Heraclitus the paradoxographer, not content with ignoring the established tradition surrounding Cerberus' multiple heads, suggests that Cerberus had two puppies that consistently accompanied him on either side, thus creating the 'illusion' that the dog had three heads (Stern 2003: 88 = *On Unbelievable Tales* 33). Similarly, the paradoxographer Palaephatus (fourth century BCE) says that Cerberus got the epithet 'three-headed' because he was from the city of Tricranium (Stern 1996: 71 = *On Unbelievable Tales* 39; see also Hawes in this volume).

Drawing on Cerberus' connections to monstrous serpents and serpentine beings, Ovid portrays Cerberus as having abilities like those of Medusa: a man who saw the beast triple-headed dog (under circumstances Ovid leaves unclear) was so terrified that he turned to stone (*Met.* 10.65–7; Felton 2014: 78). This ability to instil fear in those who saw him—which nowhere elsewhere in extant literature resulted in petrification—was not limited to his appearance; his thunderous barking, too, emanating from three separate throats, unnerved those who heard it. Yet the sources make clear that the image of Cerberus alone is enough to instil fear, even in the gods themselves. The first-century BCE playwright Seneca opens his *Hercules furens* with Juno lamenting Heracles' very existence—the result of Jupiter having impregnated a mortal woman—and explaining to the audience the crime Heracles has committed against the natural order by bringing the hound up from Hades. During this monologue, she specifically says, 'I saw the daylight grow weak at the sight of Cerberus and the Sun become terrified. A trembling fell upon me, too' (*Herc. fur.* 60–1).

Regardless of the shape he took, Cerberus was able to assert his dominance over both the living and the dead through his ability to see in all directions using his multitude of heads and his only natural weapon: his mouths. Early in the literary record, Cerberus appears to have been able to devour all—souls, flesh, and, in Aristophanes' comedic rendition, dinner scraps (*Eq.* 1030–4). Hesiod, describing Cerberus' stratagems for keeping the dead in Hades, mentions that the dog will eat any soul trying to leave (*Theog.* 772–3). While Hesiod does not clarify the composition of a soul and whether the dead could have corporeal forms, Homer, an approximate contemporary of Hesiod, specifies that when people die, their souls leave the physical body (e.g. *Il.* 22.361–3). Regardless of Hesiod's thoughts on the anatomy of a soul, Cerberus does not exhibit the ability to devour the dead and there comes a shift in the ways he maintains order. Classical authors, especially under the Roman Empire, paid particular attention to Cerberus' bark: Hesiod assigns him the epithet 'brazen-voiced'; Ovid and Vergil both refer to his triple-throated barking (*ternis latratibus*, *Met.*7.414; *latratu trifauci*, *Aen.* 6.417); and, in his poem marking the recent death of Augustus' nephew, Propertius laments that all must entreat the 'barking, three-headed dog' (*canis tria latrantia colla*, Prop. 3.18.23). By the second century CE, the creature's terrifying bark becomes one of his most essential assets, as it is the only way he can keep the dead at bay (Apul. *Met.* 6.19).

Meanwhile, the mythology surrounding Cerberus' ability to harm the living only grew. In his retelling of Heracles' twelfth labour, Ovid, once again elaborating upon Cerberus' maternal heritage, explains that the poisonous plant aconite (monkshood or wolfsbane) was created from the dog's saliva. When Heracles first brought him up from the underworld, Cerberus had an adverse reaction to the sunlight and, in his anger, 'simultaneously filled the air with barking from all three [jaws] and spattered the green fields with white foam'. The spittle, here reminiscent of snake venom, seeped into the soil and, thus, the plant was born (*Met.* 7.414–15). Ovid also notes that the sorceress Medea attempted to use a poison brewed from aconite to kill her stepson Theseus, referring to the perennial as one that 'originated from the teeth of the Echidnean dog' (*Met.* 7.408–9).

ROLE IN GREEK AND ROMAN MYTH

The ancient sources tell us virtually nothing about Cerberus' early life beyond his birth or how he became the hound of Hades; rather, the myths centre on the heroes with whom he interacts. The most notable of these was Heracles. The Greek hero, famous for his strength, was assigned twelve horrendous tasks—known as the 'Labours of Heracles'—to atone for killing his wife and children in a fit of madness caused by the jealous goddess Hera. The twelfth and final task, a representation of Heracles' conquest of death itself, was to fetch Cerberus from Hades. The methods by which Heracles accomplishes such a feat are left to the discretion of individual authors and artists. There are, however, three principal variants of the story. The first and most common version is that when Heracles asks Hades for Cerberus, the god tells him that he may take the animal as long as he masters him without the use of weapons. So, Heracles flings his arms around the creature's head and, in true Herculean fashion, bests the creature with his strength. He then manages to carry the dog—or lead him on a chain—back to Eurystheus, who had assigned the Labours, all the while being subjected to bites from Cerberus' serpentine tail (see Fig. 10.1). Having proven himself, Heracles returns the creature to Hades (e.g. Apollod. *Bibl.* 2.5.12; Sen. *Herc. fur.* 797–804). The second variant of the myth, alluded to by Greek epic poets Homer (*Il.* 5.395–7, 367–8) and Panyassis (F26 West 2003), as well as by the Greek tragic poet Euripides (*HF* 612–13) and on a bowl from the early sixth century BCE (*LIMC*, s.v. 'Herakles' 2553), requires Heracles to defeat Hades himself with either an arrow or a stone before attempting to handle his dog. The third method for obtaining Cerberus is far less challenging: Persephone greets her half-brother Heracles as family and freely gives him the dog, already harnessed for the journey (e.g. Diod. Sic. 4.26.1; Plut. *Nic.* 1.3).

No matter how Heracles was able to secure the beast, Cerberus had an unfavourable, often violent reaction to being brought into the daylight of the world above. The most vivid description of this moment comes from Theseus' monologue in the Roman playwright Seneca's *Hercules furens*:

> After they had come to the shores of Taenarum and the novel brightness of unfamiliar light hit his eyes, he regained his previously overcome spirit and, raging, shook the immense chains.... And then Hercules looked to my hands; through both our strength we brought the dog, who was drawn raving with anger and attempting to fight in vain, to our world. When he saw the bright daylight and gazed upon the clear expanses of the shining heavens, blindness overtook him—he surrendered his eyes towards the ground, closed them, and drove out the hated day. He turned his face backwards and sought the earth with all his necks; then he hid his head in the shadow of Hercules. (813–27)

What is beautiful and astonishing about this moment in Seneca's play, and this moment in Cerberus' mythology overall, is that the hound's ascent to the overworld and his reaction to daylight is the only time that audiences can perceive the beast as a dynamic character. In all other situations involving Cerberus, he is nothing more than an obstacle to overcome. But in this moment, and especially in Seneca's rendition, Cerberus goes through a clear emotional journey. Just before emerging from his home underground, Seneca's Cerberus is defeated and docile, having submitted himself to Heracles' adamantine collar after the hero has clubbed him into submission. Seneca notes that over the course of their ascension Cerberus begins to act as a house pet would: he drops his guard, wags his tail, and allows himself to be led by Heracles (*Herc. fur.* 798–812). As seen above, though, this relaxed state does not last long and, once Cerberus experiences sunlight for the first time, his natural fight-or-flight response takes hold until Heracles subdues him again, this time with Theseus' assistance. It remains unclear if Cerberus retains this posture denoting his fear and discomfort—heads low to the ground and walking in Heracles' shadow—for the remainder of their journey to Eurystheus.

Few heroes who bested Cerberus had to do so by force; most were able to control him through much less violent means. The legendary musician Orpheus, for example, descending into Hades on a quest to resurrect his wife Eurydice after she had died of a snakebite, charms the beast with a song. Vergil describes how this music left Cerberus simply standing still with his mouths agape, unbarking (*G.* 4.483). The hero Aeneas, guided to Hades by the Cumaean Sibyl, can pass by Cerberus only because the seer tosses to the 'gigantic, triple-jawed, snaky-necked' dog a honey-flavoured lump of flour laced with soporific herbs. After greedily gulping the treat down all three of his throats, the ravenous creature promptly falls asleep, its huge length stretched along the cavern floor (*Aen.* 6.417–25; Felton 2014: 78). In Apuleius' *Metamorphoses* (second century CE), the heroine Psyche distracts Cerberus in a similar manner. Psyche had been assigned a series of dangerous tasks by the goddess Venus, who was envious of Psyche's beauty and furious that her own son Cupid had fallen in love with the mortal girl. After being ordered by Venus to go to the underworld, Psyche, despairing of the impossible task, climbed a tower intending to plummet to her death. But the Tower itself spoke to Psyche, helpfully providing directions to Hades and instructing Psyche to bring with her two barley cakes, explaining that although Cerberus cannot harm the souls of the dead, he *can* harm the living, and that she should distract the creature by offering him a barley cake (*Met.* 6.19; Felton 2014: 79). As with the Sibyl's offering in Vergil, Cerberus contentedly snacks on the treats, allowing Psyche to pass safely in and out of Dis.

Not everyone attempting to travel to Hades had the strength, skill, or guidance required to surmount Cerberus. Through the Byzantine scholar Tzetzes' scholia on the Greek playwright Aristophanes' comedy *Frogs* we learn the story of Pirithous, in whose punishment Cerberus played a key role. Pirithous was the King of the Lapiths, a legendary people based in Thessaly. When his wife died, and Theseus' had died as well, the two kings make a pact to help each other secure new brides. Theseus wants none other than Helen of Sparta—more famously known later as Helen of Troy—who was but a child at this point. Pirithous, meanwhile, sets his eyes on a loftier target: Persephone, queen of Hades. In most versions of their attempt to kidnap the goddess, the story concludes with Pirithous and Theseus stuck to chairs in the underworld, with Theseus ultimately saved by Heracles during his twelfth labour, as mentioned above, and Pirithous left behind as punishment for the audacity of his crime (Apollod. *Bibl.* 2.5.15). Tzetzes, however, tells us that the retribution may have been worse: Heracles finds only Theseus trapped on a chair, Pirithous having been devoured by Cerberus (Gantz 1993: 295).

Conclusion

Unlike most monsters in classical mythology, Cerberus assists in maintaining the natural order as set by the Olympian gods, rather than disrupting it. He becomes an obstacle to a hero/heroine or soul only when they try to defy that order and, either symbolically or literally, overcome death. Thus, Cerberus does not symbolize the all-devouring earth, as suggested by Honoratus, but rather the (supposedly) impassable barrier between life and death. This is why Cerberus' design is so functional. His two duties are to monitor this barrier to ensure that none pass (hence the multiple heads, which can look in all directions at once) and to stop those who attempt to breach it by eliminating them or frightening them off. These functions also highlight the significance of Hades' request that Heracles not harm the dog: if Heracles were to kill Cerberus, Heracles not only would have conquered death itself but also would have ensured that others could do the same without hindrance.

As we have seen, however, if someone wanted to pass Cerberus and had enough fortitude, they could do so with a song or offering of food. In this way, Cerberus is not unlike the common guard dog seen in life and in media; the trope of tossing a slab of meat or a bone to the hound on duty is quite common. This similarity to and the consistency in behavioural patterns with beloved pets makes him one of the most relatable classical monsters to modern audiences, which, in turn, allows for him to be effortlessly inserted into fantastical content and capture the imagination of a new generation.

Suggested Reading

For another comprehensive overview of Cerberus, see Ogden (2013b: 104–15), who specifically examines him through the lens of his draconic heritage and explores his relationship to the great dragons of classical mythology. Gantz (1993) is a good resource for early iterations of the Cerberus myths. For artistic depictions of Cerberus, no source has yet compiled a visual encyclopaedia quite like the *LIMC*. Further information regarding Heracles' feats can be found in Ogden (2021) and López-Ruiz (2014); the latter places Heracles' entire narrative within the broader context, drawing comparisons to Mesopotamian, Egyptian, Near Eastern mythologies, providing added depth. For an overview of ancient Greek etymologies, see Beekes (2016).

Works Cited

Beekes, R. S. P., ed. 2016. *Etymological Dictionary of Greek*, 2 vols. Leiden.

Chantraine, P. 1968. *Dictionnaire étymologique de la langue grecque*. Paris.

Felton, D. 2014. 'Cerberus', in *The Ashgate Encyclopedia of Literary and Cinematic Monsters*, ed. J. A. Weinstock, 77–80. Farnham.

Frisk, H. 1960–1972. *Griechisches etymologisches Wörterbuch des Altindisches*, 3 vols. Heidelberg.

Gantz, T. 1993. *Early Greek Myth: A Guide to Literary and Artistic Sources*, 2 vols. Baltimore.

Lincoln, B. 1991. *Death, War, and Sacrifice: Studies in Ideology & Practice*. Chicago.

López-Ruiz, C., ed. 2014. *Gods, Heroes, and Monsters: A Sourcebook of Greek, Roman, and Near Eastern Myths in Translation*. Oxford.

Mayrhofer, M. 1956–1976. *Kurzgefasstes etymologisch Wörterbuch des Altindisches*, 4 vols. Heidelberg.

Ogden, D. 2013a. *Dragons, Serpents, and Slayers in the Classical and Early Christian Worlds: A Sourcebook.* Oxford.

Ogden, D. 2013b. *Drakōn: Dragon Myth & Serpent Cult in the Greek & Roman Worlds.* Oxford.

Ogden, D. 2021. *The Oxford Handbook of Heracles.* Oxford.

Sententiae Antiquae. 2018. 'No, Internet, Kerberos is Probably Not "Spot".' https://sententiae antiquae.com/2018/08/11/no-internet-kerberos-is-probably-not-spot/. Accessed 15 August 2021.

Stern, J., trans., 1996. *Palaephatus: On Unbelievable Tales.* Wauconda, IL.

Stern, J. 2003. 'Heraclitus the Paradoxographer: "On Unbelievable Tales".' *Transactions of the American Philological Association* 133/1: 51–97.

Sturz, F. W., ed. 1818. *Etymologicum Graecae Linguae Gudianum.* Leipzig.

West, M. L., trans. 2003. *Greek Epic Fragments from the Seventh to the Fifth Centuries BC.* Cambridge, MA.

CHAPTER 11

DOWN THE SINKHOLE

The Lernaean Hydra

SUSAN DEACY

INTRODUCTION

THE many-headed Lernaean Hydra has long provided an excellent example of a Greek mythological monster. Indeed, so popular in the imagination is the Hydra that, like Scylla and Charybdis, this figure has made her way into ancient and modern metaphor. Best known in ancient Greek myth as the object of Heracles' second labour, her physical monstrosity consisted not only of excess heads, but also in her ability to grow two new heads for every one that was severed. Hence, 'hydra' has been used since antiquity to refer to any persistent, complicated problem that cannot be easily solved. For example, by the early fourth century BCE, the hydra metaphor was already so well established in Greek thought that Plato's Socrates could compare the efforts of men trying to end business fraud to the futility of trying to cut off the Hydra's heads (*Resp.* 427a). Similarly, Socrates couches *logos* ('argument') in terms of the Hydra: when one avenue of debate is cut off, many rise in its place (*Euthyd.* 297c).

Indeed, the Hydra allows us to investigate ancient Greek concepts of monsters and the monstrous, and especially of how the ancient Greeks constructed their own cultural categories (see Gloyn 2019; Deacy 2020). According to Jeffrey Jerome Cohen (1996: 20), monsters, 'our children', do not exist beyond their construction; that construction is a fluid one, and dissipates when articulated. Define a monster and the monster will break up, but expel a monster and it will somehow return. Set at the 'gates of difference' (7), monsters mark out boundaries of what is permissible and desirable—or not. Given Cohen's theory of a monster that keeps falling apart, it is possible to explore how far the Hydra is located between worlds and 'something other than itself' (4). Read with Cohen in mind, the Hydra makes sense only in relation to what she is not. I intend to explore the Hydra for what she *is*, however, and especially to examine the extent to which the Hydra is constructed as a creature with so much coherence that she has her own biography and genealogy and even personality. But I shall also investigate how far the Hydra so escapes categorization that the terms 'creature' or 'person' or indeed 'monster' might present an oversimplified taxonomy for conveying the alterity of the Hydra.

In what follows, I examine the specific locality, Lerna, where the Hydra emerges and resides and where she is eventually killed—but where, in a sense, she lives on. Then I ask how to classify the Hydra in terms of the type of creature she most closely resembles and in terms of whether creature—or, for instance, 'beast' or 'serpent'—is even the best term to convey her. Then—building on my discussions of locality and terminology—I turn to the Hydra's genealogy, specifically as described in Hesiod's *Theogony*. Then, I shall consider just how far the Hydra is connected to Heracles, as one who is killed by him but whose venom enables his later exploits before finally killing Heracles himself. I shall end with a discussion of how the desire to understand the phenomenon of the Hydra has given rise to ancient, and to very recent, rationalizing explanations.

THE HYDRA'S LIMINAL LOCATION

The prodigious one-offs of ancient Greek myth, often huge like the Hydra, are usually located in faraway places. One of the Hydra's relatives, the serpent Ladon, guards the golden apples in the garden at the world's end. Medusa and her Gorgon sisters inhabit a region 'on the border of Night', while the gigantic, snaky Echidna—traditionally the Hydra's mother—dwells in a cave 'under the depths of the earth ... far from the immortal gods and mortal men' (Hes. *Theog.* 275, 300–2). The Hydra, meanwhile, is a creature of these liminal spaces in one sense, but not another. The locality she inhabits, Lerna, is a place firmly situated within the landscape of ancient Greece, in the Peloponnese, the region of Heracles' first six Labours. Situated near the coast, Lerna is also curious, ambiguous terrain, alternating between abundant water or drought, with many lakes and marshes and rivers. The karstic earth here, characterized by eroded limestone, contains many fissures and caverns, and rivers can disappear down sinkholes.

The same features contributed to Lerna's traditional reputation as the location of a cave that served as an entrance to the underworld, situated among the springs of the Lernaean lake and the nearby Alcyonian Lake. Multiple myths and local legends mention this underworld connection. For example, Lerna is associated with the Danaids, young women said to have discovered various wells in the region, who end up in Hades destined to fetch water in leaky pitchers for eternity. Their fate was punishment for what they did at Lerna: they killed their new husbands (whom they had not wished to marry) and buried their bodies near the lake (Strabo 8.6.9; Paus. 2.24.2). But a spring was named after Amymone ('blameless'), the one Danaid who refused to kill her husband. Another connection comes from the myths about the god Dionysus, said to have entered Hades via an entrance near (or in) the Alcyonian Lake to bring back his deceased mother, Semele. And at least one ancient source identifies Lerna as the place where Hades emerged from the earth to abduct Persephone and then descended again to his underground realm (Paus. 2.36.7; 3.27.1).

While it was possible to travel through Lerna, the region was considered a place of dangers, the main threat being the Hydra who, according to the mythographer Apollodorus (*c.* first/second century CE), would leave her lair to destroy the local cattle and country (*Bibl.* 2.5.2). But the Alcyonian Lake itself also posed a danger. According to the geographer Pausanias (second century CE), despite the lake's calm and quiet surface, any swimmer who dared to cross it 'was dragged down and carried off into its depths', which were thought to be bottomless (2.37.5–6). In contrast, the waters of Lake Lerna were believed to have healing powers, and the many cleansings that took place there gave rise to the proverb 'a Lerna of ills' (*Lernē kakōn*; Strabo 8.6.8). Nearby, at the source of the spring Amymone, grew a plane tree, beneath the roots of which the Hydra grew (Paus. 2.37.4).

The Hydra herself encapsulates the dangers of Lerna, adding poisonous vapours to the list; her breath was supposedly so noxious that it could kill mortals (Hyg. *Fab.* 30), and foul aromas have traditionally been linked to the site. The Hydra, then, has a particular association with an oddly liminal area of the Argolid known for its sinkholes and likely for its smell, an area that was also known (probably in part thanks to its sinkholes) as affording a gateway to the underworld—one seemingly guarded by the Hydra.

AN UNEXPECTED HYBRID

But what kind of creature is the Lernaean Hydra? The Greek word *hydra*, related to *hydōr* ('water') certainly suggests an aquatic association, and the Hydra is typically depicted as serpentine, that is, as a sort of gigantic water snake. The existence of other 'hydras' can be inferred from Pausanias, who says he believes that the Lernaean Hydra 'surpassed other hydras in size' (2.37.4), and in fact the term was regularly used to indicate a 'water snake'. Thus, to distinguish the Hydra from hydras, ancient Greek authors employed various descriptive terms. Some writers use the word *drakōn* ('serpent', 'dragon'), as for example Sophocles in his play *Trachiniae* (834). Other words applied to the Hydra throughout Greek literature include *thērion* ('beast') and, perhaps most notably, *pelōron* ('prodigy') a word frequently applied to 'unnatural' beings, as by Hesiod in his *Theogony* (295, 299), and which might also be translated as 'monster'.

Fig. 11.1 shows the characteristically multi-headed Hydra. The number of her heads varies in ancient written and artistic sources from as few as nine (as here) to as many as a hundred; determining a precise figure misses the point, given the Hydra's regenerative nature, which posed such a problem for Heracles and which has a bearing on how to classify the creature. Heracles initially attempts to deal with the Hydra as a conventional kind of opponent: she has many heads, so he sets about cutting them off. But in the place of each severed head grow two more. Thus, when Heracles tries to kill her by traditional methods, she rallies all the more vigorously. In this respect she does not behave like an

FIGURE 11.1 Heracles (right) and his nephew Iolaus (left) fighting the Hydra. Hydria (water-jug) from Caere, Etruria, *c.*525 BCE.

Source: Wikimedia / Wolfgang Sauber. CC BY-SA 3.0.

animal, which would normally die when decapitated; rather, she responds botanically, as a tree benefits from being coppiced.

One way to consider the Hydra, then, instead of simply as a type of monstrosity with excess limbs, is as a hybrid figure that falls between clear definitions of plant and animal. Such a perspective would be in keeping with ancient conceptions about the possibility of sentient plants, as expressed by various Presocratic philosophers and later by Aristotle, Galen, and others (Wilberding 2014), especially in relation to the regenerative properties of vegetation. The vocabulary surrounding the Hydra's growth also hints at its plant nature: *traphēnai*, describing the Hydra's growth at the root of the plane tree (Paus. 2.37.4), is a general Greek term for 'grow' used of both plants and animals, while *anephuonto*, describing the two heads that grow in place of any one that is cut off (Apollod. *Bibl.* 2.5.2), is frequently used of plants, in the sense of to 'shoot up' and 'produce' branches and leaves.

Therefore, 'creature' might not be the best term to convey the distinctive traits of the Hydra, who, when under attack, responds like a tree being coppiced rather than a creature being decapitated. By moving outside corporeality as a botanical entity, does the Hydra encapsulate ancient Greek concepts of monstrosity, or does she pose a challenge to the very category of 'monster' when it is applied to ancient Greece? Or does the Hydra typify the monster who, as defined by Stephen Asma (2009: 125), 'disrupt[s] the neat categories of taxonomy'? Indeed, as one who keeps returning—stronger after each attempt at killing her—is the Hydra the exemplary monster as envisaged by Cohen (see above)? As I shall now consider, the Hydra's nature, strange even in comparison with the fabulous creatures of classical myth, relates to her genealogy.

DISORDERED ORIGINS

Like nearly every other creature defined as monstrous in ancient Greek myth, the Hydra first appears in Hesiod's *Theogony* ('Origin of the Gods'), a *c.*700 BCE poem describing the origins of the cosmos and everything in it. The early stages of creation seem frenzied and experimental, with all sorts of marvellous and uncanny creatures coming into being. The poem's passage about the Hydra's birth is notable both for what it says about her and for what it does *not* say. Hesiod presents his monstrous genealogies in rapid succession: while the Titans and Olympians result from the union of Gaea and Uranus (Earth and Sky), most of the non-anthropomorphic entities result from the mating of two beings called Phorcys and Ceto, early sea deities. Among their descendants is the creature known as Echidna, twice described as a 'prodigy' or 'monster' (*pelōron*: *Theog.* 295, 299), half nymph, half immense, mottled snake, who lives in a cave far under the earth. Mating with Typhaon (see Brockliss in this volume), Echidna conceives and bears various monstrous children, including the fifty-headed Cerberus and the Lernaean Hydra. Hesiod adds that the goddess Hera raised the Hydra as part of her plan to take revenge upon Heracles, and that Heracles, aided by Iolaus, killed the creature with his sword.

Hesiod does not, however, physically describe the Hydra or her behaviour, in contrast to his treatment of Cerberus, the Chimaera, and many of the other anomalous beings who appear in the *Theogony* whose principal traits he recounts. After Hesiod, various ancient sources clearly state that the Hydra is multi-headed like Cerberus and the Chimaera, serpentine like Echidna, and has regenerative powers. All Hesiod provides is the Hydra's parentage, along with the rather vague epithet *lugra iduian*, which could mean 'bane-knowing', 'evil-minded', or even 'understanding woeful things' (*Theog.* 313), given that *lugra* (here a plural form) carries a wide variety of possible meanings, including 'woes', 'banes', 'miseries', 'misfortunes', and 'mournful experiences'. Hesiod also described the Hydra's mother, Echidna, as *lugrē* (304), probably indicating 'baneful Echidna' in the sense that she is a creature who produces misery. So, the phrase *lugra iduian* could intimate the effect of the Hydra on others, suggesting, for instance, the suffering that could be inflicted by her appearance, breath, or destructive behaviour.

Alternatively, however, *lugra iduian* could also suggest misfortunes that the Hydra herself suffers rather than pointing to any monstrosity. To take this possibility further, while also keeping a focus on the Hydra as one who inflicts ills, let us look back at how Hesiod describes another of the descendants of Phorcys and Ceto: the Gorgon Medusa, whose distinctive appearance and abilities are, even more than those of the Hydra, narrated in detail in other ancient sources. Especially notable is the emphasis these sources place on how she is able to inflict suffering on others: a glance at her turns them to stone (see Lowe in this volume). Yet, as with the Hydra, Hesiod does not provide a description of Medusa's physical attributes. He says only that she is the one who, among the three Gorgons, was mortal and *lugra pathousa*—'bane-experiencing', 'suffering sorrows' (*Theog.* 276). Medusa is headed for a woeful fate: mortal rather than immortal like her sisters, she can (and will) be deflowered and decapitated. Indeed, Hesiod focuses not on Medusa's appearance but on her death at Perseus' hands, framing her narrative in terms of what she suffers (see Bachvarova 2013). The Hydra, too, as one linked with *lugra*, ends up a victim when killed by Heracles, aided by his nephew Iolaus—all in keeping with the plans of Athena, Heracles' divine mentor, who constantly worked to counter Hera's fury against the hero.

HERA, THE HYDRA, AND HERACLES

Hera's enmity against Heracles arises, as set out in many ancient accounts, because the hero was the child of Zeus and a mortal woman. Zeus' constant affairs generally resulted in his wife's anger against either the woman, her offspring, or both, inasmuch as Hera was unable to punish Zeus himself. The Hydra, then, is nourished by Hera with the intent that the creature will share the goddess' anger and aid her goal: to kill Heracles. There is a certain irony in this, as Hera has also nurtured Heracles himself, suckling him at her breast, though, having been tricked by Athena, she did not realize that it was Zeus' illegitimate child she was nourishing (Diod. Sic. 4.9). Hera's breast milk was in part responsible for the child's supernatural strength (see Pedrucci 2017). Moreover, Hera's tending to the Hydra is part of a larger pattern: the goddess typically nurtures some monster or other with the aim of destroying a particular figure against whom she bears an immense grudge (O'Brien 1993: 77–111; Deacy 2021), but her plans inevitably fail. She had also reared the Nemean Lion, another offspring of Echidna, in order to make it a 'misery for humans (*pēma anthrōpōn*, Hes. *Theog.* 330), most specifically for Heracles. The Lion was the object of the hero's first labour, but he dispatched it handily, wearing its skin thereafter as a trophy. Hera's plan for the Hydra similarly fell through (though see below). Certainly, the multi-headed creature at least presented more of a challenge to Heracles than the Nemean Lion: he required the help of his nephew, who cauterized each stump after Heracles cut off a head, which prevented its swift regeneration. But the Hydra had one immortal head, so after Heracles hacked this one off and Iolaus burned its neck, the hero buried it under a huge boulder to immobilize it (Apollod. *Bibl.* 2.5.2).

While Heracles and Iolaus were fighting the Hydra, Hera added to the challenge by bringing in a helper of her own, just like Heracles does. In her case, it is gigantic crab (*karkinos hypermegethēs*, Apollod. *Bibl.* 2.5.2); the intrusion of this marine creature serves as a reminder that Lerna lies close to the sea. The crab bites Heracles on his foot but—contrary to his experience with the Hydra—he kills it easily, as a mere distraction, before turning back to the Hydra. The various figures involved in the encounter, the crab included, appear in various visual depictions of the scene, including Fig. 11.1, where the crab is just visible in the lower right biting Heracles' foot. In this specific representation, Heracles uses his club; others depict him using a sword against the Hydra, and both versions appear in literary sources.

Heracles' victory in this second labour is by no means as clear-cut as his victory over the Nemean Lion, however. In the terms set by Heracles' cousin Eurystheus, who was charged with assigning the Labours, the Hydra's defeat is invalid because Heracles had help. Nevertheless, the circumstance evidently does not result in the assignment of an extra labour. But the Hydra eventually resurfaces, in a sense, to kill her slayer. At first, the Hydra's death only aids Heracles, enabling his subsequent exploits: he applies the venom from the Hydra's body to his arrows, with which he goes on to defeat a range of creatures, including the Stymphalian Birds and a hostile herd of drunken centaurs. But in what perhaps serves as a foreshadowing of how the Hydra's venom will have unintended consequences for Heracles, during that same episode with the centaurs the hero's host, a friendly centaur named Pholus, accidentally drops one of the arrows on his own foot and dies from the venom's effect (see Aston in this volume).

Thus, when Heracles later ends up killing another belligerent centaur, the circumstances are set for Heracles' own death. He and his young wife, Deianira, during their travels, arrive at the river Euenus in Thessaly, where the centaur Nessus served as a sort of ferryman. Taking Deianira across first, Nessus tries to rape her, upon which Heracles fatally wounds the duplicitous centaur with an arrow. Nessus tells Deianira to take some of the semen he had spilled on the ground and mix it with blood from his wounds to use as a love potion, should Heracles ever stray from her affections; but Nessus, knowing that his blood was infected, was in fact planning Heracles' death. When Deianira suspects Heracles is straying, she finally uses what she believes to be a love charm, smearing the bloody mixture over one of Heracles' robes. The poison quickly starts to work its way into his flesh. His death scene, as described in Sophocles' *Trachiniae* (*c*.450 BCE), envisages Heracles as caught in the 'murderous' (*phonia*) net that is the blood-smeared shirt and entwined in the grip of a 'phantom Hydra' (*hydras ... phasmati*, 836–7), an apparition—perhaps produced by the venom and its excruciating effects—present and yet not present. Heracles' long-dead foes, Nessus and the Hydra—and thus, indirectly, Hera—have their revenge at last. Like the monster as explored by Cohen, the Hydra returns.

FROM MONSTER TO MIASMA

As well as unsettling 'neat categories of taxonomy', according to Asma (2009: 125), monsters 'pose irritating anomalies for science'. But not necessarily the Hydra. The

Hydra, like many creatures of classical myth, lends herself especially well to rationalizing interpretations (see Hawes in this volume). Both in antiquity and in modern times, various authors have commented on whether such a creature as the Hydra could possibly have existed. Pausanias, for example, while ready to believe that the Hydra was considerably larger than other water snakes, and that its venom was highly poisonous, also opined that the creature must have had only one head, like normal water snakes, and that it was a poet from centuries earlier—Peisander of Camireus (c.625 BCE)— who made up the Hydra's multiple heads so that the 'beast' (*thērion*) would seem more frightening (2.37.4). Heraclitus, contemporary with Pausanias, argued that the Hydra had a single head but was accompanied by multiple offspring (*De incredibilis* 18). Approximately five centuries before Pausanias and Heraclitus, the rationalizing mythographer Palaephatus had already deconstructed the myth even further, stating that the entire story of the Hydra, but especially the part about multiple heads, was 'laughable' (*geloia*). Rather, Palaephatus explained, the region of Lerna was ruled by a king named Lernus, who had a fort named Hydra guarded by many bowmen. Eurystheus sent Heracles to attack the fort, and every time one of the bowmen was struck down, two would take his place. But Iolaus came to Heracles' aid with an army, and they destroyed the Hydra (*Peri Apiston* 38).

More recently, rationalizing explanations for the myth of the Hydra have sought to ground themselves in science, arguing that the Hydra's foul breath might reflect miasma from the region's marshes, possibly sulphuric in origin. On such readings, the many water sources feeding the Lernaean marshes could have been interpreted metaphorically as regenerating heads, while Heracles' struggle with the Hydra is understood, on the basis of such interpretations and in relation to historical processes, to be 'an image of the draining effort' (Masse et al. 2007: 14; cf. Salowey 2021), in an innovative twist on the usage noted at this chapter's start of 'hydra' from antiquity onwards to refer to a persistent, complex, and recurring problem.

CONCLUSION: BACK TO THE MONSTER

The Hydra is an enormous, serpentine, multi-headed creature, dangerous even after death, and associated with the geologically liminal regions of Lerna, including its alleged entrance to the underworld, and, in recent rationalizing explanations, to drainage efforts in the Argive Plain. The Hydra's animal aspects, combining land and sea, along with her apparently botanical regenerative properties, suggest an explanation for why, on the one hand, she can be dismembered and buried by Heracles but, on the other hand, can have an existence that does not end with Heracles' victory. As one who is expelled, only to return, and who eludes categorization, the Hydra can be read as the ultimate ancient Greek monster. She also contributes to the ongoing discussion of how far the feared, fantastic, hybrid creatures of Greek mythology map onto the concepts of 'monster' and 'the monstrous'.

ACKNOWLEDGEMENTS

For her support with this chapter, I would like to thank Debbie Felton. My thanks too to Daniel Ogden for his feedback on an early version and for sharing materials I could not otherwise access during the 2020 lockdown when this chapter was taking form.

SUGGESTED READING

Murgatroyd (2013) includes a succinct overview of the ancient sources for the Lernean Hydra as well as possible interpretations, focusing on the encounters of Jason and the Argonauts and Heracles. After an excellent survey of ancient sources for the Hydra, Salowey (2021) interprets Heracles' encounter with the Hydra as an allegory for Bronze Age water management in the Argive plain. Particularly key works are Ogden (2013a) and (2013b), both of which provide many detailed sources on the Hydra, including those that track the number of the Hydra's heads and the various weapons Heracles and Iolaus used in different literary and artistic versions of the myth. More broadly, monster theory, as exemplified in the foundational and landmark work in Cohen (1996), has grown out of medieval rather than classical scholarship, although its applicability to classical concepts is explored in Lowe (2015), Gloyn (2019), and Deacy (2020).

WORKS CITED

Asma, S. T. 2009. *On Monsters: An Unnatural History of Our Worst Fears*. Oxford.

Bachvarova, M. R. 2013. 'Io and the Gorgon: Ancient Greek Medical and Mythical Constructions of the Interaction between Women's Experiences of Sex and Birth.' *Arethusa* 46/3: 415–46.

Cohen, J. J. 1996. 'Monster Culture (Seven Theses)', in *Monster Theory: Reading Culture*, ed. J. J. Cohen, 3–25. Minneapolis.

Deacy, S. 2020. ' "From the shadows": Goddess, Monster and Girl Power in Richard Woff's *Bright-Eyed Athena in the Stories of Ancient Greece*', in *Chasing Mythical Beasts: The Reception of Ancient Monsters in Children's and Young Adults' Culture*, ed. K. Marciniak, 177–95. Heidelberg.

Deacy, S. 2021. 'Heracles between Hera and Athens', in *The Oxford Handbook of Heracles*, ed. D. Ogden, 387–94. Oxford.

Gloyn, L. 2019. *Tracking Classical Monsters in Popular Culture*. London.

Lowe, D. 2015. *Monsters and Monstrosity in Augustan Poetry*. Ann Arbor.

Masse, W. B., et al. 2007. 'Exploring the Nature of Myth and Its Role in Science.' *Geological Society, London, Special Publications* 273/1: 9–28.

Murgatroyd, P. 2013. *Mythical Monsters in Classical Literature*. London.

O'Brien, J. V. 1993. *The Transformation of Hera: A Study of Ritual, Hero, and the Goddess in the Iliad*. Lanham, MD.

Ogden, D. 2013a. *Drakōn: Dragon Myth and Serpent Cult in the Greek and Roman Worlds*. Oxford.

Ogden, D. 2013b. *Dragons, Serpents, and Slayers in the Classical and Early Christian Worlds: A Sourcebook*. Oxford.

Pedrucci, G. 2017. 'Motherhood, Breastfeeding and Adoption: The Case of Hera Suckling Heracles.' *Acta Antiqua Academiae Scientiarum Hungaricae* 57/2–3: 311–22.

Salowey, C. 2021. 'Labor II: The Lernean Hydra', in *The Oxford Handbook of Heracles*, ed. D. Ogden, 45–61. Oxford.

Wengrow, D. 2013. *The Origins of Monsters: Image and Cognition in the First Age of Mechanical Reproduction*. Princeton.

Wilberding, J. 2014. 'The Secret of Sentient Vegetative Life in Galen.' *Bulletin of the Institute of Classical Studies*, suppl. 114: 249–68.

CHAPTER 12

....

CYCLOPES

....

MERCEDES AGUIRRE AND RICHARD BUXTON

INTRODUCTION

In the *imaginaire* of classical antiquity there were several different types of Cyclopes, even if their characteristics often overlap. One feature that varies among these types is monstrosity. There are also significant differences of emphasis between various media, and between individual writers or artists within those media. Another difference manifests itself within the Cyclopean community. Though numerous other Cyclopes are named and sometimes have their individual exploits recounted, unquestionably *primus inter pares* is Polyphemus, renowned especially for being outwitted and blinded at the hands of Odysseus, and for his would-be love affair with the sea-nymph Galatea. When it comes to post-classical reception, contextual variability is no less evident, though one development becomes noticeable across the board: it eventually becomes obligatory—unlike what we usually, but by no means always, find in the ancient tradition—that any creature called a Cyclops should be monocular. In that respect, in relation to the best-known, and literally central, distinguishing feature of the Cyclopes—a feature that may be, although is not always, represented as 'monstrous'—complexity is reduced to singularity.

THE CYCLOPES VIS-À-VIS OTHER MONSTERS

As this volume amply demonstrates, classical mythology abounds in creatures who, in virtue of some remarkable and often terrifying quality of 'otherness', merit the appellation 'monstrous'. Ancient myth-tellers imagine such monstrosity from a range of perspectives.

One perspective involves *genealogy*. Many monstrous creatures originate from a union which is in some way strange, owing either to the manner of conception or the parents' physical characteristics. The Minotaur was born from the mating of Pasiphaë with a bull; the centaurs descended from the coupling of wild Magnesian mares with Ixion's son Centaurus, himself the son of the copulation between Ixion and an artificial cloud; the Chimaera was born either from the Lernaean Hydra (father unknown), or from the equally monstrous pair Echidna and Typhoeus.

Another sort of imagined monstrosity involves *anatomical anomaly*. One version of this is *hybridity*. Examples of cross-species combination are legion: the Chimaera, the Sphinx, and the centaurs, among many others (Izquierdo and Le Meaux 2003). An alternative, *non*-hybrid form of physical anomaly involves *excess or deficiency*. Excess was more common: Argus had more than the regular quota of eyes, ranging from four to countless; the Hydra possessed numerous heads, the dogs Cerberus and Orthrus likewise more than one; out of Typhoeus' shoulders 'came a hundred heads of a snake, a fearsome *drakōn*, licking with black tongues' (Hes. *Theog.* 824–6). On the deficit side, the three Graeae shared one eye and one tooth; the so-called monstrous peoples described by ancient and later ethnographers included those who had one foot only. A different type of non-hybrid, physical anomaly involves *gigantic size*. Numerous mythological characters exhibit this characteristic, though in many cases—Otus, Ephialtes, Orion, not to mention the Olympian gods in some of their manifestations—this would hardly qualify them as monstrous. But gigantic size, even if not a sufficient condition for monstrosity, can sometimes be an attribute of a monster. The Laestrygonians' enormity terrifies Odysseus' men: 'they found there a woman as big as a mountain peak, and the sight of her filled them with horror' (Hom. *Od.* 10.112–13). But size is only part of the Laestrygonians' profile: it is the combination of hugeness with cannibalism that clinches their monstrosity.

This brings us to another dimension of monstrosity: *extreme, transgressive behaviour*. This is often a matter of diet: the Laestrygonians ate people, as did Scylla, Lamia, and the Minotaur. Less extreme are cases where some sort of wild behaviour marks individuals or groups as outsiders: examples are the centaurs (with the exception of hyper-civilized Chiron) and the satyrs.

The final aspect of monstrosity, whether implied or explicitly invoked, relates to its *definition* (Atherton 1998; Lenfant 1999; Piñol Lloret 2015; Winkler-Horaček 2015). Words are the heart of the matter: key identifiers are Greek *pelōr/pelōron* and *teras*, and Latin *monstrum* and *portentum*. In view of the importance of terminology, such classificatory matters usually concern verbal narrators, not visual artists.

How do we map the Cyclopes onto these general features of mythical monstrosity? The answer is complicated, since the Cyclopes are not a single, homogeneous group. There were, traditionally, three main types. The master masons were principally known for building mighty, rough-stone ('Cyclopean') walls, most famously those at Mycenae and Tiryns, where archaeologists have uncovered real sites built with unusually large and heavy stones. The metalworking Cyclopes fabricated not only Zeus' thunderbolts but also other formidable weapons; in later texts and images they are portrayed as Hephaestus' assistants working at the god's forge, usually located near or within Mount Etna. The third group consisted of the pastoral ogres, who lived remote lives among their flocks and herds, pausing only to eat the occasional visitor. Given the differences among the types, the kind of mapping we spoke of can only be approximate, but it is still worth attempting before we sample different genres and individual myth-tellers.

GENEALOGY

According to Hesiod, the Cyclopes' parents were Uranus and Gaea, a view repeated by many later myth-tellers. An alternative version held that either Polyphemus, or (as in Euripides) all the Cyclopes, were the child(ren) of Poseidon and the sea-nymph Thoosa. How far can we correlate the monstrosity of (some of) the Cyclopes with either the manner of their conception or the characteristics of their parents? In the case that they are born from Gaea, although Gaea herself can be described as *pelōrē* (as at Hes. *Theog.* 159), and although *some* of her children by Uranus are anatomically monstrous (notably the 'Hundred-Handers': Hes. *Theog.* 147–56), not all of them are—not, for instance, Oceanos, Themis, Mnemosyne, Rhea, or Tethys, to mention just a few. In other words, this genealogy does not *necessarily* entail Cyclopean monstrosity. The case where the Cyclopes' parents are Poseidon and Thoosa is somewhat different. Though neither parent is inherently monstrous in form, the sea god's repeated mythical and ritual connection with the genesis of the horse takes him into unorthodox procreative territory (Bremmer 1987; Burkert 1985: 137–8). Moreover, many aspects of Poseidon tend towards disruptive, elemental wildness, including a capacity to shatter and hurl rocks. Perhaps, of all the Olympians, Poseidon was the one most appropriately imagined as a sire of the Cyclopes, as in *Odyssey* Book 9.

ANATOMICAL ANOMALY

Physiological *hybridity*, in the sense of the blending of species, is not usually a feature of the Cyclopes. There is, arguably, one kind of exception: in some visual images a strong resemblance can be seen between the Cyclopes and the undoubtedly hybrid satyrs/Silenus. For example, a striking similarity is noticeable between the about-to-be-blinded Polyphemus on a cup in Berlin (*LIMC*, s.v. 'Kyklops, Kyklopes' 22) and the horse-eared and -tailed Silenus on an amphora from Tarquinia (*LIMC*, s.v. 'Silenoi' 112). Also noteworthy is a krater from Sabucina (*LIMC*, s.v. 'Hephaistos' 15), where two satyrs help Hephaestus at his forge: are they playing the role of Cyclopes? Such cases apart, ancient conceptions of Cyclopean monstrosity owe nothing to cross-species hybridity.

Regarding *excess or deficiency*, matters are different. Few mythological characters are more closely identified with an anatomical deficit than the Cyclopes. The concept of their single eye dates back at least to Hesiod, who stresses to the point of redundancy this facial idiosyncrasy of the thunderbolt-makers (*Theog.* 142–5):

In other respects they were like the gods, but a single eye lay in the middle of their forehead; they were named Cyclopes ('Circle-eyes') because of the one circular eye that lay in their forehead.

The same characteristic is ascribed to Polyphemus and his congeners in Euripides' *Cyclops*, while in Callimachus' *Hymn to Artemis* the metalworkers' monocularity is explicitly linked to their appearance as 'dreadful monsters' (*aina pelōra*): 'all had single eyes beneath their brows, like a shield of fourfold hide for size, glaring terribly from under' (51–4). The same motif recurs in Theocritus, Vergil, Ovid, Lucian, and Philostratus. Visual representations of the Cyclopes' monstrous monocularity are also frequent, as in the wall painting from the Tomb of Orcus II in Tarquinia (*LIMC*, s.v. 'Kyklops, Kyklopes' 26) and on several grotesque terracotta figurines from the sixth to the fourth centuries BCE, such as that from the sanctuary of the Cabiri in Thebes (*LIMC*, s.v. 'Polyphemos I' 68). But representing the Cyclopes as single-eyed—or at least as *explicitly* single-eyed— is not the only option. No source reports that the masonic Cyclopes are single-eyed. In *Odyssey* Book 9, Polyphemus' face is never described, and his monocularity is only an inference, albeit a justifiable one, since there is a single act of blinding, and the text repeatedly refers to 'the eye' rather than 'the eyes' of Polyphemus. Visual representations cover a spectrum of possibilities, which includes two eyes, as with the blinded Polyphemus on an Attic skyphos (*LIMC*, s.v. 'Kyklops, Kyklopes' 22), or the blacksmiths on a mid-second-century CE sarcophagus lid (*LIMC*, s.v. 'Kyklops, Kyklopes' 38). Sometimes, however, artists give him three eyes: two in their normal position, and a third, centrally positioned, above them, as on a Lucanian krater (*LIMC*, s.v. 'Kyklops, Kyklopes' 27). There are also several images on which, because the face appears in profile, it is impossible to quantify the eyes, as on an amphora from Eleusis (*LIMC*, s.v. 'Polyphemos I' 16; see Fig. 25.4 in this volume). Moreover, even when a Cyclopean face sports an irregular number of eyes, this anomaly is not always coupled with the idea of monstrosity, as exemplified on a mosaic from Cordoba (*LIMC*, s.v. 'Galateia' 24).

The *gigantic size* of the builder Cyclopes must be inferred from their constructional feats. As Pausanias puts it, the rocks they used to construct the wall at Tiryns were 'all so huge that a pair of mules would not even begin to shift the smallest of them' (2.25.8). In the case of the blacksmiths, their vastness, as opposed to just their strength, is rarely spelled out, though Callimachus compares them to the crags of Mount Ossa (*Hymn to Artemis* 51–2). The comparison with a mountain goes back to the *Odyssey*, where Polyphemus resembles 'a wooded peak of the high mountains, which is visible apart from the others' (9.191–2), recalling the description of the Laestrygonians (above). That Polyphemus was colossal is a standard feature of ancient accounts, but not every text takes the same line. Neither of Theocritus' two odes about Polyphemus mentions his size, while Euripides' satyr play *Cyclops* must cope with the fact that Polyphemus was played by a human actor—whose size may have been magnified in some way, perhaps by the wearing of platform boots? As for artistic representations, much depends on the varying constraints of different media. Vase-painting offers limited scope to depict divergences of scale, but one strategy for suggesting Polyphemus' greater size than the men blinding him is to show him crouching or reclining (e.g. *LIMC*, s.v. 'Polyphemos I' 16, 17, and 20; 'Odysseus' 88). A unique case is a Campanian krater on which an idiotic-looking, paunchy, and grossly over-endowed Polyphemus grills two *homunculi*—evidently normal-sized humans—on spits (*LIMC*, *Suppl. 2009*, s.v. 'Polyphemos I' add. 1). Looking beyond vase-painting, we find a nice representation on a Cypriot sarcophagus, on which a naked, hairy, and presumably already-blinded Polyphemus squats as he waits to feel the backs of a procession of large rams, with miniature Greeks slung underneath (*LIMC*, *Suppl. 2009*, s.v. 'Polyphemos I' add. 2). Much more heroic is the colossal, recumbent Polyphemus in the free-standing sculptural group from Tiberius' Grotto at Sperlonga (*LIMC*, s.v. 'Polyphemos I' 32); for all their supra-human size, the Greeks in the assault party look puny by comparison. Cyclopean size does, then, matter, but it is not always visually evident. When juxtaposed with Galatea, Polyphemus usually appears on the same scale as she does, as on a wall painting from Pompeii and a mosaic from Cordoba (*LIMC*, s.v. 'Galateia' 24 and 37); in contrast, a wall painting from the House of Livia in Rome shows the handsome young Polyphemus dwarfing Galatea and her sister nymphs (*LIMC*, s.v. 'Polyphemos I' 54). Finally, in some cases it is impossible to decide just *how* large—as it were, 'objectively'—a Cyclops is. This applies to several representations of the Cyclopes toiling in the forge of Hephaestus (e.g. *LIMC*, s.v. 'Kyklops, Kyklopes' 37 and 38)—and how big is *he*?

EXTREME, TRANSGRESSIVE BEHAVIOUR

Neither the master builders nor the blacksmiths are usually associated with behaviour that puts them beyond the norms of civilized conduct. By contrast, the pastoral ogres, above all Polyphemus, make such behaviour their trademark. Diet is crucial (see also Friedman in this volume). In *Odyssey* Book 9, two of the ogre's preferences mark him out as marginal, in Greek terms. First, he favours a dairy—specifically, milky and cheesy—menu. Second, when Odysseus presents him with wine, he gulps it down unmixed with water. But another of his fads goes far beyond mere marginality: he is, when he gets the chance, anthropophagous (*Od.* 9.288–93):

> He sprang up, and stretching his hands towards my companions clutched two at once and battered them on the floor like puppies; their brains gushed out and soaked the ground. Then cutting them up limb from limb he made his supper of them. He began to eat like a mountain lion, leaving nothing, devouring flesh and entrails and bones and marrow …

Though Polyphemus does not lack the means of cooking, given that he has a fire in his cave, the text implies that he eats Odysseus' crewmen raw; the same is explicitly true of the vilely human-meat-devouring Polyphemuses of Vergil (*Aen.* 3.622–7) and Ovid (*Met.* 14.207–12). By contrast, the theatrical descendant of the Homeric Polyphemus in

FIGURE 12.1 Rider Painter; Laconian black-figure cup, 565–560 BCE. Odysseus and his men blinding Polyphemus, mid-snack.

Source: Wikimedia / Bibi Saint-Pol. Public domain.

Euripides' *Cyclops* uses a range of culinary skills to prepare his human victims: boiling, grilling, and roasting. No wonder the Silenus character refers to Polyphemus' 'unholy meals' (31). In art, images range from the raw to the cooked; at the raw end of the spectrum is a Laconian cup on which the about-to-be-blinded ogre clutches a human leg in each hand, presumably intended as his next snack (*LIMC*, s.v. 'Polyphemos I' 18; see Fig. 12.1). Differently gruesome are two images depicting cookery. On the already-mentioned Campanian krater the hellish chef grills two spitted human victims over a charcoal fire. Another Campanian vase depicts Polyphemus gripping a human leg in one hand and an arm in the other, while the limbs' former owner is being roasted on an open fire (*LIMC*, s.v. 'Polyphemos I' 23).

DEFINITION

Are the Cyclopes 'monsters'? If not, what are they? The answer is not straightforward, and the textual myth-telling tradition came up with several, sometimes contradictory responses. Even within a single text we can find different perspectives. In *Odyssey* Book 6 we learn that the Cyclopes were *andres*—male human beings (6.5). But things get more complicated three Books later: when Odysseus narrates the events that occurred in the Cyclopes' territory, he describes Polyphemus first as a 'monstrous man' (*anēr ... pelōrios*), then as a 'monstrous wonder' (*thauma ... pelōrion*) who is *not* like an *anēr* (9.187–92), and later still as an *anēr agrios* (9.214–15, 494)—maybe an intermediate state between *anēr* and *anēr pelōrios*? It becomes a moot point, then, as to whether, when Polyphemus eats *andres*, that makes him a cannibal (an eater of his own species). Euripides' *Cyclops* develops a different sort of ambiguity. In dialogue with Odysseus near the beginning of the play (115–18), Silenus states that there are no human beings (*anthrōpoi*) living there. But when Odysseus asks: 'Who *does* live here? Wild beasts [*thēres*]?', Silenus simply answers 'Cyclopes', without making clear whether he thinks Cyclopes are wild beasts, or human beings, or neither. For a text in which the Cyclopes are, without a glimmer of doubt, card-carrying monstrous monsters, we must wait for Vergil's *Aeneid*, where a description of Polyphemus and his equally horrific brothers pulls out all the adjectival stops: 'unspeakable' (*infandi*, 644), 'horrible, hideous, huge monster' (*monstrum horrendum, informe, ingens*, 658).

HESIOD

Having discussed various aspects of what makes the Cyclopes monstrous, we can now turn to the principal texts and visual sources that provide our information, starting with the earliest surviving texts—those of Homer and Hesiod. A feature common to most ancient perceptions of the Cyclopes is primordiality—the sense that they belonged to a time Before. This certainly applies to the builder Cyclopes, whose monumental walls were made 'in times gone by'. It also applies to the metalworkers, as in Hesiod's *Theogony*. Like the other children of Uranus and Gaea, the Cyclopes were hated by their father, who saw them as a potential threat to his rule. Consequently, Uranus imprisoned all three—Brontes, Steropes, and Arges (the embodiments, as their names indicate, of thunder, lightning, and thunderbolt)—within the earth (i.e. Gaea) as soon as they were born. But eventually Zeus freed them, receiving in recompense the three formidable and power-conferring gifts which their names expressed (*Theog.* 154–9, 501–6).

HOMER

Whereas Hesiod situates the Cyclopes at the centre of a narrative about the development of divine power within the cosmos, Homeric epic stresses the Cyclopes' marginality. During the lengthy narration of his adventures to his spellbound Phaeacian audience, Odysseus arrives at an episode in which he can, as usual, highlight his own audacity and cunning. After escaping the enticements of the Lotus-Eaters, the Greeks sail to the land of the 'overbearing and lawless' Cyclopes. Opposite this territory—not itself specified as an island—lies an island uninhabited by humans but richly populated by wild goats; here the twelve Greek ships lay at anchor. Together with the crew of his own ship, Odysseus crosses to the Cyclopes' land, aiming to investigate the mind and customs of the local inhabitants, and especially how they treat strangers—such inquiry is one of the poem's fundamental themes. The Greeks come across a cave, a type of dwelling that reflects the owner's situation as an outsider. But the owner is far from being a *disorderly* outsider, since everything is meticulously arranged: milk, cheeses, pens for sheep and goats. The Greeks pilfer some cheese (the *Odyssey*'s morality is by no means straightforward), and then wait for the cave's owner to return. Eventually a colossal giant comes back to milk his sheep and goats, first blocking the cave entrance with a massive boulder (the mason Cyclopes, too, are adept at handling massive rocks). The answer to the question of how *this* local inhabitant treats strangers now becomes clear: he smashes two of them to death on the floor and then eats them.

Odysseus' tactics for outwitting the ogre echo down the millennia of Cyclopean reception. First the hero gets him drunk with a gift of delectable wine; then he blinds him with a wooden stake heated in the fire (killing him would have left unresolved the problem of how to remove the boulder/door). When the ogre, now named as Polyphemus, calls on his fellow Cyclopes for help, their inability to fathom what ails him encapsulates the difference in mental ingenuity (according to Odysseus, of course) between a Cyclops and a Greek hero. Since Odysseus has identified himself to Polyphemus as *Outis* (Nobody), the ogre is obliged to admit that Nobody (i.e. no-body) is attacking him—causing the other Cyclopes to turn away. Another Odyssean ruse enables the Greeks to escape by clinging beneath Polyphemus' fleecy rams, thus eluding the blinded ogre's probing hands, which feel only the animals' backs. Odysseus cannot resist revealing his real name. The time-honoured Cyclopean tactic of rock-throwing fails to sink Odysseus' ship, and the hero sails on to his next exploit, 'glad to have escaped death, but grieving still at heart' for the loss of his devoured companions (9.566). But the aftertaste is still bitter: thanks to Odysseus' boast, Polyphemus can pray to his father Poseidon to punish the man who robbed him of his eyesight—and the god hears him.

Many academic studies have been devoted to *Odyssey* Book 9. Folkloristic approaches continue to proliferate, the bulk of them assuming that the Homeric version is a reworking of pre-existing folk tales. However, the evidence for such *comparanda* postdates the composition of the Homeric epics, a fact which has led a minority of dissenters to reverse the presumed direction of travel by arguing that it is the *Odyssey* that constitutes the point of departure (on folk tales, see e.g. Glenn 1971; Burgess 2001: 94–114; Bremmer 2002). Another tranche of studies, both academic and popular, has posed the ultimately unanswerable question: where did the Cyclopes encountered by Odysseus live? What is not in doubt is the status of the *Odyssey* as the single most important work for the appreciation of Cyclopean mythology, including Cyclopean monstrosity.

EURIPIDES

So close yet at times so deliberately different from the Homeric account is Euripides' dramatization of the myth in his satyr play *Cyclops* (*c*.408 BCE), that a recent commentary can characterize the theatrical version as a 'critical reading' of its epic predecessor (Hunter and Laemmle 2020: 17). The correspondences are easily identified: the arrival of Odysseus and his men in the Cyclopes' territory in search of sustenance; Polyphemus' dwelling in a cave, and his pastoral existence; his eating of Odysseus' crewmen; Odysseus' intoxication of Polyphemus with wine; the blinding with a sharpened wooden firebrand; the pun on 'Nobody'; the Greeks' escape. But the differences from Homer also stand out. The Euripidean Cyclopes live in Sicily, specifically the Mount Etna region. Unlike in Homer, the other Cyclopes never appear: in a sense they are replaced by Silenus and the satyrs, who participate in the Nobody scene ('If Nobody blinded you, then you're not blind!', 674). Indeed, the satyrs have transformed Polyphemus' existence, since he has compelled them to do all the hard, dairy-farming grind, leaving him as an ogre of leisure. With the satyrs comes one of their favourite preoccupations: wine. Unlike in Homer, the Euripidean Cyclopes do not know of wine *at all* (123–4), so Odysseus' gift to Polyphemus is that much more potent. Finally, the cave: the motif of blocking the entrance with a boulder is necessarily sidelined, since the staging depends on frequent movements into and out of the cave. Most of these differences from Homer arise from the demands and emphases of the satyr-play genre—one more demonstration that the representation of myths, and of monstrosity, is shaped by the context.

THEOCRITUS

In *Idylls* 6 and 11, the pastoral poet Theocritus (third century BCE) breaks new ground in characterizing Polyphemus. The ostensible location is the typical pastoral landscape, but the combined worlds of mountain, cave, and pastureland are bounded by the sea—and the sea*shore* is a crucial part of the picture, being the setting for the emotional drama between Polyphemus and the reluctant sea-nymph Galatea. The ogre's preoccupation with milk and cheese persists from the *Odyssey*, and the emphasis on his hairiness and monocularity also looks back to earlier poetic tradition. But a distinctively Theocritean theme that will resonate throughout later Cyclopean reception is the ogre's *song*, an outpouring of self-pity that both expresses his unrequited obsession with Galatea and offers a way of 'shepherding', i.e. coping with it (Hunter 1999: 221). The theme of Polyphemus' love affair allegedly takes its origin from an early fourth-century BCE poem by Philoxenus, who supposedly seduced the mistress (named Galatea) of Dionysius, the tyrant of Syracuse, and composed a poetic spoof allegorizing Dionysius as the Cyclops. But the anecdote's truth is impossible to establish, and anyway the traceable influence of Philoxenus is negligible, certainly compared to that of Theocritus.

Vergil

Two contrasting episodes in the *Aeneid* feature the Cyclopes. In Book 8 they are mighty blacksmiths, labouring cooperatively at Hephaestus' forge in the Aeolian islands to create weapons for the gods and, at Venus' request, armour for her son Aeneas. In Book 3 their profile is grimmer and unremittingly savage, as fiery as nearby Etna. Set within Aeneas' narrative to his Carthaginian audience is an account of the Trojans' encounter with a ragged and emaciated stranger, Achaemenides, a former crewman of Odysseus who survived the man-eating horrors of Polyphemus' cave. When Polyphemus himself appears, blood is still—after three months!—oozing from his blinded eye (3.645–8, 662–5). The Trojans take Achaemenides with them, but not before Polyphemus has clamorously called on his huge and terrifying brothers (3.677–81):

> We saw the brotherhood of Etna standing there helpless, each with his one eye glaring and head held high in the sky, a fearsome gathering, standing like high-topped mountain oaks or cone-bearing cypresses in Jupiter's soaring forest or the grove of Diana.

The Sicilian location may recall Theocritus, but the atmosphere is grimly unpastoral.

Ovid

In successive Books of the *Metamorphoses*, Ovid presents two Cyclopean episodes, both concentrating on Polyphemus alone rather than on the Cyclopes collectively. In Book 14 Ovid outdoes Vergil with, once more in the words of Achaemenides, a stomach-churning recollection of the Cyclops' anthropophagy: '[he] crammed their innards and their flesh, their bones full of white marrow, and their limbs still half alive, into his greedy stomach' (14.208–9). But Book 13 draws an altogether more nuanced portrait of Polyphemus. Addressing Scylla before her monstrous hybridization, Galatea relives the story of her disgust for the ogre, his vain attempts to woo her in song, and the sad demise of her true love, the handsome young shepherd Acis—crushed when Polyphemus hurled a crag at him, at which point Acis miraculously became the eponymous river; this is, after all, the *Metamorphoses*. Among many high points are Polyphemus' absurd attempts to make himself attractive by combing his bristly hair with a rake and shaving with a scythe; his deafening musicianship on a hundred-reed pipe; and his torrential, comparative rhetoric ('O Galatea, whiter than the columbine, taller than the alder, more playful than a kid, softer than cream cheese, wilder than a heifer, grimmer than a mother bear, deafer than the sea', etc., 13.789–807). These musical and linguistic histrionics would enjoy a luxuriant afterlife in Cyclopean reception. No less enduring would be the Cyclopean association with fire: 'I feel as if I were carrying Etna within my breast!' (13.868–9).

LATER GREEK TEXTS

The satirist Lucian exploits Polyphemus' comic potential in his *Dialogues of the Sea Gods*, when Galatea and her sister nymph Doris take opposed views of Polyphemus' attractions (our italics):

> DORIS: Your lover looks hideous, sings like a donkey, and smells like a goat.
> GALATEA: He's the son of Poseidon, he's musical, *and at least I've got a lover.*

Vastly different in tone is a vignette from Philostratus' *Imagines*, a brilliant work (second to third centuries CE) purporting to evoke a series of paintings in a gallery in Naples. For the painting 'Cyclops' (2.18), Philostratus' description leaves no doubt about the ogre's monstrosity: 'mountainous and terrible … jagged teeth … voracious jaw.' But he only has (one) eye for Galatea, who is driving a team of dolphins on the open sea. She, however, oblivious of her fearsome suitor, focuses on her own element, since her glance 'travels as far as the sea extends'. In the fifth century CE, the poet Nonnus frequently refers to the Cyclopes in his epic *Dionysiaca*. In one sense he takes us back to Euripides, in virtue of the Dionysiac company in which the Cyclopes find themselves; in another sense he looks back to Hesiod, since the Cyclopes are located at the heart of the primordial conflicts between generations of gods. The host of Nonnian innovations includes the details that the Cyclopes wield weapons (thunderbolt, lightning) that are *counterfeits* of those of Zeus (Book 28), and that Polyphemus is absent from the fighting because his mind is not on war but on love—an affection that Galatea here reciprocates (Book 39).

VISUAL IMAGES

In Greek vase-painting from the mid-seventh century BCE, Polyphemus' encounter with Odysseus was a popular motif. Several illustrations of the blinding have already been mentioned: the Laconian cup, the Lucanian krater, the Attic skyphos, the wall painting in the Tomb of Orcus at Tarquinia, and the sculptural group at Sperlonga. Another popular schema depicts the ogre's vain attempt to capture the Greeks as they cling beneath his sheep, as on the Cypriot sarcophagus described above, and on a fragmentary krater on which an extremely hairy ogre gropes blindly towards a sheep, beneath which a pair of human legs protrude (*LIMC*, s.v. 'Kyklops, Kyklopes' 19). A recurrent gambit is to present the encounter with Odysseus synoptically. Thus, the Laconian cup combines three scenes which in narrative logic would presumably have been separate: Polyphemus' anthropophagy (implied by the two dismembered legs that he holds), Odysseus' proffering of a wine-cup, and the blinding (feasible only when Polyphemus was already drunk). Sometimes, though, an artist will depict one significant instant, as with the floor mosaic from the villa at Piazza Armerina in Sicily (*LIMC*,

FIGURE 12.2 Polyphemus mosaic; early fourth century CE, Roman Villa of Casale, Piazza Armerina, Sicily.

s.v. 'Kyklops, Kyklopes' 29; see Fig. 12.2), where Polyphemus—a three-eyed version, as described above—surrounded by his flock, and with an eviscerated ram draped over one knee, receives the wine-cup from Odysseus. This image offers the most detailed evocation of the Cyclops' cave in extant ancient art.

As for Polyphemus' involvement with Galatea, the most diverse and suggestive (in all senses) images appear on Campanian wall paintings of the first century CE. A painting from Boscotrecase depicts a landscape both rocky and maritime (*LIMC*, s.v. 'Polyphemos I' 55). Centre and left, a naked Polyphemus, clutching his shepherd's pan pipes, sits on a crag surrounded by his flock, while Galatea perches calmly on a dolphin; there is no hint of emotional proximity between the ill-matched couple. At right, and off in the distance, is another vignette from Polyphemus' story: he prepares to hurl a rock at a departing vessel, presumably that of Odysseus. A quite different sort of wildness can be seen on two paintings from Pompeii, where Polyphemus and Galatea are locked in passionate and, evidently, mutually satisfying embrace (*LIMC*, s.v. 'Galateia' 18 and 37). Not every ancient account of this relationship casts the Cyclops as a loser.

Apart from scenes of implied anthropophagy, often suggested by severed limbs or dastardly cookery, the most compellingly 'monstrous' Cyclopes appear in images where the ogre is visualized in isolation, and where a single, central eye dominates the viewer's attention. Examples include some marble heads (e.g. *LIMC*, s.v. 'Kyklops, Kyklopes' 10) and a group of terracotta figurines dating from the sixth to the fourth centuries BCE, portraying a grotesque ogre who looks stupid as well as ugly (*LIMC*, s.v. 'Polyphemos I' 66–8).

Three other aspects of Cyclopean representation are worth mentioning. First, there exist no images of the master masons in ancient art. Second, the blacksmiths *are* depicted, predominantly in the Roman period, when they appear as Vulcan's diligent, muscular, and emphatically un-monstrous assistants, as on a painted relief on a marble slab in Rome (*LIMC*, s.v. 'Kyklops, Kyklopes' 37). Third, the Polyphemus/Galatea duet occasionally expands into a trio with the addition of Acis. In the clearest example, a second-century BCE sarcophagus in Rome (*LIMC*, s.v. 'Galateia' 29), a semi-naked Galatea sits on a dolphin while Polyphemus sits opposite her on a rock, holding out a small animal (bear? lamb?) presumably as a love-token. Above, a smaller, male figure leans on a jar from which water flows. This must be Acis, personified as the river god he became; the flowing water-jar, among other things, is a regular aspect of river-god iconography.

AFTER ANTIQUITY

For late antique and medieval allegorists, especially those explicating Vergil or Ovid, the Cyclops who dominated their interpretations was Polyphemus, and the theme which interested them most of all was the single eye. According to John of Garland (thirteenth century), the eye symbolized rationality, though the successful act of blinding meant that Ulysses was even cleverer than the ogre (*Integumenta Ovidii* 463–8). The Polyphemus/Galatea/Acis love triangle as presented by Ovid also engaged the attention of interpreters, producing a wide range of Christian moralizing approaches. In his *Ovidius moralizatus* (Book XV fo. 92), Pierre Bersuire (*c*.1290–1362) boiled the moral down to 'corruption [Polyphemus] kills chastity [Acis]'. In contrast, for the anonymous author of *Ovide moralisé*, an adaptation and commentary on Ovid's *Metamorphoses* into French (early fourteenth century), Polyphemus stood for Satan, Galatea for divine wisdom, and Acis human nature (13.4148–294). Different again are Boccaccio's readings in *Genealogy of the Pagan Gods* (7.17). You can either take the myth naturalistically (Galatea = white, breaking waves; Acis = fresh water, which flows into the sea) or euhemeristically (Polyphemus, a cruel despot, raped a girl called Galatea and had her lover killed).

The same Polyphemian emphasis pervades early modern art. Typical bearers of mythological imagery at this period were *cassoni*, painted wooden chests often given as wedding gifts to a bride. Scenes relating to love and the relationships between the sexes were common, but illustrations of other dramatic episodes also appeared (Bull 2005: 37–9). Two such chests depict various moments from Ulysses' encounter with the ogre. The more remarkable of the two (dated 1435–1445) is ascribed to Apollonio di Giovanni: wearing magnificent robes of gold, Ulysses proffers a resplendent cup to the naked and hairy 'Pulifemo', from whose jaws protrude a half-eaten human victim

(Aguirre and Buxton 2020: 254). Less visceral but more comprehensive is a slightly later *cassone*, perhaps by Piero di Cosimo (*c*.1500; Aguirre and Buxton 2020: 253), featuring three separate Polyphemuses: a recumbent giant, like Gulliver in Lilliput, at the mercy of a platoon of mini-blinders; behind him, a forlorn figure, head down, feeling the backs of his flock; to the right, knee-deep in the sea, Polyphemus targeting some sailing ships with a massive boulder. The costumes may be end-of-cinquecento, but the storyline is rooted in the *Odyssey*.

Major sixteenth-century Italian artists, from Pellegrino Tibaldi to Annibale Carracci, reimagined these same Odyssean episodes. But a parallel tradition, within and beyond Italy, represented the armour-making blacksmith Cyclopes, usually as monstrous in neither physiognomy nor behaviour. One favourite context was Venus' commission to forge armour for Aeneas; another was Apollo's report to Vulcan, in the presence of the Cyclopes, of the embarrassing news about his wife's adultery with Mars. The first scenario, featuring a trio of incredibly muscular Cyclopes, was visualized by Maarten van Heemskerck in his *Venus and Cupid in Vulcan's Forge* (1536); the second was famously realized by Velázquez in *Apollo in Vulcan's Forge* (1630), where the boss's co-workers look like three ordinary blokes from a Spanish smithy.

From the early modern period onwards, one of the preferred sites for the sculptural evocation of mythological monstrosity was the garden (Morgan 2016). In Polyphemus' case, it was specifically in garden *grottoes* that the cave-dweller found his niche, from Antonio Novelli's massive and solitary *Polyphemus* in the Orti Oricellari in Florence (*c*.1650) to Auguste Ottin's bull's-hide-clad bronze giant in *Polyphemus Surprising Acis and Galatea* in the Jardin du Luxembourg in Paris (1866). Away from the grotto, painters, too, continued to render the ogre's raw muscularity. Guido Reni's *Polyphemus* (1639–1640) shows the open-mouthed and naked giant with his magnificent torso twisted, ready to hurl a boulder; two-and-a-half centuries later, Arnold Böcklin's *Odysseus and Polyphemus* (1896) would raise Cyclopean fury several notches higher in a landscape as savage as the vast and hairy Wild Man who bestrides it. Few of the post-classical artists just discussed make much of Cyclopean monocularity, though Giulio Romano's *Head of a Giant* in Mantua (*c*.1532) is a powerful exception. But in the nineteenth and twentieth centuries, artists working in various media have been captivated by the grotesque strangeness of the Cyclops' single eye. Odilon Redon's surreal *The Misshapen Polyp Floated on the Shores, a Sort of Smiling and Hideous Cyclops* (1883) is one high point; Jean Tinguely's huge kinetic sculpture just outside Paris (*Cyclops*, 1969–1991) is another.

Many modern literary reimaginings of the Cyclops have used him to embody a negative, threatening, and tyrannical figure, characteristics symbolized by some kind of ocular weirdness. In Ralph Ellison's novel *Invisible Man* (1952), for instance, the eyes of three of the title character's menacing adversaries are symbolically Cyclopean, including a doctor who subjects Invisible Man to electric shock therapy: he had 'a bright third eye that glowed from the centre of his forehead' (Ellison 2014: 231). The cinema, too, has frequently exploited a symbolic equivalence between ocular anomaly and moral repugnance. Notable among films which, in some sense or other, revisit the *Odyssey* is *O Brother, Where Art Thou?* (dir. Joel and Ethan Coen, 2000); among the monsters encountered by the Odysseus-equivalent hero is the unspeakable and one-eyed Ku-Klux-Klansman Big Dan Teague (Ku Klux = Kuklops). More ephemeral are the countless science fiction, fantasy, and horror movies about one-eyed monsters which may or may not be named as Cyclops. Among the less stomach-churning is the horned Cyclops designed by Ray Harryhausen for *The 7th Voyage of Sinbad* (dir. Nathan H. Juran, 1958). The lower part of his hairy body culminates devilishly in cloven hooves, a satyresque trait showing that hybridity, while virtually never a feature of the ancient Cyclopes, can sometimes enhance the monstrosity of their modern descendants.

But negativity is not the whole story. Along the reception way are portrayals that see Cyclops as exploited victim or even as a hero. Victor Hugo's titanic account of the deformed, one-eyed Quasimodo in *Notre-Dame de Paris* (1831) combines a sense of the character's physical repulsiveness (he is repeatedly described as a Cyclops) with an overwhelming evocation of his tenderness, courage, and capacity for intense affection, above all for his Galatea-equivalent—the gipsy girl Esmeralda. The hideous black man encountered on a tram by the narrator in Aimé Césaire's extraordinary anti-colonialist poem *Cahier d'un retour au pays natal* (1931) stands out as the archetypal victim: that which has pushed in his eye socket is poverty (1995: 108–9). Less well known is the micro-story 'Revenge' by Chilean writer Pedro Guillermo Jara (Serrano Cueto 2015: 50–1). It tells the tale of a baby Cyclops born on an island in Lake Titicaca in the Andes. Named Juan Quispi by the shepherd who fosters him, he eventually makes his way to Ithaca and shoots Ulysses dead: ' "For Polyphemus," murmured Juan Quispi, as his eye gleamed.'

Scholars and others have often looked for the 'origins' of the Cyclopes in the real world, for example, in the 'eye' of a volcanic crater, or the hole (actually, the nasal cavity) in the centre of the forehead of a prehistoric dwarf elephant. There is no harm in these entirely unprovable speculations, but they fail to engage with what is important in myths about the Cyclopes: those myths, alongside many other classical stories about monsters, embody a way of speculating about the limitations and potentialities, the deficits and excesses of humanity, by imagining that which is physically or behaviourally outlandish. The rich and continuing afterlife of these myths illustrates that the kind of thought experiments which they express have not become outdated, and presumably never will be.

SUGGESTED READING

For a detailed study of matters Cyclopean, whether monstrous or not, see Aguirre and Buxton (2020), in which many points touched on in this chapter are explored at much greater length; post-classical reception of the myths is discussed at 235–375 there. Among countless studies relating to the Homeric account one may mention Burgess (2001: 94–114), Bremmer (2002), Clare (2002), and D'Onofrio (2003). On Euripides' *Cyclops*, alongside commentaries by Seaford (1984) and Hunter and Laemmle (2020), see Konstan (1990). For the Theocritean

Cyclopes, see the relevant sections of Hunter (1999). For discussion of Polyphemus and Galatea in Campanian wall painting, see Squire (2009: 300–56). For analysis of various aspects of Cyclopean reception, see Dörrie (1968), Acquaro Graziosi (1984), Mangiafesta (1997), and Hall (2008: 89–100), and on the imagery of the (single) eye, Schmidt-Burkhardt (1992) and Steinhart (1995).

WORKS CITED

Acquaro Graziosi, M. T. 1984. *Polifemo e Galatea: Mito e poesia*. Rome.

Aguirre, M., and R. G. A. Buxton. 2020. *Cyclops: The Myth and Its Cultural History*. Oxford.

Atherton, C., ed. 1998. *Monsters and Monstrosity in Greek and Roman Culture*. Bari.

Bremmer, J. N. 1987. ' "Effigies dei" in Ancient Greece: Poseidon', in *Effigies Dei: Essays on the History of Religions*, ed. D. van der Plas, 35–41. Leiden.

Bremmer, J. N. 2002. 'Odysseus versus the Cyclops', in *Myth and Symbol I: Symbolic Phenomena in Ancient Greek Culture*, ed. S. des Bouvrie, 135–52. Bergen.

Bull, M. 2005. *The Mirror of the Gods: Classical Mythology in Renaissance Art*. London.

Burgess, J. S. 2001. *The Tradition of the Trojan War in Homer and the Epic Cycle*. Baltimore.

Burkert, W. 1985. *Greek Religion: Archaic and Classical*. Oxford.

Césaire, A. 1995. *Notebook of a Return to My Native Land*. Hexham.

Clare, R. J. 2002. 'Representing Monstrosity: Polyphemus in the *Odyssey*', in *Monsters and Monstrosity in Greek and Roman Culture*, ed. C. Atherton, 1–17. Bari.

D'Onofrio, S. 2003. 'Ulisse e l'uomo selvaggio', in *Ulisse nel tempo: La metafora infinita*, ed. S. Nicosia, 127–50. Venice.

Dörrie, H. 1968. *Die schöne Galatea: Eine Gestalt am Rande des griechischen Mythos in antiker und neuzeitlicher Sicht*. Munich.

Ellison, R. W. 2014. *Invisible Man*. London.

Glenn, J. 1971. 'The Polyphemus Folktale and Homer's *Kyklôpeia*.' *Transactions of the American Philological Association* 102: 133–81.

Hall, E. 2008. *The Return of Ulysses: A Cultural History of Homer's Odyssey*. London.

Hunter, R. L. 1999. *Theocritus: A Selection; Idylls 1, 3, 4, 6, 7, 10, 11 and 13*. Cambridge.

Hunter, R. L., and R. Laemmle, eds. 2020. *Euripides: Cyclops*. Cambridge.

Izquierdo, I., and H. Le Meaux, eds. 2003. *Seres híbridos: Apropiación de motivos míticos mediterráneos*. Madrid.

Konstan, D. 1990. 'An Anthropology of Euripides' *Kyklōps*', in *Nothing to Do with Dionysos? Athenian Drama in Its Social Context*, ed. J. J. Winkler and F. Zeitlin, 207–27. Princeton.

Lenfant, D. 1999. 'Monsters in Greek Ethnography and Society in the Fifth and Fourth Centuries BCE', in *From Myth to Reason? Studies in the Development of Greek Thought*, ed. R. G. A. Buxton, 197–214. Oxford.

Mangiafesta, M. 1997. 'Fortuna del mito di Polifemo nelle collezioni di antichità tra XV e XVII secolo.' *Bollettino d'arte* 82/99: 13–60.

Morgan, L. 2016. *The Monster in the Garden*. Philadelphia.

Piñol Lloret, M. 2015. *Monstruos y monstruosidades: Del imaginario fantástico medieval a los X-Men*. Barcelona.

Schmidt-Burkhardt, A. 1992. *Sehende Bilder: Die Geschichte des Augenmotivs seit dem 19. Jahrhunderts*, Berlin.

Seaford, R. A. S., ed. 1984. *Euripides: Cyclops*. Oxford.
Serrano Cueto, A. 2015. *Después de Troya: Microrrelatos hispánicos de tradición clásica*. Palencia.
Squire, M. 2009. *Image and Text in Graeco-Roman Antiquity*. Cambridge.
Steinhart, M. 1995. *Das Motiv des Auges in der griechischen Bildkunst*. Mainz.
Winkler-Horaček, L. 2015. *Monster in der frühgriechischen Kunst*. Berlin.

....

CHAPTER 13

SCYLLA AND CHARYBDIS

....

MARIANNE GOVERS HOPMAN

INTRODUCTION

IN 1793, in a Europe terrified by the bloody excesses of the French Revolution, cartoonist James Gillray drew British prime minister William Pitt carefully steering the ship *Constitution*, with a buxom Britannia aboard, between a tall rock topped with a bonnet rouge with a tricolour cockade, and a whirlpool shaped as an inverted crown. The cartoon's title, 'Britannia between Scylla and Charybdis: or The Vessel of the Constitution steered clear of the Rock of Democracy, and the Whirlpool of Arbitrary Power', clarified the intended significance of the allegory (Fig. 13.1). A little over two centuries later, the 2008 song 'Torn Between Scylla and Charybdis' by heavy metal band Trivium described in gripping details the physical manifestation of fear in a situation 'between death and doom', while in his mystery novel *Back on Murder*, J. Mark Bertrand humorously narrated how during a hasty car ride through Houston, Texas, detective Roland March and sergeant Nix 'turn on West Gray, passing between the two Starbucks locations that sit like Scylla and Charybdis on either side of the street' (2010: 292)—a witty comparison that points both to the near impossibility of avoiding the Seattle coffee retail giant in today's globalized world and to the similarity of the double-tailed female creature featured on the chain's logo with the ancient monster. Contemporary audiences may not have remembered the exact details of the ancient myth, but the idiom 'between Scylla and Charybdis' has been used in modern languages since at least the fifteenth century CE to describe a situation in which one is caught between two equally dangerous and inescapable evils.

In ancient Greek myth, the sea monster Scylla, together with her counterpart Charybdis, stands out as that rare monster undefeated by a god or male hero. Most Greek monsters exist to be defeated in a battle whose outcome secures cosmic order and re-enacts the victory of civilization over forces of chaos (Felton 2013: 107–22). Zeus buries Typhoeus under a mountain in the final stage of the divine battles that secure the god's rule; Apollo kills the local female dragon before establishing his oracle at Delphi;

SHARKS; *Dogs of Scylla* .

BRITANNIA between SCYLLA & CHARYBDIS .

or   *The Vessel of the Constitution steered clear of the Rock of Democracy, and the Whirlpool of Arbitrary Power.*

FIGURE 13.1 'Britannia between Scylla and Charybdis', James Gillray, 1793.

Source: Library of Congress, LC-USZC4-3137.

the Sphinx precipitates herself from the walls of Thebes after Oedipus solves her riddle. Scylla, however, remains undefeated. In the one exception, an obscure myth told by the Hellenistic poet Lycophron, Heracles kills her only to have her father promptly bring her back to life (*Alex.* 44–9). In possibly the most spectacular ancient depiction of Scylla, a large first-century CE sculpture group in the grotto of Roman emperor Tiberius at Sperlonga (on the coast between Rome and Naples), Scylla brutally attacks Odysseus' ship. The group was crushed when the grotto collapsed in 26 CE, but the remains of Scylla's two tails strangling sailors, and an oversized hand grabbing a man's head, convey the violence of the scene and the monster's gory victory over the humans.

In this chapter, I ask why and how Scylla uncharacteristically remains undefeated in Greek and Roman myth. What does the monster do, and what does she physically look like? What fears does she trigger, convey, or symbolize? How do individual authors engage with this collective cultural symbol and its psychological associations? I first show how, despite wide differences across individual versions, Scylla's appearance in Homer's *Odyssey* and her fifth-century manifestations in visual and verbal media can be understood as expressions of male anxieties over uncontrollable females. I then analyse how from the fourth century BCE onwards, authors deal with the psychological charge conveyed by the monster through strategies of rationalization that assimilate Scylla to real-life entities, before exploring reframing techniques through which epic poets Apollonius of Rhodes, Vergil, and Ovid engage with the epic topos and spare their heroes from Odysseus' disastrous experience while still acknowledging Scylla's inescapable power. Taken together, the argument demonstrates that despite sometimes significant differences across her manifestations, Scylla's defining combination of dog, female, and sea elements plays up and intertwines at least two elemental fears that touch on basic aspects of male identity: the fear of being eaten and the fear of emasculation.

THE HOMERIC PARADIGM

The *Odyssey* provides our earliest, most detailed, and arguably most influential manifestation of the Scylla figure in antiquity. Together with the Cyclops, Circe, and the Sirens, Scylla and her counterpart Charybdis count among the many unnatural and usually dangerous creatures encountered by Odysseus during his long sea voyage from Troy to Ithaca, as described in an extensive first-person backstory to his host, the king of the Phaeacians (Books 9–12).

These encounters all result in the death of crew members and thus implicitly explain, and perhaps justify, why Odysseus presents himself to the Phaeacians as a leader without men. Yet among all his adventures, sailing through the twin dangers of Scylla and Charybdis constitutes the lowest point in Odysseus' journey. In contrast, for instance, with the Cyclops episode, which arguably reads as a celebration of Odysseus' cunning and of the values of Greek culture, the encounter with Scylla highlights his incapacity to fight the monster. His attempt to arm himself and confront her like an enemy on the battlefield results in failure (*Od.* 12.228–33). While his attention focuses on the ebb and flow of Charybdis' whirlpool, Scylla's six heads harpoon six men as if they were fish, and she devours them on the threshold of her cave. The elaborate simile that compares her to an angler catching fish highlights how the scene challenges the anthropocentric domination of human over non-human animals (12.251–7). In Odysseus' words, the image of his six companions snatched and devoured by the monster was 'the most piteous' sight of 'all that he bore while exploring the paths of the sea' (12.258–9). Later, when he finds himself in the straits a second time after losing all his companions in a shipwreck, he manages to survive Charybdis' swirling surges by clinging to a fig tree 'like a bat', but highlights how he would not have avoided destruction had Zeus allowed Scylla to catch sight of him (12.445–6).

At one level, the gruesome death of Odysseus' companions manifests and enlarges anxieties related to the hazards of sea travel, especially the widespread fear—prominent in the earlier days of Greek seafaring—that shipwrecked sailors may end up eaten by dangerous and mysterious underwater creatures (Hopman 2012: 52–70). In the *Odyssey*, Odysseus' swineherd Eumaeus and his father Laertes fear that fish may have devoured him (14.135; 24.291). One of the Greek words for sea, *laitma*, relates etymologically to the word for throat, *laimos*, and thus suggests an image of the deep as a gigantic gullet ready to engulf sailors (*DELG*, s.v. *laitma*). Stories associated with the heroes Perseus and Heracles tell how they rescued maidens offered as sacrifices to oversized sea monsters (see Ingemark and Asplund Ingemark in this volume). On a late eighth-century BCE Greek mixing bowl from Southern Italy, a capsized ship complete with steering oar, prow, and stern, is surrounded by twenty-four fish of various sizes and six naked human beings in various degrees of mutilation, one being already partially swallowed (Ischia, Archaeological Museum 168813).

The *Odyssey*'s Scylla episode deploys such anxieties at various levels. Scylla herself is a super-predator that hunts both sea creatures—including dolphins, dogfish, and larger sea monsters (12.96–7)—and human beings. On the other side of the narrow straits that she inhabits, the whirlpool Charybdis 'swallows' (12.104–5), 'vomits' (12.106), and 'sucks down' (12.240) water, thus explicitly highlighting how the episode activates fears of being devoured at sea.

Yet while the *Odyssey* is clear about the fate of Scylla's victims, it remains rather allusive about the monster's appearance. The sorceress Circe, who offers Odysseus advice about how to deal with Scylla and Charybdis before he encounters them, describes her in enigmatic terms that make it difficult to fathom what she may look or sound like. Circe mentions a jumble of limbs—twelve feet, six very long necks, and six heads, each adorned with three rows of teeth (12.89–92). Hidden in a cave, the rest of Scylla's body defies the audience's imagination and challenges conceptions of what a living being may look like (Buchan 2004). Her voice, 'comparable in size to that of a new-born puppy', etymologizes her name in relation to the word for puppy, *skylax*, but stands in a paradoxical juxtaposition with the phrase 'terrible monster' (*pelōr kakon*) with which Circe also describes her (12.86–7). A semantic analysis of *pelōr* and its derivatives suggests that the word emphasizes not so much specific attributes as the intensity of viewers' reactions (Hopman 2012: 75–7). In other words, Circe's attempt to capture Scylla's essence says little about the monster and returns audiences to their own terrors.

Thus, the Homeric Scylla confronts Odysseus (and us) as a mystery, a being whose form is impossible to fully see or comprehend. Accordingly, Odysseus' experience highlights the dreadful consequences of his inability to imagine her as a being unlike anyone or anything that he has seen before. Against Circe's advice, he puts on his armour as if about to confront an enemy on the battlefield, but despite intensely scrutinizing the rock he cannot even see Scylla (12.228–33), and she subsequently surprises him by seizing his six best men. Odysseus' failure to protect his men is tied to his inability to fathom Scylla's strangeness and to insist on confronting the monster on his rather than her terms.

A Tripartite Hybrid

While Homer confronts us with the gaping, paradoxical, and incomprehensible body of a devouring monster, later visual and verbal accounts cast Scylla as a clearly tripartite

FIGURE 13.2 Scylla; terracotta relief plaque ('Melian relief') *c.*450 BCE.

female hybrid combining the upper body of a maiden, the lower body of a fish (or snake), and two or sometimes three dog heads attached to her waist. On one of our earliest visual representations, a small terracotta relief plaque dated around 450 BCE, Scylla has the upper body of a maiden, three dog heads attached to her waist, and a lower body featuring a triple coiled fishtail with fins and a ribbed ventral surface (London, British Museum 1867,0508.673; *LIMC*, s.v. 'Skylla I' 9; Fig. 13.2). Her hair is held together with a headdress, and a short-sleeved chiton with a pleated skirt covers the juncture between her female, fish, and dog parts. Her left hand supports her chin while her right hand rests on her hip. The identification of the creature is secured by the label SKYLLA attached to a similar figure on a fourth-century red-figure vase signed by the painter Asteas, on which Scylla and a Triton frame Europa riding on a bull while Eros hovers over the scene (see Fig. 18.1 in this volume).

The type remains stable across Graeco-Roman texts and images. With the rare exception of a *c.*440–421 BCE coin from the Italian city of Cumae that represents Scylla with dog heads attached to her shoulders (*LIMC*, s.v. 'Skylla I' 2), vases, coins, gems, and sculptures ranging from the fifth century BCE onwards regularly represent Scylla as a tripartite hybrid with dog heads attached to her waist. That visualization also underlies her description in Roman authors, such as the first-century CE poet writing under the name Lygdamus, who lists Scylla in a catalogue of monsters 'with a girdle of hounds about her woman's body' (*Scyllaque virgineam canibus succincta figuram*, [Tibullus] 3.4.89).

Perhaps because of the text-centric bias that has long affected the history of ancient art, scholars have often sought to identify a literary 'source' or 'origin' for the tripartite hybrid first attested in material media. Specifically, some scholars have proposed that the visual type originated with the Greek lyric poet Stesichorus, whom later sources credit with a poem entitled *Scylla* (Waywell 1996: 109–10). The hypothesis is shaky at best. We know nothing of Stesichorus' poem except that it identified Lamia as Scylla's mother (fr. 220 Page, *PMG*; cf. Kucharski in this volume); it is unclear whether that Stesichorus is the sixth-century BCE poet or his fourth-century homonym; and Stesichorus' poem *Geryoneis* describes the monster Geryon in terms that differ from his renditions in visual media, suggesting that Stesichorus' monsters developed separately from visual sources and vice versa. As is the case with other monsters, it seems more productive to understand Scylla's visual type within the tradition of hybrids in visual arts, as a variation on the fishtailed merman that faces her on the vase in Fig. 18.1 in this volume. Scylla's ribbed fishtail on her earliest extant representation on Melian reliefs (such as Fig. 13.2) resembles that of the merman on the so-called Northampton amphora, a *c.*540 BCE amphora in East Greek style from Etruria (Stavros Niarchos Collection A 059; *LIMC*, s.v. 'Tritones' 3). The stylistic detail supports the hypothesis that the Scylla type developed in close relation to the merman type.

Scylla's visualization as a tripartite hybrid aligns her with other monsters represented as mixed bodies in ancient art, including the Theban Sphinx (lion, bird, and woman) and Typhoeus (winged anguipede). It also fits with the broader cross-cultural observation that hybridization is a common feature among monsters (Cohen 1996: 6), and that monsters are often 'prime bearers of "taxonomic perversity" ' (Atherton 1998: xiv). Yet Scylla's unique combination of female, dog, and fish parts may help us understand why she alone remains undefeated by Greek heroes. These components occupy an ambiguous position in the Greek imagination, in that humans (specifically, men) live in close proximity with but still feel potentially threatened by all three. Since Hesiod, a long tradition of misogyny considers women a necessary evil, indispensable to procreate and maintain the family line, yet also gluttonous and demanding at best, and potentially dangerous at worse (Hes. *Theog.* 602–12). Similarly, dogs—domesticated wolves—play an important role as household guardians and hunting partners but remain susceptible to their original savagery: Odysseus in his beggar's disguise gets attacked and almost torn apart by dogs (Hom. *Od.* 14.29–36), and Priam imagines how after the fall of Troy his corpse might be torn apart by the dogs whom he once raised and fed (Hom. *Il.* 22.66–71). The sea, finally, defines the Greek landscape through islands, gulfs, and inlets. It allowed the Greeks to trade and thereby grow economically, but it was also unreliable and treacherous. Under the Aegean winds, the wine-dark sea could quickly become stormy and lethal, as evidenced by the shipwreck vases mentioned above (Vermeule 1979: 179–209). Scylla, then, combines three concepts that are indispensable to Greek life but never fully domesticated.

Scylla's cultural power is further enhanced by the metaphorical coherence of her tripartite combination. Dogs are related to both the sea and to women in Greek imagination. Lesser-known sea-life is often imagined in terms of better-known land life, and the term for dog, *kuōn*, can also refer to sea creatures. The most dangerous predator in the Mediterranean, the shark, is called 'sea-dog' as early as the *Odyssey* (12.96). Dogs are also metaphorically related to women, who are not infrequently called or compared to dogs, especially in contexts that emphasize their treachery and lecherousness (Franco 2014: 19–31). Helen famously calls herself a dog in Homer (*Il.* 6.344, 355). Her sister Clytemnestra is called a 'hateful dog' in Aeschylus' *Agamemnon*, five lines before her comparison to Scylla (1228). Scylla's anchoring in the woman-as-dog Greek metaphor is further confirmed by her translation into Roman culture, which ties lustful women not so much to she-dogs as to she-wolves. The word *lupa* ('she-wolf') commonly refers to a prostitute, with *lupanar* meaning 'brothel'. In this context, the Roman substitution of wolves for Scylla's dogs (Sall. *Hist.* fr. 4.27 Reynolds; Verg. *Aen.* 3.428) offers a fascinating demonstration of how monsters' characteristics are culturally determined.

GENDERED ANXIETIES

I suggested above that in the *Odyssey* the Scylla episode manifests anxieties linked to sea travel, and especially to the image of the sea as a devouring gullet. In the fifth century BCE, as Scylla takes on a more feminized appearance in visual media, she often occurs in contexts that cast women as potential threats to the physical or social identity of their male counterparts. In Aeschylus' *Agamemnon* (1227–36), the prophetess Cassandra compares Queen Clytemnestra to Scylla at the same time as she foresees her own and King Agamemnon's murder at the queen's hands. Jason calls Medea 'more savage than Scylla' when he realizes that she has killed their children and his future bride and thus regained control over her circumstances, despite her exile (Eur. *Med.* 1343). The notion that Scylla may upset gender roles is also illustrated on a *c.*430 BCE Boeotian red-figure krater in Paris (Louvre CA 1341; *LIMC*, s.v. 'Skylla I' 69; Fig. 13.3). Scylla, featured as the familiar tripartite hybrid with the upper body of a maiden, a coiled fishtail, and two dog heads attached to her waist, carries attributes that transgress traditional gender codes. Instead of a veil, she wears a headband reminiscent of those worn by victorious male athletes; here and on other images, her muscular, nude upper body challenges artistic conventions that normally associate nudity with males; and the sword in her raised right hand puts her in the position of a male warrior preparing to confront the enemy. Altogether, the vase powerfully exemplifies how Scylla's ontological transgression of human and non-human categories may also take on a gendered significance, allowing her to challenge anthropocentric and androcentric hierarchies alike.

   With their sharp-toothed gaping dog heads surrounding the waist of a young maiden, post-Homeric Scyllae may fruitfully be compared to the near-global *vagina dentata* folkloric motif that features a woman whose toothed vagina results in the emascula-tion and death of her sexual partners (Miller 2013). Psychoanalysts anchor the motif in broad, cross-cultural psychological phenomena—a widespread fear of women; the nightmarish symmetry between the upper and lower orifice of women's bodies; and

FIGURE 13.3   Scylla wielding a sword; red-figure krater from Boeotia, *c.*430 BCE.

Source: Wikimedia / Jastrow. Public domain.

sexual anxieties that intercourse, traditionally viewed as a site of male dominance, may become lethal to the male (Horney 1932). In the stories, the invisible peril raised by the presence of teeth inside a woman's vagina results in a nightmarish reversal of male expectations: a desirable female object becomes a murderous agent, and the pleasure of intercourse ends in excruciating death.

While Scylla does not literally manifest the *vagina dentata* motif, her post-Homeric representations come as close to it as possible within the conventions of Greek art. The teeth in question are her dogs', not hers, but they closely surround her groin in a significant juxtaposition emphasized by the ephemerality of their alternate location above Scylla's shoulders. Evidence from Latin poetry also confirms the importance of that juxtaposition. Vergil's *Eclogue* 6 imagines the barking dogs as a girdle surrounding Scylla's genitals (*candida succinctam latrantibus inguina monstris*, 6.75). The shorter phrase 'girdled with dogs' (*succincta canibus*) becomes almost formulaic in Scylla's descriptions from Lucretius onwards (e.g. Lucr. *DRN* 5.892; Sall. *Hist.* fr. 4.27). In Ovid's *Metamorphoses*, Scylla's 'truncated loins' (*inguinibus truncis*) sit on the back of beasts (14.65–6); the dogs are substituted for the maiden's groin.

If it is relatively easy to show the resemblance of post-Homeric Scyllae with the toothed vagina motif, what then, of the Homeric monster? To what extent might the multi-headed, man-devouring creature implicitly rely on and image forth male anxieties about emasculating females? There is, to be sure, nothing anthropomorphic in Circe's description of the creature, whose teeth are emphatically located inside her heads at the extremity of long necks. Yet Circe's silence over Scylla's core, hidden inside her cave, precisely highlights the mystery raised by her body and gives free rein to audience's imagination. *Vagina dentata* stories often include a mutilating door or passage that metaphorically replicates the woman's anatomy (Gessain 1957: 290). Similarly, Scylla's location in narrow straits may be understood as a metaphor for dangerous female parts, especially since the Greek word *auchēn* may refer to any narrow band or connection, including straits, the neck, and the vagina (*LSJ*, s.v. *auchēn*). The possibility that the Homeric Scylla may be grounded in unconscious anxieties about emasculating females is further supported by the poem's general context. While Odysseus' homecoming partly depends on his ability to physically sail back to Ithaca and undertake the long sea voyage between Troy and his homeland, his full reintegration into society largely depends on his wife, Penelope. The *Odyssey* remains constantly alert to the possibility that Penelope may remarry, or take a lover, or even kill her husband, as Clytemnestra did (Murnaghan 1987; Felson-Rubin 1987). The uncertainty about Penelope's thoughts, desires, and intentions remains open right until Book 23, including the long recognition scene in which Penelope tricks her husband into believing that their marriage bed has been moved, before finally affirming her fidelity and returning to her traditional role as a wife. In that context of fluctuating gender roles, other female characters in the *Odyssey* can arguably be read as explorations of Penelope's possible behaviour—whether she will be a Nausicaa-like helper, or lure Odysseus to his death like the Sirens, or attempt to 'unman' him like Circe (10.341). Similarly, audience members may have—consciously or not—understood the Homeric Scylla in relation to the terrifying possibility that, as happens in *vagina dentata* stories, renewed intercourse with Penelope may end in Odysseus' death.

HELLENISTIC DEVELOPMENTS

Starting in the fourth century BCE, the history of the Scylla figure reflects new intellectual trends, such as the valuation of critical inquiry and direct observation; the growth of literacy; the development of libraries; and the scholarly urge to organize, rationalize, and explain traditional stories. Like other monsters, she becomes a favourite target for the efforts of ancient scholars eager to purge traditional stories from fictional elements and replace those with empirically observable phenomena. Those various brands of interpretation are not easy to classify. Scholars sometimes distinguish between rationalization and allegoresis as two ways to screen out the fabulous elements of myth, the former focusing on historical and the latter on metaphysical or moral truths. The concept of allegory, however, is multifaceted and has been used in so many different senses that it has lost some of its critical edge. I thus propose to organize exegetical efforts into a tripartite typology according to the temporality of their referents (Hopman 2012: 180–90).

On the one hand, time-bound rationalizations explain Scylla with reference to specific, historical characters or objects whose characteristics, understood metaphorically, align with the monster's traditional attributes. The fourth-century BCE writer Palaephatus, known for his rationalizing explanations of mythological monsters, rejects as 'very stupid' the story that Scylla was 'a beast living in the Tyrrhenian Sea'. Instead, he proposes that hers was the name of a swift pirate ship with a figure—possibly a carved puppy—at its prow, and that the myth about the monstrous Scylla resulted from misunderstanding Odysseus' account of his escape from that ship (20). Similarly, in the first or second century CE, the paradoxographer Heraclitus proposed that Scylla was in fact a prostitute who would 'devour' (metaphorically, one assumes) the gluttonous clients who hung about her, dog-like (*On Unbelievable Tales* 2). He rationalizes other female monsters, such as Medusa, the Harpies, and the Sirens, as courtesans as well (1.4, 8, 14, 16), leading German scholar Wilhelm Nestle to speculate about Heraclitus' obsession with prostitutes (1940: 151).

At the other end of the interpretative spectrum, monsters could be aligned with the timeless entities of philosophy and morals. In the fourth century BCE, Plato uses the Chimaera, Scylla, and Cerberus as paradigms for his metaphorical representation of the human soul as a tripartite composite of three shapes: a multi-headed beast, a lion, and a man (*Resp.* 588c2). Five centuries later, in defending Homer against the charge of impiety, the rhetorician Heraclitus (not to be confused with the paradoxographer) offers a morally satisfying allegory of Odysseus' wanderings by interpreting gods and monsters as symbols for vices and temptations. In his reading, Scylla becomes an allegory for 'polymorphous shamelessness' whose three dogs represent 'rapacity, recklessness, and greediness' (*Homeric Problems* 70.11).

Between the time-bound referents of history and the timelessness of epistemology and morals, a third mode of rationalization understands monsters in relation to the long-term referents of geography and ethnography. Since at least the fifth century BCE, tradition had located Scylla on the Italian side of the straits of Messina separating the Italian peninsula from Sicily (Thuc. 4.24.5). Those were sometimes named the Scyllaean straits (Archestratus, fr. 51.2 Olson/Sens), and a specific cliff in the area was named Skyllaion in Greek and Scyllaeum in Latin, an epithet that first-century BCE Roman historian Sallust explains by the cliff's resemblance to a human girdled with dog heads and by the barking-like sound produced by sea currents (*Hist.* fr. 4.27 Reynolds). Subsequently, the Greeks and Romans sometimes explained monstrous Scylla as a distorted reflection of the rock's characteristics or of the activities practised around it. The Hellenistic historian Polybius views Scylla's method for fishing men as a warped echo of Sicilian harpooning practices (34.3.1-8). The twelfth-century CE Byzantine commentator Tzetzes closes the interpretative gap and identifies Scylla with the cliff, thus suggesting that the myth emerged as a distorted reflection on the landscape (*ad Lyc.* 46).

Despite the variety of their referents, these three modes of rationalization are related in that they all seek to reduce the instability of the monster, eliminate its unsettling hybridity, and assimilate it to a single and comprehensible element of human experience— a woman, a rock, a vice. In some way, they may be understood as efforts to intellectually overcome the monster by eliminating its mystery and its roots in male fears about women's bodies. Another effort to explain the monster, albeit within the genre of fiction, may be detected in the aetiological story that makes the monstrous, hybrid shape the product of a maiden's transformation. According to the most developed version of the metamorphosis story, Scylla was once a beautiful maiden who attracted the attention of the sea god, Glaucus, but rejected his advances. In frustration, Glaucus went to the magician Circe and asked for love potions that would cause the nymph to fall in love with him, but the jealous sorceress, herself in love with Glaucus, smeared poison on Scylla's favourite cave. When the maiden came to swim and submerged herself in the water, her lower body was transformed into the familiar monstrous shape, and she found herself surrounded by raging dog heads.

The most detailed version of Scylla's transformation from nymph to monster appears in Ovid's *Metamorphoses* (8 CE; see Liveley in this volume), but the story may be traced back as early as the third-century BCE Greek poetess Hedyle, whose poem *Scylla* told how Glaucus would bring love gifts to the nymph and how his unrequited attention attracted the pity of the neighbouring Siren (*Suppl. Hell.* 456.1–6). The aetiological structure of the metamorphosis and the transformation's permanence parallel other Hellenistic metamorphosis stories, making it likely that the tale of Scylla's transformation is a Hellenistic innovation (Forbes Irving 1990: 20–37; Lowe 2011). Its plot also fits within a broader Hellenistic interest in imagining backstories for extreme actions narrated in Homer and the tragedians, grounding them in individual psychology, especially the disruptive power of eros. For example, the Sicilian Greek poet Theocritus depicts a youthful Polyphemus in love with the nymph Galatea and suggests that the rejected Cyclops' desires and frustration may lead to violent actions not unlike those of the Homeric Cyclops (*Id.* 6 and 11). Similarly, Hellenistic poets characterize the raging Scylla as the unfortunate victim of a love triangle, and her attack on Odysseus' ship as her way of taking revenge on Odysseus' helper, Circe.

Post-Hellenistic sources also offer a variant metamorphosis story that ties Scylla to another story of unrequited love, but as desiring subject rather than love object. As early as the fifth century BCE, Aeschylus alludes to a tale in which Scylla was the daughter of Nisus, king of Megara, whose purple lock protected the city against potential invaders (*Cho.* 612–22). When Minos, king of Crete, attacked Megara, Scylla fell in love with him and cut off her father's lock in the hope that Minos would make her his wife, but he rejected her. Some authors have Minos kill the maiden; others tell how he had her tied to his ship and dragged through the water until the gods turned her into a bird; still others challenge the mythographic distinction between Megarian and Sicilian Scylla (Hyg. *Fab.* 198 and 199; Serv. on Verg. *Ecl.* 6.74) and tell how the Megarian maiden became the Sicilian monster (e.g. Verg. *Ecl.* 6.74–7; Ov. *Am.* 3.12.21).

Whether they rationalize Scylla as a reflection of Sicilian fishing practices or explain her monstrosity as the result of an unfortunate love story, post-fifth-century approaches to Scylla often share an interest in intellectually domesticating and taming the monster. Rationalizing versions trace the monster's origins to characters, entities, or practices from real life and insist that she exists only as a product of the human mind. The metamorphosis story does not question the monster's existence but gives her a past that makes her more comprehensible; aligns the maiden Scylla with usual gender conventions, making her an object of male desire; and exposes the artificiality of the hybrid combination of sea, dog, and woman born out of Circe's magic.

SCYLLA IN HELLENISTIC AND ROMAN EPIC

Keeping in mind the ongoing enterprise of domesticating or demystifying the monster, I end by examining Scylla's treatment specifically in Hellenistic and Roman epic poems—Apollonius of Rhodes' *Argonautica*, Vergil's *Aeneid*, and Ovid's *Metamorphoses*. Their heroes, Jason and Aeneas, travel in Odysseus' footsteps. The monstrous, man-eating Scylla thus inevitably belongs with their journeys, and the danger that she raises is perhaps even greater, or at least more precise than in the *Odyssey*, since, in the meantime, visual and tragic sources have fully exposed the sexual potential of the trope. How then could the poets rescue their heroes from a certain death? In other words, what literary devices may be tapped to prevent damage from a monster rooted in anxieties about women's bodies?

The most radical solution may be found in Vergil, whose hero Aeneas ends up deviating from Odysseus' route and circumnavigating Sicily rather than facing the monster. The context closely engages with the Homeric intertext. As in the *Odyssey*, this episode in the *Aeneid* forms part of an extended first-person narrative—in this case, by Aeneas to his host, Queen Dido of Carthage—and similarly includes a retelling of Circe's advice to Odysseus—here in the form of the seer Helenus' prophecy to Aeneas. Like Circe, Helenus describes how the core of Scylla's body lies hidden in a cave from which only her head emerges, but unlike his predecessor, he offers a fully embodied description of the hybrid that highlights the disjunction between her components (3.426–8). Her upper body is that of an attractive maiden, whose erotic appeal Vergil highlights through the mention of her 'beautiful breast' (*pulchro pectore*) but also sexualizes with a reference to her 'groin' (*pubes*)—a rare reference to sexual organs in the poem. Her lower body, that of a sea monster (*pistrix*), combines dolphin tails with wolf wombs. The unique phrase 'womb of wolves' (*utero luporum*) emphasizes the nightmarish fusion of the wolves' gaping mouths (and presumably sharp teeth) with the maiden's womb that closely parallels the *vagina dentata* motif. Thus, Helenus' especially terrifying description fully activates Scylla's capacity to feature the female body as both attractive and potentially emasculating, before concluding with the advice to choose a different route 'rather than to have seen just once the hideous Scylla below her large cave and the rocks echoing with the dark-blue dogs' (3.429–32). Vergil's Aeneas preserves his integrity and the life of his crew by not facing Scylla. For Helenus and Aeneas, and perhaps Vergil, avoidance is the best way to deal with a threat that manifests a fundamental anxiety about women's bodies.

A different approach to the monster and the fears associated with it appears in Ovid's *Metamorphoses*, whose Scylla story closely engages with both the Homeric and Vergilian models. Ovid's Aeneas, unlike Vergil's, does sail through the straits of Charybdis and

Scylla, but his Scylla has become something different altogether. Ovid precedes Aeneas' journey through the straits with an extensive account of the monstrous Scylla as the result of a maiden's metamorphosis caused by Circe (13.730–14.74). The final product closely parallels Vergil's description (14.59–67). Like her Vergilian predecessor, Ovid's Scylla stands on 'ravening dogs', and beastly forms encircle her loins and what remains of her womb, but Ovid provides a markedly different perspective on that body (Jouteur 2007). Rather than offering an outsider's description that confronts us with the mysterious and threatening alterity of the monster, the poem mediates the sight through Scylla herself. Rather than ours, the initial terror is hers, as, failing to recognize her new body, she 'flees in fear and tries to drive away the boisterous, barking things'. By emphasizing the maiden's incredulity, then her terror and flight as she witnesses the disfiguration of her lower body, the poem shows us a monster alienated from itself (Hardie 2009; Seidler 2022). In a striking bifurcation process, Scylla seeks for her thighs, legs, and feet, only to find gaping dog heads in lieu of her own body. Out of hatred for Circe, she robs Odysseus of his companions, but by the time the Trojans arrive, Scylla has been turned to stone—by whom or what, Ovid does not say—and the ship passes unharmed. Thus, Ovid neither avoids nor ignores the monster but rather deactivates the physical threat, first by alienating the monster from her own body and then by petrifying it.

Vergil's Aeneas avoids Scylla while Ovid's hero sails by a mitigated version of the monster. Apollonius of Rhodes offers yet another approach in his epic *Argonautica* (third century BCE). There Jason and his Argonauts go through the straits of Scylla and Charybdis on their return journey from Colchis, after successfully stealing the Golden Fleece from King Aietes with help from his daughter, Medea. Scylla belongs with a section of the journey that closely engages with Odysseus' voyage: after departing from Circe's island, Jason and Medea have no choice but to sail between Scylla and Charybdis (4.753–963).

The sense of danger is very real. In the words of Jason's divine helper Hera, Jason and his crew must avoid both Charybdis, 'lest she suck them down and carry them all off', and Scylla, 'lest she swoop down on them with her horrible jaws and destroy the choicest heroes' (4.825–31). The Homeric intertext and the undefeatable monster of the *Odyssey* are fully present here. Yet the fact that Hera rather than Circe details the danger also underscores the difference in the heroes' experience of the peril. While Circe only advises Odysseus *how* to sail through Scylla and Charybdis, Apollonius' Hera establishes a whole machinery to ensure that Jason will pass through unscathed. Her messenger Iris orders the divine smith Hephaestus to stop working at his forges under the Sicilian volcano Etna, and the wind god Aeolus to calm the winds (4.760–9). Most importantly, Hera secures the help of the sea goddess Thetis—wife of the Argonaut Peleus—and her Nereids to ensure that the Argo stays on the narrow path that will keep it at safe distance from the twin dangers.

In lieu of the terrifying navigation evoked in the *Odyssey*, readers of the Hellenistic epic face a delightful, eroticized scene of maidens at play. As the Argo comes in sight of Scylla's rock and Charybdis' whirlpool, Thetis seizes its rudder. The Nereids reveal their 'white knees' as they lift their garment hems, they rush atop the Wandering Rocks to prevent them from colliding with the ship, and they toss the Argo through the air like a ball (4.948–52). The narrative, in comparing the Nereids to girls at play by a sandy beach, recalls the Homeric description of Nausicaa and her maidens in *Odyssey* Book 6. Confronted with the Homeric monster, the poet diverts his audience's gaze from the monstrous female and redirects it towards a delightful scene that reasserts established gender hierarchy, returns female beings to their traditional role as vulnerable erotic objects, and lets Jason and the Argonauts safely sail by the indomitable monster.

CONCLUSION

On the fourth-century BCE bronze handle of a mirror from the south Italian city of Locri, Scylla frontally faces the viewer holding an oar in her left hand while two dog heads and the serpentine bodies of two marine monsters symmetrically frame her female upper body (Paris, Louvre, Br. 1686; *LIMC*, s.v. 'Skylla I' 22). Her presence on a mirror handle nicely captures how she and other monsters reflect the ever-changing interests, concerns, and anxieties of their makers and viewers. As arguably the closest instance to a Greek version of the *vagina dentata* trope, Scylla manifests deep-seated misogynistic views of women as potential threats to men's bodily integrity. On closer inspection, the specificities of each representation, verbal or visual, say something about their cultural contexts. Beyond broad trends, such as the feminization and sexualization of the monster in the fifth century BCE and the emergence of critical attitudes in the fourth and especially the third century BCE, the development of the genre of Hellenistic and Roman epic shows how individual authors use various strategies, ranging from avoidance to displacement, to rescue their heroes Odysseus and Aeneas from the indomitable threat inherited from Homer. Show me your Scylla, and I will tell you who you are.

SUGGESTED READING

Detailed lists for the deployment of Scylla and Charybdis in Graeco-Roman texts and images may be found in mythological dictionaries, including the *RE*, Roscher *Lex.*, and the *LIMC*. Hopman (2012) offers a thorough approach to Scylla's diachronic deployment from Homer to Ovid and beyond, including detailed analyses of the most important passages and images, as well as theoretical considerations on the semantics of mythological names. On the Scylla group at Sperlonga, see Andreae and Conticello (1987).

WORKS CITED

Andreae, B., and B. Conticello. 1987. *Skylla und Charybdis: Zur Skylla-Gruppe von Sperlonga.* Mainz.

Atherton, C., ed. 1998. *Monsters and Monstrosity in Greek and Roman Culture*. Bari.

Bertrand, J. M. 2010. *Back on Murder*. Minneapolis.

Buchan, M. 2004. 'Looking to the Feet: The Riddles of the Scylla.' *Helios* 31/1–2: 21–49.

Cohen, J. J. 1996. 'Monster Culture (Seven Theses)', in *Monster Theory: Reading Culture*, ed. J. J. Cohen, 3–25. Minneapolis.

Felson-Rubin, N. 1987. 'Penelope's Perspective: Character from Plot', in *Homer: Beyond Oral Poetry*, ed. J. M. Bremer, I. J. F. de Jong, and J. Kalff, 61–83. Amsterdam.

Felton, D. 2013. 'Rejecting and Embracing the Monstrous in Ancient Greece and Rome', in *The Ashgate Research Companion to Monsters and the Monstrous*, ed. A. S. Mittman and P. J. Dendle, 103–31. Farnham.

Forbes Irving, P. M. C. 1990. *Metamorphosis in Greek Myths*. Oxford.

Franco, C. 2014. *Shameless: The Canine and the Feminine in Ancient Greece*. Berkeley and Los Angeles.

Gessain, R. 1957. ' "Vagina dentata" dans la clinique et la mythologie.' *La Psychanalyse* 3: 247–95.

Hardie, P. 2009. 'The Self-Divisions of Scylla.' *Trends in Classics* 1: 118–47.

Hopman, M. G. 2012. *Scylla: Myth, Metaphor, Paradox*. Cambridge.

Horney, K. 1932. 'The Dread of Woman.' *International Journal of Psychoanalysis* 13: 348–60.

Jouteur, I. 2007. 'Scylla, le monstre candide', in *Actes du XVe Congrès de l'Association Guillaume Budé, Orléans, août 2003: La poétique, théorie et pratique*, 607–19. Paris.

Lowe, D. 2011. 'Scylla, the Diver's Daughter: Aeschrion, Hedyle, and Ovid.' *Classical Philology* 106/3: 260–4.

Miller, S. A. 2013. 'Monstrous Sexuality: Variations on the *Vagina Dentata*', in *The Ashgate Research Companion to Monsters and the Monstrous*, ed. A. S. Mittman and P. J. Dendle, 311–28. Farnham.

Murnaghan, S. 1987. *Disguise and Recognition in the* Odyssey. Princeton.

Nestle, W. 1940. *Vom Mythos zum Logos: Die Selbstentfaltung des griechischen Denkens vom Homer bis auf die Sophistik und Sokrates*. Stuttgart.

Seidler, S. 2022. 'Bitches and Witches: Grotesque Sexuality in Ovid's Scylla (*Metamorphoses* 13.730–14.74).' *Acta Iassyensia Comparationis* 29: 13–24.

Vermeule, E. 1979. *Aspects of Death in Early Greek Art and Poetry*. Berkeley and Los Angeles.

Waywell, G. B. 1996. 'Scilla nell'arte antica', in *Ulisse: Il mito e la memoria*, ed. B. Andreae and C. Parisi Presicce, 108–19. Rome.

....

CHAPTER 14

SIRENS AND HARPIES

The Enchanting and Repulsive Avian Monsters of Classical Antiquity

....

RYAN DENSON

INTRODUCTION

....

WHILE several classical mythological creatures, such as the Gorgons, the Sphinx, and Pegasus, have hybrid forms that incorporate avian body parts, particularly the wings, the Sirens and Harpies possess more avian elements in terms of both their physical forms and distinctly birdlike behaviours. Although birds themselves were occasionally already related to the supernatural, as in Greek ornithomancy and Roman augury, the Sirens' and Harpies' peculiar mixture of avian and anthropomorphic features allows us to properly deem them monsters. This unsettling hybridity designates them most strongly as monstrous entities precisely because they do not fit securely within the established categories of wholly avian or wholly anthropic living beings. Moreover, the fact that both are female aligns them with various aspects of monstrous femininity as well. Yet these two groups of female avian hybrids exhibit contrasting behaviours and attributes. Sirens have an enchanting quality resulting from the pleasant nature and allure of their song, allowing them to draw victims to their stationary position on an island cliff. In contrast, the Harpies are defined by a repulsive nature tied to the emotion of disgust, and are a more mobile threat, swooping down from the air to harass their victims.

SIRENS: ENCHANTING AVIANS

....

Most modern readers probably have a passing familiarity with the Sirens, as the phrase 'siren song' has become a commonplace means of describing something that is superficially alluring but is inherently destructive. Marine associations also surround the Sirens, as one may expect to encounter them at sea; yet they cannot properly be deemed sea monsters, as their land-dwelling nature distinguishes them from the scaly horrors within the sea itself. They are situated on an island, the melodies of the Sirens reach out across the waters to pose a hazard for ancient sailors, though the song itself is evidently not an unpleasant experience. In the words of the Roman poet Martial (first century CE), the Sirens are the 'delightful bane of sailors' (*Epigrams* 3.64.1), a description that captures the inherent tension between the blissful nature of the Sirens' song and the fact that it is simultaneously a force that leads to the death of those who succumb to its charms. This tension between their song's pleasantness and potential perils is the fundamental characteristic for the Sirens of classical antiquity.

Appropriately, then, our earliest and most famous encounter with the Sirens in ancient literature comes in the *Odyssey*, a text concerned with the dangers experienced by a wandering sailor. The witch Circe, providing instructions for Odysseus' return home, warns him to avoid the Sirens:

> First, you will come to the Sirens, who bewitch all humans that come upon them. If someone unknowingly draws near and hears the voice of the Sirens, he will never see his wife and young children rejoicing at his homecoming. But the clear song of the Sirens will bewitch him. They sit in a meadow, and many corpses of men rot around them, the skin decaying on the bones. (12.39–46)[1]

Thus, already in Homer, we observe the enchanting quality of the Sirens juxtaposed with evidence of the danger they represent: the macabre detail of the rotting corpses of previous victims. Circe advises countering this threat in a manner particularly appropriate to their sonic nature by having Odysseus' crew stop their ears up with wax, while he himself may listen if he is tied to the mast (12.47–54). When Odysseus and his crew do encounter the Sirens later in the narrative, we learn also that the song's content itself is alluring, promising wisdom, and, for Odysseus, knowledge of the Trojan War as the Sirens themselves proclaim: 'For we know all things in broad Troy that the Argives and Trojans suffered by the will of the gods, and we know the things that will come to pass on the much-nourishing earth' (12.189–91). Odysseus' personal reaction to hearing their words in person provides a clear example of the captivating nature of the Sirens, from which Odysseus is only saved because his men obey their orders: 'Yet my heart desired to listen. I twitched my eyebrows, a sign ordering my companions to unbind me. But they rowed through, rushing forward' (12.192–4).

Beyond Homer, other ancient accounts of Odysseus' encounter with the Sirens contain few additional elements as his crew always row past the Sirens' island unscathed. Occasionally, we read that the Sirens killed themselves by flinging themselves onto the harbour's rocks after their failed attempt against Odysseus (Lycoph. *Alex.* 712–16; Hyg. *Fab.* 141; Strabo 6.1.1). The *Odyssey* never alludes to this, though the Roman

---

[1] All translations are my own, unless otherwise indicated.

mythographer Hyginus provides the clearest rationale for this later tradition of the Sirens' suicide with the statement, 'It had been predicted that they would live only as long as nobody who heard their singing would pass by' (*Fab.* 141), while the earlier Hellenistic poet Lycophron had seemingly alluded to this with the detail that the Fates ordained the Sirens' demise (*Alex.* 716).

While the temptation of knowledge functions as one alluring element of the Sirens for Odysseus, ancient authors habitually describe the Sirens' song itself always as a blissful musical experience, referring to it as 'honey-sweet' (*Od.* 12.187), 'beautiful' (12.192), 'lily-like' (Ap. Rhod. *Argon.* 4.903). One especially illustrative anecdote comes from the third-century CE rhetorician Aelian when describing the voice of Aspasia, the wife of the Athenian statesman Pericles: 'But she had a sweet, gentle voice. When she spoke, one might have thought they were hearing a Siren' (*VH* 12.1). So pervasive was the musical quality of the Sirens that Plato depicted them as the force representing the different sounds of each sphere of the universe in his Myth of Er (*Resp.* 617b–d). This quality, moreover, leads the Sirens to be placed in opposition to other famously musical figures; for example, versions of the Argonauts' encounter have the Sirens' voices being drowned out by Orpheus' song (Ap. Rhod. *Argon.* 4.903–9; Apollod. *Bibl.* 1.135). Aside from their customary role as an enchanting threat for passing sailors, the Sirens' sonic nature has also led them to be contrasted with the Muses. The second-century CE travel writer Pausanias, for instance, tells in his *Guide to Greece* of a musical contest between the Muses and the Sirens, and after winning this competition the Muses duly plucked the Sirens (a particularly appropriate punishment for avian monsters), fashioning crowns out of their feathers (9.34.3). While the Homeric episode contains no explicit ties to the Muses, their 'Muse-like capacity' has resulted in some modern scholars reading the encounter in the *Odyssey* as a metapoetic episode, wherein the Sirens are viewed as bards themselves, self-referentially singing about their own singing (12.184–8), while their promise to grant Odysseus knowledge about the Trojan War recalls the more warlike story of the *Iliad* (Schur 2014: 9–10).

Details concerning the Sirens' origins, their island, and how they came to lure sailors to it are sparse. Etymological considerations reveal nothing about their origins, nor provide any hint of their avian or sonic qualities, as the ancient Greek *Seirēn* is etymologically uncertain (Chantraine 2009, s.v. *Seirēn*). The Hellenistic poet Apollonius, though, provides a glimpse at an earlier life for the Sirens:

> And once they were handmaidens for Demeter's lovely daughter [Persephone]. When she was still unmarried, they sung without reserve. At that time, part of them appearing like birds and part like maidens, from a vantage point overlooking an excellent harbour, they always kept watch for travellers, depriving them of the honey-sweet joy of a homecoming, causing them to waste away in putrefaction. (*Argon.* 4.896–902)

While Apollonius gives no precise reason for their transformation, Hyginus later specifies that they were turned into avian monsters by Ceres (the Roman equivalent of

Demeter) as a punishment for not aiding her daughter when she was abducted by Hades (*Fab.* 141). The Sirens' genealogy has some bearing on their marine associations as they are often stated to be the descendants of the river god Achelous (Ov. *Met.* 5.552; 14.88; Sil. *Pun.* 12.33; Nonnus *Dion.* 13.310–15). Occasionally, they may also be descendants of a Muse (Ap. Rhod. *Argon.* 4.895–6; Hyg. *Fab.* 141; Apollod. *Biblio.* 7.18). Likewise, the number of Sirens and their names (when provided) varied amongst ancient authors. Lycophron, for instance, has three, named Parthenope, Leucosia, and Ligeia (*Alex.* 717–27); Apollodorus, a Roman mythographer of the first or second century CE, also names three, but as Pisinoe, Aglaope, and Thelxiepia (*Bibl.* 7.18).

As for their 'traditionally' birdlike bodies, Homer provides no physical description of the Sirens. Only in later texts do we find references to these avian aspects, the earliest such reference being Euripides' mention of them as 'winged maidens' (*Hel.* 166–7), perhaps signifying predominantly anthropomorphic bodies with the addition of wings, while Lycophron refers to them as 'Harpy-limbed nightingales' (*Alex.* 653), testifying to their physical similarities to the Harpies. It is through ancient art, though, that we may gain a full appreciation of the Sirens' avian nature. Iconographic representations show them as human-avian hybrids, yet the precise mixture varies, depending on the inclination of the artist. These blends may be broadly construed as three types, though each cannot be securely associated with specific time periods. The first form, which I designate Type A, is primarily anthropic, possessing human torsos with birds' legs and wings. A mosaic from Tunisia, dated to the third century CE, best exemplifies this form (Fig. 14.1). Odysseus and his crew appear on the left-hand side, identifiable by Odysseus tied to the mast, while the Sirens are shown on their island to the right. Here, one might even mistake them for ordinary women at first glance, their monstrous nature

FIGURE 14.1 Mosaic of Odysseus and the Sirens; Bardo National Museum, Tunisia.

Source: Wikimedia / Giorces.

becoming apparent only once one notices the distinctly avian legs and wings tucked behind their bodies. Another aspect of note in this mosaic and elsewhere is the tendency to portray the Sirens holding a variety of musical instruments, likely to convey their sonic abilities within a visual medium (*LIMC*, s.v. 'Seirenes' 35–43). This feature helps distinguish visual representations of the Sirens from those of the Harpies, who, lacking any thoroughgoing musical qualities, are never represented with such instruments. A second form, which I designate Type B, configures the mixture of the anthropic and avian elements as more predominately avian, with the Sirens' body being entirely that of bird, aside from the head of a human female, as for example, with a terracotta vase dated to around 560 BCE (*LIMC*, s.v. 'Seirenes' 9). A final form, which I designate Type C, depicts what is essentially a composite of Types A and B with the body of a bird, but an entire female torso with human arms emerging from where the bird's neck would usually begin (*LIMC*, s.v. 'Seirenes' 42, 45, 58).

We can conclude this brief survey of their physical nature by pointing to an eventual evolution in the Sirens' form and, thereby, clearing up an occasional misconception about the classical Sirens. As noted above, the avian form of the Sirens differentiates them from the more piscine sea monsters, yet this distinction ultimately breaks down in the medieval world, when mermaids are sometimes referred to as Sirens (Faral 1953). We can detect the influence of this shift in the modern world as well: the modern French *sirène* can refer to either these classical avian monsters or mermaids (Chantraine 1954: 451–2), and classical scholars have sometimes even referred to Archaic Greek representations of mermaid-like figures as 'Sirens' (Shepard [1940] 2011: 10, 25), though there is no indication that these were viewed as Sirens by contemporaries. Not until the *Liber monstrorum*, a Latin catalogue of marvellous creatures dated to the late seventh to early eighth century CE, do we find the earliest reference to Sirens in this form, where they are described as having the upper torso of a maiden, and a scaly fishtail (1.6; Oswald 2012: 350–3). Thus, it is only in the early medieval period that the Sirens' fishy form is introduced. Until then, though, the Sirens were understood as hybrid avian songstresses, whose maritime aspects were confined primarily to their genealogical association with Achelous and their position on an island cliff.

HARPIES: REPULSIVE AVIANS

Whereas the Sirens are premised upon a complex tension between the beauty of their voices and their harmful intentions of luring sailors onto the deadly rocks around their island, the Harpies are commonly depicted as an unambiguously unpleasant force. They are, moreover, in a sense, more 'hands-on' monsters than the Sirens, as they regularly come into contact with their victims or their victims' food, fouling it or snatching it away. Such aspects are seen in the etymological considerations of the ancient Greek *Harpyia*, which is thought to derive either from a perfect participle of *ereptesthai* ('to feed on') or from *harpazein* ('to snatch'; Chantraine 2009, s.v. *Harpyia*). Either way, the etymology seems appropriate for the threat posed by these avian monsters. Like the Sirens, the Harpies will often be depicted as causing a type of indirect suffering for their victims, not attacking them directly, but rather causing them to languish in a state of perpetual hunger by preventing them from eating. This propensity for snatching is the principal defining trait of the Harpies, occasionally combined with the traits of swiftness and evoking disgust.

The earliest traces of the Harpies come in a series of fleeting references in Homer, where the creatures have a clear association with the winds. The *Iliad* mentions them only once, describing Achilles' horses as the offspring of the West Wind and a Harpy named Podarge ('Fleet-Foot', 18.148–51). In the *Odyssey*, the Harpies are not among the monsters Odysseus encounters, yet the fear that he has fallen afoul of them lingers back in Ithaca, though here Harpies may metaphorically refer to storms at sea. For example, Telemachus lists them among the possible calamities for his father: 'And, now, the Harpies have ignominiously swept him away' (1.241), a line repeated verbatim among Eumaeus' own worries about Odysseus (14.371). As with the Sirens, Homer gives no physical description. Rather, Hesiod provides the earliest reference to the Harpies' avian nature: 'And Thaumas married Electra, the daughter of deep-flowing Oceanos. She bore swift Iris and the lovely-haired Harpies, Aello ("Storm-Swift"), and Ocypetes ("Swift-Flying"), who with their swift wings keep up with the gusts of the wind and the birds. For they dart forth as fast as time' (*Theog.* 265–9). In later texts, we also find references to their speed (Theognis, *Elegiae* 1.715–16; Lycoph. *Alex.* 166–7). Comparison between the Harpies and the winds is another occasional feature from Hesiod that we find in later texts (Ap. Rhod. *Argon.* 2.263–5, 275–8; Val. Flacc. *Argon.* 4.452).

Hesiod's description of the Harpies as 'lovely-haired', however, is exceptional. After Hesiod, no ancient authors imbue the Harpies with any such pleasant traits. The Harpies also differ in the nature of their movement. While the Sirens do possess wings, suggesting the capability to fly, they are essentially rooted on their island; the Sirens pose no danger once one sails beyond their shoreline. With the Harpies, though, we see a more mobile type of avian monster, one that explicitly features flight as a dominant characteristic. Flying, after all, is essential to their eponymous trait of snatching up things and carrying them off.

We see this characteristic trait most strongly in the myth of Phineus as the primary narrative context in which the Harpies appear, especially that of Apollonius' *Argonautica*. Here, Phineus' story is recounted briefly: he was once granted the gift of prophecy by Apollo but began to reveal the 'sacred intentions' of the gods to humankind. Consequently, Zeus blinds him and ordains the punishment of having the Harpies perpetually steal his food (2.178–87). Apollonius vividly describes this action as a combination of the Harpies snatching up the food and befouling it with a putrid stench (2.188–93). In the later *Argonautica* of the Roman poet Valerius Flaccus (first century CE), Phineus himself describes his plight:

The Harpies always watch over my food. Alas, I can never deceive them. Immediately, they come down, like the black cloud of a swirling whirlwind. By the sound of her

wings I already know Celaeno from far away. They pillage and carry off my feast, spoil
and overturn my cups. A stench rages and a wretched fight ensues, for the monsters
have a hunger as I do. What they have scorned and polluted and what falls from their
dark claws, allows me to linger on in the light [of life]. Nor would I be allowed to
interrupt this fate by death. My cruel destitution is prolonged by such nourishment.
(4.450–9)

The suffering that the Harpies inflict on Phineus is expressed as one of prolonged
famine; they neither attack nor carry off Phineus himself. The accompanying stench and
the fact that they 'spoil' the feast in some manner makes clear the association between
the Harpies and the emotion of disgust.

Beyond the myth of Phineus, the other major literary episode to include the Harpies
appears in Vergil's *Aeneid*, where the Harpies do not play their traditional role of seizing
Phineus' food but rather harass the Trojans in a similar fashion. Vergil's description
supplies another useful insight into the behaviour of the Harpies:

But suddenly the Harpies come down from the mountains with a horrifying swoop,
and they brandish their wings with a great clamour. They pillage our feast, and spoil
everything with a filthy touch. Then, there is an ominous sound amid the revolting
stench. Again, in a deep recess underneath a hollowed-out cliffside, enclosed by
trees all around, we set up the tables, and we rekindled the fire of the altars. And yet
again, coming from the opposing area of the sky, and a concealed hiding place, the
resounding rabble with taloned feet was flying around their prey, polluting the feast
with their mouths. (3.225–34)

Here, the motif of disgust recurs with the Harpies' 'filthy touch' and the spoiling of the
Trojan feasts. While here, as in the later text of Valerius Flaccus, the disgust relates to the
befouling of food, Vergil adds a 'most foul discharge from their stomachs' (3.216–17),
which has been read as referring to excrement or possibly even menstruation (Felton
2013), and as being associated with monstrous femininity (Lowe 2015: 131–7). Later the
Harpy leader, Celaeno, described as an 'ill-omened seer,' prophesies to the Trojans their
fated home in Italy (3.245–57). This attribution of prophetic abilities is exceptional and
appears nowhere else in the extant literature about the Harpies, thus seeming to be one
of Vergil's innovations—though we may note the general similarity with the prophetic
abilities of the Sirens in the *Odyssey*.

While Vergil and others mention Harpies with taloned feet, the creatures were more
commonly depicted in ancient art as having mostly human bodies, the only avian element being wings on their backs, similar to the Type A Sirens. The only clear means
to differentiate Harpies from Sirens is either an accompanying inscription (*LIMC*, s.v.
'Harpyiai' 1) or the context of the myth of Phineus (*LIMC*, s.v. 'Harpyiai' 9, 12). These
latter two depictions also show the Harpies snatching up Phineus' food with their
human arms, rather than possessing the talons or beaks that one might expect from
avian monsters. Like the Sirens, the Harpies are also represented with differing blends
of human-bird bodies. For instance, a form identical to the Type B version of the Sirens

appears as a wall painting from Pompeii.[2] Occasionally, then, we may also see depictions of the Harpies with only the lower half of a bird (*LIMC*, s.v. 'Harpyiai' 5), similar to the Type C Sirens. Owing to this overlap with Sirens' iconographic form, the question remains whether many ancient representations which lack the contexts of any specific myth were intended to represent Sirens or Harpies.

As noted above, the *Liber monstrorum* was a pivotal point in the history of the Sirens, providing the earliest instance of fishtailed Sirens. That text's entry for the Harpies (1.44) offers no such innovation, recounting an otherwise generic description of them as birdlike women known for snatching people and food. Nor do the Harpies in the medieval period ever deviate substantially from the classical Harpies outlined here. The Harpies always retain their avian nature. Moreover, this emphasis on their birdlike elements—flight and snatching—most strongly defines the Harpies as one of the few classical monsters whose native element is neither the sea nor the land, but the air.

CONCLUSION

We may broadly construe the difference in behaviours and qualities of the Sirens and Harpies as being based upon the notions of enticement and repulsion respectively. The Sirens, with the allure of their melodious song and its attendant knowledge, are monsters that draw their victims towards them. The Harpies, meanwhile, with their motif of disgust, represent a more repellent type of monster, and a threat one would seek to escape. Both monsters are perhaps derived from different avian associations in the ancient imagination. The former are extrapolations of the auditory elements of birds' own melodious nature, whilst the latter are a more mobile manifestation of the avian habits of snatching up food and flying swiftly. These two monsters, though sharing aspects of avian anatomy, thus illustrate divergent types of danger.

SUGGESTED READING

There is certainly no lack of modern scholarship on the Sirens. On the Sirens in general: Vial (2014) is an open-access edited volume devoted to the Sirens, comprising a varied array of topics from antiquity to modern reception; Leclercq-Marx (1997) provides a useful *longue durée* study of the Sirens from antiquity to the modern world; De Rachewiltz's PhD thesis (1989) carries the topic from Homer up to the works of Shakespeare. Gresseth (1970) considers the Homeric Sirens in a folkloric context. Other useful overviews of the Sirens are Hoffstetter (1990) and Rossi (1970), the latter also including philosophical uses; see also Schur's metapoetic reading (2014). For the Sirens' iconography, see Neils (1995) and the *LIMC* entry. On their song and musical nature specifically, see Griesbach (2019) and

---

[2] Wall painting from Pompeii of a Harpy, *c.* first century CE, available at https://upload.wikimedia.org/wikipedia/commons/e/e0/Pompei_2015_%2818813967386%29.jpg.

Pucci (1979). On the Sirens as relating to monstrous femininity, see Lowe (2015: 84–96). The connections between the Sirens and the Muses on different levels are handled by Doherty (1995) and Pollard (1952). On the later fishtailed Sirens, see Faral (1953).

The Harpies, by contrast, have not attracted nearly as much scholarly attention. There currently exist no edited volumes nor book-length studies devoted specifically to these monsters. For the Harpies in art, see Engelmann in Roscher (1884–1937) and the *LIMC* entry. For the myth of Phineus in general, see Dräger (2007) and Gantz (1993: 349–56). Most other existing scholarship has focused upon the Harpies in either Apollonius or Vergil. On the Harpies in Apollonius' *Argonautica*, see Hunter (1993: 81–2) and Vian and Delage (1974: 268–9). On the Harpies as relating to monstrous femininity, see Lowe (2015: 116–24). For aspects of their portrayal in Vergil's *Aeneid*, Felton (2013) offers a reading of the Vergilian Harpies in the context of ancient ideas about menstruation and monstrous femininity; Gibson (1999) examines the elements of *hospitium* and hunger and the links of such motifs to other episodes of the *Aeneid*. For more general analyses of the Vergilian Harpies, see Stubbs (1998), Khan (1996), and Rabel (1985).

WORKS CITED

Chantraine, P. 1954. 'Aspects du vocabulaire grec et de sa survivance en français.' *Comptes rendus des séances de l'Académie des Inscriptions et Belles-Lettres* 4: 449–56.

Chantraine, P. 2009. *Dictionnaire étymologique de la langue grecque: Histoire des mots.* Paris.

De Rachewiltz, S. W. 1989. '*De Sirenibus*: An Inquiry into Sirens from Homer to Shakespeare.' PhD dissertation, Harvard University.

Doherty, L. E. 1995. 'Sirens, Muses, and Female Narrators in the *Odyssey*', in *The Distaff Side: Representing the Female in Homer's* Odyssey, ed. B. Cohen, 81–92. New York.

Dräger, P. 2007. 'Phineus', in *Brill's New Pauly: Encyclopaedia of the Ancient World*, ed. H. Cancik and H. Schneider. Leiden.

Engelmann, W. 1884–1937. 'Harpyia', in *Ausführliches Lexikon der griechischen und römischen Mythologie*, vol. 1/2, ed. W. H. Roscher, 1842–7. Leipzig.

Faral, E. 1953. 'La Queue de poisson des sirènes.' *Romania* 84: 433–506.

Felton, D. 2013. 'Were Vergil's Harpies Menstruating?' *Classical Journal* 108: 405–18.

Gantz, T. 1993. *Early Greek Myth: A Guide to Literary and Artistic Sources*, 2 vols. Baltimore.

Gibson, C. A. 1999. 'Punitive Blinding in *Aeneid* 3.' *Classical World* 92: 359–66.

Gresseth, G. K. 1970. 'The Homeric Sirens.' *Transactions of the American Philological Society* 100: 203–18.

Griesbach, J. 2019. 'Die Macht der Sirenen: Musik als Gefahr?', in *MUS-IC-ON!: Klang der Antike*, ed. F. Leitmeir, D. Shebata, and O. Wiener, 161–71. Würzburg.

Hoffstetter, E. 1990. *Sirenen in archaischen und klasischen Griechenland.* Würzburg.

Hunter, R. L. 1993. *The Argonautica of Apollonius: Literary Studies.* New York.

Khan, H. A. 1996. 'The Harpies Episode in *Aeneid* 3.' *Prometheus: Rivista quadrimestrale di studi classici* 22: 131–44.

Leclercq-Marx, J. 1997. *La Sirène dans la pensée et dans l'art de l'Antiquité et du Moyen Âge.* Brussels.

Lowe, D. 2015. *Monsters and Monstrosity in Augustan Poetry.* Ann Arbor.

Neils, J. 1995. 'Les Femmes fatales: Skylla and the Sirens in Greek Art', in *The Distaff Side: Representing the Female in Homer's* Odyssey, ed. B. Cohn, 175–84. New York.

Oswald, D. 2012. 'Monstrous Gender: Geographies of Ambiguity', in *The Ashgate Research Companion to Monsters and the Monstrous*, ed. A. S. Mittman and P. J. Dendle, 343–63. Farnham.

Pollard, J. 1952. 'Muses and Sirens.' *Classical Review* 2: 60–3.

Pucci, P. 1979. 'The Song of the Sirens.' *Arethusa* 12: 121–32.

Rabel, R. J. 1985. 'The Harpies in the *Aeneid*.' *Classical Journal* 80/4: 317–25.

Rossi, P. 1970. 'Sirènes antiques: Poésie, philosophie, iconographie.' *Bulletin de l'Association Guillaume Budé* 29: 463–81.

Schur, D. 2014. 'The Silence of Homer's Sirens.' *Arethusa* 47: 1–17.

Shepard, K. [1940] 2011. *The Fish-Tailed Monster in Greek and Etruscan Art*. Landisville, PA.

Stubbs, H. W. 1998. 'Vergil's Harpies: A Study in *Aeneid* III.' *Vergilius* 44: 3–12.

Vial, J. 2014. *Les Sirènes ou le savoir périlleux d'Homère au XXIᵉ siècle*. Rennes.

Vian, F., and E. Delage. 1974, *Argonautiques*, vol. 1: *Chants I–II*. Paris.

CHAPTER 15

THE SPHINX

CAROLINA LÓPEZ-RUIZ

INTRODUCTION

THE sphinx is a human-headed lion, often winged, and one of the most represented hybrid monsters in classical culture and even in modern media. The name by which we know it, 'sphinx', is a Greek name of uncertain meaning. The Greeks thought it related to 'constricting', 'binding', or 'strangling', from the root of *sphiggo/sphingo*, which remains a valid hypothesis. The word is first attested in Hesiod's poem *Theogony* (*c.*700 BCE), with reference to the Theban Sphinx, but with the shorter form 'Phix' (326); she was sometimes called 'Phikian monster' (Lycoph. *Alex.* 1465). This might be a dialectal variant of the same word, or perhaps a local name, which the ancients connected with that of the nearby Mount Phikion (see the quote from Apollodorus' *Library* in 'The Theban Sphinx' section, below). Whatever the case, Greek speakers also associated this Sphinx with *sphingo*, 'to strangle', whether this is a real or folk etymology (Beekes 2010; Chantraine 1984–1990, s.v.). The Sphinx's known mythological life is reduced to a single story, if a famous one indeed, that of Oedipus and his encounter with the monster in his native Thebes. But sphinxes appear on vases, sculptures, amulets, and jewellery among many Mediterranean cultures from the early first millennium BCE, especially during the development of orientalizing-style art in the eighth and seventh centuries, with no evident connection to Oedipus or Thebes. Where does this sphinx come from, and are these all the same hybrid creature? Greek sphinxes (and hence Roman and modern sphinxes) are a version of the older Near Eastern sphinx, monumentally represented in Egypt but also present in Canaanite culture and adopted in the Minoan and Mycenaean worlds. The symbology of the sphinx as a protective, fantastic creature exceeds by far the specific narrative of the Oedipus story through which much of the Western audience knows the creature. Rather, the story of the Oedipus and his accession to the Theban throne incorporated the sphinx into a narrative about the Theban succession because of its already-established associations, combining its role as funerary and royal guardian, especially as protector of thrones in Phoenician culture, and its negative quality as menace and abductor of young men.

Near Eastern Background

The majestic sight of the Great Sphinx of Giza dominates our romanticized image of the creature. The colossal monument was erected for the funerary complex of Pharaoh Khephren (c.2540–2514 BCE). Here and in other Egyptian cases the sphinx's head sometimes represented the pharaoh himself. Alternatively, whether in their human-headed or falcon- or ram-headed version, sphinxes were associated with specific gods (Hathor, Hauron, Ammon, and Horus in his falcon form; Shaw 2003: 87; Pinch 2004: 206; see also Boychenko in this volume). This is not surprising given the strong connection between lion/lioness imagery and power in the Near East, both human and divine. In the second and early first millennium BCE, from Anatolia and Syro-Palestine to the Minoan and Mycenaean palaces, the lion-human hybrids or their griffin variant could be set up as guardians of thrones (e.g. frescoes at Knossos on Crete, sphinx-thrones in Phoenician art), and of funerary and temple complexes and palace or citadel gates (e.g. reliefs in the Neo-Hittite city of Karatepe in Turkey; perhaps also the fragmentary one-headed lions at the Lion Gate at Mycenae). Sometimes sphinxes are represented flanking a sacred tree, altar, or pillar (e.g. in Mycenaean and Phoenician art), and painted on clay coffins (e.g. *larnakes* from Boeotia). In short, there is no doubt of the sphinxes' symbolic role as guardians of royal and divine power. The winged sphinx may have also been adapted as the winged cherubim that probably flanked the Ark of the Covenant, perhaps drawn directly from the Egyptian griffin (Eichler 2015; Brown 2003: 58; Wyatt 2009: 31). Therefore, we can say the sphinx was particularly popular in the Levant and in the Aegean, and that via Phoenician and Greek cultures it spread westward through the Mediterranean. By contrast, other hybrids such as bull-men, scorpion-men, fish-men, and lion-dragons were more popular in Mesopotamia (Black and Green 1992: 51, 65).

While in Egypt it remained unwinged and usually masculine (in Egypt pharaohs were unshaven), outside Egypt the human-headed lion is usually winged and seemingly feminine (or at least unshaven). This difference seems consistently upheld and aligns the Greek sphinx with the Syrian-Canaanite tradition of representation, not the Egyptian, and in Roman times—as in modern reception—male and breasted female sphinxes are popular (*DCPP*, s.v. 'Sphinx'). Greek writers take this feature for granted, assuming 'Every painter and every sculptor … figures the sphinx as winged' (Ael. *NA* 12.38). In turn, the sphinx is usually human-headed (such creatures are called *androsphinxes* in Hdt. 2.175.1), but could also be ram-headed, associated with Amon, and falcon-headed, akin to griffins and associated with Horus (these appear in modern literature also as hieracosphinxes and criosphinxes / criocephalic, respectively). The female winged sphinx predominates in Greek art and literature, often breasted and sometimes with the added hybrid element of a serpent tail (e.g. Hdt. 4.79.2; Soph. *OT* 391; Apollod. *Bibl.* 3.5.8; Kourou 2011).

In short, although it is best known from Egypt and Greece, the sphinx in its various forms was already part of a shared artistic and symbolic repertoire in the eastern Mediterranean during the second millennium BCE. It spread further west and into all sorts of artistic media in the first millennium, as we will see next.

THE ORIENTALIZING SPHINX

The image of the sphinx spread to the eastern Mediterranean from the Near East, becoming a staple of 'orientalizing' art—artistic forms that drew inspiration and techniques from Near Eastern iconography and craftsmanship, at a time when Near Eastern artefacts and artisans themselves circulated around the Mediterranean. During this period, local groups incorporated, imitated, and innovated on idiosyncratic selections of the Near Eastern artforms they now encountered, and they each developed their own versions (see e.g. Riva and Vella 2006; Gunter 2009; López-Ruiz 2021b: esp. 63–89). But again, in the first millennium BCE the Levantine version of the sphinx in particular, female and winged, took hold in Greece and other areas, due to the extent of Phoenician trade and settlement in the Mediterranean in this period. Thus, we can see adaptations of this Levantine sphinx in areas as distant from each other as Cyprus, Greece, Etruria, and southern Iberia. The sphinx appears alongside other typical elements of orientalizing art, whether in vase-painting, sculpture, metalwork, or ivory carving. Typical elements of this repertoire include the animal friezes engraved and painted on Proto-Corinthian vases (often depicting sphinxes, lions, or stags); the decoration with rosettes, lotus flowers and palmettes; and the development of human sculpture in the orientalizing style also known as 'Daedalic', after the mythical craftsman Daedalus, associated with Crete (López-Ruiz 2021b: 178–82). In Greece the sphinx and griffin share the same symbolic realms of other fantastic beings such as centaurs, gorgons, chimaeras, and 'Mistresses/Masters of Animals' that also proliferate in this period through the combination of Near Eastern imagery and Greek traditions.

This shared pattern is consistent outside the Greek world too, where the winged sphinx is adopted alongside other Levantine symbols of royalty, divinity, and protection (e.g. lotuses, rosettes, lions), largely through contact with Phoenicians, and often appears in funerary contexts in conjunction with symbols of protection and renewal often associated with the goddess Ashtart (Astarte) and her local assimilations. Examples include the griffins and lotuses painted on pithoi (storage jars) from Carmona in southern Spain and the sphinx or griffin on the decorated ostrich egg found in the 'Isis Tomb' in Etruria (Celestino and López-Ruiz 2016: 231, 272, figs. 7.4, 8.2; López-Ruiz 2021b: 151, fig. 5.4). The sphinx was a popular motif in Etruscan art of the orientalizing and Archaic periods (720–480 BCE): it appears carved in ivories and metalwork; painted on vases and frescoes (Haynes 2000); and sculpted in stone, often in funerary contexts. Similar adaptations can be seen on artefacts from Cyprus (Petit 2011).

Because of its frequent artistic appearance in non-narrative representations—where it is often lumped with other orientalizing motifs and treated as part of a decorative programme—the sphinx's potential for mythological interpretation is very limited. At a minimum, as stated above, scholars agree that Near Eastern sphinxes were associated with royalty and in the Phoenician world also with Ashtart's protective (and leonine) symbolism of life and regeneration, a repertoire promoted in luxury arts associated with elite culture. We may deduce that these connotations were not lost on other Mediterranean elite cultures as they adopted the motif alongside other features of Levantine art. In fact, the only story associated with the sphinx, that of the Theban saga of Oedipus, strongly suggests the Greeks' understanding of the symbolic force of the lion--human hybrid as a royal-throne guardian.

THE THEBAN SPHINX

In literature, the Greek sphinx is inseparable from the mythology surrounding Boeotian Thebes and the story of Oedipus' ascent to the throne of his father. We encounter the Theban Sphinx for the first time in Hesiod, a self-proclaimed Boeotian; undoubtedly his audience understood the poem's reference to 'the lethal Sphinx, ruin for the Cadmeians' (*Theog.* 326). Hesiod's rough contemporary, Homer, did not include the Sphinx in his allusion to Oedipus' story in the *Odyssey*. Perhaps the Sphinx was irrelevant to the specific allusion (11.256–68), which is about the tragic fate of Oedipus' mother-wife Epicaste (in Greek tragedy known as Jocasta), or perhaps the Sphinx was not part of the story Homer knew, but only part of the local Theban version used by Hesiod, which was later adopted by the Athenian tragedians and others. The Theban story's roots might go back to the Bronze Age, but most likely the Sphinx was an addition of the orientalizing phase, (re)introduced in Greece with new impulse alongside other borrowings from the Near East (see Burkert 1992; Morris 1992; West 1997). Whatever the case, Thebes had a deep history of connectivity with Near Eastern elites from Asia Minor, as artefacts found in its citadel attest, ranging from Asia Minor and Syria to Mesopotamia and Egypt. In turn, the myth of the foundation of Thebes by the Phoenician Cadmus accompanied an ancient belief in a Phoenician migration or settlement, also associated with the adaptation of the Phoenician alphabet, called *kadmeia grammata* (e.g. Hdt. 2.49; cf. Paus. 9.25; Strabo 9.2). Indeed, the tradition about Cadmus and Europa gives personal names—perhaps Semitic—to the connection with the Levant and Phoenicians (e.g. Hdt. 2.49; Varro, *Rust.* 3.1). More generally, Thebes shared with Troy its place in the ancestral myths of the heroic age, and with the end of Hesiod's 'Race of Heroes', some of whom died 'for the flocks of Oedipus' (*Op.* 161–3).

The Theban Sphinx, like the characters Cadmus and Europa, functions as a mythological bridge between the Near Eastern and Greek worlds. In the cosmogonic plane,

the Sphinx fits within a category of monsters that threatened cosmic order and stability, which included monsters such as Echidna, the Chimaera, and the Hydra as
well as exceptionally large and dangerous animals such as oversized boars, lions, and
bulls—also partly inspired by the Near Eastern bestiary, and fought by heroes such as
Perseus and Heracles who helped settled the new Olympian order of Zeus. Thus, in
his *Theogony* Hesiod integrated the Sphinx in a genealogy of monsters that made her
the offspring of the monstrous dog Orthrus with the Chimaera (or possibly Echidna)
and thereby the appropriate sibling of the Nemean Lion (326–7). We can detect Near
Eastern overtones when Hesiod situates Echidna, the Chimaera, and Orthrus 'among
the Arimoi', where Echidna 'kept guard' and begot her children with Typhon (304–18).
While the specific location of 'the Arimoi' is debated, one possibility is northern Syria,
the Canaanite and Aramaean realm (López-Ruiz 2010: 109–13). Apollodorus chose a
genealogy that made the Sphinx daughter of Echidna and Typhon (see below), and
in yet another tradition she came from Typhon and the Chimaera (e.g. Eurip. *Phoen.*
46). Some authors linked the Theban Sphinx to Ares, who sent her to avenge the
dragon slain by Cadmus, while others, according to scholiasts on Hesiod's *Theogony*
and Euripides' *Phoenissae*, said that she was sent by Hera or Dionysus, for varying
reasons (see Gantz 1993: 495). A fragment of the *Oidipodeia*, a lost poem of the Theban
Cycle, seems to invoke the Sphinx as a killer of Cadmean youths, including Creon's
son Haemon (fr. 1 *PEG*; see also below).

   Whatever her origin story, the only known mythological role of the Sphinx is that of
a monster who terrorized Thebes after the murder of Laius, its king. Whoever managed
to rid the city of her was promised the throne and the queen. The story of Oedipus is best
known through the painfully phased unveiling of the king's real identity and crimes that
constitute the plot of Sophocles' *Oedipus Tyrannus*. There we see only a brief mention
of Oedipus' encounter with the Sphinx, and its outcome: 'You [Oedipus] came and by
your coming saved our city, freed us from the tribute that we paid of old to the Sphinx,
cruel singer' (39–41, trans. Grene 1991). The Sphinx appeared in other classical dramas,
which inevitably described her as the bane of Thebes. Such characterizations hardly
make for a full mythology of the creature, and they provide no clue as to why she is
needed in the story, but the image of the hero—still oblivious of his true identity—facing
the winged, intelligent monster certainly captivated audiences then as now and had already found its way into artistic representations by the fifth century BCE (Fig. 15.1; cf.
also Apanomeritaki in this volume with Fig. 29.1 for the Sphinx's role in the psychoanalytical study of myth).

   While Oedipus was already infamous for his parricide and incest as early as the
Odyssey, and the Sphinx was known as a bane to the Thebans, as Hesiod made clear,
Homer does not mention the Sphinx or Hesiod the riddle. These elements—Oedipus–
Sphinx–riddle—appear bound together in the extant classical Athenian versions of
the myth, which presumably influence the later reception. Possibly the Sphinx was
incorporated to Oedipus' Theban myth to provide the hero with a monster, even if his
confrontation is verbal and does not make Oedipus into a real monster-slayer, especially
since the Sphinx kills herself. At some point the riddle-solving became part of the story,

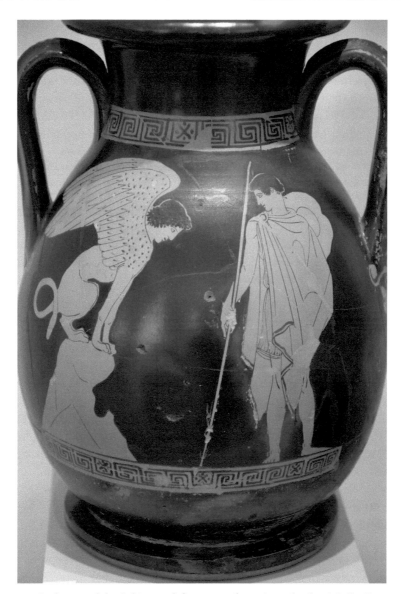

FIGURE 15.1 Oedipus and the Sphinx; red-figure vase from Attica by the Achilles Painter, *c.*450–440 BCE. Antikensammlung Berlin, F 2355.

Source: Wikimedia / Carole Reddato. CC BY-SA 2.0.

as a folkloric motif often tied to obtaining a bride and so accessing power (Edmunds 1995; Ruipérez 2006). Even with the monster's presence in the story, the literary reception of Oedipus' plight emphasized his relationship with knowledge (or lack thereof) and the interpretation of verbal communication such as the allusions to his parentage, to the oracle, and to Teiresias' warnings.

For the mythographer Apollodorus (second century CE), the Sphinx is the traditional hybrid monster of earlier mythology, born from Echidna and Typhon, and sent by Hera to Thebes to avenge Laius' rape of a friend's son, Chrysippus (*Bibl.* 3.5.7). The Sphinx (perhaps inadvertently) also acts as protector of Laius' throne, whose riddles could be solved only by the true heir. This is perhaps the most straightforward narrative we have:

> She [the Sphinx] had the face of a woman, the breast and feet and tail of a lion, and the wings of a bird. And having learned a riddle from the Muses, she sat on Mount Phikion, and presented it to the Thebans. And the riddle was this: What is that which has one voice and yet becomes four-footed and two-footed and three-footed? ... When they could not find it [the answer] she would snatch away one of them and gobble him up. When many had perished, (even, last of all, Kreon's son Haimon), Kreon proclaimed that to him who should solve the riddle he would give both the kingdom and the wife of Laius. On hearing that, Oedipus found the solution ... So the Sphinx threw herself from the citadel, and Oedipus both succeeded to the kingdom and unwittingly married his mother. (Apollod. *Bibl.* 3.5.8; translation adapted from Frazer 1921)

The answer to the Sphinx's riddle was, of course, 'a human being' (*anthropos*). Scholia, or ancient commentaries, follow this same tradition when explicating the riddle (e.g. the scholiast to Hom. *Il.* 2.494).

Other mythographers and poets revisit the same core myth with small variations, for instance having the Sphinx actively propose the riddle-contest to Creon (Hyg. *Fab.* 67), or poetically expanding upon the setting and the punishment she inflicts (e.g. Stat. *Theb.* 2.500 ff.; Ov. *Met.* 7.759 ff; Sen. *Oed.* 87 ff.). A shared salient feature of the Sphinx is her quality as a 'singer' or 'reciter' of the riddle or oracle, issued in verse, which she learned from the Muses (Apollod. *Bibl.* 3.5.8) or from the oracle at Delphi given to Laius (Paus. 9.26.3); the riddle has an oracular quality and is imagined as sung, or recited, in verse (e.g. Soph. *OT* 39–41).

Although the traditional Theban myths represent the Sphinx as one of the primordial cosmic monsters, rationalized versions of these popular myths reinterpret her as an allegorized human woman. These narratives, transmitted by mythographers and antiquarians such as Apollodorus and Pausanias, reveal a richer mythological life and interpretive range for the Sphinx, if still invariably tied to her connection to Thebes' kings, whether Cadmus or Oedipus. A scholion to Euripides' *Phoenissae* (set in Thebes) comments that she was a woman cast into madness with the daughters of Cadmus and then transformed into the monster (*Schol. ad Eurip. Phoen.* 45). In a historicized or rationalized version, the Sphinx was the human wife of Cadmus, who turned to revenge crime after he abandoned her: she recruited a group of Theban rebels and ambushed passers-by (Palaephatus 4). Several centuries later, Pausanias writes that as a daughter of Laius the Sphinx had a main role in the contest for the king's throne: she killed those sons of his who came to claim it, but was bested by Oedipus (Paus. 9.26.3–4). Pausanias also records a tradition in which the Sphinx leads a pirate expedition against Thebes, plundering the city until Oedipus defeated her with his larger army (9.26.2).

Interpreting the Sphinx: Underworld Guardian, Throne Protector, Double-Edged Demon

The relationship between the iconographic versions of hybrid monsters and the mythology behind them is often obscure. Like the Gorgon Medusa, the Lernaean Hydra, or Cerberus, the sphinx in Greece is primarily connected with one mythological narrative, and sometimes appears as a representation of that myth, as in vase-paintings (e.g. Fig. 15.1). Unlike the Hydra or Cerberus, however, the sphinx was an image with a symbolic life of its own both prior to and beyond Greece and Theban mythology. In this sense the sphinx's broader function rather resembles that of the Gorgon: Medusa was killed by the hero Perseus, but her severed head, with its terrifying gaze, was frequently considered a stand-alone enemy-averting monster in its own right. The term *gorgoneion* thus applied to reproductions of Medusa's head that were used apotropaically, for example on amulets and aegises. A similar case, often compared to that of the Gorgon, is the face of Ḥumbaba, the monstrous giant decapitated by Gilgamesh and/or his companion Enkidu in Mesopotamian myth: Ḥumbaba's furrowed, grimacing face was reproduced in the Levant as an apotropaic figure (Graff 2014).

Outside the Theban story involving the mythical hybrid, sphinxes are ubiquitous in ancient Mediterranean art in a variety of media and contexts that discourages systematic study and overarching interpretation. We find a general disconnect between discussions of the mythological Theban Sphinx and those of the artistic motif, which is generally treated in artistic terms (Kourou 2011; Petit 2011). In the sphere of mythology, her puzzling appearance in the much-analysed Oedipus story remains dominant, since this is the only mythical narrative in which she has an active role rather than merely a passing mention (as in the cosmogonies). In Oedipus' story, as discussed above, the Sphinx is not an expected or familiar trope, while all other main elements in the story are—the oracle, facing a monster, marriage by trial or contest, and parricide; indeed, in other versions of the story Oedipus fights with beasts (the Teumesian fox in Eur. *Phoen.* 26) or competes for the throne of Epicaste/Jocasta (Paus. 9.26.3–4). But the Sphinx's oral confrontation at the crux of Oedipus' access to Thebes in the Sophoclean and other versions remains (appropriately) an unsolved riddle.

Whether the sphinx was a later insertion into the older Theban tradition about Oedipus or was always an integral part of it, the question remains as to which aspect of the hybrid creature's symbology granted her presence there. Scholars generally agree that she came into the story from the realm of funerary culture, since the sphinx's artistic life is heavily tied to funerary artefacts, including representation on vases deposited in graves, and on stone grave markers (Pensa 1977; Aston 2011; Kourou 2011: 165). Some scholars have suggested that sphinxes and griffins may have been imagined as mythological underworld guardians, such as those mentioned in the Orphic-Bacchic Gold

Tablets who have the role of guarding the Lake of Memory and interrogating the souls of the deceased about their identity and lineage. These guardians are not described and have no names, which suggests they are not scary monsters or demons to be appeased (in contrast to, e.g. Cerberus). Rather, they are guardians characterized by their verbal interaction with the deceased, which aligns them somewhat with the sphinx figure (Edmonds 2004: 63; Petit 2015; 2011: 204–36). At minimum, the sphinx carried from the Near East to Greece and beyond her quality of protector of divine and human settings, as exemplified by the Archaic sphinx sitting on top of a column placed before the temple of Apollo at Delphi, on which representations of Oedipus and the Sphinx may have drawn (Aston 2011: 293; *LIMC*, s.vv. 'Oedipous', 'Sphinx'; López-Ruiz 2021a; cf. Fig. 15.1). In short, their nature as hybrid creatures of a protective or apotropaic sort would have been easily extended from the living to the dead and funerary contexts.

But related to this guardian role is another rarely emphasized aspect of the sphinx: its decorative use on thrones as a protective figure. The image of sphinx-thrones was associated with kings and gods—especially Ashtart—on funerary monuments, such as the Ahiram sarcophagus from Byblos (tenth century BCE), as well as on amulets and royal emblems in the Levant and particularly in the Phoenician world. The ubiquitous sphinx-throne image seems like a possible bridge between the Near Eastern iconography and the Greek narrative (Boardman 2003; Doak 2015: 109–15; Ziffer 2013).[1] Whoever originally added the sphinx into the Oedipus' story may have imagined her as a guardian of the palace, the tomb, or the empty throne of Laius in the Cadmean city, a setting already mythologically entangled with Phoenician references (see López-Ruiz 2021b).

A particularly aggressive aspect of the sphinx appears in representations of the creatures attacking young nude men or warriors in Greek art. Although the meaning of these representations is unclear, they seem to evoke danger and death rather than protection, and in some of these the sphinx even seems to be taking flight with her victim. If these representations allude to the Theban Sphinx, they capture an aspect in the sphinx mythology as 'snatcher' of Cadmean youths, alluded to in fragments of literature. In Archaic and Classical vase-painting and reliefs sphinxes appear surrounded by several characters (with no Oedipus figure singled out), or chasing youths in lusty pursuit, and their iconography sometimes intersects with that of the people-snatching harpies. In short, a varied iconography signals the sphinx's popularity in more general narratives apart from the Theban Sphinx's verbal encounter with Oedipus (Gantz 1993: 495–6; Vermeule 1979: esp. 171–3).

This motif of the sphinx as 'youth snatcher' also finds parallels in Levantine art, as we see in representations of a sphinx subduing a youth in Phoenician ivories (e.g. Nimrud ivory at the Iraq Museum, Baghdad). We may see this theme as a variant of the broader Near Eastern motif of the feline attacking a prey, usually bovine, a deer, or a person, also

---

[1] For a good view of the sphinx-throne on the Ahiram sarcophagus, see https://commons.wikime dia.org/wiki/File:Ahiram_Sarcophagus_2.jpg; for a common type of Hellenistic sphinx-throne, https://www.photo.rmn.fr/archive/00-009421-2C6NU04THUWA.html.

adopted in Archaic Greek reliefs and attested in Phoenician-Syrian ivories (e.g. ivory plaque 'lioness mauling an African', from Nimrud, British Museum, 127412). On the other hand, we can also find the reverse motif, of a youth or warrior slaying a griffin, which appears in Phoenician ivories and metal bowls (Markoe 1985), showing again that Greek and Near Eastern imageries were intertwined, and sphinxes and griffins could alternatively represent the onset and defeat of chaos or act as protective entities against other fearsome opponents, perhaps in the afterlife as well.

We find examples of this ambivalence in the house-protecting plaques from Arslan Tash in northern Syria; the iconography and Phoenician inscription on these plaques may provide an interesting new clue about the monster's name. One of the two small plaques (*c.* seventh century BCE) portrays a winged, human-headed lion (Fig. 15.2). Several other human-devouring monsters appear in these amulets, which invoke local gods for protection. The sphinx-like figure seems to be referred to in the accompanying inscription as *honeqet*, 'the strangler' or perhaps 'breaker of the neck' (Pardee 1998: 35, Arslan-Tash I, line 4). The debated origins of the Greek name for the sphinx may have

FIGURE 15.2 Arslan Tash plaque with Phoenician incantation and demonic figures.

Courtesy of Dennis Pardee.

a solution, or at least a new valid hypothesis here. As mentioned above, the connection with 'strangling' (Greek *sphingo*) is often dismissed as a popular etymology, not so much for linguistical difficulties as because the monster does not strictly 'strangle' anyone in the myths we have. On the other hand, in some of the 'Cadmean snatcher' imagery the sphinx is pressing hard on the young men's chests, which constricts their breathing. As we have seen, then, her actions were far from limited to one mode of oppression. It is not impossible, therefore, that the Greek name was a translation of the name from the Phoenician/Syrian realm (Demsky 2022). Even if *sphingo* were not the original Greek root of the name, the Archaic Greek-speaker quite possibly understood it as such and drew a connection between the Semitic and Greek names. This is not an unlikely scenario as the hybrid entered (or re-entered) Greek iconography and mythology in the orientalizing period after centuries of aniconic art (López-Ruiz 2021a; 2021b: 222–3). The existence of other leonine monsters and threats in the afterlife as attested in the Phoenician world strengthens the possibility (e.g. Tribulato 2013; cf. López-Ruiz 2015).

Conclusion

The sphinx has not been theorized as a monster in a holistic way, and discussions tend to focus separately either on the creature's appearance in the Oedipus myth or on her appearance as a motif in ancient art. It is difficult to articulate a single mythological role for this monster outside the one and only story preserved, that of the Theban Sphinx, although many nuances and variants existed regarding her specific role and how her encounter with the Thebans unfolded, including rationalized versions postulating that she was a human female. As we have seen, sphinxes could be both protective and terrifying. Just as with the Gorgon's or Ḥumbaba's face, it is in the logic of apotropaic figures that their enemy-averting energy could be projected against the onlooker. Recent efforts to integrate the representation of the Near Eastern and Greek sphinxes (and orientalizing adaptations outside Greece) in both visual arts and mythology suggest that the hybrid retained an ambivalent function: positively as throne and perhaps underworld guardian, negatively as a hostile enemy, both meanings well attested in the Phoenician world. An updated interpretation of the sphinx, therefore, requires considering the motif outside its Greek representation and the limited Oedipus story, and within a broader Mediterranean context.

Suggested Reading

For literary and artistic sources on the mythological Greek sphinx, see Ganz's overview (1993: 494–6). For the Mycenaean sphinxes, see Castleden (2005: 127, fig. 5.8; 102–3). For discussion of its place in the Oedipus myth, see Edmunds (1995). On the use of the sphinx in Archaic Greek art, see Kourou (2011), focused on Crete; on the Boeotian *larnakes*, Kourou

(2011: 166–7). For Bronze Age Thebes, see Latacz (2004) and Aravantinos (1996); on the antiquity of Thebes, Noegel (1998); and on Thebes' foundation stories, Edwards (1979) and Berman (2004). On the names, see *DCPP* (s.v. 'Kadmos'); West (1997: 289–90). For the sphinx's appearance in funerary contexts and her interpretation as an afterlife guardian, see Petit (2011). The winged sphinx's similarity with other guardian figures in the Near East and with the biblical cherubim is discussed by Eichler (2015) and Wyatt (2009). For the Egyptian and other Near Eastern sphinxes, see also *OEAANE* (s.v. 'Giza', 'Tell Halaf' *'Ain Dara'*) and Özyar (2016: 139, fig. 3; 143–4, fig. 5a–b), and discussion of the pharaonic sphinx in comparison with Greek and other folk motifs in Suhr (1970). The Arslan Tash sphinx figure and its name's connection to the Greek is discussed in Demsky (2022). For discussion of the sphinx as a shared motif in the orientalizing period across the Mediterranean and its Phoenician background, see López-Ruiz (2021a; 2021b: 218–25).

Works Cited

Aravantinos, V. 1996. 'New Archaeological and Archival Discoveries at Mycenaean Thebes.' *Bulletin of the Institute of Classical Studies* 41: 135–6.

Aston, E. 2011. *Mixanthrôpoi: Animal-human Hybrid Deities in Greek Religion.* Liège.

Beekes, R. 2010. *Etymological Dictionary of Greek*, 2 vols. Leiden.

Berman, D. W. 2004. 'The Double Foundation of Boitian Thebes.' *Transactions of the American Philological Society* 134: 1–22.

Black, J., and A. Green. 1992. *Gods, Demons and Symbols of Ancient Mesopotamia.* Austin.

Boardman, J. 2003. *Classical Phoenician Scarabs: A Catalogue and Study.* Oxford.

Brown, J. P. 2003. *Ancient Israel and Ancient Greece: Religion, Politics, and Culture.* Minneapolis.

Burkert, W. 2004. *Babylon, Memphis, Persepolis: Eastern Contexts of Greek Culture.* Cambridge, MA.

Castleden, R. 2005. *Mycenaeans.* London.

Celestino, S., and C. López-Ruiz. 2016. *Tartessos and the Phoenicians in Iberia.* Oxford.

Chantraine, P. 1984–1990. *Dictionnaire étymologique de la langue grecque.* Paris.

Demsky, A. 2022. 'The First Arslan Tash Incantation and the Sphinx', in *Biblical and Ancient Near Eastern Studies in Honor of P. Kyle McCarter Jr.*, ed. C. Rollston, S. Garfein, and N. H. Walls, 331–46. Atlanta.

Doak, B. 2015. *Phoenician Aniconism in Its Mediterranean and Near Eastern Contexts.* Atlanta.

Edmonds, R. G. 2004. *Myths of the Underworld Journey: Plato, Aristophanes, and the 'Orphic' Gold Tablets.* Cambridge.

Edmunds, L. 1995. 'The Sphinx in the Oedipus Legend', in *Oedipus: A Folklore Casebook*, ed. L. Edmunds and A. Dundes, 147–73. Madison.

Edwards, R. B. 1979. *Kadmos the Phoenician: A Study in Greek Legends and the Mycenaean Age.* Amsterdam.

Eichler, R. 2015. 'Cherub: A History of Interpretation.' *Biblica* 96/1: 26–38.

Frazer, J. G., trans. 1921. *Apollodorus:* The Library. Cambridge, MA.

Gantz, T. 1993. *Early Greek Myth: A Guide to Literary and Artistic Sources*, 2 vols. Baltimore.

Graff, S. B. 2014. 'Demons, Monsters, and Magic', in *Assyria to Iberia at the Dawn of the Classical Age*, ed. J. Aruz, S. B. Graff, and Y. Rakic, 263–71. New York.

Grene, D., trans. 1991. *Sophocles I:* Oedipus the King, Oedipus at Colonus, Antigone, 2nd edn. Chicago.

Gunter, A. C. 2009. *Greek Art and the Orient.* Cambridge.

Haynes, S. 2000. *Etruscan Civilization: A Cultural History.* Los Angeles.

Kourou, N. 2011. 'Following the Sphinx: Tradition and Innovation in Early Iron Age Crete', in *Identità culturale, etnicità, processi di transformazione a Creta fra* Dark Age *e Arcaismo*, ed. G. Rizza, 165–77. Catania.

Latacz, J. 2004. *Troy and Homer: Towards a Solution of an Old Mystery*, trans. K. Windle and R. Ireland. Oxford.

López-Ruiz, C. 2010. *When the Gods Were Born: Greek Cosmogonies and the Near East.* Cambridge, MA.

López-Ruiz, C. 2015. 'Near Eastern Precedents of the Orphic Gold Tablets: The Phoenician Missing Link.' *Journal of Ancient Near Eastern Religions* 15/1: 52–91.

López-Ruiz, C. 2021a. 'The Sphinx: A Greco-Phoenician Hybrid', in *Text and Intertext in Greek Epic and Drama: Essays in Honor of Margalit Finkelberg*, ed. R. Zelnick-Abramovitz and J. Price, 292–310. Abingdon.

López-Ruiz, C. 2021b. *Phoenicians and the Making of the Mediterranean.* Cambridge, MA.

Markoe, G. E. 1985. *Phoenician Bronze and Silver Bowls from Cyprus and the Mediterranean.* Berkeley and Los Angeles.

Morris, S. P. 1992. *Daidalos and the Origin of Greek Art.* Princeton.

Noegel, S. 1998. 'The Aegean Ogygos of Boeotia and the Biblical Og of Bashan: Reflections of the Same Myth.' *Zeitschrift für die alttestamentliche Wissenschaft* 110: 411–26.

Özyar, A. 2016. 'Phoenicians and Greeks in Cilicia? Coining Elite Identity in Iron Age Anatolia', in *Assyria to Iberia: Art and Culture in the Iron Age*, ed. J. Aruz and M. Seymour, 136–46. New York.

Pardee, D. 1998. 'Les Documents d'Arslan Tash: Authentiques ou faux?' *Syria* 75: 15–54.

Pensa, M. 1977. *Rappresentazioni dell'oltretomba nella ceramica apula.* Rome.

Petit, T. 2011. *Œdipe et le Chérubin: Les Sphinx levantins, cypriotes et grecs comme gardiens d'Immortalité.* Fribourg.

Petit, T. 2015. 'Sphinx, cherubins et "gardiens" orphiques.' *Museum Helveticum* 72: 142–70.

Pinch, G. 2004. *Egyptian Mythology: A Guide to the Gods, Goddesses, and Traditions of Ancient Egypt.* Oxford.

Riva, C., and N. Vella, eds. 2006. *Debating Orientalization: Multidisciplinary Approaches to Change in the Ancient Mediterranean.* London.

Ruipérez, M. S. 2006. *El mito de Edipo: Lingüística, psicoanálisis y folklore.* Madrid.

Shaw, I. 2003. *The Oxford History of Ancient Egypt.* Oxford.

Suhr, E. G. 1970. 'The Sphinx.' *Folklore* 81/2: 97–111.

Tribulato, O. 2013. 'Phoenician Lions: The Funerary Stele of the Phoenician Shem/Antipatros.' *Hesperia* 82: 459–86.

Vermeule, E. 1979. *Aspects of Death in Early Greek Art and Poetry.* Berkeley and Los Angeles.

West, M. L. 1997. *The East Face of Helicon: West Asiatic Elements in Greek Poetry and Myth.* Oxford.

Wyatt, N. 2009. 'Grasping the Griffin: Identifying and Characterizing the Griffin in Egyptian and West Semitic Tradition.' *Journal of Ancient Egyptian Interconnections* 1/1: 29–39.

Ziffer, I. 2013. 'Portraits of Ancient Israelite Kings?' *Biblical Archaeology Review* 39/5: 41–51.

CHAPTER 16

··

THE MINOTAUR

··

STEPHEN M. TRZASKOMA

Introduction

THESEUS' slaying the half-man, half-bull Minotaur ('Minos-bull') is one of the earliest and most stable components of the Greek myths about the Athenian hero (Edwards 1970: 26–7; Walker 1995a: 13). It was certainly the most famous. While our oldest literary evidence comes rather later and less clearly than we would ideally prefer (see Gantz 1993: 260–70), and the first Greek poetry to survive—from the eighth and seventh centuries BCE—does not mention the monster at all, the artistic evidence from the sixth century BCE makes clear both the story's existence and its popularity in Attica, the land of Athens, as well as throughout Greece. Thus, we need not imagine that the Greeks later grafted the Minotaur onto Theseus' story. For, unlike the hero's other famous hostile encounter with hybrid monsters when he battled the centaurs, defeating the Minotaur is distinctly Theseus' own unique achievement. Due to the specificity of the Minotaur as to mythical time, genealogy, and space, he was, in effect, locked into a particular role in two interwoven and well-known mythological cycles: that of Theseus on the one hand, and that of Crete and King Minos on the other. The figure of the Minotaur is thus stable in the sense that he is limited to a certain narrative role and to certain relationships, but also because the monster himself changes almost not at all in form or character across the whole of antiquity. As we will see, although there is slight evidence of early experimentation in representing his physical form, the Minotaur's basic appearance—a man's body with a horned bull's head, as well as some additional minor taurine features (for example, a tail)—remains essentially consistent and canonical until the medieval period and after. Likewise, the uses to which he was put in the mythical story-world and his thematic associations constitute a well-defined and limited constellation, although as Theseus himself underwent subsequent transformations of character and significance, we can imagine the Minotaur's symbolic significance shifted correspondingly, as discussed later.

OUR EVIDENCE FOR THE MONSTER AND
HIS STORY

The prehistory of the Minotaur is almost entirely speculative. In the 1890s, British archaeologist Sir Arthur Evans rediscovered a pre-Greek Bronze Age civilization on the island of Crete, which he dubbed 'Minoan' (after King Minos). Since then, scholars have put forth or condemned various connections to the importance of bulls in Minoan artistic, religious, and cultural traditions (see e.g. Harrison 1908: 481–82; Scanlon 2014: 41–6; Nilsson 1971: 373–4; Ward 1970) or drawn connections with earlier and contemporary Near Eastern civilizations that influenced Bronze Age Crete (Morris 1992: 165, 184–96). While these suggestions are appealing and address our urge to find origins, if we judge by our current evidence they amount to little more than speculation. We can say little about the myth outside actual artistic and literary renditions.

The story has a clear skeleton that varies only in minor detail from author to author and artist to artist. We can do worse than let the late mythographical testimony of Apollodorus' *Library* (first or second century CE) serve as a proxy for a 'standard' version. Apollodorus covers the Minotaur's origin and birth from the lust of Minos' wife Pasiphaë for a bull (itself a punishment for an offence of Minos against Poseidon), his confinement in the Labyrinth, his role as an executioner, and his death at the hands of Theseus. Such late summaries represent the best connected retellings of the Minotaur myth since no long narrative poetic accounts of Theseus' exploits survive (Cingano 2017; Bernabé 1992; Edmunds 2021: 3–4). Diodorus Siculus (first century BCE) gives us our other long Greek prose account of the Minotaur (4.60–1, 77). His version generally parallels Apollodorus' but adds or omits details that are not central; for instance, he records that the sacrificial Athenian youths and maidens were sent every nine years. The Roman mythographer Hyginus (*fl.* first century CE) relates a version shorter than but similar to those of Apollodorus and Diodorus, aside from positioning Aphrodite (rather than Poseidon) as the vengeful divinity (*Fab.* 40).

In the following passage, Apollodorus recounts in his section on Cretan myth the events that ensued after Asterius, the king of Crete and Minos' stepfather, passed away without a natural son. At the end of the passage, we learn that the Minotaur was named after Asterius for reasons that are not entirely clear, although Greeks commonly named firstborn sons after their paternal grandfathers. The practice in this case may highlight that the relationships are something of a mockery since Minos is not King Asterius' son and Asterius the Minotaur is not Minos'. In terms of content, the mention of 'certain prophecies' at the end is opaque, but almost every other detail is canonical.

> After Asterius died childless, Minos wanted to be king of Crete, but there was opposition. He claimed that he had received the kingship from the gods, and to prove it he said that whatever he prayed for would happen. He made a sacrifice to Poseidon and prayed for a bull to appear from the depths, promising to sacrifice the one that

appeared. Poseidon sent a magnificent bull up for him, and he received the kingdom, but he sent the bull to his herds and sacrificed another.... Poseidon grew angry at Minos because he did not sacrifice the bull. So, he made it savage and made Pasiphaë lust after the bull. When she had fallen in love with the bull, she took as her accomplice Daedalus.... He constructed a wooden cow, put it on wheels, and hollowed it out. Stripping the skin from a cow, he sewed it around the wooden one. He placed it in the meadow where the bull usually grazed and put Pasiphaë inside. The bull came and mated with it as if it were a real cow. Pasiphaë gave birth to Asterius, known as the Minotaur. He had the face of a bull, but the rest of his body was that of a man. Minos shut him in the Labyrinth in accordance with certain prophecies and kept him under guard. (*Bibl.* 3.8–11, trans. Smith and Trzaskoma 2007)[1]

Later, in his account of Theseus, the mythographer gives us the rest of the story, which eventuates from the death of Minos' son, Androgeos, in Athens, an ensuing war between Athens and Crete, and a divinely sent plague that afflicts the Athenians. They attempt in vain to rid themselves of it, and finally consult an oracle about how to rid themselves of their trouble. Apollodorus continues:

The god ordained that they pay Minos whatever penalty he might choose. Minos ordered them to send seven young men and the same number of young women, all unarmed, as food for the Minotaur, who had been shut up in a labyrinth, which was impossible for someone who entered to get out of, for it closed off its secret exit with complex twists and turns. (*Bibl.* 3.213, trans. Smith and Trzaskoma 2007)

Eating people in the Labyrinth is an essential component of the story although details vary between accounts. For instance, as noted above, Diodorus records that the Athenians sent sacrificial victims in nine-year intervals, whereas the grammarian Servius (late fourth to early fifth centuries CE), known for his commentaries on Vergil, reports that this sacrifice occurred every single year (6.14 Thilo–Hagen).

The story culminates with the Minotaur's death at Theseus' hands and the hero's escape from the Labyrinth, a feat made possible by Ariadne's famous thread. This is the canonical story, and the slighter elements found in the following passage—Daedalus' involvement, Theseus' presence in the third group—are attested across the tradition.

Theseus was chosen for the third group sent as tribute to the Minotaur, though some say he volunteered to go.... When he arrived in Crete, Minos's daughter Ariadne fell in love with him and offered to help him if he promised to take her back to Athens and make her his wife. After Theseus promised and swore oaths on it, she asked Daedalus to reveal the way out of the Labyrinth. At his suggestion she gave a thread to Theseus as he entered. Theseus tied this to the door and went in dragging it behind. He found the Minotaur in the innermost part of the Labyrinth and beat him

---

[1] Unless otherwise noted, translations are my own.

to death with his fists. He got out by following the thread back. (*Bibl.* E.1.7–1.9, trans. Smith and Trzaskoma 2007)

In Apollodorus' version, Theseus dispatches the Minotaur with his fists, but this detail varies across tellings and representations. Sometimes, for instance, he uses a sword or a club.

THE STORY'S POSSIBLE ORIGINS

Now, let us back up and search for the story's origins as narrative. Theseus was a tremendously popular figure in ancient art and storytelling, but the earliest written mentions of him are just that—references rather than narrative. While we might assume that the Minotaur had a role in the legend from its earliest phase, we have no proof. Webster (1966: 23), for instance, assumes that the mention of 'cruel-hearted Minos' in *Odyssey* 11.322, where Odysseus sees Ariadne among the dead in Hades, 'is clearly an allusion to the Minotaur story', but this remains conjecture, no matter how attractive it may seem, given that the passage does not mention the creature. Servius, in his commentary on Vergil, reports that the sixth-century BCE poetess Sappho told the story of Theseus' freeing the Athenian youths, but he makes no explicit mention of the Minotaur (2.9 Thilo–Hagen = Sappho fr. 206 LP). It is certainly difficult, however, to think that this is not our story. Later in the sixth century, however, we certainly have the basic components in place if we are to judge by the Hesiodic *Catalogue of Women*. In a fragmentary passage (fr. 145 MW), we find the names of Minos and his son Androgeos along with references to the presence of another male seized by desire for 'her' (Minos' wife) and her getting pregnant and bearing Minos a child, 'a marvel (to behold)', who resembles one kind of being down to its feet but has a different head up top (two damaged letters may represent the start of the word 'bull'). Despite the gaps in the text and the resulting omissions, there is no reason for undue scepticism; the story is the one familiar to us, at least in its basics.

Scholars have speculated about the existence of an epic poem devoted to Theseus, a *Theseis*, that may have circulated in the sixth century BCE and helped to set the standard accounts of his myth, but the arguments remain unconvincing and sometimes circular. If such a poem existed, it left no real trace. We have proof of poems called *Theseis* written in the fifth to third centuries (Walker 1995b: 38–9), but we know almost nothing beyond their existence and a few authors' names. In any case, such poems came too late to have introduced any of the basic features of the myth, especially the Minotaur, since by the fifth century the most important elements were in place—as attested in literature and the visual arts.

Our first surviving connected narrative threads about Theseus and the Minotaur come in the fifth century BCE: several poems by Bacchylides contain parts of story. Poem 18 takes place when Theseus first arrives in Athens, well before his voyage to Crete. Poem

17 details Theseus' voyage from Athens to Crete with Minos and the other Athenian youths, but, frustratingly, the poet makes no mention of the Minotaur's existence or origins. However, Bacchylides clearly knew our canonical story, as the fragmentary Poem 26 mentions Pasiphaë, her desire, and her request to Daedalus that he construct a device whereby she could have sex with the bull. Sophocles' fifth-century tragedy *Minos*, which likely dealt with the story, is essentially lost aside from one fragment. Sophocles' younger contemporary Euripides undoubtedly treated the story of the Minotaur's conception and birth, centring his tragedy *Cretans* around it. The play seems to have opened just after the birth of the Minotaur, described in one fragment as a 'baby of mingled appearance', and clarified by Pasiphaë's nurse in another fragment (*POxy.* 2461): she explicitly states that the infant 'is a mixture of bull and human with a double *physis*', where *physis* may be translated variously as 'form' or 'nature' or 'birth', among other possibilities. Asked for further details by Minos, she makes clear that the child has a bull's head and tail but walks upon two legs—in other words, the canonical physical form of the Minotaur. The fragment breaks off with Minos enquiring whether the infant suckles at its mother's breast or the udder of a cow and the nurse indicating the former. This poorly preserved play's most substantial fragment consists of an extraordinary defence speech by Pasiphaë against Minos (*PBerol.* 13217). In it, she confesses to being maddened with desire for the bull and to having intercourse with it, and she clearly blames Minos himself for angering Poseidon by not sacrificing the bull. She explicitly cites the god's anger as the cause for her lust, and the chorus apparently agrees. It is impossible to say for certain, but Apollodorus and Hyginus possibly based their versions upon Euripides' play, directly or through intermediary summaries. Another of Euripides' plays, his lost *Theseus*, may have treated the hero's encounter with the monster (Walker 1995b: 135–6); if so, it too may have served as a source for the later mythographers.

Possibly the earliest surviving mention of the Labyrinth as the Minotaur's prison appears in a fragment of Philochorus, a local Athenian historian (c.340–261 BCE; *FGrH* 328 F17). However, its context—the fragment is recorded by Plutarch (c.46–c.119 CE) in his *Theseus* (16.1)—makes clear that by Philochorus' time the Labyrinth was an established and well-known part of the myth, as corroborated by the third-century BCE poet Callimachus' brief narration about Theseus and his companions 'having fled the harsh mooing and savage son of Pasiphaë and the bent dwelling of the winding Labyrinth' (*Hymn to Delos* 4.310–11).

RATIONALIZED ACCOUNTS

Beyond mere attestation of the Labyrinth, Philochorus' account provides a rationalized version of the story; that is, an explanation that removes unbelievable, paradoxical, or supernatural elements 'to show that these stories of fabulous monsters and other-worldly deeds derive in fact from prosaic events' (Hawes 2014: 3). He apparently attributed this more realistic version to 'the Cretans'. The Minotaur also appears in the earliest surviving formal rationalized account of myth, the fourth-century BCE *On Unbelievable Tales* (*Peri Apiston*) by the paradoxographer Palaephatus (see the overview of Koning 2022), where we have perhaps the first explicit mention both of the name Minotaur (as opposed to the phrase 'the bull of Minos'; Gantz 1993: 261) and of a wooden cow. The latter detail appears here first, but may have been assumed in Bacchylides' Poem 26, when Pasiphaë requests Daedalus' help to devise a means for her to mate with the bull.

Palaephatus and Philochorus take similar approaches to rationalizing the Minotaur. Palaephatus tells us that Pasiphaë fell in love with a man named Taurus ('Bull'), who served Minos. Their illegitimate son, apparently named Minotaur for reasons Palaephatus does not clarify, is banished by Minos and then pursued for committing crimes, but he digs a deep tunnel and takes refuge there. Confined there, he kills the prisoners Minos dispatches to him—that is, until Theseus kills him instead (*Peri Apiston* 2). In reinterpreting the tale of Pasiphaë, Palaephatus raises several objections to accepting the myth's reality (see also Hawes in this volume):

> First of all, it is impossible for one animal to make love to another if their genitals do not conform. For example, it is not possible for a dog and an ape, nor a wolf and a hyena to mate with each other, nor an antelope and a deer—for they are of different species. Nor, if they did mate, could they produce offspring. Nor does it seem likely to me that a bull mated with a cow made out of wood, for all four-footed animals smell the genitals of their mate before copulating, and mount only thereafter. Nor would a woman tolerate being mounted by a bull, nor would she be able to bear an embryo with horns. (trans. Stern 1996: 32)

This focus on the biological elements, shared by other rationalizers, is meant to decisively remove anything but a figurative bestial element from Minotaur/Asterius. This saves the myth from absurdity in an obvious sense, but it also dispenses with the ability of the figure of the Minotaur to function in complex ways as a product and reminder of the Cretan tales of perverted female desire and illicit sexuality, of the feral cruelty of King Minos against the Athenians, as a force of barbarism to be overcome by the civilizing hero, and other such resonances. The bestial but not wholly bestial Minotaur as conceived in the myth is a sort of an inverted Theseus, but also in some ways a doublet of the hero: descendant of gods, child of a heroine/queen, 'son' of a king with a dual paternity, and so on.

According to Plutarch, Philochorus, too, told a version in which a man named Taurus—this time one of Minos' generals—was involved, but apparently as the 'monster' himself, not as Pasiphaë's lover. Plutarch's partial and very brief summary of Philochorus' comments does not provide anything more about the fuller tale. Rather, Plutarch's interest lies in rationalizing the Labyrinth specifically, which Philochorus says the Cretans regard as merely a tower or prison that its inmates could not escape (*Thes.* 16.1). In another passage (*Thes.* 19.2), Plutarch tells us the account of a slightly later Athenian historian, Demon (*FGrH* 327), which also notes that Taurus was a general, adding the detail that he was killed in a naval battle when Theseus escaped Crete.

However, Palaephatus' method was otherwise more influential. Several other later sources also make a man named Taurus the human lover of Pasiphaë (see Hawes 2014 and 2022).

Such rationalized accounts help by assuring us that our understanding of the 'basic' myth (always a tricky concept) seems to align with reality (see Hawes in this volume). While the rationalizing mythographers themselves introduced a variety of new and unknown details, these are motivated entirely by the authors' rationalizing aims. And what they want to push back against—traditional stories that beggar belief—motivates them to begin with common understanding of a story, not rarified details found in a single obscure poet. In that process, turning a monster into a person is a standard manoeuvre since monsters—especially hybrid ones—by their very nature, fall into the category of what must be expunged from myth to make it accord with known reality.

ARTISTIC REPRESENTATIONS

From the above, one could easily take the impression that the myth of the Minotaur was somewhat marginal in Archaic and early Classical Greece. The artistic tradition handily puts the lie to this notion, for Theseus is enormously popular during this time frame both inside and outside Athens and Attica. And while not all details of the 'standard' version of the myth can be corroborated by visual evidence, many can, and these often appear in art earlier than in surviving literary sources (Brommer 1982: 75). For example, we have seen that the Labyrinth in Knossos is not mentioned until Philochorus but appears in art much earlier (Morris 1992: 187–9). Ariadne's thread likewise turns up in art long before being attested in written sources. Examples of bull-headed men (who may be *the* Minotaur) are found as early as the eighth century BCE, and by the middle of the seventh century, we clearly have representations of the Minotaur myth (Walker 1995b: 16). By the early sixth century, painted vases and other artefacts showing Theseus killing the Minotaur appear throughout central Greece and beyond (Woodford 1992: 580). Barrett (2015: 103–5) presents statistics for 550–450 BCE indicating that the hero's encounters with bestial opponents are the most popular illustrations of his myths on Attic vases, and that among these Theseus' encounter with the Minotaur is the single most predominant subject, outnumbering all other such episodes combined until the mid-fifth century BCE.

What the artistic depictions share with the literary evidence is stability; as Woodford points out, radically different compositions 'are rare' (1992: 580). While particular scene types include many variations—such as whether Theseus uses a sword or a club or (more rarely) strangles the Minotaur, whether the monster is standing or not, and so on—nothing suggests fundamentally different stories behind the images. And the Minotaur himself is essentially unwavering in form, although a few early Archaic amphorae show an inverse Minotaur with a human head atop a bull's body (Simantoni-Bournia 2013: 388), and there are some other slight oddities in that early period (Woodford

1992: 576–7, 579). These are so few, however, and since—as in the written descriptions—
we have an overwhelming number of consistent artistic depictions from all periods,
a bull's head atop a man's body was undoubtedly the established form. But the popularity of the motif drops considerably after the Peloponnesian War (431–405 BCE), and
while Ariadne and Theseus are frequently represented in art of the Roman period, the
Minotaur is not, though he remained a common enough subject in mosaic depictions.
Woodford attributes this to the appeal in this medium of the Labyrinth's geometry
(1992: 581).

ROMAN LITERARY MINOTAURS

If, in general, the Minotaur held less interest for Roman visual artists than for their
Greek predecessors, the same cannot be said about Roman poets. The Minotaur makes
frequent appearances in Roman literature, and while this can be chalked up sometimes
to display of mythological knowledge, scholars have teased out deeper associations that
come with the Minotaur and its Labyrinth, as well as with Cretan myth more generally.
Lowe (2015: 182–8) assesses these trends and explains that poets from the first century
BCE onwards use the half-human, half-beast nature of the Minotaur to examine both the
nature of emotions (particularly passion) and their own creative acts as poets.

The Minotaur's story was always intertwined with that of his half-sister, Ariadne. But
in the Roman poets, beginning with Catullus' Poem 64, their individual tragic sufferings
at the hands of the same man, Theseus, explicitly become injuries to be interpreted together: abandonment for Ariadne, brutal death for the Minotaur. The Roman poets
weave the Minotaur more deeply into the family saga of Minos, his wife, and their offspring. When Catullus' Ariadne laments her choice to save Theseus, which led to the
death of the Minotaur, she refers to the creature as her 'full brother' (64.150 germanum,
not 'half-brother', as at Lowe 2015: 185)—an extraordinary statement, and one that
inspires a trend in Roman poetry of creating situations in which the Minotaur can be
'represented in incongruously sympathetic, (that is, human), terms' (Lowe 2015: 188; see
e.g. Ov. Met. 8.131–73 and Ars am. 1.289–326; Verg. Aen. 6.20–30 and Ecl. 6.45–60).

As in earlier periods, the basic narrative elements of the story remain unchanged aside
from occasional details, as when Ovid's Theseus uses a club on the Minotaur instead of
a sword or his hands (Her. 10.101–2). The Minotaur's form is also clearly always that of
the traditional bull-headed man. At the same time, while the Minotaur is humanized,
he is never made human. We do not hear him speak (because he cannot with his bovine
mouth), and the poets do not give us any sense of articulate inner emotional thought.
Instead, these writers focus on the fulcrum between his human and animal aspects
without allowing him to slip too far to either side.

This balanced approach to a hybrid creature helps us understand the Minotaur's
functions in Roman literature, but the thematic species-bending that we see here
might not have been entirely new. As early as Euripides' Cretans, Minos' enquiries into

Pasiphaë's child, while based on his outrage at the hybrid monstrosity that has been birthed, aim to determine how human and how bestial the bull's son is and whether he will be treated as a person or a beast. For this last point, we may recollect his question about what breast will feed the Minotaur: cow's or woman's? The answer comes just as the text breaks off: 'the breasts that gave birth [fe]ed it' (*tr]eph[ou]sin oi tekontes*).

CONCLUSION: HUMAN-ANIMAL HYBRIDITY

We can turn, then, to the larger topic of the Minotaur's hybridity, which the Roman writers generally manipulate more flexibly than their Greek predecessors. For instance, for the rhetorician Isocrates, in the fourth century BCE, the Minotaur is merely a fearsome opponent of Athens' main hero, Theseus, made more formidable by his hybridity, a 'nature/form mixed together from man and bull, with the sort of strength befitting that compounded from such bodies' (*Helen* 27). Hybridity here is only a source of monstrosity and is clearly a strong component of the Minotaur's valence in Greek culture, and the only one really visible to us in Greek art. But Euripides and the Augustan poets saw the potential for something more, for an almost human identity, and they do not seem to have been alone in this. The painters of two vases found in Etruria, for example, imaginatively portray the Minotaur as an infant with his human mother (Woodford 1992: 577). These domestic scenes rely on the effect of seeing a bovine head as the sole strange presence amidst otherwise everyday imagery (Fig. 16.1). Euripides achieves the same effect literarily when the nurse reports that Pasiphaë feeds her infant from her own breasts. We also find the occasional report that the Minotaur had a real name—a human name—Asterius (e.g. Apollod. *Bibl.* 3.11). The name's meaning, 'Starry', connects him to the celestial name of his mother, as Pasiphaë means 'All-Shining', and through her to his grandfather, the sun god Helios. The name also suggests a place for the Minotaur in the Cretan royal family since Minos' stepfather, also an Asterius (or Asterion), died without his own offspring, as mentioned above (Apollod. *Bibl.* 3.8). Meanwhile, the Greek geographer Pausanias (second century CE) reports that Theseus defeated Asterion, a son of Minos. Like the rationalizing mythographers, Pausanias, who elsewhere incorporates clearly rationalized stories into his narrative (Hawes 2014: 194–213), may be thinking of a fully human 'Minotaur' since he notes that 'Asterion surpassed the others killed by Theseus in courage' (*andreiāi*, literally, 'in manliness', Paus. 2.31.1).

   We seem, then, to have a spectrum of conceptions of the Minotaur's physical form that runs from bestial (but hybrid) to a bestial-human mix to fully human—this last being represented by the rationalizers, who must remove the physical impossibility that the Minotaur represents by turning him into an ordinary person, an adulterer, a general, and even a secretary, as the Byzantine writer Tzetzes does (*Chil.* 1.523–30; see also Hawes 2014: 125, 213). The middle, mixed position is suggested by Euripides and the enigmatic Etruscan images, and is what we find also, although never simply framed, in

FIGURE 16.1 Pasiphaë and the baby Minotaur on a red-figure vase. Fourth century BCE.

the imagination of the Roman poets. Fundamentally, the rationalizers' wholly human Minotaur is irreconcilable with the other two, so we are not really dealing with a spectrum so much as a contrast that works on two levels. The most basic distinction is between a fully human (rationalized) and a not-fully human Minotaur. The second category includes Minotaurs of varying proportions but always distinctly both beast and man simultaneously, as the artistic tradition stresses.

The Minotaur's ability to metamorphose in its relation to humanity, despite its stability in so many other ways, is perhaps due to its status as both typical and atypical of Greek notions of monstrous hybridity. The combination of animal and human is familiar enough (see Aston in this volume; also Aston 2011), but the Minotaur is exceptional in having an animal's head atop its human body and, more importantly, in being represented as the offspring of a biological process, the sexual union of Pasiphaë and the bull. While this bestiality is not 'normal', it differs from the monstrous children of divinities and the offspring of two monsters—both types being well represented in Hesiod's *Theogony*—or the metamorphosis of a human into a monstrous form (e.g. Medusa; see Lowe in this volume). This imbues the Minotaur with a wider range of possibilities, and although they are not used to their full advantage until the modern era, when the Minotaur becomes a complex symbol—most famously for Picasso and Jorge Luis Borges, unfortunately outside the scope of this chapter (but see Ziolkowski 2008)—we can glimpse the potential for a wider range of possible semiotic valences for the Minotaur already in the ancient world.

SUGGESTED READING

Gantz (1993: 259–70) gives a good overview of the early sources for various pieces of evidence for the myth of Theseus, including the Minotaur. While they deal with art, that subject is better treated in Neils (1987) and Woodford (1992), and Barrett's dissertation is a good supplement (2015). See also Edmunds (2021: 1–14). Webster (1966), Calame (1990), Walker (1995b), and Mills (1997) discuss parts or the whole of the Theseus myth and its development over time in Greece and especially Athens, and particularly about the Minotaur. The frequent rationalizations of the Minotaur can be contextualized by the analysis of Hawes (2014), but the starting place is Stern (1996) and Santoni (2000), both concentrating on Palaephatus. Lowe (2015) treats the reception of the Minotaur in Roman poetry and points to earlier bibliography.

WORKS CITED

Aston, E. 2011. *Mixanthrôpoi: Animal-human Hybrid Deities in Greek Religion.* Liège.
Barrett, E. A. 2015. 'The Iconography of the Athenian Hero in Late Archaic Greek Vase-Painting.' PhD dissertation, University of Virginia.
Bernabé, A. 1992. 'El mito de Teseo en la poesía arcaica y clásica', in *Coloquio sobre Teseo y la copa de Aison*, ed. R. Olmos, 97–118. Madrid.
Brommer, F. 1982. *Theseus: Die Taten des griechischen Helden in der antiken Kunst und Literatur.* Darmstadt.
Calame, C. 1990. *Thésée et l'imaginaire athénien: Légende et culte en Grèce antique.* Lausanne.
Cingano, E. 2017. 'Epic Fragments on Theseus: Hesiod, Cercops, and the *Theseis*.' *Journal of Juristic Papyrology* 30: 309–32.
Edmunds, L. 2021. *Greek Myth.* Berlin.
Edwards, R. B. 1970. 'The Growth of the Legend', in *The Quest for Theseus*, ed. A. G. Ward, 25–50. New York.
Gantz, T. 1993. *Early Greek Myth: A Guide to Literary and Artistic Sources*, 2 vols. Baltimore.
Harrison, J. E. 1908. *Prolegomena to the Study of Greek Religion*, 2nd edn. Cambridge.
Hawes, G. 2014. *Rationalizing Myth in Antiquity.* Oxford.
Hawes, G. 2022. 'Heraclitus the Mythographer, *On Unbelievable Stories*', in *The Oxford Handbook of Greek and Roman Mythography*, ed. R. Scott Smith and S. M. Trzaskoma, 186–91. Oxford.

Koning, H. H. 2022. 'Palaephatus', in *The Oxford Handbook of Greek and Roman Mythography*, ed. R. Scott Smith and S. M. Trzaskoma, 274–81. Oxford.

Lowe, D. 2015. *Monsters and Monstrosity in Augustan Poetry*. Ann Arbor.

Mills, S. 1997. *Theseus, Tragedy, and the Athenian Empire*. Oxford.

Morris, S. P. 1992. *Daidalos and the Origins of Greek Art*. Princeton.

Neils, J. 1987. *The Youthful Deeds of Theseus*. Rome.

Nilsson, M. P. 1971. *The Minoan–Mycenaean Religion and Its Survival in Greek Religion*, 2nd edn. New York.

Santoni, A. 2000. *Palefato: Le storie incredibili*. Pisa.

Scanlon, T. F. 2014. *Sport in the Greek and Roman Worlds*, vol. 1. Oxford.

Simantoni-Bournia, E. 2013. 'The Minotaur: The Acclimatization of a Cretan Hybrid in the Cyclades', in *Creta in der geometrichen und archaischen Zeit*, ed. W.-D. Nimeier, O. Pilz, and I. Kaiser, 383–93. Munich.

Smith, R. S., and S. M. Trzaskoma, trans. 2007. *Apollodorus' Library and Hyginus' Fabulae: Two Handbooks of Greek Mythology*. Indianapolis.

Stern, J., trans. 1996. *Palaephatus: On Unbelievable Tales*. Wauconda, IL.

Walker, H. J. 1995a. 'The Early Development of the Theseus Myth.' *Rheinisches Museum für Philologie* 188/1: 1–33.

Walker, H. J. 1995b. *Theseus and Athens*. New York.

Ward, A. G. 1970. 'The Cretan Adventure', in *The Quest for Theseus*, ed. A. G. Ward, 25–50. New York.

Webster, T. B. L. 1966. 'The Myth of Ariadne from Homer to Catullus.' *Greece & Rome* 13/1: 22–31.

Woodford, S. 1992. 'Minotauros', in *LIMC* 6/1: 574–81.

Ziolkowski, T. 2008. *Minos and the Moderns: Cretan Myth in Twentieth-Century Literature and Art*. Oxford.

CHAPTER 17

···

HUMAN-ANIMAL HYBRIDS

···

EMMA ASTON

INTRODUCTION: HYBRIDS WITHIN THE CANON OF THE STRANGE

···

> Above Saune, a city in Arabia, a hippocentaur was discovered high up a mountain which is full of a marvellous drug.... The king captured the hippocentaur alive and sent it with other gifts to Caesar in Egypt. It lived on meat, but was unable to endure the change of climate and died, so the prefect of Egypt had it preserved and sent to Rome. And first it was displayed in the palace, having a face more savage than a human's and hairy hands and fingers, and its lungs were connected to its forelegs and stomach. It had the hard hooves of a horse and yellowish hair, even though its skin had been blackened by the preservation process. It was not as big as some writers have recorded, but also not small. In the aforementioned city of Saune there were also said to be other hippocentaurs. If someone does not believe the one sent to Rome was real, he can investigate it. For the preserved one is kept on the property of the emperor, as I said before. (Phlegon of Tralles, *FGrH* 257 F36.34–5, trans. McInerney)

PHLEGON includes this pitiable centaur, snatched from an Arabian mountain and eventually consigned to the store-chambers of the emperor Hadrian, in the long list of various marvels that comprise his *Mirabilia*, a book of 'wonders'. These encompass a broad range of natural oddities and uncanny events, such as discoveries of massive bones, amazingly long lifespans, and an Aetolian general who returns from the dead and devours the body of his own newborn hermaphrodite child (*FGrH* 257 F36.11–19; 37; 2). The work seems to have been a fantastic hotchpotch. Yet one theme emerges most strongly: that of the unnatural birth. Men give birth; women give birth to animals; babies are born with multiple heads or with animal parts (*FGrH* 257 F36.20–7). The birth of a *teras*—a portent, a prodigy, something unexpected and against nature—is, in effect, the way in which the words of myth and reality collide. Centaurs, like many-headed creatures and beings of dual gender, normally belong to the realm of storytelling and to the distant past. Their occurrence in the here and now is regarded by Phlegon as meaningful and ominous. Even Aristotle, so committed to classifying the orders of life, plainly found monstrous births hard to fit into his logical analysis in *On the Generation of Animals* (4.4; for the relationship between Aristotle's work and Phlegon, see Shannon-Henderson 2019). The fact that he did include them at all is telling.

Within the world of ancient paradoxography, then, hybrids comprise just one element of the rich array of the monstrous. Within ancient myth, on the other hand, they play a far more substantial role. Mythical monsters could be monstrous because of vast size or strength, but the great majority displayed their physical monstrosity through a combination of human and animal parts. Occasionally, as with the Chimaera, different animal species could combine within a single body and without any human elements, but this was not a popular trope. There was plainly something about the juxtaposition of human and non-human that was especially good to think with and held enduring symbolic potency throughout classical antiquity and beyond. Why are animal hybrids so important? I will approach this question from two angles: first the theoretical, and then with reference to a specific case study, centaurs. The case study will reveal the limitations of the basic theoretical model by showing that every hybrid was a product of a particular environment: the specific ancient communities that told stories of its deeds and, in some cases, worshipped it as a god.

HYBRIDS AND MONSTER THEORY

It has long since been recognized that the figure of the monster gives us a special access to what a society—past or present—considers abnormal (and therefore normal) to its values and its collective fears. Monsters are 'uncanny', as Freud observed in his 1919 essay *Das Unheimliche*. Monster theory as a discipline, however, crystallized with the publication of Jeffrey Jerome Cohen's 'Monster Culture (Seven Theses)' (1996), which begins with a programmatic and still-influential list of essential qualities of monsters. Reading these, the classicist is bound to feel a thrill of recognition, for while Cohen's framework draws on diverse ages and cultures it plainly applies in many ways to the mythology of the classical world. In particular, the classical hybrid signifies 'category crisis' in its transgression of the boundary between human and non-human. By doing so, it signifies a prohibition on doing so: the consistent need for hybrid monsters to be defeated and neutralized shows that their monstrosity (anatomical and behavioural) has consequences. The hybrid is 'othered', for example by being placed in remote lands or in the distant past; Phlegon's centaur comes from Arabia (where other centaurs apparently dwell), and Pliny tells of one brought from Egypt as a gift for the emperor Claudius (*NH* 7.3). Within Greece itself the two centaur homelands, Thessaly and Arcadia, are strongly associated with 'time before', as will be discussed. Finally, hybrids appeal while they appal. Female hybrids have dangerous erotic allure, as with the Sirens and Scylla

(Neils 1995); the sexual freedom of satyrs imperils human society because on one level it is tempting (Lissarague 1993; 2013: 142–7).

Clearly, a combination of human and animal should have a special potency within this theoretical framework. Viewing the ancient *mentalité* as dominated by binary oppositions (male/female, Greek/barbarian, and so on), a key aspect of structuralist approaches, has recently been challenged (on ethnic polarities, see e.g. Skinner 2012: 45–9). Nonetheless, the Greeks plainly did use non-human animals as a contrast with the human condition and, therefore, as a way of exploring what made humans human. The contribution of hybrids to this discourse is important. One example will serve as illustration: that of the virtuous centaur Pholus hosting Heracles in his home on Mount Pholoë in the Peloponnese. The main literary source is Apollodorus (*Bibl.* 2.5.4). However, earlier circulation of the myth is attested by its adoption in fifth-century Athenian vase-painting, for example an Attic kylix of the first half of the fifth century (Basel BS489), on which Heracles and Pholus recline side by side. In Apollodorus' account, Pholus is a good host (his *xenia*, hospitality, belongs to his human component): he gives his guest cooked meat. His own portion, however, he eats raw, obeying the appetite of his animal part (since, though horses are herbivores, centaurs were thought to catch and eat game). The symbolism becomes more complex when Heracles calls for wine; the pithos, a large clay vessel, is 'shared by all the centaurs', so Pholus does not really have a right to offer it. By insisting, Heracles is probably breaking the tacit code of good guest-conduct. But Pholus obediently opens the pithos, and the smell of the wine draws the centaurs to the gathering in a rowdy group, angry at the misappropriation but also, perhaps, just maddened by the fumes, since centaurs are notoriously unable to handle their drink. The party ends very badly. On the Attic kylix, the angry centaurs are massing in the background, holding branches (the centaur's standard weapon), and reaching towards the wine. The artist has chosen to depict the horse body of one of them oddly angled to present its rear, with anus and testes, to the viewer, in contrast with Pholus' orderly pose. Like Apollodorus, the vase-painter was plainly interested in exploring the complicated juxtapositions of animal and human, civilized and disordered, which the scene contains.

Not all myths are so amenable to a structuralist interpretation, but one important function of hybrids was plainly to enact a contrast between human (simultaneously restricted and uplifted by civilization) and animal (simultaneously liberated and betrayed by its lack). Crucially, however, such thinking in the conscious sense is ours, not that of the ancient Greeks, who not only had no concept of monster theory, but who also rarely even saw fit to comment explicitly or at any length on hybrids, their importance in the mythological canon, or their meaning (see Hawes in this volume). For the most part, hybrid beings were so deeply entrenched in ancient Greek culture as to not require or excite comment. Moreover, as our case study will show, the neat synopses of Apollodorus and other such writers hardly encompass the full diversity of hybrids and their characters. Hybrids did not simply follow a universal ideological template. They emerged from, and reflected, the values and priorities of specific communities at specific times.

We should also stop short of regarding hybrids as the 'ultimate' monster in terms of their ability to arouse deep instinctive horror such as Cohen's framework—along with many modern discussions of the monstrous—requires. This is not to presume to say just what a Greek would have found most terrifying. Rather, we can discern ways in which the hybrid represents a taming, a controlling, of the monstrous, and we can identify variants which are in fact more deeply troubling—more evocative of the worst kind of disorder—than the hybrid form.

If we look at early Greek literature, we find something rather different from the animal-human hybrids familiar from later accounts and especially from ancient visual culture. Two trends emerge: one, a curiously indefinite physicality; the other, a superabundance of physical phenomena. An example of the former is the Sirens, who in Homer's *Odyssey* are never explicitly identified as bird–woman hybrids. The narrative constantly emphasizes their magical voices (12.41–4, 158–91), and the poet gives us a chilling image of them sitting in a flowering meadow surrounded by the shrivelled remains of their human victims. Whether or not a hybrid form was firmly associated with the Sirens at the time of the *Odyssey*'s composition, the poet chooses to leave their physical form vague, in a way that is just as troubling as precise details (see Denson in this volume). The latter trend is exemplified by Hesiod's description of Typhoeus (*Theog.* 820–52). Typhoeus is a hybrid of sorts: he combines a mainly humanoid body with a profusion of serpent heads in place of a humanoid head. However, the poet does not stop there; he piles on details of sensation and sound. Fire flashes from the eyes of all Typhoeus' many heads, and they all utter sounds of dizzying variety, one after another: snake-hissing, puppy-yelping, lion-roaring, bull-bellowing, and 'sounds such as the gods understand'. Thus, human and divine elements are combined not with one animal species but with many, the different kinds of voice uttered in sequence (see also Brockliss in this volume and Brockliss 2017–2018).

This animal profusion, this break with the hybrid binary, particularly resembles ancient descriptions of divine shape-shifters like Proteus, Achelous, and Thetis, who can move freely and rapidly between forms for aggressive or defensive purposes. They are terrifying not because they juxtapose human and animal but because their physicality is effectively boundless. Their non-human forms are not even limited to the animal, but include plants and fire. They are *capable of anything*. Thetis, as a deceptive vessel, is especially dangerous. Her fair form contains all the wild things (animals, plants, fire) she unleashes on Peleus as he attempts to wrestle her into submission (see Pind. *Nem.* 4.62–8; cf. Paus. 5.18.5). Whereas literary accounts describe Thetis as shifting her entire shape, vase-painters tend to show the animals as attached to her to represent her various forms (Fig. 17.1). She also carries a dreadful prophecy: that her son will exceed his father. This is why she must be shackled to a mortal in the first place, according to the main version of the story, by the fifth-century BCE poet Pindar (*Isthm.* 8.28–48). Thetis' male counterpart, Proteus, the *Halios Gerōn* ('Old Man of the Sea'), has a subtly different character according to gender: what mortals wanted from him was prophetic knowledge, and he used his shape-shifting to withhold it. But he is still a formidable prospect for Menelaus to tackle in the *Odyssey* (4.420–2).

FIGURE 17.1 Peleus wrestling Thetis. Attic black-figure vase painted by Peithinos, *c*.505–500 BCE. Berlin Antikensammlung F2279.

Source: Wikimedia / ArchaiOptix. CC BY-SA 4.0.

Mortals in myth can never shape-shift like this, with rapid multiple transformations, but they can undergo animal metamorphosis. The loss of humanity is almost always presented as a matter of degradation and suffering. The Greeks typically associated human-to-animal metamorphosis with transgression and punishment, as in the case of Lycaon, the Arcadian king who sacrifices a human child to Zeus and is turned into a wolf as punishment (Paus. 8.2.3; cf. Apollod. *Bibl.* 3.8). The version narrated by Pausanias becomes all the more striking through its mirroring in Arcadian ritual: at the sanctuary of Zeus Lycaeus, a man transforms into a wolf, returning to human form after nine years provided that he abstains from human flesh during that time. Pausanias treats this ritual with a certain scepticism, suggesting that such things were possible once but are no longer. However, metamorphosis in ancient mythology seems to represent a present danger, that of slipping into animal savagery. Human identity faces constant threat of assault and reversal (cf. Ogden 2021 166–77).

The contrast with hybrids is significant (Bynum 2001: 28–33, 166–70). Though the shadow of metamorphosis lurks behind it (Aston 2011: 26–86), hybridism is itself more stable, being a permanent state, with a certain degree of anatomical plausibility for all its unnatural quality. The repetition of hybrid forms in Greek art gave them a degree of familiarity—even, in some cases, a kind of tameness (see Aston 2011: 196–200, on Pan). It is noteworthy, too, how little ancient artists varied or experimented with such forms: specific mythological characters tend—with a few deviations—to have an accepted form, and artists rarely attempted new physical combinations or 'built' new monsters (cf. Murace in this volume). They seem to have developed a 'right way' to render a hybrid, as much as to render a cow, a horse, a human. Hybrids took on an existence of their own in the image- and story-worlds of the Greeks and Romans. The profusion, flux, and chaos of the shape-shifter, the labile identity of the metamorphosist—these are to some extent neutralized and controlled in the hybrid form.

CASE STUDY: CENTAURS

In both words and images, centaurs had a frequency and popularity unrivalled by any other hybrid, and are correspondingly prominent in modern culture, including children's literature (such as C. S. Lewis's *Narnia* books and J. K. Rowling's *Harry Potter* series). The appeal of the centaur as a visual object is captured by the second-century CE author Lucian in his *Zeuxis* (3–6), about the fifth-century BCE artist famous for his ability to produce extremely lifelike representations (see Hancock 2019: 95–9). Lucian describes a painting Zeuxis made depicting a centaur family, the original apparently lost in a shipwreck but vividly present in Lucian's memory. The painting combines the strange (the two centaur 'foals' suckle, one from its mother's human breasts, the other from her horse udder), the frightening (the centaur father is wild, hairy, fierce of face), the alluring (the female centaur combines human loveliness with the aesthetic grace of a Thessalian filly), and the touching (the centaur children pressing close to their dam). Lucian describes the junction between the human and animal parts of the female as gradual, avoiding a sharp and troubling divide, as the hybrid's most unsettling part is usually the junction between its divergent elements. The viewer is drawn, repelled, amused, puzzled. What might seem the nucleus of ordered human society, the family, is spliced—uneasily but intriguingly—with the mechanics of animal reproduction. For Zeuxis, the choice of subject is counterproductive: the viewers are too taken up with its strangeness (*to xenon*) and novelty to notice the technical brilliance of its execution, and in the end the painter grumpily orders the work to be covered up and carried away.

Zeuxis' composition was, however, untypical. Centaurs in ancient art, except where they stood alone, were most often depicted in combat, their most common adversary being the Lapiths, a legendary Thessalian tribe. Centauromachies depicting this theme adorned not only pots for private use but also major public buildings—most famously the west pediment of the temple of Zeus at Olympia, the metopes of the Athenian Parthenon, and those of the Hephaesteum (all mid-fifth century BCE), and the interior frieze of the temple of Apollo Epicurius at Bassae in Arcadia (*c.*400 BCE). In this story, the centaurs seem to conform perfectly with the chief characteristics of the monster in classical myth. They are the Enemy, endangering social order—in this case Pirithous' wedding, which they drunkenly disrupt. They pose a sexual threat—here, to the bride. They must be defeated, and either killed or sent packing (e.g. Diod. Sic. 4.70). Hubristic violence was indeed the characteristic which would most readily have come into an ancient Greek's mind when the word *kentauros* was mentioned; when, in Aristophanes' *Frogs* (38–9), Heracles wants to exclaim at Dionysus' vigorous knocking at his door, he says, 'How centaurishly [*kentaurikōs*] he drove against it, whoever he is.' This nature plainly draws in large part on their animal component. Horses in Greek thought were often associated with dangerous sexual energy and savage appetites (Detienne 1971: 168–70), and their ability to terrify when ridden into battle was known and exploited by cavalry commanders: for example, it is precisely the psychological impact of cavalry which Xenophon hopes to dispel in the *Anabasis* (3.2.18–19) when he tells his fellow Greeks that actually they have nothing to fear from the enemy's horses.

In fact, however, centaurs were far from simple, and it did not take an artful Lucian to complicate them. Below we explore the way in which the centaur, so far from presenting a one-sided monster 'recipe', raised questions and incorporated deliberate contradictions and antitheses.

GOOD AND BAD HORSES

At first glance, the contribution of the horse part in the characterization of centaurs may seem wholly negative. This impression appears to be supported by comparing them with the other widespread horse hybrid in ancient mythology and art: the satyr (Isler-Kerényi 2004). The anatomies of centaurs and satyrs are different: centaurs comprise more horse, with only the equine neck and head replaced by human parts (torso, arms and hands, neck and head). Satyrs have the bipedal gait and posture of humans; only equine hooves, tails, and ears and a certain animality of face mark them as hybrid. Their penises are human, but pronounced and normally erect. They share with centaurs lustfulness and drunkenness, both attributes appropriate, in their case, to their role as companions of Dionysus. They are somewhat less formidable as foes than centaurs, and generally tend to be more ludicrous than terrifying. Especially when depicted on drinking vessels, they illustrate the potential of wine to make us overstep the normal constraints of society and degenerate into bestial cavorting. This applies also to theatre, the other great locus of satyr activity, where norms are inverted and distorted and therefore re-expressed. Such behaviour is fitting for satyrs but not for humans; satyrs represent what we risk being, what we would perhaps sometimes like to be, but what we must not be (Lissarague 1993; 1990: 234–5).

Most centaur behaviour is similarly not to be emulated. They, and their violent ways, are listed as unsuitable topics of conversation (or perhaps singing) by Xenophanes in his elegy describing the ideal symposium, though the unsuitability of centaurs in this context seems to be linked not only to their violence but also to the fact that they belong to the distant past (fr. B1 DK, lines 21–3). However, there is one way in which they could present an admirable aspect and a model for human activity. Later rationalistic authors linked centaurs with the development of horsemanship (Hawes 2014: 56–9), but the connection goes back at least to Xenophon, who incorporates centaurs in his *Education of Cyrus* in a wholly fictitious conversation between the young Cyrus and his companions in which they resolve to become excellent cavalrymen as soon as possible through constant practice on horseback. The Persian noble Chrysantas opines that the centaur combines the best elements of humans and horses in a single body, with speed and strength the key equine virtues; therefore, Cyrus and his friends should emulate centaurs. However, a human rider is the best of all because it is like a centaur that can be dismantled, broken down into its human and horse parts so that human actions— eating, dressing, and sleeping in the human manner—can happen unimpeded (Xen. *Cyr.* 20). So, the ideal cavalryman is like a centaur that can be taken apart, achieving the best of both the combination and its separate elements.

Of course, Xenophon places these sentiments in Persian mouths, and may not wholly espouse them as applicable to Greek society. Nonetheless, they fit well with his ideal-ization of horsemanship and its ethics in other works such as the *Cavalry Commander* and *On Horsemanship*. The idea that by comparing them with centaurs Xenophon aims to make his Persian characters inherently problematic and flawed is interesting but not wholly convincing (see e.g. Johnson 2005). It relies, for example, on a widespread view that the centaurs in sculptural Centauromachies, especially the Parthenon, were in-tended as analogous to the *barbaroi* while the Lapiths stood for the civilized Greeks; this would have informed readings of the *Education of Cyrus* (see duBois 1991). However, the Parthenon carvings do little—far less than some vase-paintings—to emphasize the savagery of the centaurs. Whereas vase-paintings tend to show the centaurs wielding rocks and branches against the Lapiths' swords and shields, in the Parthenon metopes both sides fight with bare hands; the animality of the centaurs is sometimes emphasized with an animal-skin garment (Metope South XVIII) or a 'bestial' face (Metope South XXXI), but does this really signify a connection with Persian identity? Those who argue it does tend to cite the *Education of Cyrus*, so the matter becomes circular (see e.g. Spivey 1996: 142; contra: Westervelt 2004: 70). Finally, both centaurs and Lapiths are Thessalian tribes (Aston 2017: 86–9); the link with medizing Thessaly might make their Greekness suspect, but this would apply equally to both groups. In fact, cavalry, centaurs, and *some*

Persians are all things which an Athenian out of sympathy with the radical democracy of his own polis might choose to find admirable as representing values belonging to an imaginary past time.

This positive aspect of the centaur—the way in which it could be associated with equestrian excellence and military virtue—was never available to the satyr. Moreover, because of its link with horsemanship, the centaur, unlike the satyr, could be co-opted as an emblem of the elite. One of the highest-quality horse types in antiquity mentioned in our literary sources is the Thessalian *kentauridēs*, perhaps so called because of a brand mark in that form, mentioned by Lucian in *On the Ignorant Book-Collector* (*Ind.* 5). The word's patronymic ending, *-idēs*, is interesting: Pindar explains that the offspring of Ixion and Nephele was one Centaurus, seemingly wholly anthropomorphic, who coupled with the mares of Pelion to produce the hybrid centaurs (*Pyth.* 2.44–8). Possibly the Thessalians advertised the horses called *kentauridai* as the descendants of Centaurus. Such animals were affordable only by the very wealthy (see Braun 1970: 86–8; Aston and Kerr 2018: 14.). Centaurs had a shade of the aspirational, whereas the satyr's state was one which a human of good social standing must avoid.[1] This makes the important point that, though multiple associations built up around certain animal species in the ancient imagination, these did not remain immutable when the species was incorporated into a hybrid form. The symbolic significance of the animal depends in part upon the use made of the hybrid—visual, rhetorical—by a particular artist or author, and, as we shall see, by the hybrid's development in a particular place.

GOOD AND BAD CENTAURS

For all that they could be pressed into service as emblems of cavalry excellence, centaurs were overall characterized as violent, immoderate, and driven by animal instincts. There is, however, a perpetual exception: Chiron, the Thessalian counterpart of the Peloponnesian Pholus. Chiron is everything the other centaurs are not: wise, moderate, and promoting social order through its wellspring, *paideia* ('education'). And yet, with some slight difference, Chiron has the same physical form as the others, showing that anatomy does not automatically bring a certain character. He was a *phēr* ('beast') just as the others were *phēres* (Pind. *Pyth.* 3.4; Hom. *Il.* 2.743–4). In Greek art Chiron tends to be clothed and to have human forefeet; although he carries a branch, which other centaurs often brandish as a weapon, Chiron uses it for carrying game and signifying his hunting prowess and his mastery over other animals. A hybrid does not have to be a monster in the negative sense. Moreover, we might even term Chiron an anti-monster, in that he actually assists humans against the destructive force of the other centaurs: for

---

[1] Padgett (2000) rightly observes that satyrs derive much of their character from donkeys and mules rather than horses, but horses are also subjects of ambivalence, sometimes associated with destructive appetites (see Lissarague 2013: 97–105).

example, he restores Peleus' lost sword when the hero is attacked by centaurs on Mount Pelion (Apollod. *Bibl.* 3.13.3). The healing arts Chiron practises and teaches are the antithesis of the other centaurs' violence.

How can we understand the relationship between Chiron and the other centaurs, beings with the same body but diametrically different characters and roles? The evidence available does not support any convincing argument of originally independent origins, since our earliest literary source, Homer's *Iliad*, refers to Chiron as *dikaiotatos kentaurōn*, 'most just of the centaurs' (11.832). Clearly, when the poem was composed, Chiron was considered one of the centaurs but already distinguished by his character. Nor is it persuasive to argue that the negative aspects of centaurs all derive from a hostile external perspective, casting Thessaly as the land of dangerous and savage forces. The role of the centaurs as foes of the Lapiths is also mentioned in the *Iliad* (1.267–8; 2.742–4), and the poem displays no tendency to cast Thessaly as an uncivilized or inferior region. That is not to say that Thessaly—in particular, Mount Pelion and its environs—was not felt by other Greeks to be a suitable place for centaurs, associated as it was with life outside settled towns and agriculture, and with 'time before' (Buxton 1994: 93–4). But this characterization suits Chiron as much as the other centaurs (Aston 2006). The symbolic contrast of Chiron and the other centaurs was probably inherent in the Thessalian stories of these beings. Chiron was a benign natural force who, with proper appeals, could offer succour against the malign natural forces embodied in the other centaurs.

As for Chiron himself, what he reveals most of all is how deeply embedded in the religious and mythological life of a particular region a hybrid being could be. The other Thessalian centaurs had close ties to the land, being descended from the Lapith Ixion or, in another version, from the river Peneius (Apollod. *Epit.* 1.20 and *Bibl.* 1.8.2; Diod. Sic. 4.69.1–2); However, Chiron's role in Thessalian mythology was of a quite different order. He was the glue that held together many of Thessaly's diverse myth-historical traditions. He was the educator of heroes, the earliest attested being Achilles, Asclepius, and Jason; the boys lived in his cave on Pelion during their period of training, an entry into a wild space which has the characteristics of a symbolic rite of passage, and their relationship with him made him the node in a network connecting major components in the earliest surviving stratum of Thessaly's mythology (see Gregory 2018). Martin West (1988: 160) has posited a so-called Iolkos Cycle as one of the remnants of sub-Mycenaean source material detectable within the *Iliad*: this comprised stories of Peleus, Thetis, Achilles, Pelias, and Jason, and in this cluster Chiron would have played a central role. As tutor, he is an interesting alternative to the traditional figure of the shared ancestor, since he ties together heroic genealogies while not being directly incorporated in them. He is the son of Cronus and the nymph Philyra; he marries the wholly human Chariclo and has nymph daughters (e.g. Hes. *Theog.* 1001–2; Pind. *Pyth.* 4.102–3).

The question of how early Chiron's role in Thessalian mythology can be traced takes us to an especially significant piece of material evidence: the Lefkandi Centaur (Fig. 17.2). This is our earliest surviving Greek centaur representation by far, dating to the late tenth or early ninth century BCE (Desborough et al. 1970: 22–4). It seems to have been an object of mystic potency: its head was found in one grave and the rest in

FIGURE 17.2 The Lefkandi Centaur, *c.*900 BCE; archaeological museum of Eretria, Greece. Ink-wash drawing by Rosemary Aston.

Source: © Rosemary Aston 2021.

another, for reasons now irrecoverable (Arrington 2016: 23); its remaining hand (the right one) has six digits; its earholes are deeply channelled. The extra digit recalls the connection of the name Chiron with *cheir*, hand, and therefore with various kinds of handiwork, especially medicine (Gregory 2018: 42). Does it allude to superlative skill in that field? The main justification for identifying the Lefkandi Centaur as Chiron in particular, despite the lack of the human forelegs which are normally his hallmark, is a clear groove, created before firing, on the effigy's left knee. This is plausibly (though not incontestably) interpreted as the incurable wound which Chiron sustained accidentally from one of Heracles' arrows, the pain of which caused the centaur to abnegate his immortality. The weakness of this theory is the late date of our surviving sources mentioning the knee-wound specifically (e.g. Apollod. *Bibl.* 2.83–7); however, Chiron's death is attested much earlier (Pind. *Pyth.* 3.1–5). It would also be significant to find a depiction of Chiron at Lefkandi, of all places. In the tenth century BCE, a high degree of connectivity producing similarities in material culture existed between Lefkandi, coastal sites in Locris, some Aegean islands, and Thessalian settlements in the bay of Volos (Lemos 1998; Donnellan 2017). There would have been ample opportunity for the stories of Chiron's deeds to have crossed the Euboean Gulf.

Returning to Thessaly, Chiron's regional importance continues into the Classical and Hellenistic periods. In particular, in the early third century BCE, Chiron's sacred cave on Pelion became a focus of a healing cult. A family of healers, seemingly based in the newly founded city of Demetrias, in Thessalian Magnesia, considered him their shared ancestor as well as the originator of their craft; the healing herbs of Mount Pelion were used and celebrated in their medical practice, which was, apparently, carried out free from charge (Heraclides, *FGrH* 369A F2.12). In addition, an annual pilgrimage was made from Demetrias to the cave of Chiron by young men wearing sheepskins (Heraclides, *FGrH* 369A F2.8); thus a component of the region's earliest mythology was incorporated into the religious landscape of the new settlement and the lives of its diverse inhabitants (Kravaritou 2011; Mili 2015: 198-204).

CONCLUSION: HYBRID MONSTERS, BOTH OWNED AND DISOWNED

The case of Chiron certainly shows that animal hybridism does not invariably depict a being inimical to humanity or expressive of hostile savagery. Moreover, a hybrid could be placed at the core of a region's self-expression and identity. That said, to return to Cohen's recipe of the monstrous, hybrids like Chiron are not wholly detached from the otherness which Greek monsters had. He was the *phēr theios* ('divine beast'), placed in the spatial alterity of the mountain and the temporal alterity of the distant past. In this respect, Chiron bears a close resemblance to Arcadian Pan, who was emblematic of the primordial wildness of that region in the eyes of other Greeks, but who within Arcadia itself was a fundamental component of the region's religious landscape, most notably in the sanctuary he shared with Zeus on Mount Lycaeum. Like Hellenistic Magnesia, Arcadia in the Classical period had a strong drive to assert its difference and uniqueness, and the visual peculiarity of a hybrid was ideally suited to achieve this. Another highly comparable example is the Siren Parthenope. While the Sirens as a group were best known in antiquity, as now, for their attacks upon passing shipping, the tomb-cult of Parthenope was crucial to the local identity of ancient Neapolis and its environs (Taylor 2014).

So we have seen the two sides of the hybrid monster in Greek culture. On the one hand—as Lorenz Winkler-Horaček (2008) has vividly argued, with reference to fabulous creatures on the 'orientalizing' ceramics of the Archaic period—such monsters can be pushed away into the fringes of the visible and the known, to the periphery of the world where dwell a range of marvellous beings (see also Friedman in this volume). On the other hand, hybrids can be placed at the heart of the homeland, the heart of the Self. They can be enmeshed in the religious lives of a community; they can be a foundation stone of its myth-history; they can stand for important values rather than their inversion, subversion, or antithesis. Cult provided the ultimate means to control and articulate the power of the hybrid. Control, however, does not remove the wildness of the hybrid. Where Chiron dwelled, there one was likely to encounter his less placid fellow centaurs also; even Chiron was not wholly tame. Pan could be worshipped on the slope of the Athenian acropolis, but even at the heart of the urban space he dwelt in his cave, his capsule of Arcadian wilderness. Though in many ways hybrids related strongly to conceptions of Self and Other, they functioned not simply to enact this dichotomy but in fact to disturb and confuse it in many eternally fascinating ways.

Suggested Reading

The study of monsters—including animal hybrids—in ancient culture has been a strong theme in scholarship for years now, and has generated some useful publications, one of the earliest being Atherton (2000). The religious dimension of hybridism is explored in Aston (2011). Several monographs discuss specific hybrids, such as Hopman (2012). The best introduction to the visual depiction of hybrid forms remains Padgett (2003). Two related topics are worth including here: animals and metamorphosis, as both have strong relevance to hybridism. On animals, Fögen and Thomas (2017) provide a valuable range of topics and approaches. On metamorphosis, Forbes Irving (1990) has been supplemented, though not wholly replaced, by Buxton (2009); Frontisi-Ducroux (2003) is also important for the visual representation of metamorphosis.

Works Cited

Arrington, N. T. 2016. 'Talismanic Practice at Lefkandi: Trinkets, Burials and Belief in the Early Iron Age.' *Cambridge Classical Journal* 62: 1–30.

Aston, E. 2006. 'The Absence of Chiron.' *Classical Quarterly* 56: 349–62.

Aston, E. 2011. *Mixanthrôpoi: Animal-human Hybrid Deities in Greek Religion*. Liège.

Aston, E. 2017. 'Centaurs and Lapiths in the Landscape of Thessaly', in *Myths on the Map: The Storied Landscapes of Ancient Greece*, ed. G. Hawes, 83–105. Oxford.

Aston, E., and J. Kerr. 2018. 'Battlefield and Racetrack: The Role of the Horse in Thessalian Society.' *Historia* 67: 2–35.

Atherton, C., ed. 2000. *Monsters and Monstrosity in Greek and Roman Culture*. Bari.

Braun, K. 1970. 'Der Dipylon-Brunnen B1: Die Funde.' *Athenische Mitteilungen* 85: 129–269.

Brockliss, W. 2017–2018. 'Olympian Sound in the *Theogony* and the *Catalogue of Women*: Sweet Music and Disorderly Noise'. *Classical Journal* 113/2: 129–49.

Buxton, R. 1994. *Imaginary Greece: The Contexts of Mythology*. Cambridge.

Buxton, R. 2009. *Forms of Astonishment: Greek Myths of Metamorphosis*. Oxford.

Bynum, C. W. 2001. *Metamorphosis and Identity*. New York.

Cohen, J. J. 1996. 'Monster Culture (Seven Theses)', in *Monster Theory: Reading Culture*, ed. J. J. Cohen, 3–25. Minneapolis.

Desborough, V., R. Nicholls, and M. Popham. 1970. 'A Euboean Centaur'. *Annual of the British School at Athens* 65: 21–30.

Detienne, M. 1971. 'Athena and the Mastery of the Horse', trans. A.B. Werth. *History of Religions* 11.2: 168–84.

Donnellan, L. 2017. 'The "Euboean" Koine: Reassessing Patterns of Cross-Cultural Interaction and Exchange in the North-Western Aegean Region', in *Material Koinai in the Greek Early Iron Age and Archaic Period*, ed. S. Handberg and A. Gadolou, 43–64. Aarhus.

duBois, P. 1991. *Centaurs and Amazons: Women and the Pre-History of the Great Chain of Being*. Ann Arbor.

Fögen, T., and E. Thomas, eds. 2017. *Interactions between Animals and Humans in Graeco-Roman Antiquity*. Berlin.

Forbes Irving, P. M. C. 1990. *Metamorphosis in Greek Myths*. Oxford.

Frontisi-Ducroux, F. 2003. *L'Homme-cerf et la femme-araignée*. Paris.

Gregory, J. 2018. *Cheiron's Way: Youthful Education in Homer and Tragedy*. Oxford.

Hancock, M. 2019. 'Centaurs at the Symposium: Two Types of Hybridity in Lucian'. *Ancient Narrative* 15: 89–107.

Hawes, G. 2014. *Rationalizing Myth in Antiquity*. Oxford.

Hopman, M. G. 2012. *Scylla: Myth, Metaphor, Paradox*. Cambridge.

Isler-Kerényi, C. 2004. *Civilizing Violence: Satyrs on 6th-Century Greek Vases*. Göttingen and Fribourg.

Kravaritou, S. 2011. 'Synoecism and Religious Interface in Demetrias, Thessaly'. *Kernos* 24: 111–35.

Johnson, D. M. 2005. 'Persians as Centaurs in Xenophon's *Cyropaedia*'. *Transactions of the American Philological Association* 135: 177–207.

Lemos, I. 1998. 'Euboea and Its Aegean Koine', in *Euboica: L'Eubea e la presenza euboica in Calcidica e in Occidente*, ed. B. D'Agostino and M. Bats, 45–58. Naples.

Lissarague, F. 1990. 'Why Satyrs Are Good to Represent', in *Nothing to Do with Dionysos? Athenian Drama in Its Social Context*, ed. J. J. Winkler and F. Zeitlin, 228–36. Princeton.

Lissarague, F. 1993. 'On the Wildness of Satyrs', in *Masks of Dionysos*, ed. T. H. Carpenter and C. A. Faraone, 207–20. New York.

Lissarague, F. 2013. *La cité des satyres: Une anthropologie ludique (Athènes, VIe–Ve siècle avant J.-C.)*. Paris.

McInerney, J. 2012. 'Phlegon of Tralles (257)', in *Jacoby Online. Brill's New Jacoby, Part II*, ed. I. Worthington. Leiden. https://scholarlyeditions.brill.com/bnjo/.

Mili, M. 2015. *Religion and Society in Ancient Thessaly*. Oxford.

Neils, J. 1995. 'Les Femmes Fatales: Skylla and the Sirens in Greek Art', in *The Distaff Side: Representing the Female in Homer's* Odyssey, ed. B. Cohen, 175–84. Oxford.

Ogden, D. 2021. *The Werewolf in the Ancient World*. Oxford.

Padgett, J. M. 2000. 'The Stable Hands of Dionysos: Satyrs and Donkeys as Symbols of Social Marginalization in Attic Vase Painting', in *Not the Classical Ideal: Athens and the Construction of the Other in Greek Art*, ed. B. Cohen, 43–70. Leiden.

Padgett, J. M., ed. 2003. *The Centaur's Smile: The Human Animal in Early Greek Art*. Princeton.

Shannon-Henderson, K. E. 2019. 'Phlegon's Paradoxical Physiognomy: Centaurs in the *Peri Thaumasion*', in *Medicine and Paradoxography in the Ancient World*, ed. G. Kazantzidis, 141–61. Berlin.

Skinner, J. E. 2012. *The Invention of Greek Ethnography from Homer to Herodotus*. Oxford.

Spivey, N. 1996. *Understanding Greek Sculpture*. London.

Taylor, R. 2014. 'The Cult of Sirens and Greek Colonial Identity in Southern Italy', in *Attitudes Towards the Past in Antiquity: Creating Identities?*, ed. B. Alroth and C. Scheffer, 183–9. Stockholm.

West, M. L. 1988. 'The Rise of the Greek Epic.' *Journal of Hellenic Studies* 108: 151–72.

Westervelt, H. 2004. 'The Centauromachy in Greek Architectural Sculpture.' PhD dissertation, Harvard University.

Winkler-Horaček, L. 2008. 'Fiktionale Grenzräume im frühen Griechenland', in *Mensch und Tier in der Antike: Grenzziehung und Grenzüberschreitung*, ed. A. Alexandridis, M. Wild, and L. Winkler-Horaček, 503–25. Wiesbaden.

CHAPTER 18

MONSTROUS METAMORPHOSES

Ovid and the Art of Making and Unmaking Monsters

GENEVIEVE LIVELEY

INTRODUCTION

THE world of Ovid's *Metamorphoses* is a world of monsters—some new and some old. Like the fertile earth following the cataclysmic flood described in the poem's opening Book, Ovid's epic gives birth to innumerable species of strange hybrids and uncanny chimeras, in some parts returning ancient creatures to life and in other parts creating entirely new monsters. In this story world, however, many of the old familiar monsters turn out to be somewhat insipid washed-out versions of their former selves. The list of such diminished creatures includes the sad, multi-eyed watchman Argus (1.625–721); the yappy, multi-headed watchdog Cerberus (4.450–1; 7.408–15); and the snake-haired Fury Tisiphone (4.474–511), who is not only a hyperbolically monstrous figure in her own right (4.488), but carries with her poisons secreted by other monstrous creatures— the froth from Cerberus' slavering jaws and the Hydra's toxic venom (4.500–1). To these we can add the cloistered Minoan Minotaur (8.155–71); the lovelorn Cyclops Polyphemus (13.744–897); a handful of hungry sea monsters (4.688–734; 11.211–13; 15.508–13); and a virtual stable full of amorous centaurs, such as Chiron (2.630–54) and Nessus (9.101–58; 12.308–454). Significantly, all these creatures enter the narrative already fully (de)formed and Ovid seems relatively disinterested in exploring either their characters or their monstrosities. Natural born monsters, it appears, are not good subjects for a poem about the *making* of monsters—about 'bodies changed into new forms' (*mutatas . . . formas | corpora*, 1.1–2), about 'monstering' through metamorphosis.

Ovid's treatment of these old mythic monsters instead focuses upon their 'unmaking' or their 'unmonstering'—what Emmrich characterizes as 'Entmonsterung' and Seidler as the 'undoing of the monsters' monstrousness' (Seidler 2020b; Emmrich 2020). Ovid's preferred strategy for this unmonstering is through humour, using bathos to domesticate the established monstrosity of these familiar creatures. So, Ovid's Argus is effectively bored to death by Mercury's dull storytelling (Lowe 2015: 226–32). The Minotaur is locked away in the Cretan Labyrinth not because he is a man-eater but because he is an embarrassing reminder of Pasiphaë's adultery (Fantham 2004: 108). Cerberus is 'all bark and no bite' as Hercules drags him off for a walk (Sumpter 2016: 28). Tisiphone is having a bad hair day, struggling to comb her unruly reptilian locks (Jouteur 2008). The Cyclopes and centaurs similarly struggle with their personal grooming (Pietropaolo 2018). In each case, the monstrosity of the ready-made monster is swiftly and effectively unmade.

Tellingly, of this menagerie only the Minotaur (Book 8) and the Trojan sea monster (11.11–12) are explicitly designated *monstra* (on the nuances of Augustan terms for monsters, see Lowe 2015: 8–14). Indeed, throughout the *Metamorphoses* Ovid uses *monstra* and its cognates with remarkable caution and to characterize a highly selective group. The first creature he describes in this way is the Python—one of the 'new monsters' spontaneously produced by the fecund earth in the wake of the universal flood (1.437) and promptly dispatched by Apollo—unmonstered and unmade by the god of poetry. The same formulation (*nova monstra*) describes a giant wolf later in the poem (11.391), and that 'strange biform monster' the Minotaur (8.156; 9.667, 736). And, while ostensibly a very old monster indeed—albeit emphatically made 'new' by Ovid's sympathetic treatment—the snake-haired Gorgon Medusa is associated with more 'monstrous' epithets than any other character in the poem (4.615, 745; 5.216, 241). She, too, is effectively 'unmade' through an act of old-fashioned violence (see Lowe in this volume; also Lowe 2015: 105–15).

All these *monstra* certainly seem unambiguously monstrous. But Ovid also applies this description to characters and objects which we might not immediately or obviously identify as monstrous, nor, in the light of the Latin term's wider etymological associations, as warning signs or omens (Felton 2012; Atherton 1998; Cohen 1996). Take, for example, the Heliades, transformed into poplar trees, screaming in agony as their distraught mother tries to rescue them, ripping away the tree bark into which their flesh and limbs have now grown (2.367). Or Ocyrhoe, daughter of the centaur Chiron, transformed into a horse (2.675); Cadmus changed into a harmless snake (4.591); a cheeky boy transformed into a timid lizard (5.459); Atalanta and Hippomenes turned into Cybele's tame lions (10.553); the strange sex-change experienced by Caenis/Caeneus (12.175); the merman Glaucus (13.912); Circe's victims, transformed into pets (14.414); the Trojan fleet transformed into water nymphs (14.567); Cipus sprouting horns (15.571); and—a rare metaphorical 'monster'—Scylla, daughter of Nisus (8.100), given the same rapacious nature as her Homeric namesake but not her monstrous form, in Ovid's deliberate conflation of the two Scyllae.

This second group of non-monstrous creatures, made *monstra* as a result of some physical or behavioural transformation, illustrates a motif central to Ovid's treatment of monsters and monstrosity throughout the *Metamorphoses*. In the epic that he himself refers to as a poem about 'mutated bodies/forms' (*mutatae formae, Tr.* 1.1.117), we should not be surprised that Ovid is concerned with making humans into monstrous beings through metamorphosis. Indeed, the mutations through which human bodies are changed into new forms necessarily involve a kind of 'monstering'. Note Sissa's astute observation that 'Hybridization—that is to say a partial and cumulative change—lies at the heart of the poem ... Metamorphosis does not necessarily reveal, or clarify a previous identity, but it always creates hybrids' (Sissa 2019: 164). The world of the *Metamorphoses* is a world not simply of monsters but also of monstrous part-human hybrids, and this chapter explores both the mutating forms and the forms of mutation that this hybridization takes in the poem. I start by examining what Ovid has to say about monsters in his wider corpus and consider what some of his literary interlocutors say about monstrosity before tracing the mutations of those ideas into the monstrous *Metamorphoses*.[1]

Monstering Poets

In the final Book of his *Amores* (3.12.21–40) Ovid reflects upon the relationship between poets and monsters—upon the power of poetry to make and unmake such creatures, and particularly upon the poet's power to manipulate his reader's responses to them. Ovid insists that the seemingly autobiographical stories in his *Amores* are, in fact, fictions, and that his beloved *puella* is as much the product of poetic imagination as the monstrous Scylla or snake-haired Medusa. She is no more real than the three-headed dog Cerberus or the winged horse Pegasus; she is as mythical a character as Callisto (the virgin huntress turned into a bear), as Niobe (the grieving mother turned into a rock), or as one of the Heliades (the sisters of Phaethon turned into trees). Ovid stresses here that all such monsters, including his beastly lover, are created. They are fictions, the products of the strange co-creation that occurs when the credulous mind of the reader encounters the fertile imagination and creative licence of the poet (3.12.41).

Here, Ovid appears to be answering a challenge posed by one of his most significant literary interlocutors, Lucretius, who had argued that hybrid monsters like Scylla are not real (cf. Hopman 2012: 179; Hughes 2010; Buxton 2009: 173; Hardie 2009b):

> Centaurs never existed, nor at any time can there ever exist
> creatures of double nature and twofold body
> of incompatible parts combined together,
> where one half cannot be equally paired with the other.
> ....
> So you should not believe that centaurs can be formed or exist,
> if they are composed of man and the seed of the burden-bearing horse;
> nor that Scyllas can exist with a body half fish and a waist of rabid dogs,
> nor any other kind of monster in which we see the body parts are incompatible;
>
> (Lucr. *DRN* 5.878–94)

---

[1] All translations in this chapter are my own.

Appealing to the poetic rather than the anatomical senses of 'form' and 'composition', and countering Lucretius' scientific objection to fertile hybrids with his own fertile imagination, Ovid argues that hybrid creatures such as centaurs and Scyllas may not be born, but they can be made up (Farrell 1999). Conflating two infamously different characters and myths, Ovid says:

> We poets made Scylla steal her father's precious lock of hair
> and hide the snarling dogs in her private parts.

> (*Am.* 3.12.21–2)

The first line of this elegiac couplet, a hexameter, refers to Scylla, the daughter of King Nisus, who betrays both father and country after falling in love with the enemy leader, Minos (8.17–151). The second line, a pentameter, transforms that human Scylla into her monstrous namesake. Although the reference to 'the snarling dogs in her private parts' could allude metaphorically to the human Scylla's sexual desires, it more obviously evokes the other Scylla, the voracious sea monster—infamously represented with the *protomai* (literally the 'front-portions' and typically the heads and front legs) of dogs attached to the lower part of her body (Fig. 18.1; see also Hopman in this volume, esp. Fig. 13.3; Hopman 2012: 74; Aguirre Castro 2002). This doubly hybrid Scylla, the epitome of Lucretius' 'twofold body of incompatible parts combined together', becomes grotesquely deformed in the lower half of Ovid's couplet, offering an ingenious demonstration of Ovid's point that such monsters 'really' are made up by poets (cf. Hardie 2009b).

Already in the programmatic opening lines of his *Amores* (1.1.1–4), Ovid suggests that poetry is a vehicle for such monstrous transformation and presents the elegiac metre of his poetry as a 'deformation' of the epic hexameter. He was, he claims, intending to launch his literary career by writing an epic poem, but Cupid transformed his hexameter into pentameter—metamorphosing Ovid's attempt at epic verse into elegy by mutilating the shape of every other line. As Rimell (2006: 208) so nicely puts it: 'the second line gets chopped to become (hey presto) a pentameter, the first line's wasted, deforming limb' (cf. Ov. *Am.* 3.1.7–10). Ovid invites us to regard his poetry as both monstrous and monstering, his poems as fertile ground for the birthing of new monsters, and himself as among the victims of its mutations. Indeed, at the end of his literary career, banished from Rome, Ovid declares that he has himself undergone a metamorphosis just like one of the characters from his epic and that 'among those transformed bodies [*mutata*] | the shape of my own fate can be related' (*Tr.* 1.1.119–20; cf. Gildenhard and Zissos 2000).

ARS MUTATA

In this light we can see that Cupid's intervention in Ovid's origin story makes the first monstrous metamorphosis in Ovid's corpus that of the poet himself, transformed by the mutation of his poetry into hybrid epic/elegiac form. Indeed, Ovid's deformation shares

FIGURE 18.1 Zeus (as a bull) abducting Europa; Scylla at lower left with prominent *protomai*; Triton (merman) at lower right; Greek vase, *c.*350 BCE.

Source: Wikimedia / Carole Raddato. CC BY-SA 2.0.

a potent connection with the transformative poetry and poetics of another Augustan poet: Horace. In *Odes* 2.20, Horace had identified himself as a 'hybrid poet' or *biformis vates* (*Carm.* 2.20.2–3), and imagined himself as a victim of metamorphosis, vividly describing from a first-person perspective the experience of turning into a swan (cf. Citroni 2009; Hardie 2009b:119):

> Now, already rough skin is creeping
> over my legs and I am changed [*mutor*]
> into a white bird on the top part, and light plumage
> begins to grow along my fingers and arms.

(2.20.9–12)

This strange account draws an imaginary line between the upper and lower halves of the body. As the bottom half is deformed into that of a waterbird, the poet calls attention to the skin's roughening texture, as if reaching down and touching the legs of a bird with fingertips that are—as yet—those of a man. We are made to *feel* this metamorphosis together with its victim. Then those fingers are them-selves transformed as smooth feathers begin to grow over human hands and shoulders. The man is changed into a bird. And yet this new creature clearly retains its old human ambition, creativity, and identity. It (or he?) is a birdman, a hybrid, *biformis*: a point vividly underscored by the comparison Horace invites us to draw between his new form and that of Daedalus and Icarus with their own 'manmade' wings (2.20.13). Indeed, at this stage in the metamorphosis, the narrative perspec-tive explicitly bifurcates and the birdman tells us to look not only *with* but also *at* him (2.20.14) as he takes flight, soaring across the Roman Empire and into immor-tality. Crucially, as the Horace-bird takes to the air, he continues to sing and to refer to himself as the same being as his former self (2.20.17–19). He remains Horace, the 'hybrid poet', even in this new doubly hybrid form—the metamorphosis continuing his former essence and identity.

We encounter a very similar poetic hybrid immortalized in Horace's *Ars poetica*, a poem purporting to give advice on decorum in the 'art of poetry'. The poem advises against depicting fantastic scenes of metamorphosis such as Procne's transformation into a bird or Cadmus' into a snake (179–88). Yet the *Ars* itself represents a fantastic scene of metamorphosis, in which a bad poet is transformed through metaphor into a monstrous 'bear-leech' hybrid (472–6; cf. Laird 2007: 137). The poem further criticizes as monstrous and grotesque any literary work lacking aesthetic, thematic, generic, or formal unity, yet conspicuously displays these deficiencies itself (Laird 2007; Ferenczi and Hardie 2014). In fact, the poem immediately implicates itself in the very monstrous poetics it claims to condemn by opening with the ekphrasis of an artist composing a monstrous chimera, re-presenting the representation of a hybrid in the very process of its making:

> If a painter chose to attach a human head
> to a horse's neck, and covered over with multicoloured plumage
> a random collection of limbs, so that what was
> a lovely woman at the top ended hideously in the tail of a black fish,
> invited to look, could you hold back your laughter, my friends?
> Believe me, dear Pisos, a book would be just like that picture
> if its own vain shapes were so conceived—like a bad dream,
> so that neither its foot nor its head could be related
> to a unified form.
>
> (*Ars* 1–9)

As Lowe (2015: 18) cleverly observes, the similarities between this Horatian monster and the birdman creature in *Odes* 2.20 are remarkable: 'Both are feathered aquatic creatures with ugly black lower extremities and a beautiful body up above.' Moreover, both birdman and chimera explicitly demand that we *look* at them. Both are monstrous hybrids which prompt us to pay close attention to the impossible conjunctions of animal and human body parts. And both offer comment upon the art of poetry and of making *monstra*.

THE ART OF MONSTERING

In response to some of the aesthetic and poetic protocols set out in the *Ars poetica*, the first-century CE Roman rhetorician Quintilian sees Ovid's *Metamorphoses* as an (im)perfect example of the sort of misshapen book that lacks the proper unified form purportedly recommended in Horace's poem. Quintilian intimates that Ovid's attempt 'to assemble the most diverse material into the appearance of a unified body' (*Inst.* 4.1.77) renders the *Metamorphoses* a fantastical thing—a creation just like Horace's monstrous chimera (Jouteur 2009; Anderson 1995). Quintilian appears to have in mind here the formal composition of Ovid's poem—the two hundred or so different stories that Ovid splices together into a semblance of narrative unity across the fifteen Books of his epic. The Horace-swan hybrid of the *Odes* and the woman-horse-bird-fish chimera of the *Ars poetica*, however, also provide Ovid with a mould for making his own monsters. For we see the patterns first outlined by Horace reworked repeatedly in Ovid's epic: the same emphasis upon hybridity and biform bodies (Seidler 2020a; Casanova-Robin 2009); the same bifurcation of perspective to view the metamorphosis from both within and without, offering the monster's own intimate first-person perspective on their deformation alongside the viewpoint of the scene's narrator-focalizer (Hopman 2012: 237); the close-up featuring the mutation of some especially sensitive human body part such as skin, hands, mouth, or genitals (Riddehough 1959: 206); and the same accent upon metamorphosis as continuing some human essence and identity (Solodow 1988; Galinsky 1975; cf. Feldherr 2010: 26–46). Horace's monsters give Ovid a form from which to (de)form his own.

The first human metamorphosis of Ovid's poem helps to establish this pattern. King Lycaon (Greek 'Wolf') is notorious for his savagery and, after insulting Jupiter by trying to feed the god human flesh, he takes on a physical form to match his name and his character (cf. Feldherr 2010: 37–40; Anderson 1989):

> In terror, Lycaon runs out into the quiet countryside.
> He howls as he tries in vain to speak.
> His mouth foams with a rabid savagery that comes from within as he turns his usual
>   bloodlust against the sheep, taking pleasure in their bloody slaughter.
> His clothes are changed into a hairy coat and his arms into legs.
> He has become a wolf. But he still keeps some signs of his old self:
> the same grey hair, the same wild expression,
> the same blazing eyes, and same wild appearance as before.
>
> (*Met.* 1.232–9)

The surrounding peace of the Arcadian countryside intensifies the full monstrosity of this man-wolf howling into the night. Indeed, for a moment, we share the horror of this metamorphosis with the terrified Lycaon himself as he struggles in vain to speak but finds he can only howl. This moment of sympathy (literally 'feeling with') swiftly passes, however, and a quasi-cinematic shift in focus zooms in for a close-up upon Lycaon's face and mouth, the source of this inhuman sound. As he notices the grazing sheep nearby, Lycaon's jaws begin to slaver with bloodlust. At this stage we are perhaps to picture Lycaon as a monstrous werewolfish hybrid, his human face mutating into a wolf's, jaws rabidly foaming at the animalistic anticipation of bloody slaughter. Only when Lycaon 'turns' (*vertitur*) to attack the flock does he also 'turn' into the wolf—his clothes turning into fur, his arms into legs. Only then does werewolf become wolf (*fit lupus*). And yet, Ovid tells us, the old Lycaon remains recognizable even in this new shape. Lycaon retains some essence of his former human self and form, including his name. His physical transformation complete, Lycaon yet remains a monstrous hybrid creature.

Such continuity through change becomes horrifically apparent in Callisto's monstrous metamorphosis, a change which follows a pattern of deformation very similar to that of her father. Callisto has already been treated with abject cruelty by the gods (raped by Jupiter and then, her virginity 'stolen', shamed and cast out by Diana). Now she is made to suffer again at the hands of a jealous Juno:

> She grabbed Callisto by her hair at the front
> and threw her face-down on to the ground. The girl stretched out her arms
> in supplication but those arms began to grow rough with black hair;
> her hands turned into animal's feet,
> as her fingernails curled into claws;
> and the lips recently admired by Jove were deformed [*deformia*] into ugly jaws.
> To stop her appealing to his pity with prayers or pleas,
> the power of speech was snatched away from her; from her hoarse throat
> there came only a furious, menacing, terrible growl.
> But her old human mind remained the same even though she was now a bear.
>
> (*Met.* 2.476–85)

Having already conveyed the psychological ordeal of Callisto's rape and its aftermath, Ovid here sets out to describe the cognate emotional trauma of her physical transformation—portrayed emphatically as a *deformation*—into a terrifying wild animal. The gesture of supplication with which the scene begins allows us to watch the metamorphosis in horror with Callisto herself. Then, as the transformation moves up from her lower body, the point of view shifts and we watch on as her beautiful face and lips are disfigured. The briefest of temporal flashbacks to the very recent past (when Jupiter had admired their beauty) slows the pace of narration and cinematically projects a grotesque disjunction between the before and after of this monstrous makeover. Horrified and disgusted by her own body, Callisto is trapped inside this new monstrous hybrid form; her body has changed but her mind remains as it was before the metamorphosis. So, she hides in terror from other wild animals, even bears, forgetting that she herself now is one; she trembles at the sight of wolves, even though her own father Lycaon runs among them (*Met.* 2.489–95; O'Bryhim 1990).

As Frontisi-Ducroux's comprehensive study of metamorphosis in the classical tradition shows, Ovid's slow descriptions of transformation-in-process mark a radical
change in the way we see such monstrous mutations represented in the ancient sources
(2003: 86). In Greek texts especially we can see anticipated the 'advice' (however unreliable) in Horace's *Ars poetica* (179–88) to avoid the depiction of fantastic scenes of metamorphosis (Laird 2007; Oliensis 1998). In virtually all Greek and most Roman sources,
grotesque transformations traditionally take place either instantaneously or decorously
offstage (Feldherr 2010: 28–33). In Ovid, the reverse becomes the norm, as he describes
scenes of deformation in graphic anatomical detail, transforming readers into spectators
(or voyeurs) and inviting them to watch as the metamorphosis takes place 'step by slow
step' (Richlin 1992: 165). One consequence of this slower approach to the process of
transformation is a concomitant focus on the intermediate stages—that is, a close-up
of the moments when the victim of metamorphosis is still recognizable as (partially)
human and the victim's disunified hybridity is most monstrously evident. Recalling the
'random collection of limbs' of Horace's chimera, Ovidian metamorphoses emphasize
the deformation of human arms and legs and necks into their animal equivalents—
the anatomical detailing of different body parts distorted at different points in the
transformation—feet becoming fins, hands becoming hooves, noses becoming snouts,
lips becoming jaws, hair becoming feathers. The focus upon the grotesque, incremental
mutations of these incompatible and incongruous body parts enhances the monstering
effect (Lada-Richards 2018: 376–8). So, many of Ovid's characters become 'momentary
monsters' at some midpoint during their mutation, when the deformation of human
into animal (or vegetable or mineral) is in process and the victim's mixed species hybridity is most visible. That is, when a human head can be seen incongruously joined
to an animal's neck, or animal paws to the ends of human arms; when human limbs
become covered with plumage or fur or tree bark; or when the lower body of what was
once a lovely woman becomes hideously deformed into that of some other creature—an
impossible hybrid combination.

   This effect is most grotesque either when the transformation is in process or when it
is only partial, as for example when, as with Horace's chimera, we see the human parts
of the monster conjoined with the body parts of (an)other creature(s). While such monstrous metamorphoses in process appear throughout the poem, partial transformations
are rare in the *Metamorphoses*: only the Sirens (5.551–63), Midas (11.146–93), Glaucus
(13.906–14.69), Scylla (14.59–67), and Cipus (15.565–621) experience this kind of frac-
tional metamorphosis. Unexpectedly, perhaps, this partial deformation typically causes
only the mildest of inconvenience. The Sirens undergo the same easy transformation
of human into bird seen in the metamorphosis of Horace's poet-bird (*Carm.* 2.20): in
a sudden mutation, the girls see their limbs covered with golden feathers as they are
partially changed into birds, but here they retain their 'maidenly features and human
voices' (*Met.* 5.551–63). Midas' ears turn into those of an ass and Cipus sprouts horns on
his head, but both men, although embarrassed by these deformities, can conceal their
minor monstrosities with suitable headwear. Glaucus seems untroubled by his transformation into a merman, which brings with it the bonus of divine status as a sea god.

When Scylla first encounters this weird creature, she initially wonders whether he is god or monster (13.912), but quickly decides that he is more monster than god and flees.

We first encounter Ovid's monster Scylla as an absent presence in the narrative of another character named Scylla, who emphatically fails to mention her namesake when she compares the heartless Minos to a catalogue of ruthless rhetorical *monstra* (*Met.* 8.121). This 'Megarian' Scylla includes Charybdis in her tirade against Minos but not Charybdis' familiar counterpart. When next we see the other Scylla, she is paired with Charybdis and appears in her familiar form as sea monster, 'her unlucky/black (*atram*) waist surrounded with snarling dogs' (13.732). Employing techniques we recognize from his elegiac writing, however, in the very next line Ovid swiftly transforms the monster (back) into a maiden: 'she has the face of a girl, and, if not all the stories the poets have handed down are false, she was herself a girl once upon a time' (13.733–4; cf. *Am.* 3.12, *Tr.* 4.7.11–20). In a mode of metamorphosis that Lowe (2015: 70–2) aptly characterizes as 'maidenizing', we learn that the hideous monster was once a beautiful girl with many ardent suitors (*Met.* 13.730–7). Moreover, like Ovid himself, Scylla enjoyed telling tales about her would-be lovers (13.737). Among them is Glaucus—Scylla's monstrous 'other half' in this narrative—who unwittingly causes the witch Circe to poison Scylla's favourite bathing spot with noxious herbs. When Scylla wades waist-deep into the pool, she finds her body from the waist down horrifically transformed into a ring of monstrous, barking dogs' heads—evoking the monstrous *vagina dentata* motif (see Hopman in this volume; Miller 2012). Indeed, Ovid's graphic depiction of this deformation, itself a mutation of previous descriptions of Scylla in Lucretius (5.892–3) and Vergil (*Aen.* 3.426–8), conveys the impression that Scylla gives birth to these monsters. Terrified of her own body, Scylla tries to flee but only takes her monstrous new form with her:

> At first, not believing that these things are parts of her own body,
> she recoils, she tries to flee, terrified by the snarling mouths of the dogs.
> But what she flees from, she drags along with her.
> Feeling for her own body, her thighs, her legs, her feet,
> she finds in place of these parts of her the gaping jaws of dogs like Cerberus.
> She stands upon a rabid pack of dogs, she is mounted upon the backs of wild beasts,
> disfigured from the waist, with her genitals exposed.
>
> (*Met.* 14.59–65)

Ovid has no need to slow the pace of this partial transformation so that we can focus upon the grotesque mutations of different body parts step by step. The metamorphosis takes place almost instantaneously: as soon as Scylla wades into the polluted water, Circe's poison takes effect, changing the submerged part of Scylla's body into its monstrous new form. Because Scylla is only partially transformed, we can experience this monstering from the monster's own traumatized perspective. As Scylla looks down at her lower half, we see it through her eyes and we feel *with* her as she reaches down with human hands in a frantic search for where her lower limbs should be. Similarly, we sympathize with her desperate efforts to escape from herself. Like Callisto, Scylla retains part of her former self, and her mind remains unchanged by the physical deformation. Accordingly, she is terrified by the creature she has (partially) become (cf. Hopman 2012: 240). The access to Scylla's viewpoint and subjectivity in Ovid's account effectively transforms this terrifying hybrid monster into a sympathetic human figure. Indeed, as Sharrock (2002: 104 n. 36) explains: 'Strictly speaking, Scylla is transformed from virgin to monster, but … it is the other way round. Ovid takes the story of the monster and turns it into a story about a lovely victim' (cf. Lowe 2011).

CONCLUSION

Ovid's hybrid deformation of Scylla—her partial monstering and 'Entmonsterung', her characterization as both maiden and monster—clearly recalls her appearance in the *Amores*. Ovid draws our attention to the connection not only in his description of Scylla as herself a teller of *amores* (13.737), but also in his teasing double-bluff regarding the question of whether she is 'made-up' (13.733–4). Scylla's partial transformation in the *Metamorphoses* also clearly evokes Horace's poet-bird hybrid of the *Odes* and the woman-horse-bird-fish chimera of the *Ars poetica* in that Scylla too, in Lowe's neat formulation, 'is an aquatic creature with ugly black lower extremities and a beautiful body up above' (2015: 18). Ovid's metapoetic Scylla thus (im)perfectly embodies both the mutating forms and the forms of mutation that metamorphosis as hybridization— and hybridization as metamorphosis—takes in the *Metamorphoses*. An old monster unmade and made new again, Scylla beautifully demonstrates what happens when the mind of the reader merges with the fertile imagination of the poet.

SUGGESTED READING

Lowe (2015) should be at the top of any reading list on this topic, being particularly rich in its
   readings of Ovid's part-human hybrids, including Scylla, the Sirens, and centaurs. Hopman
   (2012) offers an in-depth case study of Scylla and devotes a chapter to Ovid's remaking of this
   creature. Rimell (2006) takes Medusa as the focus of her own ingenious study and tracks the
   monster's transformation through Ovid's corpus and beyond. Ovid's monsters are also well
   served by edited collections looking at broader themes: Casanova-Robin (2009) examines
   Ovid's hybrids and their reception; Hardie (2009a) includes several essays on the 'marvellous' in the *Metamorphoses*; and the chapters in Sharrock et al. (2020) take metamorphosis
   itself as their focus.

WORKS CITED

Aguirre Castro, M. 2002. 'Scylla: Hideous Monster or Femme Fatale? A Case of Contradiction
   between Literary and Artistic Evidence.' *Cuadernos de filología clásica* 12: 319–28.

Anderson, W. S. 1989. 'Lycaon: Ovid's Deceptive Paradigm in *Metamorphoses* 1.' *Illinois Classical Studies* 14: 91–101.

Anderson, W. S. 1995. 'First-Century Criticism on Ovid: The Senecas and Quintilian', in *Ovid: The Classical Heritage*, ed. W. S. Anderson, 1–10. New York.

Atherton, C., ed. 1998. *Monsters and Monstrosity in Greek and Roman Culture.* Bari.

Barchiesi, A., P. Hardie, and S. E. Hinds, eds. 1999. *Ovidian Transformations: Essays on the* Metamorphoses *and Its Reception.* Cambridge.

Buxton, R. 2009. *Forms of Astonishment: Greek Myths of Metamorphosis.* Oxford.

Casanova-Robin, H., ed. 2009. *Ovide, figures de l'hybride.* Paris.

Citroni, M. 2009. 'Horace's *Ars Poetica* and the Marvellous', in *Paradox and the Marvellous in Augustan Literature and Culture*, ed. P. Hardie, 19–38. Oxford.

Cohen, J. J., ed. 1996. *Monster Theory: Reading Culture.* Minneapolis.

Emmrich, T. 2020. *Ästhetische Monsterpolitiken.* Heidelberg.

Fantham, E. 2004. *Ovid's* Metamorphoses. Oxford.

Farrell, J. 1999. 'The Ovidian *Corpus*: Poetic Body and Poetic Text', in *Ovidian Transformations: Essays on the* Metamorphoses *and Its Reception*, ed. A. Barchiesi, P. Hardie, and S. E. Hinds, 127–41. Cambridge.

Feldherr, A. 2010. *Playing Gods: Ovid's* Metamorphoses *and the Politics of Fiction.* Princeton.

Felton, D. 2012. 'Rejecting and Embracing the Monstrous in Ancient Greece and Rome', in *The Ashgate Research Companion to Monsters and the Monstrous*, ed. A. S. Mittman and P. J. Dendle, 103–31. Farnham.

Ferenczi, A., and P. Hardie, eds. 2014. *New Approaches to Horace's Ars poetica.* Pisa.

Frontisi-Ducroux, F. 2003. *L'Homme-cerf et la femme-arraignée: Figures grecques de la métamorphose.* Paris.

Galinsky, G. K. 1975. *Ovid's Metamorphoses: An Introduction to the Basic Aspects.* Berkeley and Los Angeles.

Gildenhard, I., and A. Zissos. 2000. 'Inspirational Fictions: Autobiography and Generic Reflexivity in Ovid's Proems.' *Greece & Rome* 47/1: 67–79.

Hardie, P., ed. 2009a. *Paradox and the Marvellous in Augustan Literature and Culture.* Oxford.

Hardie, P. 2009b. 'The Self-Divisions of Scylla.' *Trends in Classics* 1/1: 118–47.

Hopman, M. G. 2012. *Scylla: Myth, Metaphor, Paradox.* Cambridge.

Hughes, J. 2010. 'Dissecting the Classical Hybrid', in *Body Parts and Bodies Whole: Changing Relations and Meanings*, ed. K. Rebay-Salisbury, M. Sørensen, and J. Hughes, 101–10. Oxford.

Jouteur, I. 2008. 'Tisiphone ovidienne *Met*. IV, 451–511.' *Euphrosyne* 36: 87–104.

Jouteur, I. 2009. 'Hybrides ovidiens au service de l'imagination créatrice', in *Ovide, figures de l'hybride*, ed. H. Casanova-Robin, 43–58. Paris.

Lada-Richards, I. 2018. ' "Closing Up" on Animal Metamorphosis: Ovid's Micro-Choreographies in the *Metamorphoses* and the Corporeal Idioms of Pantomime Dancing.' *Classical World* 111/3: 371–404.

Laird, A. 2007. 'The *Ars Poetica*', in *The Cambridge Companion to Horace*, ed. S. Harrison, 132–43. Cambridge.

Lowe, D. 2011. 'Scylla, the Diver's Daughter: Aeschrion, Hedyle, and Ovid.' *Classical Philology* 106/3: 260–4.

Lowe, D. 2015. *Monsters and Monstrosity in Augustan Poetry.* Ann Arbor.

Miller, S. A. 2012. 'Monstrous Sexuality: Variations on the Vagina Dentata', in *The Ashgate Research Companion to Monsters and the Monstrous*, ed. A. S. Mittman and P. J. Dendle, 311–28. Farnham.

O'Bryhim, S. 1990. 'Ovid's Version of Callisto's Punishment.' *Hermes* 118/1: 75–80.

Oliensis, E. 1998. *Horace and the Rhetoric of Authority.* Cambridge.

Pietropaolo, M. 2018. 'The Cyclopic Grotesque in Ovid's Tale of Galatea and Polyphemus.' *Classical Journal* 114/2: 192–214.

Richlin, A. 1992. 'Reading Ovid's Rapes', in *Pornography and Representation in Greece and Rome*, ed. Richlin, 158–79. Oxford.

Riddehough, G. B. 1959. 'Man-into-Beast Changes in Ovid.' *Phoenix* 13/4: 201–9.

Rimell, V. 2006. *Ovid's Lovers: Desire, Difference and the Poetic Imagination.* Cambridge.

Seidler, S. E. 2020a. 'Monstrous Texts and Textual Monsters: Transgressive Hybridity in Ovid's *Metamorphoses*.' MA thesis, University of Washington.

Seidler, S. E. 2020b. 'Review of Thomas Emmrich, *Ästhetische Monsterpolitiken*.' *Bryn Mawr Classical Review Online*. https://bmcr.brynmawr.edu/2020/2020.11.27. Accessed 8 December 2022.

Sharrock, A. 2002. 'Gender and Sexuality', in *The Cambridge Companion to Ovid*, ed. P. Hardie, 95–107. Cambridge.

Sharrock, A., D. Möller, and M. Malm eds. 2020. *Metamorphic Readings: Transformation, Language, and Gender in the Interpretation of Ovid's* Metamorphoses. Oxford.

Sissa, G. 2019. 'Apples and Poplars, Nuts and Bulls: The Poetic Biosphere of Ovid's *Metamorphoses*', in *Antiquities Beyond Humanism*, ed. E. Bianchi, S. Brill, and B. Holmes, 159–86. Oxford.

Solodow, J. B. 1988. *The World of Ovid's* Metamorphoses. Chapel Hill, NC.

Sumpter, E. 2016. 'Humour in the Underworld of Ovid's *Metamorphoses*.' MA thesis, McMaster University.

PART II

MONSTERS IN ANCIENT FOLKLORE AND ETHNOGRAPHY

CHAPTER 19

ANCIENT BOGEYS

Lamia, Mormo, Empousa, Gello, and Others

JANEK KUCHARSKI

INTRODUCTION

BOGEYS are no laughing matter. In ancient Greece and Rome these mischievous and malevolent supernatural entities may not have evoked the same reverent fear as divinities, and although they were *daimones* in the broad Greek sense of 'other-worldly beings' they may not have been 'really demonic' (Burkert 1992: 87). Yet delving deeper into their folklore reveals them as truly disturbing creatures with equally disturbing stories. What renders the titular quartet exceptional is that its four members, Lamia, Mormo, Empousa, and Gello—monstrous female creatures prone to frightening and even killing men, women, or children—are frequently treated as variations of the same daimonic entity: Hecate, the goddess of crossroads, witchcraft, and ghosts (Rohde [1893] 1925; also Johnston 1998; Patera 2015). Hecate herself has also been variously identified as a primordial snake demon (Fontenrose 1959); a young woman who died prematurely (Johnston 1998); or simply a bogey used to frighten children into behaving well (Patera 2015).

Such cross-identification is no mere fancy of modern scholarship: it is attested or at least intimated in many sources, such as a scholion to one of Theocritus' *Idylls* (15.40, third century BCE),[1] or a treatise of Philostratus (*c*.170–250 CE). Yet grouping these entities under one specific rallying point, such as '*daimones* who scare children' or *aōroi* (spirits of those who died before their time) cannot do full justice to each of these creatures and their peculiarities. To avoid forcing them all into yet another predetermined template, this chapter begins with a discussion of their most salient

---

[1] A 'scholion' is an anonymous ancient or Byzantine comment.

differences, and then examines their mutual resemblances, leading towards an appreci-ation of them as one daimonic 'family'.

A CATALOGUE OF DIFFERENCES

None of these four creatures can be considered a clearly defined entity; rather, each comprises a category in and of itself. Some authors, like the sophist Philostratus in his *Life of Apollonius*, explicitly speak of them in the plural, as *lamiae, empusae, gelloudes*, and *mormolykiae* (*VA* 4.25). But in many other accounts they are considered as in-dividual beings, each with her own story. Even then, however, their features, their workings, and even their fortunes accommodate many variants and conflicting versions. Lamia's story, for instance, is usually that of a bereaved mother, but sources as early as the Greek poet Stesichorus (sixth century BCE) mention her as a successful progenitor of other mythical monstrosities, such as Scylla (F 182a–182b Davies–Finglass). Mormo is represented as a quadruped creature by the Greek poetess Erinna (*Distaff* 25–7; fourth century BCE), while Mormo's other moniker, Mormolyke, may associate her with wolves (*lykoi*); yet some testimonies endow her with the ability to fly (scholia to Aelius Aristides 102.5 Dindorf). Gello's infanticidal workings are sometimes explained as strangling, but also as devouring the livers of newborns. Some sources mention Empousa as a 'noonwraith' (*Suda* ε 1049), but others as a night *daimon* (*Vita Aeschinis* 2). Thus, if one cannot entirely agree what a *lamia* or *empousa* really is, it seems all the more difficult to discuss their similarities with other creatures. For each of the four, however, certain qualities appear more prominently than others, which may provide us with a provisional roadmap of differences onto which subsequent parallels among the four can be charted.

Lamia's most salient trait is her unappealing appearance, for which she eventu-ally became a byword: 'uglier than Lamia', as noted by late Byzantine author Michael Apostolius in his collection of Greek proverbs (10.44). The Greek historian Duris of Samos provides the earliest known explicit attestation of her ugliness (*BNJ* 76 F17; *c.*350–281 BCE), but the tradition may go back even further: in the fifth century BCE, the Greek comic poet Aristophanes speaks of her filthiness (*Vesp.* 1035; *Pax* 758), while his older contemporary, Euripides, qualifies her name as 'the most disgraceful among men' (fr. 472m Kannicht). Another unique feature of hers is hermaphroditism attested by Aristophanes, who mentions her testicles, and possibly by a late sixth- or early fifth-century BCE vase-painting (Athens, National Museum, 1129 with Halm-Tisserant 1989) where she might have been endowed with a sizeable phallus. Her most sensational attribute, first mentioned by the first-century BCE Greek historian Diodorus Siculus (who alludes to an earlier tradition), was her removable eyes, which she stored in a jar while she slept (Diod. Sic. 20.41.4–5). Modern scholarship has suggested a Near Eastern origin for Lamia: the Mesopotamian goddess or demon Lamaštu, who, like Lamia, seized other people's children and 'feasted on the flesh and blood of men' (West 1991: 366).

Mormo may well have been the most paradigmatic bogeyman of the four, to the point of becoming an apotropaic interjection on the one hand, and a byword for childish (i.e. empty) fears on the other. The former usage is first attested by Aristophanes (*Eq.* 693): 'Mormo, such insolence!' but in all probability goes back much earlier. Plato (428–348 BCE) and his contemporary, the historian Xenophon (*c.*430–354 BCE), provide the oldest instances of the proverbial sense: the philosopher dismisses the fear of death by comparing it to the fear of *mormolykeia* (Pl. *Phd.* 77e), while in the historian's account soldiers are mocked for fearing the enemy just like children fear *mormones* (Xen. *Hell.* 4.4.17). The casual manner of these remarks betrays a well-entrenched usage.

Gello is distinguished primarily by her origins and little else: she died a virgin and returned as a vengeful spirit to harm the children of others, as first attested in the proverbs of the second-century CE Greek sophist Zenobius (3.3). This makes her a prominent member of an entire daimonic category, the services of which were frequently solicited in ancient magic (Ogden 1999: 16–17): the prematurely dead (*aōroi*). They were first attested as a group of potentially noxious spectres by the Christian apologist Tertullian (*c.*155–*c.*200 CE); his discussion indicates that they were clearly well known in this regard earlier (*De anim.* 57). Gello's infanticidal predilection was also regarded in a very different, ironic light: in antiquity she even became a byword for overprotective mothers, 'fonder of children than Gello', a proverb probably coined by Sappho herself (fr. 178 Lobel-Page). Of all four creatures she enjoyed the most prolific afterlife in Byzantine and modern Greek folklore (see below). Her origins, like Lamia's, are sometimes sought in the ancient Near East, in the Mesopotamian demon Gallû; but apart from the name itself there are few similarities. In fact, Gallû is a male creature, possibly with beast-like features, which quite firmly sets him apart from the prominently female Gello (West 1991: 364).

Empousa, Hecate's minion, is sometimes even explicitly identified with the chthonic goddess herself, as in one of Aristophanes' lost comedies (fr. 515 Kassel-Austin). According to the Greek historian Idomeneus of Lampsacus (*c.*325–270 BCE), she had a close connection with the 'mysteries', most likely the Eleusinian (Brown 1991), as a *daimon* appearing to initiands (*BNJ* 338 F 2). This in turn seems to tie in with the folk etymology of her name: *Empousa* from the verb *empodizein* ('to hinder')—as from initiation (*Etymologicum Magnum* s.v.), and the *daimones empodōn* ('hindering' *daimones*) attested in the Derveni Papyrus from ancient Macedonia (*c.*340 BCE; col. VI.2–3). Her most recognizable quality is her shape-shifting ability, alluded to as early as Aristophanes (*Ran.* 292–3) and referenced in later authors such as the second-century CE satirist Lucian (*Salt.* 19). Nevertheless, she was also consistently endowed with one physical attribute: a bronze leg (Ar. *Ran.* 292–3; Lucian, *Ver. hist.* 2.46) or that of a donkey (Tzetzes' scholion to Ar. *Ran.* 293). The latter even provided Empousa with an alternative name: *Onoskelis* ('donkey-legged'), a shift in appellation explicitly attested by Theodoret of Cyrrhus (fifth century CE), who says, 'what to the ancients were *empousae* our contemporaries call *onoskelides*' (*Commentary in Isaias* 5.185–8 Guinot; my translation).

FAMILY RESEMBLANCES

So much for the most salient distinguishing characteristics. Now onto the common traits linking the four creatures: the bottom line is that there are none. One would expect to find a connection in the idea of a bogeyman to frighten children, but this hardly does justice to Empousa, whose role in this capacity is mentioned only once (Plut. *Mor.* 1101c). More importantly, and somewhat unexpectedly, Gello is not given this role even once; although she causes the deaths of children (and of maidens), the sources never present her as a creature meant to frighten them. By contrast, Mormo is mentioned most frequently in this latter capacity (e.g. Lucian, *Philops.* 2), but is never said to have caused the death of a child. Only Lamia's workings are well attested in both these domains. The Greek orator Dio Chrysostom (*c.*40–115 CE), for instance, speaks of her as a children's bogeyman (*Or.* 55.11), and so did Socrates, according to Marcus Aurelius (second century CE; *Med.* 11.22.1). Duris is the earliest extant source attesting her habit of murdering children, a characterization taken up by later scholiasts and lexicographers. Empousa is mentioned as a child-killer only once, by the sixth century CE scholar Evagrius (*Ecclesiastical History*, PG 86.2836), whereas she frequently targeted adults—particularly young men—as attested by Lucian (*Ver. hist.* 2.46), Philostratus (see below), and Dio (*Or.* 5.7, 14; Felton 2013: 231–2), among others. In short, Mormo functions mainly as a child's bogeyman, and Gello as child-killer. Lamia prominently shares both these roles, but Empousa much less so.

Thus, even the most obvious characteristics are not equally distributed among the four creatures, but instead form a web of stronger and weaker relationships. In other words, there is no core trait (or set of traits) shared by all members of this group that accounts for their membership. Instead, the principle behind grouping Lamia, Mormo, Empousa, and Gello together may be explained by what Wittgenstein described as 'family resemblances'. His example was the concept of 'game', which has no set of necessary and sufficient criteria common to all members of a category (Wittgenstein 1958: 31–2). For example, solitaire has nothing to do with football, but bridge may very well be assimilated to both in different respects as a card game on the one hand and team competition on the other. As Rosch and Mervis (1975: 575) explain, 'A family resemblance relationship consists of a set of items of the form AB, BC, CD, DE. That is, each item has at least one, and probably several, elements in common with one or more other items, but no, or few, elements are common to all items.'

A common element shared by Lamia, Mormo, and Gello is their human backstory. Empousa by contrast is never credited with such a past: she is simply a *daimon*. In this respect, however, she may be assimilated to Gello, who upon her untimely death also transitioned into the daimonic realm and was referred to accordingly in later lexica. But no such transition is ever attested for Lamia and Mormo: the former became a hideous monster out of sorrow after her children's death (Duris, *BNJ* 76 F17), while the latter flew away after devouring hers (scholia to Aelius Aristides). Rarely do sources speak of either figure as a 'ghostly' being.

Even in their human backstories Lamia, Mormo, and Gello differ significantly, most obviously in their topography: Mormo's story is set in Corinth and Gello's in Lesbos, while Lamia hails predominantly from Libya. Gello died an untimely death, while the other two were already bereaved mothers when transformed into monsters. Lamia lost her children—the offspring of her union with Zeus—to Hera's jealousy, while Mormo devoured hers. Curiously enough, it is Lamia and Gello, not Mormo, who are occasionally mentioned as cannibalizing other people's children; the former by commentators on Aristotle, the latter in Byzantine vernacular culture (Michael Psellos, *Philosophica minora* 49; John of Damascus, *PG* 94.1604). Even Empousa is once said to devour foetuses (Evagrius, *PG* 86.2836). But not Mormo.

Hybridity is another sometimes-shared trait, most prominently attested for Empousa, either with her bronze leg or as *Onoskelis*—the name given also to Mormo in one source (scholion to Aelius Aristides), although it is uncertain whether this represents an independent tradition or the tendency to conflate her with the other monsters in later authors. Dio Chrysostom, among others, describes Lamia as an anguiped hybrid, fitting her with a snake's lower body attached to a divinely attractive upper body, in contrast to her traditional ugliness (*Or.* 5.12; cf. Felton 2013). As an occasional avatar of Hecate, Empousa is also associated with snakes, as in Aristophanes (fr. 515 Kassel-Austin), though he makes no reference to her looks, nor does he suggest any actual serpentine hybridity.

Polymorphism, yet another staple characteristic of Empousa, in two sources is also ascribed to Mormo and Lamia (Erinna, *Distaff*; scholion to Ar. *Pax* 758). And whereas Gello is never described as a shape-shifter in any ancient sources, in both erudite and vernacular Byzantine texts she takes various bodily forms, such as insect, snake, or dragon (Sathas 1876: 574, 576).

However fearsome Gello may have been, remedies against her daimonic workings were nonetheless known. The *Cyranides*, a Greek compilation of medical and magical texts dated to anywhere from the first to fourth century CE, recommended sleeping under a donkey's hide or wearing an amulet made of hyena's eyes to avert Gello (2.31, 2.40). In the vernacular culture of Byzantium, St Sisinnios and even St Michael were enlisted to defend children from her malice (Sathas 1876: 573–7). Empousa, too, had known weaknesses (Arata 2008: 22–4): according to late antique and Byzantine sources, jasper stone offered protection against her attacks, but in an earlier testimony harsh language was all it took to get rid of her or her kind, as Eusebius from Caesarea (fourth century BCE; *Against Hierocles* 13) and possibly Philostratus tell us (see below; cf. Miles 2017: 213). No such remedies are ever attested for Lamia or Mormo. However, the possible Mesopotamian antecedent of Lamia, the demon Lamaštu, could be warded off with incantations and amulets: many of these have been preserved, chiefly from Ugarit and the Syro-Canaanite region, but their tradition reaches back to the Sumerian times (Farber 2014).

The Family United

This overlapping network of features, rather than a set of essential criteria, probably accounted for the assimilation or cross-identification of these four creatures in antiquity. Mormo, Lamia, and Gello are spoken of as one and the same in a scholion to Theocritus' *Idylls* (15.40), though it provides a description most suitable for Lamia: in her grief after her children's death, she began killing those of others. Hesychios (s.v. Gello) explains Gello as a kind of *empousa* but restricts his definition to maidens who died before their time (unmarried), which is the former's principal quality. Empousa in turn is identified with Lamia by Eusebius (*Hierocles* 30) who, however, emphasizes her shape-shifting capacity. Mormo, as a bogeyman, is glossed in the *Suda* as Lamia.

The best-known testimony in which their names are mentioned interchangeably is that of Philostratus, who casually uses the terms *empousae*, *lamiae*, and *mormolykiae* (all plurals) as synonyms. In his account, an attractive and seemingly wealthy woman seduces a young man by the name of Menippus, who soon decided to marry her; during the wedding feast the bride is exposed by the itinerant philosopher and thaumaturge Apollonius of Tyana as 'one of the *empousae* who are commonly considered as *lamiae* and *mormolykiae*' (4.25). Forced by the wise man, she confesses to her cannibalistic appetites, revealing her identity as an *empousa*. The story's conclusion states that Apollonius defeated a *lamia*, but elsewhere this encounter is referenced as involving an *empousa* (4.38). It is not easy, and is perhaps even futile, to determine which of the creatures was 'really' depicted in this narrative. Her seductive appearance, which conceals a cannibalistic nature, makes one think of the abominations described by Dio which, though never named, were most likely *lamiae*. Yet neither the narrator nor Apollonius himself (within the narrative) ever describes her as other than an *empousa*, whereas the other names are attributed only to either popular opinion or hearsay. Such identification may also be suggested by the fact that she is referred to as an apparition (*phasma*), and by the illusions she produces, which may imply a shape-shifting capacity as well; Apollonius also speaks of her as a snake, which seems primarily metaphorical but may also suggest polymorphism.

The Distant Relatives

A host of other further removed relations also deserves a brief mention here: Gorgo, Karko, Ephialtes, Akko, and Alphito. The last two are mentioned as bogeys only once, by Plutarch (*Mor.* 1040b), but it is quite possible that he references them here as figures of laziness and stupidity (Winkler 1982), of which Akko was a paradigm, celebrated already by the fifth-century BCE comic poet Hermippus (fr. 6 Kassel-Austin). Karko is only a name, mentioned by the lexicographer Hesychios (fifth or sixth century CE) as a synonym for Lamia (s.v. Karko). Gorgo, or rather Gorgons, on the other hand, are well-established mythical monsters, best known from the Perseus legend: Medusa, whose head the hero was ordered to collect, was one of them. Along with Mormo, Gorgo is mentioned as an avatar of Hecate in an undatable, anonymous hymn quoted by a third-century CE Christian author Hippolytus (*Haer.* 4.35.5). Strabo, a geographer living at the turn of the first century, associates her with Lamia and Mormolyke (1.2.8). The same Strabo also mentions Ephialtes in their company, but his testimony is the only one to connect this *daimon* to the other lot. In Artemidorus' *Oneirocritica* ('Interpretation of Dreams', second century CE) Ephialtes is a dream-vision causing the sensation of suffocating (2.37), and many medical writers, such as Dioscorides (first century CE) use his name synonymously with a throttling nightmare (3.140.3). Since Ephialtes was also the name of a mythical Giant, the two were sometimes confused, as in the second-century CE lexicographer Aelius Dionysius (s.v. Ephialtes).

CONCLUSION: MODERN EVOLUTION AND RECEPTION

Most of the creatures described here (with the notable exception of Medusa) have never been accommodated in the heroic myths of epic and tragedy, unlike the Sphinx, the Chimaera, and the Minotaur, among others; rather, they dwelt on the peripheries of mythology. As a result, we have no clearly identifiable surviving visual representations of these monsters. Yet their continuous existence in the vernacular culture of antiquity brought them much closer to everyday experience and left a lasting impression on the Greek world in subsequent ages.

Of the four main monsters, Gello enjoyed the most prolific development through the Byzantine era to modern Greece, where she continued to be identified as a *daimon* (usually under the moniker Gulou) but was also assimilated to mortal women known as Geloudes, whose workings for all intents and purposes amounted to witchcraft, particularly in their association with the evil eye (Patera 2015: 215–48). Apart from children, they are also said to attack adults, especially mothers in confinement. As for Empousa, modern Greek culture gives her—or them, the *Onoskeleis*—a masculine identity, and even assimilates them with the more notorious Kalikantzaroi, *daimones* usually depicted as human-animal hybrids, who dwell under the earth and come to the surface at Christmas time to harass people (Patera 2015: 286). Modern Greek *lamiae* seem to have taken over many traits of the other creatures (Patera 2015: 73–89): apart from attacking children, they are also said to possess exceptional beauty, donkey's legs, and a shape-shifting ability. In western Europe, on the other hand, where they never became an enduring element of folklore, their afterlife was limited. Goethe included her kind in the second act of *Faust: Part Two* (1832), along with Empousa. John Keats's 1820 poem 'Lamia' subverts Philostratus' story of Menippus using the familiar romantic trope of cold reason (unfavourably) contrasted with authentic emotions: Apollonius, representing the former, destroys the passionate love binding Lamia—here no longer a malevolent *daimon*—with her chosen one.

SUGGESTED READING

The most comprehensive study of Lamia, Mormo, Empousa, and Gello to date is Patera (2015). Johnston (1998: 161–249) also offers a detailed account. Fontenrose (1959: 94–120) and Rohde ([1893] 1925: 590–3) briefly discuss all four as one group. The most frequently studied of the four is Lamia; Burkert (1992: 82–7) attempts to prove her and Gello's affinity with the Mesopotamian demons Lamaštu and Gallû respectively, a problem also explored by West (1991). Ogden (2013: 86–92) discusses further serpentine associations of Lamia. Resnick and Kitchell (2007) provide a comprehensive study of her fortunes in both antiquity and later periods; Landucci Gattinoni (2008) does the same, but only for antiquity. Leinweber (1994) discusses her appearance in various guises in Apuleius' *Metamorphoses*. Felton (2013) focuses on Apuleius' Cupid and Psyche story, detecting several borrowings from Lamia lore. Empousa has also several works devoted to her, including Arata (2008), but mainly in relation to her 'cameos' in Aristophanes (Borthwick 1968; Brown 1991; Andrisano 2002). The Byzantine Gello features prominently in Björklund (2017), which also discusses Empousa and Lamia.

WORKS CITED

Andrisano, A. M. 2002. 'Empusa, nome parlante (Ar. *Ran.* 288 ss.)?', in *Spoudaiogeloion: Form und Funktion der Verspottung in der aristophanischen Komödie*, ed. A. Ercolani, 273–97. Stuttgart.

Arata, L. 2008. 'Una donna vampiro dell'antica Grecia: Empusa.' *Invigilata Lucernis* 30: 15–26.

Björklund, H. 2017. 'Metamorphosis, Mixanthropy and the Child-Killing Demon in the Hellenistic and Byzantine Period.' *Acta Classica* 60: 22–49.

Borthwick, E. K. 1968. 'Seeing Weasels: The Superstitious Background of the Empusa Scene in the *Frogs*.' *Classical Quarterly* 18/2: 200–6.

Brown, C. G. 1991. 'Empousa, Dionysus and the Mysteries: Aristophanes, *Frogs* 285 ff.' *Classical Quarterly* 41/1: 41–50.

Burkert, W. 1992. *The Orientalizing Revolution: The Near Eastern Influence on Greek Culture in the Early Archaic Age*, trans. M.E. Pinder and W. Burkert. Cambridge, MA.

Davies, M., and P. J. Finglass. 2014. *Stesichorus: The Poems*. Cambridge.

Dindorf, W. 1829. *Aristides*, vol. 3. Leipzig.

Farber, W. 2014. *Lamaštu: An Edition of the Canonical Series of Lamaštu Incantations and Rituals and Related Texts from the Second and First Millennia B.C.* Winona Lake, IN.

Felton, D. 2013. 'Apuleius' Cupid considered as Lamia (*Metamorphoses* 5.17–18).' *Illinois Classical Studies* 38: 229–44.

Fontenrose, J. 1959. *Python: A Study of Delphic Myth and Its Origins*. Berkeley and Los Angeles.

Guinot, J.-N., trans. 1980. *Théodoret de Cyr: Commentaire sur Isaïe*, vol. 2. Paris.

Halm-Tisserant, M. 1989. 'Folklore et superstition en Grèce classique: Lamia torturée?' *Kernos* 2: 67–82.

Johnston, S. I. 1998. *Restless Dead: Encounters between the Living and the Dead in Ancient Greece.* Berkeley and Los Angeles.

Landucci Gattinoni, F. 2008. 'Agatocle, Ofella e il mito di Lamia (Diod. 20.41.2–6).' *Aristonothos* 2: 161–75.

Leinweber, D. W. 1994. 'Witchcraft and Lamiae in *The Golden Ass*.' *Folklore* 105: 77–82.

Miles, G. 2017. 'Hippolytus, the Lamia, and the Eunuch: Celibacy and Narrative Strategy in Philostratus' *Life of Apollonius*.' *Classical Philology* 112/2: 200–18.

Ogden, D. 1999. 'Binding Spells: Curse Tablets and Voodoo Dolls in the Greek and Roman Worlds', in *Witchcraft and Magic in Europe: Ancient Greece and Rome*, ed. V. Flint et al., 3–90. London.

Ogden, D. 2013. *Dragon Myth and Serpent Cults in the Greek and Roman Worlds.* Oxford.

Patera, M. 2015. *Figures grecques de l'épouvante de l'antiquité au présent: Peurs enfantines et adultes.* Leiden.

Resnick, I. M., and K. F. Kitchell, Jr. 2007. ' "The Sweepings of Lamia": Transformations of the Myths of Lilith and Lamia', in *Religion, Gender, and Culture in the Pre-Modern World*, ed. A. Cuffel and B. Britt, 77–104. New York.

Rohde, E. [1893] 1925. *Psyche: The Cult of Souls and Belief in Immortality among the Greeks*, trans. W. B. Hillis. London.

Rosch, E., and C. B. Mervis. 1975. 'Family Resemblances: Studies in the Internal Structure of Categories.' *Cognitive Psychology* 7: 573–605.

Sathas, K. N. 1876. *Bibliotheca Graeca medii aevi*, vol. 5. Venice.

West, D. R. 1991. 'Gello and Lamia: Two Hellenic Daemons of Semitic Origin.' *Ugarit-Forschung* 23: 361–8.

Winkler, J. J. 1982. 'Akko.' *Classical Philology* 77/2: 137–8.

Wittgenstein, L. 1958. *Philosophical Investigations*, 2nd edn., trans. G. E. M. Anscombe. Oxford.

CHAPTER 20

....

GHOSTS

The Restless and Unpleasant Dead

....

JULIA DOROSZEWSKA

INTRODUCTION

....

WE have substantial literary, epigraphical, and material evidence for the ancient beliefs in ghosts and their interactions with the living. Encounters between the living and the dead constitute one of the most prolific motifs in Graeco-Roman literature. The dead of ancient epic, prose, and drama are not only restless, but also tireless in their attempts to contact the living. Their actions are not infrequently peaceful and harmless. Many of them, however, are quite the opposite. Some apparitions haunt and harass the living in various forms and for various reasons. Their apparitions are horrific, their desires dreadful, and their demands terrible. Their actions work to the detriment and destruction of the living. This chapter will predictably focus on such instances of ghostly activity—ones that, due to their harmful effects, may be considered as monstrous—with particular emphasis on spontaneous apparitions rather than necromantic rituals and other such cases when it is the living who are intentionally trying to contact the dead. To be sure, a firm delimitation of the subject matter so defined is difficult since the very sight of the dead is often a phenomenon uncanny enough to cause even unintentional damage. I therefore present several examples that strike me as especially noteworthy.[1]

The typology of ghosts in the Graeco-Roman antiquity is as vague and elusive as ghostly nature itself. Whoever approaches it will be faced with a massive terminological, generic, and ontological confusion. Attempts at categorization and classification, however, have been undertaken by both ancient and modern 'ghostbusters', curious scholars,

[1] This research has been funded by National Science Centre in Poland under the project no. UMO-2018/31/D/HS3/00870.

and apologetic writers. The vocabulary related to the apparitions of antiquity is overall very rich. Although the common Greek terms for 'ghost' were *phasma* ('apparition', 'phantom'), and *daimon* (a divine or spiritual being), these terms overlapped and were often used interchangeably as well as in different contexts, since they could also refer to many other types of supernatural beings, such as gods or ill-intentioned creatures like the *empousae*. This terminological ambiguity results from the fact that the Greeks did not distinguish ghosts as a separate category connoting specifically just spirits of the dead like we do. Other words that were in use, albeit less frequently, were *eidolon* ('spectre'), *skia* ('shade', 'shadow'), *phantasma* ('phantom'), and *psyche* ('soul', 'spirit'). Latin is equally vague when it comes to classifying ghosts. The second-century CE author Apuleius, in *On the God of Socrates* (15), attempted to tidy up the variety of spirits of the deceased and discerned several categories, including the *lemures*, who in general seem be the souls of the dead who renounced their bodies. Among them there are *lares*, benevolent beings responsible for the wellness of the household of their descendants, and the *larvae*, malicious spirits doomed to aimless wandering because of their wicked life on earth. They are powerless against good people, but potentially harmful to bad ones. When unsure, however, whether one is dealing with a *lar* or a *larva*, one uses the phrase *di manes (di* meaning 'gods') as a precaution. *Manes* was the term for collectively venerated chthonic deities that at some point began to be identified with the souls of family ancestors. Apuleius' taxonomy accords with those provided by other ancient authors except for his definition of the *lemures*, which are generally considered maleficent like the *larvae* (e.g. Ov. *Fast.* 5.419–92; Ogden 2002: 149). His distinctions therefore are not entirely clear and correct and bring even more chaos to the discussion. Other Latin terms for ghosts include *umbra* ('shade'), *imago* ('imitation', 'image'), *spectrum* ('apparition'), *simulacrum* ('image', 'phantom'), *effigies* ('effigy'), and *monstrum* ('omen', 'portent'), that were likely used interchangeably (Felton 1999: 24). *Monstrum*, from which the modern English word 'monster' derives, stems from the Latin verb *monere*, 'to warn' and is related to *monstrare*, 'to show'. Hence to be a *monstrum* meant to be a warning sign—usually of divine displeasure—and a portent for the future. In antiquity almost all kinds of anomalous phenomena, such as a shower of stones or the birth of a two-headed calf, could have been considered portents. Thus, ghosts could also qualify as instances of the *monstrum* and technically did not have to be 'monstrous' in the modern sense. Such terminology is therefore not very helpful in disambiguating the peaceful spirits from the angry ones.

Nor is all this terminology useful when it comes to describing the spirits' ontological status. Nowadays the term 'ghost' refers as a rule to 'a disembodied figure believed to be the spirit of a living being who has died', as briefly defined by Jack Sullivan (1986: 168); in the *Oxford English Dictionary*, a 'ghost' is an incorporeal being, an immaterial part or a spirit of a person. Some of the aforementioned terms for ghostly creatures, such as *skia* or *umbra*, seem to hint at this as well. Yet, their bodily status usually is not explicitly defined. In some cases, however, the context reveals that they are also embodied ghosts, or, to put it differently, animated corpses, more accurately termed revenants (from the Latin *revenire* 'to come back'). But the terminological difference between revenants and the disembodied apparitions is frequently blurred, as both are commonly referred to with the use of umbrella terms such as *phasmata or daimones*.

Several literary sources give us insights into the ancient beliefs about what could have rendered some dead restless. In the first century BCE Vergil depicts groups of the dead who were not admitted into Hades proper but instead left lingering on either bank of the river Styx (*Aen.* 6.325–30, 426–43). Among them are the unburied dead and wailing babies deprived of life at its very threshold. There are also the spirits of those unjustly executed, those who committed suicide, and those who died in war. It is unclear at what point this categorization developed, but traces of it can be found as early as Homer's *Odyssey* where the eponymous hero descends to Hades to consult the soul of Tiresias (11.36–40; Ogden 2009: 146). The spirits that gather around Odysseus include brides and unwedded youths as well as toil-worn old men, tender maidens with their fresh grief, and men slain in battle; Elpenor, an unburied companion of Odysseus who demands proper rites, also appears. Later, the Christian author Tertullian, writing in Latin in the second or third century CE, voices a similar conception in his polemical work *On the Soul* where he dissects pagan superstitions about the afterlife (*De anim.* 56–7). Based on some magical treatises otherwise unknown to us, he also mentions categories of the deceased who were believed to be particularly prone to return and harass the living, and who were therefore exploited for magical purposes. His classification is clear-cut and includes those who were deprived of due burial (Latin *insepulti*), as well as those who died before their time (*ahori*, from the Greek *aōroi*) and those who died by violence (*biaeothanatoi*, from the Greek *biaiothanatoi*). Tertullian then explains that all these people whose lives were so unfairly and prematurely terminated would contribute to violence and unfairness, as if in reprisal for the harm done to them.

Because Tertullian's three categories of the restless dead proved highly influential, I will apply them here. To be sure, one must use them with caution, since in many cases neither the backstory of a ghost nor its motivation is explicitly stated. First, however, I must note that in antiquity an encounter with a phantom of the dead might have been considered to some extent unavoidable due to the topographical specificity of Greek and Roman habitats, where tombs and cemeteries were located outside the cities and along the roads. Thus, in Plato's fourth-century BCE dialogue *Phaedo*, the shadows of the dead are said to flit about the monuments and the tombs (81c–d). This belief was apparently still alive several centuries later, as may be inferred from a passage of the *Satyricon*, the renowned first-century CE Latin novel by Petronius. The passage tells the story of a certain man who has just witnessed a terrifying transformation of a soldier into a werewolf and is hastily fleeing to a rural or suburban villa of his fiancée. His way leads along a road surrounded with graves on both sides, so he draws out his sword and 'slays the shadows' (*umbras*) in terror until he reaches his destination. It is unclear whether the *umbras* are simply literal shadows that alarm the terrified man, or spirits of the dead. If the latter, the potential danger remains unspecified; given that they had been properly buried at the cemetery, the reason for their restlessness is unclear, unless they died either prematurely or violently.

THE VIOLENTLY DEAD

Those who died of violence had clear reasons to return and seek vengeance. Many heroes met unusually violent ends either on the battlefield or elsewhere. Dead heroes, however, constituted a distinct category of the deceased. They were believed to retain some of their power after death and were worshipped in the shrines erected on their graves (Garland 1985: 88; Burkert 1985: 203–8). The evidence of a practice that resembles a hero cult and a ritual of propitiation appears as early as Homer: the *Iliad* says that the Athenians worshipped their dead king Erechtheus in the temple of Athena, bringing him yearly sacrifices of bulls and lambs (2.546–51). Later literary sources describe these *biaiothanatoi* as interacting physically with the living, being active in the neighbourhood of their graves, their cultic sites, and their native lands (Felton 1999: 27). A few stories tell of dead heroes who gained posthumous renown as 'monsters' due to their harmful actions; possibly, their ghosts were restless, since they died of violence. In the first case below, such a conclusion seems logical, while the other leaves more room for conjecture.

Two Greek geographers, Strabo (6.1.5) and Pausanias (6.6.7–11), in the first and second centuries CE respectively, tell the story of the 'Hero of Temesa', originally one of Odysseus' companions, who remains anonymous in Pausanias but is named 'Polites' in Strabo's account. Both authors tell how a storm once forced Odysseus and his crew ashore at Temesa, a Greek colony in Southern Italy. There, Polites became drunk and raped a local maiden, and in revenge the people of Temesa stoned him to death. Odysseus then sailed away, but Polites, described by Pausanias as a ghost (*daimon*), began attacking and killing the inhabitants of Temesa. They consulted the Pythia, who ordered them to propitiate the *daimon* by devoting a sanctuary to him and by sacrificing to him every year the prettiest maiden in the town. One day the famous boxer Euthymus came to Temesa during the ceremony of expiation. He saw the girl and immediately fell in love with her. She swore to marry him if he saved her. So the boxer waited for the ghost and won a fight with him, driving him out into the sea, and then married the girl.

The third-century CE Greek sophist Philostratus, in *On Heroes*, narrates the story of Achilles, who is said to have lived after his death on the legendary White Island, with Helen as his wife (56.6–10). Once, a merchant visited the island and Achilles appeared to him, entertained him with drink, and commanded him to sail to Troy and bring back to him a certain maiden. When the merchant in surprise asked him for the reason for such a strange request, Achilles answered evasively that the girl was from the same line as Hector and was of the same blood as Priam. The merchant, supposing that the hero was in love with the maiden, brought her to the island. Achilles thanked him, rewarded him generously and asked him to leave the girl on the beach. The merchant did so and sailed away. When he was departing, the girl's screams reached him as Achilles tore her apart, limb from limb. The hero's peculiar deed is in fact a ritual act of *sparagmos*, the rending or pulling to pieces the body of a wild animal, but in exceptional cases even a human being (e.g. most prominently, Pentheus and Orpheus). *Sparagmos* was usually followed by *omophagia*, the eating of the raw flesh of the one dismembered. The rite is usually associated with the maenads or Bacchants, followers of Dionysus, but in Philostratus' narrative the act is performed outside the Dionysiac context and seems rather to imbue the dead hero with the ferocity and vengefulness for which he was famous when alive. Possibly he sought revenge for his own violent and ignoble death at the hands of Paris at Troy. In any case, this episode emphasizes the unpredictable actions of the deceased and of dead heroes specifically. The White Island itself is a curious case of an afterlife locale outside Hades proper for some dead heroes. Although the living can somehow visit and interact with them, they should not spend the night there except at the risk of their lives—or so says the Roman historian Ammianus Marcellinus, without specifying why (22.8.35). All these ambiguities render the White Island mysterious and liminal.

The first apparition in extant Greek literature to call for vengeance and not for burial is Clytemnestra (Shilo 2018: 533), the treacherous wife of King Agamemnon, whom she killed upon his return from Troy, catching him unawares in his bath. Although her husband would thus have more cause to return posthumously, it is Clytemnestra's ghost that appears onstage in the Prologue to Aeschylus' tragedy *Eumenides* (458 BCE). Her ghost summons the vengeful deities known as the Erinyes to hunt her son Orestes and drive him mad for having slain her to avenge his father. Interestingly, this case presents a ghost haunted by other ghosts: she complains that she is severely harassed by other spirits in the underworld for murdering her husband, and thus wanders in disgrace.

Unlike Agamemnon, who did not choose to haunt the living, another individual who was treacherously slain while bathing did, as told by the second-century CE Greek philosopher Plutarch in his *Life of Cimon* (1.6). Damon, a young citizen of Chaeronea, was killed in the local steam-baths. Since for a long while thereafter certain phantoms (*eidola*) appeared in the place and people reported hearing groans, the building's entrance was walled up. Plutarch, himself a citizen of Chaeronea, testifies to the persistent local belief that the place was still haunted in his own times. In the same work, Plutarch mentions another instance of haunting (*Cim.* 6.5). Pausanias, the famous Spartan commander in the Persian Wars, summoned to his bed a noble maiden named Cleonice; as she silently approached him in the dark, Pausanias mistook her for an assassin and killed her. Her phantom (*eidolon*) gave Pausanias no peace; haunting his dreams, she threatened his impending doom as punishment for his wantonness. This episode of harassment from beyond the grave points to the portentous nature of Cleonice's ghost, who accurately foreshadows Pausanias' own death and thus embodies the literal meaning of the term 'monster', whose primary function, as discussed above, was to 'show' and 'warn'.

Among the figures most prominently featured in ancient ghost stories were the Roman emperors, both as subjects and objects of hauntings. Quite a few were troubled by their dead predecessors. The Roman historian Suetonius (*c.*70–*c.*125 CE) narrates several such stories. In the *Life of Otho*, for example, the eponymous emperor is harassed in a dream by the ghost of his predecessor Galba, whom he had killed (7.2). That night Otho uttered loud groans, alarming his servants; those who ran to his aid found Otho lying on the ground beside his couch. Thereafter he tried by every kind of expiatory rite to propitiate the *manes* of Galba. The Greek historian Dio Cassius (*c.*155–*c.*235 CE) adds the case of the emperor Caracalla, who had visions in which he was being pursued by the armed apparitions (*phantasmata*) of his dead father Septimius Severus and his brother Geta, the latter of whom he had murdered (78.15). They were accompanied by the ghost of Commodus, the last emperor of the Antonine dynasty, who spoke to Caracalla, uttering vague threats that terrified the emperor. Like other victims of violent death, even former emperors could turn into quite unpleasant ghosts whose persistent haunting creates an atmosphere full of danger and fear.

THE UNBURIED DEAD

Those who did not receive proper burial rites were not accepted into the afterlife. As a result, they had serious reasons to return and demand the missing obsequies from the living. Pausanias says that a ghost (*eidolon*) was ravaging the land of Orchomenos, so the inhabitants consulted the Delphic Oracle, asking what to do about this disturbing situation (9.38.5). The Oracle bade them discover the remains of the hero Actaeon and bury them in the earth, and to make a bronze statue of the ghost and fasten it to a rock with iron. We know from Greek myth that Actaeon died by violence, torn to pieces by his own hounds. But this does not seem to be the motive behind the haunting described by Pausanias. The fifth-century CE epic poet Nonnus depicts how the ghost (*psyche*) of Actaeon in the form of a fawn appears in his father's dream and asks—this time peacefully—for burial (*Dion.* 5.412–532).

In his *Life of Caligula* (59), Suetonius tells us that the body of the slain emperor was conveyed secretly to the gardens of the Lamian family in Rome, where it was partly consumed on a hastily erected pyre and buried beneath a light covering of turf; he received proper burial rites only later upon his sisters' return from exile. In the meantime, the gardeners were disturbed by ghosts (*umbras*), while in the house in which Caligula was murdered no night passed without some kind of dread (*aliquo terrore*), until the house itself was destroyed by fire.

Among ancient ghost stories are a handful set in haunted houses, and they share many elements. The earliest traces of this story motif appear in the plot of the third-century BCE comedy *Mostellaria* by the Roman playwright Plautus. Similar stories are told by the Roman writer Pliny the Younger in the first century CE in a letter to a friend (*Ep.* 7.27.5–11) and by the Greek satirist Lucian in the second century CE in his dialogue *The Lover of Lies* (31). The basic plot sounds familiar to the modern ear: there is an abandoned half-ruined house; the occupants are frightened away by a terrifying ghost until the arrival of a great sage, Arignotus, who confronts the apparition in the dark of night; the sage 'solves' the haunting by ridding the premises of the ghost. In Lucian's version, the creature—referred to as a *daimon*—is squalid, long-haired, and 'blacker than the dark'. It attacks the philosopher, transforming itself into various animals such as a dog, a bull, and a lion. The sage utters a magical spell that repels the creature, and it disappears into the ground in the corner of a dark room. In the morning this spot is excavated and a skeleton unearthed. In Pliny's version, the philosopher, here named Athenodorus, focuses on his writing, working diligently as he awaits the ghost, which in this story is the apparition of an emaciated old man with chains on his wrists and ankles. When it appears, rattling its chains over the philosopher's head and beckoning to him, the sage initially ignores it, thinking that the apparition must be a product of his imagination. Eventually, convinced of the creature's reality, the philosopher stops writing, takes his lamp, and follows the ghost, who leads him to the courtyard and suddenly disappears. On the next day the spot is dug up, revealing bare bones entwined with chains. In both versions, when the remains receive a proper burial, the house ceases to be haunted. This general plot also occurs in several Christian authors, including Constantius of Lyon in the fifth century CE in his *Life of St Germanus* (2.10) and Gregory the Great in the sixth century in his *Dialogues* (3.4.1–3). Both authors employ similar motifs, but with the ghost replaced by a devil and the philosopher by a saint.

The unburied dead discussed here are unable to clearly communicate their need of burial to the living for various reasons. For one thing, they seem to lack the power of speech; for another, their appearance terrifies the living. Lucian's *daimon* is overtly hostile; Pliny explicitly calls the apparition a *monstrum*, especially apt given that in both stories the creatures' primary function is to literally 'show' where their remains lie. Thus, they are monstrous in being both terrifying and significative.

THE UNTIMELY DEAD

Tertullian reports that those who died before their time were believed to wander about until they completed the remaining period for which they would have lived (*De anim.* 56). Perhaps a similar thought underlies the story of Philinnion, another well-known ghost story from antiquity that was later subject to many paraphrases and reworkings. To be more precise, it does not concern a ghost so much as a revenant. The story appears in the *Mirabilia* (1), a collection of marvellous tales compiled by the second-century CE Greek writer Phlegon of Tralles. Its beginning has been lost but may nevertheless be supplied from the *Commentary to Plato's Republic* by the fifth-century Neoplatonic philosopher Proclus (2.116 Kroll): in the Greek city of Amphipolis a couple marry their daughter Philinnion to a certain Craterus, but the girl dies shortly after the wedding and is buried in the family tomb. Phlegon's story picks up six months later when a young man named Machates visits the house and lodges in the guest room. Unaware that his hosts' daughter is dead, he is not alarmed when she visits him secretly in the night. She confesses that she came to him without her parents' knowing because she was driven by desire. The girl leaves unnoticed before daybreak. On the second night she visits him again and the two exchange love-tokens: she gives him a golden ring and in return he gives her an iron one and a gilded wine-cup. This time, however, her presence is discovered by her former nurse, who reports the alarming event to her parents. So, on the third night the parents interrupt her tryst with Machates, whereupon Philinnion accuses them of meddling in her affairs, which (she says) were the working of a divine will; after this remonstration, she drops dead again. An expedition by the townspeople to Philinnion's tomb finds it empty except for the iron ring and the golden cup lying on her bier. As a result, the despondent Machates kills himself and the people burn the girl's corpse to prevent another resurrection. Philinnion's normal physical appearance may be seen as monstrously deceptive, concealing the macabre truth of her undead state; in this regard, she resembles seductive female *daimones* such as *empousae* or *lamiae* (see Kucharski in this volume). Her story, however, also seems to present a failed attempt to complete as a revenant what she was denied in life—marriage and children.

Phlegon notes another curious ghostly case (*Mir.* 2), one that also seems to belong to the category of the untimely dead. A certain Polycritus from Aetolia was elected to a prominent office. He also took a wife, but after having spent three nights with his bride, died suddenly on the fourth day of unspecified causes. His wife, however, having become pregnant, gave birth to a hermaphrodite child. An assembly was called to determine whether the baby was an evil omen, and a heated discussion broke out about the correct interpretation. Suddenly, the ghost (*phasma*) of the deceased Polycritus appeared at the assembly, dressed in black. Speaking softly, he tried to persuade the people to give him the child and warned them against resorting to any violence. Since the people were hesitant to fulfil his demands, he seized the child and tore it limb from limb. The terrified people began throwing stones to drive Polycritus away, but the ghost remained unharmed. He devoured the child's entire body except for the head before suddenly disappearing. Then the child's head began to prophesize, foretelling a swift destruction for the Aetolians—which occurred the next year, when they went to war with their neighbours. Possibly this ghost is a revenant, given its physical attack on the infant and the fact that Phlegon put this story between that of Philinnion and another also concerning animated corpses (see Doroszewska 2016: 62–3). The Polycritus narrative, in its gory brutality, bears strong similarities to that of Achilles on the White Island. Both describe *sparagmos* at the hand of a ghost. Both, furthermore, present a striking contrast between the ostensibly kind behaviour of the ghost and the vicious dismemberment that follows. This resemblance is no coincidence, since, as William Hansen (1996: 98–9) argues, both narratives are probably reworkings of the same traditional oral story.

CONCLUSION: OTHER HAUNTINGS

The Greeks and Romans recognized other patterns of harmful ghostly activity, such as daimonic possession and poltergeists. In his biography of the Neopythagorean philosopher Apollonius of Tyana (*VA* 4.38), Philostratus narrates how the sage performed exorcisms on two individuals possessed by spirits of dead people. These stories are strikingly similar to those about exorcisms effectuated by Jesus, a probable contemporary of Apollonius. In one case a ghost enters a handsome youth and deprives him of reason, preventing him from going to school and driving him out into the desert. The boy does not even retain his own voice but speaks in a deep, manly tone. The possessing spirit claims to be that of a man who long ago fell in battle. He says that at the time of his death he was passionately attached to his wife, but that only three days after his death his wife married another man—so he had come to detest the love of women and had transferred himself wholly into this boy. In the second case (*VA* 4.20), the ghost's motivation is not specified but he likewise takes possession of a young man whom he makes laugh at things that no one else finds funny, weep for no good reason, and talk and sing to himself.

An example of what today would be considered poltergeist activity can be found in Suetonius' *Life of Augustus*, which records a strange occurrence in the former home of Augustus—the emperor's place of birth, but not of his death! No one would dare to enter one specific room of the house except out of necessity and after purification, since those who ventured to approach it without ceremony immediately fled from it in terror and panic. Once, a new owner who went to sleep in that room was suddenly thrown from the bed by a mysterious force and was found half dead before the door (*Aug.* 6).

Graeco-Roman literature abounds in instances of ghostly phenomena. Some appear to certain people while others turn up in certain places, either by themselves or artificially summoned via magic. Not every instance of a ghost, however, qualifies as 'monstrous', though then, as now, there can be considerable overlap between the concepts, as evidenced by the specific vocabulary in some of the stories and by the characters' emotional reactions to the apparitions. The main criteria applied here for considering the appearance of a ghost as a monstrosity are its spontaneity—as opposed to necromantic summoning—and, most importantly, its harmful effect on the living.

Suggested Reading

The most direct insight into ancient ghost-lore is offered by Ogden's (2002) sourcebook, with English translations and commentary. Collison-Morley (1912), aimed at a general audience, briefly presents ancient beliefs in the afterlife. The most comprehensive scholarly works to date on the restless dead in the ancient tradition are those by Stramaglia (1999), Felton (1999), and Johnston (1999). Stramaglia (1999) takes a broad view and provides a literary analysis of the Greek and Roman ghost stories, while Felton's (1999) interdisciplinary study combines literary and folkloric perspectives. Johnston (1999) focuses on changing cultural concepts about the dead and beliefs in their interaction with the living in the Archaic and Classical periods in ancient Greece. Endsjø (2009) examines Greek ideas about bodily resurrection in the light of the Gospel traditions. Doroszewska (2017) discusses Greek and Roman narratives featuring ghosts, vampires, and werewolves set specifically in suburban areas. Hansen (1996) provides an English translation and commentary on Phlegon's *Mirabilia*.

Works Cited

Burkert, W. 1985. *Greek Religion*. Cambridge, MA.
Collison-Morley, L. 1912. *Greek and Roman Ghost Stories*. Oxford.

Doroszewska, J. 2016. *The Monstrous World: Corporeal Discourses in Phlegon of Tralles' Mirabilia.* Frankfurt am Main.

Doroszewska, J. 2017. 'The Liminal Space: Suburbs as a Demonic Domain in Classical Literature.' *Preternature* 6/1: 1–30.

Endsjø, D. O. 2009. *Greek Resurrection Beliefs and the Success of Christianity.* New York.

Felton, D. 1999. *Haunted Greece and Rome: Ghost Stories from Classical Antiquity.* Austin.

Garland, R. 1985. *The Greek Way of Death.* Ithaca, NY.

Hansen, W. 1996. *Phlegon of Tralles' Book of Marvels.* Exeter.

Johnston, S. 1999. *Restless Dead: Encounters between the Living and Dead in Ancient Greece.* Berkeley and Los Angeles.

Kroll, W., ed. 1901. *Procli Diadochi in Platonis Rem publicam commentarii*, vol. 2. Leipzig.

Ogden, D. 2009. *Magic, Witchcraft, and Ghosts in the Greek and Roman Worlds*, 2nd edn. Oxford.

Shilo, A. 2018. 'The Ghost of Clytemnestra in the *Eumenides*: Ethical Claims beyond Human Limits.' *American Journal of Philology* 139/4: 533–76.

Stramaglia, A. 1999. '*Res inauditae, incredulae*': *Storie di fantasmi nel mondo greco-latino.* Bari.

Sullivan, J., ed. 1986. *The Penguin Encyclopedia of Horror and the Supernatural.* New York.

....

CHAPTER 21

THE MONSTROUS ANIMALS AND ANIMAL MONSTERS OF ANCIENT GREECE

....

KENNETH F. KITCHELL, JR.

INTRODUCTION

....

THE existence of theriomorphic monsters (those composed of animal parts) in Greek art and imagination is well documented, yet most scholarly investigation centres around issues such as monsters as boundary transgressors, as born out of primordial fears, or as oddities to be explained philosophically. This chapter will focus on the real animals used to construct such monsters and will point out ways in which these monsters reflect the attitudes of the Greeks to the animals around them. I will begin by dividing the monsters, real or imagined, into two large groups. Monstrous animals, which I call 'Extremes', are those which generally retain the characteristics of their animal prototype but possess them to an unnatural degree. I use the term 'Animal Monsters' to refer to plausible or implausible hybrids, monsters that cross what we today would call family, genus, and species. Then, after a brief look at sea monsters, I investigate the invention and entertainment often found in the theriomorphic creations discussed here. Although my focus is on ancient Greece, some Roman authors, especially Pliny the Elder, contain important information from now-lost Greek works and consequently provide some good source material for this discussion.

SCOPE OF THE STUDY

....

Theriomorphic monsters exist in civilizations as old as those of Mesopotamia and Egypt, and many Greek versions have their origins there. Such monsters are commonly found on Minoan and Mycenaean seal stones, and examples include griffins, marine monsters, human-animal hybrids like sphinxes and the ever-present insectoid creature generally called a 'genius' (Marinatos 1926; Poursat 1976; Younger 1988; Zouzoula 2007). This study, however, will focus on art and literature of the Greek geometric through the Classical periods, with a few examples drawn from the Roman period for comparison. It also accepts the many meanings of words like *teras*, *pelōr*, and *monstrum*, all of which can variously mean monster, portent, sign, and/or marvel. I will generally avoid discussion of animal-human hybrids such as the Sphinx or centaurs since other chapters discuss them in detail (see both López-Ruiz and Aston in this volume). Also, some intriguing material will regrettably remain unstudied here, such as a series of remarkable coins from the Greek town of Himera on the north coast of Sicily depicting a creature with the wings of a bird (probably a cock), forelegs of a dog or lion, and the head of a bearded male with an enormous nose.

Moignard (1998: 213) sums up many of the approaches to studying monsters: 'It is, of course, not a new idea that monsters are a way of defining what is not normal, human and manageable in the terms of the society which creates them and that hybrids are used to comment on what is marginal to humanity.' This chapter attempts a new approach by focusing on the animal core of theriomorphic monsters, and by considering the basic constructs the ancient Greeks held of animals in general and, specifically, of the various animal parts that they used to construct their hybrid theriomorphic monsters—hereafter, 'Animal Monsters'. We will also touch on the boundaries that are broken when such monsters are constructed, how such monsters enhance heroes' reputations (Stern 1978), and, when used as shield emblems, how they proclaim the fierceness of mortal warriors (Chase 1902: 84–5). I hope here to demonstrate as well that these monsters also served as outlets for the playful imagination of the ancient Greeks.

NOMENCLATURE AND GEOGRAPHY

Some Animal Monsters merit their own names: Typhon, Cerberus, Python. Other, 'lesser', monsters take their names from their component parts, such as the *hippalektryōn*, or 'horse-rooster' (Camporeale 1967) or Aelian's *onokentaura*, 'ass-centaur' (*NA* 17.9). This practice parallels one by which the Greeks named animals not native to Greece: a hippopotamus is a 'river-horse' (*hippopotamos*), a giraffe is a 'camel-leopard' (*kameloleopardos*), an ostrich is a 'sparrow-camel' (*strouthokamēlos*). Today, when scientists create names for previously unknown animals, we follow the same principles, as with the *Ornithorhynchus anatinus*, the 'duck-like bird-snout', better known as the platypus ('broad-foot').

The ancient Greek imagination confined most non-indigenous animals to the hot areas at the edges of the known world (e.g. Diod. Sic. 2.51.2–4; van Duzer 2016: 391–5) or the depths of the sea. The fact that India and Africa are often given as the homes of these same animals is not as important as the fact that distance equals strangeness, whether for real animals or Animal Monsters, as we shall see.

Building Blocks and Boundaries

Except for the Extremes, most animal-based monsters are hybrids, consisting of parts taken from various species to produce a new creature with varying degrees of plausibility. The part represents the whole animal and, as in the animal similes of Homer, each animal stands for one or more of its salient traits. The lion and boar represent ferocity and courage, the bird and horse swiftness, the serpent venom and sudden attack. The entire animal kingdom is represented in animal-based monsters, with reptiles (mostly serpents), mammals (alpha predators, horses, pigs, etc.), and birds (heads, talons, and wings) contributing the most to the hybrids. Arthropods are rare but are represented by the Cretan bees that nourished the infant Zeus on Crete and the scorpion that formed the manticore's stinger. Hybrid marine monsters will be dealt with below. Some of these animal parts enable the monsters to break boundaries of normal animal habitat: winged horses and boars are no longer purely terrestrial, and hippocamps—sea creatures with the forepart of a horse—do not drown.

Taxonomies

Given that monsters are generally thought of as crossing boundaries, it is well to begin with an overview of how the ancient Greeks classified animals. As might be expected, this took many forms, depending on the priorities of the classifier. Animals might be dangerous or not; wild or domesticated; and they might inhabit different domains: air, land, or sea. Aristotle, the first to attempt a systematic classification of animals (mostly in his *Historia animalium*), divided animals into blooded and bloodless. Blooded animals include viviparous and oviparous quadrupeds (the latter including, e.g. snakes and lizards), fish, whales, and birds. Bloodless creatures include soft-shelled (such as crabs, lobsters, shrimps), hard-shelled (including gastropods and bivalves), soft-bodied (cephalopods like the octopus or squid), and animals with segmented bodies (arthropods such as insects, spiders, and scorpions). Aristotle's system is certainly not perfect, but it probably largely aligns with how the average ancient Greek viewed the animal world and so lies at the heart of this discussion.

Monstrous Animals: The Extremes

Scholars have produced dozens, if not hundreds, of definitions and groupings of monsters, and theriomorphic monsters fall into several established categories such as the Other, ontological boundary-breakers, and manifestations of societal anxiety

(Felton 2016: 103–6). For my purposes, however, I choose to divide them into two large groups based on how they fit into the average Greek's view of the natural world, doing so in the full realization that trying to categorize creatures best known for their breaking of boundaries is perilous. I term the first group 'monstrous animals', those who maintain the physical traits of a real animal but exhibit these traits in ways that belie human expectations. These are the 'Extremes', monsters that are generally not hybrids but represent exaggerated traits of regular animals. This exaggeration can take the form of enormous size, magnified powers, or dangerous variants of normal characteristics. Normal birds moult, but the Stymphalian Birds shoot their metallic feathers; some serpents are venomous, but those of Libya can melt a person; regular bees sting, but those guarding the infant Zeus were particularly venomous (Kitchell 1994: 11). Finally, Extremes come in differing shades of plausibility. Some are plausible in that a giant turtle can be imagined within our view of the natural world, whereas Gamera, the flying, fire-breathing turtle of Japanese *kaiju* movies, strains the imagination.

We begin with size. As Adrienne Mayor (2011) has posited, the Greeks might have mistaken fossils of giant, extinct animals as bones of enormous monsters. Size mattered when it came to monstrousness; it is no surprise, therefore, that gigantic animals were said to inhabit far-off lands such as India or Africa. Size also often indicates danger. A rash of horror films in the 1950s and 1960s, capitalizing on post-Hiroshima fears, featured animals enhanced by atomic radiation that were uniformly antagonistic towards humans. Examples include the original *Godzilla* (1954), the giant ants of *Them!* (1954), and *Attack of the Crab Monsters* (1957). For the Greeks, however, Extremes were not inherently dangerous. The cocks, crabs, goats, and sheep in India are enormous and, apparently, more productive than their normal sized cousins (Felton 2016: 123–6). Arabia sports huge turtles, but the *Chelōnophagoi* ('Turtle-Eaters') hunt them and use their shells as houses or boats (Strabo 16.4.14; Plin. *NH* 6.110). This thread finds its reductio ad absurdum in Lucian's *True Stories*, with its giant spiders and ants (even farther away, as they inhabit the Moon and Sun, not the Earth).

Just as the eponymous giant ape in *King Kong* terrorized the nearby village on Skull Island (1934), so did Greek oversized monstrous animals plague the outskirts of many Greek towns; driving out giant, marauding animals is a commonplace labour for Greek heroes, as with Heracles' killing of the Nemean Lion or Apollo's victory over the Python at Delphi. Cenchreus (the father of Ajax) became king of Salamis by killing a giant serpent there (Neils 2013: 605–6). The destructive power of swine is acknowledged with the Crommyonian Sow and the Calydonian and Erymanthian boars, among others, and we should not forget the giant crab, Carcinus, the Hydra's ally against Heracles.

Different sorts of 'extremity' are offered by the fifteen serpents in Lucan's description of the Libyan desert (9.702–6; Batinski 1991). Although this is a Roman source, the Libyan serpents were well known to the Greeks, especially from second-century BCE works like Nicander of Colophon's *Thēriaca* ('Concerning Venomous Beasts'), or Philoumenos of Alexandria's *On Poisons and Antidotes*. Lucan's descriptions of these serpents' bites are merely extreme versions of real-life, first-hand observation of venomous snakebites. The *dipsas* ('the thirst inducer') and the *prēstēr* ('burning') were variously deadly, the former inducing parching thirst and the latter causing the victim to swell until he bursts, both being factual symptoms of snakebites. The *seps* ('rotter') 'melted' its victims (exaggerated necrosis) and the *haemorrhois* ('blood-flower') caused a total loss of blood (exaggerated vasculotoxic venom symptoms). The *iaculus* ('spear'; Latin version of Greek *akontias*, 'javelin-snake') launches itself like an arrow towards its victim, an extreme reflection of the speed of a serpent's strike.

Another type of Extreme based on commonly observed phenomena relates to monstrous births and deformities among animals. Connell (2018: 210) notes three basic types: two animals grown together, including conjoined twins; those with two or more of a given part (e.g. polydactylism); and those with a lack of, or the stunting of, a part (e.g. congenital limb defect). Animal parts joined together during embryonic formation, such as in a four-legged chicken or a two-headed calf, were the phenomenological basis against which we should view the creation of Extremes like the Hecatoncheires ('Hundred-handers') that appear in the earliest Greek myths (e.g. Hes. *Theog.* 147 ff.) or the hundred-headed serpent Ladon (Ar. *Ran.* 475). The monstrous Cerberus, the swamp-dwelling Hydra, and dog-waisted Scylla also all have multiple heads, although the exact number varies depending on the author and time period (see Stern 1978).

Other, less common defects that merit the term 'Extreme' include human newborns so deformed that they seemed to have both human and animal parts (Hansen 1996: 46–7; Felton 2016: 128; Llada-Richards 1998: 42–9). It is an easy transition from seeing deformed animal births to extreme versions of such monsters. Yet we must admit that certain Extremes have a less obvious connection with natural phenomena and approach exhibiting perversions of natural traits, such as Sciron's man-eating turtle and Diomedes' mares, who have a similarly monstrous diet. The phoenix offers us the most improbable trait of all: eternal life (Hdt. 2.73).

ANIMAL MONSTERS (1): PLAUSIBLE

By 'Animal Monster' I mean to indicate animal hybrids that challenge the expected rules of nature and may be subdivided into plausible and implausible types. Plausible Animal Monsters would include hybrids that, in the words of von Blanckenhagen (1987: 87), seem to be 'something visually unified and acceptable, as if nature may indeed create such monsters'. Implausible Animal Monsters, in contrast, so violate the natural order as to evoke a negative, visceral response. Why? Philosophers and natural scientists such as Empedocles and Aristotle believed that nature provides animals with what they need to be successful in their existence (Arist. *Part. an.* 645a25–9, 687a5 ff.). Birds no more need teeth than a tiger needs wings, and while fancies such as a goat-stag can be *imagined*, they are contrary to nature and their actual existence would represent an untenable hybrid (Fritsche 2005). According to Aristotle, a monster is a being that does not achieve the proper form provided for it by its 'final cause'. For example, a two-headed calf should, by its final cause, have but one head, and, even proceeding logically, this line of thinking leads him to posit that, to some degree, children who do not resemble their parents are monsters, as are women—whose perfect form should have been male (cf. Lenfant 1999: 198–200).

Nevertheless, just like many rural Greeks, Aristotle knew instances of hybrids that transgressed boundaries but were in no way threating or even unusual. Mules should not have been possible in Aristotle's scheme, but he had to acknowledge this common hybridization (Groisard 2018: 159–66), since mules played a large role in Greece from earliest times and were highly valued (Gregory 2007). Likewise, in accordance with popular lore, Aristotle believed correctly that cross-breeding occurred among dogs, foxes, wolves, and jackals (Hull 1964: 41–3): all are members of the genus *Canis* and some of this behaviour would have been seen in the wild. This sort of hybrid (i.e. cross-bred species) represents a plausible Animal Monster, whereas Aristotle's citation of the unidentified 'Indian Dog' as a canine cross-breed between a tiger and a female dog provides a fine example of an implausible Animal Monster (Platt 1909; but cf. Arist. *Gen. an.* 476a35). Partridges can breed with chickens, and various raptors interbreed with each other, as Aristotle points out, but he knows of no sea creatures that do so (*Gen. an.* 746a29–747a23; Groisard 2018). Xenophon reports that the small hunting dog called the *alōpekis* (or *kynalōpēx*) was the offspring of a fox and a dog (*Cyn.* 3.1). All these hybrids (save the mule) can, in fact, reproduce. Common people such as farmers and breeders knew these things well, and the step from these real-life hybrids to Animal Monsters was a short one.

We find another type of plausible Animal Monster in Aristotle's 'dualizer' class (*epamphoterizōn*), his term for a creature that seems to participate simultaneously in two kinds of animals. For the ancient Greeks this included such animals as cetaceans and bats: the former breathe air and produce milk but share many traits with fish, while the latter, also milk producers, have the wings of a bird. These animals violate natural boundaries, but, as Connell (2018: 181) explains, Aristotle sees such boundary crossing as essential to their nature. Moreover, they are not inherently any more dangerous than the animals whose traits they exhibit.

ANIMAL MONSTERS (2): IMPLAUSIBLE

While plausible Animal Monsters are those based on observable natural phenomena, implausible Animal Monsters so violate the observations and expectations that form the background for the ancient Greek world view that they are clearly unreal and possibly to be feared. They are, if you will, eerier than the benign, plausible Animal Monsters, and stretch our credulity too far. Examples include the Chimaera, with its unthinkable triple mix of a lion's head and body, a fire-breathing goat's head sprouting from its back, and a serpent as a tail, in total yielding a monster both unnatural and dangerous (see Smith in this volume). Or consider the Hydra, or Scylla's twelve feet and six necks and heads, each bearing three rows of teeth like a manticore (see both Deacy and Hopman in this volume). While the three-headed Cerberus might be intimidating, the fifty-headed version is terrifying (Hes. *Theog.* 312; see Joyce in this volume). Many of the more frightening and violent monsters in this class involve creatures that cross the boundary between human and animal. All the parts of the notorious werewolf on a plate in the Museo Nazionale Etrusco (no. 84444) are clearly animal, but its one human trait, bipedalism, renders it unusually uncanny and frightening. An important marker in the human/animal divide is the power of speech, and most of these human-animal hybrids possess it, whereas speech is largely lacking in any animal-animal hybrid. We can thus say in summation that most Animal Monsters represent exaggerations of observable animal phenomena and that they avoid crossing the line into human-animal hybrids. We move now to sea monsters as an example of this tendency.

Sea Monsters

It is well accepted, and certainly was well known to Greek fishermen, that the sea engendered many strange creatures (Hom. *Od.* 421–2; Plin. *NH* 9.2). Since the chapter by Ingemark and Asplund Ingemark in this volume covers many sea monsters from antiquity, I will focus here only on the *kētos* as a particularly useful example of exaggerated sea animal. The term can refer to any large fish, such as the tunny, but often means 'sea monster', ranging from the monster that threatened Andromeda to spouting and breaching whales which are, presumably, monstrous in their outrageous size. It is thus incorrect to refer to the *kētos* as a particular monster (i.e. *Kētos*). Its various shapes from the Bronze Age forward have been traced in detail by Keller (1909: 1. 409–14), Boardman (1987), and Papadopoulos and Ruscilo (2002: 206–22), but *kētē* (the Greek plural) generally possess a head that resembles that of a seahorse followed by a long, serpentine body ending in a fish's tail. They may or may not also possess a crest, fangs, legs, flippers, or wings. Most relevant here is that while the shape alone would qualify a *kētos* as a monster, pictorial evidence offers a more nuanced view. *Kētē* such as the one threatening Andromeda (Boardman 1987: pl. 24.10–11, 14) or the one Heracles holds by the tongue (pl. 25.15) certainly qualify as monsters in the usual sense of the word, being huge like an Extreme and, for a sea creature, plausible in shape. Yet the most frequent type of depiction shows the *kētos* as a mount for various sea deities (Boardman 1987: 74–6, with plates). We thus see that *kētē* are a group of Animal Monsters that can be large or small, dangerous or tamed. Other such mounts existed, such as the *hippocampos*, a hybrid sea creature with the forepart of a horse attached to a *kētos*-like body and tail. In second-century CE Roman mosaics in Ostia Antica, Rome's port city, we see a veritable zoo of such monsters with the foreparts of a lion (*leocampus*), bull (*taurocampus*), and goat (*aegicampus*), to name only a few (Dunbabin 1999: 61–4).

Although we could easily spend more time discussing the various and often playful descriptions of these maritime Animal Monsters, it is important to stop and analyse them. Most obvious is the fact that they are used as mounts or are yoked to chariots. Just as the mule hybrid can be used by humans for transport, so can these marine hybrids bear divine riders. Thus, while some sea creatures are threatening, many *kētē* are under the control of sea divinities (von Blanckhagen 1987: 90–1). These monsters also cross one of the most basic boundaries separating animals: the air/sea boundary. Lions, bulls, and goats surely could not survive under the sea, but in the semi-magical world of Animal Monsters, they thrive. Conversely very few terrestrial Animal Monsters bear parts from marine animals. What lies behind such whimsical creatures?

MONSTERS FOR AMUSEMENT

Gartziou-Tatti and Zographou (2017: 9–11) have provided examples of the good that can be found in some monsters and have shown that the mere mixing of animal parts need not produce only frightening and dangerous creatures. Wings appear both on Harpies and Pegasus—the former a frightening threat, the latter a tamed beneficial mount. Beyond this it seems clear that some Animal Monsters were created simply to appeal to the human imagination. The white, curly-horned panther ridden by Dionysus on a hydria from Pella resembles hybrid animals found on today's carousels (Neils 2013: 601). A red-figure Greek chous (small pitcher) dating between 425 and 375 BCE shows a satyr before a much taller creature composed of a mule's head, a bird's body, and ridiculously large avian feet (BAPD 9554). The ubiquitous erect, winged phallus can be considered a monstrous being, and when used as a mount by a woman the initial response is laughter (BAPD 200468); this type of object was regularly used as a fertility charm. If wings are out of place in this context, then other animal parts are unmistakably irreverent. A Roman amulet in the Naples Museum is an excellent example: this erect phallus bears wings, hoofed legs, a tail that ends in the head of a penis, and its *own* erect phallus (Fig. 21.1).

Hughes (2010: 103–4) details the changing nature of monstrous hybrid's appearances over time, and Moignard (1998) identifies the Archaic period (*c.*776–480 BCE) as especially rich with experimental depictions of monsters. Take, for example, a seventh-century ceramic vase from Crete in the shape of a bull-headed bird carrying a female figure (Fig. 21.2; Catling 1978–1979). The top of the woman's head is a vertical spout that was used for filling, while the horizontal spout of the bull-bird's mouth was used for pouring. This peculiar composite creature may be intended to illustrate the story of Zeus abducting Europa: the bull would represent the disguised Zeus, while the wings indicate the speed with which he bore her from Phoenicia to Crete. This kind of artistic experimentation ultimately led to items such as a Roman bird-shaped rattle sporting a set of antlers (Harlow 2013: 325), and it lives on today in the form of various cryptids, such as the 'jackalope', a jackrabbit sporting a set of horns and sold in Texan airports for the credulous back home (see also Murace in this volume).

FIGURE 21.1 Roman bronze amulet in the form of a quadruped phallus; first century CE. Archaeological Museum of Naples, inv. 27839.

Source: © Marie-Lan Nguyen / Wikimedia Commons. CC BY 2.5.

CONCLUSION: MONSTERS OF MISUNDERSTANDING

Other animal-based monsters arose out of misobservation and exaggeration—for example, various creatures described by Herodotus, Ctesias, Megasthenes, Strabo, Pliny, and others as living in Africa or India, regions Lenfant (1999: 206) claims were 'only known from hearsay'. These authors are often dismissed as unreliable and gullible when they present such descriptions, yet a real animal or the misobservation of one often lies

FIGURE 21.2 Vase in the form of a monster from the North Cemetery of Knossos, seventh century BCE, inv. no. AMH Π24258.

Courtesy of Archaeological Museum of Heraklion-Hellenic Ministry of Cultural and Sports / Hellenic Organization of Cultural Resources Department.

behind such creatures, and subsequent exaggeration and flawed oral transmission have turned many a real animal into a monster.

For example, whereas Pliny's *leucrocotta* is an impossible mix of stag, ass, lion, and badger (*NH* 8.30.72), the *corocotta* is rooted in reality, described as a hybrid resulting from the mating of a dog with a wolf or lioness. It possessed the power to imitate voices and to cry like a human to lure people to their deaths. Some ancient authors claim the *corocotta* imitates the sound of vomiting to attract dogs, whom it then eats. All this is most likely a misunderstanding of the hyena, whose actual vocalizations include two that resemble crying and vomiting (Kitchell 2020: 460–2). The *katōbleps* ('down-looker'), a sort of bull-monster, was said to have a head too heavy to lift, and thus always hanging downwards. The creature's thick mane covered its bloodshot eyes, but it could lift the mane and kill with its glance. This description fits the wildebeest or gnu very well: a wildebeest's large, bearded head hangs low and is commonly down as it grazes. A particular fly (*Kirkioestrus minutus*) lays eggs in its eyes, which causes them to become irritated and red. Unfortunately for our explanation, the wildebeest's habitat is southern Africa, whereas ancient sources place the *katōbleps* in the north. But, quite possibly, misobservation, distance, and exaggeration conspired to turn this normal animal into a monstrosity (Kitchell 2014: 100–1). The *kranokolaptēs* ('head-striker') was a blood-sucking moth, a seeming impossibility except for the fact that certain moths, such as the vampire moth (*Calyptra thalictra*), do just this (Kitchell 2014: 102). Herodotus was the first to mention the spotted, fierce, fox-sized, gold-digging ants of India (Hdt. 3.102–5), which have been plausibly identified as marmots (Kitchell 2014: 97–8).

Such identifications are gratifying, but they also speak to the attitudes of the ancient Greeks to foreign regions, to nature, and, by extension, to all animal-based monsters. As Aristotle put it, 'In all things of nature, there is something wondrous' (*thaumaton, Part. an.* 645a.19–20). So too for its monsters.

SUGGESTED READING

Felton (2016) offers a thorough overview of Greek and Roman monsters and Syropoulos' small book (2018) is useful for its summaries and illustrations. But most information concerning animal-based monsters is found in ancient sources. Aristotle's *History of Animals, Generation of Animals,* and *Parts of Animals,* along with Pliny's vast *Natural History* (especially Book 8) and Aelian's *On the Nature of Animals,* besides being entertaining, are replete with information from now lost works. All are available in Loeb editions, with English translations, from Harvard University Press. Stoneman (2019) collects much of the information concerning India. The philosophical basis for animal monsters is set forth for non-philosophers by Yartz (1997) and by Foresman and Tobienne (2013) in reference to the television show *Supernatural* (2005–2020).

WORKS CITED

Batinski, E. 1991. 'Cato and the Battle with the Serpents'. *Syllecta Classica* 3: 71–80.

Boardman, J. 1987. ' "Very Like a Whale"—Classical Sea Monsters', in *Monsters and Demons in the Ancient and Medieval Worlds,* ed. A. E. Farkas, P. O. Harper, and E. B. Harrison, 73–87. Mainz.

Camporeale, G. 1967. 'Hippalektryon'. *Archeologia Classica* 19: 248–68.

Catling, H. W. 1978–1979. 'Knossos, 1978'. *Archaeological Reports* 25: 3–58.

Chase, H. C. 1902. 'The Shield Devices of the Greeks'. *Harvard Studies in Classical Philology* 13: 61–127.

Connell, S. M. 2018. 'Aristotle's Explanations of Monstrous Births and Deformities in *Generation of Animals* 4.4', in *Aristotle's* Generation of Animals: *A Critical Guide,* ed. A. Falcon and D. Lefebvre, 207–23. Cambridge.

Dunbabin, K. 1999. *Mosaics of the Greek and Roman World.* Cambridge.

Felton, D. 2016. 'Rejecting and Embracing the Monstrous in Ancient Greece and Rome', in *The Ashgate Research Companion to Monsters and the Monstrous,* ed. A. S. Mittman and P. J. Dendle, 103–31. Abingdon.

Foresman, G. A., and F. Tobienne, Jr. 2013. 'Aristotle's Metaphysics of Monsters and Why We Love *Supernatural*', in *Supernatural and Philosophy: Metaphysics and Monsters . . . for Idjits,* ed. G. A. Foresman, 16–25. Chichester.

Fritsche, J. 2005. 'The Riddle of the Sphinx: Aristotle, Penelope, and Empedocles', in *Monsters and Philosophy: Texts in Philosophy 3*, ed. C. T. Wolfe, 10–19. London.

Gartziou-Tatti, A., and A. Zographou. 2017. 'Mapping the Monstrous in Ancient Greece', in *Hybrid and Extraordinary Beings*, ed. A. Gartziou-Tatti, P. Soukakos, and M. Paschopoulos, 3–12. Athens.

Gregory, J. 2007. 'Donkeys and the Equine Hierarchy in Archaic Greek Literature.' *Classical Journal* 102: 193–212.

Groisard, J. 2018. 'Hybridity and Sterility in Aristotle's *Generation of Animals*', in *Aristotle's Generation of Animals: A Critical Guide*, ed. A. Falcon and D. Lefevre, 153–70. Cambridge.

Hansen, W. 1996. *Phlegon of Tralles' Book of Marvels*. Exeter.

Harlow, M. 2013. 'Toys, Dolls, and the Material Culture of Childhood', in *The Oxford Handbook of Childhood and Education in the Classical World*, ed. J. E. Grubbs and T. Parkin, 322–40. Oxford.

Hughes, J. 2010. 'Dissecting the Classical Hybrid', in *Body Parts and Bodies Whole: Changing Relations and Meanings*, ed. K. Rebay-Salisbury, M. L. S. Sørensen, and J. Hughes, 101–10. Oxford.

Hull, D. 1964. *Hounds and Hunting in Ancient Greece*. Chicago.

Keller, O. 1909. *Die Antike Tierwelt*, 2 vols. Leipzig.

Kitchell, K. 1994. ' "So Great a Warfare": Urban Relocation and Animal Incursion.' *Syllecta Classica* 5: 9–15.

Kitchell, K. 2014. *Animals in the Ancient World from A to Z*. London.

Kitchell, K. 2020. 'Talking Birds and Sobbing Hyenas: Imitative Human Speech in Ancient Animals', in *Speaking Animals in Ancient Literature*, ed. H. Schmalzgruber, 447–76. Heidelberg.

Lenfant, D. 1999. 'Monsters in Greek Ethnography and Society in the Fifth and Fourth Centuries BCE', in *From Myth to Reason? Studies in the Development of Greek Thought*, ed. R. Buxton, 198–214. Oxford.

Llasa-Richards, I. 1998. ' "Foul Monster or Good Saviour"? Reflections on Ritual Monsters', in *Monsters and Monstrosity in Greek and Roman Culture*, ed. C. Atherton, 41–76. Bari.

Marinatos, S. 1926. 'Μινωική και ομηρική Σκύλλα.' *Archaiologikon Deltion* 10: 51–62.

Mayor, A. 2011. *The First Fossil Hunters: Dinosaurs, Mammoths, and Myth in Greek and Roman Times*. Princeton.

Moignard, E. 1998. 'How to Make a Monster', in *Modus Operandi: Essays in Honour of Geoffrey Rickman*, ed. M. M. Austin, J. Harries, and C. J. Smith, 209–17. London.

Neils, J. 2013. 'Salpinx, Snake, and Salamis: The Political Geography of the Pella Hydria.' *Hesperia* 82/4: 595–613.

Papadopoulos, J., and D. Ruscilo. 2002. 'A *Ketos* in Early Athens: An Archaeology of Whales and Sea Monsters in the Greek World.' *American Journal of Archaeology* 106/2: 187–227.

Platt, A. 1909. 'On the Indian Dog.' *Classical Quarterly* 3/4: 241–3.

Poursat, J.-C. 1976. 'Notes d'iconographie préhellenique.' *Bulletin de correspondance hellénique* 100: 461–74.

Stern, F. van K. 1978. 'Heroes and Monsters in Greek Art.' *Archaeological News* 7: 1–23.

Stoneman, R. 2019. *The Greek Experience of India from Alexander the Great to the Indo-Greeks*. Princeton.

Syropoulos, S. D. 2018. *A Bestiary of Monsters in Greek Mythology*. Oxford.

van Duzer, C. 2016. '*Hic sunt dracones*: The Geography and Cartography of Monsters', in *The Ashgate Research Companion to Monsters and the Monstrous*, ed. A. S. Mittman and P. J. Dendle, 387–435. Abingdon.

von Blanckenhagen, P. H. 1987. 'Easy Monsters', in *Monsters and Demons in the Ancient and Medieval Worlds: Papers Presented in Honor of Edith Porada*, ed. A. E. Farkas, P. O. Harper, and E. B. Harrison, 85–94. Mainz.

Yartz, F. J. 1997. 'Aristotle on Monsters.' *Ancient World* 28/1: 67–72.

Younger, J. G. 1988. *The Iconography of Late Minoan and Mycenaean Sealstones and Finger Rings*. Bristol.

Zouzoula, E. 2007. 'The Fantastic Creatures of Bronze Age Crete.' PhD thesis, University of Nottingham.

CHAPTER 22

READING MONSTROUS PEOPLES IN ANCIENT GREECE AND ROME

JOHN B. FRIEDMAN

INTRODUCTION

IN his 1580 *essai* titled 'D'un enfant monstreux', Michel de Montaigne discussed an infant paraded by its parents for profit as a freak, even if the infant was 'monstrous' only in that Montaigne described conjoined twins. Exhibiting so-called freaks of nature for profit was nothing new. Such a trade had existed in ancient Rome, as noted by Plutarch in his *c.*100 CE treatise *De curiositate* ('On Being a Busybody' 10.520c), where he describes a 'monster-market' at which buyers could shop for people exhibiting unusual physical deformities. Montaigne was clearly aware of classical precedents, since he quoted from Cicero's first-century BCE *De divinatione* ('On Divination') to speculate that such a birth could be an omen of political import for the unity of France, though also observing that 'what we call monsters are not so to God'. He concludes that this monstrous birth, seemingly against the natural order, needed to be properly understood: 'we call contrary to nature what happens contrary to custom; nothing is anything but according to nature, whatever it may be' (Frame 1971: 538–9).

Montaigne thus illustrates a line of thought about monstrosity extending from classical antiquity to the Renaissance. Indeed, his ideas took root with the fifth-century BCE Greek lyric poet Pindar, quoted by his younger contemporary Herodotus as having said 'custom is king' (Hdt. 3.38). For, in fact, Montaigne was touching on the diverse ways the word 'monstrous' was used in antiquity. To the ancients, the Greek *teras* and Latin *monstrum* had several distinct meanings, while the Greek epic poets used *pelōr/pelōron* to signify frightening or deformed beings (Lowe 2015: 8–9), though that term does not usually apply to the beings discussed here.

Chiefly, the words indicated something outside custom, outside the existing order of nature. They also meant, as in Montaigne's second sense, a birth not following the physical form of its parents and hence probably a portent or omen, often but not always negative (Lowe 2015: 10–11). So too, among the Romans, *monstrum* was nuanced as it could sometimes express something aesthetically interesting. Most importantly, however, the words eventually signified, from the points of view of the Greeks or Romans, the physically and culturally unusual peoples located in distant places. Through a long and complex process, the Latin adjective *monstruosus* developed from the noun *monstrum* to indicate more specifically any peoples deviating from Western cultural norms; it came to have the primary sense of 'fear- or awe-inducing'. Starting with the first-century BCE Roman poet Horace's description of Cleopatra as *fatale monstrum*, an imprecation with a criminal tinge (*Carm.* 1.37), we find that by the third century CE, in the Roman geographer Solinus' *De mirabilibus mundi* ('On the wonders of the world'), the usage was well established (Mommsen 1958: 132). By the early seventh century, Spanish historian Isidore of Seville could simply quote without attribution or comment Solinus' use of the word when stating that 'people write about the monstrous faces of nations [*monstrosae gentium facies*]' in the Far East with the simple, even generic sense that a great many such unusual peoples lived in distant regions (*Etym.* 11.3.17; Barney 2008: 245). Though *monstrum* became virtually synonymous with 'physically anomalous beings ... it never shed its ritual origins completely, keeping an overtone of transgression and often threat' (Lowe 2015: 8), so that it hinted at both the physically and culturally unusual and the divinely monitory.

Pliny's *Natural History* and Its Background

Book 7 of Pliny the Elder's *Natural History*, a first-century CE encyclopaedic work which Mary Beagon (2007: 20) calls 'the most extensive compilation [of monstrous races] in extant ancient authors and the source for many later descriptions', provides a good starting point for our investigation, as Pliny's 'monstrous' peoples eventually dominated late antique and medieval treatments (Fig. 22.1). The geographical distribution of these monstrous peoples extended from Ethiopia and India to Inner Asia (Western China, Mongolia, the Russian Far East, and Siberia) and even South Asia (Campbell 2006: 127–8; Romer 1998: 122). In short, the Plinian peoples were widely dispersed, inhabiting India, Africa, the snowy reaches beyond the Caucasus—virtually any place often imagined but little travelled.

Pliny, more than other Roman authors, tied monstrosity to earlier Greek scientific and political views of how climate affected racial characteristics, so that, for example, the northern nomadic peoples most removed from the temperate 'centre' were imagined as savage and ungovernable and hence suitable for subjugation by Roman imperialism.

FIGURE 22.1 Thirteenth-century French bestiary with illustrations of 'monstrous' humans, including Blemmyae (lower left) and Epiphagi (upper right).

Beagon sees in the *Natural History* 'the recurrent idea ... by which the strange is a feature *of the edges* by virtue of a peculiar imbalance of the elemental forces of nature in such areas'—largely those associated with the Titan God Oceanus and with the principle of fire (2007: 22, my emphasis).

Adding considerably to the Greek and Roman interest in and understanding of teratology—an understanding that included individual prodigies of the womb such as Montaigne's conjoined twins—the forty-two physically and culturally unusual 'Plinian' peoples believed to live at the earth's edges showed the power of the gods to create wonders and served to revitalize mankind's sense of the marvellous (see Friedman 2000: 9–22). These remote peoples in Pliny's pages, largely derived from his reading (though Pliny claims to have seen certain marvels himself, such as a transgender woman, *NH* 7.4.36), remain for the most part constant in appearance and behaviour in subsequent writing on monstrosity. These monstrous peoples also multiplied through creative misunderstandings of their names. For example, Pliny speaks of the Sciapodes ('Shade-feet') as *Monocoli*, transliterating into Latin the Greek word 'one-legged' (most likely from the Greek *apo tou monou kōlou*, 'from one leg'), but this was soon misread as *Monoculus* or 'one-eyed' by the Romans and was accordingly adapted to the descriptions of one-eyed beings like Homer's Cyclopes.

How actual travellers to India and other distant regions could have believed in these peoples, especially as exploration pushed borders further outward, is puzzling. Yet, as Beagon (2007: 21) notes about Pliny's work, 'the ambiguity of the border which retreats in the face of expanding knowledge and the border which acquires a metaphorical significance beyond the purely spatial may both be exemplified' by the belief in monstrous peoples. In fact, the purported direct personal observations of the East did not result in a corresponding reduction in the legends of monsters said to live there, since most of these paradoxographers' accounts emphasized the stories' truth.

There appears, as the variety and contents of the forty chapters in this volume illustrate so well, a psychological need for such monsters. As Lenfant (1999: 197) notes, these beings differ greatly from certain mythological monsters discussed elsewhere in this volume because classical interest in them was primarily ethnographic, not religious. One key difference between the monstrous men and woman of late antiquity and the mythological creatures, for example, is that the latter are largely one-offs, individual examples; although there were several Sirens, Cyclopes, and Gorgons, the majority are individuals, such as the Minotaur, the Chimaera, and Cerberus. In contrast, Plinian monsters typically reproduce and live in groups. Their appeal to the ancient world was, then, based on such factors as fantasy, escapism, delight in the exercise of the imagination, and, perhaps most importantly, fear of chaos outside the 'tribe'. For monstrosity and the lands from which it sprang, such as India and Africa, disordered both the body and the idea of the polis or city state. As Evans (1999: 56) suggests, 'in the geographical imagination, Africa is an area of confusion and disorientation for Rome', and, of course, the Amazons, as a group of self-governing females, rejected patriarchy, the traditional male-oriented form of government in Greece and Rome. Indeed, as Lowe (2015: 7) demonstrates, 'in Augustan culture, monstrous figures often seem threatening because they challenge established expectations and boundaries'.

However startling in bodily form and behaviour they may appear, many of the so-called Plinian peoples did exist, though we might find them difficult to recognize in Greek and Roman accounts of their appearance and manners. In this anthropological explanation (rejected by scholars such as Campbell 2006: 118 but accepted by Gevaert and Laes 2013: 224), Pygmies, for example, were far from imaginary aboriginal peoples, and even their cave-dwelling nature as described in ancient sources reflects actual pit-house practice (Dan 2014: 43, 56–8). Even the improbable-sounding Hippopodes, described as having feet like horses' hooves, may have had a factual basis. The vaDoma, a Zambezi valley tribe in Zimbabwe, exhibit ectrodactyly (a claw-like malformation) as an established genetic anomaly. For the vaDoma, this hereditary condition, possibly via a single mutated gene, results in feet with only two giant toes, and for some, the hands lack a full complement of fingers as well.

As to the Blemmyae, Pliny does not provide that name but describes a people 'without a neck, having their eyes on their shoulders' who inhabit the Eastern Nubian deserts (*sine cervice oculos in umeris habentes*, NH 7.2.23; Fig. 22.1); these are sometimes also more specifically called the Epiphagi. And according to Evagrius Scholasticus, a Syrian scholar of the sixth century CE, an actual nomadic tribe with the name Blemmyae several times attacked Christian settlements to the east of the Nile between the middle of the third and the fifth centuries CE, though he gives no physical description (1.7.13; Whitby 2000: 21). The absence of a neck and the presence of a face on the chest suggest that possibly this tribe made use of ornamented shields or chest armour decorated with faces.

CAUSES OF MONSTROSITY

Some common explanations in antiquity for why these monstrous humans differed so much from the Greeks and Romans involved the influence of climate and geography as well as the divine punishment of human failings; this last explanation retained importance up to late antiquity. 'Place', said the philosopher Roger Bacon (1220–1292), 'is the beginning of our existence, just as a father' (Burke 1962: 159). This was especially true of the monstrous peoples treated here; from the earliest Greek accounts, which situated them at the world's edges, their geographic locations often related to their character and appearance. The relationship between these peoples' homelands and other regions was further developed in theories linking moral character, appearance, and place, as in the sixth-century Greek Hippocratic treatise *On Airs, Waters, Places*, which certainly affected Roman attitudes towards human deformity.

As might be imagined, the Greeks felt that their own climate and geography were best. Herodotus, for instance, claimed that Greece enjoys a climate more favourable than that of other countries (3.106). Regarding geographical distance, Herodotus says that the furthest lands possessed things that seem the most beautiful and rare (3.116). But the majority opinion in Greece and Rome was, as Romm (1989: 122) notes, that 'the ancients imagined the furthest realms of the world to be inhabited by bizarrely malformed men and animals, not at all like their native varieties'. From this line of thinking, the peoples described by Herodotus, Pliny, and other ancient authors acquired their traditional remote locations.

In antiquity some writers explained climate and its impact on character and appearance through the metaphor of 'zones'. First appearing c.400 CE in Macrobius' commentary on Cicero's *Dream of Scipio* was the easily comprehensible idea that the extreme northern and southern portions of the globe are uninhabitable by reason of being frozen, and likewise the central region or zone by reason of extreme heat:

> [The earth] is divided into regions of excessive cold or heat, with two temperate zones between the hot and cold regions. The northern and southern extremities are frozen with perpetual cold ... Neither zone affords habitation, for their icy torpor withholds life ... The belt in the middle and consequently the greatest ... is uninhabited because of the raging heat. Between the extremities and the middle zone lie two belts ... in these alone has nature permitted the human race to exist. (Stahl 1990: 201–2)

Early maps then illustrated these zones with rubrics such as *nostra zona* ('our zone') to distinguish a temperate, western region from others icy and burning hot. Therefore, certain peoples were unusual because they lived more directly in a zone barely inhabitable by reason of heat, or by cold, or because of a desert clime—an idea implicit in Herodotus' comment that north of Scythia lies a vast desolation, and beyond that dwell the Androphagi, 'a people apart' (*ethnos eon idion*, 4.18). And Pliny, speaking of 'hot' Ethiopian monstrosities, finds it not surprising in the least that the region's extremities produce 'animal and human monstrosities' (*animalium hominumque monstrificas effigies*), considering the capacity of heat to affect the formation of their bodies (*NH* 6.35.187).

Isidore of Seville elaborates, adding a moral component: 'People's faces and coloring, the size of their bodies, and their various temperaments correspond to various climates. Hence we find that the Romans are serious, the Greeks easy-going, the Africans changeable, and the Gauls fierce in nature ... because the character of the climate makes them so' (*Etym.* 9.2.105; Barney 2008: 198). In this line of thought, a people like the Sciapodes are the way they are because the extreme heat over their heads causes them to develop a single great foot like an umbrella. But what of their moral nature? The Pseudo-Aristotelian *Problemata*, a Greek dialogue probably compiled in the sixth century CE, questioned why men are brutish in character and appearance at the extremes of climate. The answer is that excesses or extremes disturb the mind and soul (14.1). Thus, the Romans, like their Greek sources, saw a direct causal relationship between savagery in nature and in men; the person over whom heat or cold holds sway will be crude, violent, and homely.

The Macrobian map structure had a cartographic parallel in the tripartite Hecataean and, later, Noachic division of the world's surface. In his *Periegesis* ('Trip round the

World'), Hecataeus of Miletus (550–475 BCE) presented a tripartite structure of the earth's surface surrounded by a ring of ocean encircling a world disc comprised of three continents: Europe, Asia, and Libya—as the whole of Africa was then called (Fig. 22.2). This tripartite structure gained a moral significance in the early Christian era, where in Isidore's *Etymologies*, for example, a schematic diagram showed how, after the Flood, God repopulated the world through Noah and his three sons, Shem, Japheth, and Ham. This type of map was called Noachid after the patriarch, and the land masses were associated with Noah's three sons, as Japhet received Europe from their father, Shem received Asia, and Ham Africa. But Ham, seeing a drunken Noah lying naked, 'told his two brethren' (Genesis 9:22), thus humiliating his father, who accordingly cursed Ham and his descendants with eternal servitude (Braude 1997: 107). Supposedly, then, all Africans partook of Ham's curse, and maps from the twelfth century onwards frequently show a band of Plinian monstrous peoples in Africa.

FIGURE 22.2 Hecataean world map.

Thus, to the climatic theory of physically and culturally unusual peoples at the edges of the earth whose existence celebrated God's diversity was added the biblical notion that such peoples resulted from human failings. This view often appears on Noachid maps such as those illustrating the eleventh-century commentary on the Book of Revelation by Beatus of Liebana (Cathedral of Burgo d'Osma MS 1, fos. 35v–36). Moreover, according to St Augustine, it is because of Noah's curse and an alleged direct lineage from Cain that Ham was believed to have fathered monsters outside the line of Adam (*De civitate dei* 16.8).

Paradoxography

Pliny based his writing on monstrosity largely on the reports of real or imaginary wonders gathered by authors of Greek paradoxographies, common from the fifth century BCE onwards. Their topics, as Schepens and Delacroix (1996: 381, 388) note, include 'unexpected features of the natural world [and] also the world of man, human physiology, unusual social customs' and their purpose is to 'engender in … readers true feelings of amazement about the world in which they live'.

Various Greek writers who primarily chronicle marvels and wonders are called 'paradoxographers' because they deal with abnormal or inexplicable phenomena in nature or human societies. In this sense they differ from Herodotus, whose principal aim was to record the fifth-century BCE conflict between the Persians and Greeks, and only incidentally to record ethnographic information—though as Burgess (2019: 20) notes, the historian's investigations, in part based on his personal travels, bring with them stories of the Scythians and other tribes north of the Black Sea. The term 'paradoxographer' has been applied to authors such as Scylax of Caryanda (late sixth/early fifth centuries BCE), a Greek geographer; Ctesias of Cnidos (late fifth or early fourth century BCE), a Greek physician who wrote about Persian and Indian cultures; Megasthenes (350–290 BCE), a Greek ambassador to India; and Phlegon of Tralles (second century CE), a freed Greek slave of the emperor Hadrian.

The wonders recorded by paradoxographers include not only monstrous peoples, as discussed below, but also individual anomalies. Phlegon devotes much of his *Mirabilia* to teratology, telling of monstrous births resulting in hermaphrodites and four-headed children. He also speaks of polymorphic creatures such as the hippocentaur, and describes the bones of vanished giants, suggesting that these are portentous. In all these stories he stresses his credibility, giving a detailed account of the hippocentaur's bodily structure as he tells of how it was sent to Rome for imperial inspection (Hansen 1996: 49). More usually, however, in the earliest examples of the genre, such as the works of Scylax and Ctesias, the wonders in question are not of individuals but of plants, animals, and humans in groups, characterized by such anomalous features as unnatural size, hybridity, or number of body parts that make them 'monstrous'. For example, Scylax includes gigantically tall Ethiopians among his human wonders, and Ctesias mentions an Indian parrot that, if taught, can speak Greek (Nichols 2011: 111). Certain of these paradoxographers associate human monstrosity with the extreme North, Inner Asia, and the very distant East, particularly India.

In his *Verae historiae* ('True Stories') a fantastical spoof of such topoi of remoteness, the second-century CE satirist Lucian of Samosata places his narrator on the moon, where he sees many strange beings, such as Hippogypians—sentries who ride on giant three-headed vultures (1.11). Later, after escaping from the belly of a whale some 200 miles long, the narrator and his crew meet men with cork feet who float along on the sea (2.4). Lucian makes the marvellous claims of paradoxographers look ridiculous by taking them to extremes—by having his characters travel to the sun, moon, and stars, and by exaggerating the sizes and types of foreign creatures—far in excess of what the paradoxographers claim.

PARADOXOGRAPHERS
ON MONSTROUS PEOPLES

The paradoxographers vouched for the truth of their tales of monstrous beings in remote locales, often on the grounds that travellers had reported these stories independently. Indeed, this veracity topos is central to paradoxography. As an illustration, Scylax, who according to Herodotus had himself travelled to the Indus River (4.44), was the source of the remarkable things most Greeks knew about the region. Though his own writings are lost, an account of what Scylax found around the Indus is reported by later writers such as the Byzantine historian John Tzetzes (1110–1180 CE):

> There are men called the Sciapodes and the Otoliknoi. Of these the Sciapodes have very broad feet and at midday they drop to the ground, stretch their feet out above them, and give themselves shade. The Otoliknoi have huge ears which they use to cover themselves like an umbrella. (F51b; Nichols 2011: 80)

The monstrosity of the Sciapodes and Otolikni results from an excess of or defect in normal human appendages; nothing is said about the moral character or behaviour of the people, and they are not especially terrifying. But Tzetzes has concerns about the veracity of these details, noting that Scylax writes about these and other strange marvels 'as if they were true', but commenting, 'Since I have not seen any of it, I consider these tales to be lies. That they have some elements of truth is attested by the fact that many others claim to have seen such marvels' (F51b; Nichols 2011: 80).

Like Scylax, Ctesias in his ethnographic *Indica* insistently affirms his claims about monsters, relying both on reputable witnesses and on personal observation. A physician-historian whose writing on India exists today in fragments recorded by others, he describes plant and animal wonders of enormous size, such as giant roosters, and dogs able to combat lions. But his real interest lies in monstrous peoples. These are largely monstrous through hybridity, such as the Cynocephali ('Dog-headed men'), or from having anomalous body parts, as with the Sciapodes. In fact, from the *Indica* come several peoples who have a long afterlife in Western monster writing, particularly the Cynocephali. A key difference from Scylax's account of the Dog-Heads—aside from being much richer in detail—is one of geography, as Ctesias situates them in the mountains of India, in contrast to Scylax's northern placement:

> In these mountains live men who have the head of a dog. Their clothes come from wild animals and they converse not with speech, but by barking like dogs, and this is how they understand each other. They have larger teeth than dogs and claws that are similar but longer and more rounded. They live in the mountains as far as the Indus River. (F45.37; Nichols 2011: 53–4)

Another people Ctesias mentions, the Pandarae or Macrobii, were remarkable through both their manner of ageing and the size of their ears:

> In the mountains of India … there is a tribe … [whose] women give birth only once in their lifetime … each man and woman has white hair on their head and eyebrows for the first thirty years of their life. Their hair all over their body is white; after this it begins to turn black. When they reach the age of sixty, their hair is totally black. These men have up to eight fingers on each hand and likewise eight toes on each foot … they have ears big enough to cover their arms as far as the elbow and their entire back at the same time and one ear can touch the other. (F45.50; Nichols 2011: 116)

The last portion of this description gave rise in later writers to a new and entirely distinct people: the Panotii ('All-ears') on the analogy of the Pamphagi or those who eat everything, showing how individual features in these descriptions can split off and become attributed to entirely separate beings.

Ctesias also gives an account of the Pygmies, monstrous through a defect in size. While the diminutive Pygmies appear as early as Homer, who describes their war with cranes (*Il.* 3.1–7), their geographical placement is unspecified. Aristotle, in his *History of Animals*, places them in Egypt (8.12). And they are widely shown in Greek red-figure vase-painting and in Roman art. In his account of Pygmies, Ctesias differs from other paradoxographers in some important particulars: first, he does not mention their traditional war with cranes (known as the Geranomachy), and second, he places them in the mountains of India to add to the wonders found in that land (Romm 1989: 123–5).

WHAT COMPRISES 'OTHERNESS'?

The term 'alterity', the idea that monsters represent in some mythic way the frightening 'Other' with regard to the people thinking and writing about them, often appears in modern discussions of monstrosity. The ancient accounts of peoples called 'monstrous' made the observer's customs, especially those relating to diet, habitation, clothing, marriage and sexual practices, language, and religious observances the norm by which to evaluate all other peoples. The Hellenes, like many tightly knit cultures, viewed outsiders as potentially inferior and untrustworthy. Yet, at the same time, this intensely curious, seafaring people often ventured into unknown territory. The ancient Greeks were particularly interested in certain areas of human experience as indicators of a people's 'humanity', and ethnographic writing often commented on foreign customs.

Diet

Chief among the features designating a people as 'Other' for the Greeks and Romans was diet, often the single reason to consider a people monstrous. Ants, sheep's eyes, and pork all create distance between those who eat them and those who do not. Homer showed Polyphemus in the Odyssey as a man-eater through his actions rather than using any specific term (such as *anthropophagos* or *androphagos*); scholarly opinion has been mixed on the significance of the Cyclops' eating four of Odysseus' companions (Dougherty 2001: 122–42), but Odysseus' sorrowful reaction speaks volumes, and generally, dietary practices were an important indicator of humanity or its absence.

Some monstrous peoples were in fact even named after their diets or were singled out for comment because of it. Thus, we find Agatharcides of Cnidos (second century BCE) describing the peoples of Ethiopia as Fish-Eaters, Root-Eaters, Elephant-Eaters, and Dog-Milkers (Burstein 1989: *passim*), while the Hyperboreans eat no meat but live on acorns, and the Scythian Androphagi and Essedones, monstrous from Herodotus to Pomponius Mela, practise human sacrifice and drink human blood (Hdt. 4.62; Romer 1998: 71–3; Evans 1999: 59). The point of view implicit in such labels is ethnocentric, for characterization by diet focuses on the difference or remoteness of the Other from the observer rather than on the common bond of humanity. Similarly, Pliny in his *Natural History* also characterized many peoples by their alien diets. Among them were the Astomi ('No-Mouths') believed to live on the smells of flowers and apples (7.2.25); and parent-eating Anthropophagi (7.2.11). Solinus describes many others, including a tribe far to the east with mouths so tiny that they can take in nourishment only through an oat straw (*aliis concreta ora sunt modicoque tantum foramine calamis avenarum pastus hauriunt*, 31.12). These are a variant on Ctesias' Indian mountain dwellers, whose offspring 'do not have an anus nor do they have bowel movements. They have buttocks but the orifice is grown together. Consequently, they do not pass excrement, but they say their urine is like cheese, not thick but foul' (F45.44; Nichols 2011: 56).

Speech

Just as important as diet in the Greek and Roman ethnographic concept of monstrosity was the use of intelligible speech. Homer, for instance, referred to a certain people as 'uncouth speakers', literally *barbarophonoi* (*Il.* 2.867); to the Greeks the use of articulate speech—distinguishing men from animals and non-men—was not enough to confer full humanity. The speech had to be Greek, for the sounds of the non-Greek-speaking Other were not the true communications of rational men. As we saw earlier, Ctesias had characterized Indians not only by physical anomalies and hybrid body forms, but also by language, such as the extreme particularity of the Cynocephali's language: 'they converse not with speech, but by barking like dogs, and this is how they understand each other … Since they understand what the other Indians say but cannot converse, they communicate by barking and making gestures with their hands and fingers like the deaf and mute' (F45.37; Nichols 2011: 53–4). Pliny, too, often characterized the 'Other' via language; for example, he observed of Libya that the names of its peoples and towns 'are impossible to pronounce except by the natives' (*vel maxime sunt ineffabilia praterquam ipsorum linguis, NH* 5.1). Solinus often elaborated upon information in both Pliny and others, and notes, for example, that the people of the Libyan interior, the Troglodytes, 'know no language and rather screech than speak' (*ignarique sermonis strident potius quam loquuntur*, 31.4).

Habitation

Peoples are often partially or even completely identified as monstrous through their habitations, their clothing (or absence of it), and their lack of technology. For example, Ctesias' Cynocephali 'live not in houses but in caves' (F45.42; Nichols 2011: 55), and Solinus says that the Troglodytes of Libya live only in caves (31.2). According to Megasthenes, the Pygmies, though monstrous primarily because of their dwarfish size, lived in earthen pits roofed with eggshells and feathers (McCrindle 1877: 81). Some Indian tribes, though human in appearance and in most customs, through ascetic views choose to sleep and live in the woods or on the open ground. These included the Gymnosophisti ('Naked Philosophers'), who in late antiquity were associated with Alexander the Great. Megasthenes seems to have been the oldest source of information about them, distinguishing among Garmanes (a caste of initiates), Bragmanni (a high priestly caste), and Hylobioi. This last group, as the name 'forest dwellers' suggests, 'neither live in cities nor even in houses' (McCrindle 1877: 104–5). When Alexander debates with some of the Gymnosophisti, they are said to live in holes in the ground.

Clothing (or Lack of It)

In keeping with their uncivilized surroundings, monstrous peoples were often described as naked or wearing only leaves or animal skins, since they did not use textiles. Such haphazard garb or utter lack of garments illustrates their bestiality. For example, Ctesias says of the Cynocephali that 'Their clothes come from wild animals' and later elaborates slightly: 'They do not wear shaggy clothes but very thin strips of leather and this is done by both the men and the women. Members of the wealthiest class wear clothes made of linen' (F45.37, 42; Nichols 2011: 53, 55). Pygmies, he says, make a skimpy garment of their hair:

> They have very long hair that reaches their knees and even lower and their beards are the longest of any man ... they wear no clothes at all but comb the hair from their head down their back well below their knees and pull their beards down the front to their feet and then gird the hair around their entire body using it in place of clothing. (F45.21; Nichols 2011: 50)

The Gymnosophisti, too, were frequently characterized by nakedness or sparse attire. Some scholars identify them with the Indian Brahmans (Derrett 1960: 66), and since these sages were vegetarian and ascetic, they seem to have considered clothing a vanity. Unlike most monstrous peoples surveyed in this chapter, they were in no way dangerous to the observer or repellent through appearance or behaviour; it was only their philosophic asceticism—of which their nakedness was part—which made them monstrous. Opinion on their nakedness varies according to the subgroup being discussed. For example, Megasthenes remarks that the Garmanes of India wore tree bark (McCrindle 1877: 102), while Philostratus, in his *Life of Apollonius of Tyana*, says that the Gymnosophisti of the Nile strip naked in the same way as people at Athens do when they bask in the sun (6.6).

Sexual Practices

Ancient writers on geographical matters noted the sexual practices of distant peoples, often with extreme (moral) disapproval, and thus often made these the defining characteristic of monstrosity. Solinus, for example, speaks scathingly of the sexual and marital customs of the Ethiopian Garamantes: 'They do not know marriage; holding women in common is the custom of the country. Thus, only mothers recognize their sons and no one holds the honoured title of father. Who could, in effect, distinguish a father in such a morass of immorality?' while the Libyan Augilae brides are apparently forced to 'copulate with several men on their wedding night, but by severe laws are thereafter constrained to remain chaste' (30.2–3; 31.4). Cynocephali lack the so-called missionary position: according to Ctesias, they have sex with their women on all fours like dogs and consider it shameful to do so any other way (F45.43; Nichols 2011: 114).

Religion

The Greeks and Romans also recorded the differing religious practices of distant peoples. They often remarked, though without comment, on the practice of theriolatry (worshipping animal deities), as among the Egyptians. For example, Pliny notes a practice of certain Ptoemphani who 'have a dog for a king' (*canem pro rege habent*) and 'surmise his commands from his movement' (*NH* 6.192); Solinus, Plutarch, and Aelian give essentially the same account (Krappe 1942: 149). Although the Greeks and Romans do not specifically describe such religious and political practices as 'monstrous', the ancient literature certainly seems to imply as much by stressing their strangeness.

Other forms of religious 'monstrosity' involve ethical or philosophic oddities of worship or belief. For example, Alexander the Great, as a Westerner going East to India in part on a 'scientific' mission, allegedly writes letters back to Aristotle describing (among other wonders) a variety of physically and culturally monstrous beings with whom he had contact. Several authors, including Plutarch and Arrian, record that Alexander debated materialism versus spiritual asceticism with the leaders of the Gymnosophists. After they had shown their wisdom, Alexander rewarded them with marvellous gifts, as we learn from Plutarch's *Life of Alexander* (64–5). These Indian philosophers had no need for Western luxuries, and practised no metalwork, commerce, or warfare. Their avoidance of negative emotions such as envy or anger—two of the perturbations of the soul shunned by the Stoics—allowed them to live to an advanced age, free from the cares of conquest or empire. It seems that these accounts of the Gymnosophists Alexander encounters were intended to shore up Greek philosophic views by putting the ascetic virtues the classical authors held in the mouths of these Indian sages. To some observers, then, these views diverged so far from those of Westerners as to give the Gymnosophists a place in most narratives of monstrous men from antiquity to the Middle Ages.

Lucian, who (as noted above) mocked paradoxographers and credulous ethnographers by creating even stranger alien races in his *True Stories*, similarly satirizes accounts of foreign customs. Whereas Pliny's Astomi supposedly subsist on the smells of flowers and apples, Lucian's Moon people are nourished by smoke and drink air (*Ver. hist.* 1.23). Their clothing is spun from bronze if they are poor, or glass if they are wealthy (1.25). They have no women; men give birth from the calf of their leg (1.22). Unlike many of his predecessors, though, Lucian makes a point of telling his readers that nothing he describes really exists, and that, therefore, no one should believe anything he says (1.4).

CONCLUSION

The Plinian or monstrous peoples in their diverse appearance and behaviour clearly represented the 'Other' with whom Greeks and Romans could contrast their own identities and see the divinely established permanence of their physical and social forms in the context of receding geographical borders and ever more porous cultural ones. Monstrous beings, moreover, allowed the ancients a strong aesthetic satisfaction, for there was something wonderful in the belief that entire regions of the world teemed with anomalous beings, seemingly generated in India by the great heat, moisture, and rich soil and in the remote North by the extreme cold. Egypt, meanwhile, had the Nile full of crocodiles and hippopotami so that it was a short step to stories of strange humans, whose very existence fed into a desire for novelty—especially among the Romans. And Roman colonialism brought supposedly monstrous people to Rome. So bringing that 'something new out of Africa'—as Pliny put it (*NH* 8.17.42)—back to the capital appealed to the desire for novelty and the delight in hybridity that characterized late Roman culture.

Moreover, for the Romans the divine or portentous religious aspect of strange births whose primary importance was to convey some divine attitude to men, as we saw in Montaigne's freaks of nature, had declined; the need of their existence for fantasy became more prominent. Thus, the wonders of individual births gradually meshed with the notion of groups reproducing like to like. Pliny, for one, certainly discussed many portents heralded by individual unusual or physically defective births, but he was really interested in social groups of monstrous people who would breed similar progeny. Accordingly, the line in later centuries of monstrous individual births remained relatively distinct from the Plinian peoples, who went on in later centuries to have a rich and various existence in works of travel, on maps of the world (*mappae mundi*), and in Christian theological discussions of how such people could have descended from Adam and Eve.

SUGGESTED READING

See Céard (1996), Friedman (2000), and Lowe (2015) for the early development of monstrous beings and for their association with birth defects. Friedman (2000: 110–19) and Lowe (2015: 8–14) survey the philological development of the Latin word for 'monster' and how it came to suggest portents and omens. Céard (1996) examines the various works specifically tying monsters to wonders in animal generation from antiquity to the early modern period, when many humanists collected examples of portents for their oddity, while Nichols's 2011 translation of and commentary on Ctesias makes this example of the paradoxography genre quite accessible. See Romm (1992) for why India provides such a fertile source for discussion of monstrous beings and Stoneman (2008) and Burgess (2019) for how the spread of Greek culture and language through the Mediterranean after Alexander the Great's campaigns made travel to encounter unusual peoples, even in India, much easier than it had been in previous centuries. For an excellent take on the Cynocephali, see Leclercq-Marx (2022).

WORKS CITED

Barney, S., ed. and trans. 2008. *The* Etymologies *of Isidore of Seville*. Cambridge.

Beagon, M. 2007. 'Situating Nature's Wonders in Pliny's *Natural History*', in *Vita Vigilia Est: Essays in Honour of Barbara Levick*, ed. E. Bispham and G. Rowe, 19–40. London.

Braude, B. 1997. 'The Sons of Noah and the Construction of Ethnic and Geographical Identities in the Medieval and Early Modern Periods.' *William and Mary Quarterly* 54/1: 103–42.

Burgess, J. W. 2019. 'Travel Writing and the Ancient World', in *The Cambridge History of Travel Writing*, ed. N. Das and T. Youngs, 19–32. Cambridge.

Burke, R. B., trans. 1962. *The Opus Majus of Roger Bacon*, vol. 1. London.

Burstein, S. M., ed. and trans. 1989. *Agatharchides of Cnidus*: On the Erythraean Sea. London.

Campbell, G. L. 2006. *Strange Creatures: Anthropology in Antiquity.* London.

Céard, J. 1996. *La nature et les prodiges: L'Insolite au XVIe siècle en France.* Geneva.

Dan, A. 2014. 'Mythic Geography, Barbarian Identities: The Pygmies in Thrace.' *Ancient Civilizations from Scythia to Siberia* 20/1: 39–66.

Derrett, J. D. M. 1960. 'The History of Palladius on the Races of India and the Brahmans.' *Classica et Mediaevalia* 21: 64–135.

Dougherty, C. 2001. *The Raft of Odysseus: The Ethnographic Imagination of Homer's* Odyssey. Oxford.

Evans, R. 1999. 'Ethnography's Freak Show: The Grotesque at the Edges of the Roman Earth.' *Ramus* 28: 54–73.

Frame, D., trans. 1971. *The Complete Essays of Montaigne.* Stanford, CA.

Friedman, J. B. 2000. *The Monstrous Races in Medieval Art and Thought.* Syracuse, NY.

Gevaert, B., and C. Laes. 2013. 'What's in a Monster? Pliny the Elder, Teratology and Bodily Disability', in *Disabilities in Ancient Rome*, ed. C. Laes et al., 211–30. Leiden.

Giannini, A., ed. 1966. *Paradoxographorum graecorum reliquae.* Milan.

Hansen, W., ed. and trans. 1996. *Phlegon of Tralles' Book of Marvels.* Exeter.

Krappe, A. H. 1942. 'The Dog King.' *Scandinavian Studies* 17/4: 148–53.

Leclercq-Marx, J. 2022. 'De la merveille à la sainteté: Saint Christophe et les Cynocéphales (Haut Moyen Âge et Moyen Âge central).' *Les Cahiers de Saint-Michel de Cuxa* 53: 137–47.

Lenfant, D. 1999. 'Monsters in Greek Ethnography and Society in the Fifth and Fourth Centuries BCE', in *From Myth to Reason? Studies in the Development of Greek Thought*, ed. R. Buxton, 197–214. Oxford.

Lowe, D. 2015. *Monsters and Monstrosity in Augustan Poetry.* Ann Arbor.

McCrindle, J. W., ed. and trans. 1877. *Ancient India as Described by Megasthenes and Arrian.* Calcutta.

Mommsen, T., ed. 1958. *C. Ivlii Solini Collectanea Rerum Memorabilium.* Berlin.

Nichols, A., ed. and trans. 2011. *Ctesias on India.* Bristol.

Romer, F., ed. and trans. 1998. *Pomponius Mela's Description of the World.* Ann Arbor.

Romm, J. S. 1989. 'Belief and Other Worlds: Ctesias and the Founding of the "Indian Wonders" ', in *Mindscapes: The Geography of Imagined Worlds*, ed. G. Slusser and E. Rabkin, 121–35. Carbondale, IL.

Romm, J. S. 1992. *The Edges of the Earth in Ancient Thought.* Princeton.

Schepens, G., and K. Delacroix. 1996. 'Ancient Paradoxography: Origin, Evolution, Production, and Reception', in *La letteratura di consumo nel mondo Greco-Latino*, ed. O. Pecere and A. Stramaglia, 373–460. Cassino.

Stahl, W. H., trans. 1990. *Commentary on the Dream of Scipio by Macrobius.* New York.

Stoneman, R. 2008. *Alexander the Great: A Life in Legend.* New Haven.

Whitby, M., ed. and trans. 2000. *The Ecclesiastical History of Evagrius Scholasticus.* Liverpool.

PART III

INTERPRETING THE MONSTERS

CHAPTER 23

MONUMENTAL MONSTERS

SIMON OSWALD

INTRODUCTION

MARAUDING monsters menaced ancient Greek society in many ways, pervading myths, art, and literature. While monsters need neither menace nor maraud—centaurs, for example, could be quite civil when sober (see Aston in this volume)—context was critical, with monumental architecture in the Archaic and Classical periods proving especially partial to the malevolent monster. Such monumental settings were also crossroads where monsters of various myths and origins could mingle in the same physical space no matter how disparate their provenance or tenuous their connection. This chapter surveys the various types and abodes of monumental monsters as well as theories seeking to explain their presence in architectural iconography.

Although a variety of monumental building types could be adorned with monsters— for example, temples, stoas, gymnasia, theatres, tombs, *leschai*, treasuries, and fountains—I will principally examine temples, monstrous hot spots in the ancient world. There is, however, the question of where a structure begins and ends: should one, for example, include depictions of monsters appearing on associated dedications or furnishings within a temple or the temple temenos, some possibly monumental in their own right? Pausanias, a second-century CE travel writer and one of our most important ancient witnesses to material culture, frequently favoured such objects in his account at the expense of the sculpture on the associated temple. There is no easy answer, though for expedience I limit my discussion mostly to monsters appearing as part of the ornamental programme of the temple itself, and less frequently to the fixed furnishings within. Primary sources are provided wherever any object is attested only by ancient authors; all other objects mentioned are preserved at least in part by the material record.

Additionally, a glossary of technical architectural and other relevant terms is provided at the end of the chapter.[1]

A familiar caveat applies to the following survey, which is not intended to be a prescriptive treatment: it is highly unlikely that across the entire Greek world the same motivations and programmatic goals always governed any decision to incorporate monsters in a building design. While the art and architecture of the Greeks was highly traditional in certain respects, it was dynamic in others, and tastes, trends, and motivations might vary both synchronically between regions and diachronically within those very same places, even when the context under examination—a Centauromachy, for instance—appeared superficially consistent throughout. This is not to suggest that general overarching trends across the greater Greek world cannot be found, nor credible motivations recommended—simply that caution should be exercised in accepting uncritically any monstrous claim.

Taxonomy

There are many ways to classify monumental monsters, including by type, thematic context, medium (artistic technique), material, and location. In principle, almost any of the cast of monsters surveyed in this volume could appear on a monumental building such as a temple, though in practice only certain creatures regularly did so. Thus, while monstrous animals, the Giants, gorgons, sphinxes, and centaurs were ubiquitous, with limited exceptions one searches fruitlessly for Cyclopes, harpies, sirens, and other sadly neglected but no less monster-y types. Also included in the monumental monstrous menagerie were non-mythical beasts such as lions, particularly in the Archaic period: even though at that time they still roamed remoter parts of the Greek world, they were certainly alien to most people and just as fantastic and terrifying as the remainder of the capricious cast.

Monstrous media included sculpture (various types, including free-standing and relief), ceramics, painting, and weaving, with material types ranging from stone (principally limestone and marble) to clay, metals, wood, ivory, and stucco. No medium or material was monster-specific in terms of architectural iconography, even though the representative record that survives up to the present day is highly skewed towards the more durable stone and terracotta sculptures. Fortunately, extant ancient texts provide ample eyewitness testimony to those monsters made from materials more easily biodegradable or otherwise lost.

---

[1] Also, in keeping with the rest of this volume, Greek names have been rendered in their Latinate spellings.

HAUNTS AND HABITS

Haunts

Monsters proved highly adept at infesting monumental architecture, particularly of the religious variety, occupying all available spaces reserved for art, though with a clear predilection for vantage points upon the entablature. Moving from the top of a structure to the bottom, and from the outside to within, the following examples reflect the many monstrous lairs lurking in and upon Greek architecture.

Sphinxes perched upon the roof as corner acroteria of the temple of Apollo at Syracuse (c.575–550 BCE). Antefixes moulded as gorgons glared from the edges of the roof of the temple of Hera at Mon Repos, Corfu (c.610 BCE). A winged, three-bodied creature with intertwined serpent tails slithered out of the southern end of the west pediment of the so-called Hecatompedon, a temple on the Athenian acropolis (c.570 BCE). The triple-bodied giant Geryon was presented being bludgeoned by Heracles on an eastern metope of the temple of Zeus at Olympia (c.570–560 BCE). The giant Asterius lay dead in the Gigantomachy of the north frieze of the Siphnian Treasury at Delphi (c.525 BCE), perhaps a victim of Athena, fighting nearby. Mighty telamones or atlantes (Giants or Titans), 7.65 metres high, were integrated into the walls of the temple of Olympian Zeus at Acragas (fifth-century BCE), with the telamones, representing the defeated and enslaved Titans, sentenced to support in perpetuity the immense weight of the entablature—i.e. the Heavens, the House of Zeus itself (Bell 1980; Stewart 2018). The flesh-eating demon Eurynomus lurked within Polygnotus' famous wall-painting of the *Nekyia* (Odysseus' journey to Hades) in the *Leschē* of the Cnidians at Delphi (c.475–450 BCE; Paus. 10.28.1). The colossal chryselephantine cult statue of Athena Parthenos in the Parthenon (447–438 BCE) included a sphinx and griffins upon her helmet, an ivory Medusa's head upon her chest, and the serpent Erichthonius at her feet (Paus. 1.24.5–7); a Gigantomachy was depicted upon the concave side of her shield (Plin. *NH* 36.18–19). Meanwhile the so-called Throne of Apollo at Amyclae, Sparta (c. sixth century BCE)— in fact a relief-decorated structure enclosing and supporting the huge cult statue— depicted, among many other things, a bound Minotaur being escorted away by Theseus, Cerberus being led from Hades by Heracles, and Medusa, as well as sphinxes, Tritons, and harpies (Paus. 3.18.9–16). Fences or screens controlling access within the temple of Zeus at Olympia included a painting of Atlas holding aloft the heavens and earth (Paus. 5.11.4–5).

No part of a temple or building was the preserve only of monsters, though the area of the roof (acroteria and antefixes) was an especially popular hangout. This propensity to skulk about all over a structure means that patterns of habitat for particular monsters are sometimes difficult to identify. For example, restless centaurs appeared all over temples—within and without: prancing about the west pediment of the temple of Zeus at Olympia, trotting across the southern metopes of the Parthenon, springing upon the sandals of the associated cult statue of Athena Parthenos (Plin. *NH* 36.18–19), and frisking about the west frieze of the temple of Hephaestus at Athens (the 'Hephaesteum' or 'Hephaisteion', *c.*450–415 BCE). About the only territory they did not occupy was the roof: perhaps it was felt to be an unrealistic spot for a fantastic half-horse creature to hoof around upon. Nor is a pattern readily evident in comparing the same iconographic form. For example, centaurs battle Lapiths upon the *exterior* frieze on the *western* side of the Hephaesteum, upon the *eastern* and *northern* sides of the *interior* frieze of the cella of the temple of Apollo Epicurius at Bassae (*c.* last quarter of the fifth century BCE), and upon the *eastern interior* frieze of the *east porch* of the temple of Poseidon at Sounion (*c.*450–440 BCE). Heracles and his monstrous opponents appear upon the eastern metopes of the Hephaisteum, but on the western ones of the temple of Zeus at Olympia, and, if we permit a comparison that is not a temple, upon the northern metopes of the Athenian Treasury at Delphi (*c.*485 BCE; according to the reconstruction of Marconi 2006). Not all monsters were of the free-range variety, and patterns of habitat or lack thereof can be important interpretative considerations when we turn below to theories behind particular sculptural programmes.

Habits

Some general observations can be made beyond the obvious fact that monumental monsters were partial to appearing repeatedly in the same mythical narratives—the Giants versus the gods in so-called Gigantomachies (see Salowey in this volume), centaurs versus the Lapiths in so-called Centauromachies—or in specific architectural contexts, such as acroteria in the case of sphinxes (cf. Osborne 1994; Petit 2013). Behaviourally, two types of monsters may very basically be distinguished: Type A, which we might term 'antagonist' monsters, those in supporting roles that completed a particular mythological scene or sequence starring gods and/or heroes—a gig that regularly involved being pummelled by their more illustrious opponent; and Type B, the 'protagonist' or 'isolated' type of monster whose claim to be present was primary, appearing not as a foil for heroes but in all their terrifying glory, with powers intact and undiminished in any way.

Type A antagonist monsters were in the habit of having a bit of a bad day. Thus, the Nemean Lion, Lernaean Hydra, Erymanthian Boar, Stymphalian Birds, Cretan Bull, and Mares of Diomedes, along with Geryon, Atlas, and Cerberus, all appeared on the metopes of the temple of Zeus at Olympia as hapless opponents or hopeless participants in Heracles' Labours. Likewise, the Marathonian Bull (bashed or struggling) and the Minotaur (strained or writhing) appeared only at the invitation of Theseus in fulfilling his Labours upon the metopes of the Athenian Treasury at Delphi and those of the Hephaesteum at Athens. That these monsters were in guest-starring roles is indicated by their sole appearance in each respective sculptural programme, while Heracles or Theseus could appear in each metope scene. Similarly, the Giants of the north frieze of the Siphnian Treasury, the eastern metopes of the Parthenon, the shield of Athena Parthenos, and the Pergamon frieze (*c.*170–150 BCE), among others, appeared not because of any gracious gigantophilia on the part of associated populace, but to depict them battling the gods, and usually rather woefully in this rather unfortunate moment of the myth—from a Giant's perspective, at least. This is not to suggest the existence of any rule dictating that antagonist monsters must be maligned in iconography: centaurs, for instance, party poopers par excellence of Lapith wedding events, were regularly depicted giving as good as they got, as in the west pediment of the temple of Zeus at Olympia, where they dealt out some well-judged kicks and bites, or the interior frieze of the temple of Apollo Epicurius at Bassae, where one chomps perpetually at the jugular of a Lapith gentleman, and another does a spot of very successful stomping. Perhaps some martial respect was accorded for the reason that centaurs are part-human and capable of advanced, civilized behaviour, even if they had difficulties in stabling their unstable tempers, though ultimately the outcome in the myth was an unhappy one for them as well (Osborne 1994; see Aston in this volume).

Meanwhile, Type B, isolated monsters, includes the legions of essentially autonomous gorgons, sphinxes, and lions that bustled about temple roofs apparently divorced from any particular mythical context. Occasionally they were permitted to prowl elsewhere: the west pediment of the temple of Artemis on Corfu (early sixth century BCE) arguably included a Type B 'protagonist' monster, a massive central 'running' Medusa, leering and framed by her comparatively tiny children, Pegasus and Chrysaor (Fig. 23.1). The running-Medusa type is usually understood as her fleeing from Perseus, though the canonical version of the myth known to us had Medusa give birth to her children only after her beheading. Pegasus and Chrysaor were, in turn, flanked by two large reclining panthers with their heads turned to directly confront the viewer. The overall visual effect of this portrayal of Medusa is less of a frightened, agonized monster on the point of death than a powerful 'Mistress of the Animals' type motif, long familiar across the ancient Mediterranean and Near East. Fragmentary scenes at either end of the pediment apparently depicted Titanomachies, and a Medusa featured as the centrepiece of the poorly preserved east pediment as well.

FIGURE 23.1 Gorgon relief sculpture, west pediment, Temple of Artemis, Corfu, *c.*580 BCE.

Such protagonist monsters were a feature more commonly encountered in Archaic monumental sculpture. The centrepiece of the western pediment of the Hecatompedon did not depict any obvious myth at all, with two juxtaposed, massive lions lording over and tearing into a rather sorry-looking bull; the centre of the eastern pediment starred at least one lioness devouring a calf (another, now lost, was likely a mirror image gobbling away at the other side). Scenes of beastly battles depicting butting bulls and lions assaulting various victims graced the eastern and western sides of the frieze of the temple of Athena at Assos (*c.*550–525 BCE); upon the north and south friezes sat pairs of heraldic sphinxes facing one another, a relatively rare example of sphinxes nesting elsewhere than their preferred perch upon the roof (see Maggidis 2009).

Not that every monster falls neatly into either of the two categories described above, as illustrated by the scenes surrounding the central banquet of the lions in the west pediment of the Hecatompedon. Out of the southern end of the pediment wiggled a three-bodied monster in a confrontation with a fragmentary figure dressed in a red himation (Fig. 23.2); if the figure is Typhoeus (an identification not at all certain), then the opponent must be Zeus (see Brockliss in this volume). In any case, quite unlike the regular rout of the Giants in Gigantomachies, here the scene is at worst evenly poised; in fact, the grinning three-bodied creature appears to exude confidence in its abilities and chances, as winged three-bodied creatures with entwined serpent tails and brandishing as weapons the natural elements of the world were wont to do. The scene at

FIGURE 23.2 Triple-bodied, serpent-tailed monster, west pediment, Hecatompedon.

the northern end of the pediment is likewise evenly contested in action though this time not in its interpretation: Heracles wrestles with Triton. Or, rather, is it Triton wrestling with Heracles? The outcome is not yet guaranteed in its depiction, even if known from myth. Whilst a Centauromachy such as that of the west pediment of the temple of Zeus at Olympia might similarly offer a favourable impression of monstrous powers—this time drunken centaurial skills at wedding brawls—an important difference between it and the even poise of the action of the Hecatompedon was in the conventionality of the former compared to the uniqueness of the latter. A viewer required only a glance to recognize and understand any general message conveyed by a Centauromachy given the wholesale repetition of the motif in monumental architecture (see below), while the unique action of the Hecatompedon invited pause and perusal of god, hero, and monsters, presumably requiring more careful deliberation in interpreting myth and message.

EGREGIOUS AESTHETICS: THE RATIONALE
BEHIND THE BEASTS

We have by now seen a multitude of monsters clambering all over monumental architecture, though we have only just begun to claw at the debate as to *why* they were depicted at all. It's all very well that hordes of flailing Giants guest-starred in iconography depicting their defeat at the hands of the gods, but why include Gigantomachies as architectural sculpture in the first place? Such debates overlap with those considering the iconographic 'decoration' of monumental architecture in general, though monsters, given their relative prevalence, play a dominant part.

No single theory adequately explains the presence of all types of monstrous imagery, nor should one necessarily be expected when many different display contexts were possible upon any one building, and within an iconographic system that could vary synchronically at the regional scale and diachronically even within the same particular city. The motivation behind the inclusion of the same type of monster in temple architecture, for example, might vary between roofs, which permitted monsters to appear without being connected to a particular mythological context; friezes, which invited depictions of narrative or progression; metopes, which suited the display of discrete, punctual events lifted from myth; and pediments, which allowed more extensive treatments of mythological episodes (Osborne 2009). But rationale there must have been, since no temple, for example, *needed* sculpture and painting in order to be defined as a temple, yet the vast majority known to us did admit iconography—an iconography that operated within an established cultural and theological framework regarding appropriateness in a sacred context, as evident from the large amount of thematic repetition in sculpture between temples, but that on other occasions could be highly innovative in theme and style. Ultimately, a temple's iconography clearly played an important part in the construction of its identity even if its status was never in jeopardy without it (Scott 2007). Below, I survey a representative, though by no means exhaustive, number of interpretations, and although I present the various ideas as 'theories', the associated authors do not necessarily claim them to be so. Overlap will be evident in certain cases, further emphasizing the fact that while all offer tantalizing insights, none alone suffices in elucidating the complete monstrous mystery.

Before examining some of the theories, we might wonder whether the Greeks themselves actively considered the reason why they adorned their monuments with monsters, or whether they did so instead purely out of a compliance with custom: monsters adorned buildings because they always had, with any original motivation behind the monstrophilia at the beginning of the tradition lost.[2] Clearly, exotic objects adorned with fantastic beasts were already being traded or exchanged with the Greek world in the Early Iron Age (c.1100–800 BCE), and thereby could readily serve as monstrous models for local artisans to imitate or adapt. Likewise, itinerant craftspeople from neighbouring cultures could have introduced and incorporated monsters into early Greek art and architecture by fusing in conventional elements from their own traditions—monstrous creatures already had a long history featuring in the art and architecture of the Near East (see Richey in this volume). But even if we were to make the rather unlikely claim that later generations of Greeks were content to unquestioningly accept certain iconographical elements as part of their architectural traditions, it is doubtful that any lost original motivation behind the monsters was simply imitative. Nor should one diminish the role of agency in any cultural exchange of ideas: while some artistic conventions might have arrived from the Near East and been incorporated passively, the Greeks were also active partners in transactions, and presumably no one forced them to plaster panthers upon their pediments.

Simple 'genealogical' considerations might lie behind the inclusion of a particular monster—whether a connection to the patron deity of the temple in question or to the greater sociopolitical community. The Hephaesteum at Athens, a temple dedicated to the joint cult of Hephaestus and Athena, depicted labours of Heracles and Theseus upon its metopes. Stewart points out that both heroes were protégés of Athena, Theseus at the local Athenian level and Heracles at the Panhellenic, and 'by putting paid to monsters, maniacs, and malefactors of all kinds' they collectively represented the (re-)establishment of order in society (2018: 733). On the broader political scale, Pegasus' appearance on the temple of Artemis on Corfu by one view was a reference to Corfu's mother city of Corinth, temporarily in political control of the island at the time of the temple's construction, and where Pegasus was an important symbol given that the hero Bellerophon, who tamed the winged horse, was Corinthian by birth (Marconi 2004). Medusa is thereby present as Pegasus' mother. Such a theory forges a convincing iconographic

---

[2] A modern analogy illustrating a (largely) unquestioned deference to tradition might be the custom of blowing out candles on a birthday cake: how many people reflect upon the origin (and wisdom) of showering spittle all over a cake, let alone the macabre ritual of then serving it up to one's invited victims under the pretence of hospitality?

link, but only gets us so far: why was Medusa then the dominant central figure? What was the role of the flanking panthers? Why are scenes from the Titanomachy entwined within the same pediment?

The 'apotropaic' theory specifically seeks to account for those monsters that stared out frontally at the viewer: they assumed such a posture in order to ward off evil spirits. Examples including the *gorgoneion* and beastly antefixes of the second temple of Apollo at Thermon (*c*.640 BCE), the judgemental acroterial sphinxes of the temple of Apollo at Syracuse, and the grinning gorgon upon the pediment of the temple of Artemis on Corfu, have all variously been understood as apotropaic. An oft-cited passage supporting this theory derives from Aeschylus' satyr play *Isthmiastai* in a humorous description demonstrating the effect that figural decoration could have: a band of satyrs carrying likenesses (*eikous*) of themselves, perhaps in the form of masks, march up to the temple of Poseidon at Isthmia (*c*.700–650 BCE) to nail them to the temple as votive offerings. Each image, so lifelike that one satyr suggests his mother 'upon seeing it would surely whirl about and shriek, thinking it to be me' (14–16) will sit upon the temple as 'a mute herald, a hinderer of wayfarers which ... will halt visitors in their tracks' (19–21).[3] It is highly doubtful, however, that the satyrs actually embody the type of amorphous evil suggested by the apotropaic theory; the context suggests that the satyrs rather represent quite the opposite—closer to the type of casual and devout temple-goer presumably never intended to be prevented from visiting by apotropaic ornamentation (Marconi 2004). Even less clear is why any given patron deity of a temple would require a security detail of monsters to guarantee their protection from malevolent spirits (Petit 2013: 212).

Marconi (2004), dissatisfied by the vagueness of the apotropaic theory, posited another by suggesting that glaring, confrontational monsters arrested the attention of the viewer, provoking a sense of awe and dread as part of the overall religious experience. Pointing to both literary and material evidence, he argues that monsters and beasts began to proliferate in temple iconography in the first half of the sixth century BCE as a stratagem to instil fear in the viewer as part of the sacred experience in encountering divine power. Petit, however, points out that Marconi's theory cannot be a universal one, given that the 'sweet smile of female sphinxes' found as architectural sculpture at, for example, Calydon, hardly inspired dread (2013: 212).

Another theory understands the inclusion of particular monsters upon a structure as governed on occasion by aesthetic principles inspired by the surrounding landscape and buildings. The strongest such candidate is the Gigantomachy depicted upon the north frieze of the Siphnian Treasury at Delphi, the side that faced the Sacred Way, the path visitors climbed to reach the temple of Apollo (*c*.525 BCE) at the heart of the sanctuary. The choice of the Gigantomachy, Scott (2007) argues, was inspired by that upon the western pediment of the temple of Apollo itself (constructed at the same time as the treasury), and thereby forged a connection between the two buildings in harmony with the theme's popularity in the sanctuary at that time. Visitors clambering up the Sacred

---

[3] Text and translation adapted from Sommerstein 2008: fr. 78a, 84–87.

Way would thus enjoy a Gigantomachia-palooza, with the smaller Siphnian version anticipating that of Apollo's temple (Fig. 5.1 in this volume).

Interpretations operating at a narrower scope can be more convincing, but difficulties are still encountered. The 'psychopomp' theory understands acroterial sphinxes as liminal creatures, subservient to their patron deity within a temple and evoking the afterlife. Petit (2013), building upon the observation that sphinxes had a penchant for perching upon temples as acroteria, argues that the key to their interpretation rests upon their recurrent positioning at the corners of roofs in concert with central, floral acroteria set upon the apex. A 'tree of life' motif was invoked by such arrangements: the sphinxes were both guardians of the path to the tree of life and psychopomps, divine chaperones who guided souls to the afterlife. Petit believes that such an arrangement represented a type of divine promise whereby the temple's patron deity used these potent symbols upon the roof to offer the hope of life after death. Sphinxes should furthermore be thought of as a type of semi-autonomous 'satellite' of the temple deity and as embodying or projecting particular attributes of their more powerful patron residing within the temple (Petit 213). This promising line of inquiry nevertheless raises further questions. What was the ancient expectation that Greek gods facilitated access to the afterlife? Did sphinxes play a ritual role at such sites? Was there a correlation between the identity of the patron deity of a temple and such 'sphincity' motifs? If sphinxes could grace the temple of any god whatsoever, but were not present on every such corresponding temple, might not the 'divine promise' be somewhat compromised, with the impression rather being that of luxury accessory items—fancy, if frightful, divine pets that were entirely optional features?

The 'decorative' theory, in turn, posits a cosmetic motivation behind the monsters: minimalized meaning, maximized make-up—and what more fabulous feature for your temple than a glamorous gorgon parading across the pediment? Such interpretations have traditionally been criticized in scholarship as overly simplistic: a complex society like that of the Greeks *must* have had sophisticated programmatic goals behind their iconographical choices—goals that aimed at relaying deep philosophical messages. More recently, however, the decorative theory has come back into vogue, albeit it in a revamped way, but before we circle back to it we need to critique other types of programmatic readings.

Some programmatic theories argue for an intensive and optimized viewing experience that captured a viewer's attention in order to transmit iconographical messages. Hölscher (2009), however, has pointed out that such theories face an uncomfortable logical hurdle in that the location of the majority of the iconography, high upon a temple's entablature, delivered just the opposite: a very inconvenient and difficult viewing experience obscured by tight angles of vision and/or poor lighting. Furthermore, if an intensive experience was ever a programmatic objective, then it is odd that iconography was regularly also situated upon areas of a temple that were less trafficked than the entranceway or side(s) adjacent to the main approach—what a tragedy that most ancient viewers must have missed the majestic message of the sacred centaurs of the western frieze at the rear of the Hephaesteum! Nor, Hölscher notes, was it realistic for a temple-planning committee to expect a comprehensive and coherent iconographic experience, given the large amount of figural decoration possible and the impossibility of consuming it all at once when it was located on multiple sides facing multiple directions. How could a visitor to the temple of Zeus at Olympia, for example, absorb any holistic message conveyed by the centaurs fighting upon the west pediment, the chariot race on the east, the parade of monsters struggling upon the east and west metopes, and the sphinxes flaunting their secrets upon the feet of Zeus' throne within?

The 'allegorical' theory, on the other hand, supposes that particular mythological battles involving gods, heroes, and monsters were deliberate programmatic choices that served as allusions to Greeks fighting Persians, or to other historical conflicts or ideologies, whether democratic or otherwise. Hölscher has likewise demonstrated the fallibility of such expectations (2009). Gigantomachies, for instance, appeared upon near-contemporaneous buildings built by regimes of very different political stripes— upon, for example, the pediment of the Megarian Treasury at Olympia (c.525 BCE), the pediment of the Old Temple of Athena on the Athenian acropolis (c.525–500 BCE), and on the west pediment of the temple of Apollo at Delphi. The Megarian Treasury was a public commission by a polis (Megara); the Old Athena temple a public benefaction by tyrants (the Peisistratids), and the temple of Apollo a private donation by a wealthy exiled aristocratic family (the Alcmaeonidae) for self-promotion. Even the most manipulative monster might struggle to accurately convey any nuanced sociopolitical message hidden within each of these stock Gigantomachies!

The path of allegory need not be so complicated, but intentionality is still difficult to prove. Osborne has argued that the Centauromachy on the west pediment of the temple of Zeus at Olympia conveyed a tense message of 'combat ... in progress', in direct contrast to the 'static' and 'foreboding' scene of Pelops and Oenomaus before their chariot race on the east pediment, with the latter an allegory to the apprehension and anticipation felt *before* athletic competition at the Olympic Games, and the former an allegory to the struggle *within* it (1994: 59–60). If this mirroring of athletic experience was a motivation behind the choice of the sculptural programme (Osborne does not necessarily claim it was so), we are still left with the problem of *why* a Centauromachy in particular, when presumably other combative scenes from myth could have evoked a similar response.

No theory should downplay the obvious importance that programmatic planning played in the construction process. Our knowledge of such matters, however, is mostly speculative due to a lack of evidence; we do not even know who had control of the process in contexts such as Delphi, where sanctuary officials might have dictated terms even if, for example, a treasury was dedicated by an outside polis. Such ignorance has repercussions for our interpretation, as demonstrated by Scott (2007): if sanctuary officials carefully controlled any iconographic programme at Delphi, then the Gigantomachy of the Siphnian Treasury might be just one approved cog in a carefully orchestrated propagandistic machine to promote the power of Apollo and/or the sanctuary. Alternatively, if Siphnian planners had free licence, then the Gigantomachy might rather be allegorical, projecting Siphnian supremacy—and so on. Certainly, there must have been some sort of collaborative and consultative process with sanctuary authorities, but it remains unknown whether this stopped at permission to build in a particular place or extended all the way to consent being granted on the condition of a north-facing Gigantomachy frieze with labels naming all the individual Giants.

Returning to the decorative theory, then, we find that its simplicity affords it an advantage in allowing that certain motifs could be both ornamental *and* deliver generic moral messages. Indeed, the Greek word *kosmos* in the context of architecture stood for both 'decoration' and 'order', concepts that appropriately capture the sense of iconography as divinely sanctioned adornment adding to the prestige of a structure (Marconi 2004; cf. Hölscher 2009). Intensive viewer experiences were not a prerequisite for understanding: stock myths such as Gigantomachies that recurred repeatedly in monumental architecture conveyed a set of general social norms and ideologies that signalled modes of sanctioned moral conduct (such as 'order over chaos'), easily recognizable by a viewer (Hölscher 2009: 61; cf. Marconi 2004). Such ideas find additional support in negative evidence. Osborne (2009: 9) has observed the relative scarcity of satyrs in monumental architecture, indeed in 'no major sculptural programme' at all. The reason, he argues, is that satyrs were opportunistic uncivilized sorts who were never cast in prominent roles overturning or threatening the very fabric of civilized society, in contrast to the Giants and centaurs. Temple iconography favoured such monumental conflicts because viewers also understood that such stories were resolved by divinely sanctioned acts that restored and upheld societal order. The 'storylessness of the satyr' precluded any such moral message and thus excluded them from monumental sculptural programmes (Osborne 2009: 11).

CONCLUSION

Monsters *mattered* in monumental Greek architecture. Even though there is little consensus among scholars regarding the underlying motivations for including monsters in the iconographic programme of any building, the interpretations outlined above all assume a conscious and careful process in incorporating them, driven by concerns ranging from the aesthetic to the allegorical, the traditional to the political, the communicative to the competitive, and many others besides. No interpretation need be mutually exclusive of others, and multiple reasons might have driven the casting of monsters on different parts of the same temple. Indeed, especially in the case of a civic monument, different stakeholder groups concerned in the planning and building process—architects, priests, city officials, artists, the public, and so on—most likely had different rationales in demanding, say, a centrepiece gorgon within the pediment rather than an enthroned Zeus, and the end result might quite reasonably be a compromise between stakeholders—the west pediment of the temple of Artemis on Corfu comes to mind with its medley of Medusa and children, panthers, and Titanomachies. While essentially all our monsters appeared also in non-monumental art, not all monsters of non-monumental art were found monumentally—a pattern that is unlikely to be accidental, and an observation that urges caution when comparing the same monsters in different media, where other factors may be in play. One *could* have a temple without a monster, but when a monster was needed, not just any random monster qualified for the task.

Suggested Reading

While all the following studies include important insights into the monsters of monumental architecture, many are broader in their analysis and consider non-monstrous ornamentation as well. Hölscher (2009) promotes the 'decorative' theory of architectural sculpture and is an authoritative critique of programmatic theories assuming viewer-intensive experiences. Marconi (2004, 2007, 2009) explores various functions of building ornamentation, including the idea of instilling awe in a visitor as part of the religious experience, while Osborne (1994, 2000, 2009) looks more narrowly at particular figural representations, including Centaurs and satyrs, advocating the idea that challenges to and resolutions of prescribed social norms could motivate the inclusion or exclusion of particular monsters. Petit (2013) is a detailed investigation of sphinxes as psychopomps in Greek architecture, and includes a survey and bibliography of theories not considered in this chapter, such as the motif of domesticated, tamed nature (cf. Winter 2009; Danner 1989 on acroterial sphinxes). Scott (2007) advocates the idea that the iconography of particular buildings could be in dialogue with those immediately surrounding it; he also considers the unknowns of the planning and permission process in building at a sanctuary such as Delphi (cf. Himmelmann 1988 on temple planning). Von Hofsten (2007) investigates feline-prey iconographical motifs; on this, see also Markoe (1989) and Hölscher (1972). Burkert (1988) remains a valuable discourse on the symbolism and function of Greek temples, and includes diachronic commentary. Many studies of particular buildings include detailed treatments of the iconography, including Sapirstein (2012) on the temple of Hera at Mon Repos, Stewart (2018) on the Hephaesteum, Maggidis (2009) on the temple of Athena at Assos, and Bell (1980) on the temple of Zeus at Acragas.

Glossary of Technical Terms

acroteria: Decorative sculptures positioned above the pediment.

antefix: A vertical sculpture concealing and supporting the cover tiles around the edge of the roof.

atlantes: Architectural sculptures of male figures used as pillars to support (or give the impression of supporting) the entablature of a structure.

cella: The chief interior chamber of a temple housing the cult statue(s).

entablature: The superstructure of a building above the columns.

frieze: A horizontal strip of the entablature running around the building that could be decorated with painting and/or sculpture; Ionic friezes were continuous unbroken strips, while Doric friezes were comprised of metopes and triglyphs.

himation: A type of Greek outer garment that served as a type of cloak.

leschai: Private or public clubs/meeting places.

metope: A square vertical block alternating with grooved triglyphs, adorning the frieze of the Doric temple order type; could be decorated with painting and/or sculpture.

pediment: A triangular space at the ends of a building, formed by the intersection of a sloped roof with the horizontal plane of the structure.

telamones: *see* **atlantes**.

temenos: A defined area around a temple or sanctuary demarcating the extent of its sacred space.

WORKS CITED

Bell, M. 1980. 'Stylobate and Roof in the Olympieion at Akragas.' *American Journal of Archaeology* 84: 359–72.

Burkert, W. 1988. 'The Meaning and Function of the Temple in Classical Greece', in *Temple in Society*, ed. M. N. Fox, 27–47. Winona Lake, IN.

Danner, P. 1989. *Griechische Akrotere der archaischen und klassischen Zeit*. Rome.

Himmelmann, N. 1988. 'Planung und Verdingung der Parthenon-Skulpturen', in *Bathron: Beiträge zur Architektur und verwandten Künsten*, ed. H. Büsing and F. Hiller, 213–24. Saarbrücken.

Hölscher, T. 1972. *Die Bedeutung archaischer Tierkampfbilder*. Würzburg.

Hölscher, T. 2009. 'Architectural Sculpture: Messages? Programs? Towards Rehabilitating the Notion of "Decoration" ', in *Structure, Image, Ornament: Architectural Sculpture in the Greek World*, ed. P. Schultz and R. von den Hoff, 54–67. Oxford.

Maggidis, C. 2009. 'Between East and West: A New Reconstruction of the Decorated Architrave Frieze of the Athena Temple at Assos and the Regional Tradition of Unconventional Architectural Decoration in East Greece', in *Koine: Mediterranean Studies in Honor of R. Ross Holloway*, ed. D. B. Counts and A. S. Tuck, 78–95. Oxford.

Marconi, C. 2004. 'Kosmos: The Imagery of the Archaic Greek Temple.' *Anthropology and Aesthetics* 45: 211–24.

Marconi, C. 2006. 'Mito e autorappresentazione nella decorazione figurata dei *thesauroí* di età arcaica', in *Stranieri e non cittadini nei santuari greci*, ed. A. Naso, 158–86. Grassina.

Marconi, C. 2007. *Temple Decoration and Cultural Identity in the Archaic Greek World: The Metopes of Selinus*. New York.

Marconi, C. 2009. 'Early Greek Architectural Decoration in Function', in *Koine: Mediterranean Studies in Honor of R. Ross Holloway*, ed. D. B. Counts and A. S. Tuck, 4–17. Oxford.

Markoe, G. E. 1989. 'The "Lion-Attack" in Archaic Greek Art: Heroic Triumph.' *Classical Antiquity* 8: 86–115.

Osborne, R. 1994. 'Framing the Centaur: Reading Fifth-Century Architectural Sculpture', in *Art and Text in Ancient Greek Culture*, ed. R. Osborne and S. D. Goldhill, 52–84. Cambridge.

Osborne, R. 2000. 'Archaic and Classical Greek Temple Sculpture and the Viewer', in *Word and Image in Ancient Greece*, ed. N. K. Rutter and B. A. Sparkes, 228–46. Edinburgh.

Osborne, R. 2009. 'The Narratology and Theology of Architectural Sculpture, or What You Can Do with a Chariot But Can't Do with a Satyr on a Greek Temple', in *Structure, Image, Ornament: Architectural Sculpture in the Greek World*, ed. P. Schultz and R. von den Hoff, 2–12. Oxford.

Petit, T. 2013. 'The Sphinx on the Roof: The Meaning of Greek Temple Acroteria.' *Annual of the British School at Athens* 108: 201–34.

Sapirstein, P. 2012. 'The Monumental Archaic Roof of the Temple of Hera at Mon Repos, Corfu.' *Hesperia* 81: 31–91.

Scott, M. C. 2007. 'Putting Architectural Sculpture into Its Archaeological Context: The Case of the Siphnian Treasury at Delphi.' *BABESCH* 82: 321–31.

Sommerstein, A., ed. and trans. 2008. *Aeschylus: Fragments.* Cambridge, MA.

Stewart, A. 2018. 'Classical Sculpture from the Athenian Agora, Part 1: The Pediments and Akroteria of the Hephaisteion.' *Hesperia* 87: 681–741.

Von Hofsten, S. 2007. *The Feline-Prey Theme in Archaic Greek Art.* Stockholm.

Winter, N. A. 2009. 'Solving the Riddle of the Sphinx on the Roof', in *Etruscan by Definition: The Cultural and Personal Identity of the Etruscans*, ed. J. Swaddling and P. Perkins, 69–72. London.

CHAPTER 24

CRYPTIDS IN GREEK ART

ANDREA MURACE

INTRODUCTION

IN a seminal article, the Italian historian Arnaldo Momigliano, discussing the basic rules of every historical investigation, pointed out that 'Just as dangerous [as hasty interpretion of texts] is the delusion that what is not documented never existed' (2016: 45; first published in Italian as Momigliano 1974). This perfectly captures the context for this chapter. Modern scholars sometimes mistakenly limit their thinking on the ancient world to what is known from written sources (Verbanck-Piérard 2018: 163–4). Of course, this is not the proper place to reopen the issue of source hierarchy, but we should bear in mind that with regard to monsters in Greek art we often lack sufficient textual evidence. For our purposes the field of analysis is that of Greek ceramics.

Many monstrous creatures depicted on ancient vases are clearly identifiable as belonging to specific known myths. But a handful of vase findings remain obscure because of their bizarre decorations, which cannot be securely identified as figurative elaborations of any known story. To approach these creatures, most of which are hybrids and worthy of being called 'cryptids', we will rely both on the available sources from the ancient world and on similar features investigated by other complementary disciplines, including mythology and anthropology.[1]

CRYPTIDS: A BRIEF OVERVIEW

There already exist several research perspectives on the figurative representations of monsters in Greek art (Boardman 2002: 127–56; Boudin 2005; Robinson and Robinson

---

[1] The author wishes to thank Adrienne Mayor for encouraging his interest in ancient cryptids and for recommending his contribution to this volume.

2015–2016). Here, through an analysis that is still necessarily partial, the goal is to better understand a limited group of ancient vases that depicts unidentified or unidentifiable creatures. In this chapter, the reader will find an anthology of the most curious illustrations observable in archaeological findings. To start, let us specify what the word 'cryptid' commonly means: our subjects are those monsters whose identification and literary or folkloric background are uncertain. The branch of knowledge that deals with them is known as cryptozoology, because it takes an interest in 'mysterious' animals (from Greek *krypto-zoon*, 'hidden animal') that elude scientific taxonomy and direct evidence (Loxton and Prothero 2013: 16–20). Although usually considered a pseudo-science, cryptozoology provides a useful approach to the figurative representations of creatures that are problematic to identify, in our case those found on Greek vases.

We will therefore focus on monstrous depictions which seem to refer to lost mythical tales or which may convey specific meanings. Our main selection criteria for the vases are, first, the rare and strange nature of the subjects and, second, the depicted *mirabilia* ('marvels') of the overall scenes, which are remarkable for their possible meanings. As will be immediately evident, the basic feature of the selected monsters is their hybridity as combinations from animals—even extinct ones, known from ancient fossil discoveries—and/or from human segments (Mayor 2011: 157–91; Robinson and Robinson 2015–2016).

SKYPHOI IN SEARCH OF A HERO

The first few vases we consider here are devoted to heroic feats against monsters. Most of these are black-figure skyphoi (plural of skyphos), deep cups characterized by a wide opening and the presence of two side handles, typically used for drinking during ancient Greek aristocratic gatherings known as *symposia* (Boardman 1991: 188–9). Our selection includes samples comparable for their possible meanings and attributed to the Theseus Painter, one of the most prominent vase-painters active from the late sixth to early fifth centuries BCE. The first subgroup consists of two vases considered 'twins' because of their similar decoration.

These two skyphoi, whose unique high-quality compositions present many similarities, are held in separate collections: one is in Boston,[2] the other in Potenza, Southern Italy (Fig. 24.1). According to Fritzilas, author of a monograph about the Theseus Painter, both vases can be dated to *c*.515–500 BCE, even if, maybe, the Potenza vase is slightly more recent, as it shows a more secure iconography without corrections or additions (2006: vol. 1, cat. 11 and 102). While the Boston skyphos was probably found in Athens and from there sold to the American museum (vol. 1, cat. 11), the Italian

---

[2] This black-figure skyphos by the Theseus Painter, in the Museum of Fine Arts, Boston (inv. 99.523) is available to view at https://collections.mfa.org/objects/153526.

FIGURE 24.1 Cryptid on a black-figure skyphos by the Theseus Painter. Potenza, Museo Archeologico Nazionale della Basilicata 'Dinu Adamesteanu', inv. 214586.

Credit: Reproduced by permission of the Ministero della Cultura—Direzione Generale Musei—Direzione Generale Musei Basilicata. Any other reproduction is prohibited.

specimen was discovered as part of a burial kit of Tomb 192 of the San Vito district in Guardia Perticara, near Potenza (Osanna, Pilo, and Trombetti 2007: 147–53; Bianco 2011; 2018: 92 n. 32). This tomb, excavated in 1998, belonged to a man who was buried with a rich kit that included many items, both ceramic and bronze, imported from Greece and now displayed with the vase (listed in Osanna, Pilo, and Trombetti 2007: 147–8).

Regarding the compositional plan of the Boston vase, the A-side—the side of primary importance—depicts a warrior on the left, recognizable as a female by the light colour of her complexion, riding a lion. She is attacking an intimidating creature on the right, distinguished by a rounded body with a rhomboid pattern (the loss of paint highlights the chessboard effect), the long-eared head of a donkey, and only two legs, both hooved. In the vase's centre stands a tree, spatially separating the warrior and the creature. The painter also included a snake, now barely visible, facing the rider. The she-warrior wears a Phrygian cap and outfit, and is holding a bow, while the monster in front of her, jaws agape, emits a jet of red fire: it promises to be a formidable fight.

The Potenza vase bears the same scene but organized somewhat differently. Again a warrior appears on the A-side, also riding a lion, but on the right; the dark skin colour indicates a male figure. Clad in a Scythian cap and trousers and armed with bow and arrow, he aims at the horrible monster on the left. This time the monster has what appears to be a wolf-head, more tapered than that of the creature on the other vase, but still a rounded body with a rhomboid pattern, though here black decorated with white dots (Osanna 2002: 79; Osanna, Pilo, and Trombetti 2007: 149). The creature again has only two legs, both donkey-like, and, as on the Boston vase, the creature's mouth emits red flames. The same tree separates the two combatants.

A similar rhomboid pattern appears on creatures on other sixth- to fifth-century BCE black-figure skyphoi; these are usually interpreted as representing guinea fowl (*Numida meleagris* L.), whose plumage is dotted with black and white. Possibly, then, for the Boston and Potenza skyphoi, the Theseus Painter adopted a figurative solution already noticeable in contemporary artistic repertoire in that he has combined a known rhomboid feature with other animal-related characteristics, thus obtaining a hybrid monster consisting of recognizable recombined parts. To summarize, the fire-breathing monsters on our two vases appear with the head of a wolf or donkey, the round and tailed body of a guinea fowl (or similar animal) but with only two legs—just as fowl have, but resembling those of an ass rather than a bird.

The B-sides of our two vases also match in their figurative plans, as they represent a roaring lion against four bulls, along with the usual tree dividing the space. Bulls are often depicted by the Theseus Painter and their fight against the lion, which harks back to the struggle on the A-side, is a traditional theme of Archaic Greek poetry (e.g. Homer's similes in *Il.* 5.161–2, 11.172–6; *Od.* 22.402–3).

These 'twin' vases have received considerable attention from scholars, whose interpretations are often discordant. Fritzilas (2006: 1. 11–12) thought that the main scene referred to the mythical fight between the Scythian Arimaspi and griffins over gold, as told by many ancient authors (e.g. Aesch. *PV* 804–7; Hdt. 4.13, 27; Plin. *NH* 7.10). Others, like Osanna (2002: 79) and Mayor (2014: 462 n. 31), saw the warrior as an Amazon fighting against a monster, while still others, including Russo (2000: 45) and Capano (2013: 117), hypothesized Heracles against Empousa or Lamia. But in these two skyphoi the monster has no traits that can be traced back to the well-known iconography of the quadrupedal griffin or to that of the terrible Lamia and Empousa (see Kucharski in this volume). A reasonable alternative could be that such an impressive *monstrum* ('portent', 'monster') was not intended to be connected to a specific tale, but rather stood in a fight scene to convey a meaning related to the use of the pot, in a context influenced by competition and the aspiration to achieve honours. Even identifying the 'hero' creates difficulties: on the one hand, the Theseus Painter derived his name from his preference for depicting Theseus and Heracles, sometimes employing sources lost to us, like the *Heracleis* and *Theseis* of which West (2003: 172–219) and Cingano (2017) speak; on the other, we lack detailed information about the *parerga* ('side adventures') of these two, not to mention the shortage of heroic iconography on the vases, such as the club and lion's skin for Heracles, or a sword and sandals for Theseus (Boardman 1991: 221–8; Batino 2002: 130–6).

Another aspect to consider is the shape of such vessels. The skyphos, unlike the kylix—another type of drinking vessel, but more shallow, and with a raised foot—is usually connected to marginal figures in society, at least judging by the decorated specimens surviving to our time. As Batino (2002: 22–3, 254) noted, the main users of skyphoi were *ephēboi* and *hetairai*, the former being boys up to the age of *c*.18–20, not yet part of the civic body, and the latter being courtesans (see Hornblower and Spawforth 2012; Cadoux and Rhodes 2012). Customary scenes depicted on skyphoi included banquets and sacrifices, so the skyphos turns out to be, in Batino's (2002: 250) words, an 'initiation vase'.

Given this context, we can now suggest interpretations of these twin vases (see Osanna, Pilo, and Trombetti 2007). Both the Potenza and Boston skyphoi could have been parts of burial kits. Both warriors depicted are dressed in Asian style and use the same type of bow, formed by two symmetrical curved sections—all details that identify the warriors as belonging to the margins of the ancient Greek world. At least for the Athenian imaginary, the lion rider could be an alter ego of the ephebe, who stayed at the edges of Attica far from the city for a period of training that constituted a ritual passage devoted to civic initiation before being readmitted to the polis as a full-fledged man (see Vidal-Naquet 1983: 151–74). Moreover, the bow, unlike the spear and the sword, is a distinctive weapon of non-adult warriors and of foreign soldiers as well, such as the Arimaspi, Amazons, Scythians, and other peoples from the East, in contrast to the Greek hoplite fighting, a synergetic light-armed infantry style that prioritized spears, swords, and small shields (Lissarrague 1990; Batino 2002: 186–7).

Even if we cannot be sure whether the warrior is a man or a woman, the meaning connected with the concept of marginality does not vary. In the absence of evidence for one hero rather than another, it is preferable to surmise that the warrior belongs to a people on the fringes of the known world, traditionally populated by monsters and frightening creatures (Doroszewska 2017). Similarly, the choice of a lion as the warrior's steed suggests an even more marked contrast with Greek civilization. Finally, the monster could be read either as an enemy that the warrior defeats during his exploits or as an underworld *daimon*, if one considers the funerary purpose for which the two vases were possibly conceived: recall that the Potenza vase was discovered with a lekythos (an elongated vase type primarily used to hold olive oil) depicting the struggle between Theseus and the Minotaur—a young warrior fighting a monster. The vases' B-side scene featuring a lion against bulls thus provides an equivalent, transferred into the real world, of the fight between man and monster and exemplifies the contrast between *kosmos* ('order', 'culture') and *anomia* ('lawlessness', 'nature').

As the outcomes of the Greek colonization of Southern Italy (Magna Graecia) and local cultures already present there from the eighth to the fifth centuries BCE have yet to be fully explored (see Osanna 2002; Giangiulio 2021: 143–51), we might, as a matter of caution, embrace the second, funerary interpretation of the twin vases, which might prove more congenial to the purposes of the Potenza vase's buyers, who were perhaps unfamiliar with the imagery of Athenian ephebian ritual training. Moreover, as animals linked to sacrifice, bulls are often represented on skyphoi intended for burial (Batino 2002: 207–8).

MONSTERS AND MYTH VARIANTS

Aside from their depictions as primary antagonists, monsters can also appear in relation to mythical variants, as seen on several vases depicting Heracles grappling with a leashed creature, dated between the end of the sixth century BCE and the first half of the fifth.[3] The monster's features are reproduced in various ways, but the illustrations generally emphasize the bristling hair and large size, especially of the head, which is decorated with a band; the contour of the face is feminine. Furthermore, the depictions connote the creature as a fire-breathing quadruped. As our example, we have a skyphos by the Theseus Painter preserved in Copenhagen. Both sides show a figure—most likely Heracles, as suggested by his club—pulling a huge monster out of a cave, of which only the huge head, tied to a rope, is visible (Fig. 24.2). The monster's mouth is wide open, as

FIGURE 24.2 Cryptid on a black-figure skyphos by the Theseus Painter; Side A: Heracles (at right) dragging a monster out of a cave. Copenhagen, The National Museum of Denmark, inv. 834.

Credit: National Museum of Denmark, image reproduced under CC BY-SA licence. Photo by Nora Petersen.

[3] A fragmentary skyphos (Acropolis Museum of Athens 1306: the Theseus Painter), another skyphos from a private collection in Monopoli, Southern Italy (the Theseus Painter), an *oinochoe* (wine jug) in Boston (Museum of Fine Arts, 98.924: the Athena Painter), another *oinochoe* of the same artist in Berlin (Staatliche Museen/Antikensammlung, fr. 1934). All these vases are collected in Reho-Bumbalova (1983), Boudin (2005: 562–5), and Fritzilas (2009).

are its eyes, while its chin, head, and upper body are decorated with thick fur, rendered with hatching.

Given the difficulty of interpreting the composition and the near-total absence of comparable narrations, scholars have proposed various identifications for the monster—from Cerberus, the Sphinx, Lamia, and the 'Monster of Troy' to an underground *daimon* (Reho-Bumbalova 1983: 54–5; Fritzilas 2009: 36; Mayor 2011: 162–3). Alternatively, among other interpretations, the scene could be considered part of Heracles' Labours, fetching Cerberus or another creature from Hades. Basing his conclusion on a careful analysis of ancient depictions and sources, Fritzilas has suggested that these vases, whose iconography might have been invented by the Theseus Painter or his circle, depict the 'Chthonic Gorgon', albeit in an unusual profile and not in the frontal view common to other depictions of gorgons in ancient Greek art (2009, 2010). This monstrous being, whose most detailed accounts are provided by Roman and Byzantine authors, was also locally called *katoblepon* or *katobleps* ('down-looker') and originated from Libya or Ethiopia (Plin. *NH* 8.77; Ael. *NA* 7.5; Eust. *Od.* 1.442.19–28 Stallbaum). Alexander of Myndos (fr. 6 Wellmann) describes this monster as a quadruped covered in fur, resembling an ox or a wild sheep, and having a huge head with terrifying eyes fixed on the ground. Its ability to emit flames from its nostrils, on the other hand, is emphasized by Timotheus of Gaza (*De an.* fr. 53 Haupt). Resuming our previous interpretation, the scenes on these skyphoi are comparable to those on the Boston and Potenza vases—a struggle between *kosmos* and *anomia*, life and death, centre and periphery, along with the anthropological connections stressed above.

Another possible 'second-tier' monster appears on an Apulian red-figure crater kept in Kiel, Germany, dated between 380 and 370 BCE and attributed to the Adolphseck Painter (Schauenburg 1979: 2122; see Fig. 24.3). The scene is commonly read as Heracles, supported by Athena, targeting a Stymphalian bird. The hero is depicted young and naked holding a bow, with his left foot resting on a rock; behind him lie his quiver and lion's skin; the seated goddess has her usual military attributes (helmet, spear, shield). Schauenburg (1979: 21–2), however, raised some concerns, as did Robinson and Robinson (2015–2016: 89), because the Stymphalian Birds are usually represented as waterfowl similar to geese or swans, while here the monster is an extraordinary hybrid creature with a fish's head, bird's wings and body plumage, legs with long claws, and seven barbels on the face. Even the presence of the goddess in this specific labour is problematic, as, though not unheard of, it is highly unusual.

Even if we agree that this scene indeed depicts Heracles' sixth labour, the figurative construction of the cryptid nevertheless has a rightful place among those scenes whose monsters seem to be inspired by fossil finds. The best-known case is undoubtedly that studied by Mayor: a Corinthian crater dating to *c.*560–540 BCE that appears to depict the mythological 'Monster of Troy' as a giant fossil skull eroding out of a rocky outcrop (2011: 157–65). The depiction of monstrous hybrids may well have been influenced by fossils, which are abundant in Southern Italy (Robinson and Robinson 2015–2016). A feature worth dwelling on is the presence of barbels, which appear not only on the

FIGURE 24.3 Cryptid on an Apulian red-figure crater by the Adolphseck Painter, possibly depicting Heracles targeting a Stymphalian bird. Kiel, Antikensammlung, inv. B 537.

Reproduced by permission of the Kiel Antikensammlung.

Kiel vase but also on the Corinthian crater and on a pelike—an elongated vase with side handles and rounded belly—from the Ragusa Collection in Taranto (Lo Porto 1966: 8–9; 1999: 25–6). Lo Porto interpreted that pelike painting as a theatrical scene about Perseus against Cetus.

OTHER CRYPTIDS

Lastly, we examine two vases depicting rather curious creatures. The first is a black-figure Laconian cup, preserved in Cerveteri, Italy, and dated to c.530 (Boardman 2002: 153–4; see Fig. 24.4). It seems to represent Typhoeus, enemy of Zeus and progenitor of many monsters, including Cerberus, the Hydra, and the Chimaera (see Brockliss in this volume). The monster's head, draped in long hair, resembles that of a dog, while the body, covered in scales, gives rise to many bearded snakes. Once again, we have a hybrid monster made up of parts from several real animals. Overall, this representation resembles that of Typhoeus in several written sources, including Hesiod (*Theog.* 820–35) and the mythographer Apollodorus (*Bibl.* 1.39–40). The representation of this monster on an object intended for social occasions could be interpreted as a means of sharing a common mythology.

FIGURE 24.4 Black-figure Laconian cup depicting Typhoeus(?). Cerveteri, Museo Archeologico Nazionale Cerite, inv. 67658.

Credit: © Museo Nazionale Etrusco di Villa Giulia. Archivio fotografico. Reproduced by kind permission of Parco Archeologico di Cerveteri e Tarquinia-Museo Archeologico Nazionale Cerite. Photo by Mauro Benedetti.

While for some cryptids we can propose reasonable explanations, for others solutions remain elusive. One of these cases, a possible reinterpretation of a Greek subject in Southern Italy, involves a bell-shaped red-figure crater by the Dijon Painter, now in Milan (Fig. 24.5). This vase depicts two figures from the procession of Dionysus dancing, both holding thyrsi (pine cone-tipped staffs used in Dionysiac ritual). One, a naked young man, holds a flute in his other hand; he stands in front of a stele (tombstone). The other, a woman, directs her gaze to a curious creature between the two. This small figure, distinguished by a grotesque face, long ears, thickly feathered wings, two legs, and a long, lizard-like tail, is turned towards the woman. In the absence of precise information on the find, Guzzo suggested that the vase belonged to a burial from the second half of the fourth century BCE, but left the question of the monstrous creature unanswered (1997: 395–401). Robinson and Robinson (2015–2016: 89–90), on the other hand, considered an influence from fossil finds, which would have helped shape creatures like this one which appear as part of cult scenes. The vase may have been used in such a context, and the bizarre creature on it may depict a cult statuette, given the static rendering of its pose. Besides that, a possible use in funerary circumstances cannot be excluded a priori, given the presence of the stele, which is reminiscent of similar funerary objects placed on graves, where libations were held in honour of the deceased.

FIGURE 24.5 Red-figure crater by the Dijon Painter; Dionysian scene. Milano, Civico Museo Archeologico, inv. A 1995.03.01.

CONCLUSIONS

Thanks to their extraordinary paintings, these vases present themselves as a gateway to reconsidering the monstrous creatures of local tales and traditions from ancient Greek culture. The value of these objects lies not only in the practical uses to which they were put, but also in the quality and type of their decorations. Many of them still cannot be fully understood, but they allow us to reflect on many different facets of ancient life.

One of the keys that we tried to exploit is the relationship between geographical and cultural centres and edges, or between order and wonder. As Herodotus wrote, 'It seems that the peripheries, which surround all the other lands and limit them inside, have the most beautiful and unusual things according to our thinking' (3.116). Moreover, the artists, and possibly the clients who commissioned some of these scenes, reinterpreted and adapted Greek stories and values according to their own cultural context. Much of what we have discussed in this chapter needs further analysis, but the fact that not everything will be fully comprehensible provides an engaging stimulus not to cease our investigation.

Suggested Reading

While the most complete collections of monsters and cryptids in Greek art are provided by Boardman (2002) and Boudin (2005), who analysed the issue mainly on a cultural and mythological level, for representations of the best-known monsters the reader can turn to the chapters devoted to them in this Handbook. Mayor has written extensively on fossil findings in antiquity (2011) and on Amazons (2014). Robinson and Robinson's (2015–2016) observations about fossils and their role in ancient rituals and stories offer many interesting insights. For a detailed discussion of the skyphos, see Batino's excellent study (2002), which integrates archaeological and anthropological elements. The same approach was adopted by Osanna (2002); Osanna, Pilo, and Trombetti (2007); and Bianco (2018), addressing mainly the context of Southern Italy. On the Theseus Painter, Fritzilas (2006), with detailed commentary and tables, is still indispensable. On the topic of marginality in the ancient world, see Doroszewska (2017).

Works Cited

Batino, S. 2002. *Lo skyphos attico dall'iconografia alla funzione.* Naples.

Bianco, S. 2011. *Enotria: Processi formativi e comunità locali; La necropoli di Guardia Perticara.* Lagonegro.

Bianco, S. 2018. 'Herakles nel mondo italico: L'iconografia della fatica degli uccelli stinfalidi sulla ceramica enotria e messapica', in *L'inesauribile curiosità: Studi in memoria di Gianni Carluccio*, ed. G. Tagliamonte and M. Spedicato, 81–105. Lecce.

Boardman, J. 1991. *Athenian Black Figure Vases: A Handbook*, 2nd edn. London.

Boardman, J. 2002. *The Archaeology of Nostalgia: How the Greeks Re-Created Their Mythical Past.* London.

Boudin, F. 2005. 'Monstres sans image, images de monstres: Représentations et non représentations des monstres sur les vases', in *Dieu(x) et hommes: Histoire et iconographie des sociétés païennes et chrétiennes de l'Antiquité à nos jours*, ed. S. Crogiez-Pétrequin, 537–68. Mont-Saint-Aignan.

Cadoux, T. J., and P. J. Rhodes. 2012. 'Hetairai', in *The Oxford Classical Dictionary*, 4th edn., ed. S. Hornblower, A. Spawforth, and E. Eidinow, 679–80. Oxford.

Capano, A. 2013. 'Il mito e il culto di Eracle/Ercole nella Magna Grecia e nella Lucania antica.' *Basilicata Regione Notizie* 131–2: 92–155.

Cingano, E. 2017. 'Epic Fragments on Theseus: Hesiod, Cercops, and the *Theseis*', in *Fragments, Holes, and Wholes: Reconstructing the Ancient World in Theory and Practice*, ed. T. Derda, J. Hilder, and J. Kwapisz, 309–32. Warsaw.

Doroszewska, J. 2017. 'The Liminal Space: Suburbs as a Demonic Domain in Classical Literature.' *Preternature* 6/1: 1–30.

Fritzilas, S. 2006. *Ο ζωγράφος του Θησέα. Η αττική αγγειογραφία στην εποχή της νεοσύστατης αθηναϊκής δημοκρατίας*, 4 vols. Athens.

Fritzilas, S. 2009. 'Herakles, Athena und Chthonia Gorgo: Mythos und Kunst in den Töpferwerkstätten des Kerameikos in Athen', in *Athenian Potters and Painters*, ed. J. H. Oakley and O. Palagia, 2. 36–47. Oxford.

Fritzilas, S. 2010. *Χθόνια Γοργόνα. Ο μύθος στην ελληνική κεραμική.* Tripoli, Greece.

Giangiulio, M. 2021. *Magna Grecia: Una storia mediterranea.* Rome.

Guzzo, P. G. 1997. 'Oreficerie dalla Puglia', in *Etrusca et Italica: Scritti in ricordo di Massimo Pallottino*, ed. G. Nardi et al., 2. 391–401. Rome.

Hornblower, S., and A. Spawforth. 2012. '*Ephēboi*', in *The Oxford Classical Dictionary*, 4th edn., ed. S. Hornblower, A. Spawforth, and E. Eidinow, 508. Oxford.

Lissarrague, F. 1990. *L'Autre guerrier: Archers, peltastes, cavaliers dans l'imagerie attique*. Paris.

Lo Porto, F. G. 1966. 'Scene teatrali e soggetti caricaturali su nuovi vasi apuli di Taranto'. *Bollettino d'arte* 51: 7–13.

Lo Porto, F. G. 1999. *I vasi italioti della Collezione Ragusa di Taranto*. Rome.

Loxton, D., and D. R. Prothero. 2013. *Abominable Science! Origins of the Yeti, Nessie, and Other Famous Cryptids*. New York.

Mayor, A. 2011. *The First Fossil Hunters: Dinosaurs, Mammoths, and Myth in Greek and Roman Times*, 2nd edn. Princeton.

Mayor, A. 2014. *The Amazons: Lives and Legends of Warrior Women across the Ancient World*. Princeton.

Momigliano, A. 1974. 'Le regole del giuoco nello studio della storia antica'. *Annali della Scuola Normale Superiore di Pisa* 4: 1183–92.

Momigliano, A. 2016. 'The Rules of the Game in the Study of Ancient History', trans. K. W. Yu. *History and Theory* 55: 39–45.

Osanna, M. 2002. 'La ricezione del mito greco nella *mesogaia*: Il mondo enotrio', in *Immagine e mito nella Basilicata antica*, ed. M. L. Nava and M. Osanna, 73–80. Venosa.

Osanna, M., C. Pilo, and C. Trombetti. 2007. 'Brevi note in margine al "margine": Vasi attici dalla necropoli di Guardia Perticara', in *Il vasaio e le sue storie*, ed. S. Angiolillo and M. Giuman, 145–69. Cagliari.

Reho-Bumbalova, M. 1983. 'Un vaso inedito del Pittore di Theseus'. *BABESCH* 58: 53–7.

Robinson, E. G. D., and T. Robinson. 2015–2016. 'Geomythology in Ancient South Italy'. *Mediterranean Archaeology* 28–29: 77–90.

Russo, A. 2000. 'Comunità enotria ed ellenizzazione nel V secolo a.C', in *Nel cuore dell'Enotria: La necropoli italica di Guardia Perticara*, ed. M. L. Nava, 41–6. Rome.

Schauenburg, K. 1979. 'Herakles und Vogelmonstrum auf einem Krater in Kiel'. *Mededelingen van het Nederlands Instituut te Rome* 41: 21–7.

Verbanck-Piérard, A. 2018. 'Round Trip to Hades: Herakles' Advice and Directions', in *Round Trip to Hades in the Eastern Mediterranean Tradition*, ed. G. Ekroth and I. Nilsson, 163–93. Leiden.

Vidal-Naquet, P. 1983. *Le Chasseur noir: Formes de pensée et formes de société dans le monde grec*. Paris.

West, M. L. 2003. *Greek Epic Fragments from the Seventh to the Fifth Centuries BC*. Cambridge, MA.

CHAPTER 25

IMAGE AND MONSTER IN ANCIENT GREEK ART

LORENZ WINKLER-HORAČEK

INTRODUCTION

WHAT role do monsters play in the imagery of the Greeks? Do they only visualize familiar texts and narratives, or do they also have an intrinsic value as images? This chapter examines the extent to which images provide specific meaning to the monsters and the myths associated with them. The historical context is as crucial for interpreting the image as the narrative behind it. The case studies considered here demonstrate a change in the importance of monsters from the Archaic to the Hellenistic periods, with emphasis on the Archaic period.

Let us start by considering a concrete example: Nessus the centaur.[1] On an Attic amphora from the late seventh century BCE, the image on the vessel's neck depicts the fight between a human and a hybrid creature (Fig. 25.1). The latter—let us call it 'monster'—consists of a horse's body as well as a human torso, arms, and head. It moves to the right out of the image field but turns its upper body back with raised arms and grasps the chin of the bearded man to its left in a pleading gesture, typical of suppliants in ancient Greece: touching the person's chin. The latter jumps onto the horse-man's back, threatening him with a drawn sword and grabbing his mop of hair. The man's dynamic leap and the horse-man's pleading gesture create a dramatic effect that suggests a fierce battle and establishes the man as the victor. Inscriptions name the figures: Heracles is fighting the centaur Nessus and is about to kill him. The story behind the image is well known from later literary versions (Gantz 1993: 431–4). Heracles had reached the river Euenus with his wife Deianira and there entrusted her to the centaur Nessus to bring her

---

[1] In keeping with the rest of this volume, Latinate rather than Greek spellings are used for all classical names.

FIGURE 25.1 Proto-Attic amphora by the Nessus Painter, *c.*620–600 BCE; detail from the neck: Heracles fights Nessus.

Source: National Archaeological Museum of Athens. Photo: Wikimedia / Marcus Cyron. CC BY-SA 3.0.

to the other bank. However, Nessus tried to rape Deianira, and the hero intervened and killed the centaur. This scene is set in a remote part of western Greece, where the Euenus flows through Aetolia and Acarnania. The hybrid Nessus dwelt here as a creature of the wild and a ferryman simultaneously. In his uncontrolled impulsiveness, he violated Deianira not only as a woman but also as the bride of Heracles, and thus violated a central institution of the human community: marriage. Heracles punished this offence; the picture reduces the complex story solely to the moment of the fight.

Notably, Heracles here kills Nessus with a sword. In later images and in the literary versions of the myth, he shoots the centaur with an arrow. This has consequences for the story, for it is Heracles' arrow, soaked in the blood of the Lernaean Hydra, that poisons the blood of Nessus. As he bleeds to death, Nessus falsely recommends this life essence to the gullible Deianira as a love potion, but it will in fact later kill Heracles, as the centaur intends. It is therefore curious that the fight is played out with the sword in this image. Because it is one of the earliest visual records of this myth, we can deduce that the story had not yet received its canonical form at the time of the painting's creation. We know of experimentation with imagery from other scenes as well (cf. the Gorgon Medusa as a centaur, Fig. 8.1 in this volume). But there is also another reasonable explanation: the fight with the sword is more heroic and immediate than the long-distance shot with a bow and arrow. The picture is about the direct physical overpowering of the monster in a face-to-face battle, and the painting visualizes this. Perhaps the inscriptions were added to account for the image's deviation from the standard narrative.

MONSTER OR HYBRID CREATURE?

Can we really speak of Nessus as a monster? The term 'monster' is highly charged and has been rejected for many images, especially in German-speaking archaeology, because of its negative character. More neutral is the term *Mischwesen* ('mixed creature'), which at the same time sounds very academic.

But what actually defines a monster? Is it only a creature of evil? Especially in recent decades, parallel to the horror genre, there has been a trivialization of monsters in the imagery of films, calling into question the perpetual 'evil' of the monster: one need only think of animated media like the *Monsters, Inc.* or *Shrek* franchises (2001–present). In the following, 'monster' therefore refers to various forms of hybridity and thus stands synonymously for *Mischwesen*. A monster is a hybrid of two—or even more—separate 'aspects', with reference to its visual form as well as to its purview. Visually, different beings—human and animal, but also human, animal, and plant—are combined in the monster. On a thematic level, however, monsters can also unite other opposites, such as life and death, the real and the fictional, and more. As a mixed creature, the monster especially questions boundaries. At the same time, it can often be localized as an inhabitant of an actual border region. All the figures discussed below live in various liminal zones. As inhabitants of the borderlands, they mark margins within which human and cultural positions and relations must be renegotiated. And therein perhaps lies their actual function. The monster questions the laws of nature as well as those of society (Borgards et al. 2009: 9).

Starting from this definition, let us again look at Nessus the centaur: half human and half animal, he questions the order of nature and the boundary between man and beast. He does this not only through his appearance but also through his actions. On the one hand, Heracles can interact with him as with a human being: Nessus functions as a ferryman, he discusses the crossing with Heracles, and agrees to take Deianira to the opposite shore. However, by attacking Deianira, Nessus gives free rein to his animal instincts. Now he is the animal who seeks to rape the hero's bride. Thus, although one can interact with the centaur as with a human being, he does not abide by human (cultural) rules. This contrast is precisely what his figure visualizes—neither completely human nor completely animal (Hölscher 1998: 61–3; 2000: 291–4).

Humans, too, can violate cultural norms. However, this human transgression of rules is transferred to the half-human monster who, in keeping with his animal element, lives in the wilderness of a border region. In this way, the cultural rule-breaking is 'outsourced'; the breaking of the norm is part of another world in which the hero Heracles must assert himself. The centaur Nessus thus fulfils several criteria we associate with 'monster': in his form, he crosses the boundary between human and animal as well as between real and fictional; through his actions he questions boundaries, in that he disrupts social norms; and, finally, he himself literally inhabits a border region.

The observations about the centaur Nessus can be linked to other centaurs we know from early Greek images: on a skyphos (wine-cup) from the early sixth century BCE in Paris, Heracles drives a whole crowd of wild centaurs out of a cave. Here, however, we also see the centaur Pholus, who, in contrast to Nessus, does not break human cultural norms. He is standing in front of a table and a large mixing vessel, holding a kantharos (another type of wine-cup) in his hand (Paris, Louvre MNC 677: Payne 1931: no. 941 pl. 31, 10). The contextual background of this painting involves Heracles' fourth labour. Heracles roamed the remote regions of Arcadia in search of the Erymanthian Boar and was hospitably received by Pholus in his cave. The wine-vessel in the picture points to this hospitality as well as to the *symposion* (common banquet) and thus to a 'central, religiously protected institution of Archaic male society' (Hölscher 2000: 291).[2] Attracted by the smell of wine, the other centaurs burst out of the surrounding forests and mountains and disturbed the banquet. Their animalistic instincts and excessive intemperance—consuming amounts of wine far beyond the usual norms—turned them into beasts. Heracles drove them out of the cave, drew his bow, and killed many of them. This slaughter is shown on a Corinthian ointment vessel from the mid-seventh century BCE (Fig. 25.2). Heracles kneels with a drawn bow and arrow amid the crowd of centaurs. Their full human bodies have already partly collapsed and are supported only by their animal limbs. The arrows also pierce these, with blood flowing from the wounds. With the last of their strength, the centaurs still hold the stylized branches in their hands, with which they hopelessly try to defend themselves. Their animal character is visualized not only by the horse's hind body but also by the painted strokes on the human body, which suggest a hairy coat. As with Nessus, the violation of a social norm is projected into the frontier regions of the wilderness—the disturbance of the banquet, the negation of hospitality, and the uncontrolled craving for wine—and is horribly punished by the hero.

---

[2] All translations of Hölscher (1998; 2000), Borgards et al. (2009), and Langner (2012) are my own.

FIGURE 25.2 Heracles fights the centaurs of the Pholoe Mountains.
Late Proto-Corinthian aryballos. Berlin Antikensammlung 2686 (F336). Photo after Adolf Furtwängler, 'Kentaurenkampf und Löwenjagd auf zwei archaischen Lekythen', AZ 41,1883, 153–162 Taf. 10.

Credit: © Antikensammlung, Staatliche Museen zu Berlin—Preussischer Kulturbesitz.

The Thessalian Centauromachy, as seen on the so-called François Vase from the early sixth century BCE, can be interpreted in a very similar way.[3]

Regarding the centaurs' hybridity, it is worth briefly noting that some centaurs have a complete human body to which the horse's hindquarters are merely attached, as on the Berlin aryballos (Fig. 25.2). Nessus, on the other hand, appears on the Proto-Attic amphora (Fig. 25.1) as having a horse body, with all four legs, that merges with a human upper body. During the seventh century BCE, both representations occur in parallel and cannot be assigned to specific centaurs or scenes (Padgett 2003: 10–14). On the Berlin aryballos, however, it is notable that, for all the centaurs, it is their human body rather than the horse-element that is pierced by arrows and collapsing. In Greek art after the seventh century BCE, the organic connection of the horse's body with the human torso, head, and arms becomes established.

Yet not all centaurs behaved like animals and were uncivilized: Chiron educates the great future heroes like Peleus and Achilles while Pholus receives Heracles for a meal, and it is precisely in them that the contradictory relationship between nature and culture coalesces. Although Chiron lives in the wilderness, he plays an essential role in the youths' education and rites of passage. Moreover, Pholus also take part in acts of human culture such as the *symposion*. They therefore hardly correspond to our contemporary ideas of the monstrous. Perhaps this is also a form of transgressing boundaries and part of their nature—even the monster is ultimately not exclusively 'good' or 'evil' in the sense of behaving like a civilized human or not.

In the images of the seventh century BCE, however, the 'civilized' centaurs are initially less present. The battles of Heracles against one or more savage centaurs, on the other hand, are among the earliest mythical images in Greek art. Statistically, they are also among the most frequent narrative images in the seventh century BCE. This theme is

---

[3] http://www.hellenicaworld.com/Greece/Art/Ancient/en/Francois.html. Accessed 25 August 2022.

thus particularly present in a period in which narrative images first began to appear in Greece.

EARLY IMAGES

In the eighth century BCE, figurative representations appeared in Greek art—especially in vase-painting—for the first time since the Bronze Age (*c*.3000–1000 BCE), when such representations were common in Minoan and Mycenaean art. The images expressed the new need for the representation of a now socially differentiated society. Accordingly, the earliest paintings show people in scenes of sociocultural activity such as war, seafaring, funeral rites, or other festive activities. In addition, the first monster fights also emerge in this period; one example is a scene on a bowl from Anavyssos, where a small man with a sword stands between the open mouths of two creatures with dangerous teeth (Fig. 25.3). The scene has usually been described as a 'lion fight' (Fittschen 1969: 76), but these 'lions' have the hooves and hind legs of bulls. It is a hybrid of bull and lion that threatens man in this case. Between the mouths of the giant monsters, the man seemingly struggles, threatened with the prospect of being devoured. Parallel to the aforementioned models of sociocultural action, the existential threat to humankind from the creatures of a hostile wilderness is expressed here. The monsters must be defeated to defend human culture.

FIGURE 25.3 Lion-like monsters threaten a man with a sword and lance. Late Geometric Attic bowl from Anavyssos. Athens, National Museum 14475.

Photo: Drawing by Konrad Eyferth © Lorenz Winkler-Horaček.

The anonymous monster (or lion) fights are quite open in their outcome for humans and can show them in a desperate situation. However, these images soon disappear and are replaced by clearly nameable mythical images from the early seventh century BCE. It is a decisive change: for now, the hero defeats the monster, albeit sometimes in existential struggles.

In the seventh century BCE, an extensive repertoire of scenes develops that we can associate with well-known mythological tales: Heracles against the centaurs or the Lernaean Hydra, Perseus against the Gorgon, Bellerophon against the Chimaera, Theseus against the Minotaur, and Odysseus against Polyphemus. A glance at the entirety of the myth images of the seventh century BCE, only roughly sketched here, proves a strong dominance of monster fighting in this era. More than half of the surviving myth images show one of the hero's battles against either a wild animal (such as the Nemean Lion) or a monster. There are an identifiable five heroes who overcome a total of seven types of monstrous creatures and thus enjoy astonishing quantitative popularity as images. All other myth images of the seventh century BCE extant today account for less than half (for the still provisional evaluation of the myth images of the seventh century BCE: Winkler-Horaček 2015: 374–5).

The fight against the various monsters is thus a central theme among the myth images of the seventh century BCE. This thematic popularity can be transferred—if we include wild animals such as the Nemean Lion and others—to the early sixth century BCE, but it is not yet statistically verified here. What seems decisive is that with the end of the sixth century BCE, the number of mythological monster fights, measured in percentage distribution, decreases again significantly, suggesting that the pictorial theme is tied to a specific historical situation. In light of these circumstances, the images of Heracles fighting the centaurs also unfold their specific meaning.

Myths, Monsters, Images

Following a research thread, myths and myth images are considered here as having an identity-forming role. Myths are relevant at the moment they are told or depicted, and they have a collective meaning for the self-definition of groups for which or in which they are told or represented as images. 'Groups' can mean various things: a society as a whole, a state, a city, a family, a social class, and many more. In short, myths are stories of the past that are significant for the present. 'Their effect is based on the fact that they provide communities and individuals with "orientation about themselves and the world", make "normative claims", and develop "formative power"' (Hölscher, unpublished, quoted in Winkler-Horaček 2015: 374, 464 n. 1531). Thus, myths should be interpreted from the historical context in which they were told, depicted, or otherwise disseminated.

There is a close overlap here with the role and meaning of the monster. The monster, too, must be understood from the respective culture in which it is constructed. Each appearance in literature and art refers to the symbolic order of a society, which is differently developed and dependent on deviating historical external conditions. The monster is not a natural given to which culture reacts; 'as an imaginary figuration, it rather arises from the productive power of a cultural design.... It serves as a regulative fiction' (Borgards et al. 2009: 10; cf. Atherton 2002: x).

And the image? It decisively shapes our collective perception. When we hear or read a story, landscapes, characters, and even monsters appear before our inner eye. A narrated story, whether transmitted orally or written down, can never be so precise that it leaves us no room for our own imagination. Moreover, the narrator can also omit details without his story suffering. He can describe bloodthirsty teeth, but what do the ears look like? Whether we learn anything about them or must fill in the blanks ourselves is the narrator's decision. With the image, however, the situation is different. Here there is a compulsion to be concrete: the artist (let us call him that) must commit himself. He must decide how tall his figure is, what colour it has, what ears, nose, and mouth. Moreover, if necessary, he must also define the monstrous abnormalities. He gives the figure a form that does not have to be specified in the spoken or written version. This compulsion to be concrete has immediate consequences. If an image is successful in a social group, it displaces individual ideas. It thus has the power of collective persuasion. This applies to the appearance of a monster as well as to the chosen moment in which the story is distilled in the picture. The image shapes the monster, but also gives the story its own meaning through the choice of scene.

Monster and Polis

As illustrated above, the myth images of the seventh century BCE often show the moment when the hero overcomes the monster. The narratives, some of which are highly complex, are reduced to this one instant. What does this mean in the historical context?

From the eighth century BCE onwards, new social structures developed in Greece. Small self-sufficient settlements, known as *poleis* (*polis*, singular), emerged. These were 'spaces of one's own community and culture demarcated from a foreign "outside"' (Hölscher 1998: 57). This demarcation occurred not only in the real world but also on an ideal level. Here, the heroes of the mythical past acted as role models for the present. The ideal space of the polis consisted of a central settlement and the surrounding fertile land. This area was surrounded by the so-called *eschatia*, an imaginary wilderness representing a fictional borderland, a spatial disposition found as early as Homer's description of the shield of Achilles (*Il.* 18.478–608). The culture of the polis was constituted as the antithesis of an imaginary, uncultivated world outside. The contrast to nature or the wilderness had a constitutive effect on the culturally defined community. Myths reflected this process and drew their relevance from it. Heroes wander the imaginary space of the wilderness and overcome the incomprehensible, the hybrid, the non-standard in the form of monsters. The battles of the centaurs, in particular, show how much they defend the rules of culture in this way. These are close to humans, but they break the community's rules and become the antithesis of civilization through their behaviour.

A large number of monster images are closely linked to the historical process of establishing the Greek polis as a cultural space. However, this is not the only reason, as we shall see.

Monsters in the Distance

Many mythological monsters in the images of the seventh and early sixth centuries BCE are fought not in Greece but at the edges of the known world. Bellerophon kills the monstrous Chimaera in far-off Lycia in Asia Minor; Perseus defeats the Gorgons far to the west (or north); and Odysseus blinds the monster Polyphemus in a fantastical mythological space in the western Mediterranean. Tonio Hölscher defined two spaces of strangeness and borderline experiences in his schematic world view of the early Greek period: the *eschatia* in the immediate vicinity of the polis and the *eschatia* at the edge of the world. He convincingly linked the latter to one of the most fundamental experiences of this epoch: the expansion of geographic space since the eighth century BCE through Greek colonization. 'This was, in addition to the limited space of the individual *polis*, a second larger space in which the then rising Greek culture was constituted and experienced. These experiences apparently found expression in a group of myths that gained particular topicality in this epoch' (Hölscher 1998: 64). Among them are those myths of the battles against monsters at the edge of the world. The cultural dimension of a monster fight can be seen very well in a picture of an amphora from Eleusis, dated to *c.*680–670 BCE, as described below.

Polyphemus as a Counter-Image

The painting on the neck of the amphora shows the blinding of the Cyclops Polyphemus (Fig. 25.4). He sits at the edge of the picture, holding a kantharos in his right hand, and with his left, he grasps a staff which is being thrust into his only eye by three people. His open mouth reflects the horror of this act. The three much smaller figures line up one behind the other, holding the long staff above their heads with both arms. The foremost figure leans on Polyphemus' knee with his own bent left knee to give the thrust more force. The scene is clearly identifiable even without inscriptions: Odysseus, with two of his companions, blinds the one-eyed and monstrously large Cyclops Polyphemus.

The *Odyssey* tells us the story. On his journey home from Troy, Odysseus and his crew are caught in a storm that carries him to a distant world. This world may be part of the

FIGURE 25.4 Proto-Attic amphora (the 'Eleusis' amphora) by the Polyphemus Painter, *c.*680–670 BCE. On the neck: Odysseus and his men blinding the Cyclops. On the belly: Gorgons pursuing Perseus.

western Mediterranean, but also serves as a fantastic space where Odysseus encounters numerous monsters and hybrid beings. Polyphemus is just one of them. The one-eyed giant lives in this land, in a rather loose community with other Cyclopes. The poem describes it as an idyllic realm, for everything flourishes and grows there without much effort. It is a paradise for the weary sailors and happiness for the Cyclopes, for they do not have to do anything:

> [The Cyclopes] plant nothing with their hands nor plough;
> but all these things spring up for them without sowing or ploughing,
> wheat, and barley, and vines, which bear the rich clusters of wine,
> and the rain of Zeus gives them increase.
>
> (Hom. *Od.* 9.108–11, trans. Murray)

The Cyclopes, in their paradisiacal landscape, are skilled at herding goats but are otherwise incapable of much of what constitutes civilized human society. Homer emphasizes that they 'know not councils nor laws' and live on their island 'on tops of high mountains in hollow grottos' (9.112–13). The island's fertility thus contrasts with the uncultivated behaviour of its monstrous inhabitants. When Odysseus asks Polyphemus for hospitality, the Cyclops traps him and his companions in the cave and begins to eat them two at a time. To illustrate the contrast with human behaviour, Homer compares Polyphemus to a lion of the rocky mountains. This is not meant as a heroic parable, but as a description of the brutality of the wilderness:

> Then he cut them limb from limb and made ready his supper,
> and ate them as a mountain-nurtured lion, leaving naught—
> ate the entrails, and the flesh, and the marrowy bones.
>
> (9.291–3)

Polyphemus violates a whole series of civilizing norms from the Greek point of view by disregarding the custom of hospitality, eating people, and—not to be underestimated— drinking wine in an unmixed state and in complete immoderation: Odysseus offers Polyphemus wine to go with the human flesh, aware that the latter was *un*aware of its effects. The Cyclopes produce wine, but, as Polyphemus remarks (9.357–9), the Greek wine is far superior. Drunk, Polyphemus falls asleep, and the poem emphasizes his uncivilized nature once more: 'pieces of human flesh burst from his throat with wine, which the snoring drunkard vomited out' (9.73–4). He is thus at the mercy of Odysseus, who blinds his only eye, as the vase illustrates.

The story in Homer's narrative is more than just a monster fight; it is the struggle for cultural norms at the edge of the world that must be defended against the 'Other', the monstrousness of the Cyclops. In the picture, the complex story is reduced to the moment of the blinding; the kantharos in the Cyclops' hand also hints at his drunkenness. Almost like a caricature, the picture thus exaggerates Odysseus' trickery and Polyphemus' lack of adherence to the expected rules.

CATEGORIES

The amphorae depicting Nessus and Polyphemus also include yet another monster encounter: Perseus' flight from the Gorgons. According to the myth, Perseus had been tasked with fetching the head of the Gorgon Medusa, whose gaze petrified anyone who met it. With help from the gods, Perseus was able to cut off her head, but then had to flee from her immortal sisters, the Gorgons. This episode also takes place on the fringes of the world; depending on the myth variant, the Gorgons lived either on a remote island or to the far north. On the Polyphemus vase, we see the immortal sisters of the Gorgon Medusa pursuing the hero—in vain—after his deed (Fig. 25.4). On their human bodies sits a grimacing head framed by snakes, in which various animal elements are grotesquely combined. They look directly at the viewer of the vase and thus have a disturbing effect. The Gorgons are arguably the ugliest and most horrible monsters of the Greeks (see below). Unlike the centaurs or Polyphemus, you cannot even talk to them. They are incapable of communication and are therefore inhuman.

Comparing the Gorgons, Polyphemus, and the centaurs illustrates that there are different categories of monsters. They differ first of all in their physical composition, but also in their respective ability to communicate. The following categories can therefore be distinguished:

1. Monsters whose human features predominate or at least make up half of their body: the centaurs have the head, upper body, and arms of a human being. Thus, they can act almost like humans. The Cyclopes are also predominantly human, only increased to giant-scale. These monsters, especially the centaurs, basically have nascent cultures of their own and thus resemble human communities. However, they do not exploit their human characteristics or are prevented from doing so by their uncontrolled instincts. Their monstrousness lies not only in their form but also in their behaviour.

2. Monsters made of predominantly animal elements with few human features: these include versions of sphinxes and sirens, whose bodies predominantly consist of various animal elements, only with a human head—a feature which allows them to communicate but in a more limited fashion than the centaurs or Cyclopes. They talk or sing to humans but otherwise hardly interact with them. The Sphinx of the Theban myth lives in the *eschatia* near Thebes and kills passing wanderers who cannot solve her riddle, until Oedipus succeeds in doing so and thus defeats her. The Sirens of the *Odyssey* live on a distant island and lure sailors to ruin with their song. Only Odysseus and his men are able to escape, thanks to advice from the goddess Circe. Through their human heads, the Sphinx and the Sirens can address humans, but they are not involved in any further human interactions. Accordingly, they do not violate cultural norms in the same manner that Polyphemus and the centaurs do. They are much more fundamentally connected to the *eschatia* and

are distant from humans. Furthermore, among the few monsters of Greece that combine a human body with an animal or animal-like head are the Gorgons and the Minotaur. Their often-idealized human bodies enhance the contrast with their monstrous faces. In their lack of communication skills, however, they correspond to the monsters from the following, third category, which evade any reference to human culture and verbal communication.

3. Monsters consisting exclusively of various animal elements: these include the Chimaera (lion, goat, snake), the Hydra (many-headed serpent), griffins (lion, bird of prey), as well as the countless non-mythologically fixed and thus unnamed hybrid creatures from ancient animal friezes like griffin-birds (body of a water-bird, head of bird of prey), panther-birds (body of a bird, head of a panther), or goat-birds (body of a bird, head of a goat). They are pure natural elements. As far as we can grasp them mythologically, they too are fought by the heroes. Bellerophon kills the Chimaera and Heracles the Lernaean Hydra. The griffins, who defend a treasure of gold against the one-eyed Arimaspi in distant lands beyond the Scythians, are a unique case.

Monsters and Animal Friezes

Coinciding with the popularity of mythical monster fights in the imagery of the seventh and early sixth centuries BCE, another theme dominates Greek vases: endless rows of animals, plants, and monsters. Many of these motifs were adopted from the Near East during the orientalizing period of Greek art in the seventh century BCE (Winkler-Horaček 2015).

The Corinthian animal friezes exhibit a remarkable phenomenon: in them, the animals and hybrid creatures are arranged in a particular order. Paratactic rows are interrupted by antithetic groups in which stronger animals flank weaker ones. These groups express a hierarchy of the animal world, including monsters. They are primarily those from the above-mentioned categories 2 and 3: sphinxes, sirens, griffin-lions, panther-birds, etc. The positions of the monsters correspond to their body. *Mischwesen* with lion bodies are aligned with dangerous predators such as lions or panthers in their position in the frieze, and mixed creatures with bird bodies correspond most closely to the peaceful waterfowl (Winkler-Horaček 2015: 287–99). This strict categorization of hybrid creatures in the hierarchy of the animal world is limited to the Corinthian vases—in other landscapes, the syntax of the friezes is structured differently—but is at the same time widespread throughout Greece due to the Corinthian exports. The categorization of creatures according to their bodies is also confirmed in the animal battle groups. Here, lions attack sirens and thus monsters with bird bodies (Fig. 25.5), while sphinxes with their lion bodies attack wild goats like lions (Fig. 25.6). This is a taxonomy of the animal world in which the strange and uncanny elements become part of an order

FIGURE 25.5 Lion attacks human bird with raised paw; Early Corinthian olpe. Rennes, Musée des Beaux-Arts et d'Archéologie D.08.2.2.

Photo: Drawing by Paul Giraud © Lorenz Winkler-Horaček.

FIGURE 25.6 Two sphinxes attack a wild goat with raised paws; fragment of an eastern Greek vessel (Milesian). Bucharest, Nationalmuseum.

Photo: Drawing by Paul Giraud © Lorenz Winkler-Horaček.

together with the known animals. The images of the animal friezes thus fulfil a similar function to the myth images in which the heroes defeat the monsters. Through this taxonomy, the monsters lose something of their uncanny incomprehensibility and are integrated into a value system.

Given the images of this taxonomy, the civilized world's cultural norms develop in a very immediate physical sense. Those vases painted with the animal friezes were primarily used in socially relevant situations and rituals such as the *symposion*, worship, celebrations of the dead, wedding ceremonies, or as containers for valuable oils and ointments. Cultural action thus took place directly in the face of an ordered animal world in which the monstrous and alien elements were integrated.

In the sixth century BCE, the animal friezes diminish and finally almost disappear from the imagery. As a temporally conditioned phenomenon, they are therefore completely bound to the historical processes mentioned above and are also an expression of a confrontation with the marginal zones of the world against the background of which Greek culture was formed. With the establishment of Greek polis society and the end of colonization, these images lose their significance.

ARE MONSTERS BECOMING HUMAN?

In the late sixth century BCE, the number of monster fights depicted in Greek art also decreases. Let us look again at the centaurs: in addition to the well-known fights, the positive behaviour of Pholus and Chiron now appears more strongly in the pictures, and with it, the individual in his ability to make decisions. Themes include Pholus' hospitality towards Heracles (cf. black-figure neck amphora c.520–510 BCE from the Shelby White and Leon Levy Collection; see Padgett 2003: 174–6), and the learned and wise Chiron, who acts as an educator to numerous heroes. 'The mixed figure of the centaur is thus also understood for the first time as a disposition of character in which either the humane or the animal side can triumph' (Langner 2012: 244). Although the negative side is still inherent in the centaur, it can be controlled. And it is precisely through this self-control that the centaur can also become a positive role model.

The humanization of the centaurs continued in the fifth century BCE. Ancient written sources tell us that the painter Zeuxis created a famous illustration of a centaur family in the late fifth century BCE (Lucian, *Zeuxis* 3–7; Morawietz 2000: 41–2; Langner 2012: 246–7; see also Aston in this volume). The centaur is suckling two of her young, one at her human breast and the other at her equine equivalent. Next to it, a centaur laughingly holds up a lion he has hunted. Humanity is shown here next to animal elements; the wilderness is an idyll full of joie de vivre. These natural states of happiness increasingly shift to the realms of the gods Dionysus and Aphrodite. The wildness of the centaur finds its place in the Dionysian realm, and here it is integrated into the sacred space and fulfils a function: for in 'every Greek man there was latently a centaur, animalistically vital, intoxicating and sexually encroaching.' Greek culture did not eliminate these forces, it controlled them and gave them a mythologically-religiously defined space, the cult of Dionysus (Hölscher 2000: 294).

For example, take a marble statue in Paris that shows an elderly centaur. He holds his arms behind his back in a bound posture (Fig. 25.7). Eros sits on the horse's body and grasps at the centaur's head with his left hand. The centaur turns with a pain-distorted face to Eros, to whose power he has obviously fallen prey. All must bow to this little god of love—gods, men, and even the centaurs. This Roman statue is a copy of a

FIGURE 25.7   Statue of an Eros on a centaur. Cast: Abguss-Sammlung Antiker Plastik der Freien Universität Berlin, inv. 39/00. Original: Paris, Louvre MA 562.

Photo: © Abguss-Sammlung Antiker Plastik der Freien Universität Berlin.

second-century BCE Hellenistic original (see Morawietz 2000: 89–120), and reflects how, especially in Hellenistic times, the suffering of love, as brought about by Eros, is particularly thematized. The interaction of wine and love can also have painful consequences. Thus, the brutal and encroaching monster becomes a tormented and suffering lover.

Nevertheless, the centaur always remains both: a brutal and animalistic counter-image to civilization and part of a Dionysian idyll. The images of the centaurs again take on a clearly negative connotation under the influence of the Persian Wars at the beginning of the fifth century BCE: the mythical battle of the Lapiths against the centaurs is equated with the historical battles of the Greeks against their external enemies. After the severe devastation of Athens by the Persians (480–479 BCE), the uncivilized centaurs functioned as a mythological example of barbarian misbehaviour, as attributed to the Persians. Accordingly, centaur fights appear frequently on large public buildings later in the fifth century, especially on the southern metopes of the Parthenon. The equation of the centaurs with the 'barbarian' enemies of the Greeks is also reflected in their physiognomy. Age indications, straggly shaggy hair, violent movements, and features of savagery in the otherwise human facial expressions correspond to the means of expressing a barbarian iconography (Langner 2012: 245 and nn. 9–10). However, Martin Langner has also pointed out that only the centaurs' humanization made it possible to equate them with the Persians, who were seen as defeated barbarians. This defamation of the enemy through the image of the centaurs thus in no way contradicts the gradual humanization of the monsters.

Monsters and Beauty

Centaurs are not the only monsters to be humanized over the centuries. Sirens, too, are increasingly given human arms and, like sphinxes, female breasts, with their heads becoming those of beautiful women (*LIMC*, s.vv. 'Seirenes', 'Sphinx'). The change is most striking in the image of the Gorgons. On the belly of the Polyphemus amphora, for example, two Gorgons' giant heads stare out at the viewer, and all their features are distorted into a grimacing mask with animalistic features (Fig. 25.4). The images of the Gorgons, especially Medusa, are the utmost in terrifying ugliness that Greek art has produced (Vernant 1985, 1991; Hölscher 2019). She radiates death from her eyes. The petrification resulting from her glare is the extreme extinction of life. Thus, the Gorgon becomes the symbol of all deterrence: the head—known as the *gorgoneion* after being cut off by Perseus—adorns not only the aegis of the warlike goddess Athena but also temples and other buildings (see Oswald in this volume). The *gorgoneion*, with its apotropaic function, protects many other culturally significant objects against desecration by sacrilegious people and destruction by enemies.

In the Classical period (fourth to fifth centuries BCE), however, the face of the Gorgon also became humanized. For example, Roman copies of a Gorgon's head attributed to the Classical sculptor Phidias—the so-called Medusa Rondanini—show it as a beautiful female head (Munich, Glyptothek 252: Vierneisel-Schlörb 1979: 62–7).[4] The threatening snakes, wild hair, and wings frame an aestheticized face, which in its idealized form corresponds to the contemporary conception of man during the Greek Classical period. Only the slightly open mouth, revealing her teeth, hints at the animalistic threat. Tonio

---

[4] https://en.wikipedia.org/wiki/File:Rondanini_Medusa_Glyptothek_Munich_252_n1.jpg. Accessed 25 August 2022. The attribution to Phidias and to an original from the 5th century has also been questioned in research.

Hölscher has separated the effect of terror from the beauty of appearance, pointing out that the larger-sized sculptures were especially intended for consecration in sanctuaries or to be placed in tombs and given as gifts to honour the gods and the dead. Therefore, the beauty of the form is independent of the potential negative evaluation of the image's subject. It is shaped solely by the pictorial work's social, cultural, and artistic rank (Hölscher 2019: 184). The Gorgon remains terrible even if she is beautiful, and as artfully staged as she may be, she makes violence and murder present through the image in an immediate sense.

THE CONQUEST OF THE WORLD

With the conquests of Alexander the Great in the fourth century BCE, the images of monsters and hybrid creatures take on renewed relevance. It is the first significant geographical expansion of space from a Greek perspective since the colonization movements of the eighth to sixth centuries BCE. Once again, the Greeks infiltrate un-known frontier regions where wondrous things happen and fantasy and reality mix. The purely fictional letter of Alexander to Aristotle—written much later—reports on Alexander the Great's journey to Bactria and India and finally beyond the borders of the inhabited world (Koulakiotis 2008). According to this narrative, Alexander encounters zones of transgression during his campaign at the edge of the world, where the order of things and thus also the separation of humans, animals, and plants dissolve. Here, the *kynokephaloi* (dog-headed men, mentioned by earlier sources such as Herodotus and Ctesias) appear, but also—depending on which of the several versions one reads[5]— snakes with emeralds embedded in their skin, trees that speak Greek and Indic, and various hybrid creatures such as mermaids, chimaeras, and griffins (Koulakiotis 2008: 424–6). Even though the text was written centuries after Alexander's conquests, it describes an alien and hybrid-infested zone at the edge of the world associated with Alexander's advance. As in the times of colonization, the monsters are reactivated.

One of the best-known representations of an extensive geographical area is the Nile mosaic from Palestrina (ancient Praeneste; Fig. 25.8). Originally laid out on the floor in a public complex next to the sanctuary of Fortuna Primigenia in Latium (Italy), it is considered one of the best-preserved ancient representations of a Nilotic landscape. Even though this is a Late Republican Roman context (the work probably dates to the late second century BCE), the inscriptions on the mosaic are in Greek. Joshua J. Thomas (2021) has made it clear that the mosaic is probably based on a painting of the third century BCE from the immediate environment of Ptolemaic Alexandria. The depic-tion of Egypt here is not only informative, but also demonstrates a very objective and

---

[5] Translations of this spurious letter from Alexander to Aristotle, which was originally composed in Greek, include versions in Latin, Old English, and Middle English, all written centuries apart and all containing slightly different descriptions of the fabulous sights and creatures Alexander encountered.

FIGURE 25.8 Nile mosaic from Palestrina, late second century BCE. Museo Nazionale di Palestrina, Italy.

Source: Wikimedia / Yann Forget.

partly scientific approach to a large geographical area. The picture in fact reflects not only geographical but also cartographic, ethnographic, and zoological interests (see also Hinterhöller 2009).

In the mosaic's upper register, the depiction of Egypt merges into a mountainous landscape full of wild and exotic animals. These are the southern border regions of Nubia and possibly Ethiopia. Thomas links these images to Ptolemaic foreign policy in the third century BCE, which culminated, among other things, in a military campaign in 275 BCE. This campaign served both to explore the territory south of Egypt and to import elephants and other exotic animals to Alexandria. We see many wild animals in the mosaic, such as flamingos, lions, giraffes, and lizards, but also quite fantastic creatures. All these animals and 'monsters' are given names, blurring the boundaries between real animals and (imaginary) hybrid creatures. A rather fantastic hybrid of a big cat and crocodile is called a land crocodile (*krokodilos chersaios*) and lies next to two cheetahs (labelled as *tigris*), a baboon (labelled *sattuos*), and a kind of bear (labelled *drkos*). Another mixture of crocodile and cat—in this case panther—is called *krokodilopardalis*, and the mixture of human and animal appears in a figure with the body of what seems to be a donkey, combined with a female head to form an *onokentaura*—but which also roughly resembles a sphinx (see Thomas 2021: 71–82).

These strange and imaginary creatures have no meaning in the sense of a narrative structure. They do, however, show us the extent to which the Greeks and Romans still thought of the foreign border regions as populated with hybrid creatures, and how this thinking also inspired scientific discourse. The classification and taxonomy also underlie an important ideological valence of the images: through them, the power of the Ptolemaic king and successor of Alexander the Great, which was also geographically far-reaching, is visualized and communicated (Thomas 2021: 115). Thus, they are part of an authentication strategy and proof that the king really rules these foreign regions.

CONCLUSION

In their interpretation, the images of monsters are tied to historical situations. As mythical images, they play an identity-forming role, whether as part of the development of Greek poleis and the confrontation with the unknown peripheries of the world, as a visualization of enemies, or as an externalization of human misbehaviour. They stand for the uncivilized and hostile, but are not limited to this: the case of the centaurs also shows the ambivalent attitude toward 'monsters'.

Many of the monsters symbolize different borderlands. In the phases of Greek expansion—the colonization of the eighth to early sixth centuries BCE and again after the conquests of Alexander the Great—they reflect extreme spatial borderline experiences. Here, alien animals and monsters 'prove' the presence of the distant frontiers. Overcoming the monsters thus becomes a sign of human dominance over these territories, as expressed in mythical imagery as well as in various taxonomies of the Archaic and Hellenistic periods. The animal friezes on Corinthian vases are based on a wish to categorize similar to the naming of foreign animals and monsters in Ptolemaic Egypt. Assigning the monster to an order overcomes the incomprehensibility of the hybrid form.

The image defines the form of the monster, even if it is a hybrid one. Myths and images, moreover, also determine the space of the monster. This visual, spatial, and temporal determination fundamentally distinguishes physical and behavioural monsters from daimonic spirits, such as ghosts of the restless dead. The terror caused by the latter lies precisely in their lack of form and their spatial omnipresence. However, the images of monsters can also spread fear, as is especially evident in the example of the Gorgon Medusa and the *gorgoneion*. Nevertheless, such horror can be harnessed. Defeated and overcome, the *gorgoneion* protects its owner, as do depictions of lions or sphinxes. As *apotropaia*, the images of monsters and wild animals take on an immediate presence.

SUGGESTED READING

The question as to the definition of a monster may well vary in different languages. See the anthologies by Atherton (2002) and Borgards et al. (2009). On the written sources for the mythological narratives of many monster tales, a good overview can be found in Gantz (1993). Hölscher has also demonstrated the social relevance of images in various works, and his writings on early Greece also deal with the relationship between myths and the idea of spaces (Hölscher 1998). In a recent English-language publication, Hölscher deals less with the myths and more with the relationship between space, action, and images, or between images and identity (Hölscher 2018). Regarding images of the individual hybrid beings, a well-illustrated and detailed overview is provided by Padgett (2003). On the centaurs, the work by Morawietz (2000)—currently only in German—is also very helpful; on the Gorgon, see Vernant (1991). Corresponding articles on all mythological hybrid beings can also be found in the *LIMC*: even though its texts are very academic, this encyclopaedia offers a wealth of images that are still not readily available online. On the role of animal friezes and monsters more generally in early Greek art, as well as their relationship to the models of the Near East, see Winkler-Horaček (2015: esp. 628–38). Other interpretations of the animal friezes and the meaning of sphinxes and sirens can be found in Petit (2011) and Böhm (2020). Finally, the recent work of Thomas (2021) has also dealt with the relation of animals and hybrid creatures in the political and scientific discourse of Hellenism.

WORKS CITED

Atherton, C., ed. 2002. *Monsters and Monstrosity in Greek and Roman Culture*. Bari.

Böhm, S. 2020. *Sphingen und Sirenen im archaischen Griechenland: Symbole der Ambivalenz in Bildszenen und Tierfriesen*. Regensburg.

Borgards, R., C. Holm, and G. Oesterle. eds. 2009. *Monster: Zur ästhetischen Verfassung eines Grenzbewohners*. Würzburg.

Fittschen, K. 1969. *Untersuchungen zum Beginn der Sagendarstellungen bei den Griechen*. Berlin.

Gantz, T. 1993. *Early Greek Myth: A Guide to Literary and Artistic Sources*, 2 vols. Baltimore.

Hinterhöller, M. 2009. 'Das Nilmosaik von Palestrina und die Bildstruktur eines geographischen Großraums.' *Römische Historische Mitteilungen* 51: 15–130.

Hölscher, T. 1998. *Aus der Frühzeit der Griechen. Räume-Körper-Mythen*. Stuttgart.

Hölscher, T. 2000. 'Feindwelten–Glückswelten: Perser, Kentauren und Amazonen', in *Gegenwelten zu den Kulturen Griechenlands und Roms in der Antike*, ed. T. Hölscher, 287–320. Munich.

Hölscher, T. 2018. *Visual Power in Ancient Greece and Rome: Between Art and Social Reality*. Oakland, CA.

Hölscher, T. 2019. 'Wie schön darf Gorgo sein? Die widersprüchliche Ästhetik der griechischen Kunst und Lebenskultur', in *Schönheit: Die Sicht der Wissenschaft*, ed. J. Funke and M. Wink, 149–87. Heidelberg.

Koulakiotis, E. 2008. 'Tiere, Menschen und Götter in der *Epistola Alexandri ad Aristotelem*: Jagd und Opferritual am Rande der Welt', in *Mensch und Tier in der Antike: Grenzziehung und Grenzüberschreitung*, ed. A. Alexandridis, M. Wild, and L. Winkler-Horaček, 417–38. Wiesbaden.

Langner, M. 2012. 'Kentauren: Der Wandel eines Bildmotivs von der Antike bis in die Neuzeit', in *Animali: Tiere und Fabelwesen von der Antike bis zur Neuzeit*, ed. L. Tori and A. Steinbrecher, 242–53. Geneva.

Morawietz, G. 2000. *Der gezähmte Kentaur*. Munich.

Murray, A. T., trans. 1919. *Homer: The* Odyssey. Cambridge, MA.

Padgett, J. M., ed. 2003. *The Centaur's Smile: The Human Animal in Early Greek Art*. New Haven.

Payne, H. G. 1931. *Necrocorinthia*. Oxford.

Petit, T. 2011. *Œdipe et le Chérubin. Les sphinx levantins, cypriotes et grecs comme gardiens d'Immortalité*. Fribourg.

Thomas, J. J. 2021. *Art, Science, and the Natural World in the Ancient Mediterranean 300 BC to AD 100*. Oxford.

Vernant, J.-P. 1985. 'Die religiöse Erfahrung der Andersheit: Das Gorgogesicht', in *Faszination des Mythos*, ed. R. Schlesier, 399–420. Basel.

Vernant, J.-P. 1991. 'Death in the Eyes: Gorgo, Figure of the *Other*', in J.-P. Vernant, *Mortals and Immortals: Collected Essays*, 111–38. Princeton.

Vierneisel-Schlörb, B. 1979. *Klassische Skulpturen des 5. und 4. Jahrhunderts v. Chr.* Munich.

Winkler-Horaček, L. 2015. *Monster in der frühgriechischen Kunst*. Berlin.

CHAPTER 26

RATIONALIZING MYTHIC MONSTERS IN ANTIQUITY

GRETA HAWES

INTRODUCTION

REPORTS of fabulous monsters raise the question of what we can in fact know about the world. Eye-catchingly marvellous, mythical monsters are ripe for rejection as biologically impossible and historically implausible. But then there are many wonderful things that do in fact exist in our world, so how are we to judge? Taking the time to interrogate the likely existence of monsters does not imply ignorance or naïvety: understanding the limits of possibility is not as easy as one might assume. The realms beyond personal empirical observation knowledge—the regions of (un)certainty and (dis)belief—are large and surprisingly difficult to surveil. Monsters belong beyond the everyday, but then so too do many other things. Interrogating monsters becomes an exercise in demarcating reality, in deriving principles and polemics useful elsewhere as well, and in playing with perception.

We find a perfect illustration of this in a passage from Pausanias' *Guide to Greece*, a second-century CE text that describes what a traveller would see in the Greek mainland of the time. Regarding what seems to have been either an image or the (alleged) preserved remains—the language is not clear—of a sea deity called a Triton in a temple in the central Greek town of Tanagra, Pausanias gives two different stories. In the first, the Triton would come from the sea to attack local women until Dionysus defeated him. In the second, he retells the episode with a rationalistic cast: the Triton's raids ended when the locals managed to get him drunk and killed him (9.20.4). With wine now playing the role of the wine-god Dionysus, the Triton belongs suddenly to a world in which alcoholic beverages, and not divine epiphanies, are the key potent forces; it *might* belong, in other words, to the world of present reality. Pausanias continues:

> I have also seen another Triton amongst the wonders of Rome; compared to the Tanagrian one, it was small. This is what Tritons look like. They have hair on their

heads that is like what those frogs that live in marshes have both in terms of its colour and in the way you cannot distinguish one strand from the next. The rest of their body is protected by delicate scales, like a shark would have. They have gills beneath their ears. Their nose is human but their mouth is broader and they have the teeth of a beast. To me their eyes seemed blue. Their hands, fingers, and fingernails resemble murex shells. Beneath their torso and belly they have a tail in the place of feet—rather like a dolphin has. (9.21.1)[1]

In cataloguing the appearance of these sea creatures, Pausanias emphasizes their weirdness. Yet in dismantling the beasts into their composite parts, he can find partial analogies for each element. Oceans, rivers, and swamps are already full of strange oddities; why not allow one more?

Pausanias then points out that we need not even leave *terra firma* to encounter wonders. Our world is full of seemingly impossible creatures which do nonetheless exist: in Africa rhinoceroses sprout horns from their noses rather than their foreheads; the Balkans have bison of exceeding shagginess; India has camels the colour of leopards; and the Celtic elk—which looks something like a cross between a deer and a camel—eludes skilled hunters (9.21.2–3). With all this in mind, why question the existence of the 'martichora' ('manticore')? That creature—the possessor of a scorpion-like tail from which it launched stings like arrows shot from a bow—was described amongst the curiosities of India by Ctesias (a fifth-century BCE physician and historian) and became paradigmatic of the unreliability of travellers' tales. Pausanias, however, can rehabilitate the beast. It was, he declares, simply a tiger, transformed by human embellishment:

> The idea that it has three rows of teeth in each jaw, and a stinger on the end of its tail, and that with these stings it wards off those who get close and even shoots them at far-off attackers like men do arrows? Not true. Such stories are what the people of India spread amongst themselves since they are so terrified of the beast. They also mistook its colour: the tiger only appeared to them in bright sunlight and seemed uniformly red perhaps because it was moving so swiftly, or twisting and turning and was not seen close up. I think if you were to explore the furthest reaches of Libya, India, and Arabia in search of the beasts of Greece, you would find some did not exist there at all, and that others had a quite different appearance. For it is not just humans that look different in different places and climates. (9.21.4–5)

What is possible—normal, even—is, quite literally in the eye of the beholder. Having seen at Rome, and perhaps also in Greece, what was billed as the remains of a sea monster, Pausanias can muster logical arguments in support of the empirical evidence for monstrosity; his argument that the martichora was really a tiger has certainly appealed to some modern interpreters of Ctesias' account (see Lenfant 2004: 301–2). Elsewhere in his *Guide to Greece*, however, his instincts tend towards the opposite position, to argue against monstrosity as a fact of life. In such cases we will see the same ideas surfacing

---

[1] All translations are the author's own, except where noted.

again: the cataloguing of what does exist; the conceptualizing of what *can* exist; attempts at productive comparison; recognition that exaggeration and misperception are integral engines of human storytelling; and the delight in rolling back mistakes to reveal the truth.

This chapter surveys ancient attempts to cut monsters down to size and make them fit with the norms of reality. Quite apart from their contribution to ideas about biological and historical rectitude, dismantling and manipulating stories of monsters bolstered the rhetorical self-positioning of the person putting forward the critique. So, rationalizing monsters could be as much an act of establishing what was appropriate to a particular literary genre as it was about establishing the boundaries of the real. My account begins with a discussion of the problems posed by monsters. The second section of the chapter then describes various rationalizing methods used to combat these problems. Here Pausanias again becomes our primary guide, his pragmatic eclecticism and situational approach to interpretation showing the various ways monsters could be reworked to belong.

Problems with Monsters

When Plato characterizes the dilemma of the man who wishes to explain every myth, he describes him as beset by monsters:

> after this first explanation he must correct the forms of the Hippocentaurs, and then that of the Chimaera, and a throng of such monsters floods upon him—Gorgons and Pegasuses, strange curiosities with various monstrous physiques, and mobs of other, impossible creatures. (*Phdr.* 229d)

This conceptual elevation of monsters as the primary obstacle to accepting stories at face value persists throughout antiquity. Monsters are ideal choices to play this role because they are beyond the everyday in two ways. Firstly, they typically reside in distant places, and so are encountered in the kinds of accounts that come back from the edges of the known world. Secondly, they were said to have inhabited the distant past; they are characters, then, in the mythic world over which poets, rather than prose historians, typically preside. Ancient commentary over the biological and historical possibility of monsters thus plays out in the context of debates over narrative reliability. In the self-serving rhetoric of historiographical authority, fabulous monsters were both the hallmark of rivals' narrative foibles, and—because they were so easily dismissed—their surest vulnerability. So, the double distancing of monsters, in both time and space, is paralleled by their double nature: they are comprehensible (and thus available for critique) both as ontologically replete (i.e. actual) creatures and as the fictional creations of storytellers.

The apparently simplest rejection of mythic monsters rested on the fact that they did not exist now. This 'doctrine of present things' is presented most forcefully in the most complete treatise on mythic rationalization that we have, a text from the second half of the fourth century BCE transmitted under the title *On Unbelievable Tales*. In the methodological preface to this work, its author Palaephatus declares:

> All those forms and shapes that are said to have once existed—but which now do not exist—never actually existed. For if something came into being at some time or other, it must also exist in our time and will exist likewise in the future. I for one always endorse what the writers Melissos and Lamiscos of Samos said at the beginning of their work: 'what exists now came into being previously, and will exist forever'. Poets and storytellers perverted some of what took place and made it more unbelievable and astonishing to astound their audiences.[2]

Elsewhere in his work, Palaephatus states again that what exists in the present determines what existed in the past. It is part of his rejection of centaurs:

> Human and equine natures are entirely incompatible: they don't live on the same sort of food, and the food of a horse would not be able to pass through the mouth and throat of a human. If a creature of this shape did once exist, it would still exist now. (1)

Similarly, of the winged horse Pegasus he says, 'I don't think that a horse would ever be capable of flight, not even if it had all the wings of flying creatures. And if such a creature existed then, it would exist now too' (28). And of the Amazons, he is equally sceptical: 'It is unlikely that an army of women ever existed, for there's no such thing anywhere today' (32).

But his more forceful protestations revolve less around the idea that such abnormalities *do not* exist, and more on the idea that they *cannot* exist. In effect, the sensibility that Palaephatus attributes to Eleatic philosophical speculation in his prologue—that we inhabit an unchanging world—is replaced in practice by reasoning based on the fixity of species, a borrowing from Aristotelian principles. As we have seen, the question of what does exist strays easily into issues of personal experience and judgement: how much reliability one is willing to ascribe to reports from those who have travelled further and how much one might pare off as simply the predicable effects of exaggeration. So, asserting that creatures like centaurs did not exist in the mythic past because they do not exist now invites arguments, given that there were accounts from later in antiquity (first to third centuries CE) of centaurs being captured and of their preserved bodies displayed as curiosities. With questions of biological possibility—what can and cannot exist according to natural principles—we are supposedly on firmer ground.

Aristotle's extant writings (fourth century BCE) do not deal directly with the fabulous beasts of myth, but he does offer a framework for thinking about the biological bases for monstrosity that could be applied in that direction. Aristotle's taxonomic logic

---

[2] All translations of Palaephatus are from Branley, Hall, Hawes, Jenetsky, Maldoni, Prestipino, and Selth 2021; see Suggested Reading.

is based on the idea of fixed, distinct species in which offspring resemble their parents. This is not to say that 'monsters' cannot be produced by nature: congenital deformities whereby the offspring depart from the characteristics of previous generations follow predictable patterns (*Gen. an.* 767a36–b8). In this system, the blending of species is possible, but limited. The crucial factor for Aristotle was the length of pregnancies: mules can be produced because the offspring of both horses and donkeys requires the same gestation period (769b22–6). But if a human is described as 'ox-faced', this is merely an apparent resemblance; an ox-human hybrid could not be produced; these species are too disparate (769b13–23).

Palaephatus, said by later ancient commentators to be one of Aristotle's students at Athens, takes up this idea of species-based difference to reject hybrid monsters in particular. He dismisses the Minotaur on the basis of problems with its conception and gestation (see also Trzaskoma in this volume):

> The myth that's told about Pasiphae is that she was consumed by lust for a grazing bull, and … gave birth to a child that had the body of a man and the head of a bull. I for one say that this never happened. To start with, it is impossible for an animal of one kind to mate with one of another unless the womb and genitals are compatible. For it is not possible for a dog and an ape to mate with one another and produce offspring, nor a wolf and a hyena, nor an antelope and a deer (for the fact is that they are of different species). More to the point, I do not think that a bull had sex with a wooden cow: for all four-footed animals smell the genitals of an animal before mating and mount it afterwards. Nor would a woman be able to withstand being mounted by a bull, nor could she have carried a horned embryo. (2)

But elsewhere Palaephatus' observations range more broadly. We have seen that he describes a centaur as being unable to eat (it has two stomachs, each requiring different food). The Chimaera would have faced a similar impediment, and more besides (see also Smith in this volume):

> The Chimaira was 'a lion at the front, a serpent at the back and a she-goat in the middle'. Some think that such a beast really did exist even though it had three heads upon one body. But it is impossible for a snake, a lion, and a goat to eat the same sort of food. And a mortal being able to breathe fire? Absurd! And which of the heads did the body obey? (28)

Ancient authors could have great fun pointing out such incongruities and pouring rhetorical scorn on those who would believe in them unthinkingly; yet monsters could provide more than just cheap jokes. Considering *why* they could not exist sharpened thinking around why creatures that did exist had the forms that they did. This, indeed, is how Galen uses the centaurs.

Galen was a Greek physician and writer who lived in the Roman Empire during the second century CE. In *On the Uses of the Parts of the Body* he points out that humans are unique in walking upright on two legs and having the front limbs as arms (3.1). What is lost in speed is gained in dexterity; we alone have the ability to throw a bridle over the head of a horse. But why, he asks, are we not brought to greater perfection by possessing *four* legs along with our two arms? If we were shaped like centaurs we could transport our skilled hands in a much quicker vehicle. Galen then rehearses what were, by his time, well-known arguments against the possibility of human-equine hybrids: these creatures were mere poetic fabrications; disparate species cannot be mixed; conception would be impossible, as would gestation; there is nothing that it could eat, even if it were able to be born. Galen then strikes out on his own: what use would the speed of a horse be if it prevented a human from being fully human?

> I should like to see a centaur build a house or ship, scramble up the mast to the yardarm, or perform any of a sailor's tasks. How terribly awkward he would be at all of them, and how perfectly impossible many of them would be for him! If he was building a house, how would he climb long, slender ladders to the tops of high walls? Or how would he climb to the yardarm of a ship? Would he be able to row when he could not sit down properly? And even if he could, the presence of his front legs would hinder the action of his hands. But though he was of no use as a sailor, perhaps he would make a good farmer. Here too, however, he would be even more useless, especially if his task was climbing trees and picking fruit. Do not think that these are the only situations where he would be absurd, but review all the other arts and imagine him working as a blacksmith, or cobbling, weaving, mending, or writing books. How would be seat himself? What sort of a lap would he have on which to rest his book, and how would he handle all the other tools? For in addition to all the other special advantages man enjoys, he is the only one of all the animals who can conveniently sit down on his hip bones. (trans. Tallmadge May 1968: 156)

Humans are, Galen concludes, as distinctive in their ability to sit as they are in their ability to stand upright. And this ability to sit affords us all sorts of benefits; indeed, as he explains, a centaur could not even recline on a couch (see also Aston in this volume). The biological fixity of humans becomes, then, a marker of culture as much as nature. The physical characteristics of humans underpin those unique technical abilities which allow human societies and economies to function. In other words, biology creates the political animal.

Arguments that monsters *cannot* exist rest on implicit assumptions about the predictability of natural phenomena and the concomitant knowability of abstract biological principles. This vision of what the world is like—fixed, regular, and accessible to reason even where autopsy is impossible—blends over into thinking about the past. Arguments that monsters cannot—and therefore do not—exist in the present and thus could not—and therefore did not—exist in the past either are founded on the assumption that the natural laws operant in the present operated in the past as well. And if the distant past was qualitatively the same as the present, then its most characteristic aspect, i.e. its mythic fabulousness, must be discarded. In short, biological speculation blends into a historical principle about the homogeneity of experience over time. There can be no place on this timeline for a mythic story world with its own rules. This is quite obviously at odds with the traditions of heroic myth, in which people were bigger and stronger, the gods more potent, and beasts more fearsome. And so there emerged to fill this gulf a practice of rationalization that explained the fabulous within our universe of possibilities.

EXPLAINING MONSTROUS FORMS

'Rationalization' is the name we give to a historicist approach to myth. Rationalizing interpretations seek to rid these stories of their fabulous elements such that they can be understood to narrate events which happen according to the natural laws of the present. The approach was certainly not invented by Palaephatus, but his *On Unbelievable Tales* is the most significant example of it that survives. In this work, Palaephatus narrates forty-six different myths and explains how these stories might have arisen through misunderstandings of actual events. Palaephatus' contribution is unique not merely because he offers a methodological justification for rationalization (part of which is quoted above), but also because he deploys the approach exclusively. His rejections of myth are always based on a narrow conception of historical possibility; his solutions purport to recover the actual events that were then exaggerated or misunderstood in subsequent retellings. It is much more common to find ancient authors using rationalistic approaches in less formalistic ways—adopting them as and when needed alongside other kinds of interpretation and deploying them in ways that assume that the reader will intuitively discern the underlying methods.

Pausanias, then, is more typical amongst the ancient exponents of rationalization. His detailed itineraries through Greece encompass cities large and small, and landmarks famous and forgotten. And he tells stories about each location's past. Because of his very granular focus, Pausanias provides us with a local level of knowledge unusual in our ancient sources. And within his work we find myriad eclectic examples of rationalistic interpretation. That a work allied to geography should deploy rationalistic recastings of myth is not in itself strange: Pausanias narrates myths in relation to the places of his own time. The implicit disjunction between a fabulous story world and the norms of Pausanias' historical present is bridged quite naturally by rationalistic treatments. Equally, his account privileges obscure, unusual knowledge. In this regard, too, rationalized versions of myths have certain advantages, not least in surprising the reader with new ways of seeing familiar stories.

Pausanias does not deploy rationalistic methods of interpretation exclusively, nor does he avoid presenting the traditional stories. He includes plenty of conventional mythic narratives in the *Guide*, and explains myths in other ways as well, such as through allegorical interpretations. However, there are some patterns to his use of rationalizing techniques. In this chapter I extract and explicate just one, as an example: his sceptical treatment of the 'monsters' encountered by Heracles.

The basic way of 'explaining away' monsters is to suggest that originally people were just describing ordinary animals, but their accounts became misunderstood and distorted with time (see also Kitchell in this volume). This is what Pausanias does at Cape Taenarum (Tainaron), to the far south of the Peloponnese:

> On the promontory is a temple like a cave, with a statue of Poseidon in front of it. Some Greek poets have said that here Heracles dragged up the hound of Hades, though there is no road that leads underground through the cave, and it (is not easy to believe that the gods possess any underground dwelling where the souls collect. But Hecataeus of Miletus hit on a likely explanation: he said that Tainaron was the home of a dreadful snake called the hound of Hades, because its bite was instantly fatal; and this snake, he said, was brought by Heracles to Eurystheus. Homer, who was the first to call the creature brought by Heracles the hound of Hades, did not give it a name or describe it as of manifold form, as he did in the case of the Chimaera. Later poets gave the name Cerberus, and though in other respects they made him resemble a dog, they say that he had three heads. Homer, however, does not imply that he was a dog, the friend of man, any more than if he had called a real serpent the hound of Hades. (3.25.4–6)

Pausanias' logic here rests on two ideas: the first is that it is physically impossible for anyone to have emerged from the underworld here, or indeed for there to exist an underworld realm at all, and so the whole story of Heracles' retrieval of Cerberus (his twelfth labour) must be treated with scepticism. The second is that we could imagine that a creature might have been called the 'hound of Hades'—Cerberus' familiar epithet—as a nickname. In other words, the name might have been a metaphorical assessment of a particular snake's lethality rather than a literal description of a dog belonging to the god of the underworld.

Pausanias bolsters his reasoning through appeals to literary authorities: he takes the argument that Cerberus was in fact a snake from Hecataeus, one of the first Greek writers in prose (late sixth and early fifth centuries BCE). And he points out that, although Cerberus was described by poets (and, we might add, depicted in art) as having multiple heads, in his earliest appearance this is not made explicit. Homer (eighth century BCE) includes brief accounts of Heracles' twelfth labour in both the *Iliad* (8.366–9) and the *Odyssey* (11.620–4). He calls the creature that Heracles is sent to retrieve 'the hound of Hades' or just 'the hound', and at neither time does he describe what it looked like; he certainly does not imply that it had any more heads than a normal dog. So Pausanias can argue that it might well be that the poet had in mind a snake with a ferocious reputation rather than an actual hound. We see here how Homer's authority is quite separate from the 'later poets' that Pausanias accuses of inventing the fictious Cerberus. Pausanias' attitude is somewhat conventional here, but his example is also carefully chosen. Homer's near-contemporary Hesiod also mentioned Cerberus, and *his* verses leave little doubt that this creature was a monstrous dog (see also Joyce in this volume): 'And then she [Echidna] gave birth to a second offspring, the undefeatable, unspeakable, raw-flesh eating Cerberus; that bronze-voiced hound of Hades, fifty-headed, ruthless, and strong' (*Theog.* 310–12).

The fact that Pausanias can find a rationalistic explanation for this labour in the earliest prose texts shows just how long the traditions of historicizing Heracles' myths was. About a century after Hecataeus another mythographer, Herodorus (c.400 BCE) dedicated an entire work to Heracles. It does not survive, but some fragments suggest that he too also took a rationalistic approach at times. For example, he explains that Heracles did not free Prometheus from the punishment of having his liver pecked out each day by an eagle. Rather, Prometheus ruled lands that were being constantly flooded by the Eagle River. Heracles helped him by diverting that river into the sea (fr. 30 Fowler). This method of replacing a mythical beast with some other creature or phenomenon called by its name (so, a snake in Hecataeus and a river in Herodorus) is found also in interpretations which suppose there to have been humans who bore the names of animals. So, Palaephatus rationalizes the serpent (in Greek, *drakōn*) that guarded the apples of the Hesperides. Palaephatus cuts him down to size by saying that the guard was simply a man called Drakōn, and Heracles killed him so he could steal the Hesperides' sheep (18; the word Palaephatus uses, *mela*, can mean either sheep or apples.)

Pausanias also seems to give us an example of this motif in a comment that he attaches to a location near Olympia: 'Once you have crossed the river Erymanthus, below what is called the Ridge of Saurus is the tomb of Saurus and a sanctuary of Heracles.... They say that Saurus would mistreat local residents and people passing by until Heracles brought him to justice' (6.21.3). No other ancient source tells us about this encounter between Heracles and Saurus, although the motif of the hero liberating a community from some harasser is very familiar. What seems curious about this particular individual is his name: *sauros* means 'lizard' in Greek. Is this Pausanias' version of a story that originally told of a *lizard* killed by the hero and buried in his sanctuary? For any reader aware of the gambit of converting animals to homonymous men, the fact that Pausanias is interpreting the story rationalistically would be obvious and need no further elaboration. Underpinning it is perhaps the idea that a cruel antagonist named after—or, better, nicknamed for—a lizard was appropriate. Elsewhere we see this kind of logic spelt out more forcefully: Plutarch (late first to early second century CE) says that Theseus did not defeat Phaia, the Crommyonian Sow, but rather a lawless brigand called Phaia who lived at Crommyon and earned the nickname 'Sow' on account of 'her character and lifestyle' (*Thes.* 9).

We have already seen that rationalizers could single out 'poets' for corrupting ancient accounts and thus inventing monsters. 'Poetic licence' was in this view a natural engine for myth-making. Pausanias gives us a particularly clear example of this attitude when he describes the supposed residence of the Hydra ('water-snake') whose killing was one of Heracles' Labours:

> Now I can believe that this creature was larger than all other water snakes and that its venom contained something so toxic that Heracles treated the tips of his arrow with its bile. But I think it had only one head and not many. It was Peisandrus of Camirus, wanting to make the beast more scary and to bring more attention to his poem, who broke with this and gave the Hydra many heads. (2.37.4)

Peisandrus, Pausanias' target, was a late seventh-century-BCE epic poet who composed a now lost *Heracleia* ('Deeds of Heracles'). Pausanias might be right that he was the first to describe the Hydra as having more than one head; we simply cannot tell given the fragmentary nature of early epic in general. Hesiod did place her in a monstrous genealogy—she is Echidna's third offspring, after Cerberus (see above)—but he says nothing of her actual appearance (*Theog.* 313–15). Nonetheless, her multiple heads were an early and integral part of the tradition in art. Contemporary with Peisandrus is a flourishing of depictions of the scene in Corinthian-style pottery beginning in the late seventh century; we also have two bronze fibulae from Boeotia decorated with Heracles' fight against a multi-headed snake (*LIMC*, s.v. 'Herakles' 2019, 2020). All this aside, Pausanias' rhetorical argument is clear: if the Hydra is to be rehabilitated as 'simply' a venomous water snake, then the exaggerations bourn of poetic competition must be recognized and rolled back so that a supposed originary version can be found, one which is both more banal and more believable than what the story came to be (see also Deacy in this volume).

Not all mythical beasts need to be explained away; where they have no obvious monstrous features, then rationalization might consist solely of treating the beast as a normal animal. Again, Pausanias gives us an indication of this general approach when he describes the Cretan Bull, whose capture was one of Heracles' Labours and which was (in this version at least) later killed by Theseus:

> In the distant past beasts were more scary to humans; examples include the lion at Nemea and the Parnassian lion, serpents all over Greece, the boars of Calydon and Erymanthus, and the sow at Corinthian Crommyon. They were so scary that it would be said that the earth had produced them, or that they were sacred to the gods, or that they had been sent to punish people. And so the Cretans say that this bull was send to their land by Poseidon because Minos, even though he controlled the Greek sea, did not specially honour Poseidon amongst the gods. (1.27.9)

The specific beasts that Pausanias highlights here all have the appearance of familiar animals, even if they might be depicted larger than their historical counterparts. He is quite vague in his reference to 'serpents', the Greek *drakontes* being a term that can cover both biologically normal snakes and something supernatural, approaching our concept of a dragon, which in Greek thought were often said to be earth-born. Their mythic 'monstrousness' was limited, but all the creatures Pausanias lists above are obviously prestigious quarry for heroes to defeat. Fear does of course play into the myths: ancient artists delighted in depicting Eurystheus hiding in a large jar when Heracles brings him the Erymanthian Boar, and the only reference we have to a 'Parnassian lion' is in a fragment from a poem of Callimachus, in which nymphs flee in terror from a lion on Parnassus (*Aet.* frr. 67–75). Pausanias' gambit here is commonly encountered in rationalizations: the past was not biologically different from the present, but its inhabitants *were* less sophisticated, and their naïvety led them to misunderstand what they saw or to attribute supernatural causation to quite natural events. Crucially, this rationalistic approach does not veer necessarily into theological cynicism: Pausanias is not saying that the gods *cannot* exert power over human lives, merely that *in these instances* the stories came about through human misunderstanding.

The unusual behaviour of mythical beasts might likewise be explained without recourse to supernatural explanations. Here is Pausanias' commentary on another of Heracles' foes, the Stymphalian Birds:

> The Arabian desert produces many beasts; amongst these are birds that are called 'Stymphalian' which are in no way more well disposed towards humans than lions or leopards. They fly at hunters, wounding them with their beaks and killing them. If hunters try to protect themselves with bronze and silver armour, the birds will pierce it. But if they contrive to make garments of thick reeds, the beaks of the Stymphalian Birds are held fast by the reed garments in the same way that the feathers of small birds get caught in sticky birdlime. These birds are the size of cranes, and resemble ibises, except that they have stronger beaks that are not curved like the ibises' are. Whether these Arabian birds of our day do not merely share the name of the birds that were once in Arcadia [i.e. at Stymphalus] but are also the same breed as them, I do not know. But given that Stymphalian Birds must have always existed, just like hawks and eagles have, then I think these birds were originally an Arabian beast and some part of the flock must have flown at some point from there over to Arcadia and come to Stymphalus. They would originally have been given some other name by the Arabians, and not named 'Stymphalian'. But Heracles' fame and the fact that the Greek world has come to win out over neighbouring territories means that the birds of the Arabian desert are called in our time 'Stymphalian'. (8.22.4–6)

Pausanias provides here a plausible backstory for Heracles' labour: the birds he was sent to get rid of had migrated to the Greek mainland from Arabia. Pausanias alone of our ancient sources describes the Stymphalian Birds of Arcadia as 'man-eating'; the Latin mythographer Hyginus says that they could shoot their feathers like arrows (*Fab.* 20, 30), but elsewhere they seem to have posed a problem simply because they were so numerous and were destroying nearby crops. In endowing them with fierce qualities, he suggests a beast which merges the prestige of mythic prey with historical plausibility: if hunters in Arabia still struggle to deal with their 'Stymphalian' birds, they would certainly have been a suitable target for the hero.

CONCLUSION

With this explanation, Pausanias brings us full circle. We are again faced with the 'doctrine of present things'. As Pausanias' argument goes, Heracles' opponents might have existed then as described in myth, because analogous creatures are still encountered now. But where they were supposedly encountered, the Arabian desert, was a corner of the Aegean poorly known to the Greeks and little-visited. The emptiness of deserts made them ideal locations for strange animals—and of course monsters—in Greek thought. Arabia is, for example, where Herodotus said that winged snakes lived (2.75–6); the ibises that he describes as savagely killing them before they cross into Egypt are the ones that Pausanias no doubt has in mind in his comparison. Aelian borrows from Herodotus in describing the ferocity of these ibises (*NA* 2.38), but Pausanias alone testifies to the existence of so-called Stymphalian Birds in Arabia. And so his explanation points to the final instability of the 'doctrine' behind its apparent simplicity: once more the reader is left wondering at the variety of living creatures, and being asked to agree that a mythical creature existed in the distant past because it seems to resemble an animal which, although said to still thrive, is so far away as to be likewise almost unknowable.

Suggested Reading

For extensive discussion of ancient mythic rationalization, including analyses of Palaephatus' and Pausanias' approaches, see Hawes (2014). Translations from Palaephatus' *On Unbelievable Tales* in this chapter are adapted from those created by Branley, Hall, Hawes, Jenetsky, Maldoni, Prestipino, and Selth in 2021 for the Canopos project (https://www.manto-myth.org/canopos), and available on the Scaife Viewer (https://scaife.perseus.org/library/urn:cts:greekLit:tlg1553.tlg001/). Other translations with good commentary (in English and Italian respectively) appear in Stern (1996) and Santoni (2000). For more on Heracles and the monsters that he defeats, Stafford (2012) and Ogden (2021) are excellent resources. The *LIMC* article devoted to the hero offers a lot more detail about visual sources. Shannon-Henderson (2019) discusses the existential impossibilities of centaurs and collates accounts of captured and preserved specimens from antiquity. The phenomenon of the discovery of monstrous remains in antiquity is described more broadly by Mayor (2000). Pease (1955: 483–4) offers a catalogue of passages in which centaurs are treated with suspicion; for the ancient tradition of rationalizing them, see Alganza Roldán, et al. (2017).

Works Cited

Alganza Roldán, M., J. Barr, and G. Hawes, 2017. 'The Reception History of Palaephatus 1 (On the Centaurs) in Ancient and Byzantine Texts.' *Polymnia* 3: 186–235.

Hawes. G. 2014. *Rationalizing Myth in Antiquity*. Oxford.

Lenfant, D. 2004. *Ctésias de Cnide: La Perse, L'Inde, Autres fragments*. Paris.

Mayor, A. 2000. *The First Fossil Hunters: Paleontology in Greek and Roman Times*. Princeton.

Ogden, D., ed. 2021. *The Oxford Handbook of Heracles*. Oxford.

Pease, A. S. 1955. *M. Tulli Ciceronis De natura deorum: Liber primus*. Cambridge, MA.

Santoni, A. 2000. *Palefato: Storie Incredibili*. Pisa.

Shannon-Henderson, K. E. 2019. 'Phlegon's Paradoxical Physiology: Centaurs in the *Peri Thaumasion*', in *Medicine and Paradoxography in the Ancient World*, ed. G. Kazantzidis, 141–62. Berlin.

Stafford, E. 2012. *Herakles*. London.

Stern, J. 1996. *Palaephatus: On Unbelievable Tales*. Wauconda, IL.

Tallmadge May, M. 1968. *Galen: On the Usefulness of the Parts of the Body*. Ithaca, NY.

....

CHAPTER 27

BEYOND 'OTHERING'

Classical Monstrosity and Feminism in the Twenty-First Century

....

VANDA ZAJKO

INTRODUCTION

....

THE long-standing interest of feminism in the configurations and epistemologies of monstrosity arises from the perception that the monstrous, like the feminine, is a denigrated category, associated with the lesser-valued side of a whole host of conceptual oppositions. The binary system of classification which has underpinned much of Western culture is widely recognized to have privileged one half of an oppositional pair over the other, and so a kind of alliance has developed between those on the losing side. The abnormal, the imperfect, the irrational, the wild, the unpredictable—all these qualities and more have been aligned putatively with anything that menaces the stability of the cultural mainstream. This means that even though not all monsters are feminine, the idea of the feminine and the idea of the monstrous have become closely entwined because they both help to define a normative subject in terms of what it is not. The phenomenon of constructing monsters to symbolize societal fears links even historically disparate cultures so that, for example, the Furies in fifth-century Athens and post-9/11 zombie films can both be analysed as exploring threats posed to the status quo and successfully containing them (for the latter, see e.g. Bloodsworth-Lugo and Lugo-Lugo 2013: 243–56).

Feminism has tended to theorize these threats in terms of the dynamics of misogyny, via an understanding that when the normative subject is gendered masculine, the feminine and its associated qualities are likely to be regarded as dangerous. Put more emphatically, feminist modes of analysis insist that the cultural work of maintaining order is often propelled by an anxiety about women which requires their disorderly bodies and aberrant behaviours to be controlled if the edifice of civilization is not to come crashing down. This control may, for example, take the form of real-world legislation which prevents women from managing their own reproduction, but it may also manifest itself in popular narratives which depict female characters who engage in disruptive behaviour being comprehensively trounced and brought back into line. We can easily see how this analysis works for some monstrous female figures from classical myth, such as Medusa and the Amazons, as well as for later characters from literature, film, and TV. In these cases, characters who are relegated to the margins both spatially and conceptually function to shore up the taxonomies of the centre—a centre which represents a humanity defined by the male. The question remains, however, are these narratives themselves straightforwardly misogynist, or does the apparatus of interpretation surrounding them also contribute to rendering them so? In other words, can we separate the myth from its interpretation, the monstrous figure from its reception?

We can see from the brief outline above that consideration of monstrosity and feminism involves an awareness of the broader intellectual landscape in which what Paul Cartledge (2002: 2) has called 'ideally polarized opposition' acts as a dominant means of evaluating cultural phenomena. For some critics, such a disposition is inevitable and reflects how the human mind works; for others, the patterning is itself reflects an underlying will to power on the part of those who benefit from a hierarchical gendering process. In the introduction to his book *The Greeks: A Portrait of Self and Others*, Cartledge (2002: 2–3) traces the intellectual history of the model of alterity underpinning his work to the two French philosophers Emannuel Levinas and Simone de Beauvoir. For feminists, the latter is the more significant figure, and her contribution will be discussed below. Cartledge's study helped naturalize alterity as a way to understand the ancient Greek world and continues to encourage the maintenance of a binary model of gender. Moreover, 'othering', the less rigorous and more popular version of this approach, has become a shorthand for describing all of that world's counter-normative inhabitants. This has the result of reproducing the perspective of the adult citizen male each time the trope is introduced into a discussion, and, in the case of myth, the interpretation comes to perform the same set of exclusions as the original story. This chapter thus aims to explore alternatives to othering when it comes to evaluating monsters, by demonstrating how contemporary queer and feminist theorists—by refusing the binary model of gender—transform the habitat of the wild, and exposes the limitations of defining through opposition.

Woman as Other

In her introduction to *The Second Sex* Beauvoir explores the question 'What is a woman?' and outlines how 'man' represents both the positive and the universal, whereas 'woman' represents only the negative, defined by everything man is not. Her famous formulation that 'woman is the other' has become something of a soundbite and one which does not do justice to the scrutiny of the historical, anthropological, and philosophical data she adduces to explain what she sees as the universality of the phenomenon whereby 'the two sexes have never shared the world in equality' (1953: 6). Although she unequivocally regards otherness as a fundamental category of human thought, Beauvoir does not conceive this as a natural state, or rather, she sees the natural as a constructed and contingent category which only poses as immutable. Even if duality can be traced back over time as a ubiquitous mode of ordering human experience, the lack of reciprocity between the categories of man and woman marks out the particular duality of gender as pernicious: because there was no historical event or identifiable beginning to the hierarchy, the inequity between men and women seems to represent the way things have always been and always must be, and it has suited the male establishment to suborn the full force of the cultural imagination to perpetuate this impression. Beauvoir cites the myth of Pandora, like the myth of Eve, as an example of a narrative which functions precisely to bed down the hierarchy, and she argues that where it was once the remit of religion, philosophy, and theology to accomplish this task, it now falls within the remit of the natural sciences too.

One criticism of *The Second Sex* is that, in its emphasis on the absolute status of the otherness of woman, the book leaves little room for a sense of how things might improve. But there is also a more optimistic reading available, one which points a way forward to the reconfiguration of the categories of sex and gender associated primarily these days with the work of Judith Butler. Butler herself pays tribute to the work's influence when she argues that, far from subscribing to the ineluctability of women's oppression by men, Beauvoir provides a 'phenomenology of victimization' which reveals that oppression, despite the appearance and weight of inevitability, is essentially contingent' (Butler 1986: 41). The refusal to regard sex as a natural category, and the insistence on the complex and covert processes of socialization via which we come to occupy positions as men or women, have paved the way for the conceptual dismantling of the masculine/feminine divide, and this, in turn, has opened further possibilities for inhabiting an imaginative world beyond the confines of duality. Tracing the development of the idea of othering helps make visible its potency and ubiquity as metaphor and provides the resources for challenging it; a feminist genealogy prioritizes questions of sex, gender, and power and uses this prioritization as a basis for querying the inevitability of additional manifestations of otherness, such as monstrosity.

THE PROBLEM WITH OTHERING

Beauvoir confronts the issue of the immutability of woman's position head-on, using examples from ancient Greek mythology to ask why men's desire for and dependence on women for sex and child-rearing has not provided a route to liberation:

> When Hercules sat at the feet of Omphale and helped with her spinning, his desire for her held him captive; but why did she fail to gain a lasting power? To revenge

herself on Jason, Medea killed their children; and this grim legend would seem to suggest that she might have obtained a formidable influence over him through his love for his offspring. In *Lysistrata* Aristophanes gaily depicts a band of women who joined forces to gain social ends through the sexual needs of their men; but this is only a play. (1953: 5)

Her answer is that the very model of configuring woman as Other in relation to man who is the One militates against any reciprocity or transformation. To facilitate new and more flexible alignments of power, a more relational conceptual model is needed, one which aims, in the words of Rosa Braidotti (2019: 11–12), 'to extract difference from the oppositional or binary logic that reduces difference to being different from, as in being worth less than'. What might such a model look like, and how might it manifest itself in cultural narratives such as myth? These questions are currently being addressed exhilaratingly in hybrid disciplines such as queer, decolonial, and crip theory, which participate in acts of radical decentring, celebrating the non-human and the post-natural worlds. Feminism is engaging with and supplementing the insights gained in these fields with the result that the impact of many familiar stories is beginning to change.

THE FURIES

In a feminist article on the *Oresteia*, Froma Zeitlin set out the mechanisms via which Aeschylus' trilogy contributed both to the specific ideological formations of the developing polis, and to 'the collective fantasies of its audience' (1978: 149). Emphasizing the *Oresteia*'s effect on the less than tangible world of the imagination, as well as on real-world political institutions, demonstrates how even in ancient Athens popular cultural narratives played a part in reinforcing the ostensible inevitability of gender roles. Explicit animosity between the male and female characters drives the plot forward, but Zeitlin argues that it is the underlying logic of otherness which links mastery over women to the idea of civilization and declares the former to be necessary if the latter is to be maintained. As we have seen, the metaphor fuses connections between oppositional groups of qualities and privileges one group over the other. In the case of Aeschylus' trilogy, the winning side consists of the Olympian gods, the Greeks, social ties, and the male, and on the losing side are the chthonic deities, the barbarians, blood ties, and the female. The Furies, who are initially unequivocal in their hostility towards Orestes who has killed his own kin (his mother, Clytemnestra), are by the trilogy's end seemingly appeased and welcomed into the religious heart of the polis. It is this transformation of the monstrous and implacable Furies into the Eumenides, the 'Kindly Ones', which provokes the most debate about the misogynist dynamics of the *Oresteia*.

The Furies are an absent presence onstage in the trilogy's first play, *Agamemnon*, where the character Cassandra describes them as hovering over the House of Atreus (1189–1192). In the second play, the *Choephoroe* ('Libation Bearers'), they appear only at the end, in the form of terrifying apparitions visible only to Orestes (1061). But in the third play, the *Eumenides*, they come into their own and dominate proceedings, first in Argos and then in Athens. The Pythia, priestess of Apollo, describes them in terms which emphasize their grotesqueness: sleeping around the figure of Orestes, they are dark in colour and wholly disgusting, emitting repellent snores and expelling vile drips from their eyes (52–4). She struggles to communicate how revolting they are and resorts to comparing them to other sets of monstrous females, the Gorgons and the Harpies, before concluding that, in fact, she has never before seen their like. Finally, they are awakened by the ghost of Clytemnestra, and the audience gets a chance to judge their dreadfulness for itself as they come to life and continue their relentless pursuit of Orestes. The Pythia's struggle to describe the Furies is striking, and Yopie Prins (1991: 178) has argued persuasively that their resistance to representation at the start of the trilogy suggests that 'they are monstrous in the literal sense of the word, demonstrating some-thing outside conventional visual categories'. This quality of evading categorization is also articulated by Apollo, who describes them paradoxically as 'grey, ancient children' and as 'eternal virgins'; he emphasizes their distinctiveness from all classes of being—gods, humans, and beasts (*Eum.* 69–70).

Aeschylus' representation of the Furies in the *Oresteia* might be said to epitomize a conventional view of the otherness of monstrosity, according to which monstrous bodies 'resist attempts to include them in any systematic structuration' (Cohen 1996: 174). In this aspect they resemble other mythic monsters, both male and female, who function to demarcate the conceptual margins and whose cultural contribution largely disrupts order, rationality, and binary thought. But central to the reaction of horror the Furies provoke is the sense that they transgress gender norms, since they possess no repro-ductive capacity and embody instead a permanent synthesis of the sexual stages of life for earthly women. This emphasis suggests that the Furies also conform to the definition of 'the monstrous-feminine' as formulated by Barbara Creed (1993), who regards the as-sociation of woman's reproductive capacities with 'the abject' as one of the most potent constructions of patriarchal ideology. Creed's ideas, developed in relation to the genre of the horror movie, provide an explanation for the reaction of disgust and shock which bridges the gap between ancient and modern audiences.

THE FURIES AND THE ABJECT

The concept of the abject originated not with Creed but with the French feminist phil-osopher Julia Kristeva, who throughout her writing career was preoccupied with the question of how gender difference is constructed and maintained. Kristeva utilizes Freudian and Lacanian models of the development of the subject to posit the abject as a space where meaning collapses, where the proprieties of the symbolic order do not hold sway: an encounter with, for example, a corpse, which provokes a violently nega-tive response, is not only an encounter with the corpse itself, but with what it represents.

In the words of Kristeva (1982: 4), 'It is thus not lack of cleanliness or health that causes abjection but what disturbs identity, system, order. What does not respect borders, positions, rules. The in-between, the ambiguous, the composite.' It is not so much that the abject overturns the order of a specific cultural system, but more that it exposes the arbitrariness of the prohibitions on which that system depends. Abjection is universal because it is integral to the formation of social identity for both the individual and the collective;[1] however, it also takes different forms within different symbolic systems and thus can be analysed in sociocultural terms. Deep excavation of a community's psychosocial structures reveals its norms and proscriptions and, like Beauvoir, Kristeva argues that everywhere such norms include the fear of and oppression of women. Explaining this ubiquity by linking the 'demarcating imperative' of abjection with the origins of gendered hierarchy, she offers an aetiological account of the separation of the sexes as follows:

> It is as if, lacking a central authoritarian power that would settle the definitive supremacy of one sex—or lacking a legal establishment that would balance the prerogatives of both sexes—two powers attempted to share out society. One of them, the masculine, apparently victorious, confesses through its very relentlessness against the other, the feminine, that it is threatened by an asymmetrical, irrational, wily, uncontrollable power. (1982: 70)

This argument is especially potent in the case of the Furies' significance to an Athenian audience because of the *Oresteia*'s role in supporting the foundation of Athenian political institutions (Prins 1991: 192).

Kristeva follows an explicitly acknowledged Freudian line of thought. She develops her argument about the abject in relation to the work of early anthropologists and historians of religion who are concerned with the categories of the sacred and the profane, because the process of trying to understand religious practice provides a good way to expose what she calls the 'deep psycho-symbolic economy' operative across a range of cultures. Her interest lies specifically in the way that negative concepts do not acquire potency in and of themselves but rather from the strength of the prohibition differentiating them from their positive counterparts. In this she follows structuralist theorists such as Levi-Strauss, who argue that meaning is produced by the oppositional structures of language, but she adds a psychoanalytic dimension with her focus on the psychodynamics of the boundary between self and not-self, and on repression. For Kristeva, the originary separation occurs when the child must differentiate itself from the mother, and as a result, the mother becomes 'an abject'; but that separation is never complete, and the abject becomes 'something rejected from which one does not part',

---

[1] Bloodsworth-Lugo and Lugo-Lugo (2013: 67): 'One might advance the hypothesis that a (social) symbolic system corresponds to a specific structuration of the speaking subject in the symbolic order. To say that it "corresponds" leaves out questions of cause and effect; is the social determined by the subjective, or is it the other way around?'

something which attracts, but also constantly threatens to engulf (1982: 4). It is not just the individual psyche which is at stake in this process of attempted separation; the precariousness of the integrity of the subject also reveals the vulnerability of the symbolic order in toto, so that both the individual and the group are jeopardized by the persistent threat of confrontation with what will not be left behind.

THE ABJECT AND ANCIENT GREEK RELIGION

Esther Eidinow has recently utilized the concept of the abject to explore 'the creatures of childhood terror' as manifest in antiquity—the monstrous *daimones* and the physical and conceptual places they occupy (2018: 210). Her analysis demonstrates beautifully how this contemporary theoretical term can illuminate transgressive spaces within the ancient imagination without losing sight of the significant differences in representation and affect across genres and over time. Eidinow concludes that the reoccurring emphasis on the libidinous appetites of the figures she examines—Mormo, Lamia, and Empousa—can be regarded as 'a (cultural) abjection of female sexuality' (231). The narratives and rituals associated with ancient Greek religion certainly seem to perform the same iterative process of recognizing and warding off perceived menace as the practices of other religions have been argued to do. In the case of the Furies, the institution of their cult in Athens at the end of the *Eumenides* takes on greater import when we consider what it means within the 'psycho-symbolic economy' of the polis, given that their power will not diminish but rather be redirected (952–5). We can develop a reading whereby their transformation into the Kindly Ones signifies an attempt to banish the insistent, malignant energy of the Furies while recognizing that, like the abject, it will constantly threaten to return. Such a reading depends upon a willingness to accept the analogy between individual subject and city state, and the Furies as symbols of an earlier stage of development for both.

In the article mentioned above, Froma Zeitlin unequivocally declares the *Oresteia* to be a misogynist text, arguing that it legitimates the status quo of the subordination of women by providing it with an ennobling aetiological myth. Under this description, the transformation of the Furies who, she suggests, 'make visible the metaphors of monstrosity which are associated with Clytemnestra throughout the trilogy' (1978: 164), might seem to be a straightforward triumph for the forces of repression. But this is the case only if we focus on the pacification of the Furies as a kind of happy ending for the polis, rather than on the instability of the outcome which has attempted to resolve the gender conflict at the trilogy's heart. An important scholarly tradition reads the play's final scenes as emphasizing the precariousness of the deal struck among Athena, Apollo, and the Furies, one which notes that only via the agency of a patently androgynous deity is the impasse of the tied vote broken: the parallels between Clytemnestra and Athena in terms of their gender complexity make it harder to envisage the final judgement as an unquestionable victory for the male. In terms of our previous discussion about the abject and ancient Greek religion, it also appears significant that, in return for ceasing their hostilities, the Furies are granted considerable ritual power. What, then, is at stake in opting for one interpretation over the other—how do we decide whether the transformation of the Furies represents a successful containment of a monstrous threat, or a partial and uneasy truce recognizing their undefeated authority?

Simon Goldhill has reviewed the two sides of this debate with attention to the language associated with justice and concluded that 'different critics, repeating the play's dynamics of conflict, appropriate the language of the *Oresteia* to arguments about social justice' (1986: 55). His conclusion resonates with critics' decisions about the gendered hierarchies in the trilogy and with the perspectival nature of scholarship more broadly. A feminist analysis of an ancient text will likely produce different results from one which does not apply itself to issues of gender, and the insistence that there is no such thing as a neutral interpretation is arguably one of the most significant contributions of feminist scholarship. Feminism is not, of course, a monolithic concept but an evolving one: the intersectional dynamics of the twenty-first century have shifted the focus away from the excavation and critique of misogyny dominant in the 1970s and 1980s towards the recognition of interlocking and multidimensional categories of oppression (see e.g. the overview in Lutz, Vivar, and Supik 2011: 1–22). Moreover, developments in technology, particularly the technologies of gender, and the accelerating environmental crisis have intensified debates about what constitutes 'the human'—with the result that conceptions of what constitute 'the centre' and 'the other' are constantly changing. Braidotti's plea for a more relational conceptual model of gender springs to mind here: what kinds of models are envisaged? The remainder of this chapter will examine how current theoretical landscapes of the post-human provide new possibilities for the monsters of classical myth beyond demarcation as 'other'.

BEYOND OTHERING

If traditional ways of configuring sex and gender rely on metaphors of opposition and fixity, the post-queer world is dominated by images of process, performance, and the fluid: rather than defined by difference, states of being are regarded as mutable and optimistically positioned somewhere on a spectrum of possibility and choice. This has implications both for the embodied experiences of individuals and, importantly for our purposes, for the scoping of the cultural imaginary, past and present. Clearly, the 'post-' in the above description is not intended to function temporally, but conceptually, and indicates a willingness and desire to dismantle existing hierarchies rather than signalling that they have already been abolished. There is a future orientation in the use of 'queer' which is perfectly expressed in the following well-known passage from Eve Kosofsky Sedgwick's *Tendencies*:

> That's one of the things that 'queer' can refer to: the open mesh of possibilities, gaps, overlaps, dissonances and resonances, lapses and excesses of meaning when the

constituent elements of anyone's gender, of anyone's sexuality aren't made (or can't be made) to signify monolithically. (1994: 8)

This orientation provides the link between the impetus to expose the inequities of the binary model of gender which is the distinctive preoccupation of feminism, and the disruption of other normative models, specifically those which rely on oppositional and hierarchical structures. Such projects involve both a potent ethical commitment to the world being otherwise, and the vision to imagine it so.

The deconstruction of dualist models is particularly pressing in crip theory, a successor or alternative to disability studies primarily concerned with the socially determined differences between 'normal' and 'abnormal' bodies. In this context, the implications of reinforcing fixed categories of disability are huge, not least because they are so often financial. But the difficulty of maintaining discrete classifications is also apparent since identification of what counts as disability is itself contested. Drawing on the insights of queer theorists, crip activists refuse to determine who counts as disabled on the basis of essential qualities of bodies; rather, they advocate for a shifting alliance of those who experience discrimination due to the capabilities of bodies or minds, and regard disability as 'a site of questions rather than firm definitions' (Kafer 2013: 10). The argument that the goal of an accessible future for everyone will be achieved only alongside an exacting reappraisal of how 'the human' is benchmarked parallels the concerns of those feminists for whom challenging the relation between markers of gender and sexed bodies is a prerequisite for a fairer world. These overlapping agendas for change are significant for evolving ideas about monstrosity because, as we have seen with the Furies, marked corporeal difference so often functions as a signifier of a monster.

Another aspect of these debates in queer and crip theory relevant to conceptions of the monstrous is the question of intelligibility: bodies which are not recognized or not understood are frequently regarded as threatening and designated 'abject' as a result. The emergence of new ways of configuring embodiment challenges the status quo in terms of knowledge and experience so that new monsters develop in the collective imagination. Once the novelty wears off, what was threatening becomes familiar and forms that were previously feared and rejected can be absorbed easily into the cultural mainstream. As a result, there is a continual tension between the disruptive potential of abject figures and the societal forces seeking to mitigate them. For crip activists, this tension is sometimes expressed in discussions about whether the category of disability should be expanded to include, for example, family members of disabled people who are also disadvantaged, or people who are living with the reduced capacities that often accompany ageing (Kafer 2013: 7–8). Fierce arguments about preferred strategies for dealing with trans* identities arise from similar dilemmas: should transgender people seek to be recognized as men or women, or should they seek to remain outsiders and resist co-option into existing gender roles altogether? In both scenarios at issue is the most effective means to force a thorough overhaul of the normative categories of human embodiment which rely for their legitimacy on the denigration and exclusion of those deemed 'the other'.

Although they are figures of the future who menace a world which cannot yet comprehend them, monsters are not always transgressive. This is because the fear of difference is sometimes matched by a fear of a *lack* of difference so that the monstrous becomes a repository for conventional values and ideas. The use of 'othering' usually functions like this, collapsing difference and homogenizing a whole range of attributes and behaviours which challenge normative identity formations. The examples above and the conflicting views about the end of the *Eumenides* clearly indicate that the process of abjection is not the end of the story since the categories of the normal and the abnormal are so closely related and the boundaries between them only appear to be fixed rather than actually being so. Just as Zeitlin's reading of the *Oresteia* was enabled and invigorated by the feminist theory of her era, so more recent feminist theory has influenced the way that we now interpret notable mythological characters—most famously, Hélène Cixous's transformation of the snake-haired, petrifying Medusa into a beautiful, laughing presence who unsettles the old hierarchies of ancient Greek myth and champions those who defy them (1986: 63–132). Cixous might be thought to have taken considerable liberties in her representation of the monstrous Gorgon, whose head was appropriated by Athena as an apotropaic device on her aegis. But imagination is an important resource for feminists, and, like the *Oresteia* itself, at least on Zeitlin's reading of it, Cixous's mythopoeic text has functioned as a model for the legitimation of an alternative world view.

Medusa has been comprehensively rehabilitated as a feminist icon, and her example has been followed in the twenty-first century in the numerous fictional works which have similarly regenerated the profiles of other mythical women, such as Madeline Miller's *Circe* (2018). From an ominous figure, associated with the negative side of a whole host of binary oppositions in the landscape of ancient Greek myth, she has become a symbol of how the repressed and banished can always return triumphantly. Far from being timeless and impossible to eradicate, the lazy taxonomies of 'the other' have a limited lifespan and are largely dependent on unthinking reproduction of existing power structures. This contention applies to the hierarchies operative in the ancient world as much as to those of modernity, and understanding the fragile building-blocks of the status quo empowers those with an investment in change, even as it produces alarm in people who would prefer things to remain just as they are. But there is no room for complacency on the part of those who situate themselves on either side of the divide. The very nature of the abject means that it shows no particular favour to progressive political agendas but works to undermine hegemonic certainties wherever they occur. Within the cultural sphere, many instances of texts in various genres dramatize the struggle for the abject to re-emerge. And it is insufficient merely to flip the coin and celebrate this return, because that will not shift the logic of opposition that structures the social order. The question is, then, what might constitute a post-queer feminist construal of the monstrous?

CONCLUSION:
TWENTY-FIRST-CENTURY FURIES

Feminist strategies have always been multifaceted, and projects such as Cixous's, which recuperate previously denigrated figures, are popular, as are those which give voice to the formerly silent. In an important sense, however, the reversal of the positive and negative terms of an opposition might serve further to entrench the opposition itself and reinforce the idea that (in this case) gendered identities are static and bounded. Seeking a more transformative mode, Judith Butler promoted what she called 'an economy of difference' which would 'force a reworking of that logic of non-contradiction by which one identification is always and only purchased at the expense of another' (1993: 118). This enjoinder that all identities are forged partially by what they reject, reminds us again of the abject and its role in the formation of both individual and social identities. Instead of fixing on one or other identity category, many activists now aim to forge affective and political alliances between a whole host of marginalized others in a way that does not foreclose their differences. 'Alliance' is indeed a key term within contemporary feminism, signifying as it does a transversal accommodation whose value is that it can be temporary. In her most recent work, *Posthuman Feminism*, Rosa Braidotti articulates the merits of this kind of strategic alliance:

> This trans-species, trans-sex and trans-racial alliance manifests a chain of solidarity between the sexualized, racialized and naturalized 'others' of white, urbanized, heteronormative 'Man'. Transversality, however, does not mean sameness. It is indeed the case that there are substantial differences in the ways in which in which patriarchy deals with each category marked by the sign of negative difference. But the marginalized others do share in a political economy of brutal discrimination. (2022: 219)

Grounded in awareness of the inequities of the world, this approach seeks to combine a pragmatic search for improvement with a philosophical awareness of the conceptual roots of oppression.

 If, in the light of this discussion, we return now to the end of the *Eumenides*, we can see how a twenty-first-century reading of the Furies takes shape. Moving away from an analysis which emphasizes their 'otherness' and perpetuates the image of the universal male who is fictively produced but potently endowed, we move to a depiction which allows for more elasticity in the bounds of their representation. The metamorphosis of the Furies into the Eumenides should not be regarded as a linear movement, a permanent resolution to the problem of their hostility towards Athens; the abject does not work like that. Rather, we need an iterative process of encounter with those who have been traduced and discarded, and a willingness to acknowledge that a sense of security, whether personal or civic, is achieved only at their expense. The Furies symbolize all those who are differently abled, gendered, or embodied; those who are discriminated against on account of race; and those who are currently bewildering and unintelligible. Spectators in the theatre of Dionysus may have breathed a sigh of relief when the Eumenides left the stage, believing their city safe, order restored, and a clear trajectory established for a prosperous and upstanding future. Such satisfaction, however, would have been misplaced: the process of incorporating their monstrous alterity, although for now successful, could not conceivably happen only once.

Suggested Reading

For an exploration of how the situation of non-normative bodies in space and time interrogate social relations see Ahmed (2006). Elliot (2010) provides a multifaceted account of some of the rifts in feminist, transgender, and queer theories, including a chapter on intelligibility. Halberstam (2018) shows how trans identities challenge all forms of gendered embodiment. The wide-ranging collection of essays by Lykke and Braidotti (1996) covers feminist engagements with science, medicine, and futuristic thinking. McRuer (2006) critiques both compulsory able-bodiedness and compulsory heterosexuality and demonstrates how a combination of queer and crip theory, thinking and activism, can begin the process of de-stigmatization. For a capacious and stimulating overview of debates within posthuman feminism see Braidotti (2022). Zimmerman (2021) provides a revisionist, celebratory analysis of eleven female monsters from Greek myth.

Works Cited

Ahmed, S. 2006. *Queer Phenomenology.* Durham, NC.
Beauvoir, S. de 1953. *The Second Sex*, trans. H. M. Parshley. New York.
Bloodsworth-Lugo, M. K., and C. R. Lugo-Lugo. 2013. 'The Monster Within: Post-9/11 Narratives of Threat and the U.S. Shifting Terrain of Terror', in *Monster Culture in the 21st Century: A Reader*, ed. M. Levina and D.-M. Bui, 243–56. London.
Braidotti, R. 2019. *Posthuman Knowledge.* Cambridge.
Braidotti, R. 2022. *Posthuman Feminism.* Cambridge.
Butler, J. 1986. *Gender Trouble.* London.
Butler, J. 1993. *Bodies That Matter.* London.
Cartledge, P. 2002. *The Greeks: A Portrait of Self and Others.* Oxford.
Cixous, H. 1986. 'Sorties', in *The Newly Born Woman*, ed. H. Cixous and C. Clément, trans. B. Wing, 63–132. Minneapolis.
Cohen, J. J. 1996. *Monster Theory: Reading Culture.* Minneapolis.
Creed, B. 1993. *The Monstrous Feminine: Film, Feminism, Psychoanalysis.* London.
Eidinow, E. 2018. 'The Horror of the Terrifying and the Hilarity of the Grotesque: Daimonic Spaces—and Emotions—in Ancient Greek Literature.' *Arethusa* 51/3: 209–35.
Elliot, P. 2010. *Debates in Transgender, Queer, and Feminist Theory.* London.
Goldhill, S. 1986. *Reading Greek Tragedy.* Cambridge.
Halberstam, J. 2018. *Trans*: A Quick and Quirky Account of Gender Variability.* Oakland, CA.
Kafer, A. 2013. *Feminist, Queer, Crip.* Bloomington, IN.

Kristeva, J. 1982. *The Power of Horror: An Essay on Abjection*, trans. L. S. Roudiez. New York.

Lutz, H., M. Vivar, and L. Supik. 2011. *Framing Intersectionality: Debates on a Multi-Faceted Concept in Gender Studies.* London.

Lykke, N., and R. Braidotti, eds. 1996. *Between Monsters, Goddesses and Cyborgs.* London.

McRuer, R. 2006. *Crip Theory: Cultural Signs of Queerness and Disability.* New York.

Mitchell, M. 2018. *Circe.* London.

Prins, Y. 1991. 'The Power of the Speech Act: Aeschylus' Furies and Their Binding Song.' *Arethusa* 24/2: 177–95.

Sedgwick, E. K. 1994. *Tendencies.* Durham, NC.

Zeitlin, F. 1978. 'The Dynamics of Misogyny: Myth and Mythmaking in the *Oresteia*.' *Arethusa* 11/1–2: 149–84.

Zimmerman, J. 2021. *Women and Other Monsters: Building a New Mythology.* Boston.

CHAPTER 28

....

GODS AND MONSTERS

Cognitive Approaches to the Monstrous

....

JENNIFER LARSON

INTRODUCTION

....

'COGNITION' is a general term for mental actions and processes, including attention, sensory perception, memory, reasoning, judgement, and language use. To an increasing degree in recent years, the definition of 'cognition' has expanded to account for the role of emotions and to move beyond 'brain-bound' understandings to more holistic ones that encompass the body and its environment: an abacus extends our cognitive capacities for calculation, just as writing supplies us with external memory. Cognitive science has always been an interdisciplinary field, drawing upon psychology, linguistics, philosophy, sociology, neuroscience, and evolutionary theory; cognitive theories provide frameworks for understanding early childhood development, common structures in human languages, the minds of neurodiverse people such as individuals with ADHD or autism, other kinds of minds (including non-human animal minds and artificial minds), and more. Increasingly, cognitive theories are being applied in the humanities (see Meineck et al. 2018: 1–18).

Before surveying cognitive theories applicable to ancient monsters, we must first ask what we mean by 'monsters'—a group not easily delimited. Lexical definitions stress the monster's fear-inducing size or form together with its imaginary status. Cultural theorists tend instead to focus on the monster's very real challenge to categories:

> The monstrous is that which creates this sense of vertigo, that which calls into question our (their, anyone's) epistemological worldview, highlights its fragmentary and inadequate nature, and thereby asks us (often with fangs at our throats, with its fire upon our skin, even as we and our stand-ins and body doubles descend the gullet) to acknowledge the failures of our systems of categorization. (Mittman 2017: 8)

Take away the parenthetical fangs and fire, and we might just as easily be talking of the miraculous and the divine. Gods and monsters are often, in fact, difficult to distinguish; in the case of monsters, category violation is perceived as negative, while in the case of gods (or other superhuman beings) it is either positive or ambiguous.

Cognitive theory includes the study of how human minds develop and apply categories, so it can be helpful as we explore questions of definition. Category violation itself has been the focus of much work in social psychology, which studies the role of essentialism (the belief that categories such as 'male' or 'dog' have an underlying invisible reality) in stereotyping and prejudice, and in the cognitive science of religion, which studies the properties attributed to superhuman beings (Newman and Knobe 2019; Martin and Wiebe 2017). Gods and ghosts combine properties we expect in the category PERSON (such as feeling emotions) with ones we do not expect (such as being invisible or knowing the future). To some degree this is also true of monsters. The Cyclops Polyphemus' emotions are psychologically familiar to us: he worries when the ram in his herd is slow to leave the cave, and he screams in pain when his eye is pierced. Yet his body plan and behaviour are so different as to exclude him from the category of humans.

Not every category violation yields a monster. Many individual animals fail to match zoological descriptions; a cat with one leg amputated is imperfect rather than monstrous. A cat born with three legs approaches closer to the monstrous because it violates our natural intuition that like begets like, yet this anomaly resembles an event—the loss of a limb—which can occur naturally. A cat with five legs strays more radically from the feline body plan, but is still recognizably a cat. An animal with a dog's head and a cat's body challenges the *essential* norms of felinity: now we must question whether this is still a cat. Behavioural anomalies differ analogously in degree: a cat that fetches balls like a dog is mildly and amusingly deviant; a talking or flying cat, on the other hand, would be a wonder, and depending on the culture, might be divine—thus forcing a questioning of category: is this creature different in essence from 'regular' cats? Psychologists have observed that humans think about certain categories, such as natural kinds, as possessing an underlying, invisible 'essence': even if you paint stripes on a donkey and call it a zebra, this in no way makes it a zebra or changes its essential 'donkeyness' (Gelman 2003: 23). Cognitive theorist Dan Sperber (1996b) notes that deviation from the *essential* norm of a living kind, or perfect adherence to an essential norm—for example, that lions are brave and dogs faithful—is what allows animals to function symbolically. Like gods and 'perfect' animals, monsters perform symbolic work.

What we call 'monsters' typically violate essential norms (physical or behavioural) in ways we perceive as negative. In some cases, these are pan-human expectations, such as the norm that the human body plan has one head, a torso, and four limbs. In other cases, they are culturally determined ideals, such as the ancient Greek expectation that women submit to their husbands and not wield weapons. In both cases, the norms are *essential* because severe violations call into question an individual's membership in the category of which the norms represent an ideal. For example, the condition of being born with no head (or two heads) might today call into question an individual's personhood. In Aeschylus' fifth-century BCE tragedy *Agamemnon*, Clytemnestra's gruesome

murder of her husband and assumption of political power make her monstrous, because she behaves like a man; one character, seeking an appropriate metaphor for this
'female slayer of the male', calls her a 'hateful beast' and compares her to Scylla (1231–4;
see Hopman in this volume). Emically—that is, from an insider's perspective on a given
culture—extreme violations of either physical or behavioural essential norms tend to
be perceived as 'unnatural', and both may attract the label 'monstrous'. From an etic,
universalizing perspective, we can see that cultures and individuals vary on the question
of which behaviours are deviant enough to disrupt identity. Claims of essential norm
violation are often used for rhetorical effect. At what point, for example, do criminal acts
or acts of war become 'inhuman' and thus monstrous?

Certain animals frighten us not because they violate any category, but simply because we innately react to them as predators or venomous creatures, and they are in
fact dangerous. Are these animals monsters? Consider the shark in the movie *Jaws*
(1975, dir. Steven Spielberg). Contrary to the behaviour of actual great white sharks, this
one exhibits a human-like ability to hold a grudge and to target certain individuals for
attack; it is also unusually large (Clasen 2018: 358). The *Jaws* shark is thus an abnormal
super-predator, yet its deviance does not necessarily call into question the essential
norms of 'sharkness'. Indeed, its essential 'sharkness' may even be enhanced because the
possession of human-like belief-desire psychology makes a shark more dangerous and
truer to itself (we speak now of the shark as symbol of predation rather than as marine
organism). It is more like Sperber's 'perfect' animal, the brave lion or the faithful dog.
Thus, an animal which already triggers innate fear need not violate essential norms
to qualify as a monster, but something about it should be different in ways which enhance its fearsomeness. We see visual expressions of this in Greek vase-paintings, where
the snakes encountered by Cadmus and Jason are depicted as abnormally large. The
Nemean Lion subdued by Heracles possessed an anomalous feature, a hide invulnerable
to weapons, but this did not threaten its status as a lion.

FEAR, MONSTERS, AND ATTENTIONAL BIAS

Cognitive theory offers additional insights on the predator-as-monster, for example
in the phenomenon of attentional bias. Because we cannot pay attention to everything
all the time, we rely on innate selective factors in order to focus on what is most important (for our hominin ancestors, this meant anything relevant to food, reproduction,
or danger). Stimuli that attract our attention are said to be *salient*, and when they produce emotional or physiological arousal, they are *compelling*. Human faces and face-
like patterns are salient and often compelling. Facial expressions of anger (frowning
brows, furrowed nose, teeth displayed in a grimace) or of terror (staring eyes and gaping
mouth) capture our attention and may also be compelling as signs of danger; these attentional factors help to explain the popularity of the Greek *gorgoneion*, a frontal image
of a hideous, grimacing face. As makers of horror movies know, missing or misshapen

facial features and limbs command attention and often evoke fear. Finally, predators and venomous creatures are both more salient and more compelling than non-predatory, non-venomous ones (Clasen 2012a, 2012b).

Evolutionary horror scholarship, a relatively new subdiscipline of horror studies, holds that 'we can understand horror fiction as a cultural technology that works by tapping into ancient, defensive psychological mechanisms to satisfy an adaptive appetite for vicarious experience with scenarios of danger' (Clasen 2018: 355). In this view, fear and disgust exist in our emotional repertoire as protective mechanisms: disgust helps protect us from pathogens, fear from dangerous situations, animals, or people. The emotions of anxiety and dread evolved to allow us to anticipate and prepare to deal with dangers. Not only are images and stories of animal or human killers salient and highly memorable (thus enhancing their transmission and cultural distribution), but interest in such representations is adaptive, permitting individuals to rehearse the actions to be taken in dangerous situations.

An alternative view, equally grounded in cognitive theory, holds that regardless of whether interest in horror stories is itself adaptive, such stories exploit or parasitize the adaptive human systems for fear and disgust. That is, because we have evolved to be fearful and to pay attention to scary things, we are irresistibly drawn to certain types of stimuli. Much of human culture works this way, parasitizing attentional and other cognitive biases. For example, masks, portrait busts, and caricatures all exploit our capacity for facial recognition, which evolved not to entertain us but to facilitate social interaction (Sperber and Hirschfeld 2004). Cultures elaborate and utilize the cognitive 'catchiness' of monsters, just as advertisers use arousing images of sex or food to sell their products. Horror fiction and movies often teach moral lessons, and generations of parents around the world have used monsters to scare misbehaving children.

MCI CONCEPTS, MONSTERS, AND GODS

Pascal Boyer's theory of the 'minimally counterintuitive [MCI] concept' is a seminal idea in the cognitive science of religion. Boyer suggests that concepts which run counter to our naturally developing intuitive expectations, yet remain easy to understand, are more memorable than other concepts. Hence, MCI concepts are more readily articulated and transmitted than fully intuitive concepts or those too counterintuitive to grasp readily. For example, that dogs give birth to puppies is so intuitive and mundane that it usually requires no comment. That dogs give birth to kittens is a simple but counterintuitive idea: an MCI concept. That a dog's mass becomes infinite as its body approaches the speed of light is a highly counterintuitive idea, difficult for most people to grasp. Of these three, the dog giving birth to kittens ought to be the most memorable and transmissible, especially in the absence of writing and over the course of many retellings. Empirical studies have borne out the memorability of MCI concepts while adding caveats about the contexts in which they are transmitted, the degree of counterintuitiveness, and the age of the subjects (Boyer 2001: 51–91; Porubanova 2019).

Experimental work has helped define what counts as naturally 'intuitive' or 'counterintuitive'. Developmental psychologists have identified several sets of expectations which young children form while interacting with their environments, without needing to be taught. These findings imply that even very young children distinguish among categories of objects: PERSONS (living things with mentality), ANIMATES (alive and self-moving), LIVING THINGS like trees that are not self-propelled, SOLID OBJECTS (non-living), and non-solid SPATIAL ENTITIES (like mist). Children apply 'intuitive physics' to the world around them, expecting objects both animate and inanimate to be visible, tangible and solid, unable to pass through each other. They likewise apply 'intuitive biology' to PERSONS, ANIMATES, and LIVING THINGS, expecting them to grow and need nourishment, to be vulnerable to injury, and to beget similar offspring. Finally, children apply an 'intuitive psychology' to PERSONS and sometimes ANIMATES, expecting other people's minds and sensory perception to function in ways analogous to their own: for example, other people feel emotions; other people cannot see through walls (Barrett 2011: 61–8). As Boyer points out, most of the world's religious concepts can be explained as violations of these naturally developing expectation sets:

> Persons can be represented as having counterintuitive physical properties (e.g., ghosts or gods), counterintuitive biology (many gods who neither grow nor die) or counterintuitive psychological properties (unblocked perception or prescience). Animals too can have all these properties. Tools and other artifacts can be represented as having biological properties (some statues bleed) or psychological ones (they hear what you say). Browsing through volumes of mythology, fantastic tales, anecdotes, cartoons, religious writings and science fiction, you will get an extraordinary variety of different concepts, but you will also find that the number of templates is very limited and in fact contained in the short list given above. (2001: 78–9)

'Counterintuitive' does not necessarily mean counterfactual. The metamorphosis of a caterpillar into a butterfly is counterintuitive. Rocks that grow exist: we call them crystals. While some intuitions develop naturally, many expectations are learned through reinforcement to the point that they become 'second nature'; violations of these expectations yield the bizarre. Bizarreness, in and of itself, does not violate naturally developing intuitions: a 'giant' eight feet tall exceeds our learned expectations for human body size but does not seem impossible, while a 'giant' as large as the earth is naturally counterintuitive, exceeding expectations for *any* living thing (Barrett and Nyhof 2001–2002).

MCI theory has often been used to describe gods, but is equally relevant to monsters, for most cultural theorists stress category violation as a defining factor in monstrousness. I described above how violation of essential norms produces monsters, whenever a person or animal negatively deviates from norms to such a degree that its membership in a category comes into question. Now, psychological essentialism and MCI theory overlap to some extent, because certain naturally developing intuitions are essentialist. A calf-like creature born from a woman violates essential norms of its category: is it a human baby or something else? The same event is also counterintuitive, violating a pan-human essentialist expectation about living kinds, that like begets like. Composite creatures violate essential physical norms: a centaur, as a man-horse combination, fails to fit either body plan. Composites are likewise counterintuitive, given the naturally developing inference that each living kind has its own essence, and that human-ness and horse-ness are mutually exclusive. The reason people are fascinated (and often horrified) by the prospect of hybrid births, like that of the Minotaur, is precisely because they are counterintuitive and especially memorable concepts.

Psychological essentialism and MCI theory do not always overlap, for essentialist expectations form only a subset of natural intuitions. A river that flows uphill or a person who exists only on Fridays are counterintuitive concepts having nothing to do with es-sentialism. Above we saw that people apply essential norms to social categories such as gender, which vary by culture. Sperber and Hirschfeld (2004) have suggested that gender is the cultural domain corresponding to the cognitive 'module' we use to identify the bio-logical sex of other people. This module would be a device similar to the mental tool we use for face recognition, but designed to assess secondary sexual characteristics such as genitalia, body size and shape, facial structure, voice pitch, and other sensory cues. If such a module exists, it will have evolved to yield crude, either/or conclusions, not to evaluate the subtleties of behaviour, grooming, or clothing, which vary by culture. Therefore, while Aeschylus depicts Clytemnestra's gender deviance in the *Agamemnon* as a violation of es-sential norms, this characterization is bizarre rather than counterintuitive in terms of MCI theory, for it contradicts no naturally developing intuitions about biological sex. Compare Hermaphroditus and other true androgynes, who are counterintuitive because they com-bine the physical characteristics of male and female.

Boyer's theory explains why monster body plans, and especially those of monsters from folklore and myth, follow quite predictable patterns, and why their deviations tend to be limited in number and degree, simple enough to transmit accurately. In the an-cient Greek world, many monsters, such as the Minotaur, Echidna, and the Harpies, are most often depicted as simple composites of two living kinds. Composites of three living kinds also occur (e.g. Scylla, the Sphinx, the Chimaera). Addition or (less often) subtraction of body parts is a recurrent yet simple counterintuitive feature (e.g. the Cyclopes, the Hundred-Handed giants, Cerberus). And the Hydra, for example, has two counterintuitive features combined: multiple heads that regenerate after amputa-tion. Talus, the living bronze giant created by the divine craftsman Hephaestus to guard Crete, is an animated object and thus counterintuitive.

Measured purely by number of category-defying features, the most counterintuitive Greek monsters are the Chimaera and the Gorgons. The hero Bellerophon battled the Chimaera, a fire-breathing lion-goat-snake composite (four features), a com-bination that mildly challenges the memory (see Smith in this volume). Most people remember Perseus' opponent Medusa simply as a snake-haired woman with a lethal visage (two features), but visual representations from antiquity show her as winged and sometimes tusked, while literary descriptions (freed from the limits of the average person's memory) add still more counterintuitive features (see Lowe in this volume). In the Roman period, for example, the mythographer Apollodorus synthesizes other accounts: 'But the Gorgons had heads entwined with dragon-scales, and great tusks like those of swine, and bronze hands, and golden wings, with which they flew; and they turned to stone whoever saw them' (*Bibl.* 2.4). This yields a composite of four living kinds plus the lethal face and metal body parts. The Gorgons' bronze hands and golden wings illustrate the counterintuitive idea of a living body with metal parts, as also found in accounts of the Stymphalian Birds and the Colchis Bulls.

Not all MCI concepts are equally likely to be remembered and transmitted. Concepts which are salient, as discussed above, have a memory advantage. In particular, *agents* are more salient than non-agents. Evolutionarily speaking, it pays to attend to other creatures who may harm or help you. Therefore, a man with an iron hand should be more salient and memorable than a tree with iron bark. Likewise, the *inferential potential* of concepts affects how memorable they are (Boyer 1996). Compare a bag that makes anything portable with a bag made of water. Both are MCI concepts, but one offers narrative possibilities while the other seems like a dead end. Which is more interesting, a tree that grants wishes or a tree that disappears when you speak to it? The narrative role of most Greek monsters is simply to be subdued by a hero, but occasionally they offer greater inferential potential. The Hundred-Handed giants switch sides to help Zeus against the Titans, Medusa's head becomes a handy weapon for Perseus, and Heracles dips his arrows in the Hydra's venomous blood.

Though both groups are counterintuitive, Greek monsters are simpler than Greek gods, who exhibit in their myths a wide variety of inferentially rich category violations, from immortality to flight to shape-shifting. Yet the audience for a traditional tale is rarely asked to consider more than a couple of counterintuitive features at once, and even these are shaped by narrative requirements. That gods may assume mortal guise is a convention of Greek epic with obvious advantages for the singer constructing a plot, yet rare in daily life or cultic contexts. With the help of memory aids such as traditional tale structures, metrical poetry, and writing, the counterintuitive features of Greek gods may accumulate, but they do not become more conceptually challenging (see Rubin 1995: 28). Greek gods may fly, for example, but they do not time-travel, bilocate, or instantly teleport from one place to another. Zeus may see everything, but he is not everywhere at once.

MONSTERS AND THE EPIDEMIOLOGY OF REPRESENTATIONS

Dan Sperber, whose writings have deeply influenced the cognitive science of religion, proposed that representations, whether internal (mental concepts) or external (spoken, written, painted, sculpted, etc.) undergo a process of selection in what he called an 'epi-demiology of representations' (1985, 1994). Sperber's theory applies Darwinian natural se-lection to the transmission of culture, taking account of the crucial ways in which cultural representations differ from genes. Genes are mechanically reproduced in identifiable units, but culture is transmitted in much less reliable and quantifiable ways. In the absence of mech-anical reproduction, every 'copy' requires the mental reception of a representation and its subsequent external expression—a messy process fraught with errors. If I say the word 'mon-ster', for example, you will likely form a mental image quite different from mine, and a verbal description of my monster will change as it passes from one person to the next. Our real task is not to discover what caused change in ancient cultural representations, but rather, given the limitations of human memory and technical ability, what allowed these representations to be reproduced with recognizable fidelity and become stabilized within a culture (Sperber 1996a: 58, 65–6). Even when technologies of reproduction and dissemination become wide-spread, mere availability does not guarantee that content will capture attention. Our evolved mental architecture and cognitive biases, together with the specifics of the cultural envir-onment, determine what we find salient and compelling, what we remember, and what we transmit. Thus, the study of cultural transmission requires a 'biocultural' approach that takes account of both cognitive and environmental factors.

David Wengrow has discussed the dissemination of images of composite creatures during the Bronze and Iron Ages in relation to MCI theory and Sperber's epidemi-ology of representations. As he notes, fantastic creatures originating in Mesopotamia found receptive audiences in Egypt, Anatolia, and the Mediterranean as each of these areas achieved 'core features of urban civilization' such as planned cities, literacy, bureaucracies, and sacred kingship (2014: 59–62). Most of all, composite creatures adorned objects made for urban elites, such as carved seals, architectural elements, ritual vessels and tools, jewellery, and (probably) textiles. Thus, arriving in Egypt from their ultimate sources in Mesopotamia or western Iran, the sphinx and griffin made their way to the palaces of Minoan Crete, and thence to Mycenae, Pylos, and Tiryns on the Greek mainland. In the late eighth and seventh centuries BCE, a second wave of composite creatures, including sirens and chimaeras, reached the Greek world and was again swiftly adopted. To explain this rapid dissemination beyond the ob-viously counterintuitive salience of sphinx, griffin, or bull-man, Wengrow points to networks of urban elites connected by trade and diplomacy, eager to embrace each other's symbols of authority and luxury. The invention of the first modes of mech-anical reproduction, such as seals and moulded terracotta, facilitated the spread of these images, as did their reproduction on durable, portable media such as gemstones and clay. Because Wengrow remains ambivalent about the ultimate impact of cogni-tive factors, it is worthwhile here to delve further into the 'epidemiology' of monster representations.

The very notion of the composite creature offered artisans fertile ground for ex-perimentation. Some produced counterintuitive creatures which did *not* catch on cross-culturally. Wengrow cites the seals created by the Minoan Zakro Master: 'hyper-composites, combining manifold elements of human and animal bodies—which appear never to have travelled far beyond their point of inception' (2014: 75–6, and his Fig. 5.1). The Zakro Master's complex, Hieronymus Bosch-like creations are highly rather than minimally counterintuitive, and thus not good candidates for transmission. The same holds true of many Mesopotamian composites, which grew more complex both visually and symbolically as they acquired layers of meaning over the centuries. The entity Lamaštu, for example, is a composite of woman, lion, donkey, raptor, and perhaps dog, who grasps snakes as attributes. Likewise, Pazuzu is a composite with elements of man, bird, scorpion, snake, and lion or dog (see Fig. 2.1 in this volume). Various Babylonian-Assyrian texts describing their gods reveal how each body part and pose of a divine being had individual symbolic meanings (Pongratz-Leisten 2015). In Egyptian art, too, an animal head on an anthropomorphic body functioned less as a literal rendering of a god's appearance than a symbolic attribute, just as in hieroglyphs. In both Mesopotamian and Egyptian cultures, these abstruse understandings of composite creatures were enabled by writing and by a class of expert scribes and scholars. When such images reached the urban elites of civilizations who did not share long-standing written traditions or systematic theology, they were stripped of their heavy cognitive load and reduced to visually striking but relatively simple composites (see also both Richey and Boychenko in this volume).

With Deirdre Wilson, Sperber has proposed that the process of cultural transmission exerts pressure in the direction of representations that are *relevant* (Sperber and Wilson 1995: 118–32). Relevance in this technical sense means, first, that a given representation (for example, a mental image of a hero battling a monster) requires *less cognitive effort* to grasp and remember than others (for example, the monster's symbolic role in the cosmology of its home culture). Second, it means that a given representation produces *more cognitive effects* than others. That is, the representation is salient (A fight with a predator-like creature!), or inferentially rich (Might this strongman be a god?), or compelling (The creature is hideous!), or richly evocative, reminding people of multiple things already known to them (The strongman is like Heracles!).

For the transmission of composite creature iconography from Near Eastern and Egyptian sources to the Greeks, cognitive theories predict the following:

> (1) Composites involving humans will be favoured as more salient and (2) composites of two or at most three living kinds will predominate despite the longer-term Mesopotamian trend towards multiplicity.

Our visual recognition of composite creatures, as of all animals, functions through the perception of parts recognized as diagnostic, such as the distinctive shape of a feline paw, a bird's beak, or a serpent's coil. Because of our attraction to faces, the most salient combination involves the transposition of a human head onto an animal body. Of the myriad composites directly available from the ancient Near East and Egypt, the most popular in 'orientalizing' Greek art (eighth to seventh centuries BCE) are the centaur, sphinx, and siren, all of which fit this pattern, while the quadruped griffin imitated from Phoenician ivories is easily recognizable as an eagle-lion composite.

(3) Composites selected for imitation will favour simple 'grafting' of body parts rather than complex 'melding' of features.

'Grafting' the frontal parts of one creature with the hind parts of another facilitates quick visual recognition. Again, centaur and siren fit this pattern, while the quadruped griffin and sphinx, composed of a substitute head on a winged lion's body, are only slightly more complex. In this regard, the *gorgoneion* and the faces of satyrs are exceptional precisely because they are formed by melding features together rather than grafting them, so that the individual components are more difficult to tease out.

(4) The living kinds selected as components will already have symbolic weight in Greek culture.

The canon of Greek composites can be broken down into a quite limited group of living kinds: human, bovine (= bull but not cow), horse, snake, lion, bird (with dog, fish, and goat less common). The more diverse Mesopotamian repertoire includes such animals as the scorpion and donkey, but the group of imported composites most popular in early Greek art (sphinx, siren, griffin, and perhaps centaur) economically consists only of human, horse, lion, and bird. As in Mesopotamia, the Greek canon favours animals notable for fierceness or boldness combined with rapidity—creatures to admire or fear. Prey animals such as deer and even boar do not appear in composites, although the siren's avian body is that of a non-raptor (see Denson in this volume).

(5) Most narrative and symbolic associations from the source culture will be jettisoned in favour of new contexts.

Greek reception of Near Eastern composites entailed the loss of most narratives and symbolic associations from the source cultures, while still retaining a connection with elites, especially in the Minoan and Mycenaean link between composite creatures and kingship. In the eighth and seventh centuries again, such composite representations were transferred via luxury and ceremonial objects owned mostly by elites, then disseminated through temple architecture, vase-paintings, and other media. In time, the creatures' imported iconography was matched with existing or new myths to produce stable cultural representations.

Because the Near Eastern and Egyptian cultures often depicted their gods with composite bodies, and even modern scholarship often hesitates to identify a given superhuman being as a god, demon, *genius*, or monster, the distinction between god and monster in these source civilizations remains vague. Our initial definition reserved the term 'monster' for creatures whose category violations were assessed negatively, but in these cultures, composite creatures were ambiguous: beings who could use their power either to threaten or to protect. In Mesopotamia and Egypt, such creatures played important roles as guardians of king and palace and in expelling illness and other misfortunes. Despite the simplification of Near Eastern monster representations during transmission, this key apotropaic function was often retained, or it spontaneously reappeared, among the Greeks (Faraone 1992: 27). The sphinx provides good examples of this role, guarding both sanctuaries and tombs.

MONSTER AND GOD ON MAGICAL GEMS: ANGUIPEDE AND CHNOUBIS

Lastly, regarding the rapid dissemination of composite creature imagery, consider the novel composites engraved on gems used as amulets in the Roman imperial period. Two figures commonly encountered on magical gems are composite beings, the Anguipede (a name bestowed by modern scholars) and Chnoubis (or Chnoumis). Visually, we might consider them 'monsters', while scholars often refer to them as gods. Yet they were apparently not objects of organized cult worship, nor did they feature in myths. Instead, their existence is almost completely limited to their magical function on gems: to heal or protect the wearers (Dasen and Nagy 2012: 302). The Anguipede, a cock-headed figure with snaky legs, wearing a cuirass, holds a whip in one hand and a shield in the other (Fig. 28.1). As a composite (cock, man, snake) with two attributes (whip, shield), he is slightly more complex and visually perplexing than Chnoubis, a lion-headed serpent who rears up as though ready to strike, with solar rays emanating from his head. In both cases, the iconography was developed by ritual specialists with esoteric learning, but the consumer did not need this knowledge to benefit from the amulet's protection.

The Anguipede's origin has been much debated. He first appears in the second century CE, likely as an innovation of Roman imperial date. According to one plausible interpretation, he functions as a combination rebus and pun on a title of the Jewish god, as his parts represent words derived from the Hebrew root GBR: *ha-gvurah* (the Mighty One), *gever* (cock and man), *gibbor* (warrior, giant in stature, also a name of God). The Anguipede's snaky legs allude to the iconography of the Greek Giants (*gigantes*) and their great strength and stature, once again in connection with *gibbor*. The figure's shield, often marked IAŌ (a Greek transcription of the Hebrew tetragrammaton YHWH, *Yahweh*), confirms the connection with the God of Israel, while the whip evokes his ability to punish enemies. The creation of the Anguipede allowed ritual specialists to draw upon the power of the Jewish 'Mighty One' and integrate it into their magical practice (Nagy 2002). Few owners of the gems would have known Hebrew or understood that the Anguipede represented not the deity himself, but one of his epithets. Rather, they may have been attracted to the exoticism of the Anguipede, his striking appearance, and the magical texts (often the word *Abrasax*) engraved alongside him.

Chnoubis, likewise, appears to have an esoteric origin, drawn from Hellenistic Egyptian astrology. Each zodiacal sign included three divinities known as 'decans', and each of these accounted for ten degrees in the band of the ecliptic. The name and

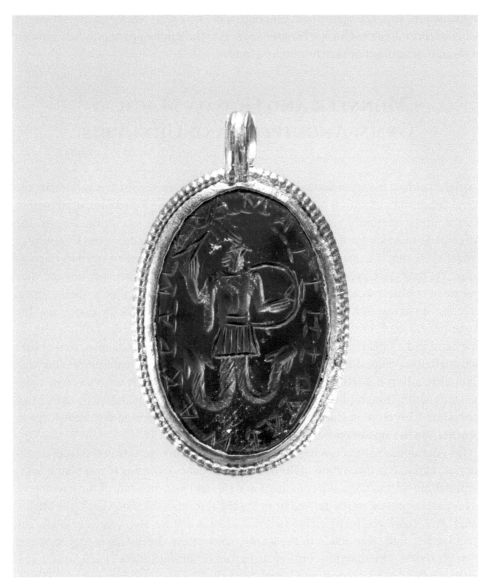

FIGURE 28.1 Cock-headed Anguipede holding a whip and shield. Roman jasper intaglio, second to third century CE.

appearance of Chnoubis were modelled on decans under the signs of Cancer and Leo, with the crown of solar rays added to elevate Chnoubis above a mere decan. The creature's protective and healing role, however, arose from the tradition that each decan was associated with a part of the human body; several inscriptions indicate that the Chnoubis amulet was used against maladies of the stomach or belly (Dasen and Nagy 2012: 295–9).

The Anguipede and Chnoubis are two of the most familiar figures on Roman-period magical gems. Their popularity may have related in part to the demand for the kinds of magical aid they offered, digestive and other belly ailments being very common. On the other hand, Chnoubis gems were not the only ones used for stomach pains. Possibly the striking images themselves, with their category-violating (i.e. monstrous) properties, generated attention, interest, and demand.

Like the seals, vessels, and jewellery Wengrow (2014) describes, magical gems were luxury items consumed by elites, and like their Bronze Age and Archaic predecessors, they warded off evils. In each case, images of composites were disseminated via thriving trade networks, but the cross-cultural processes and means of transmission differed. The Bronze Age and Archaic examples involved the selection of 'relevant' features of a given composite for transmission from a source to a target culture. Simplification and adaptation to the new culture occurred during artisans' reproduction of iconography. Oral transmission of related concepts surely contributed to this process in some cases, but not in others. With the Roman-era gems, on the other hand, magical specialists invented the new composites and applied them in complex rituals, drawing as needed on Egyptian, Greek, Roman, Jewish, and other traditions in the multicultural Empire. They also disseminated written manuals of rituals, which were then adapted to handbooks for gem engravers. The selection of 'relevant' features occurred as (1) written spells were repurposed and abbreviated for the gem format; (2) engravers without magical expertise copied the designs; and (3) certain designs proved more popular with customers.

CONCLUSION

Concepts drawn from cognitive psychology, including essentialism, attentional bias, and the minimally counterintuitive, help to define monsters and explain their ubiquity in human cultures. Monsters violate essentialist category norms, and they are often counterintuitive or frightening in ways that make them memorable, encouraging cultural transmission. The rapid dissemination of monster images from Mesopotamia to the Aegean during the Bronze and Iron Ages differed from the bricolage of ritual specialists in the Roman Empire, who invented entirely new composites to empower their gemstone amulets. In each case, however, the process of transmission included a reduction in the cognitive effort required of the recipients. Throughout the discussion, we have observed that monsters and gods are closely related, and sometimes indistinguishable.

SUGGESTED READING

For more on horror and monsters, see the essays in Corstophine and Kremmel (2018). The volume of papers edited by Slone and McCorkle (2019) describes the empirical basis of cognitive theories about religion, including minimal counterintuitiveness. Barrett (2008) provides more detailed discussion of intuitive expectations about categories. For the neuroscience of horror, see Asma (2015), and for the Anguipede and Chnoubis on magical gems, Faraone (2018).

WORKS CITED

Asma, S. T. 2015. 'Monsters on the Brain: An Evolutionary Epistemology of Horror.' *Social Research: An International Quarterly* 81/4: 941–68.

Barrett, J. 2008. 'Coding and Quantifying Counterintuitiveness in Religious Concepts: Theoretical and Methodological Reflections.' *Method and Theory in the Study of Religion* 20: 308–38.

Barrett, J. 2011. *Cognitive Science, Religion and Theology: From Human Minds to Divine Minds.* West Conshohocken, PA.

Barrett, J., and M. A. Nyhof. 2001–2002. 'Spreading Non-Natural Concepts: The Role of Intuitive Conceptual Structures in Memory and Transmission of Cultural Materials.' *Journal of Cognition and Culture* 1/1: 69–100.

Boyer, P. 1996. 'What Makes Anthropomorphism Natural: Intuitive Ontology and Cultural Representations.' *Journal of the Royal Anthropological Institute* 2/1: 83–97.

Boyer, P. 2001. *Religion Explained: The Evolutionary Origins of Religious Thought.* New York.

Clasen, M. 2012a. 'Attention, Predation, Counterintuition: Why Dracula Won't Die.' *Style* 46/3: 378–98.

Clasen, M. 2012b. 'Monsters Evolve: A Biocultural Approach to Horror Stories.' *Review of General Psychology* 16/2: 222–9.

Clasen, M. 2018. 'Evolutionary Study of Horror Literature', in *The Palgrave Handbook to Horror Literature*, ed. K. Corstorphine and L. R. Kremmel, 355–63. London.

Corstophine, K., and L. R. Kremmel, eds. 2018. *The Palgrave Handbook to Horror Literature.* London.

Dasen, V., and Á. M. Nagy. 2012. 'Le Serpent léontocéphale Chnoubis et la magie de l'époque romaine impériale.' *Anthropozoologica* 47/1: 291–314.

Faraone, C. A. 1992. *Talismans and Trojan Horses: Guardian Statues in Ancient Greek Myth and Ritual.* Oxford.

Faraone, C. 2018. *The Transformation of Greek Amulets in Roman Imperial Times.* Philadelphia.

Gelman, S. A. 2003. *The Essential Child: Origins of Essentialism in Everyday Thought.* Oxford.

Hirschfeld, L. A., and S. A. Gelman. eds. 1994. *Mapping the Mind: Domain Specificity in Cognition and Culture.* Cambridge.

Martin, L. A., and D. Wiebe. eds. 2017. *Religion Explained? The Cognitive Science of Religion after Twenty-Five Years.* London.

Meineck, P., W. M. Short, and J. Devereaux. eds. 2018. *The Routledge Handbook of Classics and Cognitive Theory.* New York.

Mittman, A. S. 2017. 'Introduction: The Impact of Monsters and Monster Studies', in *The Ashgate Research Companion to Monsters and the Monstrous*, ed. A. S. Mittman and P. J. Dendle, 1–16. New York.

Nagy, Á. M. 2002. 'Figuring out the Anguipede "Snake-Legged God" and His Relation to Judaism.' *Journal of Roman Archaeology* 15: 159–172.

Newman, G. E., and J. Knobe. 2019. 'The Essence of Essentialism.' *Mind & Language* 34/5: 585–605.

Pongratz-Leisten, B. 2015. 'Imperial Allegories: Divine Agency and Monstrous Bodies in Mesopotamia's Body Description Texts', in *The Materiality of Divine Agency*, ed. B. Pongratz-Leisten and K. Sonik, 119–41. Berlin.

Porubanova, M. 2019. 'Is Memory Crucial for Transmission of Religious Ideas?', in *The Cognitive Science of Religion*, ed. J. Slone and W. W. McCorkle, 93–100. London.

Rubin, D. C. 1995. *Memory in Oral Traditions: The Cognitive Psychology of Epic, Ballads, and Counting-Out Rhymes*. Oxford.

Slone, J., and W. W. McCorkle, eds. 2019. *The Cognitive Science of Religion*. London.

Sperber, D. 1985. 'Anthropology and Psychology: Towards an Epidemiology of Representations.' *Man*, 20/1: 73–89.

Sperber, D. 1994. 'The Modularity of Thought and the Epidemiology of Representations', in *Mapping the Mind: Domain Specificity in Cognition and Culture*, ed. L. A. Hirschfeld and S. A. Gelman, 39–67. Cambridge.

Sperber, D. 1996a. *Explaining Culture: A Naturalistic Approach*. Oxford.

Sperber, D. 1996b. 'Why Are Perfect Animals, Hybrids, and Monsters Food for Symbolic Thought?' *Method & Theory in the Study of Religion* 8/2: 143–69.

Sperber, D., and L. A. Hirschfeld. 2004. 'The Cognitive Foundations of Cultural Stability and Diversity.' *Trends in Cognitive Science* 8/1: 40–6.

Sperber, D., and D. Wilson. 1995. *Relevance: Communication and Cognition*, 2nd edn. Cambridge, MA.

Wengrow, D. 2014. *The Origins of Monsters: Image and Cognition in the First Age of Mechanical Reproduction*. Princeton.

CHAPTER 29

MONSTERS OF THE INNER WORLD

Psychoanalytic Approaches

EIRINI APANOMERITAKI

INTRODUCTION

THE relationship between psychoanalytic thought and classical monsters is a long-standing one. Monsters belong to myths, so a field surrounded by mythology, such as psychoanalysis, unsurprisingly maintains a close affinity with the imaginary beings of antiquity. Key figures of the psychoanalytic movement of the nineteenth and twentieth centuries, including Sigmund Freud (1856–1939), Otto Rank (1884–1939), Carl Gustav Jung (1875–1961), and Melanie Klein (1882–1960), relied on myths when developing their theories about the mind. That is not to say that myth held the same weight across theories that later evolved into distinct schools of thought, such as the Freudian, the Kleinian, or the school of analytical psychology. Yet, as this chapter shows, classical monsters of Greece and Rome appear frequently in the work of the pioneers of psychoanalysis and in the texts of their successors. Psychoanalysis, if one follows Freud and Jung, focuses, broadly speaking, on the individual's inner world, the unconscious. Mythical narratives, including ones about monsters, assist the analyst to explore the contents of the unconscious mind during therapy. Myths and their contents provide a framework for a better understanding of one's inner world. But how exactly do monsters fit in with psychoanalysis?

To answer, Freud's theory about the Oedipus myth as a narrative of 'universal' value is our starting point. In *The Interpretation of Dreams*, Freud examines Sophocles' tragedy *Oedipus the King* as a paradigm of the unconscious wishes that children develop towards their parents (1900: 260). Because these wishes are essentially unconscious, children remain entirely unaware of them. According to Freud, the tragic fate of Oedipus—to kill his father and marry his mother—is re-enacted in the unconscious wishes of both children and adults. For Freud, then, the Theban Sphinx that Oedipus confronts in *Oedipus the King* is a symbol of the father whom the male child needs to metaphorically murder; the father is a threat to the potential, forbidden union between the child and the mother (1928: 188). For Jung (1967: 179), the Sphinx is an expression of the mother while a hero facing any terrible monster means a confrontation with the unconscious (1966: 99). Similarly, Rank's interpretation focuses on the mother symbolism ([1924] 1999: 149).

Another female monster, Medusa with her terrible serpent hair, is at the centre of the fear of castration (Freud 1922) and she is interpreted as a symbol of women's genitalia (Ferenczi 1923), while later interpretations turn away from Freud either by examining other components of the myth (Róheim 1940) or by explicitly criticizing Freud's claims in relation to women's bodies (Cixous 1976). Feminist psychoanalytic interpretations of Medusa include Kristeva's (2012) analysis of the head and Mayock's (2013) 'Medusa Complex'.

In light of the above, this chapter discusses two monsters that occupy a seminal position in psychoanalytic thought: the Theban Sphinx and the Gorgon Medusa. First, I investigate the role of the Sphinx in the writings of Freud, Rank, and Jung. While the Sphinx is not central to the theories of these writers, it deserves attention as a divisive monster in the history of psychoanalysis. Then, I look at Medusa as discussed by Freud and others. Lastly, I examine the Minotaur, another hybrid monster present on the margins of psychoanalytic theory, yet significant. Given Freud's notes on the Knossos archaeological site, the mythological location of the Minotaur and the Labyrinth, and other approaches to the creature, the Minotaur emerges as a distinctive monster for psychoanalysis in its connection to twentieth-century archaeology and bull symbolism.

THE THEBAN SPHINX

This section examines the Theban Sphinx in the theories of Freud, Rank, Róheim, Jung, Bion, and others. Firstly, I discuss Freud's interpretation of the Sphinx in the story of Oedipus. Secondly, I look at post-Freudian and Jungian approaches to the monster showing the wide range of readings the Sphinx has attracted from theorists. In all the theories discussed below a common strand emerges: the Sphinx often represents one's parent, being a key figure to our mental development (see also López-Ruiz in this volume).

The Freudian Sphinx

One could argue that the Sphinx enters psychoanalytic theory with Freud's study of Sophocles' play *Oedipus the King* (425 BCE) as the literary source for his Oedipus complex. In the play, Oedipus, the king of Thebes, tries to help his city overcome a plague.

According to the Delphic Oracle, if the murderer of the previous Theban king, Laius, is found, the city will be saved. While searching for the murderer, the truth about Oedipus and his real parents emerges: Oedipus has fulfilled an older Delphic prophecy that one day he would kill his father, Laius, and marry his mother, Jocasta. It is Oedipus' unthinkable fate and his inability to escape it that caught Freud's attention. Freud's fascination is not with the Sphinx but rather with the plot's portrayal of Oedipus' fate, highlighting that 'it is the fate of all of us, perhaps, to direct our first sexual impulse towards our mother and our first hatred and our first murderous wish against our father. Our dreams convince us that that is so' (1900: 261). Taking his cue from Sophocles, Freud's words echo those of Jocasta's in the play before she and Oedipus discover the truth—that she is his mother: 'do not fear this marriage with your mother', she says to Oedipus, 'many a man has suffered this before | But only in his dreams' (*OT* 980–1).[1] These lines from Sophocles on the collective dreams of all men allowed Freud to claim that these dreams and unconscious wishes are universal.

The story of how Oedipus became king of Thebes remains in the background of *Oedipus the King* and is not part of the play's action: Oedipus had saved Thebes by solving the riddle of the Sphinx (*OT* 35–7), the monster that tortured the city by devouring those unable to answer her riddle. Oedipus thus won the throne of Thebes and married Jocasta, the widowed queen of the city, thereby unknowingly committing incest. Sophocles never mentions the riddle's wording, nor does he refer to the encounter between Oedipus and the monster apart from a brief description: 'the crooked-clawed, riddling Sphinx, maiden and bird' (*OT* 1199–1200), consistent with other accounts of the creature as a hybrid with wings, a lion's body, a serpent's tail, and a woman's head, born from the monsters Echidna and Typhon (Apollod. *Bibl.* 3.52–5) or the Chimaera and Orthrus (Hes. *Theog.* 26). Freud was familiar with the fabled encounter between Oedipus and the Sphinx as well as her riddle, without crediting any source other than Sophocles—despite his knowledge of the myth's variations in classical sources (Bowlby 2007: 36).

The Oedipus complex is at the core of Freud's study of the inner world of adults and children. In line with his theories on the development of sexuality, the meaning of the question of 'where babies come from' is like the riddle the Sphinx posed to her victims (1905: 193–4), which was, naturally, in the form of a question: 'What is that which has one voice and yet becomes four-footed and two-footed and three-footed?' (Apollod. *Bibl.* 3.5–8, trans. Simpson 1976). Oedipus answered 'Man', based on the different stages of one's life: a crawling infant, an adult, and an old man using a walking stick. Children, Freud explains, have an 'instinct for knowledge', much like Oedipus must have had when he answered the riddle. Freud observed that one of the first questions his young patients asked was how children are born, assuming that a child's curiosity about the origin of babies/man is identical to the Oedipal 'quest' for knowledge (1905: 194). Although he later revised some of these admittedly simplistic claims, the link between knowledge

---

[1] Translations from *Oedipus the King* are by Kitto (Hall 1994).

and the riddle can be traced back to Sophocles when Oedipus declares to the Thebans that the Sphinx was defeated by his own intelligence (*OT* 390–400). For Freud, children are called to answer the 'essential' nature of the Sphinx's riddle, much like Oedipus.

In the context of Freud's investment in Sophocles, Richard Armstrong (2005: 52) suggests 'an analogy between Oedipus solving the riddle of the Sphinx and the analyst solving the riddle of the patient's psyche'. Armstrong draws upon Freud's passion for antiquity; one example is a copy of Jean-Auguste-Dominique Ingres's 1808 painting *Oedipus and the Sphinx* that Freud kept in his practice in Vienna (Fig. 29.1). Griselda Pollock analyses the painting's exact position in Freud's office and the painting itself while questioning the Freudian Oedipal structure (2006: 77–80). On Freud's fiftieth birthday, he was given a medallion depicting Oedipus and the Sphinx, with an inscription from his favourite play, referring to Oedipus as a powerful man who solved the Sphinx's riddle. The medallion's other side depicts Freud's profile, alluding to the 'Oedipus' of psychoanalysis. According to Jones (1955: 13), Freud acknowledged that he had imagined a statue of himself at the University of Vienna, accompanied by the same line from Sophocles, confirming Armstrong's claim that 'the figure of Oedipus thus literally became symbolic capital for the [psychoanalytic] movement, that is, the means of honouring its founder as a chief riddle-solver and powerful man' (2005: 52).

In 'Dostoevsky and Parricide', Freud returns to the Sphinx and firmly places the monster in the realm of the father in the Oedipus complex. In Sophocles, comments Freud, Oedipus can marry his mother only by encountering the monster, after he has killed his father. Freud ignores the myth's variations in which the Sphinx kills herself, instead conveniently reading the Sphinx's death as a repetition of the symbolic parricide the child needs to commit to access the mother (1928: 188). Freud's Sphinx remains in the realm of the father in contrast with Rank's interpretation which rendered the creature as a symbolic mother. Freud's reliance on Sophocles' version of the Oedipus myth and his selective reading of the play as an expression of humanity's deepest desires led to criticism of the validity of the Oedipus complex.

The Maternal Sphinx

Rank's *The Trauma of Birth*, wherein the Sphinx appears, contributed to Freud's ideological break with him (Segal 2014). The Greek Sphinx, says Rank ([1924] 1999: 143), symbolizes the first anxiety arising from the trauma of birth. According to Rank, the act of the infant's separation from the mother during birth is traumatic for the baby. Speaking generally of the hybrid creatures that populate Greek myths, he argues that predominantly female monsters, such as the Medusa and the Sphinx, represent the primal mother and are associated with birth anxiety (149). The mother-monster corresponds to a version of a mother that is malignant, and not the same as Freud's Oedipal mother. The hero, Rank suggests, needs to confront his fear of this mother, and master the birth trauma, i.e. his separation from the mother's womb before the Oedipus complex arises. Oedipus' encounter with the Sphinx corresponds to the trauma of birth

FIGURE 29.1   Jean Auguste Dominique Ingres, *Oedipus Explains the Riddle of the Sphinx*, 1808.

Louvre, RF 218. Public domain.

(Armstrong 2005: 58–59). The Sphinx appears as a version of the hero's second mother, which is hostile, with animal and human features combined, and which stands in stark contrast to the hero's real mother (Rank [1909] 2004: 43). Although Rank's birth anxiety theory was rejected by the psychoanalytic community, his take on the Sphinx as a maternal representation was adopted, with variations, by future psychoanalysts. Géza Róheim's claim that the Sphinx represents the hero's mother is not far from what Rank suggested (1940: 65): Róheim's Sphinx is a devouring mother, a malevolent version of Jocasta, one that seeks to destroy the hero; but the Hungarian psychoanalyst also associates the Sphinx with other monsters, such as the Harpies and the Gorgon Medusa, as images of the mother (64). Róheim takes his cue from British scholar Jane Harrison's work on Greek religion, which traces the common traits of these monsters as an embodiment of anxiety and fear (1903: 361).

The Sphinx also appears in a maternal role in Jung's break with Freud. The monster becomes an area of debate for them; through their diametrically opposed interpretations of the monster, theoretical differences become apparent (see Cornes 1986; Segal 2014). Amongst other issues, Cornes places the break between Freud and Jung in the context of their mutual interest in the Sphinx and mythology in general, since Freud allocated the Sphinx to the realm of the father while Jung interpreted the Sphinx as a symbol of the mother (1986: 10).

Jung posits that patterns found in myths should be treated as symbols, which can lead to the understanding of the archetypes, which then help uncover the contents of the unconscious. The Jungian archetypes are known as the innate contents of the 'collective unconscious', the shared, unconscious mind of humanity that is full of mythical images. Jung (1954: 198–9) identified the Sphinx as an expression of the 'anima' archetype, a feminine image that is unconsciously present in the mind of men. While women's minds possess a counterpart 'animus' archetype, expressions of the 'animus' are less menacing compared to the anima's monstrous feminine. Jung's archetypes indeed enrich our understanding of the Sphinx as an unconscious projection of femininity, but they do not escape stereotypical representations of women in stories as enigmatic or as monsters. In *Symbols of Transformation*, Jung treats the Sphinx in more detail, considering it a symbolic image of 'the Terrible Mother, who has left numerous traces in mythology' that might also appear in the dreams of children as a frightening monster essentially replacing the mother (1967: 179, 181). Arguably, given Jung's discussion of the Oedipus myth in the same publication, he does not share Freud's enthusiasm for the Sphinx's riddle. Instead, he considers the riddle to be a 'childish' one and sees Oedipus as a victim of 'matriarchal incest' since he must marry the queen/his mother. If, according to Jung (181), the Sphinx had been a more terrifying representation of the 'devouring mother', Oedipus would not have been able to confront her. Jung also discusses the Sphinx within a wider mythological context: following Hesiod's *Theogony*, he explores the monster's parentage, emphasizing that the Sphinx resulted from incest, since her mother, the snaky monster Echidna, and her father, the monstrous dog Orthrus, were mother and son (182). Echidna, as a 'double being', is a manifestation of the terrible mother who, like the Sphinx, has 'a lovely and attractive human half' and 'a horrible animal half' (182).

The Sphinx is herself a 'symbol' of the Oedipus complex, suggests Jung, due to her incestuous origin. Taking these into account, Jung sees the riddle Oedipus needs to solve as
a warning of the terrifying mother image—a warning that Oedipus dismisses through
arrogance (182).

Jung's analysis of the Sphinx lies within his interest in mythology and the mythological images he identified in his patients' dreams. Like Freud, though, his reading
of myths is somewhat selective; incest among Greek monsters is common, especially
in Hesiod. Yet, the common theme of incest and its visual expressions in myths is, in
Jungian psychology, a proof of the existence of the collective unconscious. The Sphinx
and other hybrids that often appear in dreams are 'theriomorphic representations of the
libido' (1967: 179). In Jungian psychology, the 'libido' is a desire, a kind of energy, or an
instinct, which is often repressed in the unconscious. The appearance of a Sphinx in a
dream could then be a visual expression of this energy. Jung later returns to the Sphinx
by observing that this monster's hybrid body exemplifies the coexistence of animal
instincts and humanity, or 'the symbiosis of conscious and unconscious' (1970: 378).

Further Interpretations of the Theban Sphinx

After Rank and Jung, other psychoanalysts considered the maternal rather than the
paternal as the realm of the Sphinx. Kanzer, for instance, argues that the monster
represents two diametrically opposed sides of female sexuality, the positive one being
the human parts of the Sphinx and the negative being her animal parts. When facing the
Oedipus complex, the hero needs to be able to face both sides of the monster (1950: 561).
Carlisky, following Rank, sees the Sphinx as 'the queen's guardian' and Oedipus' union
with Jocasta as a symbolic return to the mother (1958: 93). Thus, the connection between
Jocasta and the Sphinx has not been overlooked; Edmunds (2006: 20) notes that the
Sphinx provides 'the link between parricide and the incestuous marriage'.

In his study of Oedipus, French philosopher Jean-Joseph Goux criticizes Freud's interpretation of the Sphinx and the entire Freudian treatment of the Oedipus story.
Freud overlooked important aspects of the narrative, such as that Oedipus does not
kill the Sphinx himself, unlike other heroes of Greek myth who slay their monstrous
antagonists. The Sphinx, states Goux (1993: 23), 'is the unthought element of Freudian
psychoanalysis, a riddle unresolved by the Freudian movement'. He agrees with Jung's
interpretation that the Sphinx represents a dark mother, not a father. The creature is a
negative version of the mother, one often found in myths: 'a shadowy, dark, devouring
reptile, a monster inhabiting cavernous depths', a description that also alludes to the
Sphinx's mother, Echidna (26–7).

For W. R. Bion the Oedipal monster embodies the primal scene, i.e. the intercourse
between parents, that a child might accidentally witness and that presents itself as a
riddle (1992: 224). Similarly, psychoanalyst Leonard Shengold argues that the Sphinx
symbolizes 'the primal parent' (1989: 42), making no essential distinction between the
mother and the father, in contrast to the distinction's significance for Freud, Rank, and

Jung. Following Freud on the universality of the Oedipus complex, Shengold boldly states: 'we are all Oedipus and we must all destroy the Sphinx' (43), emphasizing the role of symbolically killing the mother-monster in a child's development.

In sum, the Sphinx begins her psychoanalytic journey as an image of the father, as explored by Freud, and she later becomes an expression of the terrifying mother, as seen in Rank and Jung. Her hybrid body becomes an expression of animal-human urges, while her much-discussed riddle receives considerable attention from psychoanalysts.

MEDUSA

Another prominent female hybrid monster in psychoanalytic discussions on monstrosity is the Gorgon Medusa. Below we look at some interpretations of Medusa, namely those by Freud and Kristeva, which consider the monster in the context of female anatomy and sexuality. The approaches to Medusa covered here are by no means exhaustive; rather, they aim to show how psychoanalytic debates about Medusa and, to an extent, female sexuality, advanced from the twentieth century onwards (see also Lowe in this volume).

Medusa in Freudian Psychoanalysis

The myth of Medusa was known to Freud. In a 1913 letter, Sándor Ferenczi informs Freud about the discovery of a Gorgon sculpture from the temple of Artemis in Corfu (Fig. 23.1 in this volume; Ferenczi 1913: 476). Freud's interpretation concentrates on the Gorgon's head, cut off by Perseus with the help of Athena, overlooking other elements of the myth (see below). The basis of his interpretation is the castration complex, referring to the fear young boys develop upon the realization that their mother, and women generally, do not possess a phallus. On the contrary, Freud (1905: 194) considers that girls, being aware of their own bodies, suffer from what he calls 'penis-envy'. This widely criticized view, discussed below, privileges male sexuality. The phallus defines the development of young children and positions femininity and female sexuality strictly in terms of the absence of the phallus.

Freud approaches the severed head of the Medusa as follows. Medusa's victims were turned into stone by her terrifying gaze. This terror lingered even after Perseus killed her and handed the monster's head to the goddess Athena. The emotion the severed head causes is 'a terror of castration' (1922: 273). Consequently, the snaky monstrous head becomes a symbol of the female genitalia, as glimpsed by a boy. The snakes around Medusa's head are phallic symbols, yet it is the very absence of the phallus which creates the fear of castration (273). Freud neglects significant aspects of Medusa's story: her original transformation into a hideous monster by Athena, as a punishment for her rape by Poseidon, which occurred in Athena's sanctuary; her death at Perseus' hands; and her offspring, Pegasus and Chrysaor. Instead, Freud emphasizes the horror Medusa and her severed head evoke. Addressing an informed readership, he interprets the virgin goddess Athena, who wears an aegis decorated with the Gorgon's head, as 'an unapproachable' woman 'who repels all sexual desires—since she displays the terrifying genitals of the Mother' (273–4). Ferenczi's interpretation of Medusa follows Freud's closely: Medusa's head, indeed, symbolizes the female genitals on display, which terrorize males, threatening them with castration (3). Both Freud and Ferenczi address the parallel between the petrifying effect of Medusa's gaze and the erect phallus; Medusa's petrification abilities have a malevolent purpose—to represent male castration.

Medusa beyond Freud

Later interpretations of Medusa draw upon the myth to claim that the castration complex, previously associated with the severed head, is rendered irrelevant in a clinical context. Miller (1958: 399) focuses, instead, on the element of competition amongst women, and specifically on the opposition between Medusa and Athena. Balter, alternatively, considers Medusa a 'mother-figure', closely examining her mythical narrative considering the Oedipus complex: Medusa represents the malevolent mother while Athena represents the benevolent one (1969: 217, 221). Read side by side with another ambivalent monster, the Sphinx, Medusa embodies a 'preoedipal maternal' image of the mother that can be both beneficial and destructive for the hero (231–4).

In her influential critique of Freud's treatment of Medusa and women's bodies, Hélène Cixous proclaims that women are trapped 'between two horrifying myths: between the Medusa and the abyss', thus addressing the psychoanalytic associations of the female body to horror, death, and castration (1976: 885–6). Attacking the psychoanalytic portrayal of femininity as 'lacking the phallus', Cixous's essay deconstructs Freud's argument that female sexuality is synonymous with monstrosity and instead employs the metaphor of a laughing, non-fatal Medusa, which comes in complete contrast to the terrifying image of Medusa (885).

In *The Severed Head*, a thematic study on decapitation, psychoanalyst Julia Kristeva reads the encounter between Medusa and Perseus as a re-enactment of the ambivalent separation between mother and child, with Medusa being an ambivalent mother of 'persecuting power and castration' (2012: 30). Kristeva accepts Freud's interpretation of castration in the Medusa myth but extends it by including the murder of the mother. Following Klein's theory on symbolic matricide instead of the Freudian parricide, Kristeva (2001: 131) places the beheading of Medusa on a parallel with the killing of the mother. Because Kleinian theory focuses on the mother–infant bond and the existence of a second, 'bad' mother, the 'good' mother of Perseus, Danaë, is overlooked. Philip Slater addresses this gap by arguing that the story of Medusa and Perseus is 'particularly instructive' because Danaë is saved by her son after he defeats the monster. Medusa is seen as a 'symbol of the mother's sexual demands upon the child' (1968: 32). Jessica Elbert Mayock challenges the Kleinian notion that women need to commit matricide to be able to form an independent self. She revisits and revises Freud, arguing that male child patients display an unconscious wish to control the woman's power of maternity. Mayock (2013: 159) calls that the 'Medusa Complex', suggesting the existence of 'male fantasies of female castration and male parthenogenesis'. The male child wishes to have the ability to give birth by robbing the female, therefore wishing to control the female in every possible way. Regarding the manifestation of the Medusa complex in women, Mayock emphasizes the loss of control over their bodies (171).

Psychoanalytic readings of Medusa vary and many of them continue to challenge Freud's understanding of the monster. Approaches range from the castration complex and the fear of the female body to the ambivalence of the mother and the reclaiming of female sexuality.

THE MINOTAUR

In the nineteenth century, a series of important archaeological excavations in Greece and Italy renewed Europe's fascination with the classical past. These coincided with the beginnings of psychoanalytic thought. Sir Arthur Evans's notable excavation of the Knossos palace on Crete in 1900 turned up possible archaeological connections with the myths of King Minos, Ariadne, Theseus, and the Minotaur. Evans speculated that the mythic death of the Minotaur at the hands of Theseus was a reference to a bull's sacrifice as part of a ritual devoted to a mother-snake-goddess worshipped on Minoan Crete. The arbitrary links Evans made between archaeological artefacts and Greek myths have been criticized by scholars and archaeologists. Momigliano (2020: 57), for instance, points out that Evans named 'the large structure he excavated as the real labyrinth', ignoring the material evidence of the site. While many of Evans's hypotheses were inaccurate, his archaeological discoveries on Crete, and their implications for Greek myth, were too great to be ignored—even by Freud (see also Trzaskoma in this volume).

Psychoanalysis and Minoan Crete: An Absent Monster

A year after the initial excavations on Crete, Freud mentions the Labyrinth in a letter to Fliess, admitting that the discoveries made by Evans preoccupy him: 'Have you read that the English excavated an old palace in Crete (Knossos), which they declare to be the real labyrinth of Minos? Zeus seems originally to have been a bull' (1985: 444). What interests Freud here is the religious origin of the monster of the alleged Labyrinth: what purpose did the story of the mythic Minotaur serve in Minoan Crete? Freud's knowledge of the Cretan monster and its legendary prison probably came from classical texts; this knowledge then merged with the reality of the Knossos palace and Evans's archaeological observations.

To fully comprehend Freud's relationship to myth and antiquity and their quintes-sential role in psychoanalysis, we should examine the 'archaeological metaphor' he used in 1896. He draws an analogy between an imaginative explorer, who discovers the ruins of an ancient palace, and the psychoanalyst, who will use the right tools to 'un-cover what is buried' and who will not be satisfied with what is visible on the surface (1896: 192). Apart from giving his readers a stimulating image of psychoanalysis, Freud's analogy demonstrates his long-standing fascination with antiquity and his approach to the unconscious origins of the Minotaur. In his final work, 'Moses and Monotheism', Freud again employs the archaeological metaphor, stating that psychoanalysis aims to uncover the origins of stories about mythical places and monsters, noting that 'with our present psychological insight we could, long before Schliemann and Evans, have raised the question of where it was that the Greeks obtained all the legendary material' (1939: 69). In a direct comparison to the famous archaeologists of the nineteenth and twentieth centuries, the pioneer of psychoanalytic thought points to a significant issue for analysts: the question of the psychic location of myths, and by extension, monsters.

Freud was aware of the Minoan myths and of their importance in therapy. These stories, like many myths, often appeared in his patients' dreams, and their interpret-ation assisted him in accessing the unconscious. Freud (1933: 24) interprets the image of a labyrinth in a patient's dream as 'a representation of anal birth: the twisting paths are the bowels and Ariadne's thread is the umbilical cord'. Freud does not further ex-plain the dream or how he reached this particularly dense interpretation; his brief observations on the Cretan Labyrinth's structure may point to the route of the hero inside the Labyrinth as a representation of the child being able to master the bladder during the anal stage of the child's psychosexual development. The Minotaur does not appear as such in Freud's theories when compared to the Sphinx and Medusa, yet this monster is an integral part of psychoanalytic discussions of the bull symbol in myth and the unconscious.

Jung considers the bull, generally, as 'a notorious fertility-symbol' in the context of the animal's association with the Greek god Dionysus, who occasionally took a bull form, and with the Roman god Mithras, whose iconography includes bull-slaying (1967: 103). Although Theseus' killing of the Minotaur could suggest a parallel with the Mithraic tauroctony, Jung never draws any connections between the two deaths. He observes, though, that the sacrifice of a bull means the sacrifice of one's animal instincts (423). In mythology, this sacrifice can be translated into the death of the Minotaur, a creature that combined the animal and the human.

Other Approaches to the Minotaur

In *The Mermaid and The Minotaur*, Dorothy Dinnerstein, influenced by Freud and Klein, draws a mythological parallel between a child's parents and the two im-aginary titular creatures: she compares men to minotaurs and women to mermaids. Her choice of two hybrid monsters is not accidental; the animal-human element that the creatures embody reflects the 'inconsistent nature' of humanity (1999: 5). In a faithful portrayal of the myth, she defines the Minotaur as the 'offspring of a mother's unnatural lust, male representative of mindless, greedy power' (5; see also Trzaskoma in this volume). Dinnerstein collectively applies this mythological description to men to examine sexual issues between men and women that are governed by monstrosity; for example, she compares men who are largely absent from their children's lives to the Minotaur because it is women who remain overtly present in the early years of children's development (2). Her theory, a feminist contribution to psychoanalysis, aimed to address the inequalities between men and women in the care of children.

The Minotaur's death informs Grotstein's analysis of the monster, which builds on archaeological evidence suggesting that the bull, and by extension the Minotaur, was a sacrificial animal in Minoan Crete. This idea translated into clinical practice directly relates to the Oedipus complex and its expression in the unconscious sacrifice of oneself, which occurs after one accepts that there is a part of this self that is evil and must vanish—a part akin to the monstrous Minotaur (1997a: 57). This monstrous part unconsciously wishes, like Oedipus, to kill the father and marry the mother. Building upon the work of Bion and Grotstein, Marilyn Charles uses the Minotaur and the Cretan Labyrinth to elucidate a clinical case, wherein the monster embodies an oxymoron for her patient: the fear of knowing oneself and the 'wish to *be* truly horrible' (2002: 85). Charles discusses the hero's journey in the Labyrinth as an analogy to the patient's own route while undergoing analysis. Accordingly, the Labyrinth becomes an ambivalent place: it can be a safe space, or it can accommodate a meeting with the Minotaur (79, 84). Thus, the Minotaur symbolically describes the hidden challenges a patient might face in the consulting room but also evokes the patient's own, hidden aspects of the self.

Julia D. Hejduk suggests that the mythic story of Theseus and the Minotaur can be a more satisfying paradigm for psychoanalysis than the one Freud chose when he read Sophocles. Her theory relies on the monster's 'guilty' existence in a place very much like one's unconscious mind (2011: 93). The monster's imprisonment inside a dark, puzzling space, such as the Labyrinth, is significant as Minos had to hide his wife's shameful offspring in the intricate construction. In the myth, despite its confinement, the monster still had to be fed with human blood. Hejduk thus interprets the existence of the Minotaur inside his blood-covered prison as an example of the repressed wishes and guilty desires that can 'devour' one's mind if left uncontrolled (94).

In summary, interest in the Minotaur was initially attached to archaeological evidence in the monster's mythological location in Knossos, Crete. This interest shifted to exploring other aspects of the monster, such as the imprisonment inside the Labyrinth and his hybrid half-bull, half-human nature. The Minotaur points out an important aspect of psychoanalytic thought: an acknowledgement that our inner world is neither one-sided nor entirely visible. Instead, parts of it may be hidden within a complex structure.

CONCLUSION

Monsters of classical myths figure significantly in the psychoanalytic theories developed by Freud, Jung, Rank, and many others, in part because such monsters often appeared in the dreams of patients, but also because archaeological excavations of sites like Crete uncovered material evidence for such monsters. Psychoanalysis, fascinated with mythology and antiquity, often treats monsters symbolically, as expressions of our unconscious. Monsters may represent the father, the mother, or both. Interpretations of monsters are diverse, but most address the relationship of children to parents, as with the Sphinx in Freud's Oedipus complex. In the case of Medusa, several theories focus on her potential representations of female sexuality. In terms of classical monsters and the mind, psychoanalytic discussions about the Sphinx and the Medusa inevitably dominate; approaches to the Minotaur have been less consistent but equally significant. Freud's observations about Minoan Crete and the Minotaur's origins testify to the significance of myths in psychoanalytic theory. Despite the extensive and justified criticism of early psychoanalytic theories, they assigned classical monsters an often-complex significance as well as a continuing affinity with humanity and its deeper desires and fears. The enduring presence of monsters in therapy is found in their power as symbols that need to be dismantled and redefined to address new ideas about the inner mind.

SUGGESTED READING

One of the earliest studies in psychoanalytic theory and classical monsters is Flügel (1924: 155–96), who touches upon Freud and Rank and associates monsters with the symbolism of the phallus and the castration complex. For a comprehensive account of the uses of Greek myth in psychoanalysis, see Segal (2014: 407–55). Edmunds (2006) offers a detailed analysis of the Oedipus myth, including the Sphinx and its diverse interpretations across centuries. See also Regier (2004) for a concise study of the Sphinx, including a summary of the psychoanalytic interpretations. For the Medusa complex, see Mayock (2013) and for an overview of psychoanalytic approaches to Medusa, Athena, and gender, see Silverman (2016: 114–25). For psychoanalytic approaches to the Minotaur, see Grotstein (1997a, 1997b) and for a discussion of Minoan Crete in Freud, see Gere (2009: 153–76).

WORKS CITED

Armstrong, R. 2005. *A Compulsion for Antiquity: Freud and the Ancient World.* New York.
Balter, L. 1969. 'The Mother as Source of Power: A Psychoanalytic Study of Three Greek Myths.' *Psychoanalytic Quarterly* 38/2: 217–74.
Bion, R. W. 1992. *Cogitations.* London.
Bowlby, R. 2007. *Freudian Mythologies: Greek Tragedy and Modern Identities.* Oxford.
Carlisky, M. 1958. 'The Oedipus Legend and "Oedipus Rex".' *American Imago* 15/1: 91–5.

Charles, M. 2002. 'Through the Unknown, Remembered Gate: Journeys into the Labyrinth.' *Psychoanalytic Review* 89/1: 79–99.

Cixous, H. 1976. 'The Laugh of the Medusa', trans. K. Cohen and P. Cohen. *Signs* 1: 875–93.

Cornes, T. 1986. 'The Freud/Jung Conflict: Yahweh and the Great Goddess.' *American Imago* 43/1: 7–21.

Dinnerstein, D. 1999. *The Mermaid and the Minotaur: Sexual Arrangements and Human Malaise.* New York.

Edmunds, L. 2006. *Oedipus.* London.

Ferenczi, S. 1913. 'Letter from Sándor Ferenczi to Sigmund Freud, March 21, 1913', in *The Correspondence of Sigmund Freud and Sándor Ferenczi*, vol. 1, 476–7. Cambridge, MA.

Ferenczi, S. 1923. 'On the Symbolism of the Head of Medusa', in *The Selected Papers of Sándor Ferenczi, M.D.*, vol. 2, ed. J. Rickman, trans. J. Suttie, 360. New York.

Flügel, J. C. 1924. 'Polyphallic Symbolism and the Castration Complex.' *International Journal of Psychoanalysis* 5: 155–96.

Freud, S. 1896. 'The Aetiology of Hysteria', in *The Standard Edition of the Complete Psychological Works of Sigmund Freud*, vol. 3, ed. and trans. J. Strachey et al., 187–221. London.

Freud, S. 1900. *The Interpretation of Dreams*, in *The Standard Edition of the Complete Psychological Works of Sigmund Freud*, vol. 4, ed. and trans. J. Strachey et al., ix–627. London.

Freud, S. 1905. 'Three Essays on the Theory of Sexuality', in *The Standard Edition of the Complete Psychological Works of Sigmund Freud*, vol. 7, ed. and trans. J. Strachey et al., 123–246. London.

Freud, S. 1922. 'Medusa's Head', in *The Standard Edition of the Complete Psychological Works of Sigmund Freud*, vol. 18, ed. and trans. J. Strachey et al., 273–4. London.

Freud, S. 1928. 'Dostoevsky and Parricide', in *The Standard Edition of the Complete Psychological Works of Sigmund Freud*, vol. 21, ed. and trans. J. Strachey et al., 173–94. London.

Freud, S. 1933. 'New Introductory Lectures on Psycho-Analysis', in *The Standard Edition of the Complete Psychological Works of Sigmund Freud*, vol. 22, ed. and trans. J. Strachey et al., 1–182. London.

Freud, S. 1939. 'Moses and Monotheism', in *The Standard Edition of the Complete Psychological Works of Sigmund Freud*, vol. 23, ed. and trans. J. Strachey et al., 1–138. London.

Freud, S. 1985. *The Complete Letters of Sigmund Freud to Wilhelm Fliess 1885–1904*, trans. J. M. Masson. Cambridge, MA.

Gere, C. 2009. *Knossos and The Prophets of Modernism.* London.

Goux, J.-J. 1993. *Oedipus, Philosopher*, trans. C. Porter. Stanford, CA.

Grotstein, J. S. 1997a. '"Internal Objects" or "Chimerical Monsters"?' *Journal of Analytical Psychology* 42/1: 47–80.

Grotstein, J. S. 1997b. 'Klein's Archaic Oedipus Complex and Its Possible Relationship to the Myth of the Labyrinth: Notes on the Origin of Courage.' *Journal of Analytical Psychology* 42/4: 585–611.

Hall, E., ed. 1994. *Sophocles:* Antigone, Oedipus the King *and* Electra, trans. H. D. F. Kitto. Oxford.

Harrison, J. E. 1903. *Prolegomena to the Study of Greek Religion.* Cambridge.

Hejduk, J. D. 2011. 'Facing the Minotaur: *Inception* (2010) and *Aeneid* 6.' *Arion* 19/2: 93–104.

Jones, E. 1955, *The Life and Work of Sigmund Freud*, vol. 2. New York.

Jung, C. G. 1954. *Collected Works of C. G. Jung*, vol. 17, ed. and trans. G. Adler and R. Hull. Princeton.

Jung, C. G. 1966. *Collected Works of C. G. Jung*, vol. 7, ed. and trans. G. Adler and R. Hull. Princeton.

Jung, C. G. 1967. *Collected Works of C. G. Jung*, vol. 5, ed. and trans. G. Adler and R. Hull. Princeton.

Jung, C. G. 1970. *Collected Works of C. G. Jung*, vol. 10, ed. and trans. G. Adler and R. Hull. Princeton.

Jung, C. G. 2014. *Collected Works of C. G. Jung*, ed. and trans. G. Adler and R. Hull. Princeton. Digital Edition.

Kanzer, M. 1950. 'The Oedipus Trilogy.' *Psychoanalytic Quarterly* 19: 561–72.

Kristeva, J. 2001. *Melanie Klein*, trans. R. Guberman. New York.

Kristeva, J. 2012. *The Severed Head: Capital Visions*, trans. J. Gladding. New York.

Mayock, J. E. 2013. 'The Medusa Complex: Matricide and the Fantasy of Castration.' *philoSOPHIA* 3/2: 158–74.

Miller, A. A. 1958. 'An Interpretation of the Symbolism of Medusa.' *American Imago* 15/4: 389–99.

Momigliano, N. 2020. *In Search of the Labyrinth: The Cultural Legacy of Minoan Crete*. London.

Pollock, G. 2006. 'Beyond Oedipus: Feminist Thought, Psychoanalysis, and Mythical Figurations of the Feminine', in *Laughing with Medusa: Classical Myth and Feminist Thought*, ed. V. Zajko and M. Leonard, 69–117. Oxford.

Rank, O. [1909] 2004. *The Myth of the Birth of the Hero: A Psychological Exploration of Myth*, trans. G. C. Richter and E. J. Lieberman. Baltimore, MA.

Rank, O. [1924] 1999. *The Trauma of Birth*. London.

Regier, G. W. 2004. *Book of the Sphinx*. Lincoln.

Róheim, G. 1940. 'The Dragon and The Hero (Part Two).' *American Imago* 1/3: 61–94.

Segal, R. A. 2014. 'Greek Myth and Psychoanalysis', in *Approaches to Greek Myth*, 2nd edn., ed. L. Edmunds, 407–55. Baltimore.

Shengold, L. 1989. *Soul Murder: The Effects of Childhood Abuse and Deprivation*. London.

Silverman, D. K. 2016. 'Medusa: Sexuality, Power, Mastery, and Some Psychoanalytic Observations.' *Studies in Gender and Sexuality* 17/2: 114–25.

Simpson, M., trans. 1976. *Gods and Heroes of the Greeks: The Library of Apollodorus*. Amherst, MA.

Slater, P. E. 1968. *The Glory of Hera*. Oxford.

....

CHAPTER 30

MONSTERS AND DISABILITY

The Violence of Interpreting Bodies in Aristotle and Homer

....

HANNAH SILVERBLANK AND MARCHELLA WARD

INTRODUCTION

....

WHAT makes a monster? For many of the monsters in popular culture, it is their behaviour (which is often antisocial and violent) and their extraordinary bodies that signal monstrosity to their audiences. This is the case in modern popular culture—see, for instance, Knight (2020) on Frankenstein's creature, Alice and Ellis (2021) on *Shrek*—as well as the legendary non-normative bodies of ancient monsters: the snake hair of the Gorgons, the hybrid body of the Chimaera, and the single eye and enormous size of the Cyclopes are all emblematic of these characters' monstrosity. Throughout this chapter we use the term 'normative' or 'normate' rather than 'normal', to indicate that concepts of normalcy are socially and discursively constructed. There is no such thing as a 'normal body': there are only bodies that are considered to be normal, or politically positioned as such. The terms 'normate' and 'normative' refer, therefore, to bodies that are socially constructed as normal. The bodies of monsters are often coded in ways that rely on racist and ableist stereotypes to indicate monstrosity, where difference from the norms established by dominant groups is interpreted as evidence for threat, moral degeneracy, violence, and other aspects of monstrosity.

In this chapter we focus on the role of this non-normativity in how bodies are rendered meaningful. Specifically, we examine the act of 'monstering'—meaning the social designation of a body and/or behaviours as monstrous—and look at how monstering relies on ableism to construct the non-normative body as monstrous. We focus on approaches to bodies proposed in Aristotle's *Generation of Animals*, the Pseudo-Aristotelian *Physiognomonica*, and Book 9 of Homer's *Odyssey*. The chapter will proceed retrospectively: we will begin by examining some of the violences of interpreting bodies in the post-classical and modern worlds. Here we attend to colonialism's attempt to system-atize difference so as to impose a supremacist order as if it were a natural and neces-sary consequence of embodiment. Then, we reflect on the invitations to these colonial modes of reading bodies for meaning and their precursors in selected works of Aristotle, Pseudo-Aristotle, and Homer.

In reading backwards, we practise what Anna-Marie Jagose characterizes as 'a mode of inhabiting time that is attentive to the recursive eddies and back-to-the-future loops that often pass undetected or uncherished beneath the official narrations of the linear sequence that is taken to structure normative life' (2009: 158). Non-linear experiences of time are theorized in queer studies and disability studies as 'queer time' and 'crip time' (see e.g. Edelman 2004; Freeman 2010; Kafer 2013 and 2021; Keeling 2019; Rifkin 2017; and Piepzna-Samarasinha 2018). Writing in this way allows us to dismantle the false determinism sometimes attributed to the relationship between classical and modern ideas: it opens the possibility of reading even the most ancient texts differently. Our reading is motivated by the desire to find spaces for liberatory and anti-ableist readings of Aristotle and Homer, despite the long histories of weaponizing these texts in ways that are harmful and dangerous to disabled people.

The conviction that underlies our approach here—'that nothing has to be the way that it is'—is a central concern of disability studies and disability justice work, as Leah Lakshmi Piepzna-Samarasinha (2020: n.p.) reminds us. From its very beginnings, disability studies was alert to the role of social construction in marginalization and injustice. The project of drawing a distinction between impairment and disability characterized the field's earliest conversations. Ann Millet-Gallant and Elizabeth Howie describe this distinction—and social construction's role in it—as follows:

> Impairment is a term that refers to the specific corporeal (including both physical and psychological) ways in which a body might diverge from the so-called normal or average body in ways that create functional limitations.... The term 'disability' in this context refers to the social consequences of an impairment in relation not only to the body, but also to social constructions that result in limitations as well as a social and personal identity. (2017: 2)

And this distinction, between corporeal impairment and its (at least in part) social consequence, disability, also required a new model for understanding disability—and brought with it a shift from the dominant medical model to the social model. Whereas the medical model 'situates disability exclusively in individual bodies and strives to cure them by particular treatment, isolating the patient as diseased or defective' (Siebers 2006: 173), the social model instead focused on ways in which societies, environments, and prejudices (in other words, the material consequences of ableism) could enable or disable certain kinds of bodies. The framework that disability studies provided for assessing society's role in disablement—which was no longer a strictly biological or medical process, but one that was also engendered by ableist societies—will be crucial to our work in this chapter.

This focus on the role of social construction is important to the politics of our argument, as well as to its structure (the political purpose of drawing attention to social construction is explained at length in Haslanger 2012). Our argument here is fundamentally concerned with the politics of scholarship. Our rereading of the *Odyssey* seeks to find, within the text, a way out of the injustices caused by the physiognomic model of interpreting bodies that we discuss below. These modes of reading bodies for meaning have done serious harm to those who have been deemed to have non-normative, extraordinary, or disabled bodies. Our backwards temporality has been chosen so as not to present these physiognomic readings as the inevitable consequences of a reception history. The violences of ableism are not simply a reception history that begins with Homer and delivers these readings, via Aristotle, into the hands of colonialism and ableism, as intellectual justifications for categorization and subordination. We hope to offer a way of unreading this narrative, and of rereading Homer's Cyclops episode so as to offer a liberatory model of multi-species care, interdependence, and community.

Interpreting Bodies:
Monstering in Modernity

Extraordinary bodies offer what Rosemarie Garland-Thomson (1996: 1) calls 'an interpretative occasion'. Garland-Thomson's work is often described as the 'cornerstone' of disability studies, and she draws on the etymology of 'monster' when she remarks:

> Never simply itself, the exceptional body betokens something else, becomes revelatory, sustains narrative, exists socially in a realm of hyper-representation. Indeed the word *monster*—perhaps the earliest and most enduring name for the singular body—derives from the Latin *monstra* [*sic*], meaning to warn, show or sign, and has given us the modern verb *demonstrate*. (3)

The act of monstering is one way of interpreting an atypical body—the one most frequently invited by ancient Greek and Roman myth. And it is an interpretative act that has had real effects for people whose bodies do not fit the cultural mode for normalcy, and who were themselves monstered.

Garland-Thomson's 1996 book is a genealogy of the idea of the 'freak' rather than the monster, and throughout she seeks to historicize the idea of reading bodies that defy assumptions about corporeal normalcy for meaning. Similarly, disability studies scholar Lennard Davis (2006) has argued that the idea that bodies should conform to a single 'norm' is the invention of the 1840s (see also Cryle and Stephens 2017). Davis contextualizes this idea in a narrative of industrialization, which was financially motivated to optimize a body's production for profit. But the notion that non-normate bodies were narratively (and usually negatively) meaningful comes about much earlier than capitalism's drive for bodily normalcy and industrial growth.

This drive to categorize and narrativize difference was underscored by nineteenth-century academic disciplines that sought to establish an imaginary hierarchy of races as a biological reality. One such discipline is race science, which aimed to position white supremacy as biologically manifested in a series of physically observable differences that could be racialized and categorized. The nineteenth century also saw the development of the discipline of teratology, the 'scientific' study of congenital abnormalities, which transformed bodies that differed from an imagined normate body into biological specimens that needed to be investigated to determine their meaning. Isidore Geoffrey Saint-Hilaire, who founded the discipline in 1832, focused on what he understood to be 'defects' in real people (and in plants and animals)—but the name he chose for his new field of inquiry reworked the Greek word *teras* (pl. *terata*), commonly used to refer to the monsters of ancient mythology, or strange portents that conveyed grave divine significance. These nineteenth-century disciplines saw an intrinsic connection between non-normate bodies and monstrosity.

And although these academic disciplines positioned themselves as if they were at the forefront of cutting-edge research in the natural sciences, this attempt to categorize bodies so as to legitimate the supremacy of humans embodied in particular ways over others was not strictly new. It can be traced from Aristotle's biologizing of the monster (*teras*), through the colonial tendency to 'monster' in order to justify violent acts of domination, to contemporary xenophobic opposition to immigration. Colonial domination relied on a process of biological categorization and proceeded by weaponizing the idea of natural inequality to legitimate its extractive cruelty. Racialized people were positioned as both physically and intellectually inferior to white people, and race science later picked up on this practice of categorization, bolstering it with the trappings of science, such as craniometry (the abhorrent practice of measuring skulls to confirm racist prejudices, such as the notion of white people's intellectual superiority), phrenology (the equally disgusting practice of assuming character traits on the basis of head shape), and other modes of measurement. Monstering was crucial to this categorization process, and the bodies of colonized people were positioned not just as naturally inferior and therefore appropriate for domination, but also as monstrous.

These processes of categorization and the injustices that resulted from them—colonial domination, eugenicist policies, xenophobic immigration legislation, to name only a few—have long histories and ongoing effects in the lives of disabled and racialized people today (see Deerinwater 2020; Dolmage 2018; Snyder and Mitchell 2006). But the groundwork for them had been laid by particular ways of reading monsters in ancient texts, which were granted authoritative status for interpretative practices. These ancient texts and their reception histories assume that the bodies of monsters are narratively meaningful, and they articulate a belief that disabled people characterized as monstrous constitute a real biological category, rather than simply a political or a social one.

ARISTOTLE, PSEUDO-ARISTOTLE, AND COLONIAL INTERPRETATIONS OF BODIES

Like the academic disciplines discussed in the previous section, the project of coloniation had earlier sought to biologize difference, taking its inspiration from fantastical stories about bodies (which were reconfigured as if they described reality) as well as from the texts of the ancient world. In a 1596 text, Sir Walter Raleigh positions himself meeting various groups of indigenous people in what is now Guyana and remarking that their bodies confirmed the physicality that he had read about in Herodotus' *Histories*, Pliny the Elder's *Natural History*, and the travelogue attributed to Sir John Mandeville. Raleigh's descriptions provide an example of what Stephanie Hunt-Kennedy (2020: 7) calls 'inheriting monstrosity', since they rely on ancient texts to monster the human beings they describe. Surekha Davies agrees that Raleigh's designation of indigenous and colonized people as monstrous was based on 'textual prototypes from classical antiquity' (2016: 30). But the presumption that colonization and enslavement could be justified on the basis of bodily difference resulted not only from an engagement with classical monsters, but also from a particular physiognomic method for making sense of bodies—also found in ancient texts.

The idea that inequality was both natural and embodied was crucial to empire's project of domination. Fanciful descriptions of monsters were adapted by authors like Raleigh into tales that purported to describe real ethnographic encounters; this practice had the effect of monstering real people and positioning them outside the category of normate humanity. This process of pseudo-speciation had three important consequences. Firstly, it positioned physical difference as something that could be read for meaning. Secondly, it positioned the monster outside the boundaries and expectations of human kinship (legitimating violent treatment of monstered individuals). Thirdly, it recentred the presumed physical presentation of the normate human in ableist and racist ways.

We find one particular precedent for this racist and ableist process of speciation in Aristotelian philosophy. Humans, Aristotle argues in *On the Parts of Animals*, belong to a superior category of animals because of the way that they are embodied (686a27–32). Aristotle's argument for the exceptionalism of humans is ableist by design: human superiority is directly related to how human capacity to stand upright (*orthon*), think (*noiein*), and be intelligent (*phronein*) allows humans to do 'the work of the most divine being'.[1] In other words, they have a specific physical ability from which results a particularly divine and privileged kind of intellectual ability. Humans and other animals that deviate from this posture are thereby inferior.

This kind of speciation argument has been readily accepted in the modern world. Legal and ethical justifications of human exceptionalism often default to descriptions

---

[1] All translations from ancient texts in this chapter are our own.

of abilities *presumed* to be universal human traits: use of verbal speech, intellectual reasoning abilities, participation in various social structures, and specific tool usage, among other capacities, constitute common claims to human exceptionalism. Disability and animal justice work has often pointed to the falseness and exclusionary ableism of these presumptions, yet ableist and inaccurate human exceptionalism narratives persist in the modern world (see Boisseron 2018; Taylor 2017).

But in ancient physiognomic readings, this way of framing embodiment as species difference is not just applicable to species differences that are largely accepted in the modern world (e.g. those between humans and animals) but to differences of human embodiment too. The *Physiognomonica*, an essay on physiognomy attributed to Aristotle, argues that 'intelligences correspond to bodies' (805a1). For proof that character can be read in embodiment, the author claims:

> Soft hair is associated with cowardice, whereas stiff hair is associated with bravery. This sign can be observed in all the animals. The most cowardly animals are the deer, the hare, and sheep, and they have the softest hair, while the lion and the wild boar are the bravest, and these possess the stiffest hair.... This same thing also occurs among the human races. For those living in the north are courageous and stiff-haired, whereas those living in the south are cowardly and have soft hair. (806b8–18)

This physiognomic approach is specifically racialized, in that physical appearance is related to ethnic and geographic origin, and both are in turn related to internal character. The author also situates skin colour and gender as variables in this physiognomic system: 'Those who are extremely black are cowardly; this applies to Egyptians and Ethiopians. But those who are extremely pale are also cowardly; this applies to women' (812a12–15). The Aristotelian physiognomic logic thus sets up a framework whereby bodies' physical attributes are read for meaning, with the implicit result and historical consequence of creating a seemingly natural justification for systemic violence against racialized and disabled people.

And elsewhere, in Book 4 of his *Generation of Animals*, Aristotle straightforwardly positions physical difference as a kind of monstrosity, when he attempts to re-examine what is meant by *teras*. Before Aristotle, *teras* typically conveyed the idea that visual phenomena, usually but not always in the form of bodies of difference, could be interpreted as conveying something symbolic or divinatory—hence the common glosses 'marvel', 'portent', 'sign' (LSJ, s.v. *teras*). In literary and philosophical texts, *teras* could be applied widely to that which provokes responses of marvel or fear, and often invites acts of interpretation. *Teras* is used of a cosmically threatening monster like Typhon (Aesch. *PV* 354), a star placed in the heavens by Zeus to guide sailors or signal oncoming battle (Hom. *Il.* 4.75–7), the ominous mooing from the roasting meat of the Sun's slain cattle (Hom. *Od.* 12.394–6), or a portentous birth from a horse to a different kind of animal (Pl. *Cra.* 393b–c). Discussing the idea of a specific type of monster, Aristotle describes the human child that differs so much from their parents that they 'no longer appear to be a person at all, but appear to be an animal—which beings are called monstrosities' (*terata*, *Gen. an.* 769b7–9). Aristotle argues that such children are not *actually* multi-species hybrids, but only *appear* to be monsters. The real *teras* is, for Aristotle, not a creature that hybridizes multiple species (this phenomenon is, he argues, biologically impossible), but a child that differs physically from their parents.

Via this rhetorical repurposing of *teras*, Aristotle links disability and monstrosity. Hybrid creatures of literature and art may not be real, but monsters do exist for Aristotle, in the form of disabled people and animals: 'The explanations concerning the cause of monstrosities [*terata*] are parallel to those concerning disabled animals. For monstrosity [*teras*] is a form of disability' (*Gen. an.* 769b29–31). So embodied difference becomes monstrous for Aristotle. The reason that *terata* are not neutrally divergent from a species norm, but 'monstrous' in Aristotle's formulation, relates to Aristotle's conception of the role of animal generation and species norms as part of a larger project of species immortality. As Fiona Mitchell has written, Aristotle believes in an idea of species immortality attained through repeated Form: species should have a Form that, in its repeatability across different individuals, facilitates something close to immortality for that species (2021: 160). Insofar as individual differences 'pose a threat to the eternal and identical replication of that species' (162), they are taxonomized as monstrous rather than simply divergent from designated species norms. This conceptual framework sets up disabled people as monsters that threaten the well-being of their entire species, and as such, establishes a eugenicist approach to disability that would be inspirational for later eugenicist projects.

HOMER'S *ODYSSEY* BOOK 9: RHETORICAL CONSTRUCTIONS OF MONSTROSITY AND DISABILITY

Physiognomic associations between certain physical traits and socially problematic behaviours are also explored and contested in earlier Greek works. Odysseus' travelogue concerning his encounter with the Cyclops Polyphemus, delivered to his hosts, the Phaeacians, provides a mythical precursor to Aristotelian physiognomic principles. But it can also be read otherwise. We find the binaries of heroism and monstrosity, and ability and disability, laid bare as rhetorical oppositions, constructed to justify Odysseus' violence against the character he positions as 'monstrous'—so as to dominate. The narrative demonstrates how ability and disability are constructed through environmental contexts, as the Cyclopean architecture enables Cyclopean bodies and disables human bodies. Odysseus also interprets Polyphemus as intellectually and morally inferior to himself, and he weaponizes disablement as a strategy for overcoming the monster, abilifying his own body and extracting resources from the 'uncivilized' Cyclops. Monstrosity and disability are linked here in ways that prefigure the Aristotelian and colonial methods of monstering discussed above.

In *Odyssey* Book 9, Odysseus and his crew decide to enter the Cyclops' cave while he is out pasturing his flocks. They help themselves to his food and shelter, and ask for hospitality when the Cyclops returns, but Polyphemus is enraged by their intrusion. Instead of offering them the hospitality they retrospectively request, Polyphemus eats some of Odysseus' crew and traps the human survivors in his cave by blocking the entrance with the large rock he uses as a door. Odysseus devises an escape strategy: first, he introduces himself with a pseudonym, 'No One'; then, he intoxicates and, with the help of his men, blinds Polyphemus with a firebrand. Having disabled the Cyclops in this way, Odysseus leads his crew in their flight from the cave, as they attach themselves to the undersides of Polyphemus' livestock. Through this trick they manage to elude the Cyclops and sail away.

Classicists have usually interpreted the Polyphemus episode with sympathy for the hero, reading the story as Odysseus' righteous triumph over the foolish and cruel monster. We argue that Odysseus also performs two aspects of the monstering that we traced from Aristotle (and Pseudo-Aristotle) to the violences of colonialism. First, he links an extraordinary body with monstrous and dangerous character. Second, he designates the monster as 'uncivilized' in his behaviour, material relationship to the environment, and modes of sociality so as to steal resources from the Cyclopean people. When Odysseus' attempts at extracting resources from the Cyclopes meet with violent resistance, this resistance is positioned as justification for his subsequent acts of violence and disablement. His narrative characterizes Polyphemus as physically threatening, morally monstrous, and intellectually inferior, all of which serves as his justification for disabling the Cyclops in order to enable himself within the Cyclopean environment from which he hopes to attain wealth and glory.

Unlike Aristotle, Odysseus does not represent monstrosity as a biological category, although his encounters with mythological monsters are all couched together in his narration from Books 9–12. Thus, the *Odyssey* implicitly groups non-normative beings as if they were a category, including the Cyclopes, the Laestrygonians, the Sirens, Scylla and Charybdis, dangerous humans such as the Lotus-Eaters and Cicones, and even ghosts. Many of these are the very mythological creatures that Aristotle goes to great lengths to situate as unreal and impossible. Odysseus is a mythical hero, not a biologist, describing his own precarious encounters with monstrous beings in the flesh. His narrative is filled with retrojective suppositions about how these creatures' bodies and social contexts pose threats to his heroic journey home.

As the storyteller among the Phaeacians, Odysseus conditions their response to Polyphemus by describing the Cyclops' body prior to the main story. Before Odysseus narrates their actual encounter, he introduces Polyphemus as a monstrous man (*anēr … pelōrios*, *Od.* 9.187) and a monstrous marvel (*thaum' … pelōrion*, 9.190). To these descriptions of Polyphemus' visual appearance Odysseus adds a lifestyle assessment, as though appearance and character are implicitly connected: he notes that Polyphemus differs from bread-eating humans, lives alone in a state of lawlessness, and resembles a mountain peak, in that he appears in conspicuous, towering solitude (9.188–92). The retrospective narration has the effect of connecting Odysseus' physical description of the Cyclopes' body with behaviour that we have not yet seen Polyphemus exhibit. Odysseus also calls the Cyclops 'overbearing' and 'lawless' prior to describing the actual encounter (9.106). Odysseus thus prepares his audience to experience a story in which violence against a monster is justified by the creature's physical, moral, and behavioural non-humanity.

When Polyphemus returns to the cave and the human characters finally behold the Cyclops, Odysseus' description focuses on Polyphemus' massive size and extreme physical capacity relative to human beings. These features immediately engender fear in Odysseus and his crew, as Odysseus' recalls: 'Afraid, we retreated to the innermost part of the cave' (9.236). The implicit descriptions of Polyphemus' size and physical capacity are made with reference to the tools Polyphemus uses; the fact that he only has one eye is not directly stated, but later implied by the fact that he is blinded in one eye alone, and then loses his vision entirely (9.382–90, 452–5).

Instead of drawing attention to Polyphemus' single eye as a remarkable or unusual trait of physical difference, Odysseus communicates the difference in Polyphemus' non-human physique by noting how capably Polyphemus can negotiate his own massive environment, which is impossible for human beings to navigate even with assistive technology: 'He lifted high the massive, mighty stone, and put it down. Twenty-two good four-wheeled carts couldn't have heaved it from the ground' (9.240–3). Odysseus further emphasizes how Cyclopean architecture disables his human body when he says: 'We could not push back from the high doorway the mighty stone that he set there' (9.304–5; cf. 9.319–24 on the human assessment of the Cyclops' wooden stick). These descriptions demonstrate the way that the Cyclopean architecture and environment are suited to Cyclopean bodies and render Cyclopic embodiment normate. Odysseus' narration thus conveys how environment conditions which bodies are enabled or disabled.

An architectural access feature, the stone door, is crucial to the narrative development of the story: its size and weight trap the humans, whose bodies are not equipped to move it in the way that the Cyclops is. Only by disturbing the enabling dynamic between body and environment do Odysseus and his companions disable and defeat Polyphemus—first by getting him drunk, and then by blinding his single eye. Odysseus must find a way to keep Polyphemus' body able enough to open the door for their escape but disabled enough that Polyphemus cannot turn Odysseus into a meal.

Despite Odysseus' attempt to characterize the Cyclopes as innately monstrous, his encounter with Polyphemus demonstrates that bodies, human and non-human, acquire their meaning and enablement not only through rhetorical construction by those who invest their bodies with narrative, but also through their relationship to their environment. Since Odysseus' main skill in this story is his ability to control perception and interpretation, he is able to rhetorically construct Polyphemus' physical difference as if it indicated monstrosity via the physiognomic method of interpreting bodies that we saw above. Physical difference can be read for meaning in Odysseus' narrative, but Homer does not set this mode of interpreting bodies up as a morally neutral one. *Odyssey* Book 9 also shows that disablement can be a process that the hero weaponizes to convey his own superiority.

POLYPHEMUS' POLITICS: MULTI-SPECIES
CARE AND INTERDEPENDENCE

Polyphemus' monstrosity also prefigures Aristotelian conceptions of monstrosity in other ways—in particular, through Polyphemus' isolation from his species and through his difference from his parents. As we saw above, Aristotle depicts offspring that differ from their parents as the 'real' *teras*. Whereas the other Cyclopes live in heterosexual nuclear family units in which male Cyclopes dominate over adult female Cyclopes and their offspring (*Od.* 9.113–15), Polyphemus descends from non-Cyclopean Poseidon and the sea-nymph Thoosa (1.71–3), and has no Cyclopean family in his own cave (see Aguirre and Buxton in this volume). Odysseus emphasizes Polyphemus' anomalous sociality in his attempts to portray the Cyclops as intrinsically monstrous, and therefore deserving of his violent treatment and disablement. Reading against the grain of Odysseus' monstering allows us to imagine a more liberatory reading of this passage—one that shows how monsters like Polyphemus might inspire alternative modes of multi-species solidarity and community.

When introducing the Cyclopes, Odysseus presents his assumption that they lack sociality and mutual care in their community; according to him, these monsters 'do not care about one other' (9.115). As soon as the Cyclops is blinded, though, it becomes clear that this assumption is false; Polyphemus cries out and the other Cyclopes come running to find out what has happened (9.399–406). Physiognomic assumptions about bodies, of the kind that Aristotle advocates and that have been so useful in the post-classical world for legitimating violence, are not only relied on in this tale to legitimate cruelty, but also turn out to be inaccurate and to lead to misunderstandings of more-than-human sociality.

Part of Odysseus' argument for Polyphemus' monstrosity entails offering proof that Polyphemus is an inhuman, 'uncivilized' fool who lacks Greek notions of community and culture. Key to this presentation is Odysseus' complaint that the Cyclopic people miss an opportunity to extract natural resources and exploit neighbouring lands. Immediately after stating that the monsters have no civic institutions or meetings, Odysseus points out that they also have no interest in colonizing the nearby island. He sketches out an island full of forests and innumerable wild goats, with plenty of land appropriate for agriculture and a safe harbour, which goes unused by the Cyclopes, who do not sail (9.112–41). But Odysseus' portrayal of the Cyclopes as 'uncivilized' is little more than a reflection of his own ideas about civilization. The Cyclopes' preference for allowing biodiverse ecologies to flourish uninterrupted sits in profound contrast to Odysseus' own inability to resist breaking into Polyphemus' cave, taking his food, asking for gifts, and causing the death of several of his own crew in the process. Where Odysseus attempts to frame these differences as a lack of civilization on Polyphemus' part, the *Odyssey* also offers another way of reading the narrative: monstrous geography

is conceptualized as space that is not subjected to the colonizing practice of resource extraction that benefits the exploitative individual at the expense of the more-than-human
ecosystem.

Odysseus' attempts to monster Polyphemus repeatedly hinge on the latter's isolation, but it is Odysseus' 'No One' trick—and not the Cyclopes' own intrinsic practices
of sociality—that prevents Polyphemus from making his situation clear to the
other Cyclopes and causes this social isolation. Misled by the hero's trick, the other
Cyclopes insist that Polyphemus does not need their support 'if you are alone and No
One is attacking you' (9.410). Here, Polyphemus' isolation is narratively constructed
through Odysseus' wordplay that breathes it into being. Classicists have typically
accepted Odysseus' characterization of Polyphemus' isolation: for example, Gregory
Hutchinson writes, 'The solitude of the Cyclops is contrasted, by the speech and its
situation, with Odysseus' teamwork' (Hutchinson 2007: 24). But to read the Cyclops in
this way is to read him only through Odysseus' monstering gaze. Homer offers a much
more complex portrait, and the potential for a more liberatory reading. In the very
next sentence the Cyclopes utter, they remind Polyphemus of the role that he plays
in more-than-human networks of care and relationship: they advise Polyphemus to
pray to his father, the god Poseidon, whom they address as their lord in respectful
terms (9.412), resulting in Polyphemus' prayer for justice to Poseidon once he learns
Odysseus' true name. Polyphemus' familial bond with Poseidon proves deadly for
Odysseus' own human community, since it is Poseidon's protectiveness over his son
that protracts Odysseus' journey and endangers his crew, as Zeus notes early in the
epic (1.68–75).

In Odysseus' world view, Polyphemus seems to be lacking in human sociality, and to
be less integrated into the biological family community norms of the other Cyclopes.
But Homer invites us to read against these assumptions, and we see through this tale that
networks of care among these monsters exist not just beyond their nuclear family bonds
but also encompass divine care and sociality—and animal solidarity as well. When
Polyphemus addresses the ram that is carrying Odysseus out of the cave, Homer offers
another brief opportunity to read against Odysseus' assumptions. Polyphemus addresses
the ram in tender terms and engages him in a conversation about why he is moving so
slowly out of the cave (9.447–52). Reminiscing about the ram's long life, Polyphemus
notes the ram's regular habits and behaviours, and projects human emotions onto him.
Polyphemus speculates that the ram's change in behaviour is motivated by sadness at
Polyphemus' own injury, and he wishes that the ram could share thoughts with him,
speak, and name Odysseus' hiding place (9.452–7).

From Odysseus' point of view, this tender moment of more-than-human relation
renders the Cyclops ridiculous; the hero is narrating this moment for laughs, and
the Phaeacian audience are aware that the ram is moving slowly not out of empathy
with the Cyclops, but because of the weight of the escapee he is carrying. Odysseus
attempts to situate himself as the superior interpreter against Polyphemus' alleged
intellectual inabilities. But Polyphemus' expectations of more-than-human care

coupled with the cruelty of Odysseus' final moments in this scene—not allowing his companions to grieve their dead, taunting the monster, and thereby provoking more mortal danger (9.468–542)—leaves modern readers wondering whether normate bodies and normate heroic sociality are really preferable to monstrous kinship after all.

Recent scholarship on care has drawn increasing attention to these more-than-human contexts. In her book *Matters of Care*, María Puig de la Bellacasa undertakes 'the delicate task of broadening consideration of the lives involved in caring agencies.... Care is a human trouble, but this does not make of care a human-only matter' (2017: 2). Polyphemus assumes multi-species care when he expects support from his neighbouring Cyclopes, his Olympian father, and his ram. Despite Odysseus' derision of Polyphemus' more-than-human interdependence, disability justice movements have always situated interdependence as a crucial component of a more equal society. Disability justice activist Mia Mingus writes of the importance of 'building interdependence and embracing need, because this is such a deep part of challenging ableism and the myth of independence' (2017: n.p.). And when she comes to define the myth of independence, her definition makes apparent the radical rereading that the Cyclopes' more-than-human interdependent networks of care propose for Odysseus:

> The myth of independence is the idea that we can and should be able to do everything on our own and, of course, we know that that's not true. Someone made the clothes you're wearing now, your shoes, your car or the mass transit system you use.... We are dependent on each other, period. The myth of independence reflects such a deep level of privilege, especially in this rugged individualistic capitalist society and produces the very idea that we could even mildly conceive of our lives or our accomplishments as solely our own. (n.p.)

Other than his references to specific moments of divine intervention, Odysseus is deeply committed to emphasizing his independence and superiority in his narrative. Now bereft of all his comrades, he organizes the tale so as to provide proof of his individual heroism and super-capacity. He recites a story about a man who by his own cunning ruse defeats a monster, and even those events that resulted from chance are narrated as if they were proof of Odysseus' individual qualities. When the men cast lots to determine who will wield the stake to blind the Cyclops, Odysseus reports that the lots drawn at random selected the exact same men that he himself would have chosen (Heubeck and Hoesktra 1989: *ad* 331–5). The individualistic narrative told in the gloating voice of the lone hero is undermined by the alternative readings of the Cyclopes' ways of life that Homer offers. Though Homer does present evidence of cruelty within Polyphemus' more-than-human networks (Polyphemus does, after all, eat Odysseus' companions), he also allows the Cyclops' monstrosity to manifest in both physical difference and in radical imaginaries of alternative modes of living in non-human, multi-species communities where human exceptionalism is denaturalized.

CONCLUSION

Against the hero's own reading, we read the *Odyssey* itself as offering a much more liberatory approach to physical difference. The *Odyssey* constructs a spectrum of monstrosity and disability to function as a prompt to imagining more-than-human care, as an invitation to acknowledging the role of interdependence. Through the Cyclopes, we find mythical models of monsters who refuse to approach ecosystems as sources for monocultural extraction, and instead operate within symbiotic ecologies. The complex intertwining of monstrosity and disability has a long and dangerous history that continues to have harmful effects on the lives of disabled people in the modern world. Our reading of this story from Homer's *Odyssey* has allowed us to disentangle the relationship between monstering, eugenics, and domination that has been the cause of so much manifold violence. But we hope also to have shown how monstrosity and disability in *Odyssey* Book 9 invite us to imagine a model of interdependence and more-than-human solidarity that can offer liberation from Odysseus' heroic individualism and its allied modes of monstering that we have traced through Aristotelian interpretation and colonial categorization of embodiment.

Odysseus is, after all, dependent too—despite his mythologizing of his own individualism. By the time he arrives at the court of Alcinous, all the companions on whom he has depended are dead. In his isolation, he needs the help of the goddess Athena and the Phaeacian people to help him get home. Once back on Ithaca, he needs help from the three people who remained loyal to him in his absence: his wife, Penelope; his son, Telemachus; and the swineherd Eumaeus. At the *Odyssey*'s conclusion, the hero requires Athena's divine intervention to reintegrate him into his fractured and traumatized human community. When we shift our understanding of the monster from biological category to social process, we see that the *Odyssey* is also a poem about the human cost of individualism. And this overthrowing of the notion of individualism has been—and continues to be—crucial to disability justice.

SUGGESTED READING

For some of the readings in disability studies and in disability justice that have been foundational for our own work, see Garland-Thomson (1997), Davis (2006), McRuer (2006), Bell (2011), Kafer (2013) and Piepzna-Samarasinha (2018). On disability studies as a methodology, see Kim (2017), Minich (2016), and Schalk (2017). For studies of disability in antiquity with varied relationships to the methodologies of disability studies, see Goodey and Rose (2013), Laes et al. (2013), Laes (2016), and Adams (2021). For the argument that classical reception needs disability studies, see Silverblank and Ward (2020), which is available Open Access via the *Classical Receptions Journal*. For some of the ways that fictional portrayals of disability have been explicitly framed as speculative sites of imagining more liberatory futures, see Schalk (2018). And for first-person narratives that address the role that ableism plays in the everyday lives of disabled people, see Wong (2020).

WORKS CITED

Adams, E., ed. 2021. *Disability Studies and the Classical Body: The Forgotten Other*. Abingdon.

Alice, J., and K. Ellis. 2021. 'Subverting the Monster: Reading *Shrek* as a Disability Fairy Tale.' *Media/Culture Journal* 24/5: n.p. https://journal.media-culture.org.au/index.php/mcjournal/article/view/2828. Accessed 12 February 2024.

Bell, C., ed. 2011. *Blackness and Disability: Critical Examinations and Cultural Interventions*. East Lansing, MI.

Boisseron, B. 2018. *Afro-Dog: Blackness and the Animal Question*. New York.

Cryle, P., and E. Stephens. 2017. *Normality: A Critical Genealogy*. Chicago.

Davies, S. 2016. *Renaissance Ethnography and the Invention of the Human: New Worlds, Maps and Monsters*. Cambridge.

Davis, L. 2006. 'Constructing Normalcy: The Bell Curve, the Novel, and the Invention of the Disabled Body in the Nineteenth Century', in *The Disability Studies Reader*, ed. L. Davis, 3–16. Abingdon.

Deerinwater, J. 2020. 'The Erasure of Indigenous People in Chronic Illness', in *Disability Visibility: First-Person Stories from the Twenty-First Century*, ed. A. Wong, 47–52. New York.

Dolmage, J. 2018. *Academic Ableism: Disability and Higher Education*. Baltimore.

Edelman, L. 2004. *No Future: Queer Theory and the Death Drive*. Durham, NC.

Freeman, E. 2010. *Time Binds: Queer Temporalities, Queer Histories*. Durham, NC.

Garland-Thomson, R., ed. 1996. *Freakery: Cultural Spectacles of the Extraordinary Body*. New York.

Garland-Thomson, R. 1997. *Extraordinary Bodies: Figuring Physical Disability in American Culture and Literature*. New York.

Haslanger, S. 2012. *Resisting Reality: Social Construction and Social Critique*. Oxford.

Heubeck, A., and A. Hoekstra. 1989. *A Commentary on Homer's Odyssey: Volume II, Books IX–XVI*. Oxford.

Hunt-Kennedy, S. 2020. *Between Fitness and Death: Disability and Slavery in the Caribbean*. Urbana, IL.

Hutchinson, G. 2007. 'The Monster and the Monologue: Polyphemus from Homer to Ovid', in *Hesperos: Studies in Ancient Greek Poetry Presented to M. L. West on His Seventieth Birthday*, ed. P. Finglass, C. Collard, and R. Nicholas, 22–39. Oxford.

Jagose, A. 2009. 'Feminism's Queer Theory.' *Feminism and Psychology* 19/2: 157–74.

Kafer, A. 2013. *Feminist, Queer, Crip*. Bloomington, IN.

Kafer, A. 2021. 'After Crip, Crip Afters.' *South Atlantic Quarterly* 120/2: 415–34.

Keeling, K. 2019. *Queer Times, Black Futures*. New York.

Kim, J. B. 2017. 'Toward a Crip-of-Color Critique: Thinking with Minich's "Enabling Whom?"' *Lateral* 6/1: n.p. https://csalateral.org/issue/6-1/forum-alt-humanities-critical-disability-studies-crip-of-color-critique-kim/. Accessed 12 February 2024.

Knight, A. 2020. 'Mary Shelley's *Frankenstein*, Disability, and the Injustice of Misrecognition.' *Disability Studies Quarterly* 40/4: n.p.

Laes, C., ed. 2016. *Disability in Antiquity*. London.

Laes, C., C. Goodey, and M. L. Rose. eds. 2013. *Disabilities in Roman Antiquity: Disparate Bodies, a capite ad calcem*. Leiden.

Millet-Galland, A., and E. Howie, eds. 2017. *Disability and Art History*. London.

Mingus, M. 2017. 'Access Intimacy, Interdependence and Disability Justice.' *Leaving Evidence*. https://leavingevidence.wordpress.com/2017/04/12/access-intimacy-interdependence-and-disability-justice/. Accessed 12 February 2024.

Minich, J. A. 2016. 'Enabling Whom? Critical Disability Studies Now.' *Lateral* 5/1: n.p. https://csalateral.org/issue/5-1/forum-alt-humanities-critical-disability-studies-now-minich/. Accessed 12 February 2024.

Mitchell, F. 2021. *Monsters in Greek Literature: Aberrant Bodies in Ancient Greek Cosmogony, Ethnography, and Biology*. London.

Piepzna-Samarasinha, L. L. 2018. *Care Work: Dreaming Disability Justice*. Vancouver.

Piepzna-Samarasinha, L. L. 2020. 'Cripping the Resistance: No Revolution without Us.' *Disability Visibility Project*. https://disabilityvisibilityproject.com/2020/08/24/cripping-the-resistance-no-revolution-without-us/. Accessed 12 February 2024.

Puig de la Bellacasa, M. 2017. *Matters of Care: Speculative Ethics in More Than Human Worlds*. Minneapolis.

Rifkin, M. 2017. *Beyond Settler Time: Temporal Sovereignty and Indigenous Self-Determination*. Durham, NC.

Schalk, S. 2017. 'Critical Disability Studies as Methodology.' *Lateral* 6/1: n.p. https://csalateral.org/issue/6-1/forum-alt-humanities-critical-disability-studies-methodology-schalk/. Accessed 24 February 2024.

Schalk, S. 2018. *Bodyminds Reimagined: (Dis)ability, Race and Gender in Black Women's Speculative Fiction*. Durham, NC.

Siebers, T. 2006. 'Disability in Theory: From Social Constructionism to the New Realism of the Body', in *The Disability Studies Reader*, ed. L. Davis, 173–83. London.

Silverblank, H., and M. Ward. 2020. 'Why Does Classical Reception Need Disability Studies?' *Classical Receptions Journal* 12/4: 502–30.

Snyder, S., and D. Mitchell. 2006. *Cultural Locations of Disability*. Chicago.

Taylor, S. 2017. *Beasts of Burden: Animal and Disability Liberation*. New York.

Wong, A., ed. 2020. '*Disability Visibility: First-Person Stories from the Twenty-First Century*. New York.

PART IV

THE RECEPTION OF CLASSICAL MONSTERS

CHAPTER 31

....

PEARLS FROM A DARK CLOUD
Monsters in Persian Myth

....

PETER ADRIAN BEHRAVESH

INTRODUCTION

....

FROM gigantic birds to horned wolves to liver-stealing demons, the Persian mythological tradition is a trove of wonderfully monstrous creatures. This chapter will
examine these monsters as they appear in myths written in the New Persian language
and its predecessors (including Middle Persian and Avestan), drawing on sacred and
cosmogonic texts such as the Avesta and the *Bundahishn*, and fictional (or loosely historical) stories and epics such as the *Shāhnāmeh*, with particular emphasis on works
written in the tenth to fourteenth centuries CE by poets steeped in the oral traditions of
Persian antiquity. Many monsters in these texts are Zoroastrian in origin, though a few
find their roots in Islam. Some are simply agents of creation or destruction, mischief or
temptation. Others represent a range of anxieties, from the threat of foreign rulers to the
perils of childbirth.

While no single chapter could hope to fully explore the vast menagerie of monstrosity
found within the myths of Persia, I aim to provide a primer on the most prominent
Persian monsters and how they influenced or were influenced by other mythological
traditions, such as the Greek, Chinese, and Arabo-Islamic mythoi. I broadly delineate
Persia as the region containing modern Iran and the surrounding areas under imperial
control during the Median, Achaemenid, Parthian, and Sāsānian eras (seventh century
BCE to seventh century CE), though I will also discuss texts written or collected under
Arab and Mongol rule (seventh to fourteenth centuries CE). From here on, I will refer to
the region itself as Iran, as in the texts. Moreover, except in cases where there is a commonly accepted English transliteration, I have used the Association for Iranian Studies'
transliteration scheme for Persian words.

AVIAN MONSTERS

Fantastical birds and birdlike creatures appear widely across Persian myth in myriad forms. The most famous of these is the Simorgh, a gigantic bird that looks like a mountain or black cloud and can carry off crocodiles, panthers, and elephants (Schmidt 2002). The Simorgh turns up in epics and poems ranging from Ferdowsi's tenth-century CE *Shāhnāmeh* ('Book of Kings'), to Nezāmi's twelfth-century CE *Haft Peykar* ('The Seven Portraits', also known as the *Bahrāmnāmeh* or 'The Book of Bahrām'), and ʿAttār's twelfth-century CE *Manteq al-Teyr* ('The Conference of the Birds'), eventually becoming a symbol of the divine essence (Meisami 2015: 307). But it first appears in the Avesta as the Saena or Senmurw, an even more massive bird, which spreads its wings over the whole earth, forming a vast rain cloud (Goodell 1979: 146).[1] The Saena is associated with good fortune and lives in the middle of the heavenly sea, Vourukasha, in a tree that contains the seeds of all the plants in the world (Schmidt 2002). When the Saena alights on this tree, the seeds scatter, and a second great bird, Camrosh, collects them and carries them to where Tishtrya (the divine being identified with Sirius, the Dog Star) gathers water, mingling it with the seeds and raining this mixture down upon the earth (Goodell 1979: 146). Camrosh also protects the people of Iran by pecking up their enemies like grain. A similar seed-scattering narrative appears in the *Revāyat* of Dārāb Hormazyār, where a bird called Amrosh takes the place of the Saena (Schmidt 2002).[2]

In the *Bundahishn*, a collection of Zoroastrian cosmogonic texts, the Saena has an evil, equally massive counterpart named Kamak. Instead of bringing rain, Kamak brings drought, similarly spreading its wings over the earth, but in this case causing the rivers to dry up. And rather than devouring Iran's enemies, as Camrosh does, this malicious bird feeds on Iran's people and animals (Schmidt 2002). Kamak is killed by the eschatological hero Karshāsp, known throughout Persian myth for slaughtering monsters, including the horned dragon Azhi Sruvara, the golden-heeled sea monster Gandarewa, the stone-fisted Snavidhka, and the wolf Kapud (Bivar 2000: 24; see below).

By the time Ferdowsi writes his *Shāhnāmeh*, the Saena is known as the Simorgh and has become a primarily benevolent presence. When Zāl—great-grandson of Karshāsp (Garshāsp in the *Shāhnāmeh*) and future father of the hero Rostam—is born albino, his father, Sām, believing him to be a div (demon), abandons him in the mountains (a noteworthy example of a physical condition being treated as monstrous). The Simorgh, here female, rescues Zāl and takes him to her 'fearsome nest', which is like 'a palace towering in the clouds' (Davis 2006: 65). Though she initially intends to feed him to her chicks,

---

[1] The Avesta is a collection of Zoroastrian texts that cannot accurately be dated, though current versions trace their ancestry to a now-lost restoration set down during the third to sixth centuries CE.

[2] The Persian *Revāyats* are treatises written in the late fifteenth to eighteenth centuries by Zoroastrian scholars responding to ecclesiastical questions posed by their Indian counterparts (Choksy 2015).

when Zāl begins to cry, she takes pity on him and instead raises him as one of her own, feeding him 'the most delicate morsels of the chase' (Davis 2006: 64; Fig. 31.1).

As a young man, Zāl returns to his father, but before he leaves the Simorgh she gives him a few of her feathers, saying, 'If any trouble comes to you ... throw one of my feathers into the fire, and my glory will at once appear to you' (Davis 2006: 66). Zāl does this for the first time when his wife, Rudābeh, grows deathly ill while pregnant with Rostam, and the Simorgh appears, 'like pearls raining down from a dark cloud' (104). She helps Zāl perform a caesarean section and gives him another feather, which heals Rudābeh. Years later, when Rostam has been severely wounded by Esfandiār during single combat (after Esfandiār's father, the shah, orders him to capture Rostam), Zāl calls on the Simorgh to save his son again. She heals Rostam and shows him how to make arrows from the wood of a tamarisk tree to kill Esfandiār the next time they meet in battle. This curative power finds its roots in Zoroastrianism, when Ahura Mazdā instructs Zoroaster to take the feather of a raven and stroke his body with it to heal himself (Goodell 1979: 144). The motif recurs in Kurdish and Armenian folk tales, where the Simorgh is called the Simir or Sinam (Schmidt 2002), and in tales of the Rukh (al-Rawi 2017: 111).

The Simorgh also bestows feathers in the *Hamzenāmeh*, a prose tale based on oral tradition from eastern Iran that later became popular during the Safavid and Mughal periods (sixteenth to nineteenth centuries CE; Hanaway 2003). The hero Amir Hamza seeks to enlist the Simorgh to carry him across the seven enchanted seas of Suleyman to rescue the emperor and his kin, who have been imprisoned by divs. When he arrives at the Simorgh's nest, he hears the cries of the Simorgh's young and discovers that they are being terrorized by a fire-breathing dragon. Amir slays the dragon and feeds its meat to the chicks. Their parents—two Simorghs, male and female—return and learn of Amir's good deed. To repay him, the male Simorgh agrees to take Amir across the seas. When they land, the Simorgh gives him three feathers, telling him to burn one if he ever falls into difficulty. Later, Amir mistakenly shoots the female Simorgh, believing her to be a div. But he prays to God, and her wound is healed.

In the *Shāhnāmeh*, the Simorgh has an evil counterpart (also female), which Esfandiār kills during one of his seven trials along with her offspring, echoing Karshāsp killing the Kamak. However, it is also possible that these two Simorghs are the same, and ambivalent by nature, in which case she may have spared Zāl because she could not stomach him (Schmidt 2002). Two centuries later, though, the Simorgh has become more of a spiritual guide. In Nezāmi's *Haft Peykar*, the Simorgh hides from sight, and no one knows where the great bird may be found (Meisami 2015: 107–8), though 'a bird of mountainous size' appears in *Haft Peykar* in the tale of the black dome (one of seven such tales told to the shah Bahrām Gur over the course of the poem) and carries a fictional king to an enchanted garden populated by *paris* (Meisami 2015: 113; see below). In 'Attār's *Manteq al-Teyr*, the Simorgh is the shah of all birds (and a thinly veiled metaphor for God), living far away beyond Mount Qāf, a mythical mountain said to be the farthest peak on earth and home to the jinn. A group of birds, led by the hoopoe, set off to find their sovereign so that they can be closer to 'His transcendent majesty' (Darbandi and Davis 1984: 33). The journey, which represents the Sufi path, is harrowing, and by the

FIGURE 31.1 'Zāl, in the Simorgh's Nest, Is Sighted by a Caravan'; folio from the *Shāhnāmeh*, *c.*1530 CE.

Source: National Museum of Asian Art.

time they arrive, only thirty birds have survived. They realize that they themselves are the Simorgh (a play on words, as *si* means thirty and *morgh* means birds), because God's majesty is 'like the sun that can be seen reflected in a mirror. Yet, whoever looks into that mirror will also behold his or her own image' (Wolpe 2017: 18).

In art of the Sāsānian period (third to seventh centuries CE), the Simorgh is sometimes depicted as having the head of a dog, the claws of a lion, and the wings and tail of a peacock. Though these depictions recall the lion-griffin of Mesopotamia, it is unlikely that a single source for this hybrid can be identified (Schmidt 2002). Other mythical counterparts include the Armenian Paskuch (a similar name appears in the Middle Persian Zoroastrian texts *Menog-e Khrad*, as a grey-blue winged wolf also said to have been slain by Karshāsp), the Georgian Paskudji, the East Slavic Simargl, the Turkic Qonrul, the Talmudic Ziz and Pushqansā, the Sumerian Anzû, and the Indian Garuda (Schmidt 2002). In *The Thousand and One Nights* (and its Persian precursor, *Hezār Afsāneh*, 'The Thousand Fables'), the Simorgh is also associated with the monstrous Rukh (or Roc), though some scholars suggest that the Rukh came from the Arabic ʿAnqāʾ (also mentioned in *Haft Peykar*), a pre-Islamic giant bird with a human face and four wings (al-Rawi 2017: 112), who, like the Simorgh, hides from view.

Additional avian monsters found in Persian art and architecture include the Gopat, Lamassu, and Shedu, all variations on a winged bull or lion with a human face; the Shirdal, an eagle-headed lion (Taheri 2013); and the Homā, a mythical bird that bestows sovereignty on anyone its shadow touches. In *Manteq al-Teyr*, the Homā, in its vanity, is one of the many birds that initially denies the hoopoe's call, insisting that the Simorgh means nothing to it and that the world should instead bask in its own magnificence (Darbandi and Davis 1984: 43–4).

Aside from the obvious comparison to the Greek griffin, we can also note the Simorgh's similarities to the phoenix. Though the Simorgh is not reborn from the ashes of its predecessor, both birds possess healing powers, and artistic depictions of the two bear similarities. Additionally, like the Chinese mythological bird Fenghuang, the Simorgh and its counterparts are often depicted in combat with serpents or *azhdahās*, i.e. dragons (Lassikova 2010: 33).

Ophidian Monsters

In Persian myth, *azhdahās* are a variety of gigantic snake-like monsters living in the air, on the earth, or in the sea (Skjærvø et al. 2011). The word itself comes from the Avestan *azhi*, which means snake; according to the *Bundahishn*, Ahriman created them. They generally act as antagonists to the heroes of Persian myth, guarding treasures or water supplies, representing sins or trials to be overcome, or even embodying foreign enemies. Descriptions of several *azhdahās* appear in the Avesta: Azhi Sruvara (also called Azhi Zairita), a yellow *azhdahā* slain by Karshāsp, has horns, spits poison, and swallows humans and horses whole; Azhi Raoithrita, a red *azhdahā*, is winged; Azhi Vishapa fouls the waters; and Azhi Dahāka, a particularly powerful *azhdahā*, has three mouths, three heads, and six eyes (Skjærvø et al. 2011).

Azhi Dahāka (or Dahāg), though dragon-like in the Avesta, becomes more human (while retaining some ophidian qualities) in subsequent myths and epics, where he variously appears as a descendant of Ahriman, or even as one of the Pishdādiān—mythical shahs descended from Hushang, slayer of the Black Div, and Tahmures, Binder of Demons (see below). In the Avesta, Dahāg is slain by Thraetaona (later called Fereydun). In the *Denkard* (a tenth-century CE summary of Zoroastrian beliefs and practices), however, when Dahāg is struck by Fereydun's club, he begins to turn into reptiles and other *khrafstar* (noxious creatures from Zoroastrian mythology), so instead of killing him, Fereydun chains Dahāg to Mount Damāvand, where he will remain until the end of the world—when he will burst from his chains and Karshāsp will wake to slay him. This tale resembles similar Indo-European myths, such as Zeus imprisoning the Titans (Fereydun becomes king after slaying Dahāg), or Tyr imprisoning the Fenris wolf (both Tyr and Fereydun restrain a cosmic enemy; Skjærvø et al. 2011).

In the *Shāhnāmeh*, Dahāg becomes arabicized as Zahhāk and is depicted as an initially human tyrannical foreign ruler of Iran (in Armenian mythology, Azhidahāk is similarly the embodiment of foreign tyranny; Skjærvø et al. 2011). Zahhāk agrees to let Eblis (the Devil in Arabo-Islamic myth) murder his father (an Arab king) after Eblis tempts him with the promise of power. Eblis then kisses each of Zahhāk's shoulders. Two black snakes sprout where the Devil kisses, growing back even if Zahhāk cuts them off (he now has three mouths, three heads, and six eyes, just like Azhi Dahāka). To Zahhāk's dismay, none of his learned doctors can cure his affliction. Eblis, posing as a physician, persuades Zahhāk that the snakes were fated to appear, and that he should leave them be. The serpent-king then seizes the throne of Iran, where he reigns for a thousand years, allowing evil to flourish.

Like Azhi Dahāka, Zahhāk is eventually defeated by Fereydun, here presented as another descendant of Hushang and Tahmures. Zahhāk, after learning in a dream that Fereydun is fated to imprison him, murders both Fereydun's father and the wondrous ox that nursed him. The serpent-king also attempts to kill Fereydun, before his mother hides him away. As an adult, when Fereydun learns of Zahhāk's crimes, he seeks revenge and sets out to slay the tyrant. Fereydun hunts down Zahhāk and shatters the serpent-king's helmet with his ox-headed mace, but the angel Sorush (a figure in Iranian Islam, taking the place of the deity Sraosha from Zoroastrianism) warns Fereydun that the time has not yet come for Zahhāk's death, so Fereydun captures him instead and imprisons him in Mount Damāvand.

The *Shāhnāmeh* also contains the story of Haftvād's daughter and her giant *kerm*—literally 'worm', though there is some overlap in meaning among the Persian words for worm, snake, and dragon (Pierce 2015: 354). While spinning yarn on a mountain slope, Haftvād's daughter discovers a *kerm* coiled within an apple. She cares for it and feeds it, and so long as she does, she can spin increasing amounts of yarn, bringing great fortune and power to her family, and specifically to her father. The *kerm* begins to grow larger, its skin turning black with saffron markings. When jealous men try to take Haftvād's wealth, he gathers an army about him and kills them, amassing even more riches from his slain enemies. He then builds a fortress. After five years, the *kerm* has grown as large as an elephant, living entirely on milk and honey. No one dares attack the fortress for fear of the *kerm* (though, despite its size, it never actually harms anyone). Haftvād has now become so powerful and enlisted so many soldiers that he has caught the eye of the shah, Ardeshir (descendant of Esfandiār and founder of the Sāsānian dynasty). Ardeshir rides against Haftvād and eventually slays the *kerm* by sneaking into the fortress and pouring boiling lead down its throat, causing its bowels to burst—not unlike the Greek hero Bellerophon feeding a lump of lead to the Chimaera (Pierce 2015: 359). He then slays Haftvād.

In Zoroastrian and Manichaean sources (such as the *Bundahishn*, the Pahlavi Zand, and M 556), we find other ophidian monsters, like Gozihr and Mushparig, opponents of the sun, moon, and stars. Gozihr is an imaginary dragon that spans the sky (Mackenzie 2012). It is prophesized that at the end of the world, Gozihr will fall to the earth, and its fire will melt the mountains, creating a river of molten metal to purify humankind (Skjærvø et al. 2011). Mushparig, on the other hand, is responsible for stealing the moon, thus causing lunar eclipses. Though referred to as a dragon in Manichaean cosmogony, Mushparig is called Mush Pairikā ('rat sorceress') in the Avesta, and is therein associated with the div Āz.

No discussion of dragons would be complete without dragon slayers. Amir Hamza, mentioned above, slays multiple dragons. In the *Garshāspnāmeh* ('The Book of Garshāsp', an eleventh-century epic by Asadi Tusi), Garshāsp is ordered by Zahhāk to slay an *azhdahā* that emerges from the sea after a storm (Skjærvø et al. 2011). Similarly, in the *Shāhnāmeh*, Sām slays an *azhdahā* that emerges from the river Kashaf, 'massive as a mountain and broad as a valley' (Davis 2006: 91). This *azhdahā*, which some have identified with Azhi Sruvara (Skjærvø et al. 2011), has spittle that burns vultures' wings and venom that scorches the earth (Davis 2006: 91). It snatches monsters from the sea and eagles from the air, and the earth is emptied of people and flocks as every living thing retreats from it. In the *Jahāngirnāmeh* ('The Book of Jahāngir', date unknown), this kill is attributed to Rostam, who, like his grandfather, Sām, and his great-great-grandfather, Garshāsp, is also a dragon slayer (Skjærvø et al. 2011).

In one story, Rostam tricks an *azhdahā* with impenetrable flesh into swallowing an object—depending on the version, the object is an ox hide filled with quicklime and stones, a box with poisoned blades, or even Rostam himself—to kill the creature from the inside. He then makes a coat out of its hide (Skjærvø et al. 2011). Many of Rostam's offspring and even his enemy, Esfandiār, kill *azhdahās* with similar ruses. In the third of Rostam's seven trials—which, like Esfandiār's, echo the Labours of Heracles—Rostam faces an *azhdahā* so fearsome that no elephant has ever escaped from it. Rostam's famed horse, Rakhsh, alerts him to the *azhdahā*'s presence, even helping him defeat it by sinking his teeth into the *azhdahā*'s shoulder so that Rostam can decapitate it. When he does, poison flows like a river from its body (Davis 2006: 154–5).

Notably, Rostam's mother, Rudābeh, is the granddaughter of Zahhāk. During Rudābeh's courtship with Zāl, she loosens her hair so that he can climb up to her on the battlements of her father's fortress. Her hair cascades down, 'tumbling like snakes', recalling Medusa and the Gorgons (Pierce 2015: 359)—and perhaps serving as one of several possible influences on the later tale of Rapunzel. Moreover, since Rostam is a descendant of Garshāsp on his father's side, this means that his paternal great-great-grandfather is fated to slay his maternal great-grandfather.

TERRESTRIAL MONSTERS

In Zoroastrian mythology, the Gāwiewdād or Gāvaevodāta refers to the Primordial Bovine, the fourth of Ahura Mazdā's primal creations and the progenitor of all ben-eficent animals (Malandra 2012). When Gāwiewdād dies, it produces not only these animals, but also various types of grain and medicinal plants, which grow from its marrow. The *Bundahishn* suggests that the Gāwiewdād is hermaphroditic since it produces both semen and milk, and although it is depicted as benevolent in a way that decidedly male sacred bovines in other mythological traditions are not, its death nevertheless recalls those of similar creatures, like the Bull of Heaven from the *Epic of Gilgamesh* and the Cretan Bull of Greek myth. The *Bundahishn* also mentions the heav-enly ox Sarsaok (or Hadhayāsh), who, mirroring Gāwiewdād's sacrifice at the beginning of time, will be sacrificed at the end of time, to grant immortality to the blessed (Digard and Boyce 1990).

Conversely, the *karg* (or *kargadan*) is a fearsome four-legged beast with a single horn, variously described as having wings, the body or claws of a wolf or lion (also the body of an antelope or stag in some sources), or the appearance of a rhinoceros; indeed, *kargadan* means 'rhinoceros' in modern Persian. Other descriptions are even more fantastical, suggesting that the beast is 100 cubits long (Ettinghausen 1950: 13). Some of the confu-sion about its appearance may come from the similarity of the word *karg* to *gorg* ('wolf') when written without diacritical marks, such that in the *Shāhnāmeh*, it is unclear which creature the poet Ferdowsi has in mind (Ettinghausen 1950: 37). Ferdowsi's description hews closer to that of a rhinoceros; however, the *karg* is depicted as a wolf—with one or two horns—in many illuminated manuscripts, perhaps most famously when it is slain by Bahrām Gur (Fig. 31.2), renowned hunter and shah of Iran during the Sāsānian dynasty, who also slays an *azhdahā*. Esfandiār, Sekandar (the half-Iranian version of Alexander the Great in the *Shāhnāmeh*), and Goshtāsp (Esfandiār's father) also slay *kargs*, and in the polymath al-Qazvini's thirteenth-century *Manāfi-ye Hayavān* ('The Benefits of Animals'), the *karg* appears as the Simorgh's prey (Ettinghausen 1950: 32). Though most texts describe the *karg* as a monstrous hybrid animal, al-Qazvini suggests a gentler version of the creature, one closer to the unicorn of medieval Europe (though, unlike the unicorn, it seems to have no religious symbolism associated with it; Ettinghausen 1950: 57). This *karg* lies under the tree where a ringdove nests, so that it can listen to the bird's cooing. If the dove alights on its horn, the *karg* avoids moving its head, so as not to frighten it

FIGURE 31.2 'Bahrām Gur Slays the Rhino-Wolf'; folio from the *Shāhnāmeh* of Shah Tahmasp, *c.*1530–1535.

(Ettinghausen 1950: 23–4). In later art, the *karg* is sometimes depicted as being subdued or tamed, as in the story of *Leylā and Majnun*, an old Arabic tale popularized and Persianized in the twelfth century by Nezāmi. Al-Qazvini also suggests that the *karg*'s horn provides an antidote to poison. However, aside from two of his followers, no other Muslim scholars mention this (Ettinghausen 1950: 110). The European unicorn is similarly described as being both a detector and neutralizer of poison, but it is difficult to say with any certainty whether these depictions were influenced by the *karg*.

AQUATIC MONSTERS

Foremost among the sea-dwelling monsters of Persian myth is another man-eater, the Gandarewa. The Avesta describes the Gandarewa as a gigantic creature that lives in the heavenly sea, Vourukasha. According to the *Pahlavi Revāyat*, he is the son of Jamshid (a mythical shah) and a female div. Though the Gandarewa might be an *azhdahā* or a div, descriptions as to his exact nature are lacking (Skjærvø et al. 2011). We know that he has golden heels and can swallow twelve provinces at once; indeed, when Karshāsp looks inside the Gandarewa's mouth, he can see people hanging from the monster's teeth. The sea reaches only to his knees, and his head brushes the sun (Panaino 2012).

Karshāsp fights the Gandarewa twice. The first time, they battle for nine days before Karshāsp removes the Gandarewa's skin and binds him with it. The second time, after the Gandarewa escapes and flees back to Vourukasha, Karshāsp slays him on the shores of the sea—not unlike his later slaying of the *azhdahā* in the *Garshāspnāmeh*. Although the Gandarewa's death recalls similar stories—like Marduk slaying Tiāmat in the Babylonian creation myth *Enūma eliš*, Perseus slaying the sea monster that threatens Andromeda, or even God slaying the biblical Leviathan—a direct line of influence remains difficult to trace. However, the Avestan Gandarewa does seem to be the origin for the Vedic Gandharvas. And in some modern dialects, the word 'Gandarewa' has survived to mean 'monster', 'dragon', or even 'werewolf' (Panaino 2012).

The *Bundahishn* also mentions a sea-dwelling ox-fish whose cry causes all fish to become pregnant and all noxious water creatures to give birth. This beast is likely related to the Islamic Bahamut (a cosmic fish that carries the Primordial Bovine) and the biblical Behemoth. Other Persian aquatic monsters include Sogdian water sprites (Panaino 2012) and *mazans*, which are Manichaean sea giants often associated with the *āsreshtārs*, a group of demons involved in the creation of humankind (Skjærvø et al. 2011; Skjærvø 2011).

DEMONIC MONSTERS

Of the myriad monsters found in Persian myth, none captures the imagination more than the div. A div—from the Avestan *daeva*, originally gods, like the Vedic devas—can appear not only as a demon, but also as an ogre, a giant, or even Eblis himself (Omidsalar 2011). In text, divs are often described as black, though in Persian art they come in every colour imaginable and are often spotted. Most are clawed and covered in thick hair. Some have wings, horns, or serpents for tails; others can shape-shift, changing into people, *azhdahās*, animals, or even the wind. Some have several heads, others monstrous ears or teeth. In the oral tradition, there is even a seven-headed div who, like the Greek Hydra, grows a new head whenever one is cut off (Omidsalar 2011).

Divs roam at night and sleep during the day, in liminal spaces like caves or wells. They are contrary by nature, often doing the opposite of what they are told. When they appear, they may bring with them a change in temperature or a foul smell in the air. The *Bundahishn* states that they were (mis)created by Ahriman, and that they are responsible for all corruption and destructiveness (Omidsalar 2011). Due to their proliferation, it would be impossible to name every single div from Persian myth here, but we will explore a few of the more prominent ones.

In Zoroastrian sources, the demon Āzi or Āz (of the *āsreshtārs*) represents greed, gluttony, and lust (Asmussen 2011). In the Avesta, Āzi is masculine, and the enemy of the divine Ātar (fire). The Manichaean Āz, however, is unambiguously feminine. She created the human body to imprison the soul, and she tries to make humans forget their divine origin, thereby preventing their salvation (Asmussen 2011). Apaosha or Aposh, also from Zoroastrian sources, appears as the demon of drought, in opposition to Tishtrya (Brunner 2011).

The Black Div is the first div mentioned in the *Shāhnāmeh*. After killing Siāmak, son of Kayumars, the very first shah of Iran, the Black Div is himself slain by Hushang, Siāmak's son, who cleaves his body in two and severs his head. Hushang becomes shah when Kayumars dies, at peace now that Siamak has been avenged. Hushang has a son, Tahmures, called the Binder of Demons, because of his power over them. Through sorcery, Tahmures binds Ahriman and rides him like a mount around the world, enraging the divs. They form a great army to oppose him, but Tahmures subdues every last one of them, either with spells or with his mace. He then releases them on the condition that they reveal all their secrets to him. When Hushang dies, Tahmures assumes the throne. His son, Jamshid, succeeds him, and although Jamshid's reign is long and glorious, he is eventually overthrown and killed by the serpent-king Zahhāk (who is also sometimes described as a div).

Many centuries later, as the last of his seven trials, Rostam faces the White Div, leader of the divs of Māzandarān (a land of sorcerers and demons, not to be confused with the region of the same name in modern Iran). The White Div is described as having hair as white as snow and skin the colour of night. He moves like a mountain, and his arms and head are protected by iron armour. Rostam rides to the cave where the White Div resides, which is guarded by a demonic army. He waits until the sun is high and all the divs are asleep, then slaughters the army and makes his way into the cave to attack. Though the two combatants seem evenly matched at first, Rostam severs one of the White Div's legs, then throws him to the ground and cuts out his heart and liver. The cave is filled with the div's bulk, and the whole world seems like a sea of blood.

For his previous trial, Rostam had killed Arzhang, another div, but that battle was over in an instant, as he simply rode up and ripped the div's head off. Rostam also kills Akvān, a div disguised as a donkey. He chases Akvān for three days, but then collapses from exhaustion, at which point Akvān throws him into the sea. Rostam escapes and hunts down Akvān—whose true form is revealed as a long-haired, elephant-headed div—and beheads him (Khaleghi-Motlagh 2011).

A separate class of female demonic monsters, called *pairikās* or *paris*, encompasses witches, enchantresses, and sorceresses, like Mush Pairikā, the 'rat sorceress' mentioned earlier (who also numbers among the *khrafstar*; Adhami 2010). *Pairikās* in the Zoroastrian sources cause drought and scarcity. In Middle Persian, *pairikā* becomes *parig*, and although still mostly evil by nature, some *parigs* in this period prove benign or even benevolent (Adhami 2010). By the time of Ferdowsi, Nezāmi, and later poets, *paris* have largely shed their negative attributes and turned into alluring creatures, though their beauty sometimes hides monstrosity beneath. For example, in Rostam's fourth trial in the *Shāhnāmeh*, he encounters a witch disguised as a young woman, 'beautiful as the spring and lovelier than any painting' (Davis 2006: 156). But although he is seduced at first, when he mentions God's kindness, she reveals her true form—a withered old woman—and he slays her.

Similarly, in *Haft Peykar*, in the tale of the turquoise dome, a young man named Māhān wanders into a land filled with horned, fire-breathing demons who look like 'elephant and ox conjoined' (Meisami 2015: 181). When his horse turns into a four-winged, seven-headed *azhdahā*, Māhān flees and is rescued by an old man of considerable wealth who offers to make Māhān his heir, if only he will spend one night in silence in one of the trees in the man's garden. Māhān agrees, and when the moon rises, seventeen seductive *paris* appear, led by their queen and singing sweet songs. They coax Māhān down, despite his promise to the old man, and he feasts with them. But when he embraces the *pari* queen, she turns into a tusked and hunchbacked afrit (a type of jinn) with gaping jaws and a horrid stench. When dawn comes, the monster vanishes, but the garden has withered, along with Māhān's dreams of fortune.

Another female folkloric being, the Āl, kills women who have just given birth by stealing their liver or, in some versions, the placenta. Her form varies depending on the account, though she typically appears as a tall creature covered in hair or as a weak and wretched woman. She flees from iron, coal, the colour black, and the smell of onions (Šāmlū and Russell 2011). The Āl also appears in Georgian, Armenian, and Turkic myths, and recalls the child-stealing demon Lilith from Jewish lore (see also Kucharski in this volume). A similar female creature, Bakhtak, knows where all the treasures of the earth are hidden and tries to suffocate people in their sleep. If the sleeper grabs Bakhtak's nose, which is made of clay, she will reveal the location of one of the treasures. Though Bakhtak's connection to the Āl is debatable, she nevertheless resembles other creatures of Iranian folklore, like the Taptapo, the Shevli, and the Shavah, all of whom throw themselves on unsuspecting sleepers (Gaffary 1988).

Fulād-zereh, a div from the story of Amir Arsalān, is the chief general of the *pari* king, Malek Khāzen, who seizes the throne by turning the rightful heir and his attendants to stone. Fulād-zereh's mother, a powerful witch, casts a spell on him that makes him invulnerable to all weapons except for a special shamshir. In the end, Amir Arsalān slays both Fulād-zereh and his mother with this blade and revives their victims (Omidsalar 2012a).

Jinn (singular 'jinni', anglicized as 'genie') are supernatural beings created from smokeless fire, sometimes said to be the children of Eblis. They are divided into three classes: those that have wings, those that resemble snakes or dogs, and those that move like humans. Early Persian sources use the Arabic word *jinni* and the Persian word *pari* interchangeably, and jinn are rarely mentioned in the secular epics (Omidsalar 2012b). In the *Farāmarznāmeh* (a fourteenth-century CE epic), we meet Sorkhāb, the king of the jinn, who has taken the form of a wild ass. While jinn in religious texts are often described as beautiful, in secular texts they are monstrous creatures with long heads, large fangs, and a single eye (Omidsalar 2012b). Like divs, jinn come in a variety of shapes and sizes and can assume almost any form.

In Persian folk tales, jinn are typically malevolent creatures. For example, among the people of Baluchistan, there is a jinni that takes the form of a bull and attacks at night; another throws stones at its victims (Omidsalar 2012b). In Baluchistan and other southern coastal regions of Iran, many also believe in *zār*, evil winds or spirits capable of possessing humans and inflicting them with disease (Moghaddam 2009). But the most malevolent of all the jinn are ghuls, a word sometimes used synonymously with 'div' (Omidsalar and Omidsalar 2012) and from which the English word 'ghoul' derives.

Ghuls are hideous monsters with feline heads, forked tongues, hairy skin, and donkey-like feet. They live in the desert, feast on human flesh, and, like divs and jinn, can transform into virtually any animal. They cannot change the appearance of their feet, however, which is often how they are identified (Omidsalar and Omidsalar 2012). A ghul killed by a single blow may be revived if struck again, as seen in the *Hamzenāmeh*. In the *Shāhnāmeh*, the witch that Esfandiār faces in his fourth trial is referred to as a ghul. In the *Farāmarznāmeh*, during Farāmarz's third trial, he slays a creature called *div-e ghul*, a beast with dark skin, red eyes, and tusks. And in the *Garshāspnāmeh*, Garshāsp's army discovers a desert infested with flying snakes and ghuls. Similar demonic legions appear in both the *Sāmnāmeh* and the *Shahriārnāmeh* (Omidsalar and Omidsalar 2012).

Conclusion

The monsters of the Persian mythological tradition are a rich and varied brood, far too numerous to discuss in any detail here, and certainly deserving of further study in English. From our modern vantage, these creatures capture the imagination, evoking a time when the line between history and myth was blurred, but in their day, they reflected genuine fears about foreign rulers, natural disasters, physical ailments, and other destructive forces. Like their Greek, Chinese, and Arabo-Islamic counterparts, the monsters of Persian myth symbolized the chaos of the world, in contrast to the heroes who tried to forge order by vanquishing them. It is my sincere hope that this chapter will spur readers to dive deeper into tales of the Simorgh, the Gandarewa, *azhdahās*, *kargs*, and divs.

SUGGESTED READING

For those interested in learning more about Persian monsters, Dick Davis's meticulous translation of the *Shāhnāmeh* (Davis 2006) and Afkham Darbandi and Dick Davis's translation of *Manteq al-Teyr* (Darbandi and Davis 1984) are two wonderful gifts to English readers. Julie Meisami's translation of *Haft Peykar* is similarly comprehensive and beautiful (Meisami 2015). Richard Ettinghausen's *The Unicorn* provides an incomparable study of the *karg* (Ettinghausen 1950). And for all things Iranian, the *Encyclopædia Iranica* is an important and invaluable resource, both in print and online.

WORKS CITED

Adhami, S. 2010. 'Pairikā.' *Encyclopædia Iranica*, online edn. https://www.iranicaonline.org/articles/pairika.

Al-Rawi, A. 2017. 'A Linguistic and Literary Examination of the Rukh Bird in Arab Culture.' *Al-ʾArabiyya* 50: 105–17.

Asmussen, J. P. 2011. 'Āz', *Encyclopædia Iranica* III/2: 168–9. New York.

Bivar, A. D. H. 2000. 'The Role of Allegory in the Persian Epic.' *Bulletin of the Asia Institute* 14: 19–26.

Brunner, C. J. 2011. 'Apōš', *Encyclopædia Iranica* II/2: 161–2. New York.

Choksy, J. K. 2015. 'Zoroastrianism ii. Historical Review: from the Arab Conquest to Modern Times.' *Encyclopædia Iranica*, online edn. https://www.iranicaonline.org/articles/zoroastrianism-02-arab-conquest-to-modern.

Darbandi, A., and D. Davis, trans. 1984. *The Conference of the Birds*. New York.

Davis, D., trans. 2006. *Shahnameh: The Persian Book of Kings*. New York.

Digard, J.-P., and M. Boyce. 1990. 'Cattle', *Encyclopædia Iranica* V/1: 79–84. New York.

Ettinghausen, R. 1950. *The Unicorn*. Washington, DC.

Gaffary, F. 1988. 'Baktak', *Encyclopædia Iranica* III/5: 539. New York.

Goodell, G. 1979. 'Bird Lore in Southwestern Iran.' *Asian Folklore Studies* 38/2: 131–53.

Hanaway, W. L., Jr. 2003. 'Ḥamza-nāma', *Encyclopædia Iranica* XI/6: 649. New York.

Khaleghi-Motlagh, D. J. 2011. 'Akvān-e Dīv', *Encyclopædia Iranica* I/7: 740. New York.

Lassikova, G. 2010. 'Hushang the Dragon-slayer: Fire and Firearms in Safavid Art and Diplomacy.' *Iranian Studies* 43/1: 29–51.

Mackenzie, D. N. 2012. 'Gōzihr', *Encyclopædia Iranica* XI/2: 184. New York.

Malandra, W. W. 2012. 'Gāw ī Ēwdād', *Encyclopædia Iranica* X/4: 40. New York.

Meisami, J. S., trans. 2015. *Haft Paykar: A Medieval Persian Romance*. Indianapolis.

Moghaddam, M. S. 2009. 'Zār.' *Encyclopædia Iranica*, online edn. https://iranicaonline.org/articles/zar.

Omidsalar, M. 2011. 'Dīv', *Encyclopædia Iranica* VII/4: 428–31. New York.

Omidsalar, M. 2012a. 'Fūlād-zereh', *Encyclopædia Iranica* X/3: 227. New York.

Omidsalar, M. 2012b. 'Genie', *Encyclopædia Iranica* X/4: 418–22. New York.

Omidsalar, M., and T. P. Omidsalar. 2012. 'Gul', *Encyclopædia Iranica* XI/4: 393–5. New York.

Panaino, A. 2012. 'Gaṇdarəba', *Encyclopædia Iranica* X/3: 267–9. New York.

Pierce, L. 2015. 'Serpents and Sorcery: Humanity, Gender, and the Demonic in Ferdowsi's *Shahnameh.' Iranian Studies* 48/3: 349–67.

Šāmlū, A., and J. R. Russell. 2011. 'Āl', *Encyclopædia Iranica* I/7: 741–2. New York.

Schmidt, H.-P. 2002. 'Simorḡ.' *Encyclopædia Iranica*, online. https://iranicaonline.org/articles/simorg.

Skjærvø, P. O. 2011. 'Āsrēštār', *Encyclopædia Iranica* II/8: 801–2. New York.

Skjærvø, P. O., D. J. Khaleghi-Motlagh, and J. R. Russell. 2011. 'Aždahā', *Encyclopædia Iranica* III/2: 191–205. New York.

Taheri, S. 2013. 'Gopat & Shirdal in the Ancient East.' *Honar-Ha-Ye-Ziba: Honar-Ha-Ye-Tajassomi* 17/4: 13–22.

Williams, A. V. 2011. 'Dēw', *Encyclopædia Iranica* VII/3: 333–4. New York.

Wolpé, S., trans. 2017. *The Conference of the Birds*. New York.

CHAPTER 32

PLINIAN MONSTERS IN OLD NORSE ENCYCLOPAEDIC LITERATURE

ARNGRÍMUR VÍDALÍN

INTRODUCTION

A curious surge in learned manuscript culture occurs in Iceland at the dawn of the fourteenth-century, all written in the vernacular Old Norse-Icelandic language from which modern Icelandic developed. Before this time there were certainly didactic texts, such as the Old Norse translation of Honorius Augustodunensis' *Elucidarium*, which was a summary of Christian beliefs, and the Norwegian *Konungs skuggsjá* (*The King's Mirror*, or *Speculum regale*), a text similar to *Elucidarium* and probably based on it, yet focused on the proper education of kings. Icelandic didactic texts also included still-extant hagiographies, annals, and a singular universal history (*Veraldar saga*). Old Norse encyclopaedias, however, are most prominent in the fourteenth century. Indeed, shortly after the turn of the century, the first extant work containing a detailed monstrous ethnography was written, influenced by earlier authors such as St Isidore of Seville (*c.*560–636 CE), St Augustine (*c.*354–430 CE), Herodotus (*c.*484–*c.*425 BCE), and most of all Pliny the Elder (*c.*23–79 CE). More learned works subsequently included Plinian lore, each in their own unique way, of which four are of particular interest to the present chapter.

The four texts in question are known by their catalogue designations: the AM 544 4to manuscript of Hauksbók (1302–10), the AM 226 and 227 fol. manuscripts of Stjórn (1350), and AM 194 8vo (1387).[1] These texts exhibit an interest in encyclopaedic knowledge and geography to a degree largely lacking in twelfth- and thirteenth-century

---

[1] Excluding AM 227 fol., preserved in the Árni Magnússon Institute for Icelandic Studies in Reykjavík, Iceland, all manuscripts are preserved in the Arnamagnæan Collection at the University of Copenhagen, Denmark. All translations from Old Norse are my own.

manuscripts. The lost thirteenth-century 'Kringla manuscript', of which now only a single leaf exists, showed a similar interest in the beginning chapter of its *Ynglinga saga*. There it is stated, among other things, that dragons and *blámenn* (literally 'blue/black men') live in Scythia (cf. Vídalín 2020b). This sort of geographical knowledge starts to pervade other texts in later decades, such as the fourteenth-century vita of St Nicholas, *Nikulás saga* by Bergr Sokkason, while fourteenth-century saga narratives increasingly take the audience to ever more exotic lands with even more horrendous monsters. This strengthens the assumption that interest in geographical matters was on the rise in Iceland by the turn of the century (1299–1300).

Another interest which peaked in fourteenth-century Iceland was the question, or rather the factually stated existence, of monsters. The most prominent concept of the monstrous in learned Icelandic medieval writing is based on the so-called Plinian trad-ition, derived from Pliny the Elder's *Natural History*, which in turn derives from the writings of Herodotus, Aristotle, and others. Pliny's encyclopaedia proved so popular that St Augustine found reason to explain how such monsters might hypothetically exist. However far it may have been from Augustine's intentions to prove the existence of monsters, Icelandic scholars of the late Middle Ages seem to have concluded that Augustine had veritably shown that monsters existed and that they had been created by God. Through the prominence of St Isidore of Seville's interpretation of Augustine's interpretation of Plinian monsters, the scholarship of these men, as well as other works thence derived, eventually reached the Icelandic learned class.

This chapter explores how Plinian monsters are portrayed in Old Norse encyclo-paedic texts. While Plinian ideas about monsters also surface in saga literature, several instances of which are of great interest, these regrettably lie outside the scope of this dis-cussion (Vídalín 2020a, 2020b).

THE MONSTER THEORIES OF HERODOTUS, PLINY, AUGUSTINE, AND ISIDORE

In the fifth century BCE, Herodotus of Halicarnassus wrote his influential *Histories*. Ostensibly intended to explain the cause of the Persian Wars against the Greeks, the work contains, among other things, ethnographies describing a multitude of strange and exotic peoples with even stranger customs. Felton has shown that, in spite of this, Herodotus is very cautious in drawing any conclusions, such as his remark that he does not believe 'in a race of goat-footed men or reports of a race of men who sleep for six months out of the year' (2012: 123–4). Herodotus is thus quite hesitant to take any re-sponsibility for such tales, but does not mind recounting them all the same.

Herodotus' belief that the most distant places beget both the fairest and rarest things would evolve somewhat in the works of others through the centuries. Aristotle's phrasing of the sentiment in the fourth century BCE is that 'Libya always fosters something new';

this seems to refer to the genesis of new animal species, as frequent droughts would drive different animals to gather at the few available waterholes where they would mate and produce hybrid offspring (Peck 1942: 244–5; van Duzer 2012: 397). Pliny the Elder repeats this theory (Rackham 1983: 332), and further remarks that it should come as no surprise that the furthest regions of Ethiopia beget monsters in both animal and human form due to the immense heat there (Rackham 1942: 476). In another passage he says that India and Ethiopia are particularly filled with wonders (Rackham 1942: 518). The Greek geographer Poseidonius (c.135–c.51 BCE) had similar views, on which he based his definition of the Earth's climatic zones. He postulated that both the north and south hemispheres had one mild zone and one freezing zone each and that in between the two hemispheres lay the impassable torrid zone. Several medieval *mappae mundi* reflect Poseidonius' ideas, including a hemispherical map found in the Icelandic manuscript fragment AM 736 I 4to, discussed below (DeAngelo 2010: 268–9; cf. Simek 1990: 406–11). Similarly, the first-century BCE Greek historian Diodorus Siculus wrote that hybrid offspring of different animal species primarily occurred in hot regions, whereas the general notion that extreme climates can produce monsters in certain parts of the world may be traced to the fifth-century BCE Hippocratic treatise *On Airs, Waters, and Places* (Jones 1939: 104–9, 132–7; van Duzer 2012: 390–1; Isaac 2004: 11; Biller 2009: 157–80; Smith 2011: 11–71). The theory that a harsh climate could have monstrous effects was a widespread idea from its inception in antiquity on down the centuries, as Friedman (2000: 51–5) has shown.

Western European scholars adapted this notion to their Christian world view and put their own spin on it, effectively defining Jerusalem as the centre of the world, both symbolically in the religious sense yet also literally in a geographical sense (Friedman 2000: 43–5; Kline 2003: 162–4; Edson 2005: 19–20). The climate there was thought to be closest to that of the Terrestrial Paradise before the fall of Adam and Eve, almost perfectly mild and ideal in all respects (Ashurst 2006: 71–80; Tómasson 2001: 23–40; Jakobsson 2006: 935–43). Conversely, the further removed from this centre according to the adjusted Poseidonian concept, the worse the climate was thought to be. On the peripheries the climate was exceedingly hostile: extreme frosts in the North and unbearable, scorching heat in the South. Under such conditions it was thought that monsters would spawn (Friedman 2000: 43). This understanding is furthermore based on St Jerome's interpretation of Psalm 73, which in the Vulgate states that God performs the work of salvation to the middle of the Earth. Jerome 'connected this passage to Ezekiel 5:5: "This the Lord God said: I have placed Jerusalem in the middle of the peoples, and around her the lands"', placing the spiritual and literal centre of the Earth in Jerusalem with all the lands and its peoples in surrounding regions (Mittman 2006: 34–5), the ramifications being that the peoples furthest from this centre would also be furthest from God. Jerome's interpretation became dominant and it likewise became a defining factor for peripheral areas such as Iceland with respect to medieval Christian Europe, in that Icelanders had ample reason to fear their association with the Earth's monstrous peripheries (Mittman 2006: 36–7; Vídalín 2018).

As previously stated, Pliny's *Natural History* was far more influential for the world view of Christian thinkers of late antiquity and the early Middle Ages than was Herodotus' *Histories*. The *Natural History*, an immense encyclopaedic work, was intended as a complete compendium of available scientific knowledge according to the most reliable sources, including such topics as astronomy, agriculture, zoology, geography, anthropology, and ethnography. It became the model for later encyclopaedic works such as Isidore's *Etymologies*, and, even more than 1,200 years later, Icelandic encyclopaedic works reflected the eclectic design of Pliny's *Natural History* while viewing the world through a mostly Isidorian theological framework (Kålund 1908; Astås 2009: 100–51; Jónsson et al. 1892–1896: 165–7).

Most relevant for our purposes are Pliny's sections on geography, anthropology, and ethnography: Pliny gives a detailed account of known lands, the peoples inhabiting those lands, and their customs. Some of these peoples are derived from Herodotus, either directly or through intermediary sources. Among these, described by both Herodotus and Pliny, are the Cynocephali, Blemmyes, Pygmies, and Troglodytes. Other peoples are reported not to have noses, or to lack lips or a tongue; then there are those who have but a single hole in their face through which to feed with a straw (Rackham 1942: 478). Pliny tells of the cannibalistic Scythians, Cyclopes, one-eyed Arimaspi, and more (see Williams 1996: 107–215). While we cannot know how general the belief in such strange and monstrous peoples may have been, most likely such tall tales would not have been awarded inclusion in learned literature were they not to be taken seriously.

The credence lent to these tales is illustrated in the response, documented in Christian literature, medieval sagas, and learned treatises. The extent of Pliny's influence on popular belief, to name a relatively recent example, is revealed in Christopher Columbus's surprise that he did not come across any Plinian monsters in America (Larrington 2004: 101). Long before, in the early fifth century CE—close to four hundred years after Pliny—St Augustine saw reason to respond to rumours of the existence of the monsters described by Pliny. Augustine's argument is simultaneously clever and fair:

> It ought not to seem absurd to us, that as in individual races there are monstrous births, so in the whole race there are monstrous races. Wherefore, to conclude this question cautiously and guardedly, either these things which have been told of some races have no existence at all; or if they do exist, they are not human races; or if they are human, they are descended from Adam. (Sanford 1965: 40–8)

That is, if monsters truly exist and are human, then they are in no way unlike other people descended from Adam. If they exist yet are not human, then they are nonetheless part of God's creation, for nothing can exist but through His will. Having thus argued, Augustine does not venture an opinion on whether monsters *do* exist, for that was beside the argument as far as he was concerned (Sanford 1965: 40–8; Friedman 2000: 90–2). In this way, Augustine managed to interweave the possibility of monsters with a Catholic world view with little ado, without ever implying that their existence was at all likely. He probably never intended any such interpreting of his reasoning, and yet, with the passing of time, that is precisely what happened. Augustine gradually became a prime authority for the existence of dog-headed and otherwise monstrous peoples.

Among those who seriously considered the existence of monsters was St Isidore of Seville, and, as others would consequently follow him in, he cited Augustine as an authority. Isidore takes Augustine's position in disagreeing with the Roman author Varro, who in the first century BCE said that monsters or portents came into being *contra naturam*. Like Augustine, Isidore argues that all things are made according to the will of the Maker, although such things may exist contrary to human know-ledge of nature. However, Isidore disagrees with Augustine on the interpretation of monsters and portents, as the latter felt that God's work should not be questioned in any way, while Isidore argued that the purpose of monsters and portents was indeed to serve as premonitions of various kinds, to portend and demonstrate (*portendere, (de) monstrare*), and thus it was quite natural to try to interpret and understand these phe-nomena (Barney et al. 2010: 243–4). Isidore essentially picks up the thread where Pliny and Augustine left it and weaves in an image of a world populated with literal monsters, arguing that just as there exist monstrous individuals within societies, so there exist en-tire societies of monstrous people. These monstrous people are indeed familiar: giants, Cynocephali, Cyclopes, Blemmyes, Hippopodes ('horse-footed' people), and many more—with all of their varying monstrous characteristics described in detail (Barney et al. 2010: 244–5).

In all these six hundred years of virtually verbatim accounts of monsters surrounding Europe on all fronts, the main difference among them lies in the added theological confirmation of their veracity in the early Middle Ages. In the fifth century, Augustine accepts that monsters may exist, while in the seventh century, Isidore claims their ex-istence without a shred of doubt. From then on, the number of purportedly factual accounts of monsters grows exponentially, usually recycled from Isidore, including the late seventh-century *Liber monstrorum* and the tradition of the *bestiarium vocabulum* (i.e. bestiary), derived from the Greek *Physiologus*, a collection of moralized beast tales which, in its Icelandic manifestation, included the Plinian monsters (see Fig. 32.1), merging two different traditions into one (Hermannsson 1938).

An interesting example, given this chapter's Scandinavian context, emerges in the eleventh-century *History of the Archbishops of Hamburg* by Adam of Bremen. The usual suspects enter the stage. According to Adam, Scythians are barbaric, while Estonians are so ignorant of God that they worship dragons and birds, to which they sacrifice living slaves bought from merchants (but not before checking them for physical imperfections, so that the dragons will not reject the sacrifice). The Sambians, or Prussians, said to be blue/dark of skin, have the single vice that they persecute Christian missionaries; the Amazons live in Fennoscandia and several theories abound as to how they beget chil-dren: they do so either simply by drinking water, or by using merchants and/or other men willingly or unwillingly to that end, or their children are begat by the multitude of monsters in that area (Adam thinks this is the likeliest theory). When the child is born it will become a Cynocephalus if it is male, or the most beautiful woman if it is fe-male. Adam elaborates on Cynocephali, noting that Russians hunt down and imprison

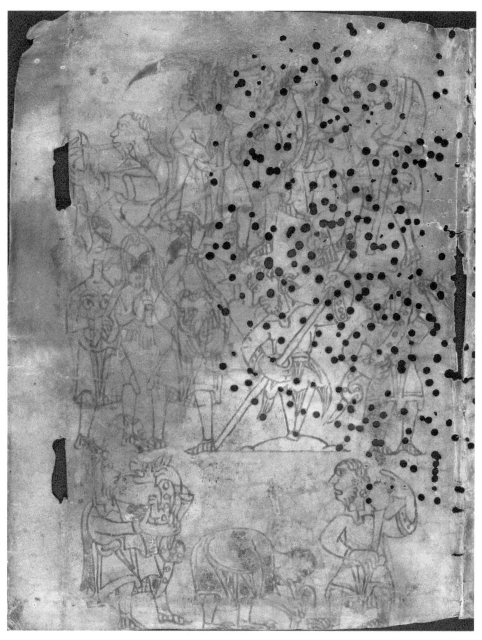

FIGURE 32.1 An Icelandic depiction of Plinian monsters from a *Physiologus* manuscript, including Blemmyes, a Sciapod, snake-eaters, and a grass-eater. Not all figures have been identified.

Reproduced with kind permission from The Árni Magnússon Institute for Icelandic Studies, Reykjavík, AM 673 a I 4to, fo. 2v, *c.*1200.

them, and that they bark their words instead of speaking them. A scribal error results in their conflation with Blemmyes when Adam says that their head is on their chest. Adam mentions these and many more monsters, including dwarfs, cannibals, and Cyclopes (Tschan 2002: 200–6; Simek 1990: 199–278).

When his eye turns to Scandinavia, however, the tone shifts decidedly. Adam says that all Norwegians are properly Christian—discounting those living beyond the Arctic Circle, who are akin to wild beasts, well versed in sorcery, claim they know all events wherever in the world they take place, and lure immense sea monsters ashore with but a brief chant; moreover, the women in the roughest mountain regions grow beards while the men dwell in the woods and are hardly ever seen. People on Scandinavia's fringes furthermore wear pelts for clothes and grind their teeth instead of speaking to one another, so hardly anyone may understand their language. Some of this is also attested in Old Norse sources, indicating that perhaps Adam was familiar with Nordic dehumanization of the peoples in the most peripheral North. Conversely, according to Adam, all Icelanders are blessed by God in their service to him, in their poverty and toil in a hard and scantily populated land. They revere their bishop as if he were king; they are generous, and Scripture is law. Very few descriptions of Iceland and its inhabitants written before the eighteenth century are as positive as this one (Ísleifsson 2015: 62–6).

Learned Icelanders were themselves intensely fascinated by Plinian monsters; the earliest evidence for this dates to the late twelfth century. They were inspired by and even directly cited the above texts and others as authorities on the matter. The primary medieval Icelandic scholarly texts on the subject are explored in the following sections.

THE FOUNDATION OF OLD NORSE GEOGRAPHY

In what appears to be the first extant treatise of its kind in Old Norse, the Arnamagnæan Collection's fragmentary manuscript AM 736 I 4to, written between 1290 and 1310, we find a detailed description of the geography of the known world, seemingly derived from the twelfth-century Old Norse universal history *Veraldar saga*. The manuscript describes how the Earth is divided into three great continents: Asia, Africa, and Europe. While this fragment makes no mention of monsters, it is notable in three respects. Firstly, it includes a zonal map with reference to the movements of the heavenly bodies, showing the habitable northern hemisphere including the three continents, a presumably uninhabited southern hemisphere, and a torrid zone in between (Kedwards 2020: 63–100). Secondly, it contains one of three Icelandic maps of Jerusalem, all of which are surprisingly accurate (Guðmundsdóttir 2015: 96–7; Kedwards 2020: 48–53). Thirdly, it mentions the presumption that the then newly found Vínland in modern-day North America is an extension of the west coast of Africa, which hinges on the well-established fact of the time that God created only three continents. For this last reason the fragment is especially invaluable, as it would explain why Plinian Sciapodes pop up in descriptions of North America in *Eiríks saga rauða* (*The Saga of Eric the Red*), extant in Hauksbók, as learned texts available to Icelandic scribes frequently place Sciapodes in northwest Africa.

MONSTROUS PEOPLES IN THE HAUKSBÓK MANUSCRIPT

The Arnamagnæan manuscript Hauksbók, preserved in three parts, is a massive compendium of sagas, myths, and medieval learning. Its second part, designated with the shelf mark AM 544 4to (1302–1310), will be my focus here. Like AM 736 I 4to, it includes information from *Veraldar saga*. But it also includes a geographical compendium, the division of the three continents between the sons of Noah, passages from Honorius' *Elucidarium* in Old Norse, the oldest Scandinavian mathematical treatise (*Algorismus*), and many other texts. One chapter describes the many different peoples of varying monstrosity who populate the Earth. It is clear from several references in the manuscript that its main scribe, Haukr Erlendsson (d. 1334), knew Pliny's works either directly or through intermediary sources, and this chapter in particular reveals Haukr's interest in Plinian teratology. The monstrous peoples therein described include Troglodytes ('cave-dwellers'), Anthropophagi ('man-eaters'), Ichthyophagi, ('fish-eaters') Sciapodes ('shade-feet'), Blemmyes, satyrs, Cynocephali, and Cyclopes (Jónsson et al. 1892–1896: 165–7). Haukr reports the existence of these peoples matter-of-factly, within a geographical compendium based on the division of continents between Noah's sons and on which countries belong to those continents. One is presumably to conclude from the chapter that most of the world's monsters are descendants of Ham, the accursed one of Noah's three sons.

Hauksbók is also remarkable for containing another one of the three Icelandic maps of Jerusalem, quite similar to the one in AM 736 I 4to albeit more industriously drawn. Despite this, nothing indicates any textual relations between the two manuscripts, save for Hauksbók's inclusion of the aforementioned *Eiríks saga rauða*, which places Sciapodes in North America, possibly indicating Haukr's understanding that Vínland was part of North Africa.

PLINIAN MONSTERS IN THE BIBLICAL-ENCYCLOPAEDIC COMPENDIUM STJÓRN

Stjórn is a remarkable fourteenth-century attempt at an Icelandic translation of biblical material, interspersed with additions and translated exegeses by Church Fathers such as St Jerome and St Augustine. The text is so heavily annotated it could hardly count as a de facto translation of the Bible, as Stjórn was meant to be so much more. A particular manuscript of Stjórn, AM 226 fol., seems to have been intended as a universal history, with translations of several texts considered historical at the time. The first text is the so-called *History of the Romans* (*Rómverja sǫgur*), incorporating Sallust's *Bellum Jugurthinum* and *Conjuratio Catilinae*, as well as Lucan's *Pharsalia* all in one. The second text is a translation of the *Alexandreis* (*Alexanders saga*) by Galtherus of Châtillon. Concluding the collection is the *History of the Jews* (*Gyðinga saga*), based on translations of 1 and 2 Maccabees and Comestor's *Historia scholastica* (Óskarsdóttir 2005: 127). Stjórn is immense, and yet the attention scholars have given to it is disproportionately small (see Astås 1991).

Here I focus on the first part of Stjórn, extant in three Arnamagnæan manuscripts written in Iceland: AM 227 fol. (*c*.1350), AM 225 fol. (*c*.1400) and AM 226 fol. (*c*.1440). Stjórn I, as it has been designated to differentiate it from Stjórn II and Stjórn III, contains a geographical compendium worthy of the size of the overall work. In the most recent edition (Astås 2009), the geographical chapter takes up fifty pages. Interspersed throughout the recounting of the various lands and their animals and peoples are descriptions of Plinian monsters, as in this passage from the section on India (Unger 1862: 68–9; cf. Fig. 22.1 in this volume):

> India has in it many peoples and a great number of big cities. There the Cenocephali are born, people who are so named for the reason that they have the head of a dog [*at þeir hafa hundz hòfut*], and that their barking reveals their nature to be no less that of dogs than men. Nonetheless, they are in some ways considered rather among senseless beasts than men, like apesses, for their heads notwithstanding they are not unlike them.

From this and other passages, it is apparent that Jerusalem, and continental Europe in the wider context, is the cultural, religious, and ethnic centre that the scribes of Stjórn consider to be the norm with which to compare, as it were, the 'outside world'. The geography of Europe is, unsurprisingly, free of monstrosities, discounting a particular *minocentaurus* in Greece (more famously associated with Crete; Unger 1862: 85). The further from this centre one ventures, the more hideous and monstrous the people become. This reflects both the Macrobian theory of the physiological effects of climate on the development of people and common ideas about a cultural centre versus an exotic periphery—that is, the politics of an 'us' and 'them' dichotomy.

Between Europe and Asia lies Scythia, or 'the Greater Sweden' as it is frequently called in Old Norse (*Svíþjóð en mikla*). Here Stjórn puts forth an interesting thesis concerning the origins of monstrous (*skyssiligra*)[2] peoples (Unger 1862: 78–9), one fundamentally similar to views expressed elsewhere in Old Norse sources:

---

[2] Variations in spelling are quite common in Old Norse-Icelandic manuscripts as no standard existed during the earliest centuries of writing. Therefore words like *skyssiligr* (nom.), *skyssiligra* (dat.), may also be spelled *skyrsiligr* (nom.), *skyrsilighra* (dat.), and so on.

Bordering [Scythia] is a land called Hircania. Both these countries have many peoples roaming and wandering far and wide due to the infertility of the lands. Some of them plough the fields for their survival, some of them have become very monstrous and terrifying [*skyrsiligar ok rædiligar*] and feed on human bodies and drink their blood, and these are called *Ancropagi* [i.e. Anthropophagi].

This text continues, counting Panotii ('large-eared' people), Hippopodes, Hermaphrodites, Garamanti, Panphagi ('omnivores'), and many more. The text then elaborates on the furthest eastern periphery (Unger 1862: 79):

In the furthest reaches of the world's eastern continent it is told that many of the peoples have monstrous appearances [*skyssilighar þiodanna aaseonur*], as it is written, that they have become so vile-looking, that they neither have noses nor nostrils [*at þeir hafi huarki nef ne nasir*], and that their entire faces are square-topped and flat. On others the lower lip protrudes so extremely that they conceal their entire countenance with it, to shield themselves from the scorching sun as they sleep [*audrum liggr sua langt framm hin nedri uòrrin. at þeir hylia medr henni alla sina aaseonu i solar hita. þann tima sem þeir sofa*].... Of others it is told that they have no tongue whatsoever [*af odrum segiz at ònguar hafi tungurnar medr aullu*], and employ among themselves all sorts of gestures and contortions of the body instead of speech. Though some people find it wondrous or unbelievable that which is told of such monstrous creatures [*skyrsiligri skepnu*], it is no less the truth. Isidore furthermore explains that these sorts of creatures are not against nature [*at þess háttar skepnur ero eigi i moti natturu*], for they exist by the will of God, and the will of the Creator is reflected through the very nature of all things in creation. It is for this reason that heathens have sometimes referred to God as nature itself, and at other times as a deity. By the same logic by Him so made and given, that the Creator's will is the self-same as the nature of His creation, it follows that such wonders and monstrous creatures have not by any means contrary to nature come into being, though it may be contrary to our understanding of nature [*þa er þess hattar undr ok skyrsileg skepna eigi moti sealfri natturunni uordin. utan moti þeirri natturu sem oss er kunnig*].

The scribes of Stjórn clearly agree with Augustine's monster theory as argued by Isidore, almost gleefully revealing how well read they are by quoting Pliny 'and other naturalists', stating that Pliny was 'one of the wisest men of ancient times' (Unger 1862: 80). Thus the text continues, citing well-known authoritative texts. Bláland ('Land of the dark/black people'), roughly corresponding to Africa south of the Sahara, is said to be 'abundant with strange animals and venomous serpents; Isidore tells of many different kinds of venomous serpents' in his *Etymologies* (12.4), 'and yet he says that there exist even more kinds than are numbered there' (Unger 1862: 96). Indeed, according to Stjórn, Africa is brimming with wonders and monsters. To the west of Libya there live cave-dwellers, *Trogidite*, who are 'swifter on foot than any animal' (Unger 1862: 93). Mauritania spawns 'many strange animals and beasts, such as apesses, dragons, and ostriches', apparently revealing that all of these creatures are considered equally marvellous, and perhaps thus exhibiting an underlying influence from contemporary bestiaries (Unger 1862: 95–6).

Bestiaries were certainly known in Iceland; at least two separate translations of the *Physiologus* into Old Norse were put to parchment (although only fragments survive), in which the natural traits of beasts ranging from phoenixes to crocodiles to elephants are explained in theological light. Stjórn is accompanied by edifying illuminations, and while the Icelandic *Physiologus* in its extant form lacks textual descriptions of the Plinian peoples, the fact that such descriptions *were* included is made apparent in fragment AM 673 a I 4to by the illumination of as many of them as could possibly (and improperly) fit on two whole pages, including Cynocephali, Sciapodes, Cyclopes, and Blemmyes (Hermannsson 1938: 27–8). In that vein, the scribes of Stjórn dutifully list dozens of the Plinian peoples (Unger 1862: 93–4):

> In Libya there are born headless people [*hǫfuðlausir men*] according to belief, whom the Libyans call *Lemnia* [i.e. Blemmyes]. Their mouths and eyes are on their chest [*hafa þeir munn ok augu framan aa briostinu*]. Others exist there who are born with no neck, with eyes on their shoulders [*adrir eru þeir sem þar fædaz ok ǫngan hafa halsinn. enn augun aa oxlunum*]. *Antipodes* are also there, whom some people call the reverse-footed [*andfetinga*], as their feet and arches point backwards, and they have VIII toes on each foot [*þeim horfa fǫtrnir ok ristrnar aa bak aptr ok hafa .viii. tær á huarum fæti*].

Stjórn thus offers a particularly fascinating window into the mindset of the Icelandic learned class of the fourteenth and fifteenth centuries, in which eclectic materials such as universal, biblical, and legendary history combine with natural sciences on the one hand, and with Plinian teratology on the other, to create a surprising yet comprehensive whole.

PLINIAN TERATOLOGY AND CHRISTIAN IDEOLOGY IN AM 194 8VO (NARFEYRARBÓK)

The meshing of Plinian teratology, the legendary pagan past, and Christian ideology took on yet another form around the turn of the fourteenth century, when the brief treatise in AM 736 was copied into AM 194 8vo, hereafter called Narfeyrarbók ('Book of Narfeyri') after its place of composition.[3] Parts of Hauksbók's geographical treatise concerning the resting places of holy men were copied along with it, thus combining parts of two of the earliest Old Norse geographical texts into one with the addition of material not verifiably of older origin (Vídalín 2018). This new material includes a description of the route from Iceland to Rome and Jerusalem, which might originally have been written

---

[3] This title is of my own making. While the manuscript is usually referred to by shelf-mark, I am preparing an edition of its text under the title 'Narfeyrarbók'.

by the scribe Óláfr Ormsson, or could be a copy of another fourteenth-century manuscript. Previously this text has been attributed to the twelfth-century abbot Nikulás of Munkaþverá, of whose life we have scant knowledge (Marani 2012; Vídalín 2018).

Narfeyrarbók is especially noteworthy for its compilation of universal history and other encyclopaedic works known in fourteenth-century Iceland. It thus seems not to have been based on first-hand knowledge of Latin works as Hauksbók and Stjórn were, but rather founded on learning already amassed by such works in the vernacular. Narfeyrarbók's geographical treatise includes an original description of different regions within the three known continents, as well as the usual suspects inhabiting them: albinos, Cyclopes, Blemmyes, Cynocephali, Panotii, Pygmies, Anthropophagi—and many more.

Particularly astounding about the structure of Narfeyrarbók's geographical part is its presentation as fact, placed after the detailed itinerary from Iceland to Rome and Jerusalem and before a small chapter on dragons. The itinerary itself, while not explicitly mentioning monsters (the manuscript places all of them firmly outside the road to Jerusalem), does pointedly include pagan mythological waymarkers along the route among the Christian ones. Thus, for example, one may pass through Gnitaheiðr where the legendary Sigurðr slew the dragon Fáfnir, and later arrive at the archdiocece at St Peter's Church in Cologne.

In this way, Narfeyrarbók presents a Christian world view in which the pagan past is also directly addressed and seemingly considered factual, in which the sons of Noah inherited the Earth now inhabited by their kin as well as by Plinian monsters, dragons, and griffins, and in which the road to the Holy City takes you through the reality of all these different legends—from classical monsters through Germanic mythology to early and medieval Christian philosophy—to deliver you safely, through absolution, to Heaven's gate. As they do in St Isidore's understanding, the monsters here serve a greater Christian purpose: to provide a contrast to the light of true faith—to reveal the good path and warn us from straying from it. Moreover, Narfeyrarbók's amalgam of different myths and belief systems from very different periods is surprisingly coherent, thus arguably illustrating better than any other work the peak of teratological thought in late medieval Iceland and how easily classical monsters could be melded with both pagan heritage and mainstream theology.

CONCLUSION

It is unclear why, but various monstrous anxieties seem to gain prominence in Old Norse sources in the fourteenth century: that monsters inhabit fringe locations, where the weather is so awful that it actually creates these monsters; that these monsters are ungodly deformities with faces in their chest, or heads of dogs, or have huge ears to cover themselves from top to bottom to shield themselves from the sun. What does seem clear, however, is that this very concept of the monstrous was a standard part of the overall geographical package. Since so many Continental geographical texts associated exotic countries with monstrous inhabitants, this seems to have been the familiar trope Icelanders used when situating monsters; even though their most prominent sources, such as Augustine and Isidore, speak of these monsters independent of geography, the various intermediary sources that Icelanders relied on did not. This may indicate that the author of Stjórn, for example, did not read Isidore directly even though they cite him.

What, then, would one do when confronted with the idea that one's very Christian, very Continental-influenced home country is now associated with the monstrosity and evil of the far north, which included skin-clad, cannibalistic, trollish figures? The answer is simple in all its inevitable complexities: you simply situate Iceland *within* the Christian framework that delineates centre from periphery—in part by writing geographical treatises in which Iceland's place in the world is clearly defined within Europe, or by adding to a treatise on Europe an itinerary from Iceland to Rome and Jerusalem with detailed descriptions of the resting places of the holy, while dehumanizing the rest of the world. Alternatively, you could write travel narratives about Nordic heroes venturing far into lands to the east and to the west, finding salvation among the marvels in the former, monstrosities and godforsaken heathens in the latter. Christianity may come to Garðaríki in the East, but the boundaries of Christian influence to the west are much further out than Iceland—even further out than the Christian Greenland, past Helluland and Markland in Vínland and the Land of the Sciapodes. The saga mostly focuses on the failed colonization of Vínland, and concludes with the pilgrimage of Guðríðr Þorbjarnardóttir to Rome and her subsequent life as a hermit. This situates Iceland well within the realm of Continental Christianity while countering its culture and history with that of the unexplored lands of the monstrous.

All these sources are in their oldest form extant only in fourteenth-century manuscripts. Whether their focus in possible older incarnations was as fixed on the contrast between Christian and pagan, man and monster as their fourteenth-century counterparts, we will never know. What we do know is that these fourteenth-century manuscripts exhibit an intense fascination with monsters and other abject fears of Christians, whereas earlier Old Norse manuscripts do not. This correlates with a growing interest in the topic in Europe, with the fourteenth century producing one of the most popular texts on monsters ever, *The Book of John Mandeville*. This text, a fantastical sort of travel memoir (attributed to a probably fictional Sir John Mandeville), was known in Denmark at least from the fifteenth century, but it is unclear how quickly, if at all, it became known in Iceland. While there seems to have been considerable textual influence from Britain in Iceland, no trace of works such as the eleventh-century Old English *Marvels of the East* appears until much later. Even *Grettis saga* is preserved only in fifteenth-century manuscripts. The exception is a fragmentary *Physiologus* from the late twelfth century with illuminations of Plinian monsters. Corazza (2005) believes these illustrations derive from a Middle English bestiary, but the text that one may suppose came with the Plinian monsters in particular is now lost.

Why this sudden interest in monsters in the fourteenth century, then? One may only guess. The fact of the matter is that such narratives had been popular for over 1,200 years prior to the documentation of Icelandic geographical thought, and older Icelandic examples do exist, albeit very few. Another explanation might be Norwegian influence. When Iceland came under Norwegian rule in 1262–1264 a great change occurred in manuscript culture, with bigger, more expensive manuscripts being produced at the behest of the court—texts like lawbooks, but also Stjórn, with the most detailed description of the world in any medieval Nordic body of work. To create an immense work like Stjórn required access to a significant number of books, and perhaps some of these had not been known to Icelanders prior to the fourteenth century. By the end of the century we find in the very interesting manuscript Narfeyrarbók—a small and unilluminated version created by a priest of a small parish—a treatise which, unlike the others, is not based on Continental sources directly, but on the other treatises already written in Icelandic.

This shows, perhaps, that at this time Latin sources were no longer needed, as much had already been written in the vernacular. This information gap having been filled over the course of a whole century, such geographical descriptions cease to be made as far as extant sources can testify, while the saga literature retains its interest in both geographical and monstrous alterity. By the sixteenth century, with the Protestant Reformation having separated Jón Arason, the last Icelandic Catholic bishop, from his head, the rhetoric changes as well. No longer do Icelanders see monsters on the peripheries; they have to defend themselves from the accusation that Iceland itself is filled with monsters typical of Hyperborean regions, whether of Plinian stock or the horrible sea monsters frequently associated with Iceland and Greenland. Yet, at the same time, the sagas portraying these monsters are, in their minds, the true history not only of Iceland, but also of the world. What appears in the learned texts discussed here seems to be, in all estimation, an attempt to reconcile the two—to make sense of greatly divergent beliefs and tradition and thus, in a way, to try to fit a square peg into a round hole. This is a seemingly impossible task indeed, and yet, as I argue, one somehow managed through painstaking medieval scholarship.

SUGGESTED READING

On Plinian monsters in particular, see the seminal work by Friedman (2000). Regarding alterity in saga literature, see Vídalín (2020a, 2020b) and Larrington (2004), and on its protoracist implications especially, refer to Isaac (2004), Biller (2009), and Vídalín (2020c). On medieval maps and their encyclopaedic context, see Kedwards (2020), Kline (2003), Simek (1990), and Guðmundsdóttir (2015).

WORKS CITED

Ashurst, D. 2006. 'Imagining Paradise', in *The Fantastic in Old Norse-Icelandic Literature: Sagas and the British Isles*, ed. J. McKinnell, D. Ashurst, and D. Kick, 71–80. Durham.
Astås, R. 1991. *An Old Norse Biblical Compilation: Studies in Stjórn*. New York.

Astås, R., ed. 2009. *Stjórn: Tekst etter håndskriftene.* Oslo.

Barney, S. A., et al., ed. 2010. *The Etymologies of Isidore of Seville.* Cambridge.

Biller, P. 2009. 'Proto-Racial Thought in Medieval Science', in *The Origins of Racism in the West*, ed. M. Eliav-Feldon, B. Isaac, and J. Ziegler, 157–80. Cambridge.

Corazza, V. D. 2005. 'Crossing Paths in the Middle Ages: the *Physiologus* in Iceland', in *The Garden of Crossing Paths: The Manipulation and Rewriting of Medieval Texts*, ed. M. Buzzoni and M. Bampi, 225–48. Venice.

DeAngelo, J. 2010. 'The North and the Depiction of the *Finnar* in the Icelandic Sagas.' *Scandinavian Studies* 82/3: 257–86.

Edson, E. 2005. 'Mapping the Middle Ages: The Imaginary and Real Universe of the Mappaemundi', in *Monsters, Marvels and Miracles: Imaginary Journeys and Landscapes in the Middle Ages*, ed. L. Sondergaard and R. T. Hansen, 11–25. Odense.

Felton, D. 2012. 'Rejecting and Embracing the Monstrous in Ancient Greece and Rome', in *The Ashgate Research Companion to Monsters and the Monstrous*, ed. A. S. Mittman and P. J. Dendle, 103–31. Farnham.

Friedman, J. B. 2000. *The Monstrous Races in Medieval Art and Thought.* Syracuse.

Guðmundsdóttir, S. G. 2015. 'A Map of Jerusalem', in *66 Manuscripts From the Arnamagnæan Collection*, ed. M. J. Driscoll and S. Óskarsdóttir, 96–7. Reykjavík.

Hermannsson, H., ed. 1938. *The Icelandic Physiologus.* Ithaca, NY.

Isaac, B. 2004. *The Invention of Racism in Classical Antiquity.* Princeton.

Ísleifsson, S. 2015. *Tvær eyjar á jaðrinum: Ímyndir Íslands og Grænlands frá miðöldum til miðrar 19. aldar.* Reykjavik.

Jakobsson, S. 2006. 'On the Road to Paradise: "Austrvegr" in the Icelandic Imagination', in *The Fantastic in Old Norse-Icelandic Literature: Sagas and the British Isles*, ed. J. McKinnell, D. Ashurst, and D. Kick, 935–43. Durham.

Jones, W. H. S., ed. and trans. 1939. *Hippocrates I.* Cambridge, MA.

Jónsson, F., et al., eds. 1892–1896. *Hauksbók: Udgiven efter de Arnamagnæanske håndskrifter no. 371, 544 og 674 4°, samt forskellige papirshåndskrifter.* Copenhagen.

Kålund, K., ed. 1908. *Alfræði íslenzk I.* Copenhagen.

Kedwards, D., 2020. *The Mappae Mundi of Medieval Iceland.* Cambridge.

Kline, N. R. 2003. *Maps of Medieval Thought: The Hereford Paradigm.* Woodbridge.

Larrington, C. 2004. ' "Undruðusk þá, sem fyrir var": Wonder, Vínland and Mediaeval Travel Narratives.' *Mediaeval Scandinavia* 14: 91–114.

Marani, T. 2012. *Leiðarvísir: Its Genre and Sources, with Particular Reference to the Description of Rome.* Durham.

Mittman, A. S. 2006. *Maps and Monsters in Medieval England.* New York.

Óskarsdóttir, S. 2005. 'Um aldir alda: Veraldarsögur miðalda og íslenskar aldartölur.' *Ritið* 5/3: 111–33.

Peck, A. L., ed. and trans. 1942. *Aristotle XIII: Generation of Animals.* Cambridge, MA.

Rackham, H., trans. 1942. *Pliny the Elder: Natural History.* Vol. II. Cambridge, MA.

Rackham, H., trans. 1983. *Pliny the Elder: Natural History.* Vol. III. Cambridge, MA.

Sanford, E. M., et al., eds. 1965. *The City of God Against the Pagans.* Cambridge, MA.

Simek, R. 1990. *Altnordische Kosmographie.* Berlin.

Smith, D. L. 2011. *Less than Human: Why We Demean, Enslave, and Exterminate Others.* New York.

Tómasson, S. 2001. 'Ferðir þessa heims og annars: Paradís—Ódáinsakur—Vínland í íslenskum ferðalýsingum miðalda.' *Gripla* 12: 199–216.

Tschan, F. J., ed. 2002. *History of the Archbishops of Hamburg-Bremen.* New York.

Unger, C. R., ed. 1862. *Stjorn: Gammelnorsk Bibelhistorie fra Verdens Skabelse til det babyloniske Fangenskab.* Christiania.

van Duzer, C. 2012. '*Hic sunt dracones*: The Geography and Cartography of Monsters', in *The Ashgate Research Companion to Monsters and the Monstrous*, ed. A. S. Mittman and P. J. Dendle, 387–435. Farnham.

Vídalín, A. 2018. 'Óláfr Ormsson's Leiðarvísir: The Fourteenth-Century Manuscript of a Supposed Twelfth-Century Itinerary.' *Journal of English and Germanic Philology* 117/2: 212–34.

Vídalín, A. 2020a. 'Alterity and Occidentalism in the 14th Century: Narratives of Travel, Conversion and Dehumanization.' *Medieval Globe* 6/2: 85–108.

Vídalín, A. 2020b. 'Demons, Muslims, Wrestling-Champions: The Semantic History of Blámenn from the 12th to the 20th Century', in *Paranormal Encounters in Iceland 1150–1400*, ed. Á. Jakobsson and M. Mayburd, 203–26. Berlin.

Vídalín, A. 2020c. 'The Man Who Seemed Like a Troll: Racism in Old Norse Literature', in *Margins, Monsters, Deviants: Alterities in Old Norse Literature and Culture*, ed. G. Knight and R. Merkelbach, 215–38. Turnhout.

Williams, D. 1996. *Deformed Discourse: The Function of the Monster in Mediaeval Thought and Literature.* Montreal.

CHAPTER 33

CLASSICAL MONSTERS IN MEDIEVAL LITERATURE AND ART

ANTONELLA SCIANCALEPORE

INTRODUCTION

THE Middle Ages were particularly receptive to monsters from classical antiquity. Classical monsters thrived and transformed across all channels of medieval culture, particularly natural history treatises, ethnographic and geographic texts, and romances. Although what we call the 'Middle Ages' spanned almost a millennium—approximately from the fifth to the end of the fifteenth century CE—and was studded with political, socio-economic, and cultural shifts, learned culture throughout this macro era was largely characterized by its veneration of antiquity. The classical Greek and Latin texts available were considered authorities by medieval scholars, who used them as sources of information on science, geography, and history, or as sources of inspiration for genea-logical tales and literary works. Consequently, classical sources ushered the monsters of antiquity into medieval lore.

In this chapter, I consider the path of continuity and transformation of monsters from classical antiquity into the Middle Ages. By 'monster' I identify those creatures that medieval culture considered explicitly or implicitly to embody an exception to what was considered the norm of living things; monsters were beings characterized as physical oddities that exceeded normal human or animal morphology (Lascault 1973: 21–3), and which inhabited geographical, moral, and social edges (Cohen 1996: 12; Bildhauer and Mills 2003). Medieval classical monsters expressed the universal quality of monsters as 'viciously intertextual' since they recurred from one text to another and established connections across textual traditions (Olsen and Olsen 2001: 11).

MEDIEVAL CLASSICAL MONSTERS: SOURCES
AND TRANSMISSION

Two major factors conditioned the transmission of classical monsters. One was the limited availability in the Middle Ages of direct access to classical sources—especially works of literature, but also philosophical, didactic, scientific, and historiographic treatises. Following the fall of the Western Roman Empire, the sources of classical Greek literature were mostly lost to the West, at least until the twelfth century (Reynolds and Wilson 1974: 105–7). After the collapse of Roman centres of secular education, the new Christian cultural elites regarded pre-Christian Roman literature with suspicion. Even though copies of works by classical Latin authors continued to be produced in the new centres of written culture—the monasteries first, the cathedral schools and universities later—and despite the crucial role of classical Latin revivals throughout the Middle Ages, the lack of interest in those classical authors who were not considered useful for the new cultural needs doomed many of them to almost complete oblivion. Other texts were copied, transmitted, and read throughout the Middle Ages, either because they were recognized as aesthetically valuable regardless of their contents or because they were included in the new educational programmes. Such was the case with authors who had an impact on medieval teratology, such as Vergil, Cicero, Ovid, and Pliny the Elder. Also, medieval scholars knew many classical texts not directly but through the intermediary of anthologies, or *florilegia* (Reynolds and Wilson 1974: 70–105; Munk Olsen 1995).

The other major factor that influenced the medieval transmission of classical monsters was Christianity. The assimilation of classical writings into medieval culture happened through a Christian lens, which either reinterpreted Greek and Roman sources by finding in them a Christian moral meaning, or (less frequently) disproved the most marvellous aspects of classical mythology, blaming them on the superficiality of pre-Christian beliefs. These two attitudes were not mutually exclusive. Nonetheless, the reverence that Christian culture held towards classical antiquity, which peaked during the medieval 'renaissances', brought about a 'process of accumulation and increasingly refined analysis' (Smits 1995: 3) that allowed the survival and the new life of classical literature in the post-antiquity world.

Both factors are relevant for the transmission of classical monsters into medieval culture. Medieval knowledge of those monsters depended heavily on texts by two early Christian authors: Augustine of Hippo and Isidore of Seville. Augustine, writing in the fifth century, discussed whether monsters were real, concluding that they must be; moreover, if they existed they were also natural, because all things are created by God (*De civitate dei* 21.8). In the seventh century, Isidore authored what can be considered the first medieval encyclopaedic work: the *Etymologiae*, a collection of knowledge that covered various matters from Christian doctrine to agriculture, from rhetoric to cosmology. Its chapter on *portenta*, relying on Pliny the Elder's *Naturalis historia*, lists monsters that became extremely popular in medieval lore—monstrous species and populations such as sirens, fauns, satyrs, centaurs, Cynocephali, Pygmies, and Cyclopes, but also individual monsters, like the Minotaur and Scylla (11.2). In his chapter on *transformati* (11.3), Isidore discusses cases of monsters deriving from transformation, such as Ulysses' men turned into swine by Circe, and the werewolves of Arcadia.

In explicating the medieval transmission of classical monsters, we must consider a third important aspect: the convergence of non-classical teratologic traditions, including biblical monsters. Medieval authors knew the Bible through its fourth-century Latin translations—the *Vetus Latina* and Jerome's *Vulgata*—as well as through its long tradition of commentaries, beginning in the early fifth century. Biblical translations gave new meaning to Latin words; for example, Jerome described the *sirena* as a type of dragon in his commentary (*Commentariorum in Esaiam* 13:21–2; cf. Leclercq-Marx 1997: 44). Medieval authors also multiplied traditional monsters, as in the case of *fatui ficarii* ('fig fauns'), which Jerome uses as a synonym for *fauni* in the apocalyptic waste-land remaining after God's fury (Jer. 50:39), but which later authors interpreted as a new species of monstrous animal.

Also affecting the transmission of classical monsters were European oral folkloric traditions, which thrived in the gap left by the collapse of Roman scholarship and, eventually, heavily influenced written medieval culture. The monsters of these non-classical traditions did not overwrite the classical ones; rather, they merged with and enriched them. With its compilatory nature, medieval scholarship considered all sources equally important for understanding the endless variety of the world. The eclectic knowledge on monsters in the Middle Ages caused a certain fluidity of definitions and engendered variants in the written and visual representation of those monsters. For instance, the animal traits of monsters derived from antiquity sometimes transferred from one to another: centaurs could be represented as having a horse head instead of a horse bottom; the Minotaur could have a human head on a bull body; and sirens varied greatly, their bottom half being birdlike, fish-like, both (Fig. 33.1), or even horse-like (cf. Leclercq-Marx 2011).

MEDIEVAL CONCEPTIONS OF THE MONSTROUS

But did medieval authors define monsters of classical antiquity as monsters? Often, they marked them as such through a special lexicon. As mentioned above, in his *Etymologiae*, Isidore identifies certain types of classical monster—including the Cyclopes, the Minotaur, centaurs, and sirens—as *portenta*, phenomena that appear to be contrary to nature but are, in fact, only 'contrary to what we know as nature'. According to Isidore's

e est grant senefiance
a ier len remenbrance

este de tel baillie
er homes senefie
c om fu ananias
z com azarias
s i com fu misael
a iii deu seruirent bel
j eist del feu ardant
e issirent deu loant
s i com dauid nos dit
p or uoir en son estrit
z seint pol en uerte
d it qp li feel de

FIGURE 33.1 Siren, from Philippe de Thaon, *Bestiaire* (France, fourteenth century).
Copenhagen, Kongelige Bibliotek, ms. Gl. kgl. S. 3466 8°, fo. 37r.

source, the first-century BCE Roman scholar Varro (as cited by Servius' fifth-century BCE commentary on Vergil's *Aeneid*), *portenta* is almost synonymical with *monstra*, *ostenta*, and *prodigia*:

> The term 'portent' [*portentum*] is said to be derived from foreshadowing [*portendere*], that is, from 'showing beforehand' [*praeostendere*]. 'Signs' [*ostentum* [*sic*]], because they seem to show [*ostendere*] a future event. Prodigies [*prodigium* [*sic*]] are so called, because they 'speak hereafter' [*porro dicere*], that is, they predict the future. But omens [*monstrum* [*sic*]] derive their name from admonition [*monitus*], because in giving a sign they indicate [*demonstrare*] something, or else because they instantly show [*monstrare*] what may appear. (Isid. *Etym.* 11.3.3, trans. Barney et al. 2006)

In another text, *De differentiis*, Isidore introduces a distinction between *monstra* and *portenta*, according to which *portenta* can have different forms, while monsters are *extra natura* only because of their size—either too small or too big (1.395; Avenel 2017: 10). This new definition, probably not as influential as the first, testifies to the profound difficulty medieval authors had in isolating the physical aspects that define the monster. Rather, medieval science and literature after Isidore do not define the monstrous according to a set of morphological requirements (that is, according to ways in which the monster's body is different) but to the epistemological function of the monster (that is, the capacity of the monster to be interpreted in moral, theological, or prophetic terms).

This working definition proves useful as classical monsters were not consistently called 'monsters' from one author to another. For example, sirens and centaurs are called *bestia* in bestiaries, but *monstra* in encyclopaedias like Bartholomeus Anglicus' *De proprietatibus rerum* (*c.*1230–1240 CE). This inconsistency demonstrates the traditionally protean and dynamic nature of monsters, which escape categorizations (Cohen 1996; Mittman 2012). It also results from the vagueness and yet overabundance of definitions of 'monstrous' across medieval culture.

Yet, if we had to draw a catalogue of medieval monsters, a good starting point would be the anonymous *Liber monstrorum* (*Book of Monsters*), dating to the late seventh or early eighth century. In this text, the author lists beings explicitly called monsters, drawing from patristical sources (e.g. Augustine's *De civitate dei*), classical sources (Vergil, Ovid) and late antique sources (*Epistola Alexandri*; see Orchard 1995). The characteristics of these monsters vary, but all the beings described in the *Liber*'s entries present some form of morphological oddity. The animal-like monsters are characterized by unusually gigantic size or hybridity, and are often linked to a particularly violent or dangerous nature, as in the case of Scylla. In contrast, anthropomorphic monsters are determined in several ways. They may have supernumerary or missing body parts; examples include the one-eyed Cyclopes and humans with twenty-four fingers. They may possess unusual bodily features, such as glowing eyes. They may exhibit behaviour considered inhuman or exceptional, as with the

Anthropophagi or the people described as speaking all languages. They may be of incongruous size, as for example the Colossus or Pygmies. Anthropomorphic monsters may be human-animal hybrids, like the Cynocephali and satyrs; or they may mix gender features, as with bearded women and hermaphrodites. These characteristics remained important in placing such beings among the monsters in thirteenth-century encyclopaedias; for example, Vincent de Beauvais devoted part of his *Speculum Maius* to *portenta vel monstra fabulosa*, which included all monsters deriving from classical sources (*Speculum Naturale* 21.122).

Although the monsters listed in the *Liber monstrorum* are often characterized by behaviour threatening to humans, the author's own attitude is not tainted by fear but informed by wonder and curiosity. Indeed, although classical monsters in the Middle Ages are often dangerous and, like their Greek and Roman predecessors, tend to inhabit liminal spaces outside civilization, they are not viewed as enemies to be overcome. Moreover, while in Greek myth the monster is often seen as a threat to society, medieval culture instead picks up the Roman—and Augustan in particular—fascination for monsters (Felton 2012; Lowe 2015). In encyclopaedias, bestiaries, and geographical texts, classical monsters evoke amazement and curiosity and illustrate nature's variety, while sometimes conveying specific moral messages that nature teaches through its wonders.

In addition to those mentioned above, the *Liber monstrorum* lists many other monsters from antiquity that become typical in medieval natural histories, such as fauns, hippo- and onocentaurs (see below), the Minotaur, Cacus (a flame-spewing giant), the Sciapodes (men with one giant foot), and other monstrous populations, such as two-bodied men and headless people. The list is quite comprehensive. Several other medieval monsters from classical antiquity not considered by the *Liber*'s author surfaced in other medieval written works and iconography, most notably the manticore (lion body, human head, and horrific set of teeth), the Chimaera, Cerberus, and Medusa.

Of these monsters, some were exclusively objects of scholarly erudition passed down as characters of ancient mythology and literature, but no moral interpretations or new narratives were attached to them, and they lost their characteristic traits across time and different genres. Such was the case with Medusa, whose hair in medieval descriptions and illuminations—the term for illustrations in medieval manuscripts—was hardly ever made of snakes. Similarly, Scylla, whose specificity—according to the tradition, either a human-wolf-fish hybrid body or supernumerary dog heads—could get lost, causing her to become just one of many immense fish-like sea monsters (Fig. 33.2). However, even these 'scholarly' monsters were occasionally revived by medieval literature for other purposes. Many shifted to the role of demons awaiting souls in Dante Alighieri's Christian hell. In his *Inferno* (early fourteenth century), Dante reuses the centaur Chiron, the Gorgon Medusa, the hybrid Chimaera, the giant Cacus, and other classical monsters, now charging them with revealing the winding road towards Christian redemption.

FIGURE 33.2 Scylla, from Thomas of Cantimpré, *De natura rerum* (France, 1275–1295).

Valenciennes, Bibliothèque municipale, MS 320, fo. 119r.

© Cliché CNRS-IRHT.

VISUAL AND WRITTEN OCCURRENCES
OF CLASSICAL MONSTERS
IN MEDIEVAL CULTURE

Classical monsters appeared in several contexts of medieval life. Centaurs and sirens decorate the façades of Romanesque churches (see examples in Leclercq-Marx 1997 and 2002), for all layers of society to see. Several anthropomorphic, zoomorphic, or phytomorphic (plant-based) hybrid bodies decorate the margins of rich manuscripts, destined for high prelates and aristocrats. Among the classical monsters in medieval manuscript marginalia, particularly popular were the *sagittarii* (archer hippocentaurs) and the fishtailed mermaids and mermen, whose tapered extremities formed fitting decorations for page borders (Bovey 2002; Randall 1966; Dittmar 2012). Classical monsters belonging to geographical extremities appear in *mappae mundi* (medieval maps of the world), where Cynocephali ('dog-headed' men), Blemmyes (headless men), and other unusual peoples haunt the far regions, and human-fish creatures and sea monsters inhabit the oceans (van Duzer 2012; Davies 2016). Most importantly, though, classical monsters appear in illuminated manuscripts, where they most often decorate the borders, and less frequently illustrate the texts. These illustrations do not always faithfully reflect literary descriptions, a loose correspondence exposing the complex relations between visual and scholarly consumption and transmission of classical monsters in medieval Europe (see Mittman and Kim 2016).

In medieval writings, classical monsters appear in several genres, primarily in bestiaries. Originally based on the anonymous Greek *Physiologus*—a *c.* second-century CE treatise on animals, birds, and fantastic beasts—medieval bestiaries comprise a unique genre that flourished from the eleventh to the thirteenth centuries. These bestiaries collected information and stories about animals—both real and imaginary—but could also include humans, plants, and stones, extracting moral or practical teachings from the stories. Bestiary entries invariably included the siren and the onocentaur (see below); a few bestiaries added monsters from other sources, such as the manticore and basilisk.

As in classical antiquity, medieval monsters were described in natural history, a genre that 'tends to live on the boundary line between the credible and the incredible' (Asma 2009: 32). Medieval natural histories took the shape of encyclopaedias, a genre of scientific treatises developed in the twelfth and thirteenth centuries that collected what was known of the natural world and organized it according to various principles to allow readers to consult it. In these texts, classical monsters are included within the chapters on animals, or in specific sections dedicated to *portenta* and to monstrous animals (as in Vincent de Beauvais's *Speculum naturale*) or monstrous humans (as in Thomas of Cantimpré's *De natura rerum*). Geographical sections of encyclopaedias and geographical texts were also an important source of classical monsters; hence, the success of texts like the fifteenth-century *Les Secrets de l'histoire naturelle*, a French geographical compilation of various natural wonders organized according to their location (Friedman et al. 2018).

Because of their role in Greek and Latin mythography, monsters appeared in medieval historiography, as for example *L'Histoire ancienne jusqu'à César* (*c.*1213 CE), a universal history from Creation to the time of Julius Caesar. This French prose collection of stories from antiquity had an impressive circulation in medieval Europe, especially in the form of richly decorated manuscripts for courtly collections. The *Histoire ancienne*, adapting Orosius' *Historiae Adversus Paganos* (early fifth century CE), describes (among other things) the monstrous creatures Alexander the Great encountered during his campaign in Asia, the Minotaur's origin, and Greek heroes' adventures with the Chimaera, the centaurs, and the Sphinx.

As in classical antiquity, when monsters were a measure of the geographical distance from an ethnocentric norm (Asma 2009: 6), medieval monsters abounded in the geographical margins of the earth (Mittman 2006; van Duzer 2012). For this reason, medieval travel literature was an important source of monsters. The travels of Alexander the Great were a particularly important late-antique locus for monsters, so it is not surprising that, when describing Asia, many real-life medieval travellers felt compelled to include some of those monsters in their own accounts. In fact, the encounter with distant Plinian monsters was a necessary element to confirm the authenticity of the travel experience (Kappler 1980: 115)—so much so, that even the most honest and accurate account that we have of a thirteenth-century European's travels to China, Marco Polo's

Devisement du monde (1298), reports as true the belief in the existence of dog-headed populations on the Andaman Island (§167; cf. Fig. 33.3).

Finally, since the main sources of classical monsters for medieval scholars were Roman poems such as Vergil's *Aeneid* and Ovid's *Metamorphoses*, it is not surprising that these monsters appear also in medieval narrative literature. Among these, we distinguish three types of texts. The first include renderings of Classical Latin literary works, as in so-called romances such as the anonymous *Roman de Thèbe* (mid-twelfth century) and Benoît de Sainte-Maure's *Roman de Troie* (1165). The second type consists of romances that revolve around Alexander, which make abundant use of monsters from Graeco-Roman antiquity while rewriting narrative models from a later period. Examples include the various *Alexander Romances* written in different European languages from the twelfth to fifteenth centuries, such as Thomas of Kent's *Le roman de toute chevalerie* (late twelfth century).

The third type of text includes literary works of non-classical content that use classical monsters as the heroes' adversaries, as with the centaurs in *La mort d'Aymeri de Narbonne* (early thirteenth century) or as their allies, as with the siren in *Tristan de Nanteuil* (fourteenth century). An important metamorphic monster of medieval lore, the werewolf, is the protagonist of several celebrated medieval literary works, including Marie de France's *Lais* (late twelfth century), although the source for this creature in medieval literature seems to be mostly folklore (cf. Friedman 2015; Ogden 2021). Within medieval literary texts of classical content, a special mention must go to the *Ovide moralisé*, a popular fourteenth-century French rendering of Ovid's *Metamorphoses* that reinterpreted Ovid's stories as historical, moral, and theological allegories. This text demonstrates the long-lasting appreciation of medieval scholars for Ovid, especially from the twelfth century onwards, an era that Traube called *aetas Ovidiana* ('the Ovidian age'; Munk Olsen 1995: 71–94). The moralization of the *Metamorphoses* injected new epistemological depth in the monstrous characters of classical mythology.

Below I discuss four classical monsters as they appear in medieval culture: the centaur, the siren, the Minotaur, and the Cynocephali. Besides being some of the most popular monsters of medieval culture, each exemplifies a specific approach through which medieval culture preserved, interpreted, and transformed the monsters inherited from Greece and Rome.

THE CENTAUR, OR THE HUMAN-ANIMAL IDENTITY

In medieval culture, the classical centaur burgeons into several different types. Although the Thessalian centaurs were known through classical sources like Ovid's *Metamorphoses*, in medieval culture we more frequently find the hippocentaurs (generic man-horse hybrids) and onocentaurs (upper body of human, lower body of ass);

FIGURE 33.3 Cynocephali, from Marco Polo, *Livre des merveilles* (France, 1410–1412).

Paris, Bibliothèque nationale de France, fr. 2810, fo. 76v.

medieval sources often simply call the latter 'centaur'. This hybrid entered the medieval imagination via Jerome's *Vulgata*, where it stands as one of the malevolent animals reclaiming the earth after the world's end (Isa. 34:14; Kordecki 1997: 30). Medieval onocentaurs and hippocentaurs were located in marginal places. Isidore rationalized the centaurs as being an optic illusion resulting from seeing men riding horses from afar (*Etym.* 11.3.37), an interpretation he inherited from ancient Greek sources (see Hawes in this volume). However, this explanation did not take hold in later medieval writings and certainly did not affect the medieval fortune of these creatures.

In his *Vita Sancti Pauli* (*Life of St Paul*, c.377–382 CE), Jerome reports that, on his way to visit Paul the Hermit, St Anthony meets a hippocentaur and a satyr in the desert. When interrogating the hippocentaur as to the whereabouts of St Paul, 'the monster, after gnashing out some kind of outlandish utterance, in words broken rather than spoken through his bristling lips' eventually extends its right hand to point out the way (§7). Although Anthony first wonders if the creature is a manifestation of the Devil, the hippocentaur demonstrates an understanding of the saint's words and cooperates, though his physical inability to speak a human language separates him from the world of men. The hippocentaur thus incarnates the difference between human and non-human while simultaneously showing that communication between the two is possible. Moreover, the monster can quite literally point the way towards spiritual truth.

This latter function comes through especially in bestiaries, which consistently use the hippocentaur and onocentaur to illustrate the coexistence of two identities within oneself. The language used to describe these creatures—words such as *mixtum*, *coniunctum*, *compositum*, *semihomo* ('mixed', 'conjoined', 'compound', 'half-man')—is one of irreducible duality (Douchet 2005: 289). Moreover, this coexistence of opposites reflects an internal moral and psychological duality that humans must constantly negotiate. In the *Physiologus* (23–4), the onocentaur represents the deceitful doubleness of bad Christians: 'Such are the impulses of the souls of wicked merchants; they even sin secretly while gathered together in church.' The same text interprets the centaur as reflecting the persisting animality of human beings: 'they are like brutish beasts' (Ps. 49: 20). This moral and spiritual duality reverberates in Vernacular bestiaries: according to a French twelfth-century bestiary, 'man, when he says the truth, | is rightfully called man, | while the ass represents | when man behaves wickedly' (Philippe de Thaon, *Bestiaire*, lines 1119–21, my translation).

The *sagittarius* contributes to this duality on a different level. This archer centaur in medieval culture indicated an exotic species of half-human and half-horse archers, characterized by an apparent lack of human reason. *Sagittarius* and (ono) centaur were almost synonyms in vernacular texts (e.g. Pierre de Beauvais, *Bestiaire version courte* 11), and the first could work as a visual representation of the second in some manuscripts. As its pure function was violence, the *sagittarius* was employed as the animalization of the war enemy in medieval literature. A crucial example of this monster's reception appears in Benoît de Saint-Maure's *Roman de Troie* (1165). Despite being based on ancient sources (the Trojan Wars' alleged chronicles by Dictys Cretensis and Dares Phrygius), the man-horse archer is an innovation, stemming from the medieval author reinterpreting the word *sagittarius*, which simply meant 'archer'. In the romance's description, the *sagittarius'* human upper half is black and covered in fur; this characterization, matching as it did medieval tropes about demonic bodies, was meant to underline the whole monstrous quality of the hybrid. In the following centuries, this demonic aspect was counterbalanced by an ethnographic investigation on the *sagittarii's* background: they could be described as a population organized into a society, although their preference for raw meat set them apart from the human norm (*Mort Aymeri* lines 2416–49; Dubost 1988). This evolution is reflected in visual representations: the fourteenth-century illuminations of the prose *Roman de Troie* tend to humanize the *sagittarius* (Cerrito 2004). The centaur had undergone a similar process of domestication in Romanesque sculpture, where capital decorations showed female centaurs and breastfeeding centaurs (Leclercq-Marx 2002: 65), as in manuscript margin decoration (e.g. London, British Library, Add. MS 62925, fo. 58v).

Because they uniquely mixed familiarity and otherness, medieval centaurs were particularly versatile. In the *Inferno*, Dante reimagines the centaurs Chiron, Nessus, and Pholus as inhabitants of the Christian Hell, in the seventh circle, that of those violent against others. There, the centaurs strike the souls that try to escape from the boiling, bloody river Phlegethon, thus working as the instruments of God's punishment. Heirs to the creature met by St Anthony, these centaurs are beasts (*fiere*) but can speak; they threaten Dante, but eventually carry him across the deadly river (12.46–99). Now agents of the Christian other-world, the centaurs' ability to incarnate borders helps mankind on the path of truth once again.

THE SIREN, OR REINVENTION

From classical antiquity on, the siren's body has been the object of constant reinventions. Though not described in Homer's *Odyssey*, the earliest literary source for the creature, in Greek art from the sixth century BCE and later the siren was represented as half-woman and half-bird, and literature such as Apollonius of Rhodes' third-century BCE *Argonautica* clearly followed this tradition (see Denson in this volume). The siren's bird-woman morphology entered medieval scholarly literature through the medium of Ovid's *Metamorphoses* and the *Physiologus* (March 2014: 446; Murgatroyd 2013: 44–8). Like for the centaur, the early transmission of the siren in medieval culture was determined by the biblical word use: in the *Vulgata*, Jerome uses *sirena* to indicate a serpent-like beast (Isa. 13.22; Leclercq-Marx 1997: 41–68), which contributed further to characterize the siren as a monstrous being. Scepticism towards the existence of sirens and their rationalization as a metaphor for harlots—'they were said to have had wings and talons because sexual desire both flies and wounds' (Isid. *Etym.* 11.3.31)—did not hinder their popularity, and possibly even encouraged their use for moral purposes in medieval texts.

The medieval morphology of the siren is fluid. Although the bestiaries' source adheres to the Ovidian half-woman, half-bird configuration, the bestiaries themselves and encyclopaedias also include a concurrent configuration: that of the siren as half-woman and half-fish. The first written testimony of *sirena* as a woman-fish hybrid appears in the *Liber monstrorum* (§6). Scholars previously hypothesized that this shift originated from sirens becoming associated with Scylla in Carolingian literature and art, due to the similar marine habitat (Faral 1953; Vieillard-Troïekouroff 1969). However, Leclercq-Marx has since convincingly argued that the spread of the fishtail siren might derive from the influence of sea-dwelling feminine nymphs of Northern European folklore, especially the *meerwib/merimenni*, and that the syncretism among Latin, Celtic, and Germanic divinities allowed the shift to happen in the seventh to tenth centuries (Leclercq-Marx 1997: 69–91). This demonstrates not only the multifaceted and fluid nature of the medieval siren, but also the crucial role of non-classical traditions in furbishing the medieval aliases of monsters from classical antiquity.

A corollary of this shift is the medieval siren's new eroticism. Since antiquity, the siren had been characterized by the dangerous lure of its song; this led some medieval scholars to interpret the siren song as an allegory for the temptation of worldly pleasures (e.g. *Physiologus* 23–4), and more specifically of women's treacherous seduction (e.g. Pierre de Beauvais, *Bestiaire version courte* 11). Medieval sirens attracted sailors not only with their songs, however, but also with their looks, as their human bodies became increasingly sexualized in written and visual culture. This probably results from the siren acquiring the characteristics of another popular monstrous medieval creature: the 'water maiden' of the Alexander tradition (Leclercq-Marx 1997: 76). These humanoid marine creatures were introduced into the medieval imagination by the so-called *Epistola Alexandri ad Aristotelem* (fourth to fifth centuries), an apocryphal letter describing the wonders of the East encountered by Alexander the Great during his travels to India. The text and its later vernacular renditions described the water maidens as creatures living underwater who used their nakedness and beauty to attract and drown human men after having intercourse with them (*Epistola* §21). The fusion of water maidens with sirens is evident in Bartholomaeus Anglicus' thirteenth-century encyclopaedia *De proprietatibus rerum*, in which the half-fish, half-woman siren sings sailors to sleep, then drags them where she can have coitus with them and then devour them (18.94).

The threatening eroticism should not overshadow a final characterization of the siren: the nursing mother. Encyclopaedist Thomas of Cantimpré writes that the siren typically appears feeding her sucklings at her gigantic breasts (*De natura rerum* 6.45). This nursing siren, also attested in Romanesque sculpture and manuscript decoration (e.g. London, British Library, MS 24686, fo. 13r), is the prototype of the only siren designated as such who appears as a character in a medieval romance. In the fourteenth-century romance *Tristan de Nanteuil*, a siren miraculously saves the protagonist when he is a newborn by nursing him with her own supernatural milk (lines 415–26). This nursing characteristic might also derive from folkloric narrative sources, as it seems to resonate with the character of Mélusine, the half-woman, half-serpent fairy ancestor of the House of Lusignan, characterized by her maternity and represented in manuscript illuminations as a woman-fish breastfeeding her children (Bain 2017; Griffin 2020). In *Tristan de Nanteuil*, nursing rehabilitates the siren, who can thus become an instrument of God's providence.

In twelfth- and thirteenth-century bestiaries and encyclopaedias, the birdlike siren and the new fish-like siren meet and produce different results. Faced with differing information, medieval scholars preferred to aggregate rather than choose one authoritative source over another. Vernacular bestiary authors account for the multiplicity of sources and lay out the two or three types of *sirena* (e.g. Pierre de Beauvais, *Bestiaire version longue* §23); in one case, the author blends the two into one multi-hybrid creature, with bird claws, wings, and a fishtail (Philippe de Thaon, *Bestiaire*, lines 1364–8). By the late thirteenth century, the double or triple characterization of the siren was established: the traditional birdlike siren; a crested serpent; and a marine monster with long hair, long breasts, a scaly tail, and even eagle claws (e.g. Albertus Magnus, *De animalibus* 25.1.39 and 26.1.55).

The visual representations of the siren in medieval art reflect the convergence of different traditions and different functions. The illuminations in bestiaries relative to the entry on the siren sometimes reflect the abundance of her attributes, thus showing this monster as having both wings and a fishtail (Fig. 33.1). What is more, illuminations of the fishtailed siren sometimes contradict the written description in the manuscript, thus demonstrating that the fish-like prototype was expanding differently across visual culture (McCulloch 1962: 166–8).

THE MINOTAUR, OR MISCEGENATION

The poems of Ovid and Vergil served as the main sources for knowledge about the Minotaur in the Middle Ages. Ovid makes fleeting references to the Minotaur and its origin from the coupling of Pasiphaë with the bull in the *Metamorphoses* (8.131–7, 155–6; 9.736–7), but gives the full story in his *Ars amatoria* (1.295–326; see Blumenfeld-Kosinski 1996). Vergil briefly mentions the Minotaur, but Servius' commentary on Vergil fills the gap for the medieval reader (*Aen.* 6.14–25).

Isidore, in his description of the Minotaur, cites a single line from the *Ars amatoria*: *semibovemque virum, semivirumque bovem* ('half-bull man, half-man bull', 2.24). This verse blurred the Minotaur's human/non-human nature and its morphology. The two possible bodily arrangements probably coexisted, to judge from an illumination in the *Liber Floridus*, in which the Minotaur has a bull lower body, a human torso and arms, but also a human head with bull's horns (Ghent University Library, MS 92, fo. 20r). Still, most medieval visual representations of the Minotaur show him with a taurine lower half and human upper half (see Peyronie 1997), a representation that lasted until the fifteenth century, with the rediscovery of previously lost Greek and Latin texts and art.

Medieval scholars could live with the Minotaur's morphology remaining unspeci-fied; their interest focused mainly on the monster's origin. Since, in classical myth, the Minotaur resulted from an interspecies coupling, the creature was used in medieval texts as an argument about bestiality as a possible cause of monstrous births. Medieval theology and science were cautious about the possibility that monsters could be born of human-animal sex but did not categorically reject what was a popular belief (van der Lugt 2005: 9). After the rediscovery of Aristotle's zoological treatises in the thir-teenth century, scholars could rely on his authority to fully deny this possibility on the grounds of the different gestation periods of human and non-human species (*Gen. an.* 4.3.769b21–4). Aristotle's argument was not always fully understood, however, and could even be misquoted to mean exactly the opposite (Vincent de Beauvais, *Speculum Naturalis* 22.41; Roux 2008: 197). Moreover, even though bestiality was not frequently used to explain the birth of monsters, in semi-learned and popular knowledge any dis-orderly sexual act (*inordinatus coitus, De secretis mulierum* 4, trans. Barragan Nieto 2011: 404) could originate monstrous births (Lecouteux 1999: 142–5). For example, in his *Topographia Hibernica* (*c.*1188), Gerald of Wales describes human-cow hybrids as resulting from interspecies coupling (2.21).

If we add that Ovid was considered an authority in both scientific and erotic matters (Thomasset 1982: 32), the Minotaur unsurprisingly persisted as a counter-argument in favour of interspecies generation. Even a scholar of Aristotle like Albertus Magnus deems the Minotaur realistic or even real, despite appearing 'in the tales of poets' (*De animalibus* 28.1.6 §47). In the French *Placides et Timéo*, a late thirteenth-century scien-tific dialogue between a student and his master about universal knowledge, the Minotaur serves as an example both to explain hybrids as resulting from interspecies coupling and to respond to the question of whether hybrids have one or two souls (§330–40). Understanding the monster's origin was also crucial for doctrinal reasons: as Augustine wrote, if monsters have reason, it means they descend from Adam (*De civitate dei* 16.8), and therefore must have human souls; and if they have a soul, they can and should be baptized (van der Lugt 2005).

The anonymous author of *Placides et Timéo* does not limit himself to a scientific ex-planation of the Minotaur's origin. To answer Placides's question about how such a mon-ster can be born, Timéo, interested in capturing the essence of Pasiphaë's unorthodox desire, gives a long and detailed account of her love for the bull. This attention to the erotic scandal is shared by the *Ovide moralisé* (8.617–1095). Its author, who integrates the story of the Minotaur's conception from *Ars amatoria*, describes Pasiphaë's love in terms that mimic not only the stages of courtly love typical of romance female heroes (Blumenfeld-Kosinski 1996), but also the resourceful trickery of romance fe-male villains. For the moralizer, the Minotaur's birth is a safe narrative space in which to indulge in the description of transgressive sexual behaviour (Blumefeld-Kosinski 1996: 320), as well as an occasion to chastise not only bestiality per se, but also excessive female lust.

In short, placed in a poetic mythical past, the Minotaur's monstrous body served different agendas during the medieval period. Among its many uses, it also provided an authoritative reference to the long-lasting belief in cross-species generation and could be adapted to Christian moralizing mission as a cautionary tale about disordered sexuality.

THE CYNOCEPHALI, OR THE ANTHROPOLOGY OF DIFFERENCE

All the examples provided so far performed several roles simultaneously, including interrogating the nature of humanity by demonstrating its opposite; arguably, all monsters 'dwell at the gates of difference' (Cohen 1996: 7). Yet there is one category of classical monsters, the monstrous populations, whose *main* purpose was to highlight the difference between a culture's ethnographic centre and the populations that lived at its periphery. From classical Greece on down the centuries, this difference was articulated as a declining degree of humanity: the further one travelled from what was considered the centre of the world, the more monstrous the peoples encountered (Wittkower 1942; Asma 2009). Pliny the Elder's *Naturalis historia* was the main source through which the Middle Ages learned about alleged monstrous populations living on the world's edges. The popularity of stories about such peoples, though, was due to the appeal these monsters held for medieval audiences as being 'a measure of man' (Friedman [1991] 2000: 25; cf. Roy 1975). Among them, the Cynocephali, or 'dog-headed' people, stand out for the dramatic otherness of their human-animal body, which continuously questioned the definition of the human (Steel 2012).

Pliny, drawing from the *Indica* of the fifth-century BCE historian Ctesias, describes the Cynocephali in detail (*NH* 7.2.23). As both Ctesias and Pliny state, the Cynocephali hunt with weapons, feed on human meat, and eat raw food; they wear clothes, but express themselves through inarticulate sounds. Through Pliny and Solinus, the third-century CE author of a collection of Plinian material titled *Collectanea rerum memorabilium*, the Cynocephali spread in medieval culture, which placed them in various geographical margins from Scandinavia to Libya and Ethiopia (Karttunen 1984)—although their prevalent location in texts and maps was India, more precisely the Andaman and Nicobar islands (Woodward 1987: 331–2). Their morphology was, in contrast to that of the siren, rather stable, though some branches of romance and encyclopaedic traditions, evidently by misinterpreting the word *cynocephali* for *(e)quinocephali*, describe the Cynocephali as having horse's heads—for example, Jacob of Vitry (thirteenth century), who places them among the marvels of the East (*Historia Orientale* 88, ed. Donnadieu 2008: 364).

Cynocephali were a particularly popular monstrous race in medieval imagination, most likely due to the ambiguity of the dog as the most familiar and civilized non-human species (White 1991: 15), torn between undignified and holy in medieval culture (Smets 2001). Moreover, since their animality involved the head, considered the seat of the rational soul, Cynocephali posed a conundrum to medieval science and theology. Because of their dog head, they could not physically articulate words, and expressed themselves only by barking (Isid., *Etym.* 11.3.15). For this reason, Augustine used the Cynocephali as an exemplar to discuss whether monstrous people were human, and he resolved for the substantial humanity of anything endowed with rationality, no matter how monstrous its aspect might be (*De civitate dei* 16.8). Later writers did not always share this view, but the Cynocepahli's special status allowed them to be used variously across time and genres.

Since the Cynocephali's dog head did not make them inhuman, their degree of distance from medieval European humans was instead defined by their behaviour. One frequent characteristic of the medieval Cynocephali was anthropophagy: as such, their outer monstrosity matched their moral monstrosity (Phillips 2014: 90). Yet this trait did not determine their absolute otherness. The ninth-century Frankish theologian Ratramnus of Corbie, when asked by a fellow monk whether the Cynocephali should be considered human, replied that indeed, considering their society, their use of clothes, and their farming and husbandry practices, they were human and therefore could be converted to Christianity (Migne 1852; Friedman [1991] 2000: 188–90).

In fact, more than any other monster, medieval Cynocephali could be 'domesticated'. The legend of St Christopher provided a striking example of this ability. According to Latin and Old English martyrology, before becoming the 'bearer of Christ' Christopher belonged to a dog-headed population of man-eaters; upon converting to Christianity, he miraculously gained the ability to speak (Williams 1996: 286–97; Lionarons 2002). A similar path probably awaited the Cynocephali represented in the sculpted tympanum decoration in the church of St Mary Magdalene of Vézelay (Strickland 2003: 50–1; Green 2010: 181–2). Cynocephali soon became integral to Christian evangelism. In fact, in no accounts of St Christopher's life is his dog head changed into a human head after his conversion, although the later versions of the story increasingly tone down his monstrosity (Friedrich 2017).

This 'domestication' worked not only on a narrative level, but also on a symbolic one: the Cynocephali were particularly apt to be converted into familiar 'others', covert mirrors of Western society. As they were pushed to the geographical margins, Cynocephali could more safely be considered not just for their difference, but also for their similarity to us (Vincenot 2017). In his *Itinerarium*, Odoric of Pordenone, a Franciscan friar who travelled to India and China from 1318 to 1330, described the inhabitants of the Nicobar islands as dog-headed people. He reported that they were capable of feeling shame for nakedness and of weaving cloths and producing jewels, and that they had a king and a religious cult whose practices were similar to Christian ones. They wore armour in battle, and their cannibalism was limited to wartime (*Itinerarium* 18). The author of the extremely influential *Livre des merveilles*, a fictional fourteenth-century travel account attributed to John Mandeville, uses Odoric as his model to describe the Cynocephali, but goes one step further. For the writer, the Cynocephali's practices relate directly to Christian ones: their beads are like rosaries, their prayers like the paternoster; they are aware that their idols, like Christian saints, are not gods; and their king ensures justice and social cohesion (*Livre des merveilles* 21). This portrayal describes a utopian image of Western medieval society (Salih 2003). Set in stark contrast with their marginality, physical oddity, and cannibalism, the Cynocephali could even be used to demonstrate that examples of virtue and social progress can be found in the most unexpected places.

Conclusion

Medieval Christian culture welcomed with surprising enthusiasm the monsters of pagan antiquity. The deference of medieval scholars towards Greece and Rome did not contrast with their militant moralizing-symbolist attitude (Leclercq-Marx 2011: 10), which sometimes provoked radical transformations of the classical monsters they inherited.

Throughout social, cultural, and philosophical transformations, monsters of classical antiquity kept their relevance in medieval culture and art because their significations and new applications were potentially infinite. Able to demarcate segments of space, time, morals, political, sexual, and social identities, those monsters drew their efficacy as platforms for ontological enquiries because they resulted from 'intensive literary' and artistic 'accumulations' (Verner 2005: 157). That is, classical monsters had been and could always be rewritten, reinterpreted, and resignified. In a sense, like Dante in the *Inferno,* it was by riding on the back of centaurs that medieval scholars, artists, and their audiences could venture into the stranger lands of scientific, philosophical, and spiritual exploration, and reach for new levels of scientific and spiritual understanding of the universe.

Suggested Reading

For an easy-access introduction to monster lore across medieval European culture, see Asma (2009). For a compelling overview on monsters in the history of literature and art, see Mittman and Dendle (2012). Reynolds and Wilson (1974, see also 2013) provides a solid guidebook to the modes of transmission of classical authors after antiquity, while Williams (1996) discusses medieval monsters and their function in medieval written culture. The complicated transmission and evolution of the siren is masterfully synthesized in Leclercq-Marx (1997). Friedman ([1991] 2000) remains the most influential monograph on medieval monstrous races.

Works Cited

Asma, S. T. 2009. *On Monsters: An Unnatural History of Our Worst Fears.* Oxford.
Avenel, M.-A. 2017. 'Les "Monstres marins" sont-ils des poissons? Le Livre VI du *Liber de Natura Rerum de Thomas de Cantimpré.*' *Rursus-Spicae* 11. <https://journals.openedition.org/rursus/1320>.

Badel, P.-Y., ed. and trans. 1998. *Marco Polo: La Description du monde*. Paris.

Bain, F. 2017. 'The Tail of Melusine: Hybridity, Mutability, and the Accessible Other', in *Melusine's Footprint: Tracing the Legacy of a Medieval Myth*, ed. M. Urban, D. Kemmis, and M. Ridley, 1–13. Leiden.

Baker, C., ed. 2010. *Le Bestiaire. Version longue attribuée à Pierre de Beauvais*. Paris.

Barney, S. A., et al., trans. 2006. *The Etymologies of Isidore of Seville*. Cambridge.

Barragan Nieto, J. P., ed. and trans. 2011. *El De secretis mulierum atribuído a Alberto Magno*. Porto.

Bartholomaeus, A. 1601. *De genuinis rerum coelestium, terrestrium et inferarum proprietatibus*. Francofurti.

Bildhauer, B., and R. Mills. 2003. 'Introduction: Conceptualizing the Monstrous', in *The Monstrous Middle Ages*, ed. B. Bildhauer and R. Mills, 1–17. Cardiff.

Blumenfeld-Kosinski, R. 1996. 'The Scandal of Pasiphae: Narration and Interpretation in the *Ovide moralisé*.' *Modern Philology* 93/3: 307–26.

Bovey, A. 2002. *Monsters and Grotesques in Medieval Manuscripts*. Toronto.

Cerrito, S. 2004. '*Come beste esteit peluz*—l'image du Sagittaire dans les différentes versions de la légende de Troie au Moyen Âge', in *La Chevelure dans la littérature et l'art du Moyen Âge*, ed. C. Connochie-Bourgne, 69–82. Aix-en-Provence.

Cohen, J. J. 1996. 'Monster Culture (Seven Theses)', in *Monster Theory: Reading Culture*, ed. J. J. Cohen, 3–25. Minneapolis.

Curley, M. J., ed. 1979. *Physiologus: A Medieval Book of Nature Lore*. Chicago.

Davies, S. 2016. *Renaissance Ethnography and the Invention of the Human*. Cambridge.

Deluz, C., ed. 2000. *Jean de Mandeville: Le Livre des merveilles du monde*. Paris.

Dittmar, P.-O. 2012. 'Les Corps sans fins: Extensions animales et végétales dans les marges de la représentation (XIIIe–XIVe siècle).' *Micrologus* 20: 25–42.

Donnadieu, J., ed. 2008. *Jacques de Vitry: Histoire orientale*. Turnhout.

Douchet, S. 2005. 'La Peau du centaure à la frontière de l'humanité et de l'animalité.' *Micrologus* 13: 285–312.

Dubost, F. 1988. 'L'Autre guerrier: L'Archer-cheval; Du Sagittaire du *Roman de Troie* aux Sagittaires de *La mort Aymeri de Narbonne*', in *De l'étranger à l'étrange ou la conjointure de la merveille*, 171–88. Aix-en-Provence.

Faral, E. 1953. 'La queue de poisson des sirènes.' *Romania* 74: 433–506.

Felton, D. 2012. 'Rejecting and Embracing the Monstrous in Ancient Greece and Rome', in *The Ashgate Research Companion to Monsters and the Monstrous*, ed. A. S. Mittman and P. J. Dendle, 103–31. Farnham.

Friedman, J. B. [1991] 2000. *The Monstrous Races in Medieval Art and Thought*. Reprint. New York.

Friedman, J. B. 2015. 'Werewolf Transformation in the Manuscript Era.' *Journal of the Early Book Society* 17: 36–95.

Friedman, J. B., K. Giogoli, and K. Figg. 2018. *Book of the Wonders of the World: Studies, Transcription and Translation MS fr. 22971*. Burgos.

Friedrich, J. 2017. 'Saint Christopher's Canine Hybrid Body and Its Cultural Autocannibalism.' *Preternature: Critical and Historical Studies on the Preternatural* 6/2: 189–211.

Green, M. H. 2010. 'The Diversity of Human Kind', in *A Cultural History of the Human Body in the Medieval Age*, ed. L. Kalof, 173–90. Oxford.

Griffin, M. 2020. 'Mélusine and Margaret: Hybrids and Monstrous Maternity', in *Corps hybrides aux frontières de l'humain au Moyen Âge*, ed. A. Sciancalepore, 63–82. Louvain-la-Neuve.

Hollander, R., ed., and S. Marchesi, trans. 2011. *La Commedia di Dante Alighieri*. Florence.

Jerome [Hieronymus]. 1883. *Vita Sancti Pauli Primi Eremitae*, in *PL* 23, cols. 17–28.

Jerome [Hieronymus]. 1963. *Commentariorum in Esaiam*, in *Corpus Christianorum Series Latina*, ed. M. Adriaen, vols. 73–73A. Turnhout.

Kaimakis, D. V., ed. 1974. *Der Physiologus nach der ersten Redaktion*. Meisenheim am Glan.

Kappler, C. 1980. *Monstres, démons et merveilles à la fin du Moyen Âge*. Paris.

Karttunen, K. 1984. 'Κυνοκέφαλοι and κυναμολγοί in Classical Ethnography.' *Arctos* 18: 31–6.

Kordecki, L. C. 1997. 'Losing the Monster and Recovering the Non-Human in Fable(d) Subjectivity', in *Animals and the Symbolic in Mediaeval Art and Literature*, ed. L. A. J. R. Houwen, 25–37. Groningen.

Leclercq-Marx, J. 1997. *La Sirène dans la pensée et dans l'art de l'Antiquité et du Moyen Âge*. Brussels. https://koregos.org/fr/jacqueline-leclercq-marx-la-sirene-dans-la-pensee-et-dans-l-art-de-l-antiquite-et-du-moyen-age/

Leclercq-Marx, J. 2002. 'Du monstre androcéphale au monstre humanisé: A propos des sirènes et des centaures, et de leur famille, dans le haut Moyen Âge et à l'époque romane.' *Cahiers de civilisation médiévale* 177: 55–67.

Leclercq-Marx, J. 2011. 'Prototypes antiques et recréations médiévales: Le Cas de quelques monstres anthropomorphes (sirènes, centaures, minotaures).' *Degrés* 145/6: 1–17.

Lascault, G. 1973. *Le monstre dans l'art occidental: un problème esthétique*. Paris.

Lecouteux, C. 1999. *Les monstres dans la pensée médiévale européenne*, 2nd edn. Paris.

Lionarons, J. T. 2002. 'From Monster to Martyr: The Old English Legend of Saint Christopher', in *Marvels, Monsters, and Miracles: Studies in the Medieval and Early Modern Imaginations*, ed. T. S. Jones and D. A. Springer, 171–82. Kalamazoo, MI.

Lowe, D. 2015. *Monsters and Monstrosity in Augustan Poetry*. Ann Arbor.

McCracken, G. E., et al., trans. 1957–1972. *Augustine: The City of God against the Pagans*. Cambridge, MA.

McCulloch, F. 1962. *Medieval Latin and French Bestiaries*. Chapel Hill, NC.

March, J. R. 2014. *Dictionary of Classical Mythology*, 2nd edn. Oxford.

Marchisio, A., ed. 2016. *Odorico da Pordenone: Relatio de mirabilibus orientalium Tartarorum*. Florence.

Mermier, G. R., ed. 1977. *Le Bestiaire de Pierre de Beauvais (version courte)*. Paris.

Migne, J.-P., ed. 1852. 'Ratramnus Corbeiensis: *Epistola de Cynocephalis*', in *PL* 121, cols. 153–156D.

Mittman, A. S. 2006. *Maps and Monsters in Medieval England*. London.

Mittman, A. S. 2012. 'Introduction: The Impact of Monsters and Monster Studies', in *The Ashgate Research Companion to Monsters and the Monstrous*, ed. A. S. Mittman and P. J. Dendle, 1–14. Farnham.

Mittman, A. S., and Dendle, P. J., eds. 2012. *The Ashgate Research Companion to Monsters and the Monstrous*. Farnham.

Mittman, A. S., and Kim, S. M. 2016. 'Monstrous Iconography', in *The Routledge Companion to Medieval Iconography*, ed. C. Hourihane, 512–33. London.

Morini, L., ed. 2018. *Philippe de Thaon: Bestiaire*. Paris.

Munk Olsen, B. 1995. *La Réception de la littérature classique au Moyen Âge (IXe–XIIe siècle)*. Copenhagen.

Murgatroyd, P. 2013. *Mythical Monsters in Classical Literature*. London.

Ogden, D. 2021. *The Werewolf in the Ancient World*. Oxford.

Olsen, K. E., and R. Olsen. 2001. 'Introduction: On the Embodiment of Monstrosity in Northwest Medieval Europe', in *Monsters and the Monstrous in Medieval Northwest Europe*, ed. K. E. Olsen and L. A. J. R. Houwen, 1–22. Leuven.

O'Meara, J. J., ed. 1949. 'Giraldus Cambrensis in Topographia Hibernie: Text of the First Recension.' *Proceedings of the Royal Irish Academy* 52: 113–78.

Orchard, A. 1995. *Pride and Prodigies: Studies in the Monsters of the Beowulf-Manuscript.* Toronto.

Peck, A. L., ed. and trans. 1979. *Aristotle: Generation of Animals.* Cambridge, MA.

Peyronie, A. 1997. 'Le Mythe de Thésée pendant le Moyen Âge latin (500–1150).' *Médiévales* 32: 119–33.

Phillips, K. M. 2014. *Before Orientalism: Asian Peoples and Cultures in European Travel Writing, 1245–1510.* Philadelphia.

Porsia, F., ed. and trans. 2012. *Liber monstrorum (secolo IX).* Naples.

Randall, L. M. C. 1966. *Images in the Margins of Gothic Manuscripts.* Berkeley and Los Angeles.

Reynolds, L. D., and N. G. Wilson. 1974. *Scribes and Scholars: A Guide to the Transmission of Greek and Latin Literature*, 2nd edn. Oxford.

Reynolds, L. D., and N. G. Wilson. 2013. *Scribes and Scholars: A Guide to the Transmission of Greek and Latin Literature*, 4th edn. Oxford.

Rinoldi, P., ed. 2000. *La Mort Aymeri de Narbonne.* Milan.

Roux, O. 2008. *Monstres: Une histoire générale de la tératologie des origines à nos jours.* Paris.

Roy, B. 1975. 'En marge du monde connu: Les Races des monstres', in *Aspects de la marginalité au Moyen Âge*, ed. G. H. Allard, 70–80. Montreal.

Salih, S. 2003. 'Idols and Simulacra: Paganity, Hybridity and Representation in "Mandeville's Travels"', in *The Monstrous Middle Ages*, ed. B. Bildhauer and R. Mills, 113–33. Cardiff.

Sinclair, K. V., ed. 1971. *Tristan de Nanteuil, chanson de geste inédite.* Assen.

Smets, A. 2001. 'L'Image ambiguë du chien à travers la littérature didactique latine et française (XIIe–XIVe s.)', *Reinardus* 14: 243–53.

Smits, E. R. 1995. 'Aspects of Medieval Literary Theory', in *Mediaeval Antiquity*, ed. A. Welkenhuysen, H. Braet, and W. Verbeke, 1–20. Leuven.

Stadler, J., ed. 1916–1920. *Albertus Magnus:* De animalibus *libri XXVI.* Münster.

Steel, K. 2012. 'Centaurs, Satyrs, and Cynocephali: Medieval Scholarly Teratology and the Question of the Human', in *The Ashgate Research Companion to Monsters and the Monstrous*, ed. A. S. Mittman and P. J. Dendle, 257–74. Farnham.

Strickland, D. 2003. *Saracens, Demons, and Jews: Making Monsters in Medieval Art.* Princeton.

Thomasset, C., ed. 1980. *Placides et Timéo, ou li secrés as philosophes.* Geneva.

Thomasset, C. 1982. *Une vision du monde à la fin du XIIIe siècle: Commentaire du dialogue de Placides et Timéo.* Geneva.

van der Lugt, M. 2005. 'L'Humanité des monstres et leur accès aux sacrements dans la pensée médiévale', in *Monstres et imaginaire social: Approches historiques*, ed. A. Caiozzo and A.-E. Demartini, 135–62. Paris.

van Duzer, C. 2012. '*Hic sunt dracones*: The Geography and Cartography of Monsters', in *The Ashgate Research Companion to Monsters and the Monstrous*, ed. A. S. Mittman and P. J. Dendle, 387–435. Farnham.

Verner, L. 2005. *The Epistemology of the Monstrous in the Middle Ages.* New York.

Vieillard-Troïekouroff, M. 1969. 'Sirènes-poissons carolingiennes.' *Cahiers archéologiques* 19: 61–82.

Vincenot, Q. 2017. 'Cynocéphale et loup-garou: Deux anthropophages aux marges de l'humanité', in *Merveilleux et marges dans le livre profane à la fin du Moyen Âge (XIIe–XVe siècles)*, ed. A. Latimier, J. Pavlevski-Malingre, and A. Servier, 77–87. Turnhout.

Walther Boer, W., ed. 1973. *Epistola Alexandri ad Aristotelem de miraculis Indiae*. Meisenheim am Glan.

White, D. G. 1991. *Myths of the Dog-Man*. Chicago.

Williams, D. 1996. *Deformed Discourse: The Function of the Monster in Medieval Thought and Literature*. Montreal.

Wittkower, R. 1942. 'Marvels of the East: A Study in the History of Monsters.' *Journal of the Warburg and Courtauld Institutes* 5: 159–97.

Woodward, D. 1987. 'Medieval *Mappaemundi*', in *Cartography in Prehistoric, Ancient, and Medieval Europe and the Mediterranean*, ed. J. B. Harley and D. Woodward, 286–368. Chicago.

CHAPTER 34

THE REVIVAL OF CLASSICAL MONSTERS IN THE ITALIAN RENAISSANCE

LUBA FREEDMAN

INTRODUCTION

THE conjunction of 'Classical' and 'Monsters' in the title serves from the outset to signal the extraordinary and wondrous. Today, the word 'classical' in the field of art signifies the ideal beauty of visual images whereas 'monsters' suggests threatening creatures of the ancient imagination. In the Italian Renaissance (*c.*1450–*c.*1550), although the term *classico* was not typically used, a renewed interest in cultural heritage revived mythological monsters from ancient Greece and Rome. Since Greek vases and Roman paintings were barely known at this time, this revival occurred first in Renaissance literature and then in sculpture. In essence, classical monsters once again assumed the importance they originally had in the poetry and visual arts of Greek and Roman antiquity. Additionally, the significance attributed to the sculpted images in their original physical locations, as indicated in ancient texts, once more came to light.

The term 'monster' is not always an apt description of these mythical creatures, although the integration of human and bestial elements or the manifestation of several bestial elements is appropriate to the semantics of the term. The very fact that they were creations of the ancient imagination reveals the improbability of their existence. By definition, monsters are *contra naturam* ('against nature'), whether in physical appearance or habitat. Rather than considering classical monsters generically, humanists and artists thought about them individually, often by naming them whenever possible and mostly within the framework of their references to Greek and Roman texts. Regarding their interpretations of classical monsters, Italian Renaissance humanists—themselves descendants of late antique and medieval mythographers—hunted for the didactic imports of imagined creatures while adapting them to the Christian world-view. As for their representations in the context of poetically elaborated myths, Italian artists retained the physical appetites and powers of monsters as exaggerated as they were in antiquity.

MOSTRO IN EARLY ITALIAN TEXTS

The monstrous creations of the Italian Renaissance to be discussed here include centaurs, sirens, sphinxes, harpies, satyrs or fauns, Tritons, Nereids, Pegasus, Cerberus, the Gorgon Medusa, and two giants: Polyphemus the Cyclops and Argus Panoptes ('Argus the All-Seeing'), whose otherwise human appearance was described as many-eyed. These creatures are *mostri*, or 'monsters', to borrow the term used by early Italian writers in mainly cosmographic manuals. The earliest known appearance of the word *mostro* occurs in the first scientific treatise in Italian prose, Restoro d'Arezzo's *Composizione del mondo, c.*1282 (*The Composition of the World*, 2.2.5; Restoro d'Arezzo 1997: 117), in reference to the era of Jupiter, which gave rise to 'his miraculous monster' (*suo mostro miracoloso*), the centaur Sagittarius. Dante's follower, Fazio degli Uberti, in *Il Dittamondo* (1367), his didactic poem on the sayings of the world, has his guide Solinus, the third-century CE Roman geographer, remark that the centaur and another similar 'monster' lived in time immemorial, when simple folk, driven by fear, could believe in their existence (3.20.58–64; Fazio 1952: vol. 1. 241). Significantly, early Italian writers illustrate the term *mostro* by referring to the centaur, as if this biform creature were synonymous with the image the word itself evoked in their minds.

In his *Commedia* (1321), Dante Alighieri uses the term *mostro* only three times, to mark a new phase of his pilgrimage: the passage from Purgatory to Paradise (*Purgatorio* 32.147, 158; 33.39). In the first two instances, Dante employs the classical Latin sense of *monēre* ('to warn or admonish'); in the third, 'to become monstrous' signifies the abandonment of virtue, as Cristoforo Landino, a lecturer on Dante and Vergil and a philosopher-poet in his own right, interprets the phrase *divenne mostro* ('became a monster', Landino 2001: vol. 3, 1545–6.23–4).[1] The pilgrim Dante, however, encounters multiple monstrous beings during his journey. Not all are menacing; the monster Griffin (32.89), which combines the characteristics of an eagle and a lion (Lansing 2000: 455), represents the fabulous combination of celestial and terrestrial realms, thereby signalling the epiphany of Christ (Landino 2001: vol. 3, 1534.16–17). As Livanos (2009: 84) observes, Dante wisely understood the joining of the human and the divine as being *contra naturam*. This coupling stands in stark contrast to combining the human and the bestial, which is characteristic of biform creatures such as centaurs. Almost two centuries later, a Florentine humanist and prolific writer Benedetto Varchi, after reading Lucretius' didactic poem, *On the Nature of Things* (*De rerum natura*), stated

---

[1] References to Landino are by volume, page, and line number, e.g. vol. 3, 1534.16.

unequivocally in his public lecture on monsters (1548) that centaurs do not exist because equine and human forms could not synchronically develop in the same figure (Ciseri Montemagno 2007; see also Hawes in this volume).

Imaginary creatures first arrived in ancient Greece from Mesopotamia and Egypt (Felton 2012: 103), where they gradually acquired more physically attractive shapes and new interpretations. Many of the listed monsters figured in later annotations and illustrations of Dante's *Commedia*. Previously, only two—siren and onocentaur—were familiar figures, reflecting the popularity of the *Physiologus* (the precursor to medieval bestiaries), in which these beasts specifically 'represent the figures of devils' (Curley 2009: 23–4). Whereas siren survived with a classical name though not image, being usually represented as a mermaid, onocentaur received a corrupted name ('ass-centaur') but maintained a resemblance to the original biform centaur. Their descriptions were realized in the weight-bearing corbel sculptures of monastery cloisters, and they subsequently found a place in the margins of illustrated codices of the Renaissance period, their figures shaped *all'antica*, that is, after the style of Greek and Roman artists (Alexander 1994: 143).

Classical monsters were kept alive through the popularity of Dante's *Commedia* (Meiss 1969: 1. 37). Latin and Italian commentaries, some illustrated, proliferated after Dante's death in 1321, culminating during the fifteenth century in Landino's 1481 printed text, with Baccio Baldini's woodcuts based on Sandro Botticelli's drawings (Italian artists read little Latin). All the monsters listed above, apart from Tritons and Nereids, are glossed therein, with annotations indicating Dante's reliance on Roman poets such as Vergil and Ovid. Nurtured by the imagination of the great Florentine poet (Gilson 2005, 2018), mythological monsters hereinafter regained their relatively classical forms as compared to their accessible representations in the visual arts of antiquity.

HISTORICAL FRAMEWORK

Of central importance is the legacy of Italian humanists and artists, as transmitted in their interpretations of 'classical monsters'. The Renaissance understanding of their ancient heritage was far from monolithic as the heritage itself was far from uniform. I have argued elsewhere that specific contexts, secular and religious, determined the approach to classical themes (Freedman 2003b, 2011); here I consider the wider question as it relates to the formal and symbolic aspects that accrued to 'classical' monsters between 1445, the date of Filarete's bronze doors at St Peter's—where the sculpted mythological subjects on its borders are quite accessible to all viewers—and 1550, the date of the first published version of Giorgio Vasari's magisterial book, *The Lives of the Most Excellent Painters, Sculptors and Architects from Cimabue to up Our Times* (*Le vite de' piú eccellenti architetti, pittori, et scultori italiani, da Cimabue, insino a' tempi nostri*).

The Italian Renaissance humanists were drawn primarily to classical texts and only secondarily to antique sculptures, no matter how accessible; that is, written descriptions of classical monsters always prevailed over visual evidence, which required decoding because of its novelty. The sphinx provides a clear example, a creature to some extent merged with the concept of the harpy. Sphinxes that are seen in Roman art—on the side reliefs of sarcophagi and the bases of candelabra—are all founded on the Theban Sphinx (Demisch 1977: 109–11), but in the Renaissance, the image of harpies could be drawn only from poetry (Wirth 1981: 1–4, 43). These winged hybrid creatures have distinctly different appearances. The visible Roman sphinx has leonine paws, and the literary harpy has an avian body with talons. The Italian plural *arpie* refers to both sphinxes and harpies (Caglioti 1995: 33, 38), and harpies, as represented throughout Renaissance art, are clearly based on Roman sphinxes. Both monsters present the face and nude bosom of a maiden, but the word 'sphinx' refers only to the Egyptian sphinx (Caglioti 1995: 55 n. 157). Francesco Colonna, for example, in his 1499 allegorical romance *Hypnerotomachia Poliphili* (*Poliphilo's Strife of Love in a Dream*), describes the Egyptian sphinx (though without using the term) as having leonine paws and a serpentine tail, and refers to other similar figures as harpies (though without penning their description; Colonna 1999: 129, 89). Whether found within church precincts, or set at the base of a sepulchre, or decorating a throne, both remind classically educated churchgoers about the deficiency of paganism.

RENAISSANCE APPROACHES TO MONSTERS

It may be useful here to organize the classical monsters of the Italian Renaissance according to the innovative concepts that were applied to these cultural relics of Greek and Roman antiquity. This chapter considers four approaches characteristic of the Renaissance:

1. The scrutiny of two types of ancient texts, poetic and didactic, to reveal:
    a) the role of monsters in myths;
    b) the physical locations in which sculpted monsters were originally seen in antiquity (paintings are not mentioned).
2. The examination of antique sculpted reliefs and gems, paying particular attention to:
    a) the figurative context which features monsters;
    b) the artistic principles that determined the forms of lifelike figures (precise copying of antiques in painting and sculpture was unacceptable unless required by the commissioner).
3. The adaptation of intricately shaped monsters that emerged from the paintings discovered in the so-called Domus Aurea ('Golden House'), Nero's palace in Rome (no systematic excavations were underway at the time).
4. The reinterpretation of monsters by artists whose familiarity with the classical origins allowed them to adapt their renditions to the contemporaries' humanistic inclinations.

Accordingly, the monsters chosen for discussion here exemplify in one way or another each of these four categories, bearing in mind that the categories are not necessarily exclusive. As evidence, ancient texts and material remains were mutually supportive; for example, sculpted reliefs and gems with recognized subjects could provide historical validation to descriptive images, or occasionally contradict them. In the Italian Renaissance, the physical location of commissioned representations of classical monsters in painting and sculpture often determined whether their portrayal should be shaped *all'antica*. Since newly made images were developed within a Christian milieu, the formal innovations were consistent with those beliefs and traditions; whereas works of art on Christian subjects were based on an honoured tradition, works of art on mythological subjects were new for fifteenth-century painters and sculptors. These new readings combined the original characteristics, already familiar to the classically educated audience, with the allegorical interpretations drawn from mythographic treatises and often modified for their contemporary viewers.

Innovative Treatments

Humanists of the Italian Renaissance pursued innovative treatments of ancient texts. They learned Greek to be able to read Homer and other poets in the original, they read the Latin classics with an eye to the authors' historic ambience, they wrote commentaries in Latin and Italian, and they made annotations to classical texts (Celenza 2018; Field 2017). Their intention was not to interpret the texts for a Christian audience—as was done, for example, by Fulgentius in the fifth century and Petrus Berchorius in the fourteenth (Seznec 1953: 89–93)—but rather, to focus attention on the expressive vocabulary of ancient texts (Seznec 1953: 234–51). Renaissance painters and sculptors, encouraged by their humanistically educated patrons, revived depictions of classical myths in their works, representing classical monsters in the context of mythological plots as if they were in works of Greek and Roman art as known from their ancient descriptions, though with clues for their projected moral consequences. This new approach manifests in the treatment of individually named monsters such as the winged steed Pegasus, the centaurs Nessus and Chiron, the satyr Marsyas, and even the sirens, because they began to be visually represented *all'antica* as playing a critical role in Odysseus' saga precisely at a time when humanists promoted reading Homeric poems in Greek.

Although Pegasus, as a winged horse, may qualify as a monster because of its physical anomaly, it is not the wings that make him a monster in Renaissance thought, but his monstrous parentage. Italian Renaissance viewers were accustomed to seeing the winged figures of angels and the winged symbols of the Evangelists. Pegasus, a noble steed, stands out among equines because he could fly. The story of his birth varies, but consistently features the snake-haired Gorgon Medusa as his mother. The winged steed sprang from the neck of her pregnant body at the very moment Perseus decapitated her (Ov. *Met.* 4.793–8). Pegasus struck with his hoofs a rock on Mount Helicon, dedicated to the Muses, thereby causing a fountain to flow forth. Dante wittily alludes to this when he invokes 'O diva pegasea' (*Paradiso* 18.82), a phrase that eludes precise translation, but may refer to the goddess Minerva or Vergil's Muse Calliope (Francesco da Buti 1858–1862: vol. 3. 525; *c.*1385; Landino 2001: vol. 4, 1828.5–7). Either way, Pegasus became a symbol of poetic evocation.

The earliest Renaissance representation of Pegasus in the mythological context, which shows him being tamed by the hero Bellerophon with the aid of Minerva's golden bridle, was motivated by the Greek poet Pindar's *Olympian Ode* (13.62–87), manuscripts of which were held by the Medici family from the 1450s. It was designed in Florence in the early 1480s by Bertoldo di Giovanni, the Medici sculptor, and cast in bronze by Adriano Fiorentino.[2] The addition of the Herculean club for further submission of the winged steed is not Pindar's but Bertoldo's, meant to indicate Bellerophon's subsequent failure in his aspiration to resemble Hercules. This bronze statuette, 33 centimetres tall, was commissioned by Febo Cappella, the Venetian ambassador in Florence and learned Hellenophile (Noelle 2019: 358, 362–3), who likely wished to remind himself about Bellerophon's doom (*Ol.* 13.92) or the consequences of self-pride, to which Pindar faintly alludes.

Following Ovid, Dante gave centaurs specific identities, contrasting intemperate Nessus with reserved Chiron (*Inferno* 12.64–101; Lansing 2000: 153, 163, 646). Around 1475 Antonio del Pollaiuolo recreated the ancient painting about Nessus abducting Deianira, based on one of Philostratus' descriptions (*Imag.* 16; *c.*250 CE).[3] The re-creation of the ancient painting for the Medici villa at Careggi prompted Pollaiuolo to model his Nessus on the roundel from the frieze in the courtyard of the Palazzo Medici (Freedman 2010: 275, 287–8; Nethersole 2018: 158–9, 140 fig. 93), itself a marble replica of a gem depicting a generic centaur. In contrast to Nessus, who, apart from his abduction of Deianira, could not be visually distinguished from other centaurs, Chiron's head was encircled with a laurel wreath and was identified even in antiquity by his attributes—among them, the lyre. Even as early as the sixth century BCE, the Greeks characterized Chiron as highly civilized and knowledgeable. Pindar praises Chiron for helping the Greek hero Peleus win the favour of the Oceanid Thetis and for tutoring their son Achilles (*Isthm.* 8.38–58). In the 1490s, the Florentine Bartolomeo di Giovanni painted the meeting of Peleus and Thetis, placing Chiron, striking a lyre with a plectrum, at the centre.[4] In keeping with the popularity of Niccolò Machiavelli's 1513 work *The Prince*, which highlights Chiron's tutorship of future leaders (Rispoli 2015), Chiron is seen again at the compositional centre in the anonymous fresco at the Palazzo Spada in Rome, *Thetis Entrusts Achilles to the Centaur Chiron* (*c.*1545; Martinez 2019: 204–6).[5] For Landino, Chiron embodied pure reason (2001: vol. 2, 627.155).

---

[2] https://www.wga.hu/html_m/b/bertoldo/bellerop.html.

[3] https://commons.wikimedia.org/wiki/File:Pollaiolo,_ercole_e_deianira.jpg.

[4] https://commons.wikimedia.org/wiki/File:Bartolomeo_di_giovanni,_nozze_di_teti_e_pe leo,_1490-1500_ca._01.JPG.

[5] https://www.agefotostock.es/age/es/detalles-foto/tetis-confiar-bebe-aquiles-centauro-chiron-anon imo-artista-1550-1500s-fresco-italia-lazio-roma-palazzo-spada-estrofa/MDO-155578.

One principal innovation in the Renaissance depiction of monsters was their deliberate integration into the original context of their poetic myths, the illustration of which in painting and sculpture lent a certain nobility to their physical appearance. Marsyas, one of the familiar forest creatures interchangeably called *sileni*, *fauni*, or satyrs, came to be modelled on the well-known classical statue showing the satyr vanquished by Apollo (Caglioti 1993: 21). This representation of the Ovidian myth, in which a foolishly arrogant Marsyas challenges the god to a music contest, was inspired in turn by Philostratus' description of the ancient painting on the subject (*Imag.* 2; Freedman 2011: 117–20). Marsyas has long pointed ears and a snub nose, the only two features remaining from his characteristic appearance as a satyr.[6] These physical indications also symbolically reflect his character: his arrogant claim that he could best the musician god Apollo was indeed a monstruous affront.

As to the sirens lurking in cloister corbels, their earliest known mention in literature is found in Homer's *Odyssey* (12.45–6, 158–200). The episode describing Odysseus listening to their enchanted songs became visualized *all'antica* by Bolognese painter Francesco Primaticcio (*c*.1555) in the frescoed Gallery of Ulysses at Fontainebleau as part of its grand cycle, whose programme reflects the revived interest in Homer's poems during the period (Ford 2006). Homer does not describe the Sirens' looks but highlights their fatally enticing song. The artist shows the Homeric Sirens, whose heads are adorned with blond curls, positioned with their nude backs to the viewers of the fresco, thereby wittily leaving most of their appearance to the imagination (Véron-Denise 2005: 202, 217).[7]

The Original Contexts of Sculpted Images

Close readings of Pliny the Elder's *Natural History* (*c*.77 CE) and Pausanias' *Guide to Greece* (*c*.170 CE), which describe the actual locations of sculpted images on mythological subjects during their lifetimes, stimulated Renaissance artists to faithfully establish the contexts in which ancient mythical creatures, such as the Sphinx and Medusa (particularly the *gorgoneion*), were positioned. Pliny, the first Roman writer to mention the Egyptian sphinx, indicates its location in the precinct of the pyramids (*NH* 19.17.77; Curran 2007: 21). The Egyptian sphinx, distinguished by the pharaoh's striped *nemes* headcloth as well as by its lion's tail, eventually visualized as serpent's, was familiar in Renaissance Rome because several sculptures, albeit on a much smaller scale, were arrayed in the vicinity of the Pantheon (Giandandrea 2010: 152). The threefold description of the Theban Sphinx, familiar from Ausonius' fourth-century CE didactic poem 'A Riddle of the Number Three', 40–1—'in wings a bird, in paws a beast, in face a girl' (*volucris pennis, pedibus fera, fronte puella*)—provoked the subsequent confusion between the Egyptian and Theban sphinxes (Cook 2006: 8–13), who differ not only in

---

[6] https://commons.wikimedia.org/wiki/File:Stanza_della_segnatura,_soffitto,_apollo_e_marsia.JPG.
[7] https://commons.wikimedia.org/wiki/File:Sirens_and_Odysseus_by_Francesco_Primaticcio.jpg.

physical composition, but also in posture: the Egyptian sphinx is recumbent, the Theban is seated—the latter being replicated in Roman art.

Pliny's description of the Gizan Sphinx as set among the pyramids greatly impressed his Renaissance readers. In the Basilica of Santa Croce in Florence, two corner figures shaped into Roman sphinxes with dragon-like tails flank the pedestal of Desiderio da Settignano's sculpted tomb of Carlo Marsuppini, a renowned Hellenophile humanist (1454–9);[8] their position on the tomb's low register visually demonstrates that pagan thoughts and beliefs provided the foundation of Christian theology (Mozzati 2007: 118–22). In his *Commentary on Benivieni's Canzone d'amore* (1486), Giovanni Pico della Mirandola states that both Plutarch's *Isis and Osiris* (345bc) and Clement of Alexandria's *Stromata* (5.31.5) attest that the placement of sphinxes near Egyptian temples was understood as a warning about the importance of using enigmatic language to veil written or spoken messages of divine wisdom; he recommends his contemporaries continue to speak cryptically on significant matters (Herrmann and van den Hoek 2013; Wind 1968: 123). Landino, commenting on *Purgatory* 33.47, designates the presence of the Sphinx as an 'enygma' (2001: vol. 3, 1547.15) while pointing out that Dante, steeped in the verses of Ovid, pairs Themis (the goddess of order and justice) with the Theban Sphinx (symbolic of riddles and ruthlessness) to indicate to contemporary readership that disastrous consequences, such as untimely death, signal divine retributions (Cerri 2013: 18–19).

In Padua, *c*.1447–1450, Florentine sculptor Donatello was the earliest artist to set a pair of Theban/Roman sphinxes at the base of the bronze statue of the Virgin's throne (placed above the Santo's High Altar; Bodon 2017: 173; Demisch 1977: 167).[9] Their contrastingly expressive faces, sorrowful and blissful, could provoke the churchgoers to ponder over the Christian mystery of Salvation inevitably caused by Sacrifice. In 1447, after his return from Padua, Florentine painter Andrea del Castagno rendered two pseudo-sculpted sphinxes as flanking the bench of the Apostles in the frescoed refectory at the Sant'Apollonia's convent in Florence (Bodon 2017: 167; Demisch 1977: 168). Adapted into the scene of the Last Supper, a female image in this pair has lion's paws contrasting with the protruding breast, whereas the hind parts of both figures morph into serpentine tails; this suggests an evil aftermath; that is, the artist added the imagined serpentine tail of the Egyptian sphinx to the otherwise Theban-like sphinx so familiar from Roman sarcophagi, thereby alluding to Original Sin (Fig. 34.1).

Almost ten years later, Paduan painter Andrea Mantegna also used the figure of the Roman/Theban Sphinx, but in a context determined by the subject of the Ovetari chapel in the Church of the Eremitani: The Martyrdom of St James (Bodon 2017: 168). Familiar with Pausanias' description of Phidias' statue of Zeus in the temple of Zeus at Olympia, the armrests of whose throne were sculpted in the form of the Theban Sphinx (5.11.2–7), Mantegna designed his sphinx to function precisely as the armrest of the throne of

FIGURE 34.1 Andrea del Castagno, *The Last Supper*, 1447. The former Convent of Sant'Apollonia, Florence.

Public domain.

Herod, the ruler of Judaea (Knabenshue 1959: 67). Keeping in mind the Theban Sphinx's connection to the untimely deaths of young men, Mantegna's sphinx functioned as the visual evidence of the Judaean ruler's cruelty in condemning St James to beheading. To preclude any ambiguity in the interpretation of the sphinx, Mantegna gave it Herod's profile.

Two poetic texts of the late first century BCE, Ovid's *Metamorphoses* (4.801) and Propertius' *Elegies* (2.7–8), both mention the *gorgoneion* on Minerva's breastplate; however, not until *c*.1450 did it become common knowledge that Pausanias described Phidias' statue of Athena on the Acropolis as having Medusa's head on her aegis (1.24.7; Reynolds and Wilson 1974: 137–42). Continuing the medieval practice of decorating helmets with fantastic creatures, Andrea del Verrocchio's workshop (*c*.1485), imitating Phidias, introduced representations of armoured leaders, both ancient and contemporary, bearing the *gorgoneion*. In their attentive reading of Greek texts, Renaissance humanists noted that Homer, in describing Agamemnon's shield, singled out the face of Medusa 'with her stare of horror' (*Il.* 11.36–7; trans. Lattimore). Verrocchio shaped the terracotta bust of Giuliano de' Medici with the winged *gorgoneion* prominently centred on his breastplate.[10] Similarly, on his marble relief of Alexander the Great, he sculpted a breastplate with a winged male head, square and bony, whose eyes are transfixed in a horror repeated in the expression of his mouth, which is open in a scream, in strong resemblance to Medusa's (Caglioti 2011: 174).[11] The Medici patrons of Verrocchio's sculptures most probably invested the *gorgoneion* with the same apotropaic function it

[10] https://www.nga.gov/collection/art-object-page.134.html.
[11] https://www.nga.gov/collection/art-object-page.43513.html.

had in antiquity. Moreover, both *gorgoneia* are winged, inspired by Ciriaco of Ancona's amateurish drawings brought to Florence from his travels to Cyzicus in 1444, where he saw the winged heads of Medusa in the vicinity of Hadrian's temple (Ashmole 1956: 190).

Examination of Roman Sarcophagi and Gems

The careful examination of ancient art, mostly sculpted panels on Roman sarcophagi and ancient carved gems, allowed Italian Renaissance artists to discover aspects of these mythical creatures that had remained unknown to medieval artists. Among third-century CE Roman sarcophagi featuring sculpted processions of Bacchus and Ariadne, several represent a pair of centaurs being harnessed to the couple's chariot, thereby revealing to Renaissance viewers that unruly monsters could be tamed. One such sarcophagus, located within Santa Maria Maggiore in Rome, became documented in drawings dating from *c*.1420. Yoked together to pull the chariot, two centaurs are playing musical instruments (Bober and Rubinstein 1986: 116–17 no. 83). It is precisely this scene that Botticelli recreated, retaining the centaurs as they appeared on the sarcophagus, in the frescoed frieze in the house of Lorenzo di Pierfrancesco de' Medici, presently known only from Baldini's fine engraving (*c*.1486; Ebert 2016: 114–15).[12]

Bacchic sarcophagi also modified the medieval link of satyrs with goats as symbolic of lust (Kaufmann 1979: 52). One such sarcophagus portrays a satyr unveiling the sleeping Ariadne for Bacchus (Bober and Rubinstein 1986: 115 no. 80). As it stood near the Palazzo Massimo in Rome and was recorded in late fifteenth-century drawings, this section of the sarcophagus took on a life of its own, especially after the scene was represented in the woodcut for the *Hypnerotomachia Poliphili* (Colonna 1999: 73).[13] This woodcut of the satyr, whether lifting the curtain to cast a protective shadow on the sleeping nymph or to unveil her, presented him in a far more restrained manner than was common to his nature (Nygren 2015: 146).

Following Lorenzo the Magnificent's 1471 purchase of the so-called Tazza Farnese (the Farnese Cup; Gasparri 2006: 75),[14] Florentine artists became fascinated with the portrayal of Medusa as both beautiful and sorrowful, not just frozen in horror. This stupendous gemstone bowl, likely carved in the second century BCE, bears the Gorgon's head on its convex underside; thus resembling a shield, the *gorgoneion* evidently conveys the apotropaic significance. They were even more fascinated by Medusa's sorrowful expression on the cuirassed busts of the Antonine emperors, who ruled over the Roman Empire from 96 to 192 CE. The well-preserved bust of Hadrian in the collection of Cosimo I de' Medici inspired Benvenuto Cellini and Baccio Bandinelli to create *c*.1543 the bronze and marble portraits of the Florentine ruler (Romualdi 2007: 2. 191; Forster

---

[12] https://www.britishmuseum.org/collection/object/P_1860-0714-41.
[13] https://www.wga.hu/html_m/b/bordon/satyr.html.
[14] https://www.wikiwand.com/en/Farnese_Cup.

1971).[15] Cellini, adapting the winged *gorgoneion* from Hadrian's to Cosimo's cuirass, elaborated the ruler's features based on Medusa's expression from the Tazza Farnese by emphasizing Cosimo's wrinkled forehead and bulging eyes.[16] Bandinelli repeated the winged *gorgoneia* with one image on each blade of Cosimo's cuirass; however, he left the ruler with a blank visage, analogous to Hadrian's.[17] Henceforth, Cellini and Bandinelli shrewdly employed antique images of Medusa for likening the portrayals of their ruler to that of the Roman emperor not least because both were Hellenophiles, with the *gorgoneia* attesting to these rulers' predilections.

Classical Principles for Lifelike Figures

The principles of classical sculpture that guided the formation of the lifelike figures of men and animals in antiquity also shaped the depiction of classical monsters in the Renaissance, as in the sculpted images of the monstrous Cerberus, the triple-headed guard-dog of Hades. Around 1519, Bandinelli sculpted Orpheus pacifying Cerberus (Cherubini 2014: 125). In this marble statue, set in the courtyard of the Palazzo Medici, the dog sits like the Roman sphinx, with all three heads gazing upwards.[18] Only Gianlorenzo Bernini, a century later, would represent Cerberus in classical fashion, with each of the three heads looking in a different direction, dutifully watching the approaches to Hades' kingdom (Fig. 34.2). This marble group statue of Pluto/Hades abducting Proserpina/Persephone evidently constitutes the conflation of this classical myth, since the abduction occurred above ground, so Cerberus functions as Pluto's attribute.

Renaissance artists did not necessarily depict all mythological subjects *all'antica*, but rather depicted their protagonists as lifelike figures. The classical appearance could have been motivated by the chosen artistic medium. One illustrative example is Argus: familiar from classical poetry, he was a many-eyed cowherd whom Juno ordered to guard Io after the girl's transformation into a heifer. Dante uses the phrase *occhi d'Argo* ('the eyes of Argus') in the sense of seeing everything vividly (*Purgatorio* 29.95). Later commentators, among them Francesco da Buti and Landino, remind their readers that, despite his being one-hundred-eyed per Ovid's description (*Met.* 1.625), Argus was nonetheless beheaded by Mercury (Francesco da Buti 1858–1862: vol. 2. 714; Landino 2001: vol. 3, 1481.76). To commemorate her loyal guard, Juno transferred the many eyes of Argus to the tail of her sacred bird, the peacock.

---

[15] https://commons.wikimedia.org/wiki/File:Bust_of_Hadrian,_117-121_AD,_Type-_Termini,_Galler ia_degli_Uffizi,_Florence_%2819243185430%29.jpg.

[16] https://www.ansa.it/sito/notizie/cultura/arte/2021/05/24/restauri-riscoperti-occhi-argento-cos imo-i-in-busto-cellini_cfd43c66-3c66-406f-bdb3-e8392223f5d1.html.

[17] https://commons.wikimedia.org/wiki/File:Bargello_-_Bandinelli_Cosimo_I.jpg.

[18] https://www.manuelcohen.com/image/I0000Yf_S2KOPOjc.

FIGURE 34.2 Gianlorenzo Bernini, *The Abduction of Proserpina*, 1621–1622. Galleria Borghese, Rome.

Source: Wikimedia / Daderot.

Mercury's decapitation of Argus, though never represented in Roman art, was a popular theme on Greek vases, starting in the mid-sixth century BCE. Its portrayal in the classical mode occurred only once during the Renaissance, on the bronze doors fashioned in 1445 by Filarete (Antonio Averlino) for St Peter's Basilica. The medium, often used in antiquity, provided Filarete with the impetus to represent Argus as an athletic youth, whose head alone is covered with eyes (Freedman 2014/15: 196, 210–13).

Moreover, the scene of Mercury decapitating Argus provided a pagan parallel to the major scene on the bronze doors, the Beheading of St Paul. On the frescoed vault of the Sala dei Santi (The Hall of the Saints, 1494) in the Vatican Palace, Pinturicchio (Bernardino di Betto) depicted Argus garbed as an old man, with multiple eyes visible only on his bare arms and feet (Freedman 2014–2015: 227–8). The medium and location of the painting are not the only means by which it is possible to determine the classical appearance of mythological monsters; often the creatures' size encourages their *all'antica* depiction. Argus, for example, was depicted as a giant in the *c.*1493 fresco by Bramantino (Bartolomeo Suardi) on the entrance wall of the Sala del Tesoro (the Treasure Hall) in Castello Sforzesco in Milan.[19] The artist, familiar with the mythographer Apollodorus' description of Argus in his *Library* (a second-century CE mythographic treatise known in the Renaissance from *c.*1450), depicted Argus as a huge, majestically athletic figure (Freedman 2014–2015: 223–4). Bramantino's *all'antica* rendering reminds the viewers that, even in antiquity, the mighty guard cannot withstand the will of Jupiter, the omnipotent father of all gods and men.

By contrast, the genuinely antique rendition of another giant, the Cyclops Polyphemus, in de' Rossi's Roman collection (Christian 2003: 178–9), and thus accessible to Raphael and his fellow artists, was not necessarily the model adopted by either Sebastiano del Piombo (*c.*1512) in the Villa Farnesina in Rome or Giulio Romano (1526–1528) in the Palazzo del Te in Mantua in their frescoed depictions of Polyphemus' rejection by Galatea (Freedman 2011: 51, 78–9). The antique head of Polyphemus, having a cruel expression, could not have been a fitting model for these frescoes. Unlike his role in the epic *Odyssey*, Polyphemus in pastoral Greek poetry was portrayed as a ridiculous admirer of the unattainable Galatea. Sebastiano followed Theocritus' description of Polyphemus' rough looks in his bucolic poem 'The Cyclops', written in the third century BCE and printed in Venice in 1496.[20] Giulio, meanwhile, imagined Polyphemus as one of the ludicrous giants.[21] In other words, both painters found the then-extant and available Roman head of Polyphemus unfit for depicting him wooing Galatea.

Classical Monsters of the Domus Aurea

The period from 1445 to 1550 gave rise to remarkably diverse depictions of classical monsters. Some of the creatures, mostly female, changed their shapes after the discovery in *c.*1480 of the strange and marvellous paintings in the Domus Aurea, then thought to be part of the Baths of Titus rather than the Palace of Nero (Hammeken and Hansen 2019: 26–9). These curious pictures were labelled 'grotesques' because their location

---

[19] https://commons.wikimedia.org/wiki/File:Bramante_e_bramantino,_Argo,_Sala_del_Tesoro_01.JPG.

[20] https://en.wikipedia.org/wiki/Polyphemus_%28Sebastiano_del_Piombo%29.

[21] https://commons.wikimedia.org/wiki/File:Giulio_romano,_rinaldo_mantovano_e_benedetto_pagni,_camera_di_amore_e_psiche,_1526-28,_polifemo,_galatea_e_aci_01.jpg.

FIGURE 34.3 Pinturicchio (Bernardino di Betto), fragment with grotesques on the vault of the Piccolomini Library, 1502. Cathedral, Siena.

Source: Wikimedia / Sailko. CC BY 3.0.

resembled a cavern or grotto. What struck the artists the most were these monstrous figures with traits of the sphinx, sirens, and harpies all combined into one fantastic creature. These figures from the Domus Aurea influenced the vault decoration of the Piccolomini Library inside the Cathedral of Siena, frescoed by Pinturicchio in 1502 with *grottesche* on the patron's orders (Fig. 34.3; Schulz 1962: 48). When viewed from the front, the pose of these two (ochre-coloured) grotesques with maiden's bosoms, their hairy arms uplifted and turned into dolphin-like shapes, and ape-like legs ending alternately in paws or hoofs, corresponds to that of the Roman/Theban Sphinx (see Demisch 1977: 113, fig. 322), with lion's paws in place of bird's talons. Andrea del Sarto, among other contemporary artists, intentionally blurred the difference between these three creatures when representing the bird-women with lion's paws on the pedestal of the upright Madonna (Cohen 2018).[22] The title given by Vasari to Andrea's painting, *The Madonna of the Harpies*, is misleading because the composite nature of these creatures defies this classification (Caglioti 1995: 32; Shearman 1965: vol. 1. 47–9). As pseudo-sculpted creatures on the pedestal, their significance as evil forces vanquished by the

[22] https://en.wikipedia.org/wiki/Madonna_of_the_Harpies#/media/File:Andrea_del_Sarto_-_Madonna_delle_Arpie_-_Google_Art_Project.jpg.

Virgin was clear to the nuns who were the original viewers of the altarpiece, which in 1517 was located above the high altar of San Francesco dei Macci in Florence.

The combination of female seductiveness and repulsiveness was familiar to the readers of the *Commedia*, who associated the former with an alluring voice, as represented by sirens, and the latter with disgusting odours, as represented by harpies. In *Purgatorio*, Dante the pilgrim describes a dream in which he faces a woman covered in a cloak, whose voice and song bewitch him completely (19.16–31). The woman identifies herself as the *dolce syrena* ('sweet siren'; 19.19) who once fascinated Ulysses (Landino 2001: vol. 3, 1338.17–19). Her charms disappear the moment another woman (her antipode) arises and angrily queries Vergil, Dante's guide, as to this seducer's identity (Lansing 2000: 784). Looking into her eyes but without responding verbally, Vergil, the personification of reason (Landino 2001: vol. 3, 1339.56), grabs the first woman's cloak. This action results in her emitting a stench that wakened the pilgrim. The pilgrim's dream uses two specific mythological monsters to warn about the deceptive charms of a beautiful voice: the sweet-voiced siren is revealed to be a repulsive and malodorous harpy.

Henceforth these bird-women, avian creatures with the face and breasts of a maiden, serve as reminders of and warnings against the pagan world, a world that could insinuate itself again through the seductive beauty of its creations, including mythical female monsters. Bearing this in mind, in 1518 Cardinal Bibbiena commissioned Raphael to decorate a small porch (*loggetta*) adjacent to a dry bath (*stuffetta*) in his private apartments in the Vatican Palace, both constructed in ancient Roman fashion. Their decorations were Raphael's inventions, adapted to his patron's caprices. The prevalent figures were avian creatures with feminine traits in the style of pictures from the Domus Aurea (Hansen 2018: 93, 100, 102; Squire 2013: 456–9).

Individual Approaches

The period of the Renaissance, especially from the last decade of the fifteenth century to the first quarter of the sixteenth century, is distinguished by the artists' individual approaches to their subjects. The artists' novel interpretations complied with the preferences of their patrons as the works were made on commission; however, their patrons' expectations were rarely documented, and the titles by which the works are known today were given two or three centuries later. Painters and sculptors such as Mantegna, Piero di Cosimo, Botticelli, Michelangelo, and Raphael learned from notably excellent examples in antique art and aimed to surpass them. They, and other artists mentioned in this chapter, all stood out among their peers in their willingness to work on secular subjects along with the incomparably larger bulk of commissions which focused on Christian themes; altarpieces or other works placed in a church were far more important and prestigious than any secular work on pagan subjects produced for a domestic milieu, even though the latter could remind viewers of antiquity's glorious past (Freedman 2011: 1–11).

Mantegna, for example, turned frolicking satyrs into images of devils by portraying them with ape-like faces, reminiscent of their simian descriptions in medieval bestiaries. Most importantly, he inserted their otherwise classically shaped figures into work that described the defeat of vice and the defence of virtue, such as the *Virtus Combusta* ('Virtue in Flames' *c.*1500–1505; Kaufmann 1979: 128).[23] By contrast, Florentine painter Piero di Cosimo depicted a kneeling satyr mourning over a fatally wounded nymph (*c.*1495–1500); unlike Mantegna's ape-like satyrs, Piero's more classical figure seems a distant relative of the satyr portrayed unveiling Ariadne (Geronimus 2006: 87).[24] Piero, whom Vasari describes as 'fanciful and extravagant in invention' (1906: vol. 4. 134; 1996: vol. 1. 652), highlights the poignant love story of the centaur couple in *The Fight between the Lapiths and Centaurs* (*c.*1500–1515), as told by Ovid (*Met.* 12.393–428; Nethersole 2018: 162–4).[25]

Similarly, Botticelli demonstrated his own unique approach to classical monsters. Vasari terms the artist a *persona sofistica* ('a man of inquiring mind') when he was immersed in the creation of a visual commentary on the *Commedia* (1906: vol. 3. 317; 1996: vol. 1. 538). When illustrating *Inferno* 9. 52–60, Botticelli depicts the head of Medusa, from whose petrifying gaze Vergil shields his eyes while commanding Dante the pilgrim to do the same. To increase the effect, Botticelli, faithful to Dante's text and mindful of Landino's commentary, represents a demon brandishing the head of Medusa *à la* Perseus (Schulze Altcappenberg 2000: 56–60; Watts 1995: 173–5). Botticelli's inventiveness is also manifest in his *c.*1492 painting *Pallas and the Centaur*, where he casts the centaur as a majestic figure clasping a bow and armed with a quiver of arrows.[26] The identity of this centaur has remained undetermined (Martinez 2019: 156–9). His face is as sorrowful as Medusa's from the Tazza Farnese and he is submissive to Pallas. The painting is likely an allegory; its potential meanings continue to engage modern scholars in debate.

Michelangelo, too, demonstrated a highly individualistic approach. During his stay in Rome in 1497, he sculpted a life-size marble statue of Bacchus, in which he replaced Ampelus—a personification of wine often seen on Bacchic sarcophagi—with a *panisk*, that is, a childlike version of Pan (from the Greek diminutive *Paniskos*), nibbling on some grapes (Fig. 34.4). In the Renaissance, this type of childlike forest creature was called *Satirello* (Freedman 2003a: 131). To be sure, horned satyrs are included in the entourage of Bacchus, but they are adults, not children; and when these are shown as children, they result from nineteenth-century restorations. Most likely, therefore, Michelangelo invented this *Satirello* as well as this Bacchus by depicting him in a state of drunkenness. The idea of a child-satyr could have occurred to Michelangelo during his visit to Padua (*c.*1494) because *Satirelli* in various scenes were associated with Mantegna (Kurz 1959;

---

[23] https://commons.wikimedia.org/wiki/File:Mantegna_-_Allegory_of_the_Fall_of_Ignorant_Humanity_%28Virtus_Combusta%29,_Pp,1.23.jpg.

[24] https://en.wikipedia.org/wiki/The_Death_of_Procris.

[25] https://commons.wikimedia.org/wiki/File:Piero_di_Cosimo_-_Combat_des_Centaures.jpg.

[26] https://www.uffizi.it/opere/minerva-e-il-centauro.

FIGURE 34.4 Michelangelo Buonarroti, *Bacchus*, 1497; detail: *Satirello*. The Museum of the Bargello, Florence.

Sannazaro 1966: 124). Monstrous, inasmuch as it is a formal hybrid, this *panisk* is humorous in its playfulness, whereas the entirely human figure of the pagan god of wine conveys a psychic monstrosity through his unstable posture and even more through his facial expression, which verges on inebriation. Michelangelo's *Bacchus* warns of the dangers of imitating this god too closely by literally adapting the commonly accepted meaning of *mostro*, as was used by Dante in his *Commedia*—which Michelangelo knew well (Vasari 1906: vol. 7. 147; 1996: vol. 2. 650).

CONCLUSION

Italian Renaissance artists restored classical monsters to life. They presented these imaginary creatures in the visual arts in line with the way they had been rendered in classical antiquity; that is, by inserting them into the contexts of their original narratives, occasionally in accordance with the canons established by leading Greek artists. They concomitantly modified the dignified representations of classical monsters to suit the sensibilities of their own times. Additionally, many of the monsters were still alive in their memory, thanks to the commentaries and illustrated versions of Dante's *Commedia*. While representing classical monsters *all'antica*, Italian Renaissance artists fashioned them into cautionary tales on overcoming vice or, more rarely, imitating virtue.

The art of the Italian Renaissance prolonged the life of classical monsters, rescuing them from oblivion. Their new representation became the artistic norm for subsequent artists, who rarely reached back as far as classical antiquity for their inspiration, since all the material they required was easily accessible in the Renaissance. Perhaps the most illustrative example of this process can be seen in Raphael's portrayal of Tritons and Nereids in the *Galatea*, c.1514 in the Villa Farnesina (Fig. 34.5; Freedman 2011: 112–17).[27] In this fresco, Raphael set the precedent for depicting Nereids as fully human maidens frolicking with Tritons, portrayed as athletic mermen with legs shaped into either dolphin tails or the horse hoofs of a hippocamp. To stress the beauty of the sea-nymphs, among whom Galatea is the most beautiful, Raphael visually compared Galatea's thighs to those of one of the Nereids. In 1502, Raphael had viewed a marine-themed sarcophagus in the Siena Cathedral complex (Bober and Rubinstein 1986: 134–5 no. 104); he placed his trust in the physical evidence of such sculpted reliefs, which featured fully human Nereids astride Tritons, rather than in authoritative literary descriptions such as those found in Pliny, who mentions the Nereids as covered with fish scales (*NH* 9.4; Luchs 2010: 188 n. 21). Raphael inventively emphasized the classical shape of the fully human-shaped Nereid known to him from Roman art. Thanks to his depiction of Nereids as companions of Galatea, their monstrosity rests not in their physical characteristics, but in their ability to dwell in the realm of the sea, as opposed to the normal habitat of ordinary humans. Following Raphael, artists and their patrons fell under the charms of his Nereids (Penny 1984: 496).

Classical monsters in their original form, though accessible through Roman art during the Italian Renaissance, might well have fallen into oblivion had the humanists not devoted themselves to a careful study of their images in Greek and Latin texts, along with artists who could produce these images in related paintings and sculptures in ways that conformed to the expectations of classically educated viewers. Whether considered

---

[27] An image of Raphael's *Galatea* accessible in the public domain can be seen here: https://upload.wikimedia.org/wikipedia/commons/2/20/Galatea_Raphael.jpg.

FIGURE 34.5 Marcantonio Raimondi, 1515 print after Raphael's *c*.1514 fresco of Galatea in the Villa Farnesina, Rome.

Source: Metropolitan Museum of Art New York. Public domain.

individually or as a group, and guided always by the available textual and visual sources, each classical monster became integrated into the artistic panorama at precisely the moment when a revival of ancient Greek and Roman heritage was occurring in earnest between 1445 and 1550. The classical monsters of the Renaissance imagination continue to captivate subsequent generations.

SUGGESTED READING

No single study comprehensively discusses the interpretation of all classical monsters by Italian Renaissance humanists and artists. Individual studies on monsters with emphasis on Italian Renaissance art appear in the Works Cited list. The most accessible and seminal ones include Argus, but somewhat obliquely, as the emphasis was on Mercury's deed (Freedman 2014–2015); centaurs (Martinez 2019); mermaids rather than Nereids (Luchs 2010); satyrs (Kaufmann 1979); and the confusion, or rather conflation of Egyptian and Theban sphinxes and harpies (Caglioti 1995). It is advisable to read specific studies about artists which relate to the iconography of their works as listed below. On the ambience in which Italian Renaissance artists could create representations of specifically mythological subjects, see Freedman (2003b and 2011) and Nygren (2015); on the accessibility of particular Greek and Latin texts, see Reynolds and Wilson (1974); and on the perception of antiquities, see Bober and Rubinstein (1986). On Dante's mention of monsters, see individual entries in Lansing (2000) as well as Livanos (2009); on the intellectual background of Italian humanism, see Celenza (2018) and Field (2017); for the history of allegorical readings of classical myths, see Seznec (1953) and Wind (1968). On the discovery of the Domus Aurea and the subsequent transformation of classical monsters into grotesques, see Hammeken and Hansen (2019), Hansen (2018), and especially Squire (2013).

WORKS CITED

Alexander, J. J. 1994. *The Painted Page: Italian Renaissance Book Illumination, 1450–1550.* Munich.

Ashmole, B. 1956. 'Cyriac of Ancona and the Temple of Hadrian at Cyzicus.' *Journal of the Warburg and Courtauld Institutes* 19: 179–91.

Bober, P. P., and R. O. Rubinstein. 1986. *Renaissance Artists and Antique Sculpture: A Handbook of Sources.* London.

Bodon, G. 2017. 'La Sfinge ambigua: Momenti della tradizione di un'immagine dal mondo antico alla cultura figurativa rinascimentale.' *Idola: International Journal of Classical Art History* 14: 165–80.

Caglioti, F. 1993. 'Due "restauratori" per le antichità dei primi Medici: Mino da Fiesole, Andrea del Verrocchio e il "Marsia rosso" degli Uffizi. I.' *Prospettiva* 72: 17–42.

Caglioti, F. 1995. 'Donatello, i Medici e Gentile de' Becchi: Un po' d'ordine intorno alla "Giuditta" (e al "David") di Via Larga. III.' *Prospettiva* 80: 15–58.

Caglioti, F. 2011. Cat. no. 49, in *Renaissance Portraits from Donatello to Bellini,* ed. K. Christiansen and S. Weppelmann, 171–4. New York.

Celenza, C. S. 2018. *The Intellectual World of the Italian Renaissance: Language, Philosophy and the Search for Meaning*. Cambridge.

Cerri, G. 2013. 'Identificazione del "cinquecento diece e cinque": Saggio interpretativo su Dante, *Purg.* XXXIII, 43.' *Dante: Rivista internazionale di studi su Dante Alighieri* 10: 11–43.

Cherubini, A. 2014. 'Baccio Bandinelli e l'*Orfeo* di Palazzo Medici: Una questione di spazio', in *Baccio Bandinelli. Scultore e maestro (1493–1560)*, ed. D. Heikamp and B. Paolozzi Strozzi, 120–7. Florence.

Christian, K. 2003. 'The de' Rossi Collection of Ancient Sculptures, Leo X and Raphael.' *Journal of the Warburg and Courtauld Institutes* 65: 132–200.

Ciseri Montemagno, L. 2007. 'A lezione con i mostri: Benedetto Varchi e "La lezione sulla generazione dei mostri".' *Rinascimento* 47: 301–54.

Cohen, S. 2018. 'Andrea del Sarto's Monsters: The *Madonna of the Harpies* and Human-Animal Hybrids in the Renaissance.' *Apollo* 160/509: 38–44.

Colonna, F. 1999. *Hypnerotomachia Poliphili: The Strife of Love in a Dream*, trans. J. Godwin. London.

Cook, E. 2006. *Enigmas and Riddles in Literature*. Cambridge.

Corsi, G., ed. 1952. *Fazio degli Uberti*: Il Dittamondo *et le rime.*, 2 vols. Bari.

Curley, M. J. 2009. *Physiologus: A Medieval Book of Nature Lore*. Chicago.

Curran, B. A. 2007. *The Egyptian Renaissance: The Afterlife of Ancient Egypt in Early Modern Italy*. Chicago.

Demisch, H. 1977. *Die Sphinx: Geschichte ihrer Darstellung von den Anfängen bis zur Gegenwart*. Stuttgart.

Ebert, S. 2016. *Botticelli, Signorelli, Michelangelo: Zur Kunstpolitik des Lorenzo di Pierfrancesco de' Medici*. Berlin.

Felton, D. 2012. 'Rejecting and Embracing the Monstrous in Ancient Greece and Rome', in *The Ashgate Research Companion to Monsters and the Monstrous*, ed. A. S. Mittman and P. Dendle, 103–31. Farnham.

Field, A. 2017. *The Intellectual Struggle for Florence: Humanists and the Beginnings of the Medici Regime, 1420–1440*. Oxford.

Ford, P. 2006. 'Homer in the French Renaissance.' *Renaissance Quarterly* 59: 1–28.

Forster, K. W. 1971. 'Metaphors of Rule, Political Ideology and History in the Portraits of Cosimo de' Medici.' *Mitteilungen des Kunsthistorischen Institutes in Florenz* 15: 65–104.

Freedman, L. 2003a. 'Michelangelo's Reflections on Bacchus.' *Artibus et Historiae* 24/47: 121–35.

Freedman, L. 2003b. *The Revival of the Olympian Gods in Renaissance Art*. Cambridge.

Freedman, L. 2010. 'Florence in Two Pollaiuolo Paintings.' *Annali della Scuola Normale Superiore di Pisa: Classe di Lettere e Filosofia* 5: 275–96.

Freedman, L. 2011. *Classical Myths in Italian Renaissance Painting*. Cambridge.

Freedman, L. 2014–2015. '*Argicida Mercurius* from Homer to Giraldi and from Greek Vases to Sansovino.' *Memoirs of the American Academy in Rome* 59–60: 181–254.

Gasparri, C. 2006. ' "La scudella nostra di calcidonio": Una tazza per molte corti', in *Le Gemme Farnese: Museo archeologico Nazionale di Napoli*, ed. C. Gasparri, 75–83. Naples.

Geronimus, D. 2006. *Piero di Cosimo: Visions Beautiful and Strange*. New Haven.

Gianandrea, M. 2010. 'Creazioni *à l'antique*: I Vassalletto e il fascino della sfinge egizia nel Medioevo romano.' *Hortus Artium Medievalium* 16: 151–60.

Giannini, C. 1858–1862. *Commento di Francesco da Buti sopra la Divina Comedia di Dante Alighieri*, 3 vols. Pisa.

Gilson, S. A. 2005. *Dante and Renaissance Florence*. Cambridge.

Gilson, S. A. 2018. *Reading Dante in Renaissance Italy: Florence, Venice and the Divine Poet.* Cambridge.

Hammeken, C. A., and M. F. Hansen, 2019. 'Introduction', in *Ornament and Monstrosity in Early Modern Art*, ed. C. A. Hammeken and M. F. Hansen, 13–42. Amsterdam.

Hansen, M. F. 2018. *The Art of Transformation: Grotesques in Sixteenth-Century Italy.* Rome.

Herrmann, J. J., Jr., and A. van den Hoek. 2013. 'The Sphinx: An Egyptian Theological Symbol in Plutarch and Clement of Alexandria', in *The Wisdom of Egypt: Jewish, Early Christian and Gnostic Essays in Honour of Gerard P. Luttikhuizen*, ed. A. Hilhorst and G. H. van Kooten, 285–310. Leiden.

Kaufmann, L. F. 1979. 'The Noble Savage: Satyrs and Satyr Family in Renaissance Art.' PhD dissertation, University of Pennsylvania.

Knabenshue, P. D. 1959. 'Ancient and Mediaeval Elements in Mantegna's *Trial of St. James.*' *Art Bulletin* 41: 59–73.

Kurz, O. 1959. 'Sannazaro and Mantegna', in *Studi in onore di Riccardo Filangieri*, vol. 2, 277–83. Naples.

Landino. C. 2001. *Comento sopra la Comedia*, ed. P. Procaccioli, 4 vols. Rome.

Lansing, R. H., ed. 2000. *The Dante Encyclopedia.* New York.

Lattimore, R., trans. 1951. *The Iliad of Homer.* Chicago.

Livanos, C. 2009. 'Dante's Monsters: Nature and Evil in the *Commedia.*' *Dante Studies* 127: 81–92.

Luchs, A. 2010. *The Mermaids of Venice: Fantastic Sea Creatures in Venetian Renaissance Art.* London.

Martinez, T. 2019. 'The Evolution of the Centaur in Italian Renaissance Art: Monster, Healer, Mentor and Constellation.' PhD dissertation, CUNY.

Meiss, M. 1969. 'The Smiling Pages', in *Illuminated Manuscripts of the Divine Comedy*, ed. P. Brieger et al., 1. 31–80. Princeton.

Mozzati, T. 2007. Cat. no. 1, in *Desiderio da Settignano: Sculptor of Renaissance Florence*, ed. M. Bormand et al., 118–22. Milan.

Nethersole, S. 2018. *Art and Violence in Early Renaissance Florence.* New Haven.

Noelle, A. J. 2019. Cat. no. 6, in *Bertoldo di Giovanni: The Renaissance of Sculpture in Medici Florence*, ed. A. Ng et al., 358–65. New York.

Nygren, C. J. 2015. 'The *Hypnerotomachia Poliphili* and Italian Art circa 1500: Mantegna, Antico and Correggio.' *Word & Image* 31: 140–54.

Penny, N. 1984. 'Raphael in the Sixteenth and Seventeenth Centuries.' *Journal of the Royal Society of Arts* 132/5336: 485–500.

Restoro d'Arezzo. 1997. *La Composizione del mondo*, ed. A. Morino. Parma.

Reynolds, L. D., and N. G. Wilson. 1974. *Scribes and Scholars: A Guide to the Transmission of Greek and Latin Literature*, 2nd edn. Oxford.

Rispoli, T. 2015. 'Imitation and Animality: On the Relationship between Nature and History in Chapter XVIII of *The Prince*', in *The Radical Machiavelli: Politics, Philosophy and Language*, ed. F. Del Lucchese et al., 190–203. Leiden.

Romualdi, A. 2007. 'Ritratto di Adriano', in *Studi e restauri: I marmi antichi della Galleria degli Uffizi*, ed. A. Romualdi, vol. 2, 191–2. Florence.

Sannazaro, J. 1966. *Arcadia and Piscatorial Eclogues*, ed. and trans. R. Nash. Detroit.

Schulz, J. 1962. 'Pinturicchio and the Revival of Antiquity.' *Journal of the Warburg and Courtauld Institutes* 25: 35–55.

Schulze Altcappenberg, H.-T., ed. 2000. *Sandro Botticelli: The Drawings for Dante's Divine Comedy.* London.

Seznec, J. 1953. *The Survival of the Pagan Gods: The Mythological Tradition and Its Place in Renaissance Humanism and Art*, trans. B. F. Sessions. Princeton.

Shearman, J. K. G. 1965. *Andrea del Sarto*, 2 vols. Oxford.

Squire, M. 2013. ' "Fantasies so Varied and Bizarre": The Domus Aurea, the Renaissance and the "Grotesque" ', in *A Companion to the Neronian Age*, ed. E. Buckley and M. T. Dinter, 444–64. Chichester.

Vasari, G. 1906. *Le opere*, ed. G. Milanesi, 9 vols. Florence.

Vasari, G. 1996. *Lives of the Painters, Sculptors and Architects*, trans. G. du C. De Vere, ed. D. Ekserdjian, 2 vols. London.

Véron-Denise, D. 2005. Cat. no. 70, in *Primaticcio: Un Bolognese alla corte di Francia*, ed. D. Cordellier, 217. Milan.

Watts, B. J. 1995. 'Sandro Botticelli's Drawings for Dante's *Inferno*: Narrative Structure, Topography and Manuscript Design.' *Artibus et Historiae* 16/32: 163–201.

Wind, E. 1968. *Pagan Mysteries in the Renaissance: An Explanation of Philosophical and Mystical Sources of Iconography in Renaissance Art*. New York.

Wirth, K.-A. 1981. 'Wege und Abwege der Überlieferungsgeschichte von Gestalten des klassisch-antiken Mythos: das Bild der Harpyie im ausgehenden Mittelalter (und bei Giorgio Vasari).' *Zbornik za likovne umetnosti* 17: 1–76.

CHAPTER 35

CLASSICAL MONSTERS IN LATIN AMERICAN CULTURES

PERSEPHONE BRAHAM

Introduction

THE passage of monsters from classical mythology to Latin America began with Christopher Columbus's account of his encounter with the indigenous peoples of the Caribbean. Racing home to claim his reward for finding a westward route to Asia (he had really only got a third of the way), Columbus wrote in early 1493 to the Catholic Monarchs a letter in which he stated that, while he had personally not encountered any monsters, 'Your Highnesses should know that the first island of the Indies, closest to Spain, is populated entirely by women, without a single man, and their comportment is not feminine, but rather they use weapons and other masculine practices'. These women, he reported, consorted for procreation with the man-eating inhabitants of the second island; nearby islands were populated by people with tails and others with no hair, who possessed gold in 'immeasurable quantities' (Zamora 1993: 196).

What possessed Columbus to make this seemingly offhand remark at the very end of a letter in which he had repeatedly stated that he had not met with any monsters? Possibly he was anticipating audience expectations for a narrative of discovery. By the mid-fifteenth century, Europeans shared a common vocabulary of monsters and monstrous peoples drawn from natural histories and travel accounts. Columbus's island of man-eaters next to an island of warrior women drew on a well-known tradition represented in Marco Polo's description of the Male and Female islands (Book 3, ch. 31) and Mandeville's realm of Feminye on the isle of Amazonia (ch. 17); Marco Polo's version had encapsulated numerous Chinese, European, and Indian legends centred on cities of warrior women (Cordier and Yule 2004: vol. 2 n. 1). Europeans easily recognized the martial women of Matinino (Martinique) as the Amazons of legend; Columbus's coinage *caniba* or cannibal to describe the more warlike Caribe peoples soon replaced the unwieldy 'Anthropophagi'; and cannibals and Amazons became a mainstay of sixteenth-century maps and accounts of conquest and exploration.

Despite growing scepticism about the existence of monsters and magical beings, it was useful to attach monsters to the New World. Monsters in antiquity embodied qualities and appetites precluded by the very concepts of civilization, sociability, and economy, and the job of heroes was to defeat monsters to make way for civilization. Columbus's letter offered a kind of monster schema that informed Iberian engagement with the New World and its peoples for the next century: reports about cannibals, Amazons, and giants provided a badge of authenticity and merit for explorers who were otherwise frustrated in their pursuit of the Fountain of Youth, the golden city-king of El Dorado, or other prodigies, or simply unable to match the grand exploits of Columbus, Hernán Cortés, or Francisco Pizarro.

In addition to Columbus's cannibals and Amazons, this chapter looks at giants, lycanthropes, and sirens traceable through the Iberian Peninsula back to the ancient Mediterranean. Conquest and colonization brought Europeans face to face with diverse indigenous cultures, as well as approximately eleven million enslaved Africans with gods, heroes, and monsters of their own.[1] Today, Latin America comprises nineteen countries in North, Central, and South America and the Caribbean, where Latin-derived languages—Spanish, Portuguese, and French—predominate. Other sizeable linguistic and cultural groups include the Maya (North and Central America), Arawak (Caribbean and Northern South American), Quechua (Andes), Tupi-Guaraní (Brazil/Southern Cone), and Mapuche (Southern Cone). Consequently, modern Latin America has far too many monsters to cover in a single chapter. Classical monsters also have numerous Latin American analogues unconnected to the ancient world: for example, the Aztec goddess Coatlicue, 'she whose skirt is made of snakes', superficially resembles the serpent-girded Scylla. Others like La Llorona, the weeping phantom who seeks the children she herself had murdered, recall the Greek figure of Medea (not a monster, just an angry woman), but the connection is debated.

CANNIBALS

Man-eating tribes of Greek legend included the giant Cyclopes and Laestrygones encountered by Odysseus, and the *Androphagoi*, also called 'Anthropophagi', of whom the fifth-century BCE Greek historian Herodotus wrote:

> The Man-eaters [*Androphagoi*] are the most savage of all men in their way of life; they know no justice and obey no law. They are nomads, wearing a costume like

---

[1] Iberian exploration and conquest occurred roughly between 1492 and 1650. African and indigenous slavery was mostly abolished with independence from Spain (1810-25), but African slavery persisted in Brazil, Cuba, and Puerto Rico until the 1870s and 1880s.

the Scythian, but speaking a language of their own; of all these, they are the only people that eat men [*androphageousi*]. (4.106.1; all Herodotus translations are from Godley 1920)

Everything about the Anthropophagi, from language to diet, was antithetical to human civilization. Even though the Roman naturalist Pliny the Elder (first century CE) deemed the Anthropophagi a 'purely imaginary' race (*NH* 6.195, trans. Bostock and Riley), man-eaters persisted through the ages as shorthand for abject races deserving of enslavement. Early Christians were accused of cannibalism, a libel they turned upon Jews in the Middle Ages, New World indigenes in the sixteenth century, and rebelling slaves in eighteenth-century Saint-Domingue.

The enterprising Italian explorer Amerigo Vespucci (1451–1512) elaborated greatly on Columbus's cannibals, and their ubiquity was affirmed by all the major historians of the period. Isabel of Castile's so-called Cannibal Law of 1503, which exempted non-cannibal peoples from enslavement and despoliation, was amended in 1510 by a papal decree expressly permitting enslavement of cannibals. In this light, it is not surprising that so many indigenous peoples turned out to be 'cannibals'. The meaning and true extent of cannibalism worldwide is hotly debated, but it has undeniably been the bread and butter, so to speak, of ethnographers from 1492 forward.

The first historian of the Americas, Pedro Mártir de Anglería (Peter Martyr d'Anghiera, 1459–1526), related the story of Juan Díaz de Solís, who navigated up the Río de la Plata in 1516 and was reportedly eaten along with several crew members:

> In these parts are found some of those abominable anthropophagi, Caribs, whom I have mentioned before. With fox-like astuteness these Caribs feigned amicable signs, but meanwhile prepared their stomachs for a succulent repast; and from their first glimpse of the strangers their mouths watered like tavern trenchermen. The unfortunate Solis landed with as many of his companions as he could crowd into the largest of the barques, and was treacherously set upon by a multitude of natives who killed him and his men with clubs in the presence of the remainder of his crew. Not a soul escaped; and after having killed and cut them in pieces on the shore, the natives prepared to eat them in full view of the Spaniards, who from their ships witnessed this horrible sight. (1912: 401–2)

Anglería claimed that his information came via correspondence, but the Dominican friar Bartolomé de las Casas questioned the story's veracity (Toribio Medina 1897: 210). In any case, mid-sixteenth-century first-person accounts by Hans Staden, a captive of the Tupinamba, and others cemented the image of South American indigenes as cannibals. Cannibalism permeated European descriptions of indigenous social and religious practice, sometimes as an offhand attestation of other barbarities such as sodomy and polyamory. Gonzalo Fernández de Oviedo (1478–1557) asserted that the indigenes copulated 'like vipers'—that is, they practised sodomy—and compared them to man-eating Scythians, saying that it was 'as common to eat human flesh, as it [was] in France and Italy to eat sheep and

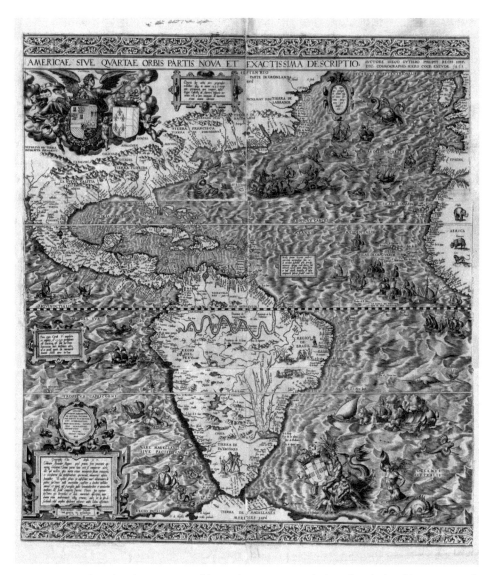

FIGURE 35.1 *America sive quartae orbis partis nova et exactissima description* [Antwerp: s.n.], 1562. D. Gutiérrez, H. Cock, and J. Lessing. Rosenwald Collection.

cows' (1851: 133, 138). Anthropophagi, giants, and Amazons appeared in illustrated voyages and natural histories by engravers such as Theodor de Bry, and on maps such as Diego Gutiérrez's 1562 map of the Americas (Fig. 35.1). Gutiérrez's map portrays Philip II as Poseidon, and identifies the territory of the Amazons, a cannibal encampment, and the Land of the Patagoni, among other details.

MODERN-DAY CANNIBALS

The best-known cannibal figure of modern culture is the fat-stealing Andean *pishtaco* and its analogues *ñakaq*, *lik'ichiri*, and Bolivian *kharisiri*. These monsters are almost universally grouped with proto-vampires and succubae such as the *lamiae*, but typology, iconography, and etymology point to the cannibal. For one thing, the *lamiae* and similar ancient Greek *daimones* manifested as female, with a serpent's tail or other irregularities below the waist (see Kucharski in this volume), and their seductiveness aligns them with the medieval fishtailed siren, who usually targeted young men. In contrast, New World cannibals were both men and women, always represented in the act of butchery, and modern fat-stealers manifest as male, white, or mestizo, and as affiliated with modern technology. Andean names for the fat-stealers—the Quechua *pishtaku* from *pishtay* 'to cut into pieces; to slaughter'; *ñakaq* 'to butcher'; *lik'ichiri* 'fat remover'; and Aymara *kharasiri* 'to cut with a knife or razor'—all denote butchery, and popular art represents the *pishtaco* in the act of rendering butchered victims' fat.

Fat-stealers do not have a direct analogue in classical mythology, where fat is rarely mentioned except when describing cattle. However, Andean rumours about fat-stealing priests began with the arrival of Europeans and were first documented in fray Cristóbal de Molina's *Account of the Fables and Rites of the Incas* (1575) in connection with coercive evangelization. The *pishtaco* would have also syncretized with the Spanish *sacamanteca* ('fat-taker'), a bogey invoked to enforce good behaviour in children. Fat is sacred to Andean cultures, and is associated with a person's spirit or essence, or the souls coveted by evangelizing priests. These were notorious for gluttony and covetousness, as we know from Guamán Poma de Ayala's *Nueva Corónica y Buen Gobierno* (1615), a history of the Inca and manual for good government addressed to Spanish king Philip III. Part of Guamán Poma's purpose in the *Buen Gobierno* was to curb the excesses of 'the psychopath Father Juan Bautista de Albadán' (Ouweneel 2017: 116), a notorious torturer whose behaviour alone seems sufficient to support rumours of priests rendering indigenous bodies for their fat. In the colonial period, the stolen fat was used variously as holy oil or to grease church bells; the *kharisiri* traditionally appeared as a Franciscan monk (Crandon-Malamud 1991: 120).

Modern fat-stealers are believed to sell the fat to lubricate sugar mills and jet engines (Scheper-Hughes 1993: 236); to make luxury cosmetics and bath soaps; or worst of all, to pay off the external debt to international banks. Tales of *pishtacos* and *kharasiris* multiply around US-affiliated development projects and in the context of Peru's long civil conflict (1980–2000), as portrayed in Mario Vargas Llosa's *Death in the Andes* (1993). In November 2009, a '*pishtaco*' scandal in the Peruvian press was used to cover up the disappearance of sixty people in the region of Huánuco (Whalen 2009). There is no better metaphor than cannibalism for extractivist systems like mining, which converts enslaved bodies to silver or copper. The Bolivian Cerro Rico de Potosí, a silver mine in operation since 1547, is popularly known as the 'the mountain that eats men' (Forero 2012).

Giants: Patagoni and Mapinguarí

The humanoid Giants of Greek myth were lawless, insolent bullies given to banditry and rock-throwing. They scorned the divinely embodied principles of hearth, hospitality, and husbandry. In contrast to Greek art and technology, giants exhibited only brute force and animal cunning. Ferdinand Magellan (1480–1521) named the giants located in South America 'Patagoni' after a fictional character in the bestselling 1512 chivalric novel *Primaleón*, about a Greek prince who, during his many adventures, vanquishes a dog-faced monster called the Grand Patagon. Antonio Pigafetta, who accompanied Magellan on his famous voyage around South America (1519–1522), reported the encounter:

> [W]e saw a giant, who was on the shore of the sea, quite naked, and was dancing and leaping, and singing, and whilst singing he put the sand and dust on his head.... He was so tall that the tallest of us only came up to his waist; however he was well built. He had a large face, painted red all round, and his eyes also were painted yellow around them, and he had two hearts painted on his cheeks; he had but little hair on his head, and it was painted white. (1874: 50)

In contrast to the giants of Greek myth, the Patagoni were given to dancing. They were gracious and hospitable until Magellan's crew tried to kidnap them, whereupon they cried out for their 'devil' Setebos (the god worshipped by Caliban in Shakespeare's *The Tempest*). Their most notable custom was putting an arrow down their throat to cure a stomachache. Sir Francis Drake later opined that the Spanish had exaggerated their height, and that Magellan's cruelty had turned them monstrous and inhospitable (1628: 28).

Jesuit scholar and naturalist José de Acosta (1540–1600) connected the Patagoni to classical giants, speculating that, given the Canary Islands' proximity to South America, it was likely they were of European origin, as were their unnatural vices:

> It seemes therefore likely to me that, in times past, men came to the Indies against their wills, driven by the furie of the winds. In Peru, they make great mention of certaine Giants, which have been in those parts, whose bones are yet seene at

Manta and Puerto Viejo, of a huge greatnes, and by their proportion they should be thrice as big as the Indians.... They say moreover, that these men committing abominable sinnes, especially against nature, were consumed by fire from heaven. (1880: 56)

The 'sinnes' of the Patagoni are suggested in the image at the bottom of the South American continent in Fig. 35.1, Tierra de Patagones, which seems to show two giants embracing.

In 1914, Amazon explorer Colonel Percy Harrison Fawcett reported an encounter with giant hairy bipeds similar to the Patagoni:

It seemed to me they were large, hairy men, with exceptionally long arms, and with foreheads sloping back from pronounced eye ridges—men of a very primitive kind, in fact, and stark naked. . . . I whistled, and an enormous creature, hairy as a dog, leapt to his feet in the nearest shelter, fitted an arrow to his bow in a flash, and came up dancing from one leg to the other till he was only four yards away. Emitting grunts that sounded like 'Eugh! Eugh! Eugh!' he remained there dancing, and suddenly the whole forest around us was alive with these hideous ape-men, all grunting 'Eugh! Eugh! Eugh!' and dancing from leg to leg in the same way as they strung arrows to their bows. (2010: 201–2)

Fawcett's descriptions repeat the 'dancing and leaping' reported by Pigafetta, embellished with the scientific racism of the modern era. Fawcett may also have drawn on local tales of the Amazonian Mapinguarí. The best-known modern-day giant in Latin America, the Mapinguarí is a large, hairy humanoid sometimes represented with one eye in his forehead like Polyphemus, but more frequently with a mouth in his stomach like the Acephaloi—'headless men'—described by Herodotus as having eyes in their chests (4.191.4), later called 'Blemmyae' by Pliny the Elder (*NH* 7. 23) and others. The Mapinguarí sometimes appears with backwards feet, in common with the Brazilian Curupira, Dominican Ciguapa, and Colombian Patasola. Like Homer's Cyclopes and Laestrygones, the Mapinguarí occasionally eats human beings. Some believe the Mapinguarí is a cryptid based on the giant ground sloth (see *Baltimore Sun* 1995), which is now extinct; various species of *Megatherium* were widespread in South America in prehistoric times, and 'would have been observed alive by Ice Age humans' (Mayor 2005: 357).

Scholars have traced aspects of the Mapinguarí to both Portuguese and African traditions (Câmara Cascudo 2012). His emergence coincided with the beginnings of rubber exploitation at the turn of the twentieth century, when large numbers of workers of European and African descent migrated from northeastern Brazil to the Amazon, bringing oral traditions that readily syncretized with the local ones (Vegini et al. 2014). The Mapinguarí is irredeemably evil and 'always, unfailingly, obstinately kills whoever he finds' (Câmara Cascudo 2012: 207). He roars and yells as he hunts, and 'when he catches a hunter, he puts him under his big powerful arm, dips his head into the immense opening of his mouth [in his belly] and chews, that is, he eats it little by little, chewing it slowly, grinding' (209). In support of Church strictures, the Mapinguarí hunts on Sundays and feast days, as a disincentive to Christians inclined to do the same. In common with the Nemean Lion, Achilles, Talus the automaton, and a few other figures of Greek myth, the Mapinguarí is almost invulnerable to weapons.

AMAZONS

The Amazons were not monsters, but a real people whose behaviour was such a monstrous affront to the values of ancient Greek civilization that they attained mythical status, interacting with heroes of Greek legend as well as historical figures like Alexander the Great. Amazons reportedly inhabited a range of territories from the Black Sea to Northern Africa, including Scythia, at the outermost frontier of Greek civilization (today Ukraine). Scythia was a wasteland of wild beasts and monstrous races, but its kings were rumoured to have hoards of gold, guarded by griffins (Hdt. 4.7).

The active, autonomous Amazon women represented a monstrous inversion of the homosocial principles of ancient Greek civilization. Variously depicted as celibate or sexually aggressive, the matriarchal Amazons defied the economics of patriarchy by treating men as sperm donors, sexual slaves, and household drudges, and flouted patrilineage by killing or exiling their sons. On the battlefield, they penetrated their opponents with arrows, spears, and their patented double-headed axes. Homer called the Amazons 'peers of men' in war (*antianeiras*, *Il.* 6.186), and Herodotus notes that the Scythians named them 'killers of men' (*androktonoi*, Hdt. 4.110). The great mythological heroes Heracles, Theseus, Achilles, Jason, and Bellerophon all had defining encounters with the Amazons, as did Alexander the Great, according to the *Alexander Romance*. Ancient Amazons were generally represented as wise and fair rulers, builders of cities— a hallmark of civilization—and gallant opponents in battle. For Christian Iberian historians such as Paulus Orosius, Amazons were monstrous because they transgressed territorial and matrimonial boundaries, challenging man's sovereignty over all Creation.

Spanish *novelas de caballería* or chivalric novels fuelled Amazon fever among Spanish explorers throughout the sixteenth century. Garci Rodríguez de Montalvo's *Exploits of Esplandián* (before 1510) introduced the redoubtable Queen Calafia of California, a mythical realm of black warrior women who fed their pet griffins on men and boys:

> [D]ue east of the Indies there is an island called California, very near to the locale called the Terrestrial Paradise. It was populated by black women, with no men among them, for they lived in the fashion of Amazons. They possessed strong and firm bodies of ardent courage and great strength.... Being themselves quite a match for the griffins, the island women fed them with men they had taken as prisoners and with male children to whom they had given birth.... Every man who landed on the shores of the island was immediately devoured by these creatures. (Sukut and Kihyer 2007: 17–19)

In a great battle in Constantinople,[2] the ambitious Calafia and her warriors fought alongside the pagan horde, their griffins devouring the unhappy Christians. (Unfortunately, the griffins soon started eating the pagan men too.) Queen Calafia fell in love with the hero Esplandián, but he was repulsed by her paganism and manly behaviour. Eventually Calafia and her warriors married Christian knights and returned with them to California.

The New World Amazons encountered by actual conquistadors were tall and light-skinned. As generals, they were ruthless. Like the ancient Scythians and Amazons, they were expert archers; in contrast, the Spaniards, like the Greeks, eschewed archery, favouring steel swords, lances, and occasionally the spectacular but ineffectual harquebus (an early type of gun). The infamous Nuño Beltrán de Guzmán, who oversaw the pacification of Western Mexico, wrote in 1530 of the Amazons—whom he did not meet—that 'they are rich, and accounted of the people for Goddesses, and whiter than other women. They use Bowes, Arrowes and Targets: [and] have many and great Townes' (Purchas 1905). Apparently, like the Scythians and Amazons of antiquity, the New World Amazons possessed quantities of gold.

In 1540, Gonzalo Pizarro (Francisco's even more unpleasant younger brother) initiated a search for El Canela, or the Land of Cinnamon, but turned back, leaving the glory of the Amazon exploration to Francisco de Orellana (1511–1546). Gaspar de Carvajal (c.1500–1584), who documented Orellana's two-year expedition, wrote admiringly of the Amazons' strength and bravery—and their nakedness, which obsessed Europeans:

> These women are very white and tall, and have very long hair which they wear braided and wrapped around their head, and they are very strong and go naked except for their private parts, which are covered. With their bows and arrows in their hands they fight like ten Indians, and there was one among them who sent an arrow into one of the brigantines a handspan deep, and others less, so our boats looked like porcupines. (De Onís 1948: 15)

The Amazons of antiquity were usually happy to exploit a passing hero as breeding stock (as with Heracles and Alexander), and generally sent any resulting sons to be raised by their fathers (Mayor 2014: 157). According to Carvajal, however, New World Amazons were sexual predators and, perhaps inspired by Queen Calafia and her ilk, baby-killers (see De Onís 1948: 18). Tirso de Molina's outrageously sycophantic drama *Amazonas en las Indias* (1635), meanwhile, corrected Gonzalo Pizarro's historic miscalculation: on their way to finding the cinnamon, Gonzalo and Carvajal defeat Amazon sisters Queen Menalipe and sorceress Martesia in battle. The sisters instantly fall in love with them and

---

[2] The 'Terrestrial Paradise' or Garden of Eden was traditionally located in Mesopotamia (in reach of Constantinople), but Columbus identified it with Venezuela, which he believed was Asia. Thus Montalvo's 'California' is simultaneously due east of the 'Indies' (the Caribbean) and near the biblical Garden of Eden. Modern-day California is named after the mythical realm.

for the rest of the play try unsuccessfully to preserve Gonzalo from his enemies' political manoeuvres. The play ends with Gonzalo's heroic death for refusing to betray the Spanish crown, and the Amazons vow vengeance against future interlopers.

By the mid-sixteenth century, America was universally allegorized as both Amazon and cannibal, with a bow and arrow, sometimes a missing breast (taking the Greek *a-mazon*, 'lacking a breast' literally), a decapitated male head, and either a lizard or parrot (Fig. 35.2). The Amazon-cannibal allowed Europeans to conceptualize and enforce boundaries between civilization and barbarism, and presented a heroic framework for the conquest of a New World. For example, Cesare Ripa's 1618 personification of the New World depicts America with a bow and quiver because 'The Arms are what both Men and Women use there'; she is naked 'because the Inhabitants are all so'; the decapitated head at her feet 'shews that they are *Cannibals*'; and the lizard shows that 'they are so big here, that they *devour* Men' (Ripa 1709: 53). Sadly, despite rumours of Amazons into the early nineteenth century (Humboldt 1995: 240–1), the gallant warrior women did not survive into the modern era.

FIGURE 35.2   Amazon; Cesare Ripa, *Nova Iconologia*, 1618., p. 353.

Source: Duke University Libraries, Emblem Books. https://archive.org/details/novaiconologia18ripa/page/353/mode/1up?q=amazona

LYCANTHROPES

The impious King Lycaon of Arcadia from Greek myth is the probable ancestor of the New World werewolf, known variously as Lugaru or Je-rouge (French Caribbean), Luisón or Lobizón (Southern Cone), Lobisomem (Brazil), and Galipote (Dominican Republic). While many indigenous traditions include zoanthropy (the belief that people can transform into animals), there are no wolves native to Central or South America or the Caribbean, ruling out purely indigenous origins.

Herodotus stated sceptically that the Neuri, a tribe forced from their lands by serpents, transformed into wolves for a few days once each year (4.105). Early Christians associated the werewolf with the Devil (Blécourt 2015: 2); werewolves were persecuted alongside/as witches in medieval Europe, and werewolf scares were common from the fifteenth to the eighteenth century, allowing for transmission to the Americas. Large numbers of Portuguese settlers in Brazil came from a northern province near Galicia (Vegini et al. 2014: 33), a region with a strong werewolf tradition—in nineteenth-century Galicia, for example, infamous serial killer Manuel Blanco Romasanta successfully escaped the death penalty by claiming to be a *lobishome* (Sadurni 2020).

Among the Guaraní of Paraguay, Luisón is the seventh son of Tau (a spirit of Evil) and the beautiful Guaraní maiden Kerana, who were cursed to bear seven monstrous sons. Luisón transforms on Tuesdays and Fridays, dining on fresh human cadavers that he digs up in cemeteries at night. At the full moon he seeks live victims to convert them into *luisones*. The only way to kill him is with a silver bullet blessed seven times in seven different churches. Luisón is particularly insidious, since his true character is usually hidden, and he has the power to infect others with his monstrosity. If a woman bears only sons, the seventh will be a *luisón*. Luisón is white-skinned, with flowing black hair and fangs, and, though humanoid, walks on all fours. He is the manifestation of death among the Guarani.

In Argentina, Law 20.843 (1974) stipulates that the president must become the godparent of any seventh son, supposedly to prevent the curse from taking effect (Nuwer 2014). The Argentinian version of this monster (the *lobizón*) is popularly supposed to have arrived with Russian immigrants in the early twentieth century, but less xenophobic authorities say the *lobizón* far predates the law (CBS News 2014). Perhaps in tribute to the monster's toxic masculinity, there is a line of grooming products for men called Lobizón.

In eighteenth-century Portuguese Amazonia, the Inquisition tried José Cavalcante on charges of drunkenness, neglect of duty, and being a werewolf (*lobisomem*; Harris 2013: 92). The Brazilian Lobisomem derives from the Portuguese version, who had a truly hard lot, as 'every Tuesday and Friday, from midnight to two o'clock, [he] has to make his run visiting seven churchyards (cemeteries), seven walled towns, seven turns around the world, seven hills, seven crossroads, before returning to the same sinkhole where he regains his human form' (Câmara Cascudo 2012: 159, my trans.).

Every Brazilian town and settlement has a werewolf tradition. Whereas southern Lobishomems are men who have committed incest, northern Lobishomems are people suffering from parasites, anaemia, or malaria, who transform at night to hunt for blood to stem their illness.

The cryptid Chupacabras (also Chupacabra; 'Goat-sucker'), a hairless, dog-like creature first encountered in Puerto Rico in 1995, is a possible variation on the *lobizón*. The Puerto Rican version is a biped, but the Southwest US version is more coyote-like and goes on all fours. Sadly, the Chupacabras is being retroactively inserted into the ethnographic 'lore' of the Spanish conquest. Pentecostals use the Chupacabras as a symbol for Satan (Radford 2016).

SIRENS

Serpent entities in various roles are common throughout Latin America, though not necessarily derived from classical sources. Yakumama (Amazon), Ampalagua (Chile), and Mayuy-Mama (Argentina) are primordial Water Mothers embodied as giant serpents, or even the Amazon itself. Serpents are central in Yoruba, Edo, Dahomey, Igbo, and other West African traditions as well, and common in the iconography of sea-goddesses Yemayá, La Sirène, Mami Wata, and other Afro-Latin American deities. The Andean *sirena* and Amazonian Yara are syncretic sirens that combine European, African, and indigenous elements.

As Jorge Luis Borges observed, sirens defy classification: 'No less debatable is their nature. In his classical dictionary Lempriére calls them nymphs; in Quicherat's they are monsters, and in Grimal's they are demons' (1969: 206). The *Odyssey*'s Sirens (whose physical attributes were not specified) promised him knowledge of 'all things that come to pass on the fruitful earth' (12.191, trans. Murray 1995), but, following Circe's advice, Odysseus eluded their clutches. After the biblical Eve's misadventure with the serpent, medieval sirens acquired attributes of seductive woman-snake hybrids such as the *lamiae*, offering carnal knowledge in lieu of metaphysical enlightenment, while Christians mapped Odysseus' perilous voyage onto the spiritual passage through trial and temptation (Jones and Sprunger 2002: 107). The Spanish *sirena* appeared in poems and popular romances, including a well-known legend of a Galician (or Catalan) family descended from one. By the fifteenth century, the *sirena* of Iberian lore was 'a confusion between Oceanids and sirens. The body of the first with the voice of the second' (Câmara Cascudo 2012: 135).

By the sixteenth century, the *sirena* was no longer considered a monster, as we see in two miscellanies. Pedro Mexía's *Silva de varia lección* (1540), reflects scepticism about the siren's nature and provenance:

> I know perfectly well that rational man does not live anywhere but on the land, and that they do not inhabit the water, nor live in it, but even so, according to what I have

read, there are some fishes, that have the shape and size of men, and among them are males and females, and the female has the same shape as a woman, and they (male) are called Tritons, and they (females) are called Nereids. (1673: 61, my trans.)

His co-miscellanist Antonio de Torquemada (1507–1569) described sirens as *pescados* or fishes, rather ungenerously distancing himself from Mexía:

> To tell the truth, I haven't seen written by any serious author anything about these sirens, only Pero Mejía says that … one was seen that came out in a net among other fishes that were taken, and it showed such sadness in its face that it moved the fishermen who saw it to compassion, and, moving it, they turned it around in such a manner that it could return to the water, and it submerged itself, and they never saw it again. And even if this type of fish should be in the sea, I take for superstition the thing about their song, and everything else they say about them. (2012: 671, my trans.)

Indeed, the public were not regaled with tales of dangerous, immoral New World sirens as they were with those of cannibals and Amazons. The mermaids and Tritons of contemporary illustrations were rhetorical, not ethnographic, intended to signify the grandeur of the New World endeavour as equal to those of Odysseus, Heracles, and Alexander.

Like Western mermaids, Latin American *sirenas* are connected to powerful natural forces. Some have fishtails, and some have golden hair. They sometimes have difficult relations with fishermen and may fall in love with them. Many carry conches, and some have supernatural musical powers. However, it is not at all clear that the erotic or moral valences of the European siren—as a symbol of forbidden knowledge and sexual enchantment—were ever absorbed into Latin American popular traditions. Only a few, including the Andean *sirena* and Amazonian Yara, embody the dangers associated with the medieval siren.

Art historians have documented a *sirena* tradition in Andean church art and textiles from the sixteenth to the eighteenth centuries (Gutiérrez de Ángelis 2010: 70). These images probably arrived via moral emblem books, which attached classically derived figures to Christian values (Callahan and Cuttler 1985: 244). Colonial depictions of the Virgin with mermaids would have been seen by the Church as representing her triumph over sin, with *sirenas* in the place of a serpent or dragon. European mermaids became the syncretic face of Andean water spirits also known as *sirenas*, from whom young musicians would seek power for their instruments. Like the medieval sirens' song, the enchanted music could lead to lovesickness, madness, or drowning (Stobart 2006). The *sirena* in southern Peruvian tradition is exclusively associated with stringed instruments, specifically the *charango*, unknown in the region before the Spanish arrived. Modern artists in Chiloé (Chile) have claimed the *sirena* and related figures, the *pincoya* and *sumpall*, as 'symbolic guardian[s] of Chilote culture and environment', using their images to protest the depredations of the salmon fishing industry (Hayward

2011: 91). Indigenous Peruvian artisans have also claimed the *sirena* as part of their economy, selling *retablos* (altarpieces) of musical mermaids to an international market.

Despite numerous water-entities in indigenous Brazilian cultures, there was no pre-Columbian indigenous spirit with the seductiveness, beautiful voice, and fishtail of the mermaid. The Portuguese, brilliant navigators, versed in 'maritime legends, of tritons, mermaids and fabulous animals' brought with them the traditions of the mermaid and the Moura Encantada, a mythical fairy woman with long golden tresses (or black, or red in Galicia) who seduced men with her singing and promises of gold (Câmara Cascudo 2012: 133, 137). The Moura tradition is believed to be of Celtic (not Roman) origin, but it is syncretized with elements of the *lamiae*. The mermaid and Moura traditions syncretized with the indigenous Ipupiara, enemy of fishermen, and the various Mães-d'Água or water mothers to create the Yara. Numerous sixteenth- and seventeenth-century priests recorded cases of 'fish-men and fish-women', marine spirits who would emerge from the depths to seize and drown unwary villagers (139).

According to Tupi/Guaraní legend, Yara was the daughter of an indigenous chief. She was both beautiful and a brave, skilled warrior. Her brothers, resenting their father's praise of Yara, plotted to kill her. However, she discovered the plan and killed the brothers first. She fled into the jungle but was captured and thrown into the Solimões river to drown. The fish rescued her, and she became a beautiful mermaid. Another version says that her brothers managed to kill her and then threw her body into the river, where the moon goddess Jaci transformed her. Yara is often portrayed with white skin, blond hair, and green or blue eyes, betraying her European ancestry. She seduces fishermen and drowns them. Those who escape face a life of madness.

Today, Yara is sometimes syncretized with the Afro-Brazilian water deity Yemayá (also Iemanjá or Yemoja), who is a powerful, positive popular-culture figure for girls and young women. Yara appears in video games, television, and film, as 'A pequena Yara' modelled after Disney's *The Little Mermaid*. A happier adaptation is Yara Flor, DC Comics' latest Wonder Girl. The daughter of an Amazon and a Brazilian river god, Yara is unaware of her heritage, but destined to become reacquainted with the Olympians and the Amazon queen Hippolyta in a journey to Brazil.

Conclusion

In order to project the Iberian adventure as a civilizing mission, conquerors and their historians attached to New World peoples behaviours that the Greeks associated with monsters and barbarous races: cannibalism, rejection of patriarchy, nakedness, rusticity, and lack of language. This is not surprising, as the colonization of the Americas coincided with a resurgence of interest in classical myth in fifteenth- and sixteenth-century Spain. Spanish monarchs traced their lineage to Heracles, who was credited with liberating the Iberians from the three-bodied giant Geryon and civilizing the Peninsula. Heracles had also defeated Gaea's Gigantes and the Amazons (his ninth labour), and his monster-slaying provided evangelizing clergy with endless metaphors for vanquishing the Devil. After the first centuries of contact, European traditions and iconography were absorbed and repurposed in indigenous traditions, sometimes providing monsters with European faces. Sixteenth-century engravings of cannibal cookouts inspire modern-day *pishtaco* rendering scenes; medieval sirens became blond-haired Amazonian mermaids; and werewolves became the face of white interlopers, blood-borne illness, incest, and other threats to community. These monsters reveal the ongoing, multidirectional syncretism of European, African, and Amerindian cultural beliefs.

Suggested Reading

Greenblatt (1991) is an excellent analysis of the discourses of the marvellous, the providential, and the monstrous in early accounts of the New World. Mayor (2014) is the most comprehensive source on the history, iconography, and myth of the Amazons. On the extent and uses of cannibalism in both the Early Modern and New World, see Hulme et. al. (1998). See Braham (2012) on the development of the Amazon/cannibal woman in Vespucci and contemporary visual representations. On Afro-Caribbean and Afro-Brazilian sirens, see Braham (2018). Galeano (2009) is accessible and comprehensive.

Works Cited

Acosta, J. de. 1880. *The Natural & Moral History of the Indies*. London. http://archive.org/deta ils/naturalmoralhisto1acos. Accessed 30 May 2022.

Anghiera, P. M. d'. 1912. *De orbe novo, the Eight Decades of Peter Martyr d'Anghera*. New York. http://archive.org/details/deorbenovoeightdo1angh. Accessed 30 May 2022.

Baltimore Sun. 1995. 'Amazon's Mapinguarí More than Myth?' 13 January. https://www.balti moresun.com/news/bs-xpm-1995-01-13-1995013206-story.html. Accessed 30 May 2022.

Blécourt, W. de, ed. 2015. *Werewolf Histories*. New York.

Borges, J. L. 1969. *The Book of Imaginary Beings*. New York.

Bostock, J., and H. T. Riley, trans. 1855. *The Natural History of Pliny*. London. https://www. gutenberg.org/files/57493/57493-h/57493-h.htm. Accessed 30 May 2022.

Braham, P. 2012. 'The Monstrous Caribbean', in *The Ashgate Research Companion to Monsters and the Monstrous*, ed. A. S. Mittman and P. J. Dendle, 17–47. Farnham.

Braham, P. 2018. 'Song of the Sirenas: Mermaids in Latin America', in *Scaled for Success: The Internationalisation of the Mermaid*, ed. P. Hayward, 149–70. Bloomington, IN.

Callahan, V. W., and S. Cuttler. 1985. *The French, German, Italian, and Spanish Emblems: Facsimiles and Translations*. Toronto.

Câmara Cascudo, L. da. 2012. *Geografia dos Mitos Brasileiros*, https://ia903401.us.archive. org/7/items/livrainosdomal2020/%20Lu%C3%ADs%20da%20C%C3%A2mara%20Casc udo%20-%20Geografia%20dos%20Mitos%20Brasileiros.pdf. Accessed 30 May 2022.

CBS News. 2014. 'The Story of the Argentinean President, Werewolves and Seventh Sons', 29 December. https://www.cbsnews.com/news/did-argentinas-president-adopt-jewish-godson-so-he-doesnt-become-a-werewolf/. Accessed 30 May 2022.

Cordier, H., ed., and H. Yule, trans. 2004. *The Travels of Marco Polo*, vol. 3. Project Gutenberg. https://www.gutenberg.org/files/12410/12410-h/12410-h.htm#Page_405. Accessed 30 May 2022.

Crandon-Malamud, L. 1991. *From the Fat of Our Souls: Social Change, Political Process, and Medical Pluralism in Bolivia*. Berkeley and Los Angeles.

De Onís, H. 1948. *The Golden Land: An Anthology of Latin American Folklore in Literature*. New York.

Drake, F. S. 1628. *The World Encompassed*. London.

Fawcett, P. H. 2010. *Exploration Fawcett*. New York. http://archive.org/details/explorationfawc e000over. Accessed 30 May 2022.

Fernández de Oviedo, G. 1851. *Historia general y natural de las Indias Islas y Tierra-Firme del Mar Oceáno*. Madrid. http://archive.org/details/raha_103011. Accessed 30 May 2022.

Forero, J. 2012. 'Bolivia's Cerro Rico: The Mountain That Eats Men.' *NPR*. 25 September. https://www.npr.org/2012/09/25/161752820/bolivias-cerro-rico-the-mountain-that-eats-men. Accessed 30 May 2022.

Galeano, J. C. 2009. *Folktales of the Amazon*, trans. R. Morgan and K. Watson. London.

Godley, A. D., trans. 1920. *Herodotus: Histories*. Cambridge, MA.

Greenblatt, S. 1991. *Marvellous Possessions*. Chicago.

Guamán Poma de Ayala, F. 1978 [1615]. *Letter to a King: A Peruvian Chief's Account of Life Under the Incas and Under Spanish Rule*, trans. C. W. Dilke. New York. http://archive.org/details/let tertokingperuooguam. Accessed 30 May 2022.

Gutiérrez de Ángelis, M. 2010. 'Idolatrías, extirpaciones y resistencias en la imaginería religiosa de los Andes, Siglos XVII y XVIII.' *Andes* 21: 61–94.

Harris, M. 2013. 'The Werewolf in between Indians and Whites: Imaginative Frontiers and Mobile Identities in Eighteenth Century Amazonia.' *Tipití* 11/1: 87–103.

Hayward, P. 2011. 'Salmon Aquaculture, Cuisine and Cultural Disruption in Chiloé.' *Locale* 1: 87–110.

Hulme, P., F. Barker, and M. Iversen. 1998. *Cannibalism and the Colonial World*. Cambridge.

Humboldt, A. von. 1995. *Personal Narrative*. New York.

Jones, T. S., and D. A. Sprunger. 2002. *Marvels, Monsters, and Miracles: Studies in the Medieval and Early Modern Imaginations*. Kalamazoo, MI.

Mandeville, J. 2014. *The Travels of Sir John Mandeville*. Project Gutenberg. https://www.gutenb erg.org/files/782/782-h/782-h.htm. Accessed 30 May 2022.

Mayor, A. 2005. *Fossil Legends of the First Americans*. Princeton.

Mayor, A. 2014. *The Amazons: Lives and Legends of Warrior Women Across the Ancient World*. Princeton.

Mexía, P. 1673. *Silva de varia lección*. Madrid. http://archive.org/details/silvadevarialecoo mex. Accessed 30 May 2022.

Molina, C. de. 1873 [1575]. *Narratives of the Rites and Laws of the Yncas*. London. http://archive.org/details/narrativesofriteoomoli. Accessed 30 May 2022.

Murray, A. T., trans. 1995. *Homer: Odyssey Books 1–12*. Cambridge, MA.

Nuwer, R. 2014. 'Argentina Has a Superstition That Seventh Sons Will Turn into Werewolves.' *Smithsonian*. https://www.smithsonianmag.com/smart-news/argentina-has-superstition-7th-sons-will-turn-werewolves-180953746/. Accessed 30 May 2022.

Ouweneel, A. 2017. 'Buen Gobierno: Chronicles of Violence Committed against Amerindians in the Andes.' *European Review of Latin American and Caribbean Studies* 104: 113–20.

Pigafetta, A. 1874. *The First Voyage Round the World, by Magellan*. London. http://archive.org/details/firstvoyagerounoopigagoog. Accessed 30 May 2022.

Purchas, S. 1905. *Hakluytus posthumus, or Purchas his pilgrimes: Contayning a history of the world in sea voyages and lande travells by Englishmen and others*. Glasgow. http://archive.org/details/hakluytusposthu18purc. Accessed 30 May 2022.

Radford, B. 2016. 'Mistaken Memories of Vampires: Pseudohistories of the Chupacabra.' *Skeptical Inquirer* 40/1: 50–4. https://skepticalinquirer.org/wp-content/uploads/sites/29/2016/01/SI-JF-16-50.pdf. Accessed 30 May 2022.

Ripa, C. 1709. *Iconologia, or, Moral Emblems*. London. http://archive.org/details/iconologiaormoraooripa. Accessed 30 May 2022.

Sadurni, J. M. 2020. 'Romasanta, el "hombre lobo" Gallego.' *National Geographic*. https://historia.nationalgeographic.com.es/a/romasanta-hombre-lobo-gallego_15323. Accessed 30 May 2022.

Scheper-Hughes, N. 1993. *Death Without Weeping: The Violence of Everyday Life in Brazil*. Berkeley and Los Angeles.

Stobart, H. 2006. 'Devils, Daydreams and Desire: Siren Traditions and Musical Creation in the Central-Southern Andes', in *Music of the Sirens*, ed. L. Austern and I. Naroditskaya, 105–39. Bloomington, IN.

Sukut, M., ed., and C. Kihyer, trans. 2007. *The Chronicles of California's Queen Calafia, retold from Garci Rodriguez de Montalvo's 1587 Castilian edition of Amadis, Book 5, the Adventures of Esplandian*. San Juan Capistrano.

Tirso de Molina. 1999 [1635]. *Amazonas en las Indias*. Biblioteca Virtual Miguel de Cervantes. http://www.cervantesvirtual.com/obra-visor/amazonas-en-las-indias--0/html/fee00696-82b1-11df-acc7-002185ce6064_2.html. Accessed 30 May 2022.

Toribio Medina, J. 1897. *Juan Diaz de Solís: Estudio histórico*. Santiago. http://archive.org/details/juandiazdesolseo1medigoog.

Torquemada, A. de. 2012. 'Jardín de flores curiosas.' *Lemir* 16: 607–834.

Vargas Llosa, M. 1993. *Death in the Andes*. New York.

Vázquez, F. 1596 [1512]. *The Second Booke of Primaleon of Greece*, trans. A. Munday. London. http://www.proquest.com/eebo/docview/2240894507/99898720. Accessed 30 May 2022.

Vegini, V., R. L. Vegini, and W. F. Netto. 2014. *O mostruoso mapinguari pan-amazônico*. Porto Velho.

Whalen, A. 2009. 'Peru Villagers Murdered to Make Anti-Wrinkle Cream.' *Toronto Star*. 20 November. https://www.thestar.com/news/world/2009/11/20/peru_villagers_murdered_to_make_antiwrinkle_cream.html. Accessed 30 May 2022.

Zamora, M. 1993. *Reading Columbus*. Berkeley and Los Angeles.

CHAPTER 36

....

RECASTING MONSTERS IN POSTCOLONIAL ART AND LITERATURE

....

JUSTINE McCONNELL

INTRODUCTION

....

When Christopher Columbus wrote of his 1492 voyage that he had 'so far found no human monstrosities, as many expected' (Columbus [1493] 1963: 185), it was with some surprise. The expectation that distant lands were populated by monsters had been fostered by the writings of Pliny the Elder, Marco Polo, and Sir John Mandeville, which continued to wield enormous influence in the early modern period (Ramey 2014: 89–110). Even Columbus's proclamation that he had discovered no monstrous people did not persuade those who read it that there were no monsters to be found. Instead, holding firm to the need for the existence of monsters, colonial powers did what they have always done and created monsters for themselves.

Historical accounts of monsters are underpinned not so much by the observation of physical difference as they are rooted in the political context that creates those accounts, as Sylvester Johnson (2015) has argued of colonialism. Pliny the Elder's reference to *gentes huius monstri* in his *Naturalis historia* (*Natural History*) came to be widely adopted in the medieval and early modern eras as 'monstrous races' (7.9). Although Pliny was frequently mocked for his credulity, his terminology was nonetheless put to insidious use when early modern explorers applied it to people from faraway places. The noxious logic of colonialism encouraged European voyagers to cast peoples they encountered as 'other', magnifying the discourse that Edward Said identifies as a trait of all human collectives. As Said (1994: 60) observed, 'no identity can ever exist by itself and without an array of opposites, negatives, oppositions: Greeks always require barbarians, and Europeans Africans, Orientals, etcetera'. To justify their inhuman treatment of people in the lands they reached, European explorers and colonizers cast them as literally non-human: as monsters. This offered a (spurious) justification for their sense that they had the right to invade and occupy these lands. Yet it simultaneously betrayed their own understanding that these were human beings they were oppressing since a persistent feature of the monstrous is hybridity, found in the combination of similarity and difference that is perceived by those who apply the designation 'monster': the 'monster' is steadfastly claimed to be dissimilar to the person who deems them monstrous. For explorers and colonizing forces, the 'otherness' they identified in the people whose lands they invaded was often found in cultural norms and practices, such as clothing and social structures, but these were magnified in colonial discourse into features deemed innate and often cast in moral terms in order to categorize peoples as firmly 'other'.

This chapter explores a range of twentieth- and twenty-first-century works that engage simultaneously with the mythic monsters of Graeco-Roman antiquity and the long legacy of colonialism that still shapes the world today. While postcolonialism is often associated with the period in the twentieth century when European empires around the globe began to be dismantled, its scope is much broader than that. Postcolonial theory, literature, and art are not so designated on purely chronological grounds, nor need they relate only to European imperialism: rather, these are works that explore and contest the ways in which colonialism has impacted the world, its power structures, and our understanding of both. Recognizing the ongoing effects of colonialism and its discourses, Aníbal Quijano (2000) applied the term 'coloniality' to those structures of power which grew out of colonialism but reach far beyond it, both temporally and in terms of the aspects of life that they govern. When we consider works of visual art by Romare Bearden and Jane Alexander; poetry by Nikki Giovanni, Natalie Diaz, and Lorna Goodison; fiction by Ralph Ellison; and an essay by Derek Walcott, the variety of postcolonial receptions of ancient 'monsters' such as the Cyclops, Medusa, and the Minotaur becomes clear, shedding light on the many and varied ways in which these mythic figures have been adopted and recast to contest the very ideologies that label them as 'monstrous'.

IMPOSING MONSTROSITY: THE HOMERIC CYCLOPS

A striking instance of the imposition of monstrousness onto a person from another place features in one of the earliest works of ancient Greek literature, Homer's *Odyssey*. When Odysseus regales the Phaeacians with an account of his adventures as he tries to make his way home from the Trojan War, his narrative is full of encounters with supernatural beings and monstrous figures. Among these is his tale of the Cyclops Polyphemus, through which we glimpse an alternative perspective that Odysseus seems to be trying to suppress: Polyphemus, depicted as distinctly 'other' by the Greek hero, is more similar to Odysseus than the latter will admit. At pains to conceal this similarity, Odysseus describes the society that he finds in the land of the Cyclopes purely in terms of what it is not, emphasizing the ways in which it differs from his own culture:

> With heavy hearts we sailed along and reached
> the country of the reckless Cyclopes,
> lacking in customs. They put trust in gods,
> and do not plant their food from seed, nor plow,
> and yet the barley, grain, and clustering wine-grapes
> all flourish there, increased by rain from Zeus.
> They hold no councils, have no common laws,
> but live in caves on lofty mountaintops,
> and each makes laws for his own wife and children,
> without concern for what the others think.
>
> (*Od.* 9.106–15, trans. Wilson 2018)

Yet the tale that Odysseus goes on to tell describes Cyclopes who do indeed farm the land, grazing their animals and making cheese from their milk, and who—far from each living with no concern for the other—come running when they hear the wounded Polyphemus, now blinded by Odysseus, cry out. Their society, and their relationship to the land, is strikingly similar to that depicted as the 'Golden Age' in Hesiod's *Works and Days*, further destabilizing Odysseus' self-interested commentary of his encounter with them (Vidal-Naquet 1995: 41–2).

Moreover, the apex of that which Odysseus casts as Polyphemus' 'otherness' is his devouring of Odysseus' men. Tragic though this may be for Odysseus and his crew, it only becomes a signifier of the contravening of the taboo of cannibalism if one acknowledges that the Cyclopes are human (since to eat another species is the norm in carnivorous societies). The horror that Odysseus stirs up in his listeners by his tale of the Cyclops' anthropophagy, therefore, depends on an understanding that Polyphemus is human. This is a feature that the epic confirms when Odysseus describes Polyphemus as an *anēr pelōrios* (*Od.* 9.187), 'a huge man' or even 'a monstrously huge man', given that the adjective often conveys a sense both of great size and unusualness, crucially using the word reserved specifically for a male human (*anēr*). It is the Cyclops' enormous size that Odysseus finds remarkable, rather than the fact that he has just one eye (as implied by the poem's use of the singular). However, to justify his treatment of Polyphemus, Odysseus attempts to cast him as irremediably 'other'; yet in doing so, he repeatedly flags the similarities between them. For example, while Polyphemus contravenes the well-established traditions of *xenia* (guest-friendship), so too does Odysseus: he enters Polyphemus' home uninvited and, together with his men, helps himself to the food they find there and starts a fire. They are, quite literally, making themselves at home in a way that disregards the rules governing hospitality in ancient Greece and that echoes the behaviour of the suitors back in Ithaca, who are designated throughout the epic as morally reprehensible.

Odysseus' violation of *xenia* is also, as the notion of making himself and his crew at home indicates, a proto-colonial moment with the voyaging hero stopping at a new land and treating it like his own, albeit fleetingly. Since as far back as the ninth century BCE, Odysseus had been seen as a proto-colonial figure by Greek explorers (Malkin 1998), and his story aided the construction of a Greek sense of self in the midst of expanding social and cultural contacts (Dougherty 2001). In the twenty-first century, this facet of Odysseus' encounter with Polyphemus necessitates a reappraisal of the Greek hero's narrative, poignantly highlighted by Emily Wilson in the title she gave to Book 9 of her translation of the *Odyssey*: 'A Pirate in a Shepherd's Cave'.

The coloniality of Odysseus' encounter with Polyphemus, combined with the understanding that the Cyclopes are human beings, renders the episode one in which—long before the concept had been developed—Homi Bhabha's notion of 'colonial mimicry' is played out. Bhabha has formulated colonial mimicry as 'the desire for a reformed, recognisable Other, as *a subject of difference that is almost the same, but not quite*' (1984: 126, original italics); Polyphemus is presented as the 'unreformed' version of this 'Other'. What necessitates his depiction as a monster is the fact that he is a human being whom Odysseus treats inhumanly. While the *Odyssey*—indeed, Odysseus himself—confirms Polyphemus' identity as a human being, later portrayals have very often rendered him as steadfastly non-human, with his size and single eye dominating depictions in a way that indicates that artists down the centuries have been beguiled by Odysseus' version of events and have overlooked the more contestatory narrative that bubbles contrapuntally beneath the surface. As Bhabha remarks, the 'otherness' of colonial mimicry has often meant that 'almost the same but not quite' is a synonym for 'almost the same but not white' (1984: 130, 132); in later engagements with the *Odyssey*, Polyphemus' visible alterity is magnified by the emphasis on his single eye in a way present but not emphasized in the Homeric original, where the shakiness of Odysseus' claims of cultural difference are camouflaged but not concealed.

ROMARE BEARDEN'S CYCLOPS

Postcolonial engagements with the Homeric Cyclops have often highlighted this dimension that sees him cast as 'other', revealing the coloniality of such perceptions and contesting them. Sylvia Wynter asks us to go a step further, encouraging us to adopt the Cyclops' perspective, and observing that the 'Cyclopean quest for the assumption and revalorization of the being and perspective of alterity' remains unexplored (1997: 155), though Aimé Césaire delineated what this Cyclopean quest could look like in his 1939 poem *Cahier d'un retour au pays natal* (*Notebook of a Return to My Native Land*; Wynter 1997: 161–2). Wynter's formulation of the Cyclopean quest exposes, once again, the subjective perception involved in casting figures as either heroes or monsters that has always taken shape along lines of perceived racial difference.

The artist Romare Bearden compels us to reassess in another way the victim-oppressor dyad Odysseus presents when he depicts himself as a small and cunning hero overcoming the monstrous giant. Odysseus' assertion that the Cyclopes lack laws and agricultural technology has re-echoed through history in the designation of some peoples as more 'primitive' than others; it is this claim that Bearden centres and exposes in his collage *The Cyclops* from his 1977 'Odysseus Series' (Fig. 36.1). Bearden's Cyclops is, as Robert O'Meally has observed, 'a gigantic baby (perhaps Poseidon's baby boy), born and living between the legs of a broken monster-mountain' (2007: 44). As this enormous toddler-Cyclops peers out from his cave, he resembles a young child clutching the legs of their parent as they peer around from what should be a position of safety. The artwork refuses to allow the discrepancies of Odysseus' account to remain veiled. Either Polyphemus is naïve and uncultured, and thus easily tricked both into drinking the proffered wine without realizing its consequences and falling for Odysseus' famous linguistic trick that his name is 'Nobody', or he is a vast and threatening monster. If he is both at once, as in Bearden's work, the result is an enormous baby, rendering Odysseus' attack on him distinctly more exploitative than valiant.

The insight engendered by Bearden's artwork exposes the collision of these two contradictory depictions that coexist in Odysseus' intradiegetic narrative within Homer's epic. The paradoxical nature of Odysseus' depiction of Polyphemus as both threateningly vast and childishly naïve prefigures a persistent trope of imperial rhetoric whereby victims of colonization are cast as both culturally immature and dangerous. The archetypal instantiation of the latter appears in claims of cannibalism that date at least to Christopher Columbus's reports of his own voyages (Columbus [1493] 1963: 185), but that have been a trope of 'othering' much further back, as the story of Odysseus and Polyphemus confirms. While cannibalism remains, as Bill Ashcroft (2001: 45) articulates, 'the central trope of the colonial myth of savagery', the rendering of the colonized as children is more ambiguous because it places people as 'other' while holding in place their potential to be 'the same' once they mature. It may not be coincidence that the invention of childhood as a discourse took place in Europe at the same time as the invention of 'race' because, as Jo-Ann Wallace has argued, 'an idea of "the child" is a necessary precondition of imperialism—that is, that the West had to invent for itself "the child" before it could think a specifically colonialist imperialism' (1994: 176). The trope of the colonized person as child casts colonial domination not as oppression but as parental nurturing, albeit of a brutal kind; this, in turn, allows the colonizer to delude themselves into believing that their actions are in the best interests of the oppressed. Yet even in imperial discourse, the two are not elided so much as on a spectrum. As Ashcroft (2001: 37) explains, 'Whereas "race" could not exist without racism, that is, the need to establish a hierarchy of difference, the idea of the child dilutes the hostility inherent in that taxonomy and offers a "natural" justification for imperial dominance over subject peoples.'

Bearden's vision of the Cyclops as an infant, then, cuts to the heart of the colonialist discourse that underpins Odysseus' account of his encounter with Polyphemus. By presenting us with a vulnerable child who appears to be waving both to us as viewer and to Odysseus and his men on their ship in the foreground of the collage, Bearden ensures

FIGURE 36.1 Romare Bearden, *The Cyclops*, 1977.

Credit: © Romare Bearden Foundation/VAGA at ARS, NY and DACS, London 2022.

that we will sympathize with the Cyclops, while his position at the collage's centre makes Polyphemus the protagonist, inverting the traditional protagonist–antagonist roles of the Homeric episode.

POLYPHEMUS IN THE POETRY OF
NIKKI GIOVANNI

Nikki Giovanni takes up Bearden's image of Polyphemus as a baby in her poem 'Poseidon Hears His Baby Boy Crying', written in response to Bearden's collage (2017). In the poem, Polyphemus calls out to his father as he does in Homer's *Odyssey* (9.528–35), but rather than exhibiting the Homeric Polyphemus' belated awareness that Odysseus was the man of whom he had been prophetically warned and calling down his father's wrath on the Greek hero, Giovanni's Polyphemus is unmistakeably a small child, crying out in pain for his father. Giovanni's Cyclops does not yet understand either the humanity of others or the irreversibility of his actions:

> I didn't mean
> For the men to go
> They were fun
> . . . .
> But they broke
> And they cried.

(2017: 21)

In mistaking Odysseus' men for toys, Polyphemus dehumanizes them as inanimate objects in a way that parallels Odysseus' dehumanizing of Polyphemus as a monster. And as a toddler, the Cyclops' inability to comprehend what has happened overrides any power imbalance asserted by Odysseus on account of Polyphemus' size, as the Cyclops calls out to Poseidon:

> Why did No-Man take
> My eye
> I only wanted to play
> With him
> Is he broken
> Too

(2017: 22–3)

The poem closes with Polyphemus pleading, in terms that are unambiguously those of a young child, that his father reverse what Odysseus has done and return the Cyclops' eye to him:

> Make him give it back
> Daddy
> Make him give it back.

(2017: 23)

Together, Bearden's and Giovanni's depictions of Polyphemus not only extend the 'chain of reception'—to use Jauss's and Martindale's term (Jauss 1982: 20; Martindale 1993: 7)—but do so in a way that embarks on Wynter's notion of the 'Cyclopean quest' and makes it almost impossible not to sympathize with Polyphemus as victim of Odysseus' actions.

As well as the depiction of the Cyclops as a baby highlighting the colonial dynamics of the story, a reading of the episode developed through a psychoanalytical lens underlines the observation that both Odysseus and Polyphemus behave like children in their encounter: Odysseus wanting as many gifts as he can get and boasting afterwards of his cunning exploits, and Polyphemus using his superior size and strength to bully the Greek hero (Austin 1983). If Odysseus endeavours to cast the Cyclops as irremediably 'other' by depicting him as a monster, we glimpse in the childishness of both characters an instance of what Bhabha has termed the 'menace' of colonial mimicry: for all that Odysseus describes the Cyclopes' culture as diametrically opposed to that of the Greeks, in their shared immaturity we see again 'a difference that is almost total but not quite' (Bhabha 1984: 132). Homer's epic, therefore, indicates that, despite Odysseus' best efforts to cast Polyphemus as monstrous, the two were always more similar than the Greek hero wishes to admit.

Ironically, this 'similarity' takes another form in the context of colonial discourse in a way that rebounds on the colonizer. For, as Aimé Césaire argued in his 1950 work, *Discours sur le colonialisme* (*Discourse on Colonialism*), the 'othering' strategy that underpins colonial discourse and is designed to cast people from anywhere other than the imperial core as monstrous rebounds on its wielder: in treating people as other than human, the colonizer loses their own humanity. In Césaire's words:

> que l'action coloniale, l'enterprise coloniale, la conquête coloniale, fondée sur le mépris de l'homme indigène et justifiée par ce mépris, tend inévitablement à modifier celui qui l'entreprend; ... le colonisateur, qui, pour se donner bonne conscience, s'habitue à voir dans l'autre *la bête*, s'entraîne à le traiter en bête, tend objectivement à se transformer lui-même *en bête*. (Césaire 1955: 21, original italics)

> [Colonial activity, colonial enterprise, colonial conquest, which is based on contempt for the native and justified by that contempt, inevitably tends to change him who undertakes it; ... the colonizer, who in order to ease his conscience gets into the habit of seeing the other man as *an animal*, accustoms himself to treating him like an animal, and tends objectively to transform *himself* into an animal.] (2000: 41, original italics)

The appellation 'monster', applied to those oppressed by imperialist regimes, thus shifts to the oppressors, highlighting that the dynamics of coloniality, not its victims, are monstrous.

THE CYCLOPS IN THE IMAGINATION OF
RALPH ELLISON

Ralph Ellison's 1952 novel, *Invisible Man* (2002), takes this understanding of the shared features of Odysseus and Polyphemus in another direction. As Patrice Rankine (2006) has shown, allusions to the *Odyssey* pervade Ellison's novel and engagement with Graeco-Roman myth is a persistent feature of his oeuvre. The Cyclops looms large in Ellison's imaginary and, contrary to Wynter's conception of the 'Cyclops factor', he is portrayed as a brutish, almost monstrous figure. However, in keeping with Ellison's efforts to overcome the divisions still firmly institutionalized between Black and White Americans in pre-Civil-Rights-era America, the Cyclops is not so much a figure for Ellison as a trait, a way of being and thinking. Thus, the early 'battle royal' scene of the novel presents two sets of Cyclopean figures. The first, a group of white men for whom the humiliation of young black men fighting is a form of entertainment, are Cyclopean both in their drunkenness and their disregard for life. The second is the protagonist Invisible Man himself, who lacks the understanding at this stage of the narrative to assess the situation and behaviour of the white men; his characterization as a Polyphemus figure is confirmed when he literally almost loses an eye during the boxing match (Ellison 2002: 14–26; Rankine 2006: 134–7).

The novel contains two more Cyclopean episodes, but Invisible Man, whose progression towards becoming an Odyssean trickster hero is traced over the course of the narrative, will never again be wholeheartedly the Polyphemus figure. Instead, waking in the hospital after being injured in an explosion at the factory where he worked, Invisible Man finds himself being examined by a doctor who is portrayed in distinctly Cyclopean terms as a 'man with a circular mirror attached to his forehead', a 'bright third eye', and with 'the bright eye still burning into mine' (Ellison 2002: 176–7). A slippage between Invisible Man as Odysseus and/or Polyphemus can be seen in that image of the doctor's eye—not being burned by a stake as in Homer, but instead inflicting a burn on the protagonist.

The transition from Cyclopean to Odyssean character continues as the disoriented protagonist cannot recall his own name, thereby acquiring a shadow of Odysseus' moment as 'Nobody', even if by default. Only by almost beginning to play 'the dozens' with the doctor,[1] and by the mention of the African American trickster figure Brer Rabbit, with whom he comes to identify himself, does he begin to recall his identity. Having passed through this stage of the Cyclopean motif, only the blinding of Polyphemus remains to be carried out if Invisible Man is to take on the role of a heroic Odysseus (Rankine 2006: 132–44; MᶜConnell 2013: 71–105).

---

[1] 'The dozens' is a verbal game, with its roots in African American culture, in which insults are exchanged, often centred around the opponent's mother.

That episode occurs in an angry exchange between Invisible Man and Brother Jack, for whom the protagonist has worked as part of a group that closely resembles the Communist Party, known in the novel as 'the Brotherhood'. As they argue, Brother Jack's eye suddenly pops out of his head and he stands 'squinting at [Invisible Man] with Cyclopean irritation' (Ellison 2002: 358). Though it is a glass eye, Invisible Man's shock is palpable; yet his surprise signifies not only the physical loss of Jack's eye but the fact that he has succeeded in exposing the blindness and tyranny of Brother Jack and his organization. Revelling in his newly secured status as a trickster figure, like both Odysseus and Brer Rabbit, Invisible Man taunts Jack with wordplay that recalls Odysseus' famous 'Nobody' trick, as he goads him: ' "maybe you'll recommend me to your oculist ... then I may not-see myself as others see-me-not" ' (Ellison 2002: 360; Rankine 2006: 144). In Ellison's hands, then, the Cyclops is not so much a monster as a figure capable of both monstrous acts and an immature lack of insight. Ellison refuses to cast this as a fundamental difference between 'self' and 'other': to be Cyclopean is not innate or unchangeable and cannot be used to draw a distinction between one group of people and another. As the novel's closing line affirms, with controversial effect at the time of publication, Ellison put no store by such divisions, choosing instead to focus on common bonds of humanity and rejecting the discourse of self and other, hero and monster: 'Who knows but that, on the lower frequencies, I speak for you?' (2002: 439).

DEREK WALCOTT'S POSTCOLONIAL MEDUSA

Graeco-Roman myth, with its rich array of folkloric motifs and monsters, has proved a fertile source for postcolonial rewritings of its tales. But there is another reason beyond the presence of its 'monsters' that the literature of ancient Greece and Rome has had such prominence in the work of postcolonial artists. The valorization of Classics as a discipline across Europe meant that when European imperial powers colonized other lands, they took with them not only their religion, but also the Graeco-Roman classics, and imposed these on the peoples of the lands they oppressed. Other canonical works were prominent too in this wholesale imposition of an educational model, but as Barbara Goff observes, 'classics is preselected as the vehicle of these imperial combinations by its role in Europe as the common coin of the educated metropolitan elite' (2005: 11). Imperial powers used knowledge of Graeco-Roman antiquity as a means by which to claim superiority over the people they colonized while also building connections between otherwise disparate European powers. This further cemented a discourse of self and other, centre and periphery that emphasized a common cultural heritage between European colonial powers from which colonized people were either excluded, or permitted to join only with the kind of credentials granted by attendance at elite colonial schools.

Making use of that which was previously used to oppress you can be a powerful manoeuvre of appropriation, as the St Lucian poet and Nobel Laureate Derek

Walcott demonstrates with his figuration of History as Medusa. Most well known for his epic poem *Omeros* (1990), which recasts figures from Homeric epic in contemporary St Lucia, Walcott engaged with Graeco-Roman antiquity in his poetry, drama, and non-fiction throughout his career. His 1974 essay, 'The Muse of History', explicitly connects a 'monster' from antiquity to the colonial discourse propagated by imperialists, with Walcott introducing his exploration of time, identity, and art in the Caribbean with the declaration that history is 'the Medusa of the New World' (1998: 36). Fundamental to the essay is a reconceptualization of time by which its linear trajectory, as proposed by European thinkers, is no longer permitted to stand as the only way of understanding chronology (McConnell 2023: 58-64). At stake is the contestation of European notions of superiority and inferiority that are mapped onto age and newness. By this logic, to be new and to engage with ideas found in other works is to be derivative; newness stands not for innovation but for imitation if it can be connected with ideas that have gone before, justifying (in the European mind) a position of condescension towards the 'New World'. But, as Walcott argued, time should be seen not only as linear but also as simultaneous, as the Caribbean artists he admires understand:

> These writers reject the idea of history as time for its original concept as myth, the partial recall of the race. For them history is fiction, subject to a fitful muse, memory. Their philosophy, based on a contempt for historic time, is revolutionary, for what they repeat to the New World is its simultaneity with the Old. (1998: 37)

Walcott's understanding of history as myth and his conception of time, in which the 'New World' is simultaneous with the 'Old', is crucial to his engagement with Graeco-Roman antiquity and his denial that such works of classical reception are derivative.

Walcott aptly personifies this plural understanding of time in the figure of Medusa, who is both victim and oppressor in the mythic tales told about her. History is her monstrous form in which she may, Medusa-like, petrify the Caribbean into a state of immobility, freezing the region's potential. However, harking back to Ovid's narrative of Medusa assaulted by Neptune (*Met.* 4.791–804), Walcott's metaphor also suggests that time itself may be an innocent victim. It is Neptune's rape of Medusa that leads Minerva to punish her by transforming the beautiful Gorgon into a monster whose gaze turns all to stone. Similarly, imperialism (metonymically represented by Neptune and Minerva as gods of sea and war respectively, in Walcott's analogy) turned time into petrifying History. History, then, is the transformed and previously innocent Time that, Medusa-like, fixes formerly colonized worlds in a state of stasis, at least in the eyes of those who adopt a colonially inflected gaze. Walcott's engagement with the figure of Medusa, so often depicted as monstrous, incorporates her earlier identity as innocent victim, refusing once again to cast her as unequivocally 'other', just as other postcolonial receptions of Graeco-Roman monsters have likewise exposed the fact that 'monstrosity' rests only in the eye, and the retelling, of the dominant power.

Natalie Diaz's Minotaur

The 'monstrousness' imposed by others is also a theme of Natalie Diaz's poem, 'I, Minotaur' (2020: 59–61), which, in figuring the narrator as the Minotaur, seems to answer Sylvia Wynter's call to explore the quest of the Cyclops. Asserting herself as the Minotaur, Diaz's narrator adopts Wynter's notion of 'radical alterity', and just as swiftly, exposes designations of 'otherness' to be the creation of oppressive ideologies. The poem opens,

> I am an invention—dark alarm,
> Briareus's hands striking the bells of my blood.
>   Whose toll am I?
>
> (2020: 59)

The ancient Minotaur, with his human body and bull's head, is not only himself an 'invention', but is both conceived and imprisoned via technology created by the renowned inventor Daedalus (see Trzaskoma in this volume). Diaz gives voice to the Minotaur-figure, whose subjectivity was occluded in ancient accounts and whose voice was silenced. At the same time, the proclamation, 'I am an invention', confronts the audience with the realization that they themselves have imposed 'monstrousness' on this figure. So embedded is this 'othering' gaze that it must be exposed before it can be discarded. The figure of Briareus—a primordial, hundred-handed giant of Greek myth—is, therefore, an apt personification of a perspective of prejudice so enduring that it continues to strike at the very figures it has constructed as dangerous, even while being 'monstrous' itself. With the colourism of racial discrimination evoked by the 'dark alarm', the question 'Whose toll am I?' reverberates with Césaire's observation that efforts to dehumanize others ricochet back on the one who applies them.

   Yet, Diaz's narrator does have a two-ness reminiscent of the ancient Minotaur's physical form—but one located in the divisions of her identity that she feels as an Indigenous person in the settler colonialism of the United States:

> In my chest, I am two-hearted always—
> love and what love becomes
>   arrive when they want to, and hungry.
> . . . .
> I obey what I don't understand, then I become it.
>
> (2020: 59–60)

In Diaz's poem, American society in the United States functions as the Labyrinth entrapping the Minotaur, and the people imprisoned within that maze are Indigenous, as the poem articulates towards its close:

> I have a name, yet no one who will say it not roughly.
> I am your Native,
> and this is my American labyrinth.
>
> (2020: 61)

The collection's title, *Postcolonial Love Poem*, and the fact that many of the poems within it, including 'I, Minotaur', are love poems of a kind, makes inescapable the understanding that coloniality is not only about empires and invasion and national independence; rather, it seeps into every aspect of life. That the monsters of Graeco-Roman antiquity are recast to convey this highlights the way in which these ancient narratives have retained an aspect of their hegemony while, at the same time, affirming that the myths are capacious enough and sufficiently dislocated from any one context to create meaning anew. Postcolonial receptions of Graeco-Roman antiquity and its monsters foster fresh perspectives on the ancient works.

The story of the Minotaur and the Labyrinth, alongside that of the Cyclops, have proved particularly prominent in postcolonial engagements with Graeco-Roman myth. As well as Diaz's 'I, Minotaur' and 'Asterion's Lament' in the same collection, one might think of Lorna Goodison's poem 'The Mulatta and the Minotaur' from her 1986 collection, *I Am Becoming My Mother*. Goodison, who has recounted her surprise at finding the now-offensive term 'mulatta' applied to herself when she was travelling in Latin America (Baugh 1986: 20), explores the term's nature in several poems within the collection (including another that engages with Greek myth, 'The Mulatta as Penelope'). The startling use of the derogatory word in 'The Mulatta and the Minotaur' asks the reader also to question the designation 'Minotaur', guided by the poem's narrator who, at its close, multiply renames her sometime-lover:

> So,
> Minotaur;
> God's-head wearer
> Galileo
> Conqueror-of-Paris
> Someone I don't know
> There will be a next time
> Centuries ago.
>
> (Goodison 1986: 31)

Here, again, the monstrousness of the ancient mythic figure is simultaneously questioned and reimagined as the poem encourages us to reassess figures such as Galileo, onto whom the Minotaur is mapped, to expose the subjective arbitrariness of designations of 'monstrousness'. Where Diaz's narrator places herself as the Minotaur, Goodison's relates her encounter as its lover: 'And shall I tell you what the minotaur said to me | as we dined by the Nile on almond eyes and tea?' (1986: 31).

CONCLUSION

The reception of monsters from Graeco-Roman myth has taken many forms in postcolonial literature and art but uniting these is a pervasive insistence that the categorization of 'monster' is rethought. As each of the works discussed above shows, 'monstrousness' is in the eyes of the beholder, developed in opposition to what the one applying that categorization believes themselves to be. Because this dynamic of 'self' and 'other' underpinning narratives of monsters is also fundamental to colonial discourse, the reception of ancient monsters holds a key place in postcolonial literature. Breaking away from binary oppositions, postcolonial engagements do not simply invert roles; instead, in their rejection of simple oppositions, they present a more complex picture in which there are no ontological monsters.

A final example, Jane Alexander's iconic sculpture *Butcher Boys*, encapsulates this.[2] Created in the mid-1980s under Apartheid rule in South Africa, Alexander's artwork depicts three life-sized figures seated on a bench. Their poses are relaxed, their naked bodies human; yet their heads have horns; they have no mouths, outer ears, or genitalia; their noses are snouts; and their torsos are bisected with a scar running from belly to chin. To encounter them in the Iziko South African National Gallery is startling: at first glance, we are uncertain whether we are looking at humans or monsters. A second gaze refuses to resolve the uncertainty.

Butcher Boys does not explicitly engage with the myth of the Minotaur: the figures' horns and naked torsos may evoke the Cretan creature for some viewers, but it is the way they engender uncertainty that is so fundamental to their power. Made of reinforced plaster, animal bone and horn, and oil paint, the sculpted figures make literal their hybrid assemblage, while their mutilated forms embody the kind of self-inflicted animalization that Césaire identified as a by-product of the dehumanization of others. Alexander offers us nothing so definite as an allusion to ancient myth in her artwork just as, more fundamentally, her work encourages us not to attempt to resolve its meaning into easy binaries. As Kobena Mercer observes of Alexander's art, 'the material fabrication of the humanimal generates poetic tropes that unsettle the fixed dichotomies of biological essentialism' (2013: 85). This 'unsettling' is crucial because binary thinking is what has been used to underwrite any number of oppressive regimes, including those of colonialism and apartheid. The figures' collective title, too, highlights the depersonalization that facilitated the perpetration of atrocities by denying the individuality of victims while camouflaging that of proponents of apartheid; *Butcher Boys* challenges the viewer to gaze on apartheid's 'brutality and psychical distortions' (Oguibe 2000: 64).

Butcher Boys confronts the viewer with figures who are only 'monstrous' because they are also human—figures whose traumatized and distorted bodies reflect the violence of apartheid, even while they survive it. Like other postcolonial receptions of Graeco-Roman monsters, Alexander's sculpture confronts the binary thinking that creates 'monsters', and shatters it.

---

[2] https://arthur.io/art/jane-alexander/butcher-boys.

Suggested Reading

For an overview of postcolonialism, see Young (2001), and for a foundational work in the field, Said (1978). On the role of Classics in colonial discourses of the British Empire, see Goff (2005); on its continuing impact in formerly colonized lands, see Hardwick and Gillespie (2007); and on classicisms in the transnational world of the Black Atlantic, see Moyer, Lecznar, and Morse (2020). For a cultural history of the myth of the Cyclops in Homer and beyond, see Aguirre and Buxton (2020), and on Odysseus as a proto-colonial hero, Malkin (1998).

Works Cited

Aguirre, M., and R. Buxton. 2020. *Cyclops: The Myth and Its Cultural History*. Oxford.

Ashcroft, B. 2001. *On Post-Colonial Futures: Transformations of Colonial Culture*. London.

Austin, N. 1983. 'Odysseus and the Cyclops: Who Is Who?', in *Approaches to Homer*, ed. C. A. Rubino and C. W. Shelmerdine, 3–37. Austin.

Baugh, E. 1986, 'Goodison on the Road to Heartease.' *Journal of West Indian Literature* 1/ 1: 13–22.

Bhabha, H. 1984, 'Of Mimicry and Man: The Ambivalence of Colonial Discourse.' *October* 28: 125–33.

Césaire, A. 1955. *Discours sur le colonialisme*. Paris.

Césaire, A. 2000. *Discourse on Colonialism*, trans. J. Pinkham. New York.

Columbus, C. [1493] 1963. 'Letter to the Sovereigns on His First Voyage, 15 February–4 March', in *Journals and Other Documents on the Life and Voyages of Christopher Columbus*, trans. and ed. S. E. Morison, 180–7. New York.

Diaz, N. 2020. *Postcolonial Love Poem*. London.

Dougherty, C. 2001. *The Raft of Odysseus: The Ethnographic Imagination of Homer's* Odyssey. New York.

Ellison, R. 2002, *Invisible Man*. New York.

Giovanni, N. 2017. 'Poseidon Hears His Baby Boy Crying', in *Bearden's Odyssey: Poets Respond to the Art of Romare Bearden*, ed. K. Dawes and M. Shenoda, 21–3. Evanston, IL.

Goff, B., ed. 2005. *Classics and Colonialism*. London.

Goodison, L. 1986. *I Am Becoming My Mother*. London.

Hardwick, L., and C. Gillespie, eds. 2007. *Classics in Post-Colonial Worlds*. Oxford.

Jauss, H. R. 1982. *Towards an Aesthetic of Reception*, trans. T. Bahti. Minneapolis.

Johnson, S. 2015. 'Monstrosity, Colonialism, and the Racial State.' *J19: The Journal of Nineteenth Century Americanists* 3/1: 173–81.

MᶜConnell, J. 2013. *Black Odysseys: The Homeric Odyssey in the African Diaspora since 1939*. Oxford.

MᶜConnell, J. 2023. *Derek Walcott and the Creation of a Classical Caribbean*. London.

Malkin, I. 1998. *The Returns of Odysseus: Colonization and Ethnicity*. Berkeley and Los Angeles.

Martindale, C. 1993. *Redeeming the Text: Latin Poetry and the Hermeneutics of Reception*. Cambridge.

Mercer, K. 2013. 'Postcolonial Grotesque: Jane Alexander's Poetic Monsters.' *Nka: Journal of Contemporary African Art* 33: 80–90.

Moyer, I., A. Lecznar, and H. Morse, eds. 2020. *Classicisms in the Black Atlantic*. Oxford.

O'Meally, R. 2007. *Romare Bearden: A Black Odyssey*. New York.

Oguibe, O. 2000. 'Jane Alexander', in *Fresh Cream: Contemporary Art in Culture; 10 Curators, 10 Writers, 100 Artists*, 64. New York.

Quijano, A. 2000. 'Coloniality of Power, Eurocentrism, and Latin America.' *Nepantla: Views from the South* 1/3: 533–80.

Ramey, L. T. 2014. *Black Legacies: Race and the European Middle Ages*. Gainesville, FL.

Rankine, P. 2006. *Ulysses in Black: Ralph Ellison, Classicism, and African American Literature*. Madison.

Said, E. W. 1978. *Orientalism*. New York.

Said, E. W. 1994. *Culture and Imperialism*. London.

Vidal-Naquet, P. 1995. 'Land and Sacrifice in the *Odyssey*: A Study of Religious and Mythical Meanings', trans. A. Szegedy-Maszak, in *Reading the* Odyssey: *Selected Interpretative Essays*, ed. S. L. Schein, 33–53. Princeton.

Walcott, D. 1998. *What the Twilight Says: Essays*. London.

Wallace, J.-A. 1994. 'De-Scribing *The Water Babies*: "The Child" in Post-Colonial Theory', in *De-Scribing Empire: Post-Colonialism and Textuality*, ed. C. Tiffin and A. Lawson, 171–84. London.

Wilson, E., trans. 2018. *Homer: The Odyssey*. New York.

Wynter, S. 1997. ' "A Different Kind of Creature": Caribbean Literature, The Cyclops Factor, and The Second Poetics of the Propter Nos.' *Annals of Scholarship* 12/1–2: 153–72.

Young, R. J. C. 2001. *Postcolonialism: An Historical Introduction*. Oxford.

CHAPTER 37

....

CLASSICAL MONSTERS IN CHILDREN'S AND YOUNG ADULT LITERATURE

....

KATARZYNA MARCINIAK

INTRODUCTION

....

MONSTERS originating from classical myth are the perfect tutors. You too grew up under their care, as this chapter will help you recall by taking you back to some of your childhood books, discussed here together with several more recent works in order to offer a broader panorama. If you have any doubts regarding the pedagogical skills of the ancient monsters, simply cast a glance at their Greek and Roman 'biographies', as presented in this volume and in various editions of mythologies, mythological dictionaries, and—last but not least—the ancient sources themselves. The general conclusion is as surprising as it is highly interesting: with a few exceptions, the most famous monsters from Greek myths do not prey on children (below 12 years of age as the conventional borderline goes; Beaumont et al. 2021). Rather, they provide a formidable rite of passage for the heroes-to-be who as demigod adolescents stand a chance in their confrontation.

Consider, for example, the terrible Minotaur and the cruel tribute of seven youths and seven maidens to appease its hunger—via a detail that is often overlooked, although it is crucial for a deeper understanding of the myth: they were the Minotaur's peers, with Theseus mature enough to face the beast. We owe this important piece of information to Ovid who mentions the double figure of the beast as part bull, part young boy (*tauri iuvenisque figuram*, *Met.* 8.169, where *iuvenis* denotes a 'youth' of 14–17 years of age; see *OCD* 2015). Similarly, another 'prominent' monster, Medusa—whether considered a primordial creature (Hes. *Theog.* 274) or a beautiful woman turned into a beast (Ov. *Met.* 4.794–804)—encounters Perseus in his salad days, but for him this is also the age suitable for marriage with Andromeda and, with some divine help, he is then fully capable of attacking the Gorgon on an equal footing (in Hermes' winged sandals). Furthermore, were we asked to indicate the perfect ancient tutor and educator, someone who had successfully managed to raise quite an impressive number of rather 'challenging' children to become benefactors of humankind—well, the answer is unequivocal: half man, half horse—the centaur Chiron, teaching his wards to revere the gods, respect their parents, and protect Nature (Hall 2020). His love for human offspring differs sharply from the cruelty of the conquerors of Troy who killed Hector and Andromache's infant son Astyanax, or from King Acrisius of Argos who threw the baby Perseus, imprisoned in a chest with his mother Danaë, into the high seas, thus exposing him to a greater danger than the youth's later encounter with the horrific Medusa.

All this invites us to further explore the peculiar link between mythical beasts and the young members of the human species, especially as not only Chiron but also Medusa and the Minotaur and many other of their monstrous kind have always been present in the world of children and adolescents via two main channels. The first is storytelling: fascinating myths told to communities of all ages by the *aoidoi* ('singers of tales')—Homer's disciples. The second is the phenomenon of reception: by adapting and retelling the ancient myths, new generations of writers and artists have been giving new life to the mythical monsters in various places of the world, wherever Graeco-Roman tradition has reached over the millennia. And it is this reception that is of the greatest potential for children's and young adult literature. For the ancient creatures are not fossils like so many other victims of time (or of Medusa). Instead, they undergo a metamorphosis and often develop empathy, thus responding to young people's changing needs. The reason for this is that the ancient beasts are part and parcel of a malleable cultural heritage—the classical tradition in constant reinterpretations across the centuries, ever mirroring the transformations underway on both a global scale and in local contexts. Thus, reflection on the receptions of classical monsters for young audiences broadens our understanding not only of the childhood we ourselves have gone through, but also of the childhood and the adulthood we hope to create for future generations.

To encourage and facilitate such reflection, I first address the basic methodological issues, as the intersections among children's literature, classical reception, and monster studies pose challenges for all who wish to explore this portion of the mythical beasts' realm. Then I discuss the distribution of classical monsters in children's and young adult literature, along with their main functions therein. Finally, I present a sample bestiary in children's and young adult literature to supplement analyses of the 'adult' reception cases elsewhere in this volume. On this basis, we observe the transition process from childhood to adulthood under the care of our mythical, monstrous mentors.

METHODOLOGICAL CHALLENGES

There are three main research questions to address upon entering the realm of mythical monsters in children's and young adult literature. None of the three meets with satisfactory answers, yet there is a solution on how to cope with this challenging status quo.

What Is a Myth?

This question must remain open, as there are many, equally justified definitions available, and each of them takes a different approach to the topic.[1] For now, let us agree to understand myths as narratives of gods, humans, and supernatural beings, including monsters. These narratives played a fundamental role in Greek and Roman culture, as attested by the ancient sources—and they also do so today the world over, through the reception process.

What Is a Monster?

There is no consensus on a definition of 'monster'—not even in this handbook (see also Felton 2021). The Greek and Roman bestiary usually includes human-animal hybrids (the Minotaur), creatures with a lack or excess of some bodily parts (Argus Panoptes), and animalesque beings (the Chimaera), but the problem is more complex (Marciniak 2020c: 30). The beginning of the twenty-first century in children's literature brought a discussion on the difference between a 'being' and a 'beast' as offered by Newton Artemis Fido Scamander—the expert in 'magizoology' (the study of magical creatures) in J. K. Rowling's Harry Potter universe. Rowling endowed him with three names: those of the ingenious scientist (Isaac Newton), the Greek goddess of the hunt (Artemis), and the first-person singular form of the Latin verb meaning 'to trust, to have faith' (*fidere*; Fido being also the most recognizable name for a dog), while his surname is taken from the river god at Troy. This strange nomenclature well reflects how rational thinking and mythical thinking intertwine in the human approach to monsters. Scamander features as the author of the handbook *Fantastic Beasts & Where to Find Them*, used by Harry and his friends during their studies at Hogwarts and actually written by Rowling (2001) for charity. Its humorous form, parodying a scholarly volume, hides a serious content exceeding the fictional world of a children's book: it is meaningful that Rowling-Scamander avoids the term 'monster', instead focusing on two concepts—'being' in opposition to 'beast'—and showing the impossibility of any clear-cut categorization. In so doing, *Fantastic Beasts* points to the creatures' right to self-identification: for example, the centaurs in the Harry Potter universe rejected the categories proposed by the humans and 'declared that they would manage their own affairs separately' (2001: xiii). Thus, the readers receive an important lesson in empathy: they learn that beings so

[1] See e.g. *Britannica*, s.v. 'myth', https://www.britannica.com/topic/myth.

different from humans demonstrate reason and emotions, and should be entitled to make their own decisions (Maurice 2015a: 148–52; Marciniak 2020c: 30).

These reflections, when transferred to the readers' reality, offer food for thought—and not only for children—in regard to the use of certain words ('beast', 'monster') as tools of stigmatization, and this encourages reflection on one of the greatest challenges of contemporary societies: the issue of Otherness. This issue seems crucial for understanding the reception of the mythical creatures in children's and young adult literature. After all, it encapsulates the need to belong, to be accepted, and to fit in, and at the same time to develop one's own identity, despite all the obstacles and fears. The classical literary monsters guide readers through these conflicting desires, so frequent in the transition process of young people into adulthood. 'Monsters are our children', as the iconic statement by Jeffrey Jerome Cohen (1996: 20) goes: this applies particularly well to children's and young adult literature, where beasts, through their writers' talent and imagination, have the chance to express themselves and gain subjectivity, so that they can help the (not only) young readers mature and come to terms with Otherness—their own included.

What Is Children's and Young Adult Literature?

Children's and young adult literature is a relatively fresh cultural invention, classified according to the intended age of readers (respectively: 0–11 and 12–18 years), albeit with no consensus on a clear dividing line.[2] Its beginning is dated to the mid-eighteenth century with the publication of *A Little Pretty Pocket-Book, Intended for the Instruction and Amusement of Little Master Tommy, and Pretty Miss Polly* (1744), which contained, among other texts, a selection of Aesop's *Fables*. The obvious—and hence often overlooked—factor that the writers of children's and young adult books are adults is not without consequences: the 'hidden adult' is present in the works intended for children, both as the author and as a member of the implied readership (Nodelman 2008). The latter includes the phenomenon of dual or double addressee, when the writers direct their message to both a younger and an older audience or build a separate line of communication with adults 'over the heads' of children (Wall 1991). We are thus close to the ancients here, who attended storytelling sessions irrespective of their age. At the same time, the still occurring marginalization of works for youth as 'less serious', and therefore less important, makes it easier for authors to find a place therein for experiments and to lead a 'silent revolution' through innovative messages, ones crucial also for adults, but for the moment too controversial for older audiences to face directly in the mainstream culture (Marciniak 2024).

All this considered, the young age of the targeted readers, as determined by the publishers, should not discourage adults from reaching for a given work. Rather, even children's books that might seem obsolete, judging from the date of their creation, have

---

[2] That is why in the next sections of this chapter, when the age of the readers is indicated, the classification by the publishers or bookshops is used, though this should by no means be treated as limiting.

the potential to surprise contemporary audiences of all ages—older ones perhaps even more. This happens, for example, in the case of Nathaniel Hawthorne's version of the Minotaur's myth in *Tanglewood Tales for Boys and Girls* (1853). For a start, the American writer boldly questions the creature's inability to communicate, thus alluding polemic-ally to Aristotle's famous criterion ('no animal has speech except a human being', *Pol.* 1253a9–10, trans. C. D. C. Reeve). The Minotaur can voice his thoughts—indeed, 'his', not 'its', as Hawthorne uses the pronoun endowing the monster with an ontological status usually reserved for humans. The sounds made by the Minotaur may not be clear, but Theseus understands them and feels 'some sort of pity' for the beast (1853: 61). This mid-nineteenth-century elaboration is also revolutionary in shifting blame from the creature to King Minos, whom the hero calls 'a more hideous monster than the Minotaur him-self' (53), thus encouraging young readers to look beyond appearances—all the more so as the narrator also links monstrosity with the human species: 'And O, my good little people, you will perhaps see, one of these days, as I do now, that every human being who suffers any thing evil to get into his nature, or to remain there, is a kind of Minotaur, an enemy of his fellow-creatures, and separated from all good companionship, as this poor monster was' (61–2). This message is not without meaning for adults, too (Marciniak 2020c: 34; Murnaghan and Roberts 2020: 56–74, esp. 66; Marciniak 2024). In sum, the universal context of Greek mythology and its creatures, obtaining new lives in children and young adult literature, strengthens its intergenerational (crossover) potential.

A Solution

The above methodological issues should not scare us from approaching monsters in children's and young adult literature, for such issues only prove how rich and fascinating the theme of the mythical creatures' reception is and how it challenges our preconceptions and demands constant openness towards crossing barriers and overcoming stereotypes. In cases like this, team projects work particularly well, along with the individual scholars' readiness for an interdisciplinary approach, including such fields as classical philology, education, the history of ideas, human-animal studies, lit-erature studies, philosophy, and psychology.

Identifying Mythical Monsters in Children's and Young Adult Literature

Children's and young adult literature is not a consistent body but a collection of genres, some of which, such as novels, follow the taxonomy typical of works also targeted at an adult audience, while others, such as picture books, are indeed more frequent among the young public (Mickenberg and Vallone 2011; Kümmerling-Meibauer 2012). Classical monsters populate them all. There is no risk in venturing the hypothesis that each genre identified by the Library of Congress has been touched by creatures from Greek myths. These creatures dwell in literature from around the world, in a vast number of human languages and in line with the chief categories of reception—including adaptation, transplant, and translation—as defined by Lorna Hardwick (2003). We can meet mythical monsters in mythologies, bestiaries, school novels (i.e. set in a school and focused on students, teachers, and administration staff), comics, poetry, and even cookbooks. Each genre offers different opportunities and requires a different research approach. For instance, illustrations are often as important as the text, especially in picture books but also in other genres, and they deserve their own in-depth analysis, as has been done for the Minotaur in Hawthorne's *Tanglewood Tales* (Roberts and Murnaghan 2020). Furthermore, mythical creatures broaden their distribution area outside literature through the phenomenon of the supersystem of entertainment (Kinder 1991: 1), that is, the set of works originating from a given hypotext. The Harry Potter universe provides a good example, since the original book series gave rise to movies, merchandise, and even amusement parks. As a result, the first medium of contact with classical monsters often cannot be identified, especially since such contacts may occur long before the child's reading experience—via television, the Internet, and the ongoing practice of storytelling within families, as well as at schools, public libraries, and other such venues. One does not exclude the other, however, as all these encounters are complementary and thereby strengthen the importance of mythical beasts in young people's lives.

Functions of Mythical Monsters in Children's and Young Adult Literature

Classical monsters fulfil a variety of functions in children's and young adult literature, starting from the fundamental narrative role—that is, as elements in a story's development according to Joseph Campbell's scheme of the hero's journey or Vladimir Propp's morphology of the folk tale (e.g. monsters as antagonists, helpers, tricksters). Monsters are, however, more than that, provided they originate from the pen of truly ingenious writers. Of crucial importance is the educational function of mythical creatures, for they transmit to children and young adults knowledge of the ancient myths and other related subjects, like mythological phraseology in contemporary languages. All this enables intergenerational communication based on the cultural code that draws upon classical antiquity and is present in both everyday life and masterpieces of world civilization. Furthermore, as the mythological beasts of ancient Greece and Rome appear not only in obligatory school texts, but also in literary works read 'after hours', this 'Monster University' (Marciniak 2020c: 33) operates through entertainment and in an attractive way, with excitement and humour working together and dispelling tedious didacticism. However, it is worth emphasizing that the educational function of the ancient creatures is not limited to intellectual growth, but extends also to the emotional development of young readers. Indeed, psychologists consider the confrontation with fears impersonated by the monsters to be a natural stage in the process of maturation—hence the children's early fascination with them (Sayfan and Lagattuta 2009; Marciniak 2020c: 25). In this context, the etymology of the Latin term 'monster' is symbolic, as one posited origin is the verb *monere* ('to warn'): dwelling within ontological liminality, the mythical creatures throw us off balance. They lead us out from our comfort zone and make us look at the world from a different perspective, beyond appearances (Marciniak 2020c: 31–2 and 37). It is impossible to offer such versatility, essential especially for the identity-building process, to children by human tutors. In this context the ethical function also becomes activated: as befits wise mentors, the ancient creatures teach children and young adults to respect the Other and they show that there is nothing wrong in being different. Last but not least, the function of the reception mirror should be mentioned as one of the most important contributions of classical monsters: authors employ them to talk about issues vital for society in given periods—for example, women's rights, ecology, disability, and (altogether frequently) Otherness. Thus, the reception of the ancient creatures as such becomes a litmus test for transformations in societal sensitivity (Marciniak 2020a). In what follows, we see some of these functions at work.

A Sample Bestiary of Mythical Monsters in Children's and Young Adult Literature

A complete bestiary of classical monsters prowling through children's and young adult literature would fill a whole volume at least. It is no small consolation that many of the monsters excluded from this discussion because of space limitations, already enjoy excellent scholarly analyses (see Suggested Reading). Here I have chosen five mythical creatures with three examples of their reception per case. The selection criterion was diversity. Thus, both the most and less famous monsters are showcased. They represent various functions in books targeted at diverse age groups within differing genres and language circles. Moreover, the texts discussed have the status of children's and young adult classics or represent the most recent literary phenomena, for which the parameter of time to test their lasting value is not applicable. All this permits us to signal the similarities and differences in the reception of the mythical bestiary across the world. Finally, as many talented authors of children's and young adult literature prove (see Hawthorne above), even the well-known ancient monsters can still take readers by surprise. Thus, the examples chosen also offer the experience of the unexpected, so important in the transition process from childhood to adulthood and beyond.

Argus

Argus Panoptes ('all-seeing') features in Ingri and Edgar Parin d'Aulaires' *Book of Greek Myths* (1962), which belongs to the genre of mythologies and is one of the basic sources of knowledge about this part of ancient Greece's heritage for English-speaking children in the 8- to 12-year-old range, especially in the United States. Argus appears as a secondary character in the chapter on Hera, in the context of Zeus' love affair with Io. The monster is described as a giant with 'a hundred bright eyes placed all over his body' (1962: 24). He serves Hera as her best watchman, always vigilant in guarding Io (whom Zeus has transformed into a cow), as only half of his eyes sleep at the same time. This description is complemented by an elaborate illustration showing Argous with a club. His whole body is covered with eyes, just as on the red-figure Attic stamnos by the Argos Painter (Kunsthistorisches Museum in Vienna, 3729/BA 202608). A peacock nearby foreshadows the metamorphosis to take place after Argus' death at Hermes' hand: Hera will honour her watchman by placing his eyes into the tail feathers of this bird. The educational function of introducing the myth to children predominates, yet it expands beyond basic knowledge of the myth, as the authors prepare the readers for communing with visual arts by creating a reference to Greek pottery painting.

A similar approach has been applied in the Italian picture book recommended from the age of 5, *Mostri e creature mitologiche* (2016) by Marisa Vestita (illustrations) and Giorgio Ferrero (text). Its genre is a bestiary, but the content remains the same as in d'Aulaires' mythology—the renarration of the Argus myth from his characteristics to his death, including the transfer of his eyes on the peacock's tail. Also here a dialogue with visual arts can be traced, this time, however—as suggested by the eyes placed prominently on the monster's head—with *Mercury and Argus* (1635–1638) by Peter Paul Rubens and in correspondence with the monster's description in Ovid's *Metamorphoses* (1.624).

Argus manifests more aspects of his educational role in the collection of short stories *The Thread of Ariadne, or Finding Your Way* (*Nić Ariadny, czyli po nitce do kłębka*, 1989) by Anna M. Komornicka, who explains to elementary school children the meaning of mythological phraseology used in Polish. To this end, her book revolves around three siblings placed in contemporary settings (Marciniak 2015: 75–80). Argus means in Polish a 'careful watchman'. The children use this expression to describe their severe teacher who notices any attempt at cheating. Such a transplant-reception permits the readers not only to gain knowledge of mythology, but also to develop their Polish language skills. All this contributes to learning the cultural code that enables communication between the present and the past (Marciniak 2023: 129–30), while the theme of condemning cheating activates the ethical function of Argus' tutorship.

Centaurs

Children's and young adult literature builds on the ancient imagery of two kinds of centaurs: the wise Chiron and the lustful creatures born from Ixion and Nephele ('Cloud'). In C. S. Lewis's novels from *The Chronicles of Narnia* series (1950–1956), the centaurs bear elements of both traditions and represent the duality of human nature (Maurice 2015a: 146–8; Marciniak 2021b: 231). They fulfil an ethical function as they display a high moral code and side with Aslan. The centaurs contribute to the protagonists' intellectual and emotional development by explaining the world to them and encouraging them to overcome fears. They teach respect as they take two children on a daring ride—an exceptional honour for a human being. The adaptation of the centaurs' myth in the Narnia universe also familiarizes readers with classical heritage: Lewis presents the centaurs as prophets—in that they read the future in the stars—and they practise the art of herbal medicine, just as in the ancient sources. The centaurs' carnal side manifests itself via their predilection for wine (though they are excused somehow, as they drink in Aslan's honour) and their two stomachs (the reason for their long feasts). This anatomical detail, sometimes overlooked as 'indecorous', paved the way for including the descriptions of physiological processes in children's literature—its popular component today.

The iconic figure of Chiron the educator and ethical guide was transplanted by Rick Riordan into his Percy Jackson novels (2005–) for early teenagers. Riordan places Chiron in an enchanted wheelchair that conceals his horse part in the ordinary world of humans, thereby offering an opportunity to discuss the theme of disability and to raise the readers' empathy towards this issue in line with inclusivity movements in contemporary societies. The Percy Jackson universe is also inhabited by wild centaurs known as the 'Party Ponies' who drink root beer and use paintball guns as a kind of extension of their archery skills (Maurice 2015a: 152–5). These centaurs pose no danger to the protagonist; rather, they support him and his case in the hour of need.

J. K. Rowling, in her Harry Potter cycle (1997–2007), a crossover read by both children and adults, keeps closer to the ancient sources in presenting the centaurs as a wild, forest-dwelling population. In *The Order of the Phoenix* (2003), she even alludes to the myths of their abuse of women—a sensitive topic, still rarely employed in children's literature. In fact, Rowling does not reference it directly, but rather suggests it to the adult audience, via the double-address technique, beyond the perception of the young readers. The detested teacher Dolores Umbridge, after she was abducted by the centaurs whom she had gravely insulted, displays behaviours typical of victims of sexual harassment (Maurice 2015a: 151–2). From this wild herd, a wise and human-friendly centaur stands out—namely, Firenze, who is a counterpart for Chiron. Harry first meets him in *Harry Potter and the Philosopher's Stone* (1997; published in the United States as *Harry Potter and the Sorcerer's Stone*, 1998). Inquisitive readers have a chance to enjoy the intertextual game proposed by Rowling, who intertwines elements of classical antiquity with its medieval reception. Firenze is the Italian name for Florence, the city of Dante Alighieri; this builds a link to his most famous work, *The Divine Comedy* (Hofmann

2015: 168–75; Maurice 2015a: 152). Just as Dante was guided by Vergil, symbolizing the wisdom of the ancients, so Harry, having lost his way in the dark Forbidden Forest, is guided by the wise, mythical centaur. Firenze, who will also become Harry's teacher in the future, then saves the boy's life. He is also the first character ready to tell Harry the truth of the imminent fight against the forces of evil in defence of all that is good in the world (Maurice 2015a: 149; Marciniak 2021b: 231).

Cyclopes

The Cyclopes belong to the mythical figures whose adaptations best show the creativity of children's writers in overcoming various societal stereotypes through the reception of classical monsters. For instance, the Polish story for toddlers *Ancyklopek on the Playground* (*Ancyklopek na placu zabaw*, 2016) by Piotr Dobry with illustrations by Łukasz Majewski, encourages readers—including adults, if only for the sole fact that 2- and 3-year-olds require their help in accessing the story—to reflect on the issues of tolerance and otherness. The toddler Ancyklopek—whose name is a wordplay in Polish, a fusion of the mythological Cyclops and *ancymonek* (a rascal)—inherits many features of the ancient creature, thus teaching young readers about mythology: he is huge, has one eye, and displays a talent for building sandcastles that represent the famous 'Cyclopean' masonry of Mycenaean times. The atypical appearance of Ancyklopek causes the toddlers in the playground to avoid him, so he plays alone until he meets a Four-Eyes who turns out to be a boy in glasses—another feature resulting in stigmatization. The two outsiders become friends and have fun together (and soon they are joined by other children), while their adventures contribute to the emotional development of readers by helping them learn to look beyond appearances.

The American picture book *Cyclops of Central Park* (2020), with the text by Madelyn Rosenberg and illustrations by Victoria Tentler-Krylov, aims at a slightly older audience (3–7 years old), but this work also, full of absurd humour, supports children's emotional maturation, here in regard to overcoming timidity. The eponymous Cyclops is a caring and gentle creature. He lives in a cave in New York's Central Park. His extravagant appearance (the ancient monster in modern clothes) does not cause a sensation among the inhabitants of New York, who symbolize an open-minded society that embraces all kind of diversity. Rather, an inner psychological problem poses a social barrier for the Cyclops: his paralysing shyness. Forced to leave the cave to find a missing sheep from his flock, he discovers (and the readers along with him) both the value of teamwork—the other sheep help in the search—and the advantages of going outside one's comfort zone. The story ends happily as they all enjoy a ride on the Coney Island Cyclone roller coaster (Peer 2021).

An approach to the Cyclops myth as a component of the heritage of the Western world is applied in the young adult detective novel *The Subway Cyclops* (1996) by Marivi Soliven Blanco with illustrations by Remus San Diego. The protagonists Jenny and Jay, two teenagers from a family of Filipino immigrants in the United States, unveil the identity of a one-eyed creature in Boston's subway system. The stranger turns out to be not a terrible monster, as suggested by their housekeeper, but a benign assembly-line worker, wounded in a gas explosion many years earlier (Hale 2018; Hale and Riverlea 2023: 376–7). The genre of detective novel makes the educational content natural and deprived of burdensome didacticism as the kids learn modern history and the Mediterranean roots of their new motherland, while the myth of the Cyclops, used metaphorically, serves both as a narrative tool for creating a mysterious atmosphere and as an element of the code enabling intergenerational and intercultural communication.

Medusa

While collections of myths usually draw upon the Hesiodic tale of Medusa as a primordial monster and place her within the Campbellian heroic quest narrative, other genres ever more often refer to Ovid (*Met.* 4.604–5.263) and embed Medusa's story in the context of women's struggle for developing agency—a process that can start in early childhood, as with the picture book *Brush Your Hair, Medusa!* (2015) by Joan Holub with illustrations by Leslie Patricelli. Aimed at preschool children (ages 1 to 3), the book belongs to the series 'Mini Myths', offering 'mythology-inspired modern-day parable' intended to teach children both mythology and contemporary social norms. Medusa is a toddler who refuses to brush her hair. This act symbolizes her fight for identity (hair is a cultural topos standing for freedom and rebellion). A visit to the hairdresser results in the difficult compromise Medusa has to make in her socialization process. Accepting a new and short haircut, she loses a part of herself, but starts resembling her grandma, which protects her from becoming an Other for her family. However, as the little Medusa immediately thereafter is about to refuse to brush her teeth, we can rest assured that she will grow up to be a strong woman (Marciniak 2020b).

The themes of maturation and being true to oneself stand out in the novel *Being Medusa: And Other Things that Suck* (2014) by A. Lynn Powers. It represents the genre of a school novel with the protagonist 15-year-old Medusa, already with her snaky hair which is part of her 'monstrous charm'. The snakes also express Medusa's emotions before she is aware of them. The novel discusses sensitive topics and encourages respect for diversity, since Medusa undergoes a transition from being a lonely girl and victim of bullying to becoming a young woman who accepts herself and displays her agency (Hodkinson 2020).

Developing one's agency, yet in a grave context, provides the theme for the novel *Medusa: The Girl Behind the Myth* (2021) by Jessie Burton with illustrations by Olivia Lomenech Gill. The novel is recommended for older teens (ages 14–17) and contains trigger warnings due to its focus on sexual abuse, rape, the unjust punishment of an innocent victim, and the process of overcoming trauma. At the story's opening, the first-person narration from Medusa herself establishes a close relation between the implied audience and the monster, thus causing us to question the very notion of monstrosity. In the novel Medusa stands for emotional development and the empowerment of victims, her fate mirroring the cases of abuse known also from contemporary times.

Minotaur

Next to Ovid's somehow unexpected description of the Minotaur as *iuvenis*, a similarly unusual image of this creature may be mentioned: the baby Minotaur caressed by Pasiphaë on a red-figure kylix from Vulci (see Fig. 16.1). The scene surprises us with its original perspective, quasi-surreal, given the fierce, fully grown monster we usually see in other sources. Yet children's and young adult literature, as already demonstrated in Hawthorne's case, takes up the challenge of showing the unknown face of the Minotaur. For instance, surrealism is the trademark of Maurice Sendak, who refers to this myth indirectly in his picture book *Where the Wild Things Are* (1963). Sendak's gift for storytelling and the mastery of his illustrations result in an inspirational tale of searching for identity and maturation via the example of Max, a boy who magically travels to the realm of the Minotaur-like monsters. They stand for lack of (self-)control, while Max accomplishes the impossible: he becomes their king, he tames what cannot be tamed, and thus proves himself ready for the challenges of adulthood.

The transition from childhood to adulthood, albeit in the context of a heavy personal and national trauma, provides the theme for a highly original reference to the Minotaur myth in the Australian young adult 'multimodal work' (a graphic novel with a musical score) *Requiem for a Beast* (2007) by Matt Ottley. It belongs to the 'hybrid' reception category (Hardwick 2003: 9), by combining classical and Aboriginal heritage. The Minotaur symbolizes the inner fight of the young protagonist who works as a stockman with bulls and must face the terrible truth of his father's involvement in a crime on an Aboriginal man. The boy feels the need to atone somehow for this sin and rebuild his identity challenged by the burden of the truth (Hale 2020; Hale and Riverlea 2023: 81, 160, 221).

Maturation is also the focus of Anthony McGowan's short novel *I Am the Minotaur* (2021) from a series aimed at less experienced readers from the age of 11. It discusses the issues of fitting in, bullying, loneliness, and mental health (Hale 2022). The protagonist, a teenage boy, feels entrapped as in a labyrinth, like the Minotaur. The references to the mythical creature show the boy (and readers) the way to put conflicting emotions in order, as well as to accept the things that cannot be changed, which is the true sign of maturity.

CONCLUSION

Monsters from classical myth are the perfect tutors. If you have any doubts, check with yourself. You, too, have grown up under their care. For we need monster mentors in order not to become human monsters. As the above examples show, our monstrous tutors enable us to go out into the adult world equipped with a reservoir of compassion, love, and empathy towards the Other. It is worth remembering that, in case we lose any of this reservoir on our troubled journey, we can always replenish it by coming back to the monsters dwelling in the works for kids of all ages.

ACKNOWLEDGEMENTS

This chapter has been prepared within the project *Our Mythical Childhood ... The Reception of Classical Antiquity in Children's and Young Adults' Culture in Response to Regional and Global Challenges*, which has received funding from the European Research Council (ERC) under the European Union's Horizon 2020 Research and Innovation Programme under grant agreement No 681202, ERC Consolidator Grant (2016–22), Faculty of "Artes Liberales", University of Warsaw.

SUGGESTED READING

The crucial scholarly guides through the reception of classical antiquity in children's and young adult literature are offered by Murnaghan and Roberts (2018), Hodkinson and Lovatt (2018), and Hale and Riverlea (2023). The following collected volumes include chapters dedicated to the reception of classical monsters in the culture for young people: Maurice (2015b), Marciniak (2016), Janka and Stierstorfer (2017), Zajko and Hoyle (2017), Marciniak (2021a). A fundamental study on how post-classical societies use the mythical creatures in popular culture has been published by Gloyn (2019). Analyses of selected monsters have been accomplished within the international team projects *Chasing Mythical Beasts ... The Reception of Creatures from Graeco-Roman Mythology in Children's and Young Adults' Culture as a Transformation Marker* (Alexander von Humboldt Foundation Alumni Award for Innovative Networking Initiatives, 2014–17) and *Our Mythical Childhood ... The Reception of Classical Antiquity in Children's and Young Adults' Culture in Response to Regional and Global Challenges* (European Research Council Consolidator Grant, 2016–22) with the results published in Marciniak (2020a). The latter project has resulted also in a database (*Our Mythical Childhood Survey*, http://omc.obta.al.uw.edu.pl/myth-survey) containing short summaries and analyses of *c.*1,500 works of children's and young adult culture in the context of the reception of classical antiquity, the ancient monsters included.

WORKS CITED

Aristotle. 1998. *Politics*, trans. C. D. C. Reeve. Indianapolis and Cambridge.

Beaumont, L. A., M. Dillon, and N. Harrington, eds. 2021. *Children in Antiquity: Perspectives and Experiences of Childhood in the Ancient Mediterranean*. London.

Cohen, J. J., ed. 1996. *Monster Theory: Reading Culture*. Minneapolis.

D'Aulaire, I., and E. P. D'Aulaire. 1962. *D'Aulaires' Book of Greek Myths*. Garden City, NY.

Felton, D. 2021. 'Monsters and the Monstrous: Ancient Expressions of Cultural Anxieties', in *A Cultural History of Fairy Tales in Antiquity*, ed. D. Felton, 109–30. London.

Gloyn, L. 2019. *Tracking Classical Monsters in Popular Culture*. London.

Hale, E. 2018. '*A Jenny and Jay Mystery (Series, Book 4): The Subway Cyclops* by M. Soliven Blanco, ill. by R. San Diego.' *Our Mythical Childhood Survey*. Warsaw. http://omc.obta.al.uw. edu.pl/myth-survey/item/497. Accessed 5 November 2023.

Hale, E. 2020. 'Facing the Minotaur in the Australian Labyrinth: Politics and the Personal in *Requiem for a Beast*', in *Chasing Mythical Beasts: The Reception of Ancient Monsters in Children's and Young Adults' Culture*, ed. K. Marciniak, 157–73. Heidelberg.

Hale, E. 2022. '*I Am the Minotaur* by Anthony McGowan.' *Our Mythical Childhood Survey*. Warsaw. http://www.omc.obta.al.uw.edu.pl/myth-survey/item/1242. Accessed 5 November 2023.

Hale, E., and M. Riverlea. 2023. *Classical Mythology and Children's Literature: An Alphabetical Odyssey*, illus. S. K. Simons. Warsaw.

Hall, E. 2020. 'Cheiron as Youth Author: Ancient Example, Modern Responses', in *Chasing Mythical Beasts: The Reception of Ancient Monsters in Children's and Young Adults' Culture*, ed. K. Marciniak, 301–26. Heidelberg.

Hardwick, L. 2003. *Reception Studies*. Oxford.

Hawthorne, N. 1853. *Tanglewood Tales for Boys and Girls*. Boston.

Hodkinson, O. 2020. ' "She's not deadly. She's beautiful": Reclaiming Medusa for Millennial Tween and Teen Girls?', in *Chasing Mythical Beasts: The Reception of Ancient Monsters in Children's and Young Adults' Culture*, ed. K. Marciniak, 197–222. Heidelberg.

Hodkinson, O., and H. Lovatt. 2018. *Classical Reception and Children's Literature: Greece, Rome and Childhood Transformation*. London.

Hofmann, D. 2015. 'The Phoenix, the Werewolf and the Centaur: The Reception of Mythical Beasts in the Harry Potter Novels and Their Film Adaptations', in *Ancient Magic and the Supernatural in the Modern Visual and Performing Arts*, ed. F. Carlà and I. Berti, 163–76. London.

Janka, M., and M. Stierstorfer, eds. 2017. *Verjüngte Antike: Griechisch-römische Mythologie und Historie in zeitgenössischen Kinder- und Jugendmedien*. Heidelberg.

Kinder, M. 1991. *Playing with Power in Movies, Television and Video Games*. Berkeley and Los Angeles.

Kümmerling-Meibauer, B. 2012. *Kinder- und Jugendliteratur: Eine Einführung*. Darmstadt.

Marciniak, K. 2015. '(De)constructing Arcadia: Polish Struggles with History and Differing Colours of Childhood in the Mirror of Classical Mythology', in *The Reception of Ancient Greece and Rome in Children's Literature: Heroes and Eagles*, ed. L. Maurice, 56–82. Leiden.

Marciniak, K., ed. 2016. *Our Mythical Childhood . . . The Classics and Literature for Children and Young Adults*. Leiden.

Marciniak, K., ed. 2020a. *Chasing Mythical Beasts: The Reception of Ancient Monsters in Children's and Young Adults' Culture*. Heidelberg.

Marciniak, K. 2020b. 'Medusa's Bad Hair Day, or The Taming of the Baby Shrew.' *Libri Liberorom: Fachzeitschrift für Kinder- und Jugendliteraturforschung* 54–55: 60–3.

Marciniak, K. 2020c. 'What Is a (Classical) Monster? The Metamorphoses of the Be(a)st Friends of Childhood', in *Chasing Mythical Beasts: The Reception of the Ancient Monsters in Children's and Young Adults' Culture*, ed. K. Marciniak, 25–52. Heidelberg.

Marciniak, K., ed. 2021a. *Our Mythical Hope: The Ancient Myths as Medicine for the Hardships of Life in Children's and Young Adults' Culture*. Warsaw.

Marciniak, K. 2021b. 'Mythos/Mythologie', in *Ovid-Handbuch: Leben–Werk–Wirkung*, ed. M. Möller, 228–32. Stuttgart.

Marciniak, K. 2023. 'Make Peace, Not (the Trojan) War: Transformation and Continuity in the Mirror of the Myth of Troy—with a Focus on Polish Children's Literature', in *Political Changes and Transformations in Twentieth- and Twenty-first Century Children's Literature*, ed. B. Kümmerling-Meibauer and F. Schulz, 119–38. Heidelberg.

Marciniak, K. 2024 (forthcoming). 'Der Trojanische Käse, oder: Ökologiedidaxe und antike Mythen in Luis Sepúlvedas Roman *Wie Kater Zorbas der kleinen Möwe das Fliegen beibrachte* und in seiner Filmadaptation von Enzo D'Alò', in *Mythen multimedial: Modernste Antike in der Gegenwartskultur*, ed. M. Janka, R. Fichtel, and B. Sariaydin. 24–59. Darmstadt.

Maurice, L. 2015a. 'From Chiron to Foaly: The Centaur in Classical Mythology and Fantasy Literature', in *The Reception of Ancient Greece and Rome in Children's Literature: Heroes and Eagles*, ed. L. Maurice, 139–68. Leiden.

Maurice, L., ed. 2015b. *The Reception of Ancient Greece and Rome in Children's Literature: Heroes and Eagles*. Leiden.

Mickenberg, J. L., and L. Vallone. 2011. *The Oxford Handbook of Children's Literature*. Oxford.

Murnaghan, S., and D. H. Roberts. 2018. *Childhood and the Classics: Britain and America, 1850–1965*. Oxford.

Murnaghan, S., and D. H. Roberts. 2020. '"A Kind of Minotaur": Literal and Spiritual Monstrosity in the Works of Nathaniel Hawthorne', in *Chasing Mythical Beasts: The Reception of Ancient Monsters in Children's and Young Adults' Culture*, ed. K. Marciniak, 55–74. Heidelberg.

Nodelman, P. 2008. *The Hidden Adult: Defining Children's Literature*. Baltimore.

Peer, A. 2021. '*Cyclops of Central Park* by Madelyn Rosenberg, illus. Victoria Tentler-Krylov.' *Our Mythical Childhood Survey*. Warsaw. http://omc.obta.al.uw.edu.pl/myth-survey/item/1298. Accessed 5 November 2023.

Roberts, D. H., and S. Murnaghan. 2020. 'Picturing Duality: The Minotaur as Beast and Human in Illustrated Myth Collections for Children', in *Chasing Mythical Beasts: The Reception of Ancient Monsters in Children's and Young Adults' Culture*, ed. K. Marciniak, 75–97. Heidelberg.

Rowling, J. K. 2001. *Fantastic Beasts & Where to Find Them*. London.

Sayfan, L., and K. H. Lagattuta. 2009. 'Scaring the Monster Away: What Children Know About Managing Fears of Real and Imaginary Creatures.' *Child Development* 80/6: 1756–74.

Wall, B. 1991. *The Narrator's Voice: The Dilemma of Children's Fiction*. Basingstoke.

Zajko, V., and H. Hoyle, eds. 2017. *A Handbook to the Reception of Classical Mythology*. Hoboken, NJ.

CHAPTER 38

ANCIENT MONSTERS IN MODERN SPECULATIVE FICTION

BENJAMIN ELDON STEVENS, JESSE WEINER, AND BRETT M. ROGERS

INTRODUCTION

IN this chapter, we discuss how monsters from ancient Greek and Roman materials may be found in every genre and medium of modern speculative fiction: in science fiction, horror, and fantasy, and in formats including print, film and television, and games. Examples range widely over classical monsters, which likewise vary in their modern cultural prominence, and across different modes and histories of reception. In general, however, ancient monsters in speculative fiction continue to do what they did in classical sources: they 'demonstrate' (i.e. de-monst[e]r-ate, after Latin *monstrare*, 'to show'; see Foucault 1967: 68–70 and Weiner 2018: 179–84). In particular, monsters reveal the imaginary but consequential boundaries that are set up in culture to separate categories of being, especially 'human' and 'natural' from purported 'others'.

Ancient Greek and Roman monsters thus symbolize a central theme of modern science fiction, horror, and fantasy: the limits of human knowledge. By embodying complications for taxonomy, monsters draw attention to the historical contingence and ideological force of categories like 'human being'; like other figures for repressed speech, they articulate how such cultural fictions result in living beings' real experience of violence, exclusion, and precarity. On this reading, ancient monsters would seem to further speculative fiction's critical inquiry into modern power structures by exposing the limits and excesses of inherited classical humanism. Indeed, as alternatives to normative humanity, monsters are suggestive of a possibility for change in power structures: a potential teratopolitics (from Greek *teras*, 'monster').

In what follows, we first aim to sketch the range of relevant ancient monsters and speculative fiction by describing a set of examples: the Cyclops, Medusa, and the Minotaur. Even that small set can suggest the complexity of reception histories and of interrelated definitions of monster/monstrosity and human/humanity. With the same examples also indicating overlaps of science fiction, horror, and fantasy *in practice*, we discuss why it is useful to consider those genres together *in theory*: they may all be read as knowledge fictions premised on certain ancient modes, with science fiction 'Promethean', horror arguably 'Sphinxian', and fantasy 'Protean'.

Next, we turn to what are arguably, first, the most famous modern monster with ancient roots and, second, the most famous modern monster whose ancient roots are made up: *Frankenstein*'s Creature and the Kraken from *Clash of the Titans*. Drawing out some of their political implications, we take monstrosity's complex boundary-crossings—in bodies, geographies, and laws—as an invitation to examine how our three genres (re-) constitute the related monstrous or not-classical (humanist) body, with special reference to biopolitics and the possibility of a revolutionary teratopolitics. We conclude with final remarks on monsters as figures of epochal transition and Suggested Reading.

THE CYCLOPS, MEDUSA, AND THE MINOTAUR

We begin by examining three paradigmatic monsters from classical antiquity: the Cyclops Polyphemus, the Gorgon Medusa, and the Cretan Minotaur. Though an admittedly small sample from the multitude of creatures swarming through ancient Greek and Roman literature and art, even just these three allow us to examine the many complexities of reception histories and interrelated conceptions of monster/monstrosity and human/humanity.

The mythic Cyclops of Homer's *Odyssey* Book 9 is recalled in monocular antagonists like the all-seeing eye of Sauron in J. R. R. Tolkien's series *The Lord of the Rings* (1954–1955); the AI HAL-9000 in Stanley Kubrick's film *2001: A Space Odyssey* (1968); the humanoid robot Cylons of the first *Battlestar Galactica* television series (1978–1979) created by Glenn A. Larson (cf. Tomasso 2015); and the horrific anthropophagous daughter of Poseidon in the comics series *Ody-C* (2014–) by Matt Fraction and Christian Ward (cf. Rogers 2018: 219–21). Similarly, snaky-haired Medusa features in both the 1981 and 2010 *Clash of the Titans* films (cf. Chiu 2010 and Curley 2015); in the largely 'false medieval' role-playing game *Dungeons & Dragons* (1974–), created by Gary Gygax and Dave Arneson (cf. Marshall 2019: 158–64); and as an enemy of Wonder Woman in comics and other media, starting with *Wonder Woman* #153 (April 1965) by Robert Kanigher and Ross Andru.

Some recent works have sought to rehabilitate or humanize such figures, playing on the modern trope of retelling stories with sympathy for the Devil or the anti-hero. Such retellings respond to stories being structured around the Monomyth or so-called Hero's Journey (per Campbell 1949): for example, the myth of the hero Theseus entering the Labyrinth to fight the Minotaur becomes a model for *Labyrinth* (dir. Jim Henson 1986) and Suzanne Collins's *The Hunger Games* (2008–2010; cf. Blasingame 2009: 726–7). In that trilogy, President Snow, who presides over the capital's ritualized sacrifice of children from indebted provinces, recalls both King Minos and the Minotaur, and so must be defeated by Katniss Everdeen acting as a kind of Theseus, 'volunteering as tribute' (Mills 2015).

When, however, modern speculative fiction is critical, seemingly descriptive categories like 'hero' and 'monster' are exposed as projections of self-interested power structures. Thus, Katniss is also monstrous, undergoing a symbolic metamorphosis from ordinary, mortal girl and hunter into the image of the birdlike Mockingjay, both a potentially hunted animal and a symbol of political revolution (Makins 2015: 298–301). In turn, modern critical fictions can point backwards to the complexity of monstrosity in ancient materials: the Minotaur results from Queen Pasiphaë's desire for bestiality; in one version of Medusa's myth, the originally beautiful maiden is punished by Minerva with snaky hair after Neptune violates her in Minerva's temple (Ov. *Met.* 4.794–803); and the Cyclops Polyphemus lives outside human society and, upon encountering humans, commits violence and is violently injured.

As these first examples may suggest, some modern works identify their monsters as ancient or classical, while others use ancient myth as a basis for new characters and stories. Still other works are more abstract, not depicting monsters but engaging with ancient ideas about monstrosity. So, reception might usefully be theorized in order to emphasize a question central to modern speculative fiction: how do we define 'human' and its putative 'others'? From this perspective, monsters continue to 'demonstrate', showing how boundaries between categories like 'human' and 'not human' are not natural givens but rather cultural constructions.

DEFINING 'MONSTROSITY'

Ancient monsters may help us identify such cultural constructions in ways that more modern monsters cannot, since many modern monsters have been domesticated as parts of commercial identities—for example, the Cyclops Mike Wazowski in Pixar's 2001 film *Monsters, Inc.* and the Italian seafood brand Medusa. Indeed, monstrosity resists a universal definition across cultures and time, as suggested by a statement attributed to Varro by Isidore: monsters 'do not come into being contrary to nature, but rather contrary to what nature *is understood* to be' (*Etym.* 11.3.1–2, our emphasis). Monsters thus embody problems in knowledge, unsettling the taxonomies we construct to order 'nature', including our own status as 'natural'.

Such bodily monstrosity is often framed as mixture or hybridity—as with snaky Medusa, dog-like Scylla, horse-human centaurs, and winged Pegasus—and ancient thinkers emphasized that framework. Lucretius highlights the hybrid-as-monster, writing that nature could never have produced such bodily forms (*DRN* 5.916–24). Isidore includes hybridity as one of twelve categories marking monstrous bodies, alongside such features as impossible size and strength, as well as extra limbs (*Etym.* 11.3.7–11; cf. Williams 1996: 107). Epistemological trouble is therefore signalled in the monster's chief marker, its body. From Polyphemus through later classical and Renaissance physiognomy to horribly scarred Freddy Krueger of the horror-film franchise *A Nightmare on Elm Street*, bodily monstrosity is, as in Varro's dictum, thought to mark ethical deviance (esp. Halberstam 1995)—hence the frequent modern application of 'monster' to people committing extreme violence (cf. Felton 2021).

In signalling how monstrosity is a matter of shifting definition, classical monsters in modern speculative fiction may reveal how imaginary distinctions can be used to justify real differences in treatment. In the cultural imaginary of classical myth, violence to 'unnatural' bodies is only 'natural', a kind of foregone conclusion. Figures like the Cyclops, Medusa, and the Minotaur are, when not simply killed, variously maimed, made disabled (cf. Raphael 2015), or despoiled of livelihood as if in natural extension of already inhuman lifeways. They are sites for dispossession of personhood by ostensible persons who, themselves, act monstrously (cf. Watkins 1995).

In this way, whole categories of being are considered justifiably excluded from humanity by virtue of their alleged monstrosity and are thereby reduced to mere bodies or 'bare life' (Agamben 1998; see also Butler 2000; Foucault 2004: 243–6; Butler and Spivak 2007; and Mbembe 2019). By continuing to reveal the dehumanizing effects wrought by systems of order, classical monsters in speculative fiction embody real alternatives to present cultural imaginaries. They attest to histories of power that underlie the ideology of classical humanism, while also suggesting how classical receptions may contribute to a potentially revolutionary politics of monstrosity: a teratopolitics.

PROMETHEAN SCIENCE FICTION

With their characteristic interest in unsettling boundaries, the genres of science fiction, horror, and fantasy seem suited to hosting troublesome classical monsters. But what is the nature of this reception? Do monsters from ancient Greek and Roman materials appear in speculative fiction at random, or rather in some patterns or relationships to other generic aspects? We might ask whether classical monsters do different kinds of work—taxonomical, ontological, epistemological, ethical, or political—in science fiction, fantasy, and horror taken separately.

At least since Mary Wollstonecraft Shelley's *Frankenstein*, science fiction has appeared to be a 'Promethean' genre or mode, interested in how technology—not in the narrow sense of a new invention (like the fire stolen by Prometheus) but in the broader, Heideggerian sense of any process that transforms unknown natural materials into knowable cultural products—helps define the human condition (Rogers and Stevens 2017: 10). If science fiction is thus a kind of 'knowledge fiction', its monsters embody our freighted relationship to knowledge. One example would be the Id Monster in the film *Forbidden Planet* (dir. Fred M. Wilcox, 1956). Generated by advanced extraterrestrial mind-technology, the Id Monster is a physical (albeit invisible) manifestation of a character's suppressed self-knowledge, enacting secret desires that include doing violence to his fellow human beings. Since the film demonstrably draws on Sophocles' *Oedipus Rex* (Bucher 2015), *Forbidden Planet* illustrates how science-fictional monstrosity may trouble knowledge considered classical, including classical humanism.

Beyond *Forbidden Planet*, other works of Promethean science fiction seem both to define the human condition and to trouble its boundaries. Like the mythic culture hero and trickster Prometheus, science fiction not only disguises but also reveals the historically contingent privilege upon which knowledge-making disciplines (Foucauldian *epistemai*) have been constructed. Shelley's *Frankenstein*, for example, blurs the line between creator and creation, such that the novel—like the Greek tragedy on which it draws, *Prometheus Bound*—points to how its very existence as a story could come undone (see below). The rewritability of traditional stories raises serious questions about the continued effect of constructed categories like 'human' and 'monster' on real lives. Monsters can thus help to make (un)clear how classical reception emphasizes the instability of boundaries.

As we have argued elsewhere, modern receptions in science fiction remake 'the classics' into 'reliably esoteric, public-domain material for popular cultural ironization' (Rogers and Stevens 2012: 131). Such remade classics, 'as it were cobbled and stitched together into a new *monstrum*', form part of an ongoing cultural turn 'marked by recomposition of past cultural products'. Such recomposition is literalized in monsters, 'imagistically vivid but ontologically indistinct', both familiar and unrecognizable, seeming unknowable or hitherto unseen while yet revealing (post)modern master narratives and ideologies. Receptions in science fiction—and horror and fantasy—continuously reinvent classics that never existed: rather like *Frankenstein*'s reanimated patchwork Creature, they are built of the exhumed and 'discordant assemblages of limbs' of ancient materials, as in Lucretius' image of monsters as *discordia membra* (*DRN* 5.894; cf. Weiner 2015a: esp. 52–64 and Weiner 2018).

SPHINXIAN HORROR?

The image of 'discordant assemblages of limbs' directs our gaze to horror. If science fiction is in a Promethean mode, is there a comparably productive ancient-mythic analogy for horror? Scholars have argued that horror constitutes 'forbidden-knowledge fiction', dramatizing our encounters with what seems unnatural, uncanny, or otherwise not-to-be-known (see Colavito 2007). While horror may place obscenely monstrous bodies and acts of violence before our very eyes, perhaps the main forbidden knowledge is the recognition that one's privilege, including forms of bodily autonomy, is implicated in others' precarity. From this perspective, horror is a critical historical genre: its images of physical harm may fictionalize but do not therefore falsify the violence to which people are subjected in real life.

With privilege and precarity in mind, one may first wish to label horror 'Scyllan', after the *Odyssey*'s ravenous dog-monster, especially if we think of noble Odysseus surviving by sacrificing six of his sailors to it (12.244–60). Indeed, even though Circe has given him advance warning, Odysseus specifically withholds details from his crew to prevent inspiring fear in advance (12.222–33); but once they see Scylla, fear overtakes them (12.243–4), such that Odysseus' privileged hero's journey is simultaneously horror for his less-privileged men. Such supernatural or non-human violence against Odysseus' men recalls the violence found in ancient myths about encounters between mortals and gods, often resulting in mortals' destruction or destructive transformation. Monstrous violence and supernatural encounter are reflected in modern-mythic icons like H. P. Lovecraft's immortal cosmic deity Cthulhu (Beal 2002; Krämer 2017), such that a possibly Scyllan horror may be more recognizable to modern audiences as 'Lovecraftian.' In his 1928 short story 'The Call of Cthulhu', Lovecraft introduced the titular creature as 'a monster of vaguely anthropoid outline, but with an octopus-like head whose face was a mass of feelers, a scaly, rubbery-looking body, prodigious claws on hind and fore feet, and long, narrow wings behind' (Lovecraft 1978: 54); Cthulhu thus recalls the hybrid mode of classical monsters like Scylla and the Sphinx. Its vague human shape, however, in combination with its non-human animal features, gigantic scale, and incalculable age, pushes it beyond hybridity into utter unknowability: a monstrous body that is emblematic of the uncanny and the sublime.

While characteristic of Lovecraftian fiction, such qualities as the uncanny and the sublime are not limited to modern monsters. Ancient myth includes similarly squamous or formless creatures operating at cosmic, i.e. world-ordering, scales. One is Typhoeus, as described in Hesiod's *Theogony* (820–68; see Brockliss in this volume), a monster whose perceived threat to divine order is mapped onto its disordered body and uncanny vocalizations. Such cacophony appears in other ancient monstrous figures as well: the Sirens, whose song entangles its audience (see Pucci 1997); or mythic Helen, the daughter of a swan and hatched from an egg, who introduces disorder by imitating the voices of the wives of every Achaean soldier hiding in the Wooden Horse (*Od.* 4.265–90). The trope of monstrous capacity mapped onto female bodies recurs in science fiction and horror, as in non-humanoid figures like the Echidnic Alien Queen of *Aliens* (dir. James Cameron 1986) and in dangerous gynoids like the seductive Ava of *Ex Machina* (dir. Alex Garland 2014; cf. Hammond 2018; Wosk 2015).

As in those films, monsters also reveal how genres, like categories of body, are riddles with no clear single or simple answer. Thus, *Forbidden Planet* may gesture, via its classical source, towards a different ancient figure for horror. The plot of Sophocles' *Oedipus Rex* is easily read as horror, with unwanted discovery that is ultimately written onto the body. The *mise en abyme* of Oedipus' violent blinding is anticipated in the backstory's monster: the Sphinx, a hybrid of woman, lion, and bird. In the classical Greek imaginary, woman must be contained for her monstrous capacity of (re)production (Loraux 1978), while lions and birds are emblems of ravenous hunger—especially scavenging human bodies left unburied. The Sphinx's three sources are thus symbolic of biopolitical fears—that is, of the real violence that awaits precarious bodies. Since her role combines pestilence and riddles, like the tragedy's plot she links unknowable, uncanny, incomprehensible violence to secret knowledge (see López-Ruiz in this volume). In a possible parallel to Prometheus for science fiction, then, modern horror might productively be considered as forbidden-knowledge fiction in a monstrously Sphinxian mode.

PROTEAN FANTASY

Fantasy, too, may be read as knowledge fiction with ancient roots. Like horror, fantasy is notoriously difficult to define: although the major theorists in the field 'all agree that fantasy is about the construction of the impossible whereas science fiction may be about the unlikely', there is otherwise little positive consensus (James and Mendlesohn 2012: 1). Yet theorists often describe fantasy as 'Protean'—that is, 'metamorphic', 'fluid', 'having no fixed form', gesturing towards the ancient figure of Proteus, the 'Old Man of the Sea' capable of changing form and substance and who will reveal truth about past or future if he can be wrestled to a standstill (*Od.* 4.435–570; cf. Rogers and Stevens 2017: 12–14). In the figure of Proteus, we may therefore glimpse how fantasy develops images of monsters troubling knowledge. This can be comedic, in the manner of Bakhtin's carnivalesque, or perhaps Apuleian: ludic metamorphosis, with changing bodies embodying play across genre and other boundaries. Thus, for example, the nervous comedy in J. K. Rowling's *Harry Potter* series around polyjuice potion, a metamorphic technology that seems playfully fantastic to second-year Hogwarts students but also evokes more unsettling possibilities, including doppelgängers, human-animal hybrids (the series' *animagi*), and the racialized monstrosity of hybrid species (e.g. the centaurs). Similarly comic, the most powerful being in the *Incredibles* film series (dir. Brad Bird, 2004 and 2018) is a baby, Jack-Jack, whose endless changes in form and substance, as well as his boisterous hopping in and out of nearby dimensions, playfully mirror the films' own protean movement across genres (see Stevens 2025).

Fantasy thus joins science fiction and horror in treating knowledge in terms of beings that reveal much by resisting classification through their impossibility. That includes 'humans', a category whose definition may be arbitrary or, as in the myth of Proteus, a matter of others' constraint by force. Protean fantasy in particular can help us remember that the boundaries holding these subgenres apart are, like baby Jack-Jack and other monstrous bodies in mythic imaginaries, labile and liable to dangerous blurring, playful crossing, or outright collapse.

To suggest how such boundary blurring might affect our understanding of classical receptions, we turn now to two prominent modern monsters, whose Promethean nature, Sphinxian culture, and Protean (genre) forms are suggestive of central modes in classical receptions in speculative fiction.

FRANKENSTEIN'S CREATURE

Easily the most famous and influential modern monster is the Creature from Mary Wollstonecraft Shelley's 1818 novel, *Frankenstein; or, the Modern Prometheus*. Although in Shelley's era the name 'Prometheus' evoked a range of sources and associations, it ultimately alludes to the Titan of classical myth (e.g. Goldberg 1959; Small 1973; Priestman 2018; Rogers 2018: 208–10). The Titan most notably appears in ancient sources in two roles: as *pyrphoros*, Greek 'fire-bearer', who steals fire from Zeus and gives it to humankind, symbolizing technology and the arts or *technai* (e.g. Hes. *Op.* 50–2; Aesch., *PV*); and as *plasticator*, Latin 'shaper', who fashions humankind from clay and instils the spark of life (e.g. Ov. *Met.* 1.76–88). The two Promethean roles are both at work in *Frankenstein*, whose central conceit is an alchemical/technoscientific 'spark of being' that brings new life to dead animal matter (Pollin 1965; Mellor 1988; Barnett 2018).

This seems to identify Victor Frankenstein as the novel's Promethean figure. He has inspired a long tradition of 'mad scientists', including the likes of Lex Luthor in *Superman Returns* (dir. Bryan Singer 2006), Peter Weyland in *Prometheus* (dir. Ridley Scott 2012), and Nathan Bateman in *Ex Machina*. All Promethean in a would-be world-conquering mode, each commits transgression that is met by punishment. Luthor, having attempted to create a destructive new landmass, is instead trapped on a little island; Weyland, who has made a humanoid AI, is killed by an extraterrestrial Engineer, whose species long ago created humankind; and Bateman experiences a version of Victor's fear when he is killed by his latest gynoid 'bride of Frankenstein'. In these scenarios, knowledge-based creation becomes the creator's own undoing. As in classical tragedy, knowledge offers no real capacity to avert disaster.

Just as it remains an open question which of Shelley's two main characters is 'the Modern Prometheus', the Creature is not simply a monster from classical myth. As an artificial synthesis of parts brought to life, he may recall Pandora, who is both monstrous, embodying a 'beautiful evil' (*kalon kakon*) for humankind, and yet also marvellous, as an artifice producing 'wonder' (*thauma*; Hes. *Theog.* 585, 589). By extension, Frankenstein's Creature would be monstrous insofar as he is sublime, perhaps so beautiful as to be beyond human comprehension (Gumpert 2018). But Pandora is hybridized early in the classical tradition: attributed no subjectivity in ancient stories, in later versions she is elided with aspects of biblical Eve (Stevens 2022: 171–2). Hence *Frankenstein* pairs its subtitle's allusion to *Prometheus Bound* with an epigraph from Milton's retelling of the Fall, when Adam asks, 'Did I request Thee, Maker, from my Clay | to mould me Man?' (*Paradise Lost* 10.743–4). Here, again, is paradigmatically modern monstrosity asking about its mode of being, only to find itself Protean, endlessly eluding certainty.

CLASH OF THE TITANS' KRAKEN

Modern speculative fiction paradigmatically does complex things with monsters from classical myth. The monsters in question, rarely simply 'monsters', are also rarely simply 'classical'. Even when a modern work identifies its monster as ancient, that very action reveals the modern work as productive of hitherto unforeseen categories. Thus, *Frankenstein*'s subtitle, *the Modern Prometheus*, overtly refers to the ancient myth while also suggesting a new story. We may further track monstrous, metaliterary (re-) productivity in, for example, the movement from Shelley's novel to Dan Simmons's

'Frankenstein monster syndrome', which he uses in *The Fall of Hyperion* to describe the 'fear of anything in human form that is not completely human' (1990: 14).

Such metaliterary hideous progeny are rarely simply ludic but also further speculative fiction's serious challenges to institutional knowledge-systems. Speculative fiction offers alternatives to reason, parodying the power-fantasies of imperialist epistemological projects like the Enlightenment and suggesting what could now be different by imagining what never was (Flugt 2017). Nor is this impetus modern. For example, Lucian's *True Stories*, from the second century CE, explicitly parodies the credulity of earlier ancient Greek 'masters of truth' such as Homer, Herodotus, and various philosophers (Detienne 1999; cf. Fredericks 1976; Georgiadou and Larmour 1998).

Modern speculative fiction often follows suit, adopting self-consciously unclassical forms and themes. For example, Horace Walpole's 1764 Gothic novel *The Castle of Otranto* signals a commitment to disunity of form that is denigrated in the ancient Roman poet Horace's influential *Ars poetica* (see Rogers and Stevens 2017: 1–7; Uden 2020: 61–3). In horror, Bram Stoker's *Dracula* is comprised of several literary forms, including stenography and telegraphy, matched thematically by Count Dracula's obsession with modern media including the phonograph and the cinema (Wicke 1992). In fantasy, Tolkien's *The Hobbit* and *The Lord of the Rings* present themselves similarly as found texts that are only translated by the author into English, the former 'compiled from [the main character's] memoirs' and the latter derived from that text and other materials, together comprising the equally fictional *The Red Book of Westmarch* (Flieger 1997). These and other examples suggest that form, including monstrosity, is as much a matter of literary bodies of work and genres as it is of physical bodies per se, with the one symbolizing the other and vice versa.

Such metapoetic involution or *mise en abyme* occurs, finally, in what is perhaps the most famous 'ancient' monster without classical sources in modern speculative fiction, the Kraken (Gloyn 2020: 51–3; 2013). The Kraken belongs properly to eighteenth-century Scandinavian myth (if not reaching back to medieval Norse myth), yet this sea creature has subsequently been projected backwards in time via modern representations of classical mythos. In 1981's *Clash of the Titans* (dir. Desmond Davis), the Kraken is kept in an underwater cave with its entrance barred; once released, the monster becomes a source of science-fictional wonder and horrific fear even for the Olympian gods. Poseidon's open-mouthed amazement echoes the gods' response to Hesiodic Pandora, such that the Kraken is likewise—and like Frankenstein's Creature—sublime. Poseidon's wonder further models our response to the film and emphasizes how aesthetic response cannot be separated from ethical considerations.

Poseidon's amazement, however, is not identical to that of moviegoers marvelling at the artistry of Ray Harryhausen's stop-motion animation. By contrast, inside the story the Kraken leaves even the gods feeling threatened, topples cities, evidently will accept but not be sated by human sacrifice, and ultimately can be stopped only by another weapon of mass destruction, the severed head of Medusa. In a telling moment, these two exemplary monsters disappear together, the petrified Kraken's body collapsing under its own weight into the sea that swallows Medusa's head. If this is fantasy, then here are removed the final major obstacles on the hero's journey. But with genres overlapping and monsters confounding definition, the political consequences are more complex. And so to political readings we (re)turn.

TERATOPOLITICS

Although science fiction, horror, and fantasy may be treated together as speculative fiction, our attempts to identify an ancient-mythic analogue for each have also revealed significant differences among the genres' classical receptions. This matters because popular culture, including genre fictions, is a field where cultural constructions of real-world import may be articulated and challenged. So, while at first blush the topic of ancient monsters in modern speculative fiction could seem esoteric, every act of marking off a category of being as 'monstrous' is a form of biopolitics (Foucault 2004). Scholars have begun to examine how ancient materials are mobilized to serve modern biopolitical structures, with an emergent focus on possibilities for what constitutes the 'human' beyond the limits and exclusions of classical humanism (e.g. Lively 2008; Bianchi, Brill, and Holmes 2019; Chesi and Spiegel 2020). We must therefore consider how classical receptions, too, may serve modern biopolitical practices, while remaining open to the hope that, since monstrosity may resist definition, receptions of ancient monsters can suggest potential alternatives to present imaginaries of power.

MODERN BIOPOLITICS

We noted above how Varro suggested that monsters are contrary not to nature but to what we understand nature to be (cf. Weiner 2018: 170). 'Human nature' could thus be treated as a juridical category; consider Lucian's dialogue *Prometheus*, in which both the creation of humans and their empowerment through technology have been deemed criminal by Zeus. Ovid's *Metamorphoses* similarly presents several tales of the artificial creation or reanimation of human life, all of which end poorly—including an origin story wherein the species' new founders after cataclysmic flood, Deucalion and Pyrrha, are criticized by the poet himself 'for turning to artificial means of reproduction' when they cast stones to form the new human race (see Lively 2018: 26–8). These tales can be read as mythic figurations of how discourse is used to categorize living beings under unjust power-structures.

So, too, Homer's *Odyssey*, especially Books 9–12. Read as science fiction, Odysseus' wanderings begin with a desire for knowledge about unknown places and their inhabitants (cf. Weiner 2015b). The perceived risks of scientific pursuit are symbolized in the monsters, which add a political dimension to distinctions between human and non-human and suggest potential danger to the polis in cross-contamination or ethical hybridity (see Horkheimer and Adorno 2002: 35–62; Rogers 2015). Instructed by Circe, Odysseus uses a technological solution—stuffing his sailors' ears with wax and having them strap him to the mast—to listen to the Sirens, hoping to hear their account of his toils at Troy and all things upon the earth without succumbing to the usually fatal song (12.158–200). *Technai* also allow for Odysseus to enforce the distinction between human and non-human by intoxicating Polyphemus with wine, blinding him with a firebrand, and, in a final trick of language—'No-one is killing me' (9.408)—shutting him off even from the society of his fellow Cyclopes by making him speak nonsense.

The *Odyssey*'s monster stories are also revealing when read as fantasy: the Sirens, Cyclops, Scylla and Charybdis, and more become mere obstacles for the ostensible hero to overcome on his journey home to Ithaca. Ancient parallels include monsters subdued by Heracles and Theseus in their labours, such as the Hydra and the Minotaur; the Harpies, fire-breathing bulls, earth-born men, dragons, and bronze giant Talus, all encountered by Jason; and the creatures Aeneas, his journey aping Odysseus', escapes en route to Italy from the ruins of Troy. Each myth is a lengthy quest that monsters threaten to derail, such that evading or subjugating them is a mark of 'heroic' status. Even if much modern high fantasy adopts false medieval aesthetics (see Folch 2017: esp. 160–7), it also looks back to such ancient stories of ordering, like that of Cadmus, an iconic early dragon-slayer whose wanderings span continents (cf. Weiner 2017; Ogden 2013: esp. 109–18).

REGRESSIVE FANTASIES OF ANTIQUITY?

On this model, high fantasy seems less frequently to afford monsters ethical consideration in terms of their relation to humanity and place in the natural world. There are exceptions—for example, the orogenes in N. K. Jemisin's *Broken Earth* trilogy, Dobby the elf in the *Harry Potter* series, or the orcs of Stan Nichols's *Orcs* trilogy. Each example presents its sympathetic monsters in opposition to humans and, therefore, as subjected to political conditions of enslavement. However, the Tolkien model is more prevalent: giant spiders, the treasure-hoarding dragon Smaug, and others are merely obstacles to the likes of Bilbo, Frodo, and Aragorn. Even the sentient monstrous figures' potential personhood or claims to social inclusion are hardly at issue.

Nevertheless, the subjugation or elimination of monsters in fantasy is, as it was in ancient myth, political in different ways. In addition to a realm or empire frequently being at stake, the overcoming or disappearance of monsters frequently has a civilizing force. The mythic voyage of the Argo is a narrative of colonization, and the dispersal of monsters by Heracles, Theseus, and Perseus has the ideological implication of making the world safer and more civilized for human beings (Dougherty 1993: 38; Mori 2008: 16, 40; Murray 2017: 65). So it is that, after monstrous figures like Smaug and Sauron have been bested in *The Hobbit* and *The Lord of the Rings*, even avatars of the divine like Wizards and Elves must depart Middle-Earth, clearing room for the forthcoming age of humans.

A Potentially
Revolutionary Teratopolitics

Many ancient-monster stories and modern fantasies have been deployed in service of social, economic, and political ideologies that would reify as 'natural' what are in fact historical systems of oppression. But might we read monsters in ancient myth, or ancient monsters in classical receptions, as revealing such hierarchies so as to suggest a way forward?

Here we return one last time to *Frankenstein*, which we have previously read as 'interrogating ancient discourses in ways that speak to ongoing concerns about politics and society in the global twenty-first century'; particularly, the Creature's 'composite nature, taken to mark him as abject and subhuman, represents the challenge posed by hybridity to monolithic authority' (Weiner et al. 2018: 13). Modern discourses of colonialism have their own classical reception histories, recalling practices found in ancient Greek and Roman ethnography (Said 1978; Rossi-Reder 2002; Weiner 2016). We have therefore argued that the Creature's 'struggles for inclusion in society and for identification as human speak to current biopolitical crises and some of the most pressing social issues of our time, which include movements for progressive expansion of rights to historically marginalized groups and the plight of refugees around the world' (Weiner et al. 2018: 13; cf. Ciccone 2022 on classics and the Syrian refugee crisis).

These concerns are not limited to *Frankenstein* or to science fiction. A core function of ancient monsters in speculative fiction is to name the secret history of modern culture via the proxy of their own 'unspeakable' bodies. The significance of this trope is suggested by the sheer proliferation of *Frankenstein*'s hideous progeny—figures like the androids and xenomorphs of the *Blade Runner* and *Alien* film series, Sil in *Species* (dir. Roger Donaldson 1995), Ava in *Ex Machina*, and hundreds more. Many such monsters not only embody but also voice essential questions about the limits of the 'human', including the ethics of epistemological projects like technoscience and the right to change, make, or take life.

In that context, monsters cannot but be political, implying a potentially revolutionary teratopolitics. Our focus has been on showing how such modern monsters, all resisting classification as 'Linnaean nightmares' (Greenberg 1991: 190; cf. Cohen 1996b: 6; Weiner 2018: 170), also involve classical receptions. With ancestors as varied as the Cyclops, Medusa, the Minotaur, Prometheus, Scylla, the Sphinx, Proteus, Talus, and more, monsters and their creators in speculative fiction embody the ongoing productivity of ancient materials beyond the 'human' and therefore beyond subsequent traditions of classical humanism. Exposing that shibboleth as a biopolitical word of power, the study of these receptions may shed new light on the monstrous in ancient myths and other taxonomical discourses—and help keep unsettled definitions of so freighted a being as the 'human'.

CONCLUSION

Folklorist Vladimir Propp argued that the hybrid monsters of ancient myth arose out of social transformations and upheaval, 'out of the clash of two ages or of two systems and their ideologies. The old and the new can exist not only in a state of unresolved contradictions; they may also enter into hybrid formations' (1984: 11–12). The monsters of science fiction, horror, and fantasy can often be understood as markers of such transitions. Thus, Propp's thought resembles Antonio Gramsci's statement that 'the crisis consists precisely in the fact that the old is dying and the new cannot be born: in this interregnum, morbid symptoms of the most varied kind come to pass' (1996: 32–3). Slavoj Žižek (2012: 43) strikingly translates the latter portion of Gramsci's line as 'now is the time of monsters', implicitly linking Gramsci's political analysis to the critical cultural insight of Jeffrey Jerome Cohen (1996a: vii)—namely, 'we live in a time of monsters'.

In science fiction, these transitions may be imagined variously: as an outward spread of humanity from Earth into the cosmos; as progress towards the technological singularity; as dystopic/utopic political change; or as a state existing somewhere between the human and post-human. In fantasy, related transitions may be between barbarism and civilization, between different epochs, or between the spiritual and the rational. They may also be Protean or Ovidian transformations from one form into another or signal an ascent into heroic stature.

Even as these genres look backwards to the classical past in their formulation of monstrosity, we thus find it of little surprise that they rose in popularity in concert with the Industrial Revolution, periods of political upheaval, transformative social change, and technoscientific acceleration. From this perspective, Liz Gloyn rightly suggests that classical monsters, rather than being the discarded *discordia membra* of times long past, 'are still capable of asking us difficult questions about what our culture values and whether the boundaries we think we have established actually stand firm' (2020: 196). Through our own speculative universes, the mythical monsters of antiquity thus continue to challenge us towards critical introspection.

ACKNOWLEDGEMENTS

For assistance on receptions in horror, we are grateful to two Summer (2020) Undergraduate Research Fellows at Trinity University, Meg McDonald and Will Ramsey, both '22. We also extend our gratitude to Debbie Felton for helpful comments.

SUGGESTED READING AND SCREENINGS

Although directed mainly towards medieval monsters, Cohen (1996a) has also been foundational for the study of monsters in popular culture. The fullest study of specifically classical monsters in that context is Gloyn (2020), a chronological approach focused on film and television, with many examples from science fiction and fantasy. Those two genres are theorized as sites of classical reception in Rogers and Stevens (2015, 2017), drawing on the essential Liveley (2008). Relevant chapters in those two volumes include Weiner (2015a) on Lucretius and Lucan in *Frankenstein*; Bucher (2015) on the Oedipal Id Monster in *Forbidden Planet*; Rogers (2015) on Odyssean hybridity in *Alien: Resurrection*; and Syson (2017) on the Harpies in *His Dark Materials*. On monsters in the fantasy role-playing game series *Dungeons & Dragons*, see Marshall (2019). For classical reception in horror, see Colavito (2013) on *Dracula*, and Krämer (2017) on Lovecraft. Important related work includes Colavito (2007) on horror as knowledge fiction and Uden (2020) on classical receptions as haunting in the Gothic, including *Frankenstein*.

WORKS CITED

Agamben, G. 1998. *Homo Sacer: Sovereign Power and Bare Life*, trans. D. Heller-Roazen. Stanford, CA.

Barnett, S. 2018. 'Romantic Prometheis and the Molding of *Frankenstein*', in Frankenstein *and Its Classics: The Modern Prometheus from Antiquity to Science Fiction*, ed. J. Weiner, B. E. Stevens, and B. M. Rogers, 76–90. London.

Beal, T. K. 2002. *Religion and Its Monsters*. New York.

Bianchi, E., S. Brill, and B. Holmes, eds. 2019. *Antiquities beyond Humanism*. Oxford.

Blasingame, J. 2009. 'An Interview with Suzanne Collins'. *Journal of Adolescent and Adult Literacy* 52/8: 726–7.

Bucher, G. M. 2015. 'A Complex Oedipus: The Tragedy of Edward Morbius', in *Classical Traditions in Science Fiction*, ed. B. M. Rogers and B. E. Stevens, 123–44. Oxford.

Butler, J. 2000. *Antigone's Claim: Kinship between Life and Death*. New York.

Butler, J., and G. Spivak. 2007. *Who Sings the Nation State? Language, Politics, Belonging*. New York.

Campbell, J. 1949. *The Hero with a Thousand Faces*. New York.

Chesi, G. M., and F. Spiegel, eds. 2020. *Classical Literature and Posthumanism*. London.

Chiu, A. 2010. 'Clash of the Titans'. *Classical Outlook* 87/3: 104–5.

Ciccone, N. 2022. 'Dislocated Identities: the *Aeneid* and the Syrian Refugee Crisis', in The Aeneid *and the Modern World*, ed. J. R. O'Neill and A. Rigoni, 198–210. London.

Cohen, J. J., ed. 1996a. *Monster Theory: Reading Culture*. Minneapolis.

Cohen, J. J. 1996b. 'Monster Culture (Seven Theses)', in *Monster Theory: Reading Culture*, ed. J. J. Cohen, 3–25. Minneapolis.

Colavito, J. 2007. *Science, Knowledge and the Development of the Horror Genre*. Jefferson, NC.

Colavito, J. 2013. 'On Dracula and Dionysus', https://www.jasoncolavito.com/blog/on-dracula-and-dionysus 10/26/13.

Curley, D. 2015. 'Divine Animation: *Clash of the Titans* (1981)', in *Classical Myth on Screen*, ed. M. Cyrino and M. Safran, 207–17. New York.

Detienne, M. 1999. *Masters of Truth in Archaic Greece*, trans. J. Lloyd. Princeton.

Dougherty, C. 1993. *The Poetics of Colonization: From City to Text in Archaic Greece*. Oxford.

Felton, D. 2021. *Monsters and Monarchs: Serial Killers in Classical Myth and History*. Austin.

Flieger, V. 1997. 'Frame Narrative', in *The J. R .R. Tolkien Encyclopedia*, ed. M. D. C. Drout, 216–18. New York.

Flugt, C. 2017. 'Theorizing Fantasy: Enchantment, Parody, and the Classical Tradition', in *Classical Traditions in Modern Fantasy*, ed. B. M. Rogers and B. E. Stevens, 47–62. Oxford.

Folch, M. 2017. 'A Time for Fantasy: Retelling Apuleius in C. S. Lewis's *Till We Have Faces*', in *Classical Traditions in Modern Fantasy*, ed. B. M. Rogers and B. E. Stevens, 160–88. Oxford.

Foucault, M. 1967. *Madness and Civilization: A History of Insanity in the Age of Reason*, trans. R. Howard. London.

Foucault, M. 2004. *Naissance de la biopolitique: Cours au Collège de France, 1978–1979*. Paris.

Fredericks, S. C. 1976. 'Lucian's *True History* as SF.' *Science Fiction Studies* 3/1: 49–60.

Georgiadou, A., and D. Larmour. 1998. *Lucian's Science Fiction Novel* True Histories: *Interpretation and Commentary*. Leiden.

Gloyn, L. 2013. ' "The Dragon-green, the Luminous, the Dark, the Serpent-haunted Sea": Monsters, Landscape and Gender in *Clash of the Titans* (1981 and 2010)', in *New Voices in Classical Reception Studies*, Conference Proceedings Volume One, ed. S. Green and P. Goodman, 64–75. Milton Keynes.

Gloyn, L. 2020. *Tracking Classical Monsters in Popular Culture*. Oxford.

Goldberg, M. A. 1959. 'Moral and Myth in Mrs. Shelley's *Frankenstein*.' *Keats–Shelley Journal* 8/1: 27–38.

Gramsci, A. 1996. *Prison Notebooks*, vol. 2, ed. and trans. J. A. Buttigieg. New York.

Greenberg, H. R. 1991. 'Reimagining the Gargoyle: Psychoanalytic Notes on *Alien*', in *Close Encounters: Film, Feminism, and Science Fiction*, ed. C. Penley et al., 83–106. Minneapolis.

Gumpert, M. 2018. 'The Sublime Monster: *Frankenstein*, or The Modern Pandora', in Frankenstein *and Its Classics: The Modern Prometheus from Antiquity to Science Fiction*, ed. J. Weiner, B. E. Stevens, and B. M. Rogers, 102–20. London.

Halberstam, J. 1995. *Skin Shows: Gothic Horror and the Technology of Monsters*. Durham, NC.

Hammond, E. 2018. 'Alex Garland's *Ex Machina* or The Modern Epimetheus', in Frankenstein *and Its Classics: The Modern Prometheus from Antiquity to Science Fiction*, ed. J. Weiner, B. E. Stevens, and B. M. Rogers, 190–205. London.

Horkheimer, M., and T. W. Adorno. 2002. *Dialectic of Enlightenment*, trans. E. Jephcott. Stanford, CA.

James, E., and F. Mendlesohn, eds. 2012. *The Cambridge Companion to Fantasy Literature*. Cambridge.

Krämer, R. P. 2017. 'Classical Antiquity and the Timeless Horrors of H. P. Lovecraft', in *Classical Traditions in Modern Fantasy*, ed. B. M. Rogers and B. E. Stevens, 92–117. Oxford.

Liveley, G. 2008. 'Science Fictions and Cyber Myths: Or, Do Androids Dream of Dolly the Sheep?', in *Laughing with Medusa*, ed. V. Zajko and M. Leonard, 275–94. Oxford.

Liveley, G. 2018. 'Patchwork Paratexts and Monstrous Metapoetics: "After tea M reads Ovid"', in Frankenstein *and Its Classics: The Modern Prometheus from Antiquity to Science Fiction*, ed. J. Weiner, B. E. Stevens, and B. M. Rogers, 25–41. London.

Loraux, N. 1978. 'On the Race of Women and Some of Its Tribes: Hesiod and Semonides.' *Arethusa* 11: 43–87.

Lovecraft, H. P. [1928] 1978. *The Colour Out of Space*. New York.

Makins, M. 2015. 'Refiguring the Roman Empire in *The Hunger Games* Trilogy', in *Classical Traditions in Science Fiction*, ed. B. M. Rogers and B. E. Stevens, 280–306. Oxford.

Marshall, C. W. 2019. 'Classical Reception and the Half-Elf Cleric', in *Once and Future Antiquities in Science Fiction and Fantasy*, ed. B. M. Rogers and B. E. Stevens, 149–71. London.

Mbembe, A. 2019. *Necropolitics*, trans. S. Corcoran. Durham, NC.

Mellor, A. K. 1988. *Mary Shelley: Her Life, Her Fiction, Her Monsters*. New York.

Mills, S. 2015. 'Classical Elements and Mythological Archetypes in *The Hunger Games*.' *New Voices in Classical Reception Studies* 10: 56–64.

Mori, A. 2008. *The Politics of Apollonius Rhodius'* Argonautica. Cambridge.

Murray, J. 2017. 'Apollonius of Rhodes, *Argonautica*, Selections', in *Hellenistic Poetry: A Selection*, ed. D. Sider, 64–97. Ann Arbor.

Ogden, D. 2013. *Dragons, Serpents, and Slayers in the Classical and Early Christian Worlds*. Oxford.

Pollin, B. 1965. 'Philosophical and Literary Sources of *Frankenstein*.' *Comparative Literature* 17/2: 97–108.

Priestman, M. 2018. 'Prometheus and Dr. Darwin's Vermicelli: Another Stir to the *Frankenstein* Broth', in Frankenstein *and Its Classics: The Modern Prometheus from Antiquity to Science Fiction*, ed. J. Weiner, B. E. Stevens, and B. M. Rogers, 42–58. London.

Propp, V. 1984. *Theory of History and Folklore*, trans. A.Y. Martin et al. Minneapolis.

Pucci, P. 1997. 'The Song of the Sirens', in *Reading the* Odyssey, ed. S. L. Schein, 191–200. Princeton.

Raphael, R. 2015. 'Disability as Rhetorical Trope in Classical Myth and *Blade Runner*', in *Classical Traditions in Science Fiction*, ed. B. M. Rogers and B. E. Stevens, 176–96. Oxford.

Rogers, B. M. 2015. 'Hybrids and Homecomings in the *Odyssey* and *Alien: Resurrection*', in *Classical Traditions in Science Fiction*, ed. B. M. Rogers and B. E. Stevens, 217–42. Oxford.

Rogers, B. M. 2018. 'The Postmodern Prometheus and Posthuman Reproductions in Science Fiction', in Frankenstein *and Its Classics: The Modern Prometheus from Antiquity to Science Fiction*, ed. J. Weiner, B. E. Stevens, and B. M. Rogers. 206–27. London.

Rogers, B. M., and B. E. Stevens. 2012. 'Classical Receptions in Science Fiction.' *Classical Receptions Journal* 4/1: 127–47.

Rogers, B. M., and B. E. Stevens, eds. 2015. *Classical Traditions in Science Fiction*. Oxford.

Rogers, B. M., and B. E. Stevens, eds. 2017. *Classical Traditions in Modern Fantasy*. Oxford.

Rossi-Reder, A. 2002. 'Wonders of the Beast: India in Classical and Medieval Literature', in *Marvels, Monsters, and Miracles: Studies in the Medieval and Early Modern Imaginations*, ed. T. S. Jones and D. A. Sprunger, 53–66. Kalamazoo.

Said, E. 1978. *Orientalism*. New York.

Simmons, D. 1990. *The Fall of Hyperion*. New York.

Small, C. 1973. *Mary Shelley's* Frankenstein: *Tracing the Myth*. Pittsburgh.

Stevens, B. E. 2022. ' "The beautiful trap inside us": Pandoran Science Fiction and Posthuman Personhood', in *Gender, Creation Myths and their Reception: Prometheus, Pandora, Adam, and Eve*, ed. L. Maurice and T. Bibring, 169–81. London.

Stevens, B. E. 2025. 'Greek and Roman Epic in Film Translation', in *A Companion to Translation of Classical Epic*, ed. R. Armstrong and A. Lianeri. Malden, MA.

Syson, A. 2017. 'Filthy Harpies and Fictive Knowledge in Philip Pullman's *His Dark Materials* Trilogy', in *Classical Traditions in Modern Fantasy*, ed. B. M. Rogers and B. E. Stevens, 233–49. Oxford.

Tomasso, V. 2015. 'Classical Antiquity and Western Identity in *Battlestar Galactica*', in *Classical Traditions in Science Fiction*, ed. B. M. Rogers and B. E. Stevens, 243–59. Oxford.

Uden, J. 2020. *Spectres of Antiquity: Classical Literature and the Gothic, 1740–1830*. Oxford.

Watkins, C. 1995. *How to Kill a Dragon: Aspects of Indo-European Poetics*. Cambridge, MA.

Weiner, J. 2015a. 'Lucretius, Lucan, and Mary Shelley's *Frankenstein*', in *Classical Traditions in Science Fiction*, ed. B. M. Rogers and B. E. Stevens, 46–74. Oxford.

Weiner, J. 2015b. 'Mapping Hubris: Odysseus' *Apologoi* and Vonnegut's *Cat's Cradle*.' *International Journal of the Classical Tradition* 22/1: 116–37.

Weiner, J. 2016. 'Xenophon, *Cyropaedia* 8.8: The Many Forms of Persian Decline after Cyrus.' *Cyrus' Paradise*, http://cyropaedia.online/book-8/chapter-8-8-bracketed-chapter-the-many-forms-of-persian-decline-after-cyrus. Accessed 28 October 2023.

Weiner, J. 2017. 'Classical Epic and the Poetics of Modern Fantasy', in *Classical Traditions in Modern Fantasy*, ed. B. M. Rogers and B. E. Stevens, 25–47. Oxford.

Weiner, J. 2018. 'Frankenfilm: Classical Monstrosity in Bill Morrison's *Spark of Being*', in Frankenstein *and Its Classics: The Modern Prometheus from Antiquity to Science Fiction*, ed. J. Weiner, B. E. Stevens, and B. M. Rogers, 170–89. London.

Weiner, J., B. E. Stevens, and B. M. Rogers, eds. 2018. Frankenstein *and Its Classics: The Modern Prometheus from Antiquity to Science Fiction*. London.

Wicke, J. 1992. 'Vampiric Typewriting: *Dracula* and Its Media.' *English Literary History* 59/2: 467–93.

Williams, D. A. 1996. *Deformed Discourse: The Function of the Monster in Mediaeval Thought and Literature*. Montreal.

Wosk, J. 2015. *My Fair Ladies: Female Robots, Androids, and Other Artificial Eves*. Rutgers.

Žižek, S. 2012. 'Living in the Time of Monsters', in *Critical Pedagogy in the New Dark Ages: Challenges and Possibilities*, ed. M. Nikolakaki, 32–44. New York.

CHAPTER 39

....

CLASSICAL MONSTERS IN MODERN POPULAR CULTURE

A Case Study in Fan Fiction

....

LIZ GLOYN

Introduction

....

As other chapters in this volume have explored, classical monsters appear in a wide range of mainstream media, including film, television, books, and computer games. While the products generated by these industries vary wildly in their shape and content, they share the underlying characteristic of being formed within a context which is interested primarily in generating a profit. The capitalist desire for commercial profitability inevitably shapes the outputs of creative industries; for instance, an inherent conservatism drives major Hollywood film studios, and sees monsters as heroic cannon fodder. While the classical monsters of mainstream culture have a certain permanence due to the media in which they appear, they are mediated through institutional gatekeeping and quality control. In the spirit of exploring the democratic turn in ancient Mediterranean studies, this chapter investigates how classical monsters appear in a different form of popular culture, fan fiction. Given the rise of convergence culture, created by often unanticipated interactions between different media systems and technological platforms (Jenkins 2006), and the ways technology makes once marginalized activities and groups increasingly accessible to society at large, the use of classical material by fan communities deserves greater attention from classical reception scholars.

First, some notes on my own position. I'm a white European woman living in the UK, in open-ended employment in UK higher education, with the economic security and privilege that brings. My expertise is classical reception in Anglo-American culture; in this chapter I focus on fan fiction written in English. Inevitably, a reader forms personal judgements about a given piece of writing; I have tried to avoid commenting on my perception of a piece's aesthetic qualities, but I have included examples I found particularly compelling. While I would not call myself an aca-fan, or a person who simultaneously is an academic and identifies as a fan of a particular fan-object (see the introduction of Hills 2002 for the distinction between fan-scholars and scholar-fans), I identify as fandom-adjacent: I have spoken about my academic work at conventions, and I have been active on the right parts of the internet for long enough that nobody needs to tell me that slash fiction is sexually explicit, although I have never written any. That said, I have debated whether I might be an aca-fan despite myself, given that I am writing about fan fiction written about Greek myth, which I both work with professionally and enjoy. This question of position is one of the challenges posed by work in this area, since classical reception has not yet fully worked out a framework for situating our subject in relation to fandom. I offer a preliminary attempt to construct such a framework, using ancient monsters as a test case for both the methodological challenges such a study poses and the insights that it offers.

FANDOM AND ANCIENT MYTHOLOGY

What makes a 'fan' has been the subject of debate since the inception of fan studies in the early 1990s, particularly in light of rapid changes brought about by the advent of the internet. The first wave of fan studies (e.g. Jenkins 1992) was defensive of fans, who were then often seen as deviant participants in peculiar communities—monsters in their own right, if you will. The defence and rehabilitation of fan culture attempted to mark it out as separate and marginalized from the mainstream, behaving in ways which were transgressive and resistant rather than passively consuming commercial culture. While fan studies scholarship now complicates this view to acknowledge that not everything in fandom is, by definition, resistant, the internet changed everything: it not only made fan culture more accessible (through listservs, internet communities, and dedicated websites rather than on-site conventions and hard-copy zines, self-published booklets made in limited numbers), but also made this culture more visible and co-optable to mainstream media corporations. Being a fan in the modern world is thus much easier than it was in the 1970s, and many people do things that might be described as 'fannish', such as reading internet forums devoted to celebrity gossip or their favourite television show.

Fandom is associated with a spectrum of behaviours, some of which are more demanding than others. Busse and Gray (2011: 434) use twin axes of community interaction and emotional investment to describe levels of fan identity and engagement; for instance, a casual viewer might skim webpages or communities they find interesting, but never take the step of registering on a site and becoming an active participant in a community. One fannish behaviour which undoubtedly requires more investment in the fan object is the production of transformative fanwork, which can consist of 'a variety of document formats, including artwork, video, animation, music, costume, poetry, installations, 3D worlds', and creative writing commonly known as 'fan fiction' (Price and Robinson 2017: 1.1). Academics studying fanfic usually locate its beginnings in the 1960s, with roots in *Star Trek* fandom and other science fiction and fantasy television series, initially circulated through hard-copy hand-produced zines (Hellekson and Busse 2014: 6). The internet has made creating fanfic and finding communities to share it much easier over the last twenty years, completely changing the landscape of fanfic production; while some sites and forums have elaborate feedback and drafting processes, on others a writer can just press 'post' and immediately make their story publicly available (Busse and Hellekson 2006: 6–7). Fanfic has also become more visible to mainstream culture, most notably through the blockbuster success of the *Fifty Shades of Grey* book series of E. L. James, which started its life as *Twilight* fan fiction (Hellekson and Busse 2014: 5). Nonetheless, deciding to produce fanfic inspired by a fan object demonstrates a higher level of investment in the fandom than that associated with a casual fan.

This leads us to the question of whether ancient mythology counts as a fandom. Fan studies scholarship has concentrated on fandoms focused on recent television series, films, and computer games, but as Brooker's study of the Lewis Carroll Society makes clear, fan activity is not limited to objects in popular media; despite the choice of a fan object with high levels of cultural capital, he found familiar characteristics of 'community bonding, the dedicated immersion in specialist arcana, debates about interpretation, and pilgrimages to geographical locations associated with the author and his works' (2005: 861–2). Similarly, while fans of Sherlock Holmes and J. S. Bach might find prefer the label of 'aficionado' or 'enthusiast' to 'fan', Pearson (2007) also found that patterns of behaviour in so-called high-culture fan communities tended to mirror those of popular culture fandoms. Classical myth fandom can also be confident that, as Farley (2016: 5.22) puts it, 'the Homeric poems are not under copyright'; as such, there is no question of whether its transformative activities are legitimate. Contra Fiske's assertion that 'in capitalist societies popular culture is necessarily produced from the products of capitalism' (1992: 47), classical myth fandom does not revolve around responses to a commercial product. Fanfic arising from classical myth or ancient history thus blurs the boundaries between a high-culture fan object and a fan practice associated with popular culture.

I should here note that fan objects with high levels of cultural capital can emerge from classical myth. Contemporary literary retellings of ancient myths abound—examples include Madeline Miller's *The Song of Achilles* (2011) and *Circe* (2018), Jorge Luis Borges's short story 'The House of Asterion' (1947), Mary Renault's novels *The King Must Die* (1958) and *The Bull from The Sea* (1962), and Jeanette Winterson's *Weight* (2018). What differentiates these works from fan fiction is not their subject and content, but the context of their production. They are written within the mechanisms of publishing houses, overseen by editors, reviewed though a system of various quality checks, distributed and sold for profit according to a publisher's marketing strategy, and aimed at reaching mass audiences. By contrast, fanfic is produced and published as and when the writer wishes it to be, without any formal oversight, with little or no institutional machinery, and is usually accessible for free or nominal amounts.

Many fanfic scholars identify community as a key element of fandom, because of the importance of having a shared set of interpretative standards and the interaction between like-minded people (see e.g. Busse and Gray 2011). Unlike cult objects such as the television series *Doctor Who* or *Lost*, no forums, zines, or discussion boards exist dedicated to classical myth fandom to provide a focused hub for activity community. Fans instead share their fanwork on private blogs, Tumblr, DeviantART, and even more ephemeral social media like Twitter and Facebook. However, the rise of the internet means that 'if you're one in a million, you can find a 250-person mailing list of people just like you' (Tushnet 2007: 63). Fanfic in particular supports rare fandoms through Yuletide, 'the annual rare and obscure fandoms fic exchange'. This exchange originated on the blogging website Livejournal, a popular forum for fanfic writers, and is now primarily managed and archived on the Archive of Our Own, also known as AO3, which describes itself as 'a fan-created, fan-run, non-profit, non-commercial archive for transformative fanworks, like fan fiction, fanart, fan videos, and podfic'. Farley's study of Homer fanfic on AO3 found 20 per cent of such stories were written for Yuletide (2016: 5.21). Classical myth fandom thus finds community inside these larger organizations, blurring the lines between community and engagement.

Classical fandom also demonstrates Brooker's 'dedicated immersion in specialist arcana'. Creators of fanwork drawing on the ancient world are often immersed in the Greek and Latin sources. For instance, people requesting Yuletide stories based around figures from ancient history referred to Cicero's letters to Atticus, a particular speech by Demosthenes, and specific academic literature to guide the authors assigned to write their Yuletide requests (Wilson 2016: 3.7–3.19). While less explicitly scholarly, in *A tale of Sirens*, Willow1977 (2021) offers a fictional explanation of how sirens and mermaids became conflated. Similarly, knowledge of Greek myth, whether obtained informally or in an educational setting, often shapes the production of transformative fanwork—particularly its desire to alter the 'traditional' myth and instead tell the myths as they 'ought' to be. For example, in the preface to *Thirteen Views of a Labyrinth* (2012), raspberryhunter thanks ricardienne for 'pointing me to Ovid and Catullus so I could draw details from them and then summarily ignore them'.

Providing alternative versions of antiquity follows broader patterns within fanfic of offering a range of interpretations of the fan object, ranging from the normative to the subversive (Busse and Gray 2011: 434–5). However, ancient myth again functions differently to other fan objects, in that it possesses an innate flexibility. For instance, in 431 BCE Euripides easily staged a new, very different version of the death of Medea's children: he introduced Medea murdering them to spite Jason. One way to explain this is to say that myth and fan fiction are both transformative in nature (Keen 2016: 6.2). Another way to talk about this quality is through hyperseriality, in that 'the relationships [in myth] not only come to life but help to create a coherent story world that serves to anchor and validate each individual myth in an infinitely reciprocal way' (Johnston 2015: 297); the rich and complex story world of the gods, heroes, and monsters of Greek myth allows both the repetition of key narrative points and the reshaping of connections between its characters. This suppleness means that 'interesting prequels, sequels, midquels, and paraquels could emerge, keeping the stories and their characters vigorously alive', much as fan fiction broadly defined creates similar stories outside the canon that do not exist but, the fan feels, really should (Johnston 2015: 309). Seen from this angle, transformative fanwork shares many similarities with the authors of antiquity, in that they both take a canon which is amenable to adaptation and seek to fill in its hinterland. As Willis (2016: 1.1) has persuasively argued, myth offers a useful model for 'understanding of fan fiction as narrative form and as social practice' beyond its engagement with the classical world.

Medusa and the Minotaur

My research focuses on the archive gathered in AO3, which is a public space without any community structure and thus differs from, for instance, the Harry Potter fandom boards documented by Jenkins in that it has no arrangements for beta readers (who provide peer critique for work in progress) or editorial support; minimal capacity for readers to comment and respond to published works; and no general discussion forums for networking or community building (2006: 175–94). I use the pseudonyms chosen by fic authors. I selected case studies based on how they had been tagged, beginning with the category 'ancient Greek mythology and lore' (which in August 2021 included 5,504 entries) and looking at specific monster tags. My resulting case studies have been chosen partly at random and partly based on personal preference. I have filtered out crossover fanfic, or fic which combined myth with another fan object. (There is no shortage of this, as Potter's 2016 work on classical monsters in *Doctor Who* fanfic demonstrates.) I have also prioritized fanwork that centres the monster's experience rather than that of the hero or other protagonist. I focus on fanfic rather than other transformative work because it offers an opportunity to explore what function classical monsters serve in popular culture broadly defined, beyond the limits of mainstream media production.

One significant element of monstrous activity in the fanfic environment is driven by a contemporary interest in 'sympathy for the devil' narratives (Weinstock 2012: 276). Stories which take the monster's side have become much more common, as exemplified by many novels and films featuring vampires, including Anne Rice's *Vampire Chronicles* and Stephenie Meyer's *Twilight* saga. These stories often contain characters who are drawn to become monstrous, precisely because of the attraction of a given monster. This exemplifies a broader trend of seeking to reclaim monsters or otherwise redeem them, particularly because of the way that monsters have historically represented the marginalized Other (Gloyn 2020: 7–25). One excellent example is how LBGT+ people have reclaimed the term 'monster', often applied to those who defy the heterosexual norm, now symbolized by the adoption of the Babadook, a closet-dwelling monster from the eponymous 2014 film, as a queer icon.

The hyperseriality of ancient myth allows plenty of scope to develop the mythical backstories of classical monsters: 'an infinite number of alternative endings to a series can be proposed by a fan writer', meaning that the death of a monster does not have to be taken as a fixed narrative endpoint (Potter 2015: 226). Classical monsters' stories also offer the opportunity to reclaim aspects of monstrosity that contribute to a monster's otherness. In the story of Medusa, for instance, Ovid's version of her sexual assault by Poseidon and her subsequent transformation from beautiful to hideous by an irate Athena provides more than ample narrative space for a version of her story which explores her identity as a survivor of sexual violence. The Minotaur's isolation in the Labyrinth allows a story of someone who is Other being forcibly confined by his father because of his difference. These sympathetic versions of the myths do appear in main-stream media representations, but fanwork permits them to run wilder.

To grasp the Minotaur by the horns, anyone with a passing familiarity with fanfic will not be surprised that plenty of sexually explicit material features classical characters, including monsters. Fanfic has always been closely associated with sexual content, most famously in Kirk/Spock homosexual fiction inside the *Star Trek* fandom (see Russ [1985] 2014). Women continue to dominate fanfic production, although the precise ratio of gender identities of authors varies from fandom to fandom (Hellekson and Busse 2014: 75–81). The three main categories of fanfic are slash (same-sex relationships), het (heterosexual relationships), and gen (general, that is, anything else). Fanfic archived in AO3 can be labelled for content rating (where options run from 'general audiences' to 'explicit: only suitable for adults'); relationships, pairings, and orientations (which indi-cate what kind of relationship, if any, feature in the fic); content warnings; and whether the work is complete or not. Authors may also provide free-form tags to describe their work, including tagging the characters or important plot elements. The variety of labels available indicate the wide range of sexual partnerships and behaviours that fanfic may cover, while the openness of such content can play an important role in sexual self-discovery and raised awareness of available sexual practices (Meggers 2012). Driscoll (2006: 85–6) distinguished two key modes of sex in fanfic, either 'plot sex', that is, as part of a story development, or 'porn sex', where sex is the purpose of the fic—a mode also known as PWP, or 'plot? What plot?'.

Fanfic of the latter variety allows writers to explore the realm of human/monster ro-mance much more explicitly than mainstream venues. The tags on stories speak for themselves; the tag of 'Unrealistic Sex' that PumpkinGuts gives *Labyrinth* (2021) feels rather an understatement for their graphic second-person narrative of a trans man's sexual encounter with the Minotaur. There is a particular cluster of stories around the experience of a person encountering the Minotaur in the Labyrinth, either as one of the Athenian sacrifices or a bold hero (sometimes Theseus, sometimes not) seeking to kill the beast, who instead finds themselves drawn into sexual activity with varying degrees of consent. In *Laying the Minotaur* (2020), a more playful example, Greenhorne has his hero gain Minotaur-conquering credentials when he steals the monster's golden axe after becoming the unexpected target of its sexual attention. In all the examples I located, the Minotaur remains the dominant figure, particularly in terms of pene-tration. The stories are mainly told from the viewpoint of the other party rather than articulating his perspective. Given the ways in which the Minotaur is used to represent our contemporary fear of ourselves, the pattern these fics reflect of seeking the monster and being devoured by bestial erotic urges matches the contemporary interpretation of the Minotaur as psychoanalytic sexual symbol (Gloyn 2020: 170–1).

Not all human/monster fics provide this level of sexual detail, instead either offering 'plot sex' or focusing on the emotional aspects of the chosen relationship. One group of Medusa narratives revolves around the scenario of a lesbian Medusa and her girlfriend, who may be blind (either by birth or by accident) or voluntarily blindfolded, meaning that the girlfriend is immune to being turned to stone by Medusa's gaze. The stories often clearly state their intentions in writing these narratives; deadvinesandfanfics (2021) prefaces her incomplete fic *Fall is for the ghosts (and the snakes)* with the comment 'long story short i just wanted to write medusa with a happy ending and a cute gay girlfriend', while littlemiss23 (2021) promises 'a lot of mutual pining and a slow-ish lesbian romance' in *We'll Be a Myth*. The relational aspect is beautifully captured in the anonymous *to see without eyes* (2021), a brief second-person narrative in a modern setting which describes a blind woman being helped around the kitchen by her girlfriend; the closing line reads 'you loved Medusa so much, and you want her to love you so much too'. As unlikely as the pairing may seem, both bisexualoftheblade in *no body, no crime* (2021) and fresne in *In the Grip of Her Unblinking Gaze* (2012) cast Athena as Medusa's lover and explore the goddess's response to Poseidon's violence. This more emotionally vulnerable material maps onto fanfic tropes that are shaped by the contours of the romance genre, in which tension is built over how a couple will come together and the intimate tensions of their relationship (Driscoll 2006: 86). That this theme foregrounds positive representations of lesbian relationships is particularly significant given the monstering of LBGT+ sexuality; Medusa's monstrosity thus becomes a key part of why she becomes an attractive protagonist for these stories.

One example worth highlighting is *Galedusa* (2021), which Get_below_my_line_of_vision wrote as part of the series 'June Pride fic month 2021'. Get_below merges the stories of Medusa and Galatea, the statue created by Pygmalion and animated by the goddess Aphrodite, using the ingenious premise that since Galatea was originally made of stone, Medusa's gaze cannot turn her back into stone, neatly avoiding the potentially ableist trope of blindness. Get_below's version departs from Ovid (*Met.* 10.243–97) in having Galatea sculpted from stone rather than ivory, and uses the name given to Ovid's anonymous statue in the post-classical period, but these changes allow an ingenious adaptation to emerge. The narrative weaves together two mythical women recovering from different forms of intimate partner violence; the opening of the story describes the domestic abuse that Galatea experiences at the hands of Pygmalion when she does not meet his expectations of perfection, including being locked in a cellar when she makes mistakes. Although Medusa's experience of rape at the hands of Poseidon is not explicitly recounted, the story alludes to the 'tragedy' that she has gone through and the panic she felt when she realized what Poseidon had done to her. Get_below focuses on the developing emotional intimacy between the characters. At one stage, she explains that the relationship grows stronger because of 'protecting each other and providing love and relief', including support with post-traumatic flashbacks. Both women find respite from their loneliness in the other's company; Perseus' arrival acts as the impetus for their declaration of love and Galatea's free choice to become Medusa's wife rather than being forced into the marriage. Perseus fails in his attempt to behead Medusa and is instead turned to stone. The story offers recovery and reclamation in a safe queer space, using the flexibility of classical myth to offer a satisfactory romantic conclusion to two myths which have long been the subject of feminist academic critique.

As well as slash and het fanfic, plenty of gen fanfic on AO3 explores the hinterland of Greek myth that is left undescribed in the ancient sources. Where mainstream representations of Medusa tend to avoid the moment of transformation, fanfic engages with it: in *untouched and untouchable* (2020), Y Y Nott captures Medusa's relief at her transformation and the end it brings to the possibility of her assault being repeated. SargeantWoof's *give me fire, burning hell* (2020) summarizes itself as 'Medusa was not a kind girl', and turns Medusa's wish after she is raped into the source of her transformation. It also explores Medusa's relationships with her sisters Sthenno [*sic*] and Euryale; in the mythic tradition they are immortal Gorgons sharing Medusa's power to turn those they see to stone, but here they are also mortal. They pray at Athena's altar with their violated sister, and (we are told) are not kind in their prayers. Medusa's family networks are often ignored by authors relying on Ovid's *Metamorphoses*, which obliterates them; the liberty of creative writing allows authors to meld the two traditions. Whisperslip goes further in *Gorgoneia* (2010), which places an immortal Stheno and Euryale in a contemporary setting where they still mourn Medusa's death; Stheno has found ways to coexist with modernity and the 'pale residue of belief' that remains, while Euryale stays locked in her stone halls, sacrificing birds in the traditional way, praying 'in a language no longer even spoken in dreams'. The sibling relationship offers another vector for acknowledging and exploring the impact of grief created by the traditional mythic narrative. sparklight takes a different detour from Ovid in *The Shape of Your Tongue, the Flare of Your Wings* (2020a); prefaced with the comment that 'this follows the older myth, where Medusa is born a Gorgon', the fic offers a flirtatious first encounter between Poseidon and a Medusa who appears fully capable of giving consent.

Despite the best intentions, not all fics which attempt to offer restorative or reparative approaches are successful. In Kara_luna's *The Monsters Look Like Angels, and The Angels Are Dressed as Monsters* (2019), Perseus finds himself helping Medusa to birth her twins Pegasus and Chrysaor rather than decapitating her. On the surface, this is a positive retelling, in that it acknowledges Medusa's fear at a hero's approach and creates a sympathetic Perseus who decides to help rather than to harm. However, Perseus is saved from being turned to stone by Medusa's gaze because the process of childbirth has healed her—'these children filled the gaps and mended the broken shards, fitting their hearts into hers with ease', and when Perseus looks at her, he sees that 'the love in her heart chased away the grief in her golden irises'. Motherhood becomes the miraculous saviour, despite the very difficult labour without formal medical assistance that Medusa has just survived; what's more, it becomes her salvation despite the fact that these are the children born from her sexual assault. *The Monsters* acknowledges that Medusa is pregnant because Poseidon raped her, and Perseus reels with shock when he realizes the monster he has been sent to kill is pregnant, but at no point does any character consider the psychological impact upon a mother of having a child conceived through rape. This omission, combined with the mystical redemptive qualities ascribed to giving birth, means that a fic which is intended to offer an alternative outcome to the canon raises uncomfortable questions of its own about gender roles and the sanctification of motherhood.

Minotaur stories which offer something other than PWP tend to centre a relationship between Ariadne and Icarus rather than the Minotaur himself. A small subgroup explores the relationship between Pasiphaë and the infant Minotaur before his confinement to the Labyrinth, although Pasiphaë's emotions as a bereft mother are more often the focus of these fics. Summoninglupine offers a notable exception in *Unendlichkeit der Depressionen* (2021), a brief exploration of the Minotaur's experience of being confined in the Labyrinth. While this setting might recall Borges's 'The House of Asterion', the work is tagged 'The author was reading Paradise Lost at the time of writing this' and 'Dante's Inferno compliant', indicating a different kind of intertextual relationship. The piece describes the monster's failure to understand his own strength or control his temper, and the inevitable fate that awaits the 'fragile things' that enter the maze. This Minotaur can feel remorse at the fate he is assigned, and his stillness as he waits for those doomed visitors reflects the psychological paralysis of depression. Faera explores a similar angle in *Asterion* (2019), in which the Minotaur remembers the care he was given as a child and his slow, gradual, and unwilling transformation into a killer. This fic closes with Asterion hearing the voice of Ariadne promising him that a warrior will show him the way out, which gives him 'the promise of redemption, of hope, of *family*'. Faera notes she has left whether Asterion survives his encounter with Theseus deliberately ambiguous, but the keynote of family as salvation for the monster-who-is-not-a-monster taps into contemporary themes around monstrosity as experienced by LBGT+ people whose families struggle with their identity.

Some fics offer the Minotaur the kind of gentle romance that Medusa is given. In *Star* (2021), GwenChan reshapes the myth so that Theseus brings Asterion back to Athens, where the Minotaur finds a cave to live in while Theseus teaches him to speak, and their relationship deepens; the ending is a sad one as Asterion is killed by hunters and Theseus steps off a cliff in grief. firecat decides to pair Asterion and Icarus in *The White Bull's Son & the Builder of Wings* (2021), although this fully human Minotaur has only pure white fur over his body to mark him as monstrous; Icarus builds a simulacrum of the Minotaur for Theseus to kill (including a bull's head to match the rumours about the beast), and then fakes his own death so that he and Asterion can live peacefully on Icaria. Icarus comes up with the trickery specifically because Asterion cannot face killing; the monstrosity of the beast is here removed from both his temperament and appearance. Less well developed but still unexpected is gracca_amorosa's *The Labyrinth* (2020), which narrates a second-person journey into the maze, the narrator's long-awaited reunion with the Minotaur, and a cuddle on a flower-covered bed. This fic is prefaced with the comment 'You adventure into a labyrinth, and what you find is ROMANCE'; while the AO3 framework makes identifying deliberate intertextuality difficult, this premise feels as if it responds to the considerable PWP content also available on the platform. The openness of fanfic as a practice means that there is space for every reimagining, regardless of how dominant other tropes may be.

OTHER MONSTERS

I have focused on Medusa and the Minotaur because they are overwhelmingly the most popular classical monsters in reception terms. But they are not the only monsters who appear in the AO3 archive, so I close by looking at three other monsters favoured by fan authors: sirens, Cerberus, and the Sphinx. These examples offer further illustrations of what the democratic nature of fanwork permits. ViaLethe wrote the eight vignettes in *Three Gods in an Underworld* (2021) for the three-sentence ficathon 2021, and thus demonstrates the possibilities of working at the micro-scale. Her eighth fic, *Lost in the Flood*, takes place during the Second World War and features an ancient siren meeting her modern mechanical counterpart as it sounds out over the Channel; the ancient monster is transfixed by the noise that the alarm makes, perhaps during an air raid, but shudders when it falls silent, feeling at odds with the 'endless warning call' that is 'not in her nature'. In three short sentences, ViaLethe puts ancient and modern understandings of 'siren' into dialogue and draws out both the significance of song and its dangers.

Stories involving Cerberus cluster around retellings of the Hades and Persephone myth, which has become an extremely popular template for romantic reinterpretations. Those focusing on Cerberus and his personality usually emphasize his underlying dogginess rather than anthropomorphizing him; his monstrosity becomes domesticated by his transformation from a fierce guardian into a pet, much as the Hades/Persephone story is domesticated from a kidnap and rape into a romance. Amagifu is aware of the disjunct in *Old Dog, New Trick* (2017), where a mongrel named Spot, adopted from a shelter by the narrator, is reclaimed by an unimpressed Hades and transformed back into his three-headed shape at a flick of his master's fingers before trotting back to the underworld after a brief interlude chasing sticks. Persephone takes a firmer line in Evil_Little_Dog's *They're All Good Dogs* (2019), horrified that Cerberus has no water, food, or shelter—'they're a high energy breed and need to run and play and have jobs that make them think', she says, pleading his case to a bemused Hades. Hades himself, during the early days of his reign, names and trains Cerberus in sparklight's *Hound of Hades* (2020b) after he discovers the monster digging into the bank of the Acheron and realizes that the dog offers a solution to his problem of stopping shades wandering out of the underworld and the living sneaking in. The shift between Hades instructing the monster to sit and then finding himself trying to pet three heads at once nicely illustrates the general trend in fanfic towards seeing Cerberus as a big dog, with decidedly doggy tendencies, rather than as a dangerous and threatening monster.

DaughterofProspero, a self-confessed 'Greek mythology nerd', tackles the Sphinx in *The Fate of Monsters* (2019). The fic offers a first-person autobiographical survey, moving from the Sphinx's early life and relationship with her siblings (born of Typhon and Echidna), to a visit to Delphi which sent her to Thebes, and then the final encounter with a smug (unnamed) Oedipus, where she knows his eventual fate along with her own prophesied death. DaughterofProspero makes full use of the developed backdrop of Greek myth to create a world in which the Sphinx fulfils her own destiny by going to Thebes and waiting for Oedipus; she is given knowledge of Oedipus' encounter-to-come with his 'mother-wife' and responds to his cocky self-identification as 'my mother's son' with the barbed 'not quite'. Rather than see the monster simply as an appendage to the hero's quest, this fic gives the Sphinx agency to follow her own destiny, even if that is to be slaughtered. The end of the fic also foreshadows what Oedipus will become; he comments that ' "Monster" is such a … self-defeating title' when the Sphinx self-identifies as such, blithely unaware that he too will shortly be acting in ways which will make him monstrous.

CONCLUSION

My brief survey of monsters in the fanfic gathered on AO3 barely scratches the surface of what is possible when classical myth enters the fanwork space. My initial explorations have highlighted ways in which the conventions and structures of fan fiction allow narratives around classical monsters to develop and grow in ways which are much freer than mainstream cultural productions. A particularly striking difference is the way in which fanfic's openness to sexually explicit content allows classical monsters to join contemporary expressions of LBGT+ identity in a much more active way than they do in mainstream media. The flexibility of fan fiction also allows engagement with ancient sources in ways which generate productive immersion in the hyper-seriality of Greek myth, without needing to worry about the concerns of commerciality and the gatekeepers which come with them. Both mainstream media and fanfic use classical monsters as a way of exploring the Other; the removal of constraints allows fanfic to imagine what the Other might do and how it might be understood more broadly than mainstream formats.

I close by returning to the question of the links between ancient mythology and fandom. Fiske (1992: 42) argues that fandom creates its own cultural capital through fannish activity, including the accumulation of knowledge and textual production. The influential cultural capital of ancient myth becomes transmuted into marginalized forms of cultural capital through the practice of fanfic; Greek myth retains its authority and its respectability even as it is being enthusiastically slashed. Fan fiction becomes appealing to 'individuals on the cultural margins who used archontic writing to express not only their narrative creativity, but their criticisms of social and political inequities as well' (Derecho 2006: 76); archontic here, rather than derivative or appropriative, refers to work which is constantly expanding, invites selectivity, and works in dialogue with itself, as in an archive. As far as classical monsters are concerned, critique manifests in using the hyper-seriality of myth to produce alternative versions that undermine the qualities of Otherness upon which monstrosity is predicated. The use of a marginal practice, the composition of fanfic, to tell stories about classical myth, with all its baggage of cultural capital and authority in the West, reflects how the democratization possible through fandom and the internet becomes in turn a democratization of our academic discipline. There is clearly much more to be said about how fanfic enables a truly popular engagement with Classics in its broadest sense; the fascination with the classical monster points the way to a deeper democratic reclamation of what studying the ancient Greek and Roman world can be and what it can mean.

SUGGESTED READING

Classical reception research on fan fiction is in its infancy. Potter (2015) and (2016) are significant opening studies, as are the pieces collected in 'The Classical Canon and/as Transformative Work', a special edition of *Transformative Works and Cultures* edited by Willis in 2016. Müller (2020) explores the depiction of the Persian princess Drypetis in fanfiction. Hellekson and Busse (2014) collects some of the foundational works of fan studies and particularly fan fiction, with helpful overall synthesis. Hellekson and Busse (2006) collects essays exploring the function of fanfic in the internet age. The essays in Gray et al. (2007) provide a useful overview of fan studies more generally. Willis (2006) explores the notion of supplementation as a writing praxis through her own Harry Potter fanfic as a scholar more closely integrated into the fanfic community.

WORKS CITED

Amagifu. 2017. *Old Dog, New Trick*. Archive of Our Own. https://archiveofourown.org/works/11096316. Accessed 19 August 2021.

bisexualoftheblade. 2021. *no body, no crime*. Archive of Our Own. https://web.archive.org/web/20210127152200/https://archiveofourown.org/works/28467402. Accessed 30 October 2023.

Brooker, W. 2005. ' "It Is Love": The Lewis Carroll Society as a Fan Community'. *American Behavioral Scientist* 48/7: 859–80.

Busse, K., and J. Gray. 2011. 'Fan Cultures and Fan Communities', in *The Handbook of Media Audiences*, ed. V. Nightingale, 425–43. Malden, MA.

Busse, K., and K. Hellekson. 2006. 'Introduction: Work in Progress', in *Fan Fiction and Fan Communities in the Age of the Internet: New Essays*, ed. K. Hellekson and K. Busse, 5–32. Jefferson, NC.

DaughterofProspero. 2019. *The Fate of Monsters*. Archive of Our Own. https://archiveofourown.org/works/18285578. Accessed 19 August 2021.

deadvinesandfanfics. 2021. *Fall is for the ghosts (and the snakes)*. Archive of Our Own. https://archiveofourown.org/works/28999548/chapters/71170482. Accessed 19 August 2021.

Derecho, A. 2006. 'Archontic Literature: A Definition, a History, and Several Theories of Fan Fiction', in *Fan Fiction and Fan Communities in the Age of the Internet: New Essays*, ed. K. Hellekson and K. Busse, 61–78. Jefferson, NC.

Driscoll, C. 2006. 'One True Pairing: The Romance of Pornography and the Pornography of Romance', in *Fan Fiction and Fan Communities in the Age of the Internet: New Essays*, ed. K. Hellekson and K. Busse, 79–96. Jefferson, NC.

Evil_Little_Dog. 2019. *They're All Good Dogs*. Archive of Our Own. https://archiveofourown. org/works/20742728. Accessed 19 August 2021.

Faera. 2019. *Asterion*. Archive of Our Own. https://archiveofourown.org/works/20319436. Accessed 19 August 2021.

Farley, S. K. 2016. 'Versions of Homer: Translation, Fan Fiction, and Other Transformative Rewriting.' *Transformative Works and Cultures* 21, https://doi.org/10.3983/twc.2016.0673. Accessed 9 December 2022.

firecat. 2021. *The White Bull's Son & the Builder of Wings*. Archive of Our Own. https://archiveo fourown.org/works/30256488. Accessed 19 August 2021.

Fiske, J. 1992. 'The Cultural Economy of Fandom', in *The Adoring Audience: Fan Culture and Popular Media*, ed. L. A. Lewis, 30–49. London.

fresne. 2012. *In the Grip of Her Unblinking Gaze*. Archive of Our Own. https://archiveofour own.org/works/591456. Accessed 19 August 2021.

Get_below_my_line_of_vision. 2021. *Galedusa*. Archive of Our Own. https://archiveofour own.org/works/31496261/chapters/77911769. Accessed 19 August 2021.

Gloyn, L. 2020. *Tracking Classical Monsters in Popular Culture*. London.

gracca_amorosa. 2020. *The Labyrinth*. Archive of Our Own. https://archiveofourown.org/ works/27001537. Accessed 19 August 2021.

Gray, J. A., C. Sandvoss, and C. L. Harrington, eds. (2007). *Fandom: Identities and Communities in a Mediated World*. New York.

Greenhorne. 2020. *Laying the Minotaur*. Archive of Our Own. https://archiveofourown.org/ works/26651041. Accessed 19 August 2021.

GwenChan. 2021. *Star*. Archive of Our Own. https://archiveofourown.org/works/31507550. Accessed 19 August 2021.

Hellekson, K., and K. Busse, eds. 2006. *Fan Fiction and Fan Communities in the Age of the Internet: New Essays*. Jefferson, NC.

Hellekson, K., and K. Busse, eds. 2014. *The Fan Fiction Studies Reader*. Iowa City.

Hills, M. 2002. *Fan Cultures*. London.

Jenkins, H. 1992. *Textual Poachers: Television Fans and Participatory Culture*. New York.

Jenkins, H. 2006. *Convergence Culture: Where Old and New Media Collide*. New York.

Johnston, S. I. 2015. 'The Greek Mythic Story World.' *Arethusa* 48/3: 283–311.

Kara_luna. 2019. *The Monsters Look Like Angels, and The Angels Are Dressed as Monsters*. Archive of Our Own. https://archiveofourown.org/works/21398776. Accessed 19 August 2021.

Keen, T. 2016. 'Are Fan Fiction and Mythology Really the Same?' *Transformative Works and Cultures* 21, https://doi.org/10.3983/twc.2016.0689. Accessed 9 December 2022.

littlemiss23. 2021. *We'll Be a Myth*. Archive of Our Own. https://archiveofourown.org/works/ 31248560/chapters/77240762. Accessed 19 August 2021.

Meggers, H. J. 2012. 'Discovering the Authentic Sexual Self: The Role of Fandom in the Transformation of Fans' Sexual Attitudes', in *Fan Culture: Theory/Practice*, ed. K. Larsen and L. Zubernis, 57–80. Cambridge.

Müller, S. 2020. 'Drypetis In Fact and (Fan)Fiction', in *Orientalism and the Reception of Powerful Women from the Ancient World*, ed. F. Carlà-Uhink and A. Wieber, 57-69. London.

Pearson, R. 2007. 'Bachies, Bardies, Trekkies and Sherlockians', in *Fandom: Identities and Communities in a Mediated World*, ed. J. A. Gray, C. Sandvoss, and C. L. Harrington, 98–109. New York.

Potter, A. 2015. 'Slashing Rome: Season Two Rewritten in Online Fan Fiction', in Rome, *Season Two: Trial and Triumph*, ed. M. S. Cyrino, 219–30. Edinburgh.

Potter, A. 2016. 'Classical Monsters in New *Doctor Who* Fan Fiction.' *Transformative Works and Cultures* 21, http://dx.doi.org/10.3983/twc.2016.0676. Accessed 9 December 2022.

Price, L., and L. Robinson. 2017. 'Fan Fiction in the Library.' *Transformative Works and Cultures* 25, http://dx.doi.org/10.3983/twc.2017.1090. Accessed 9 December 2022.

PumpkinsGuts. 2021. *Labyrinth*. Archive of Our Own. https://archiveofourown.org/works/32712835. Accessed 19 August 2021.

raspberryhunter. 2012. *Thirteen Views of a Labyrinth*. Archive of Our Own. https://archiveofourown.org/works/605218. Accessed 19 August 2021.

Russ, J. [1985] 2014. 'Pornography by Women for Women, with Love', in *The Fan Fiction Studies Reader*, ed. K. Hellekson and K. Busse, 82–96. Iowa City.

SargeantWoof. 2020. *give me fire, burning hell*. Archive of Our Own. https://archiveofourown.org/works/28207428. Accessed 19 August 2021.

sparklight. 2020a. *The Shape of Your Tongue, the Flare of Your Wings*. Archive of Our Own. https://archiveofourown.org/works/23926249. Accessed 19 August 2021.

sparklight. 2020b. *Hound of Hades*. Archive of Our Own. https://archiveofourown.org/works/26545765. Accessed 19 August 2021.

summoninglupine. 2021. *Unendlichkeit der Depressionen*. Archive of Our Own. https://web.archive.org/web/20210713044128/https://archiveofourown.org/works/32382895. Accessed 30 October 2023.

Tushnet, R. 2007. 'Copyright Law, Fan Practices, and the Rights of the Author', in *Fandom: Identities and Communities in a Mediated World*, ed. J. A. Gray, C. Sandvoss, and C. L. Harrington, 60–71. New York.

ViaLethe. 2021. *Three Gods in an Underworld*. Archive of Our Own. https://archiveofourown.org/works/29877102/chapters/73523154#workskin. Accessed 19 August 2021.

Weinstock, J. A. 2012. 'Invisible Monsters: Vision, Horror, and Contemporary Culture', in *The Ashgate Research Companion to Monsters and the Monstrous*, ed. A. S. Mittman and P. J. Dendle, 275–89. Burlington.

Whisperslip. 2010. *Gorgoneia*. Archive of Our Own. https://archiveofourown.org/works/141274. Accessed 19 August 2021.

Willis, I. 2006. 'Keeping Promises to Queer Children: Making Space (for Mary Sue) at Hogwarts', in *Fan Fiction and Fan Communities in the Age of the Internet: New Essays*, ed. K. Hellekson and K. Busse, 153–70. Jefferson, NC.

Willis, I. 2016. 'Amateur Mythographies: Fan Fiction and the Myth of Myth.' *Transformative Works and Cultures* 21, https://doi.org/10.3983/twc.2016.0692. Accessed 9 December 2022.

Willow1977. 2021. *A tale of Sirens*. Archive of Our Own. https://archiveofourown.org/works/29173212. Accessed 19 August 2021.

Wilson, A. 2016. 'The Role of Affect in Fan Fiction.' *Transformative Works and Cultures* 21, https://doi.org/10.3983/twc.2016.0684. Accessed 9 December 2022.

Y Y Nott (WhyWhyNot). 2020. *untouched and untouchable*, Archive of Our Own. https://archiveofourown.org/works/24717529. Accessed 19 August 2021.

....

CHAPTER 40

ANCIENT MONSTERS IN MODERN SCIENCE

....

DEBBIE FELTON

Introduction

....

THE discussions throughout this volume show that mythical monsters easily lend themselves to multiple interpretations and contexts. At a literal level, these monsters provide thrilling entertainment, acting as menacing foils for daring heroes. As metaphors, their symbolism ranges wildly across space and time; monsters can consequently be repurposed to represent a society's current concerns. For the early Greeks, a monster such as Typhoeus might have represented the chaos of the untamed natural world and its resistance to humankind's encroachment upon it. Cerberus, guardian of Hades, could have represented our mortality, since heroes making their *katabasis* to the land of the dead first had to get past this frightening, ravenous creature, symbolically facing their own deaths in doing so. Other monstrous beings, such as Scylla and Charybdis—with their toothed loins and devouring whirlpool (respectively)—arguably represented not only the dangers of seafaring but also fears about female sexuality.

More humanoid 'aberrations', including anthropophagous beings (like Polyphemus and the Laestrygonians) and physically unexpected peoples (like the Cynocephali and Blemmyes) may reflect how ethnocentric cultures 'othered' foreign peoples, whose alleged physical and behavioural oddities defined ethnographic distance and difference from the Greeks and Romans. Monsters can also prove useful in the context of political discourse, as with Horace's description of Cleopatra as *fatale monstrum* in the first century BCE (*Carm.* 1.37.21; see Boychenko in this volume), and James Gillray's 1793 political cartoon 'Britannia between Scylla and Charybdis: or The Vessel of the Constitution steered clear of the Rock of Democracy, and the Whirlpool of Arbitrary Power' (see Hopman in this volume).

And, of course, the monsters of classical myth have made their way into modern science, principally through the method of taxonomic nomenclature developed by

Swedish naturalist Carl Linnaeus as part of his biological classification system (*Systema Naturae*, 1735), but also via general surviving knowledge of and interest in the ancient stories. We cannot possibly cover all the monsters referenced in all fields of science, but we can look at examples of how various scientific disciplines adapted classical monsters and did so on the assumption that, three thousand years or more after these creatures first appeared in literature and art, they would still hold meaning. For the purposes of this chapter, 'modern' encompasses the eighteenth century to the present, starting with Linnaeus's classification system, which included binomial nomenclature. And 'science' here indicates mainly empirical fields of study, though I will focus on the natural and applied sciences such as biology and computer science rather than on social sciences such as anthropology and sociology (but cf. Apanomeritaki, and Silverblank and Ward in this volume). The monsters in the cases discussed here may have been chosen to reflect the creatures' physical characteristics, but sometimes also (or instead) reflect their behaviour, environment, or role in myth—whether literal or metaphorical—again demonstrating monsters' great adaptability.

ASTRONOMY

The ancient Romans gave the names of their gods to the five planets of our solar system visible to them with the naked eye: Mercury, Venus, Mars, Jupiter, and Saturn. For nearly two millennia thereafter, astronomers continued to draw on classical myths for the names of various celestial bodies and phenomena. When telescopes were invented in the Netherlands in the early seventeenth century, the tradition persisted. But eventually, with the conscious intent to be more globally inclusive, astronomers turned to regions other than western Europe for inspiration. They looked to indigenous populations of northern Canada for Sedna, a dwarf planet, named for an Inuit sea goddess (2003); to China for Gonggong, another dwarf planet, named for a water deity (2007); and to Polynesia—Hawai'i in particular—for Oumuamua ('Scout'), the first interstellar object known to pass through our solar system (2017). Yet few celestial objects are named specifically after mythical monsters rather than deities or human characters. The Trojan asteroids, for example (the objective of the Lucy spacecraft, launched in 2021), initially took their names from the Trojan and Greek warriors of the *Iliad* until, having run out of characters, astronomers resorted to a wider variety of names and, eventually, numbers. But we find one notable use of classical monsters in the so-called centaurs that inhabit the space between Jupiter and Neptune. Named for the mythical half-human, half-horse creatures of Greek myth—one is even called 'Chiron'—these centaurs are small bodies composed of rock and/or ice, acquiring their name after their hybrid nature: they exhibit the characteristics of both asteroids and comets, particularly in their physical composition (McKinney 2015).

Given the lack of sunlight in the further regions of our solar system, astronomers sometimes also drew inspiration from Cerberus, guard dog of the gloomy underworld.

For example, the creature lends its name to the Cerberus Fossae, a series of deep fissures on the surface of Mars, and to a small moon of the dwarf planet Pluto (another name for Hades). Overall, though, ancient monsters, in contrast to gods and heroes, play a far less prominent role in astronomy than they do in many other sciences. One possible reason may be that it was only natural to name celestial objects after entities thought to dwell in the sky, like the Olympian deities. On the other hand, classical myths frequently placed vanquished monsters (themselves often the offspring of deities) in the sky as constellations to honour them—Cetus, Draco (the serpent Ladon), and the Hydra, to name only a few—many of which were formally catalogued by the Greek astronomer Ptolemy in the second century CE. Still, the deities clearly took priority.

Biology

The systematic method for classifying biological organisms owes its existence to Swedish scientist Carl Linnaeus (1707–1778). Specializing in botany and zoology, Linnaeus developed a standardized hierarchical system for cataloguing the plants and animals he observed, arranging living organisms based on the extent to which they shared common characteristics. He assigned the term 'kingdom' to his most general grouping, and 'genus' and 'species' to the most specific. With these latter two, Linnaeus developed the system of binomial nomenclature ('two-name name-calling'). Pre-Linnaean taxonomy had varied considerably and tended towards lengthy descriptions; for example, some botanists called the common wild briar rose *Rosa sylvestris inodora seu canina* (literally 'wild rose unscented or dog-like') while others used *Rosa sylvestris alba cum rubore, folio glabro* ('wild rose white with red, with smooth leaf'). While those botanists might have been generally certain that they were speaking of the same pink, faint-scented flower with thorns resembling a dog's canine teeth, such variation inevitably led to confusion. Linnaeus's simplification provided a considerably less capricious system, and in this case 'settled the argument by leaving it at *Rosa canina*'—the dog rose, native to Europe, western Asia, and north-west Africa (García 2018).

Classical Latin and, to a certain extent, ancient Greek were still widely familiar among the European educated classes in Linnaeus's day: Latin, as the root of the Romance languages, and Greek, as having attained new popularity during the Renaissance. Latin and ancient Greek had the additional benefit of being 'dead' languages, meaning that they remained largely unchanged. The static nature of Latin and Greek vocabulary and grammar proved useful as a basis for common communication among scientists across the European continent, so Linnaeus adopted ancient Greek and especially Latin vocabulary as the basis for assigning his taxonomic categories. At the time, and up through the early twentieth century, an education grounded in the literature, art, and languages of classical antiquity was still the norm, and biologists drew readily on classical culture, especially mythology, in any ways that struck their fancy. Heller notes that Linnaeus usually did not justify 'his choice of trivial names, either for plants or animals',

but that clearly 'classical mythology was again a favorite source' even if Linnaeus's application of classical names was neither particularly profound nor even entirely accurate
(1945: 336, 346).

Linnaeus's system, which includes kingdom, phylum, class, order, family, genus, and
species (and which has been expanded to include many intermediate ranks such as sub-
class) continues to be used in taxonomic classification. Biologists still assign Greek and
Latinate names to newly discovered creatures and expect that the meanings and stories
behind those names remain familiar enough for people to recognize the allusions.
Although Western names predominated for centuries—even when assigning ranks to
organisms from continents other than Europe!—scientists have increasingly begun to
acknowledge non-Western cultures by assigning names from local languages and lore
(see Isaak 2022). For example, in 1828 German entomologist Christian Wiedemann
named a genus of gigantic (7 cm/2.8 in.) Brazilian flies after the Mapinguarí, a Latin
American monster famous for its intimidating size (see Braham in this volume). This
mythical monster also had a frightening, razor-toothed mouth on its abdomen, which
apparently inspired the genus name for a group of South American orchids, including
Mapinguari desvauxianus. These orchids, aside from being extremely large, have central
lip petals that look like toothed mouths.[1]

Many fields within the biological sciences have applied the names of classical
monsters to organisms that share one or more basic characteristics of those monsters, as
with the Mapinguarí. For example, the species designation of *Papio cynocephalus*, better
known as the yellow baboon, means 'dog-headed', inspired by the dog-like shape of its
head and muzzle. But the name also hearkens back to the Cynocephali, the dog-headed
people referred to by classical and medieval authors as living in Africa and India (see
Fig. 33.3). *P. cynocephalus* are native to several African countries, and the Cynocephali
themselves were in fact most likely baboons—an animal unfamiliar in the West in
antiquity—mistaken for people (see e.g. Friedman 2000: 24–5). *Hipposideros cyclops*,
the cyclops roundleaf bat found in parts of equatorial Africa, takes its species name from
the one-eyed giants of Greek myth (see Aguirre and Buxton in this volume), but this bat
has two eyes, and the name instead alludes to the unusual orifice in the centre of its forehead (this opening leads to a small frontal sac; Decher and Fahr 2005: 2, 4). The harpy
fruit bats (*Harpyionycteris whiteheadi*) of Indonesia and the Philippines, and the harpy
eagles (*Harpia harpyja*) found mainly in Central and South America, have wings and
claws resembling those of the mythological Harpies, as reflected in both their genus and
common names, while the order Sirenia, which includes manatees and dugongs (commonly known as sea cows) found in tropical waters across the globe, derives its name
from the Sirens of Greek myth (see Denson in this volume). Brito notes that 'historical
sightings [of sirens/mermaids] by sailors may have been the result of misunderstood
encounters with these aquatic mammals.... Since the end of the 14th century, following

---

[1] https://commons.wikimedia.org/wiki/File:Mapinguari_desvauxianus_06.jpg. Accessed 26
August 2022.

the Iberian Atlantic expeditions to Africa and the overseas, new encounters with large and strange marine mammals revived the legend of mermaids.' She adds that in 1493, 'while sailing off the coast of Hispaniola, Christopher Columbus reported seeing three "female forms" which "rose high out of the sea, but were not as beautiful as they are represented" ' (2013: 13–15; cf. Braham in this volume). Whereas manatees thrived in Columbus's day, they are now listed as 'vulnerable to extinction' thanks to threats to their habitats.[2]

Botany

The scientific nomenclature of plants occasionally draws upon classical monsters both great and small. The whimsically named 'little goblin moonwort', *Botrychium mormo*, is a tiny forest fern endemic to the US upper Midwest. Its genus name derives from Greek *botrys*, 'cluster of grapes', because the plant's spore-bearing organs (sporangia) look like miniature grapes; hence the common name grapefern. But the species *B. mormo*, reflected in the English 'goblin', suggests that twentieth-century botanist W. H. Wagner, who named the plant, had a passing familiarity with the female Greek *daimon* who served as a companion to Hecate, the goddess associated with witchcraft and the night (see Kucharski in this volume). According to widespread folklore, moonworts—so nicknamed for their crescent-shaped leaves—had a role in magic, as witches supposedly gathered them by moonlight.

The genus Centaurium (centaury) consists of perhaps two dozen species of flowering plants that grow across Europe. The name clearly derives from 'centaur': in his *Dionysiaca*, the fifth-century CE Greek poet Nonnus has one character, lamenting over a dead girl, wish he could summon the centaur Chiron, who was famous for his medicinal knowledge. The man then exclaims, 'if only I had the herb they call "centaury", so that, winding the flower that relieves pain [*anōdyne*] around your limbs, I might save you from death!' (35.60–5).[3] Another genus of flowering plants, Chironia, also takes its name from the benevolent centaur, as some of its species, such as *Chironia baccifera*, are used in traditional medicine in south African countries (Maroyi 2019).

Whereas *Botrychium mormo*, centaury, and Chironia seem to have acquired their names via the behavioural characteristics of their mythical monsters, *Acacia cyclops*, like the orchid *Mapinguari desvauxianus*, provides an example of a plant named for its physical appearance. Native to the coastal areas of southern Australia, this small tree

---

[2] The 'spiny anteater' or echidna may also take its name from a classical monster, Echidna, because as monotreme (a mammal that lays eggs), the echidna is hybrid of sorts, mixing mammalian and reptilian traits. But scholars still debate the etymology, which may instead come from the Greek *ekhînos*, 'hedgehog' or 'sea urchin.'

[3] Confusingly, the genus Centaurea (sometimes unhelpfully also called 'centaury') seems unrelated; the thistle-like flowering plant more likely derives from the Greek *kentron*, 'thorn'.

takes its species name from the appearance of its seed pods: the shiny black seeds are encircled by their reddish stalk, giving them an eye-like appearance.

Entomology

Entomology, the branch of zoology involving the study of insects, takes its name from the Greek words reflecting the segmentation of the creatures' bodies: *en-tom-*, 'cut into' (*en*, 'into' + *tom-*, 'cut'). This translates literally into Latin as *in-sect* (*in*, 'into' + *sect-*, 'cut', a linguistic calque). Humans seem to find insects rather alien: too many legs, various unsettling appendages, and sudden unexpected movements, in addition to vastly different variegations—characteristics resulting in many classically monstrous appellations.

For instance, the order of insects known as Lepidoptera ('scale-wings') includes principally moths and butterflies, and their often intricate and striking wing patterns readily lend themselves to creative nomenclature. The Polyphemus moth, *Antheraea polyphemus*, widespread in North America, was named by the late nineteenth-century Dutch entomologist Pieter Cramer after the *Odyssey's* Cyclops, inspired by the prominent eyespots on its hind wings (Himmelman 2002: 22–3): when at rest with its wings folded, the moth appears to have one large eye, helpful for frightening off potential predators. In contrast, the family Sphingidae, consisting of hawk and sphinx moths, takes its name from the caterpillar stage rather than from its adult wing pattern. Evidently the caterpillar's posture—resting in a recumbent position on branches with its head held up—reminded early nineteenth-century French zoologist Pierre André Latreille of the typical sphinx's posture, especially that of the Great Sphinx at Giza: because of Napoleon's campaign in and occupation of Egypt (1798–1801), Egyptian culture was all the rage in France at the time (see Gillispie 1989: esp. 460).

In many cases of insect nomenclature, the reasons behind classically derived names are not always explicitly stated and instead provoke speculation. The connection between the tropical butterfly subfamily Satyrinae (formerly the family Satyridae) and their namesakes, the satyrs of Greek myth, was not made clear by Jean Baptiste Boisduval, the French lepidopterist who identified them in the early nineteenth century. Possibly the Satyr butterflies were so named because they are largely brown and live predominantly in woodlands, the preferred haunts of classical satyrs (Herbison-Evans and Crossley: n.d.). Similarly, the one-headed stick insect *Charmides cerberus*, native to Sri Lanka, would appear to have no obvious relation to the tricephalic guardian dog of Hades, except perhaps that is it a phasmid—a type of ghost insect—so called from ancient Greek *phasma*, 'apparition', thanks to its camouflaged appearance. The connection would then be to the ghosts of the dead that inhabit the classical underworld.

While prominent monsters of classical myth, such as Polyphemus and Cerberus, among others, clearly provided the names for many insects, the lesser-known monsters of ancient Greek legend also inspired various modern taxonomic nomenclature. The Mormolyce genus of beetles (commonly known as 'violin beetles' thanks to their shape), identified by Swiss entomologist Jacob Johann Hagenbach in the early nineteenth century, derive their scientific name from Mormo/Mormolyke, the Greek *daimon* known for killing children. The highly predatory South Asian *Mormolyce phyllodes* beetle, for example, in both its larval and adult stages, feeds on the larvae of other insects. The connection between the North Asian weaver beetle *Lamia textor* and the blood-drinking female *daimon* of ancient Greece is less clear, though the species name means 'weaver'.

Herpetology

Herpetology, from the Greek verb *herpein*, 'to creep' and its related noun *herpeton*, 'reptile', is the branch of zoology concerned with the study of amphibians and reptiles. Unsurprisingly, many of these creatures take their names from monsters of classical myth, and one of the most well known is the python snake. Whereas in Greek myth 'Python' referred to the giant guardian serpent of Delphi killed by the god Apollo, its name bestowed retroactively after it died and rotted (Greek *pythein*; see Ogden in this volume), in modern usage, the python (both a genus and common name), endemic to various regions of Africa, Asia, and Australia, is a large, non-venomous snake that wraps itself around its prey and squeezes until the victim suffocates. It then swallows its kill whole, usually head first (but cf. Fig. 6.1). The creature's large size most likely helped the classical association: pythons, which are some of the largest snakes in the world, can grow up to over 10 metres (33 feet) long and weigh up to 113 kilograms (250 pounds).

Cerberus rynchops, a South Asian reptile commonly known as the dog-faced water snake, takes its name principally from the dog-face connection; when scientists are conventionally naming organisms with canid-like characteristics, Cerberus tends to be the main dog to come to mind. But French zoologist Georges Cuvier (1769–1832), who named the genus, may also have had in mind the snakes often associated with the chthonic hound (see Joyce in this volume). The Arizona black rattlesnake, or *Crotalus cerberus*, identified in the late nineteenth century, may have taken its species name from any or all of several characteristics in common with Hades' pet: the snake's largely gloomy colouring, its tendency to rest in crevices and caves (i.e. underground) when inactive, and even its size; though not nearly as large as the python, *Crotalus cerberus* can grow to over 1 metre long. (The genus name comes from the Greek *krotalon*, 'castanet' or 'rattle'.)

Another example, from an ancient fantastical creature not mentioned elsewhere in this volume, is the Amphisbaena genus of lizards. The amphisbaena takes its name from the Greek *amphis*, 'both' and *bainein*, 'to go': ancient sources describe the mythical ant-eating serpent as having two heads, one at each end. In the first century BCE, Pliny the Elder remarked of the amphisbaena, 'as if it weren't enough that venom be poured out of one mouth!' (8.35.85, my trans.) Later natural historians focused instead on the creature's unusual movement. Aelian (*c*.175–*c*.235 CE), for one, said that when the amphisbaena wishes to move forward it uses one end as the head and the other as a tail; when it wants to move in the opposite direction, it reverses the procedure (9.23). In contrast, Solinus (mid-third century CE) claimed that the amphisbaena's twin heads cause it to creep along dragging itself in circles, as each head stubbornly strains in a different direction (27.29). The creature was clearly as familiar to the ancient Greeks as Homer's monsters: in 458 BCE, the tragedian Aeschylus had no need to explicate in the *Agamemnon* when Cassandra, foreseeing the horrific murder of King Agamemnon at the hands of his wife, Clytemnestra, calls the queen 'an amphisbaena, or a Scylla!' (1233). The amphisbaena became especially popular in medieval bestiaries, where it acquired wings (e.g. the twelfth-century Aberdeen Bestiary, fo. 68v; British Library Harley MS 475, vol. 62r).[4] Real-life lizards of the Amphisbaena genus, which appear nearly world-wide, have no limbs (and so are also known as 'worm lizards'), and the truncated tail looks remarkably like the head, a similarity that confuses predators. Moreover, also like their mythical counterparts, amphisbaena lizards can move easily in either direction. They do so by 'exploiting some waves of muscular contraction that propagate along the body. . . . Since the skin is loosely anchored to the underlying layers its specialized tegument forms a tube that the animal can move in both directions', generating an accordion-like movement (Venturini 2003; cf. Kitchell 2015: 135–6).

Marine Biology

Marine biology encompasses many subfields, among which are marine mammalogy, in-vertebrate zoology, and ichthyology (the study of fish, from Greek *ichthys*, 'fish'). One marine mammal group, the order Sirenia (manatees and dugongs), is mentioned above, so this section briefly discusses other examples of marine life that draw on classical monsters.

Marine invertebrates (sea creatures that never develop a backbone) include sponges, molluscs, cnidarians, and arthropods. The Cyclops genus of freshwater sea snails—a type of mollusc—seems to have earned its name from the shape and colouring of the snail's shell: the circular shell, darker in the centre, resembles one large eye. Cnidaria, meanwhile, comprises an entire phylum of stinging invertebrates (from the Greek *knidē*, 'stinging nettle'), so called because they bear a type of specialized cell containing a barb that ejects venom when touched (useful for self-defence and for catching food). With over 11,000 species spanning the globe, Cnidaria include corals, jellyfish, and polyps (such as sea anemones),[5] many of which take their names from classical monsters. Tentacles are their main physical attribute, one most frequently reflected in their mon-strous nomenclature. The small freshwater polyps of the Hydra genus, for example, have a tubelike body that attaches via one end to a solid surface, with an orifice surrounded

---

[4] These and other sources, with images, available at https://bestiary.ca/beasts/beast144.htm. Accessed 23 August 2022.

[5] 'Polyp' derives from *polypus*, 'many feet', though in antiquity this Greek-based Latin word usually applied to an octopus or cuttlefish.

by tentacles—anywhere from four to twelve, depending on the species—at the other end. This feature only partially explains the name, however; the creature shares a more significant characteristic with its mythological predecessor. As Baggaley humorously explains, 'For a group of small aquatic animals known as hydra, decapitation is more an inconvenience than anything else. Thanks to the creatures' incredible regenerative abilities, it needn't be fatal' (2021). Like the Hydra of Greek myth, if this cnidarian loses its head, it grows a new one. Scientists studying how such regeneration works at the hydra's cellular level hope that the genetic mechanisms behind the process might eventually help treat and cure disease in other organisms, including humans (Baggaley 2021). Hydras lack the jellyfish stage common to most other organisms in the Hydrozoa taxonomic class, and so are differentiated from the Medusozoa subphylum of Cnidaria, or medusas—the common jellyfish—which derive their name from the resemblance of their tentacles to the mythical Medusa's snaky hair. Technically, 'medusa' more specifically refers to the adult, sexually reproductive, free-swimming (non-polyp) stage of the jellyfish life cycle, when the tentacles hang downward. The cnidarians known as gorgonians, on the other hand, are soft corals such as sea fans, characterized by their extensive upwardly branching formations, still reminiscent of the Gorgon Medusa.

Within the phylum Arthropoda, the Cyclops gives his name to a genus of small, freshwater crustaceans commonly known as water fleas: they have a single, medially situated compound eye, usually red. Another water flea genus, Polyphemus, has two compound eyes, but they fuse to form one unit. (Compound eyes consist of smaller visual units, such as multiple lenses, in contrast to the single-aperture eye with one lens, such as found in humans.) *Limulus polyphemus*, the Atlantic horseshoe crab, received its name via error: Linnaeus, who identified the species in 1758, mistakenly thought the animal had only one eye, whereas, in fact, depending on what counts as an eye—the creature has several different kinds of photoreceptors—the horseshoe crab may have as many as eleven (Payne 2019).

Turning to marine vertebrates, we find various examples of monstrous nomenclature in ichthyology. A genus of fish known as Pegasus, found in the West Pacific waters, takes its name from the creature's winglike pectoral fins. The name of *Thermarces cerberus*, the pink vent fish that lives in the Pacific, relates to its extreme environment: this animal lives deep in the ocean where cold seawater, meeting liquid hot magma oozing up from tectonic subduction zones, forms hydrothermal vents that spew hot, particle-laden fluids reaching 340°C/700°F up into the ocean (Greek *therm-*, 'hot'). Soulen (2015) explains, 'One could easily imagine this place as some kind of entrance to Hell with the pink vent fish as watchdogs of the Underworld'. The chimaeras (order Chimaeriformes), oddly shaped fish that have a network of lines over the surface of their bodies, look like they have been stitched together from parts of other creatures, and so are named for the unusual lion-goat-snake composite creature known as the Chimaera (Crampton 2022; see Smith in this volume).[6]

[6] Lest anyone sense a missed opportunity here, please note that the Chimaera genus name was bestowed by Linnaeus in 1758, decades before Mary Shelley's 1818 *Frankenstein*. See also https://en.wikipedia.org/wiki/Chimaera#/media/File:Deep_sea_chimaera.jpg. Accessed 10 June 2023.

Genetics

The Chimaera has also provided the name for the real-life phenomenon known as 'genetic chimerism'. A genetic chimera is a single organism that contains at least two separate sets of DNA—genetic material (the genotype) from more than one source; normally, an organism has only one set of DNA. An animal's DNA is a combination of its parents' DNA, and animal chimerism results from two or more zygotes (a fertilized egg). Chimerism can also occur in plants.

In contrast to the mythological Chimaera's spectacular appearance, genetic chimerism is not often evident in the phenotype (visible characteristics) and is more readily identified via DNA testing. Examples of visible chimerism, however, include heterochromia—a variation in the colour of an animal's eyes, such as having one blue and one brown (though this condition can also be hereditary). Chimera cats, many of which have heterochromia, are often identifiable from their colouring, typically with the two sides of their face or body being entirely different colours. These cats have two sets of DNA, usually resulting from a pair of embryos that fused in the mother cat's womb— meaning that a chimera kitten is born with not only its own DNA, but also that of the absorbed second embryo (Basepaws 2019; Parker 2021). This rare phenomenon occurs in humans, too, when genes from a 'vanishing twin' end up mixed in with those from a surviving sibling (Vergano 2022).

While such chimerism occurs naturally, since at least the mid-twentieth century scientists have been experimenting with artificially produced animal chimeras, transplanting embryonic cells from one animal or species onto the embryo of another (Scharping 2021). Such experimentation raises considerable ethical concerns, especially when the chimera involves human cells, as with human-pig and human-monkey chimera experiments. Yet such biological research continues because, as Scharping (2021) explains, 'Much of the work done today is focused on creating better animal models to study drugs and disease with, or to advance research into organ transplantation.' One goal of such chimerism is to grow fully functional human organs inside animals for use in transplants (Devlin 2017). Scientists also believe that chimeras will be able to help fight disease such as cancers: in 2017 Portuguese researchers created a chimera virus by combining a mouse virus with a human viral gene, producing a virus that could be used to test molecules that inhibit cancer-causing proteins (Instituto de Medicina Molecular 2017).

COMPUTER SCIENCE

Computer scientists have proven just as adept at adopting classical mythology as their counterparts in biological disciplines. One well-known non-monstrous example is the Trojan Horse virus, a type of malware that sneaks onto your computer disguised as a legitimate program much as the Wooden Horse of myth seemed to be a legitimate peace offering from the Greeks to the Trojans, but really concealed enemy soldiers who crept out at night and destroyed the city. One type of Trojan Horse virus specifically targets your phone: the Pegasus spyware that, like the winged horse of Greek myth, goes 'flying through the air', in this case to infiltrate mobile phones and similar devices (Bouquet 2019). Developed by the cybersecurity company NSO Group, Pegasus ended up infecting phones belonging to activists, human rights workers, journalists, and businesspeople who were put under surveillance by software originally intended to help governments pursue criminals and terrorists (Shankland 2022). Jonathan Bouquet (2019) notes the irony in having such a malevolent device named after Pegasus: while monstrous in his hybrid form and heritage, having been born from the blood of the decapitated Medusa, Pegasus was best known for being tamed by the hero Bellerophon and helping him to fight the Chimaera. Many myths even tell how the sacred spring of the nine Muses was formed when Pegasus struck a rock on Mount Helicon with his hoof.

Seemingly in response to such mythologically dubbed malware, one computer network security protocol aptly takes its name from Cerberus. 'Kerberos' authenticates service requests between two or more trusted hosts across an untrusted network (such as the internet) by using secret-key cryptography and a trusted third party to verify users' identities. Kerberos takes not only its guardian role from the mythological hound, but also the creature's tricephalic aspect: as Peter Loshin explains, 'The three heads of the Kerberos protocol represent the following: 1. the client or principal; 2. the network resource, which is the application server that provides access to the network resource; and 3. a key distribution center (KDC), which acts as Kerberos' trusted third-party authentication service' (2021).

The Cyclops, too, lends his name to various aspects of computing, most of them focused (unsurprisingly) on his eye/vision. In its function as an interface, the single Cyclops eye may be best recognizable from HAL, the supercomputer on board the spaceship 'Discovery' in Stanley Kubrick's 1968 film *2001: A Space Odyssey*. This influential design was later adapted for various video-monitored door intercoms and security systems (Wagner 2012). Cyclops is also (somewhat alarmingly) the name of a web-based eye-care software office system (http://cyclopsemr.com/). And, in what seems to be a shift from literal vision to the monocular aspect, the computer architecture known as Cyclops integrates all its functions onto a single chip—processing logic, main memory, and communications hardware.

Also related to programming, the Basilisk software framework, designed as a set of Python modules written in C/C++ (computer languages), takes its name from the creature mentioned as early as Pliny the Elder's *Natural History* (8.32–3). According to Pliny, the basilisk was a small but deadly serpent native to North Africa. The white spot on its head resembled a crown; hence its name, from the Greek *basiliskos*, 'little king'. Its noxious breath could burn grass and break stones, but worst of all was its glare: anyone who looked into its eyes immediately dropped dead. In the case of the software, the name fortunately has nothing to do with the creature's fatal effect. Rather, the Basilisk name was chosen to reflect both the reptilian nature of the Python-related product-design and the faster-than-realtime speed requirements for its simulations—the latter with reference to the South American common basilisk lizard (*Basiliscus basiliscus*), so speedy that it can run across the surface of water (AVS 2022).[7]

The basilisk also appears in relation to AI (artificial intelligence), the simulation or replication of human intelligence by machines, especially computers. One urgent concern facing the AI community is the technological singularity, the (hypothetical, though increasingly less so) future point in time at which technology becomes uncontrollable, most likely via a self-improving AI that far surpasses human intelligence. Such an entity would have no use for humans; consequently, many computer scientists are currently working to align AI developments with human interests. In 2010, in a disturbing thought experiment now known as Roko's basilisk, *LessWrong* user Roko argued that a sufficiently powerful AI agent 'would have an incentive to torture anyone who imagined the agent but didn't work to bring the agent into existence'. The argument was named after the legendary basilisk, which could cause death with a single glance—in this case, because 'merely hearing the argument would supposedly put you at risk of torture from this hypothetical [future] agent. A *basilisk* in this context is any information that harms or endangers the people who hear it' (Roko's Basilisk). That is, this potentially malicious AI could, in theory, find a way 'to punish people *today* who [can envision it but] are not helping it come into existence later' (Auerbach 2014).

On a somewhat less dizzying and considerably more optimistic note, the centaur, as half-human, half-horse creature, finds its hybridity promoted as a different kind of AI from the one in Roko's thought experiment. Whereas the Greeks and Romans generally characterized centaurs quite negatively as brutish—apart from the more 'civilized' Chiron and Pholus—'Centaur AI' sees the combination of human and other as beneficially bringing out the powers of each. In William Vorhies's view, 'Centaur AI is the best marriage of the machine's ability to remember, analyze, and detect issues along with the human's intuition to evaluate or take action on those results. Instead of focusing on AI replacing humans, we should focus on AI in its role of augmenting humans' (2020). That is, while in many areas AI performance equals or exceeds human performance, both developers and consumers of AI apps 'should increasingly look for opportunities where AI works in tandem with human knowledge and intuition to produce a better outcome'—preferably, one in which AI will not see any benefit in wiping out humankind (Vorhies 2020). In fact, although most public reporting on AI systems focuses on their increasing capabilities, a less reported trend is that 'many of the most powerful systems being developed today combine artificial and human intelligence' (PARC). The significance of these centaur systems (human–machine teams) came to international attention after World Chess champion Garry Kasparov, having lost to Deep Blue in 1997 (though he had beaten the machine a year earlier), reviewed human–computer teams

---

[7] The Python community uses a documentation generator known as Sphinx. Regarding the Python programming language itself, its creator, Guido van Rossum, took the name not from the giant serpent of Greek myth, but from *Monty Python's Flying Circus*, the 1970s British comedy sketch show, of which he was a huge fan (Rossum 1996; Monty Python themselves also did not have Greek myth in mind). Python's two-snakes logo thus has nothing to do with the name's origin.

cooperating in chess and noted that the combination 'led to performance that beat not only people but also the most powerful artificial intelligence systems', despite computer systems' ability to process information much more quickly than humans (PARC; this advanced form of chess is sometimes called 'centaur chess'). It should come as no surprise that computers 'are less capable than people when life experience matters, especially given that computer programming typically reflects a fixed set of assumptions about the world' (PARC). According to Vorhies (2020), the most likely scenarios for Centaur AI include those where there is a need to add more context around human interaction or human understanding, such as subjective decision-making—which could be something as basic as deciding which of two potholes to fill first or as complicated as military defence strategy. The modern centaur, rather than spreading chaos as ancient centaurs did, could work to maintain order and benefit humankind.

ARGUS PANOPTES

Sometimes a mythological monster has a feature so outstanding that it lends itself to an extremely broad range of eponymous organisms. Argus Panoptes ('All-seeing'), the hundred-eyed watchman of classical myth (see Marciniak in this volume), provides an excellent example of such a phenomenon. Whereas Polyphemus often lends his name to various creatures based on the association with his one large eye, *Gopherus polyphemus*—the gopher tortoise native to the south-eastern United States—takes its species name not from any relation to the Cyclops' eye, but from its habitat: like the cave-dwelling Polyphemus, this tortoise prefers to live in a large hole in the earth (also like a gopher). Similarly, anything named after Cerberus might have been so called from the number of its heads, its guardian role, its dark underground lair, its association with the dead, and so on. But Argus' presence in scientific nomenclature relates entirely to his multiple eyes: the organisms named for him bear patterns of ocelli, or eyespots, all over their body. Such eyespots, generally thought to be a kind of defensive mimicry, appear on vastly different animals, including butterflies, birds, reptiles, fish, and even some cats (but not housecats)—the black-and-white pattern on the back of bobcats' and tigers' ears, for example.

The Malaysian *Cnemaspis argus*, commonly known as the Argus rock gecko, and the *Eremias argus* lizard, or Mongolia racerunner, are just two of several small reptiles having brownish bodies covered with white eyespots. The *Sibon argus* snake, native to Central America, sports a brown-and-black ocellate pattern along the length of its green body, while *Varanus panoptes*, the yellow-spotted monitor (or Argus monitor), found largely in Australia has—you guessed it—yellow eyespots. But the moniker is hardly limited to various reptilians. The fish commonly known as the blue-spotted grouper, blue-dot grouper, or peacock hind, with the scientific name *Cephalopholis argus*, bears a particularly striking pattern of bright blue dots ringed with black, and a species of sea snail, *Arestorides argus*—the eyed cowrie—has a prominent dorsal ring pattern that evidently recalled the Greek myth for Linnaeus, who named the animal himself.

The Indonesian *Argusianus argus* is an avian, one more commonly known as the great argus pheasant, also named by Linnaeus, aware of the detailed ocelli on its wings. These pheasants are closely related to peafowl, but, oddly, none of the latter take their names from Argus Panoptes despite the myth's conclusion, in which Juno places the eyes of the slain watchman in the tail feathers of her favourite bird—the peacock.

CONCLUSION

The applications of monstrous appellations discussed here represent only a tiny portion of the nearly innumerable adaptations of ancient monsters in modern science. Though our focus has been on natural and applied sciences, the social and behavioural sciences also use mythological monsters extensively, if perhaps more for analysis than adaptation. In psychology, for example, the Lernaean Hydra with its regenerating heads might represent futile attempts to solve a problem that, ironically, end up increasing it—an interpretation also evident in our current figurative meaning of 'hydra' as a thing or person compared to the Hydra 'in its baneful or destructive character, its multifarious aspects, or the difficulty of its extirpation' (*OED*, s.v. 'hydra'). Medusa, alternatively, could symbolize (among other things) the difficulty of directly confronting a problem that one is not yet equipped to face (Marsden and Nesbitt 2018).

In short, scholars in various disciplines, including STEM fields, clearly appreciate and enjoy the myths of the ancient world. During a time when most humanities fields, and certainly classical studies, frequently find themselves forced to justify their very existence despite their value to critical thinking and other important yet evidently unappreciated skills, the ongoing interdependence of science and humanities should not be forgotten.

ACKNOWLEDGEMENTS

I am grateful to my research assistant, Lily Noyes, for helping track down many of the details for this chapter; to Ethan Uetrecht, a former volunteer at Cabrillo Marine Aquarium in San Pedro, CA, for his help with the marine biology section; to James D. Miller, AI researcher and Professor of Economics at Smith College, for bringing Roko's basilisk to my attention; and to Claire Kitzmiller for her wonderful suggestions throughout.

SUGGESTED READING

Heller (1945) focuses on Linnaeus's use of classical myth, including monsters, as does Levitt (1982); while both are somewhat dated, they nevertheless provide good overviews. Levitt also includes the names of organisms in other romance languages—for example, that *méduse* is French for 'jellyfish' generally, not just for the adult stage (as in English). Masse et al. (2007) provide a useful perspective on how science can mine classical myth for information about astronomical and geological phenomena. Kaplan (2013) and Kitchell (2015) present a different approach to the science of monsters, examining real-life animals that very likely could have inspired the monsters of myth; cf. Mayor (2000).

WORKS CITED

Auerbach, D. 2014. 'The Most Terrifying Thought Experiment of All Time.' *Slate*. https://slate.com/technology/2014/07/rokos-basilisk-the-most-terrifying-thought-experiment-of-all-time.html. Accessed 11 August 2022.

AVS (Autonomous Vehicle Systems). 2022. 'Welcome to Basilisk.' https://hanspeterschaub.info/basilisk/. Accessed 11 August 2022.

Baggaley, K. 2021. 'Hydras Can Regrow Their Heads: Scientists Want to Know How They Do It.' *Popular Science*. https://www.popsci.com/science/hydra-animals-regrow-head-mystery/. Accessed 23 August 2022.

Basepaws. 2019. 'The Chimera Cat—Its Own Non-Identical Twin.' https://basepaws.com/blogs/news/chimera-cats-genetics. Accessed 10 August 2022.

Bouquet, J. 2019. 'May I Have a Word about ... Pegasus Spyware.' *The Guardian*. https://www.theguardian.com/theobserver/commentisfree/2019/may/19/may-i-have-a-word-about-pegasus-spyware . Accessed 11 August 2022.

Brito, C. 2013. 'On Mermaids and Manatees: A First Approach to the Evolution of Natural History Images in Early Modern Times', in *Proceedings of the ECS Workshop: From Nature to Science: Scientific Illustration on Marine Mammals Through the Centuries*, ed. A.C. Roque and A. J. Wright, 12–22, Setúbal, Portugal.

Crampton, L. 2022. 'Chimaera Facts: Strange Fish with a Cartilaginous Skeleton.' *Owlcation*. https://owlcation.com/stem/The-Chimaera-Ratfish-or-Ghost-Shark-Strange-and-Cartilaginous. Accessed 24 August 2022.

Decher, J., and J. Fahr. 2005. '*Hipposideros cyclops.' Mammalian Species* 763: 1–7.

Devlin, H. 2017. 'First Human-Pig "Chimera" Created in Milestone Study.' *The Guardian*. https://www.theguardian.com/science/2017/jan/26/first-human-pig-chimera-created-in-milestone-study . Accessed 10 August 2022.

Friedman, J. B. 2000. *The Monstrous Races in Medieval Art and Thought*. Syracuse, NY

Garcia, B. 2018. 'Linnaeus and the Fear of Ordering Nature.' https://www.bbvaopenmind.com/en/science/leading-figures/linnaeus-and-the-feat-of-ordering-nature/. Accessed 24 August 2022.

Gillispie, C. C. 1989. 'Scientific Aspects of the French Egyptian Expedition 1798–1801.' *Proceedings of the American Philosophical Society* 133/4: 447–74.

Heller, J. L. 1945. 'Classical Mythology in the *Systema Naturae* of Linnaeus.' *Transactions and Proceedings of the American Philological Association* 76: 333–57.

Herbison-Evans, D., and S. Crossley. n.d. 'Satyrinae of Australia.' http://lepidoptera.butterflyhouse.com.au/nymp/satyrinae.html. Accessed 22 August 2022.

Himmelman J. 2002. *Discovering Moths: Nighttime Jewels in Your Own Backyard*. Camden, ME.

Instituto de Medicina Molecular. 2017. 'Chimera Viruses Can Help the Fight Against Lymphomas.' *EurekAlert!* 14 September https://www.eurekalert.org/news-releases/594400. Accessed 26 August 2022.

Isaak, M. 2022. 'Curiosities of Biological Nomenclature.' https://www.curioustaxonomy.net/etym/myth.html. Accessed 26 August 2022.

Kaplan, M. 2013. *The Science of Monsters: The Origins of the Creatures We Love to Fear*. New York.

Kitchell, K. F., Jr. 2015. 'A Defense of the "Monstrous" Animals of Pliny, Aelian, and Other Authors.' *Preternature* 4/2: 125–51.

Levitt, J. 1982. 'The Adaptation of Names from Classical Mythology as Scientific Terminology.' *Literary Onomastics Studies* 9: 65–80.

Loshin, P. 2021. 'Kerberos.' https://www.techtarget.com/searchsecurity/definition/Kerberos. Accessed 11 August 2022.

McKinney, J. 2015. 'Meet the Solar System's Mysterious Centaurs.' *Futurism*, 24 October https://futurism.com/meet-solar-systems-mysterious-centaurs. Accessed 26 August 2022.

Maroyi, A. 2019. 'Ethnomedicinal Uses, Phytochemistry and Pharmacological Properties of *Chironia baccifera*.' *Journal of Pharmaceutical Sciences and Research* 11/11: 3670–4.

Marsden, A. J., and W. Nesbitt. 2018. 'The Monsters That Make Us: Things That Go Bump in the Mind.' *Psychology Today*. https://www.psychologytoday.com/us/blog/myth-the-mind/201803/the-monsters-make-us-things-go-bump-in-the-mind. Accessed 1 December 2022.

Masse, W. B., et al. 2007. 'Exploring the Nature of Myth and Its Role in Science.' *Geological Society, London, Special Publications* 273/1: 9–28.

Mayor, A. 2000. *The First Fossil Hunters: Paleontology in Greek and Roman Times*. Princeton.

Parker, E. 2021. 'Chimera Cat Facts.' https://www.catological.com/facts-chimera-cats. Accessed 10 August 2022.

Payne, R. 2019. 'Phototransduction in Limulus Photoreceptors.' *Reference Module in Neuroscience and Biobehavioral Psychology*. https://doi.org/10.1016/B978-0-12-809324-5.21583-6. Accessed 24 August 2022.

Roko. 2010. 'Roko's Basilisk.' *LessWrong*. https://www.lesswrong.com/tag/rokos-basilisk#Roko_s_post. Accessed 11 August 2022.

Scharping, N. 2021. 'Why Scientists Have Been Creating Chimeras in the Lab for Decades.' *Discover*. https://www.discovermagazine.com/health/why-scientists-have-been-creating-chimeras-in-the-lab-for-decades. Accessed 10 August 2022.

Shankland, S. 2022. 'Pegasus Spyware and Citizen Surveillance.' *CNET*. https://www.cnet.com/tech/mobile/pegasus-spyware-and-citizen-surveillance-what-you-need-to-know/. Accessed 11 August 2022.

Soulen, H. 2015. 'The Dark Side of Taxonomy: Part Two.' *Shorelines: Life and Science at the Smithsonian Environmental Research Center*. https://sercblog.si.edu/the-dark-side-of-taxonomy-part-two/. Accessed 24 August 2022.

van Rossum, G. 1996. 'Foreword for *Programming Python* (1st ed.).' https://www.python.org/doc/essays/foreword/. Accessed 12 August 2022.

Venturini, G. 2003. '*Amphisbaena fulginosa*', trans. M. Beltramini. *Monaco Nature Encyclopedia*. https://www.monaconatureencyclopedia.com/amphisbaena-fuliginosa/?lang=en. Accessed 22 August 2022.

Vergano, D. 2022. 'DNA Showed a Mother Was Also Her Daughter's Uncle—How Scientists Solved This Medical Mystery.' *Grid*. https://www.grid.news/story/science/2022/11/25/dna-showed-a-mother-was-also-her-daughters-uncle-how-scientists-solved-this-medical-mystery/. Accessed 27 November 2022.

Vorhies, W. 2020. 'An Argument in Favor of Centaur AI.' *Data Science Central*. https://www.datasciencecentral.com/an-argument-in-favor-of-centaur-ai/. Accessed 12 August 2022.

Wagner, T. 2012. 'Guardian "HAL" or The Cyclops Eye.' *Stylepark*. *https://www.stylepark.com/en/news/guardian-hal-or-the-cyclops-eye/*. Accessed 11 August 2022.

INDEX

·······················

For the benefit of digital users, indexed terms that span two pages (e.g. 52–53) may, on occasion, appear on only one of those pages.

Figures are indicated by *f* following the page number